INDUSTRIAL ORGANIZATION AND PUBLIC POLICY

Industrial Organization and Public Policy

SECOND EDITION

Douglas F. Greer
San Jose State University

MACMILLAN PUBLISHING COMPANY
New York

Collier Macmillan Publishers
London

Macmillan Publishing Company
866 Third Avenue, New York, New York 10022

Collier Macmillan Canada, Inc.

Library of Congress Cataloging in Publication Data

Greer, Douglas F.
    Industrial organization and public policy.

    Includes index.
    1. Industrial organization (Economic theory)
2. Industry and state.   I. Title.
HD2326.G73   1984   658   83–14956
ISBN 0–02–347070–4

Printing 1 2 3 4 5 6 7 8   Year: 4 5 6 7 8 9 0 1 2

TO THE MEMORY OF F.A.G. AND C.D.E.

Preface to the
Second Edition

The 1982 volume of the *Review of Economics and Statistics* alone probably justifies the revision this book represents. But there is much more. The old data have been updated where appropriate. The old examples have in many cases been retired in favor of new and better examples. Statements of prevailing public policy have been changed to incorporate such modifications as the new Department of Justice Merger Guidelines and the dismissal of the famous IBM case.

Besides freshening in these standard ways, I have tried to improve the book in response to helpful commentators and my disturbed conscience. Among other things: (1) The theoretical model of monopoly is introduced much earlier in the present edition (Chapter 2), facilitating comparison and contrast to the model of perfect competition on such particulars as excess profits and welfare loss. (2) The theory of dynamic competition is set forth and contrasted with the theory of static, perfect competition. The idea of anticompetitive strategic behavior is also explored in this connection to point out the possibility that "dynamics" need not always imply procompetitive outcomes. (3) Performance measures of market power are developed earlier now, in conjunction with structural and conduct measures. (4) The importance of "first mover" advantages is now noted. (5) The concept of "strategic groups" within industries has edged its way into the discussion at several points. (6) Cournot's model of oligopolistic interdependence has been added along with a separate segment on multinational firms. (7) Refinements on the impact of advertising on prices and profits have been incorporated, refinements giving greater recognition to differences in manufacturer versus retailer advertising. (8) Several passages that have proven particularly difficult for students have been rewritten or deleted. (9) The book has been shortened by overall tightening and by stripping it of two relatively little-used chapters, namely those on health, safety, and environmental problems.

Left untouched are features that seem to be popular among readers. In particular, it retains its flexible, two-chapter—abstract and concrete—treatment of topics.

The circle of contributors to this second edition is as wide as that for the first. For this I am grateful. Comments from Samuel Loescher, Arthur Woolf, Jon Mosle, and Robert E. Smith, plus many students, have improved the book substantially. In addition I would like to thank W. J. Lane, Texas A & M University; James W. McKie, the University of Texas at Austin; and Jon P. Nelson, Pennsylvania State University, for their review of the first edition and suggestions for the revision. Flaws remain only because I have been too bull-headed to follow every suggestion to the letter. Finally, at the center of this circle of contributors is my wife, Wendy, with typing and editing talents that sparkle.

D. F. G.

Contents

Part One: Introduction

Introduction and Overview

Because we live in a market-run society, we are apt to take for granted the puzzling—indeed almost paradoxical—nature of the market solution to the economic problem.

—ROBERT HEILBRONER and LESTER THUROW[1]

Markets comprise the central nervous system of our economy. We rely on them for most of what life is all about—food, entertainment, fuel, transport, shelter, and so forth. Still, markets are neither widely understood nor greatly appreciated. Most people seem to think of markets as places where fish, produce, or shares of equity stock are bought and sold. They fail to recognize the economist's broader use of the term, which encompasses an enormous variety of markets, including those for stereos, apparel, autos, steel, gasoline, soap, beer, motion pictures, and air travel. Moreover, people tend to ignore the large diversity of firms populating most markets, ranging from such pygmies as Harvey Aluminum and Star Gas to such giants as ALCOA and ARCO. On top of all this is a hodgepodge of government regulations, many of which escape most people's notice.

The purpose of this book is to give the reader a broad understanding of markets and their regulation. In particular, we shall attempt (1) to bring some *order* to this almost chaotic diversity by developing a systematic way of looking at markets; (2) to *analyze* how markets function; (3) to *evaluate* how well various markets function in light of society's desires; and (4) to *explain* and *assess* many of the policies governing markets. Among the numerous issues that will be addressed along the way, the following are apt to be of greatest interest to the reader: Why are markets so important to the economy? What factors determine price and output? Why do just a few huge firms dominate some of our key markets, such as those for computers, steel, and aluminum? What are the effects of such dominance on profits, wages, innovation, and effi-

[1] Robert Heilbroner and Lester Thurow, *The Economic Problem,* 4th ed. (Englewood Cliffs, N.J.: Prentice-Hall, Inc.), p. 12.

ciency? Why are soaps, cereals, and cosmetics heavily advertised, whereas sugar, cement, and coal go largely unpromoted by Madison Avenue? Does advertising foster market power? Has market power contributed to inflation or high unemployment? What do policy makers hope to accomplish with measures like grade rating and product standardization? Should the government take action to break up big corporations or subsidize small ones? What has the government done about mergers, price fixing, false advertising, and inflation? Are there such things as "natural monopolies"? If there are, can they be regulated effectively? In a nutshell, under what conditions do our markets best serve the public interest?

First, a few words need to be defined, including the word "market." Second, we shall briefly explore the place markets occupy in the scheme of things. Third, because evaluation is one of our objectives, a discussion of certain values held by our society is needed for later use in evaluating various types of markets and regulations. Fourth, to facilitate understanding and analysis, we need to devise a systematic way of looking at markets. Finally, we shall explain our particular methodology and indicate the organization of the remaining chapters.

I. SETTING THE SCENE

Simply put, a **market** is an organized process by which buyers and sellers exchange goods and services for money, the medium of exchange. Notice that every market has two sides to it—a demand side (made up of buyers) and a supply side (made up of sellers). Notice also that markets can be local, regional, national, or international in scope. When the exchange alternatives of either buyers or sellers are geographically limited—as is true of barbering and grocery retailing, for example—then exchange and competition are correspondingly limited in geographic scope. Strictly speaking, the word "industry" denotes a much broader concept than market because an industry can include numerous local or regional markets. When we speak of the construction industry or the banking industry, we usually refer to something more than local business. In practice, however, "market" and "industry" are often used synonymously, without careful distinction, a practice we too will follow when precision is not required. Indeed, economists commonly use the term "industrial organization" rather than "market organization" to describe the areas of study we cover.

The crucial importance of markets can be fully appreciated only after it is recognized that the "market" is the basic economic *institution* upholding our private free-enterprise capitalist system. An **institution** may be defined as selected elements of a scheme of values mobilized and coordinated to accomplish a particular purpose or function.[2] This definition implies that "markets" have two principal aspects—a *value* aspect and a *functional* aspect.

---

[2] Talcott Parsons and Neil Smelser, *Economy and Society* (New York: Free Press, 1965), p. 102.

INTRODUCTION

A. The Functional Aspect

With respect to function, we rely on markets to cope with the fundamental problem of scarcity, which is what economics is all about. Scarcity would be no problem if desires were severely curtailed. Scarcity would be no problem if our productive capabilities knew no bounds. But, alas, neither of these conditions holds for our society. We have neither limited desires nor unlimited resources. Quite the contrary, Americans are the most prosperous people who have ever lived; yet we still want more goods and services—more than our limited resources of land, capital, labor, energy, and time can produce. Proof of this statement is easy: markets, prices, wages, and all the other trappings of our economy would not exist save for scarcity.

To be a little more specific about the *function* of markets, scarcity rudely forces us to make certain decisions:

1. *What goods and services shall we produce and in what amounts?* At first glance the answer may seem obvious. We need such basics as food, clothing, and shelter. But even in this context our limitations impose trade-offs. Shall it be more "Twinkies" and less "Granola"; more apartments and fewer single-family dwellings; more sweaters and fewer jackets? Similarly, if we commit more of our resources to autos, trains, and planes, sacrifices will have to be made elsewhere. What combination of goods is most desirable?

2. *How are goods and services to be produced?* Many different methods of production are possible for most goods. Cigars, for instance, can be made by man as well as by machine. What mixture of the two will it be? Should coal be mined by strip or underground methods? In short, what combination of resource commitments is most efficient?

3. *Who shall get and consume the goods and services we produce?* There are two aspects to this question. One aspect relates to income distribution—what share of our total national income should each household receive? At present, some enjoy riches and others suffer poverty, while most of us hold down the middle. The other aspect relates to rationing of specific goods. Not enough gasoline can be produced for all people to get as much as they would like. Hence some form of rationing is required.

4. *How shall we maintain flexibility for changes over time?* No condition of scarcity is unchanging. Advances in technology and better educational attainments continually expand our productive capabilities. Consumer tastes also alter. Thus we are confronted with questions of change. Shall we convert to solar power, steam autos, and nine-track tapes? Decisions affecting change must be made continually. The question involved here is "What's new?"

Although every human society has had to arrive at answers to these fundamental questions, only three basic institutional devices (or answer machines) have so far evolved to handle them—tradition, command, and the market. *Tradi-*

4

tion is typical of most primitive societies, wherein each generation merely emulates its ancestor's pattern of life-support. *Command* involves centralized decision making, usually by government authorities (as in Communist China) but also by high priests, war lords, and the like. Elements of tradition and command can of course be found in our own economy. But, by and large, we entrust these decisions to the *market,* to millions of consumers, workers, employers, land owners, investors, and proprietors, each pursuing self-interest in the market place. *Thus, the function of markets is to coordinate and control this decentralized decision-making process, which answers these four crucial questions.* It should also be noted that private property and contract assist markets in this task. *Private property* provides material incentives for individual actions and enables decentralized decision making. *Contract* allows individuals to determine their own terms of exchange and permits stabilizing, long-run commitments.

B. The Value Aspect

As far as its values are concerned, our society generally believes that markets tend to perform the function of coordination and control very nicely. That is to say, the market system accords well with many of our society's values by (1) typically providing fairly good answers to the four questions and (2) arriving at these answers in a particularly appealing way. Exactly what these answers are and exactly how the market system goes about arriving at them will be discussed in subsequent chapters. Right now we need to explain which values we refer to and thereby specify what is meant here by "good" and "appealing."

In the present context, **values** are simply generalized concepts of the desirable. They are objectives or aims that guide our attitudes and actions. Among the most generalized concepts of the desirable are such notions as "welfare and happiness," "freedom," "justice," and "equality." These may be called **ultimate** values because they reign supreme in the minds of most of us. Indeed, they even justify occasional bloodshed.

Although these are undeniably noble aims, they are too vague and too ill-defined to provide a basis for specific institutional arrangements and policy decisions. So, for purposes of actual application, they can be translated into more specific concepts—like "full-employment" and "allocation efficiency"—which may be called **proximate** values. Table 1–1 presents a summary list of proximate values that are relevant here, together with the ultimate values from which they are derived. Allocation efficiency, full employment, clean environment, and health and safety, for example, are several proximate values that convey the spirit of "welfare and happiness." The list is intended to be more illustrative than exhaustive, so only a brief discussion of it is warranted.

Freedom. Proximate values reflecting freedom include such notions as "free choice in consumption and occupation," and "free entry and investment." They imply active, unhampered participation in the economic decision-making process by all of us. The market furthers these objectives because, unlike tradition or command, the market affords free expression to individual choice in answering

5

TABLE 1–1. Some Proximate Values and the Ultimate Values from Which They Derive

Ultimate Values ~Fundamental	Proximate Values
① Freedom	Free choice in consumption and occupation Free entry and investment Limited government intervention Free political parties National security
② Equality	Diffusion of economic and political power Equal bargaining power for buyers/sellers Equal opportunity Limited income inequality
③ Justice and fairness	Prohibition of unfair practices Fair labor standards Honesty Full disclosure
④ Welfare and happiness	Allocation and technical efficiency Full employment Price stability Health and safety Clean environment
⑤ Progress	Rising real income Technological advancement

the key economic questions outlined earlier—what, how, who, and what's new? Unfettered individual choice is possible *only* under favorable circumstances, however. For if markets are burdened with barriers to entry, monopoly power, price fixing, or similar restraints of trade—imposed *either* by government *or* by private groups—then this freedom is sharply curtailed. Although the government has often imposed these and other restraints (usually under the influence and for the benefit of special interest groups), most people in our society favor "limited government intervention" and "free political parties," both of which tend to inhibit centralized command and coercion. Thus, to the extent government intervention is properly called for, most would probably agree that it should be for purposes of *preventing* private restraints of trade rather than for *imposing* official restraints.

Equality. When one person's freedom encroaches upon another person's freedom, some criterion is needed to resolve the conflict. In our society the

6

ideal criterion is "equality" or "equity."[3] This usually means that everybody's preferences and aspirations are weighted equally, as in the political cliché: one man, one vote. In economics, the notion that each individual's dollar counts the same as anyone else's dollar reflects a similar sentiment. Among the more important proximate values stemming from equality are "a wide diffusion of economic and political power," "equal bargaining power on both sides of an exchange transaction," "equal opportunity, regardless of race, religion, or sex," and *"limited in*equality in the distribution of income.*"* Under favorable conditions, the market system can further these objectives.

Justice and Fairness. The market is often given high marks for justice and fairness because, under ideal circumstances, it generates answers to the key economic questions that are not arbitrary, imperious, or despotic. Adam Smith's metaphorical "invisible hand" eloquently illustrates this deduction. Unfortunately, real world circumstances often fall short of the ideal, so that free pursuit of profits in the market place may not always yield fair or just results. As Vernon Mund has written, "Profit can be made not only by producing more and better goods but also by using inferior materials, by artificially restricting supply to secure monopoly profits, by misleading and deceiving consumers, and by exploiting labor."[4] Thus, to account for these sad possibilities and to introduce several forms of market regulation that will be discussed in later chapters, we have listed "full-disclosure," "honesty," and "prohibition of unfair practices" among the proximate values of Table 1–1.

Welfare, Happiness, and Progress. The foregoing discussion of freedom, equality, justice, and fairness helps to explain our earlier statement that the market system arrives at answers to the key economic questions in a *particularly appealing way,* but it remains to be demonstrated that the answers themselves are *fairly good answers.* In other words, as far as markets are concerned, the foregoing values relate more to the decision-making process than to the decisions made—to *means* rather than to *ends.* So, what about ends? Fortunately for us, the answers provided by the market system (again under favorable circumstances) comport fairly well with our society's concepts of welfare, happiness, and progress. As already indicated, a thorough exploration of these answers is deferred until later chapters, especially Chapter 2, when we can elaborate on the meaning of the phrases "favorable circumstances" and "ideal conditions" that have echoed interchangeably across these pages. Nevertheless, for a prelude, we can note briefly that the market system is generally efficient and flexible. Thus, markets answer the question "what will be produced" by allocating labor and material resources to the production of goods and services yielding the

[3] Robert A. Dahl and Charles E. Lindblom, *Politics, Economics, and Welfare* (New York: Harper & Row Publishers, 1963), p. 41.
[4] Vernon A. Mund, *Government and Business,* 4th ed. (New York: Harper & Row Publishers, 1965), p. 24.

greatest social satisfaction. And, with respect to the question of how goods are produced, markets encourage the use of low-cost production techniques that consume the least amount of scarce resources possible for a given bundle of output. Finally, flexibility: the market is generally receptive to good new ideas and new resource capabilities so that, with each passing year, we can produce more and better goods with less and less time, effort, and waste; all of which implies progress.

Although these ultimate and proximate values are widely shared and vigorously advocated by most people in our society, they are also sources of conflict, frustration, and disappointment simply because they are not always consistent with each other. Among the more obvious examples of inconsistency are the following:

1. "Health and safety" may be furthered by requiring seat belts and a collapsible steering wheel in every auto, but this requirement would inevitably interfere with "free choice in consumption."
2. Measures designed to procure a "clean environment," such as banning the use of sulfur laden coal, may seriously diminish what we can achieve in the way of "rising real income."
3. Enforcement of "honesty" and the "prohibition of unfair practices" in the marketing of products may conflict with many people's concepts of "limited government intervention."
4. Patents may be deemed the best means of encouraging "technological progress," but each patent confers monopolistic privileges that run counter to both "free entry" and "diffusion of economic power."

Lest the picture painted by these examples look too bleak, we hasten to add that in many instances there may not be inconsistencies among values, and in other instances the inconsistencies may be so mild that they are readily amenable to resolution and compromise. Still, inconsistencies do exist and are often sharp, which helps to explain several important facts of political-economic life.

First, for various reasons (including material self-interest, educational background, and emotional empathy) each individual gives differing *weights* and *definitions* to these values. It is the particular weight and definition that guides each person's judgment of conflicts among values, precluding unanimous agreement on almost anything.

Second, several "economic philosophies" or "schools of thought" have evolved that differ primarily in terms of the weights they apply to these values and the definitions they give to them. Thus, for example, "conservatives" generally believe that "freedom" is superior to "equality" and "fairness." They prefer less government intervention. In contrast, "liberals" often stress "equality" and "fairness" over "freedom," and their list of preferences is consequently quite different from that of "conservatives."

Third, people's definitions and weights are by no means static or immutable. They obviously change with time and events. Indeed, economic policy formulation has been described as "a trial and error process of self-correcting value judgments."[5] *Knowledge* and *policy* have within them and between them certain irreconcilable inconsistencies. They are both undergoing continuous review and revision, and opinions about both are strongly influenced by values. For these several reasons, we shall frequently return to this matter of value judgments.[6]

II. A SYSTEM FOR ANALYSIS

Having examined the place markets occupy in our economy and having described the basic ideals that will be applied in our evaluation of markets, we are ready to develop a systematic way of looking at markets and categorizing their characteristics. Such a system is necessary if any headway is to be made in analyzing market operations or evaluating how well various markets perform their function. In essence, all that is required is (1) a workable categorization of the principal attributes of markets and (2) a theoretical scheme tying these attributes together. The process is analogous to analyzing the operation of an automobile—the categorization of attributes (or parts) would distinguish between the electrical system, fuel supply system, and so on, and the theoretical scheme would relate each of these attributes to the others to explain how a car works. This "modeling" of the problem not only helps us organize our thoughts, it also helps us formulate testable hypotheses about how markets work. For example, one obvious and familiar hypothesis is that an unregulated monopoly sets higher prices than would prevail under competitive conditions.

The traditional model of markets is outlined in Figure 1–1.[7] As indicated there, the principal components of market analysis are the basic conditions, structure, conduct, and performance. The **basic conditions** may be thought of as characteristics that are either inherent to the product (as is largely true of price elasticity of demand, purchase method, and product durability) or relatively impervious to easy manipulation by policy (as is largely true of growth rate, technology, and historical background). The elements of market **structure** also tend to be stable over time, but they can be affected by either private or government policy. Among the more important variables of structure are the number of sellers and their size distribution (both of which can be altered by antitrust divestiture and dissolution), product differentiation (determined chiefly by private

[5] H. H. Liebhafsky's entire book *American Government and Business* (New York: Wiley and Sons, 1971) is devoted to this theme, but see especially Chapters 1, 2, 6, and 18.

[6] For more extensive discussions of values and their importance see Liebhafsky, *ibid;* Donald Watson, *Economic Policy* (Boston: Houghton Mifflin, 1960), Chapters 2–6; Duncan MacRae, Jr., *The Social Function of Social Science* (New Haven: Yale University Press, 1976); and Scott Gordon, *Welfare, Justice, and Freedom* (New York: Columbia University Press, 1980).

[7] Basic sources include Edward Mason "Price and Production of Large-Scale Enterprise," *American Economic Review,* Supplement (March, 1939), pp. 61–74; Joe Bain, *Industrial Organization* (New York: Wiley & Sons, 1959); J. M. Clark, *Competition as a Dynamic Process* (Washington, D.C.: Brookings Institution, 1961); and F. M. Scherer, *Industrial Market Structure and Economic Performance* (Chicago: Rand McNally, 1970).

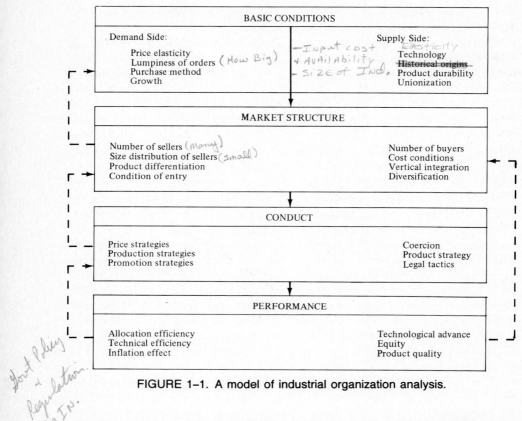

FIGURE 1-1. A model of industrial organization analysis.

advertising and promotion), and the condition of entry (which is affected by patents, licensing, and product differentiation, among other things). The word **conduct** denotes behavior and strategy on the part of firms in the market, so the several items listed under conduct in Figure 1-1 reflect action, not static condition. Finally, **performance** relates to achievements or end results as determined by such variables as efficiency, technological advances, and product quality. In short, structure and conduct relate to *how* the market functions within the limits of its basic conditions, whereas performance relates to *how well* the market functions.

The arrows of Figure 1-1 indicate possible relationships among these attributes. In particular, traditional theory assumes a causal flow running from the basic conditions and structure to conduct and performance. Technology and growth, for instance, could greatly influence the number and size distribution of firms in the market. In turn, the structural characteristics of number and size distribution might determine price and production strategies (conduct) that cause good or bad allocation and technical efficiency (performance). The broken lines of Figure 1-1 represent causal flows running in the opposite direction from those of the traditional model. As recent research has increasingly turned

10

its attention to these latter possibilities, they too will occasionally attract our attention.

Sticking with the traditional model for now, a more explicit portrayal of structure-conduct-performance relationships is contained in Table 1–2. Four traditional market types are summarized there—**perfect competition, monopolistic competition, oligopoly, and monopoly.** Among the more obvious theoretical relationships depicted is that between the number of firms and price strategy. Notice first that under perfect competition the large number of firms prevents any one firm from being large enough to influence price. These many firms thus have no price strategy. They take prices as given by the market and independently determine their production with an eye to maximizing profits. Under oligopoly, however, with just a few sellers, each firm knows that its price and output actions are likely to affect its rivals' behavior. Hence "recognized interdependence" is said to prevail in oligopoly. Only the monopolist enjoys full independence in *both* price and production because he is the sole supplier in his market.

Another simple example of causal flow concerns the relationship between product type and promotion strategy. Intensive brand name advertising is likely to arise only for products that are differentiable; that is, products that people *believe* can have significant brand differences, whether or not the differences are real. Examples include drugs, cosmetics, soft drinks, and autos—each of which is vigorously advertised by brand. In contrast, standardized products— like milk, wheat, and potatoes—might be promoted on an industry-wide basis or by large segments of the industry (for example, Idaho peddles aristocratic potatoes), but the perfect substitutability of various suppliers' offerings of these products makes brand advertising and promotion by individual producers unprofitable. Table 1–2 also acknowledges the possibility of institutional or political advertising, which is generally practiced by firms self-conscious about their public image, as seems especially true of large oligopolists and monopolists.

The relationship between condition of entry and profits also deserves mention. According to the traditional model, industry profits (averaging all member firms) can be excessively high in the long run only if the entry of new firms into the industry is at least partially impeded. Otherwise, such high profits would attract newcomers seeking a piece of the profitable action. The new competition would in turn expand production, lower prices, and reduce profits. Thus, Table 1–2 specifies a positive, direct relationship between the height of barriers to entry (structure) and the likely level of industry profits (performance).

On the whole, then, it may seem that perfect competition provides the "ideal circumstances" and "favorable conditions" alluded to earlier. To some extent it does, but, as we shall explain in the next chapter, this is only partly true.

Table 1–2 also serves to illustrate the two principal methodologies employed by industrial organization economists to analyze structure-conduct-performance relationships and test their significance—the "case study" approach and the "cross-section" approach. Under the former approach, the researcher narrows his focus to one industry for his "case study"; at the same time he usually considers almost all important aspects of the industry's structure, conduct, and

TABLE 1-2. Basic Market Types

Market Type	Structure			Conduct			Performance		
	Number of Firms	Entry Condition	Product Type	Price Strategy	Production Strategy	Promotion Strategy*	Profits	Technical Efficiency	Progressiveness
Perfect Competition	Very large number	Easy	Standardized	None	Independent	b	Normal	Good	Poor perhaps
Monopolistic Competition	Large number	Easy	Differentiated	Unrecognized interdependence		a	Normal	Moderately good	Fair
Oligopoly	Few	Impeded	Standardized or differentiated	Recognized interdependence		a, b, c	Somewhat excessive	Poor perhaps	Good
Monopoly	One	Blocked	Perfectly differentiated	Independent		a ≡ b c	Excessive	Poor perhaps	Poor perhaps

* Key: a = promotion of firm's brand product; b = industry or market wide advertising and promotion; c = institutional or political advertising.

12

performance. This approach is like viewing Table 1–2 *horizontally,* concentrating on only one row (for example, oligopoly), and moving from left to right across all the columns. In contrast, the cross-section approach is more inclusive of industries covered but less comprehensive in its study of attributes or variables. With this approach one can usually focus on only a few items of structure, conduct, or performance (for example, the number of firms and profits). Thus the cross-section approach is like viewing Table 1–2 *vertically,* concentrating on relatively few columns, but including as many industries as the available data permit.

The two approaches have different advantages and disadvantages, so their contributions to our fund of knowledge are complementary. In particular, each industry is in some ways unique in its basic conditions, structure, or regulation. The case study approach can take these unique characteristics into account and assess their impact on conduct and performance. The main shortcoming of case studies, however, is that generalizations cannot reliably be drawn from them—that is, their conclusions may not be applicable to industries other than those under study. By contrast, the cross-section approach cannot include all the unique attributes of all the industries under its purview (because of data limitations and measurement problems), but with this approach the researcher can test the *general* validity of certain hypotheses by estimating statistically the relationships between the variables of structure, conduct and performance. For example, cross-section evidence indicates that industry profits are generally associated positively with the height of barriers to entry. However, certain unique features of a particular industry may have been left out of the cross-section analysis, thus precluding a direct and accurate application of this generalization to its specific case. Public pressure, flaccid demand, or some other factor that could only be accounted for by a thorough case study might cause low profits in a certain industry despite the presence of quite formidable barriers to entry. In sum, then, neither approach by itself is foolproof.

The case study and cross-section approaches differ not only in their substantive strengths and weaknesses. They also offer alternative ways to learn about the field of industrial organization, each of which has its pedagogical advantages and disadvantages. To most students' eyes, case studies appear concrete and lifelike, but the abstract overall view tends to be obscured by the wealth of detail they contain. On the other hand, cross-section evidence has opposite qualities—it provides an overall abstract view but lacks the concrete and often engrossing details one finds in case studies. Although this book is based primarily on the cross-section approach, it includes large doses of case study material. To blend approaches, we treat each major attribute of markets outlined in Figure 1–1 and Table 1–2 with a *pair* of chapters rather than just one chapter. As a glance at the table of contents will show, the first chapter of each pair presents "abstract" theories and cross-section evidence, whereas the second presents "concrete" case study illustrations and relevant policy provisions. Each pair of chapters is classified under the broad heading to which it corresponds, beginning with structure and ending with performance.

III. AN OVERVIEW OF POLICIES

Government policies concerning markets can also be classified within the structure-conduct-performance framework because, generally speaking, the focus or impact of such policies is limited to just one or a few of the market attributes outlined in Figure 1–1 and Table 1–2. Indeed, a chief reason for organizing this book into a sequence on structure, conduct, and performance was the integrated treatment of policies and economics that could be achieved by such an organization. Most of the major policies that will be reviewed are outlined in Table 1–3, according to where they fit in this three-part scheme. Each policy has also been crossclassified in terms of how the policy relates to one important summary attribute of markets—*competition*. Thus, the left hand side of Table 1–3 shows three designations concerning competition: (1) maintenance of competition, (2) setting the plane of competition, and (3) reliance on a "public utility" type of regulation instead of competition. It must be stressed that the resulting alignment of policies and market attributes is only a very loose representation of reality. Moreover, space limitations prevent the mention of numerous other policies, particularly those that constitute exemptions or special privileges. Nevertheless, the table serves as a lofty perch from which to catch a panoramic view of the overall landscape that lies ahead.

Setting details aside until later, we may illustrate these points by highlighting some of the contents of Table 1–3. Mergers between firms in the same market, for example, are prohibited by the Clayton Act (as amended by the Celler-Kefauver Act of 1950) if their effect "may be substantially to lessen competition." The courts, when judging whether a given case produces this effect, examine the number of firms in the market, the trend in numbers over time, and the market shares of the merging firms, all of which obviously relate to two attributes of market structure, namely, the number and size distribution of firms. Thus, Table 1–3 lists "merger laws" under the column headed "Structure." And, since prosecutions of monopolization under the Sherman Act are grounded on similar types of evidence, particularly size of market share, monopoly law joins merger law under "Structure" in Table 1–3. Without further reference to judicial considerations, it should be fairly clear that the remaining policies listed under structure belong there, for they relate primarily to product differentiation.

Under the column headed "Conduct," are laws governing price fixing (collusion), price discrimination, exclusive dealing, tying, and false advertising. There can be no question that, among these, price fixing and false advertising policies should be classified under conduct. Price fixing's *per se* illegality (regardless of the extent of market power behind it or its effect on performance) illustrates the reasons for this. On the other hand, as will be shown later, simply designating price discrimination, tying, and exclusive dealing policies under "Conduct" may be somewhat misleading. Standards of illegality in these cases require that structural circumstances be taken into account before violation can be determined.

"Performance" is the third classification. It will be recalled that allocation

14

TABLE 1–3. Basic Government Policies Concerning Markets

Policy Type	Structure	Conduct	Performance
Maintenance of competition	1. Monopoly law 2. Merger laws	1. Price fixing law 2. Price discrimination law 3. Exclusive dealing law 4. Tying law	
Setting the plane of competition	1. Disclosure of information, truth-in-lending 2. Grading and standardization agricultural products, general weights and measures 3. Trade mark and copyright protection	1. False advertising 2. Deceptive practices	1. Health and safety disclosures 2. Health and safety regulation in products, transportation, etc. 3. Pollution limitations
"Public utility" regulation		1. Price regulation in railroads, telephone, electricity and gas, banking and insurance 2. Abandonment of service	1. Profit regulation 2. Service requirements 3. Safety 4. Innovation regulation

efficiency, technical efficiency, macroeconomic stability, and technological progress are attributes of major concern here. Performance measured by these attributes lies largely outside the purview of policies designed to maintain competition. Hence, the first cell of the "Performance" column in Table 1-3 has been left blank. The remaining performance policies are divided into two categories: (1) those policies that apply to almost all industries, regardless of competitive structure (since structure may have no effect on these particular forms of performance), and (2) those policies that apply to specific industries regulated by government commissions rather than by competition.

The first category includes such policies as pollution control, minimum safety requirements, and standards of purity for food and drugs (undeniably important matters of performance not hitherto mentioned because their connection to the traditional variables of structure and conduct is tenuous). The second category includes similar policies to some extent, but its main contents are profit regulation, service requirements, investment control, and supervision of innovation and technological change, for these policies typically lie within the jurisdiction of numerous independent commissions that regulate these aspects of specific industries—for example the Interstate Commerce Commission and the Federal Communications Commission. Instances of such direct performance regulation are usually rationalized on the ground that competitive structure cannot be attained or, if attainable, cannot be relied upon to provide desirable performance. For this reason the last structural policy cell of Table 1-3, corresponding to public utility type regulation, has been left blank even though these industries are subject to certain forms of structural supervision.

IV. VALUES, ATTRIBUTES, AND POLICIES TOGETHER

This chapter cannot be concluded without an explicit acknowledgement of the links between all three of its major components—value judgments, market attributes, and public policies. The ties connecting the latter two have just been dealt with, so all that remains is a brief exploration of whatever correspondence they may have to value judgments. To state the obvious: All public policies have some *purpose* or *objective,* usually (or hopefully) the furtherance of one or more social values. And, broadly speaking, the purpose of most policies governing markets is to further one or more of the ultimate and proximate values listed earlier in Table 1-1. This observation may be comforting but it is not really very illuminating. We need to know a few specifics. In particular, which policies are designed to further which objectives? And which objectives are associated with which market attributes?

To best understand the answers to these questions, the reader must use his mind's eye to divide Table 1-1 into three main groups of ultimate values— (1) freedom and equality, (2) justice and fairness, and (3) welfare, happiness, and progress—retaining within each group the appropriate proximate values listed under each broad heading. Now (without straining your mind's eye too

TABLE 1–4. Overall Correspondence Among Values, Policies, and Market Attributes

Values	Policies	Market Attributes
Freedom and equality	Maintenance of competitive opportunity	Structure and (to a lesser extent) conduct
Justice and fairness	Rules regarding pricing, promotion, tying, etc.	Conduct
Welfare, happiness, and progress	Direct regulation of performance	Performance

much), align the resulting three groups of values next to the three categories of market attributes outlined in Figure 1–1 that are, in principle, readily amenable to policy change—that is, (1) market structure, (2) conduct, and (3) performance. By this procedure it is possible to gain a loose appreciation for the fact that, generally speaking, (1) policies dealing primarily with market structure have as their main purpose the furtherance of "freedom and equality," (2) policies dealing primarily with market conduct are typically designed to enhance "justice and fairness," and (3) policies dealing chiefly with performance usually have as their objective the enrichment of "welfare and happiness" or the encouragement of "progress." Finally, if tilted properly, the policy outline of Table 1–3 could join this rough conceptual alignment of values and market attributes to complete an overall pattern of correspondence among values, market attributes, and policies, as indicated in Table 1–4. This summary alignment is of course only a very crude representation of reality, for numerous overlaps and inconsistencies could easily be pointed out. Still, for introductory purposes, it has the benefit of brevity.

The interrelationships between values, policies, and market characteristics, together with some qualifications, may be illustrated with special reference to the antitrust laws, which have been labeled "Maintenance of competition" policies in Table 1–3, and which may be the most important of all policies considered in this book because they constitute the "general rule" applying to most industries. Regarding values, antitrust policy could serve one or more of a wide variety of possible aims, nearly all of which may be grouped in the following three classes:[8]

1. *Maintenance of competition and limited business power:* This broad objective would draw its justification from the desirability of having (a) free entry and investment; (b) a large number of alternatives for exercising free choice in consumption and investment; (c) limited business power, or a diffusion of economic power; and (d) equal bargaining power on

[8] For a more thorough treatment of antitrust objectives see Carl Kaysen and Donald Turner, *Antitrust Policy* (Cambridge: Harvard University Press, 1965), pp. 11–22.

both sides of the market. These aims embody certain desirable *economic* traits or conditions descriptive of *markets*, but antitrust could help to achieve certain *political* or *social* aims as well, for political and social power are often grounded on economic power. Many if not most of us believe that furtherance of these several aims tends to foster "freedom" and "equality" as defined earlier.

2. *Fair conduct:* The foregoing relates primarily to the *mere possession* of power, not to its *exercise*. In contrast, aims of "fair conduct" relate more to the way business power is used rather than its mere presence. Should large buyers be charged less than small buyers? Should a seller be allowed to tie the sale of two products together, like computers and punch cards, one of which is monopolistically controlled by patents or trade secrets? Also, what about group boycotts and aggregated rebates? Antitrust could attempt to lay down certain standards of fair business conduct that would curtail these kinds of practices without necessarily attacking the economic power that makes them onerous.

3. *Desirable economic performance:* Because market structure and conduct greatly affect market performance, antitrust policy could be concerned with structure and conduct *only* in so far as they might produce poor performance, while overlooking any concentrations of power or unfair practices that had no discernible effect on performance or promised potential improvements therein. Indeed, despite ample evidence to the contrary, a few economists believe that bigness brings about efficiency, stability, and progress; that cartels are relatively harmless; and that "restrictive practices" are not really restrictive at all. Hence they emphatically favor having performance as the only goal, arguing that "the *process* of choice itself must not be a value,"[9] and that our policy objectives should be confined to "maximizing economic benefits, *whatever* the number of firms may turn out to be."[10]

Which of these three broad aims actually predominates? Notwithstanding the views of the performance minded minority, the general consensus among economists, legislators, and jurists seems to be that our antitrust policy should be aimed primarily at the maintenance of competition as an end in itself and secondarily at the enforcement of fair conduct. To quote a few authorities:

The greatest common denominator in antitrust decisions is a commitment to smallness and decentralization as ways of discouraging the concentration of discretionary authority.—Donald Dewey[11]

[9] C. E. Ferguson, *A Macroeconomic Theory of Workable Competition* (Durham: University of North Carolina Press, 1964), p. 56 (emphasis added).
[10] John McGee, *In Defense of Industrial Concentration* (New York: Praeger Publishers, 1971) p. 21 (emphasis added).
[11] Donald Dewey, "The New Learning: One Man's View," in *Industrial Concentration: The New Learning,* edited by H. J. Goldschmid, H. M. Mann, and J. F. Weston (Boston: Little, Brown and Co., 1974) p. 13.

The grounds for the policy include not only dislike of restriction of output and of one-sided bargaining power but also desire to prevent excessive concentration of wealth and power, desire to keep open the channels of opportunity, and concern lest monopolistic controls of business lead to political oligarchy.—Corwin Edwards[12]

Throughout the history of these [antitrust] statutes it has been constantly assumed that one of their purposes was to perpetuate and preserve, for its own sake and in spite of possible cost, an organization of industry in small units which can effectively compete with each other.—Judge Learned Hand[13]

As for the views of laymen, the reader need merely ask: Would most people like to see each and every industry turned over to the control of two or three firms and the economy as a whole (including mining, manufacturing, transportation, finance, and wholesale and retail trade) subjected to the overwhelming dominance of only fifty corporations, assuming for the sake of illustration that economists believed this massive restructuring would eventually yield 5% greater efficiency, 3% less cyclical instability, and slightly faster growth in GNP? In all probability, the answer is no (or NO!). Moreover, the same answer would most likely greet a similar question regarding unfair or restrictive business practices. Thus our major antitrust policies have been assigned to the "Structure" and "Conduct" sections of Table 1–3, and it is not inappropriate to draw an association between these policies and certain broad classes of values addressed at the outset—freedom, equality, justice, and fairness. If, for one reason or another, the antitrust approach fails to satisfy these objectives in a specific industry, or if the approach is irrelevant to certain performance objectives (like clean air), or if the approach is considered *too* costly in terms of poor performance in an industry, then direct regulation of performance often ensues. But this step is usually taken only with great reluctance and often in response to crisis.

SUMMARY

A few first steps toward an understanding of markets have now been taken. In a nutshell, the market system should be looked upon not only as the organized process by which buyers and sellers exchange goods and services but as an *institution*—the key institution upholding our private free-enterprise capitalistic economy. Because markets are institutional by nature, they embody certain social values, they perform an essential economic function, and they are the target of many governmental policies. In function, markets coordinate and control the largely decentralized decision-making process that provides answers to the four fundamental questions scarcity forces upon us: (1) What should be produced? (2) How should goods and services be produced? (3) Who shall get the benefits of our productive efforts? (4) How can we maintain flexibility for changes over time? Given their assigned task, markets may be analyzed

[12] Corwin Edwards, *Maintaining Competition* (New York: McGraw Hill, 1949), p. 9.
[13] *United States v. Aluminum Company of America*, 148 F.2d 416 (1945).

and evaluated by both the specific *answers provided* and the *process by which the answers are obtained*. If the decision process seems "bad" but the answers themselves are considered "good," society might want to reject the system despite its considerable "goodness." Indeed, the way decisions are made may be important enough to people to make them willing to suffer an occasional bad answer in order to maintain a system or process to their liking. Ideally, of course, both the process of choice and the answers produced should conform to society's concepts of the desirable—that is, society's values.

Translating "process" and "answers" into a model of markets, we come up with a four-part categorization of market attributes—the basic conditions, structure, conduct, and performance. The last three command special attention because structure and conduct comprise the market's decision-making process, whereas performance consists of the achievements, outcomes, or answers provided by the process. In other words, structure refers to such factors as the number and size distribution of the decision makers (buyers and sellers), the condition of entry, and product differentiation. Conduct includes, among other things, price strategy, production strategy, promotion activity, and coercive tactics. Last, the principal attributes of performance are allocation and technical efficiency, progress, and aggregate economic stability.

Returning to goodness and badness, value judgments furnish standards for assessing market structure, conduct, and performance. Moreover, value judgments guide policy formulation and enforcement. Antitrust policy provides an apt illustration of this junction of market attributes, value judgments, and public policies: (1) antitrust focuses most intently on structure and conduct, (2) its principal purpose is the maintenance of competition as an end in itself, and (3) maintenance of competition is, in essence, a shorthand way of saying freedom, equality, fairness, and justice, together with most of the relevant proximate values they represent.

2

Perfect Competition vs. Monopoly, Dynamic Competition vs. Monopoly, and Workable Competition

"Competition may be the spice of life, but in economics it has been more nearly the main dish."
—GEORGE STIGLER

Chapter 1 described, in very general terms, the linkage between market structure, conduct, and performance. We now move from the general to the particular. The first part of this chapter surveys traditional theories of structure, conduct, and performance as they relate to perfect competition and pure monopoly. These traditional theories introduce market *analysis.* That is to say, they demonstrate how sellers make market decisions under certain conditions. Moreover, these traditional theories offer an opportunity to review some basic concepts that will be useful later, concepts like elasticity of demand, marginal cost, and marginal revenue. Finally, these traditional theories open the door to market *evaluation* because they generate definitions of "allocation efficiency" and "equity."

Though instructive, these traditional theories of perfect competition and pure monopoly are limited. In particular, they are *static* theories that more or less misrepresent the competitive and monopolistic behavior that occurs in the real world. Hence this chapter goes on to outline what may be called *dynamic* competition and monopoly. Technological change plays a major role in this dynamic view.

Finally, the chapter offers a standard for evaluating markets that draws upon both static and dynamic theories, namely the standard of *workable competition.* It is workable competition that provides the best guide for public policy.

I. PERFECT COMPETITION VERSUS PURE MONOPOLY

A. The Perfectly Competitive Model

Economic theory's conventional ideal is perfect competition. In this section we (1) specify the structural conditions that must be met to obtain perfect competition; (2) show how these structural conditions affect market conduct; and (3) elaborate on the performance produced by this combination of structure and conduct. Emerging from this exercise is an understanding of a market's two essences—demand and supply.

1. Perfect Competition: Structure and Demand. Perfect competition is defined by four main structural conditions. First, perfect competition requires a very large number of small buyers and sellers. Indeed, each buyer and each seller must be so small relative to the total market that none of them *individually* can affect product price by altering their volume of purchases, if they are buyers, or their level of output, if they are sellers.

Second, the product of any one seller must be a perfect substitute for the product of any other seller. In economists' jargon, the product is homogeneous or standardized.

Third, perfect competition requires that productive resources be freely mobile into and out of markets. Of course any such movement will take time, and in the short run some factors like land and capital are said to be "fixed" because of their short-run immobility once they are committed to production. However, in the long run, all factors are variable and perfectly mobile. This means an absence of barriers to new firm entry—that is, an absence of patents, economies of scale, and the like.

Finally, perfect competition requires that all market participants have full knowledge of the economic and technical data relevant to their decision making. Buyers must be aware of the price and product offerings of sellers. Sellers must know product prices, wage rates, materials costs, and interest rates.

Under these several conditions the demand curve facing each individual firm will be infinitely elastic with respect to price. This is a supremely important statement, yet its specific content is meaningless without an understanding of two of its key terms: "demand" and "elasticity." In the very broad sense, **demand** refers to the quantity of product that would be purchased at various possible prices during some given period of time, holding all determinants of demand other than product price constant. Specifically, demand can refer (1) to the demand *of an individual buyer,* (2) to the demand *of all buyers* in the market taken together, or (3) to the demand *facing an individual seller* in the market. Generally speaking, structural conditions do not influence demand in the first two respects. That is to say, the purchases of a single buyer are only a function of product price, income, tastes, prices of substitute goods (for example, coffee for tea or vice-versa), prices of complements (for example, coffee and donuts), and expectations. Individual demand, as your own experience should tell you, is *not* a function of the number of sellers in the market or the condition of new firm entry. Similarly, since total market demand is simply the summation of all the demands of the individual buyers' in the market, total market demand is a function of the same variables that determine individual demand (price, incomes, tastes, prices of related goods, and expectations), plus one additional factor—the number of buyers in the market. Now the number of buyers was

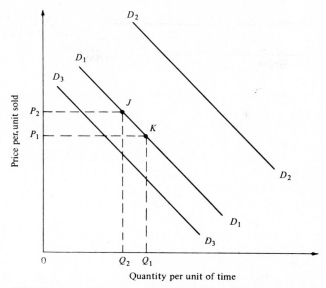

FIGURE 2–1. Examples of market-wide product demand.

mentioned as a structural element. But the number is typically large, so in all but a few instances we are safe in saying that *market structure does not directly affect market-wide demand.*

Figure 2–1 illustrates several **market-wide** demand curves. According to the conventional "law" of demand each demand curve must have a negative slope because price and quantity are inversely related. Thus, on curve D_1D_1, an increase in the price of the product from P_1 to P_2 causes quantity demanded to drop from Q_1 to Q_2, resulting in a movement along the demand curve from point K to J. Such movements along the demand curve, under the impetus of price changes, should not be confused with *shifts* of demand, which are caused by changes in variables *other* than the product's price. An increase in income, for instance, is likely to shift demand outward from D_1D_1 to D_2D_2. Conversely, a reduction of income is likely to shift demand down from D_1D_1 to D_3D_3, resulting in fewer purchases than before at each possible price.

Later, it will be important to know just *how responsive* demand is to variations in price. To measure such responsiveness, economists rely on the **elasticity of demand** in relation to price, which is defined as follows:

$$\text{price elasticity of demand} = \frac{\text{percentage change in quantity demanded}}{\text{percentage change in price}}$$

Strictly speaking, the negative slope of demand always yields a negative elasticity, but the negative sign is usually suppressed for simplification. When the percentage change in quantity demanded exceeds the percentage change in price for some

23

given price change, quantity demand is highly responsive to price and the elasticity ratio will be greater than 1, or *elastic*. Conversely, if the percentage change in quantity demanded is less than the percentage change in price, demand is relatively *un*responsive to price variations and the elasticity will be less than 1, or *inelastic*.

Market-wide demand cannot be the same view of demand held by the typical *individual firm* selling in the market, unless, of course, there is only one firm in the market (a monopolist). In the case of perfect competition the number of sellers is very large, and each seller is so small relative to the total market that it views its demand as in Figure 2-2—a horizontal line running parallel to the quantity axis and intersecting the vertical axis at the going market price. This demand is infinitely elastic.

Thus, market structure is a *crucial determinant* of demand as viewed by the typical firm in the market, even though structure generally does *not* influence the market-wide demand curve. In and of itself this finding may seem meaningless, but it is precisely through this influence on the firm's view of demand that structure subsequently influences firm conduct and, thereby, market conduct as well. How does the firm's view of demand influence firm conduct? By influencing the way firms in the market go about maximizing their profits—assuming that firms want to maximize profits. In summary,

$$structure \rightarrow firm's\ view\ of\ demand \rightarrow firm\ conduct$$

$$profit\ maximization$$

And the next step, before explicitly taking up conduct, is to extract the element of demand particularly relevant to the firm's profit maximizing calculation.

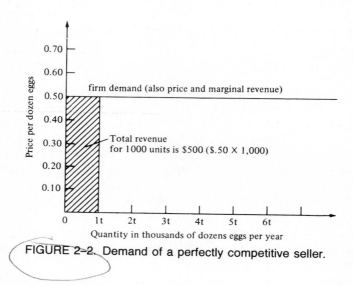

FIGURE 2-2. Demand of a perfectly competitive seller.

There are numerous profit maximizing rules of thumb (for example, "never give a sucker an even break"). The formal economic principle is, in essence, *equalize marginal revenue and marginal cost.* Because demand determines marginal revenue, we shall discuss the revenue portion of the formula first, postponing consideration of marginal cost until the next section. **Marginal revenue** *is the change in total revenue attributable to the sale of one more unit of output.* ✗ *MR*
Indeed, "incremental revenue" might be a better name for it. As price and quantity are always the two basic components of demand and as total revenue is always price *times* quantity sold, there is a very intimate relationship between demand and marginal revenue. In the purely competitive case, the firm's total revenue will rise directly with quantity sold at a constant rate of increase because, according to the firm's demand curve, price is constant over the firm's range of product sales. In other words, the additional sale of one unit of output always adds to total revenue an amount that *just equals the price.* Hence, price and marginal revenue are equal when, as shown in Figure 2–2, the demand curve of the firm is infinitely elastic. Using that figure's data, an additional sale of 1 dozen eggs adds 50 cents to the firm's total revenue regardless of whether it is the first dozen sold or the 3000th dozen sold. Hence, marginal revenue is 50 cents.

2. Perfect Competition: Supply and Conduct. **Marginal cost,** the second portion of the profit maximizing rule of thumb, may be defined as *the addition to total costs due to the additional production of one unit of output.* What are "total costs"? In the short run, total costs are made up of two components—total fixed costs and total variable costs. The short run is a time period short enough for certain factors of production—such as land, buildings, and equipment—to be immobile. Those immobile factors generate **total fixed costs**—such as rent, debt repayments, and property taxes—that *in terms of total costs* do not vary with output. In terms of *cost per unit* of output or "average fixed cost," however, these costs actually decline with greater output because average fixed cost is the total fixed cost (a constant) divided by the number of units produced. Thus, as output rises these fixed costs are "spread" over a larger and larger number of units.

Total variable costs, on the other hand, are those costs associated with variable factors of production such as labor, raw materials, and purchased parts. In terms of *total* costs these costs *always* rise with greater amounts of output, but in terms of *per unit* or "average costs" these may fall, remain unchanged, or rise, depending on the prices and productivity of these variable factors as they are variously applied to the fixed factors. Average, or per-unit, variable cost is the total variable cost at some given level of output, divided by the number of units in that quantity of output. Thus, functionally speaking, if total variable cost rises less rapidly than quantity, per unit variable cost will fall; if total variable cost rises one-for-one with quantity at a constant rate, per unit variable cost will be constant; and, if the total rises more rapidly than the quantity, per unit variable cost will rise.

25

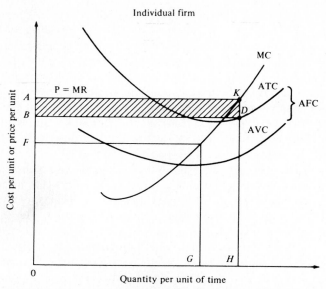

FIGURE 2–3. Short-run cost curves of the firm together with perfectly competitive demand.

Figure 2–3 depicts this family of cost curves on a per-unit or average basis, according to conventional forms. ATC indicates short-run average total cost, and AVC indicates short-run average variable cost. Average fixed cost, AFC, constitutes the difference between ATC and AVC. When ATC is falling, marginal cost, MC, will be below ATC. Once ATC begins to rise, however, MC exceeds ATC. If the P = MR (price equals marginal revenue) line represents the individual firm's demand curve for a prevailing price of *OA*, profit maximization is achieved by producing *OH* units of output because, at that level of output, marginal cost just equals marginal revenue at point *K*. Bearing in mind that total profits are simply total revenue less total cost, the profit-maximizing firm will add to its output so long as the added revenue thereby obtained, MR, exceeds the added cost thereby incurred, MC. This is true of all output levels up to *OH*. However, once the added cost of added output, MC, exceeds the added revenue obtained, MR, total profits will begin to fall. Hence, the astute firm will not produce an output greater than *OH*. At output *OH* total economic profit is the shaded rectangle *BAKD*, which is the economic profit per unit, *KD*, times the number of units produced *AK*. This is called **economic profit or excess profit** because the average total costs *includes* a "normal" profit for the investors that is just sufficiently large, say 7% per year, to pay the cost of capital. Provision of this normal profit rate discourages the investors from withdrawing their capital in the long run and investing it elsewhere.

At price *OF* there would be neither excess profit nor normal profit; there would be a loss. Still, in the short run, the firm would continue to produce

26

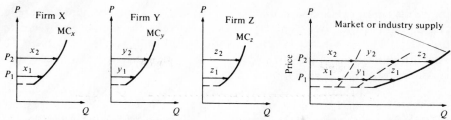

FIGURE 2–4. Horizontal summation of firm supply curves for industry supply.

an amount *OG*, which would again equate marginal revenue (now *OF*) with marginal cost. The firm will thus minimize its losses. Only if price were to drop so low that the firm could not recover its variable cost AVC on each unit would it minimize loss by closing down. The firm should *never* lose in total dollars more than its total fixed cost. If it cannot even cover its variable cost on each unit, then its continued operation will result in losses exceeding total fixed cost.

Two major conclusions emerge from this analysis. First, since price equals marginal revenue for the perfectly competitive firm, the **MR = MC** profit rule of thumb causes price to equal marginal cost and fulfills the optimal welfare requirement to be explained shortly. Second, the supply curve for the firm is identical to its marginal cost curve above the AVC curve. Over the range of possible prices, the quantity offered for sale by the firm may be read from the MC curve. It follows, then, that market-wide short-run supply is determined by simply adding up the short-run supplies of all individual firms in the market at each possible price, as is illustrated in Figure 2–4.

The ties between the typical firm and the market may now be seen in Figure 2–5. Figure 2–5(a) shows the major short-run cost curves of a typical firm; Figure 2–5(b) depicts market-wide supply and demand curves. The first thing

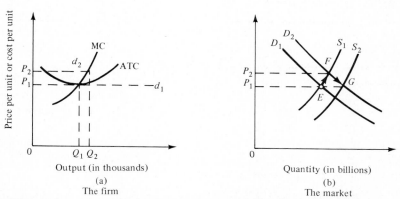

FIGURE 2–5. Long-run adjustment and equilibrium for the firm and market.

to note is that price in the market is determined by the interaction of supply and demand. Thus, given demand D_1 and supply S_1, the market will generate a price of P_1. As viewed by the individual firm in Figure 2–5(a), price P_1 establishes the demand curve $P_1 d_1$, which is infinitely elastic. Short-run profit maximization leads to an output of Q_1.

Of course changes in tastes, income, and other factors will cause demand to shift. If demand shifts from D_1 to D_2, point E will no longer represent equilibrium. In the short run, the enhanced demand will boost prices to P_2, inducing existing firms to move up along their short-run marginal cost curves (MC) to an output level Q_2. This translates into a movement *along* the short-run industry supply curve S_1 from E to F when viewed in the market-wide perspective of Figure 2–5(b). With price greater than short-run average total cost, ATC, economic or excess profits mount up. New firms will enter the market and shift the supply curve to the right to S_2. Entry continues until price falls low enough to wipe out the prospect of excess profits for new entrants. In Figure 2–5 it is assumed that price returns to P_1, a movement that implies that, in the long run, industry supply has increased from E to G without any long-run change of price.

3. Demand, Supply, and Performance. Figure 2–6 completes the perfect competition story. Note that the intersection of demand and supply, E, is an equilibrium position because price at that point, P_1, will not be budged up or down by discrepancies between demand and supply. A price higher than P_1, such as P_2, could not last because a glut of quantity supplied (Q_2) over quantity demanded (Q_0), measured by distance AB, would with competition press price

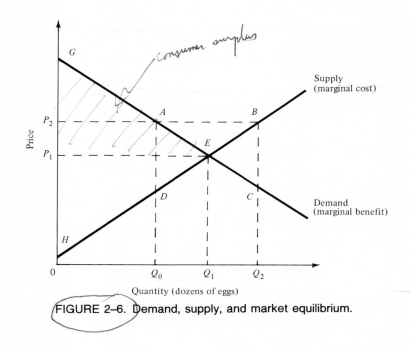

FIGURE 2–6. Demand, supply, and market equilibrium.

down until demand matched supply. Conversely, a price below P_1 would tend to rise as the excess of demand over supply bid price up until equilibrium was reached. That is, price is determined by the mating of demand and supply.

In the short run, price P_1 might mean excess profits for firms in the market, due, perhaps, to a recent boom in demand. Losses are also possible in the short run, due for instance to depressed demand. In the long run, however, entry would wipe out excess profits and exit would tend to erase any losses. Entry implies expanding supply and downward price adjustment, while exit contracts supply and bolsters price. In the long run, after all adjustments are completed, equilibrium implies only "normal" profit, with average total costs and marginal costs equaling price. Thus entry and exit are essential to competitive control.

To assess *how well* this market performs we must evaluate its answers to the basic questions raised by scarcity—namely, what, how, who, and what's new. The questions of "what" and "how" receive answers—namely, allocation efficiency and technical efficiency—that are highly desirable. These are desirable answers because they give society as much economic well being as possible within the bounds imposed by scarcity.

Allocation Efficiency (re What?): The nice answer to "What should be produced in what amounts?" is seen through an appreciation of the fact that Q_1 in Figure 2–6 is just the right amount—not too much, not too little. The demand curve indicates the **benefit** society gains from the production of this good, say eggs, both at the margin and overall. For example, distance Q_1E, which is the same as price OP_1, indicates the benefit of the last dozen eggs at Q_1, so-called *marginal benefit,* because that is the amount people *are willing to pay* for that *last dozen* at Q_1. Area $OGEQ_1$ indicates the benefit of all dozens over the range of OQ_1, or *total benefit,* because that is the amount people *would be willing to pay* for the *entire* quantity OQ_1. Given a price of OP_1, they actually pay only amount OP_1EQ_1, which is price times quantity. The difference between what they are willing to pay, $OGEQ_1$, and what they actually pay, OP_1EQ_1, is triangular area P_1GE, which is like a gift and which accordingly is called *consumers' surplus.*

For its part, the supply curve in Figure 2–6 represents society's **cost** of producing eggs—that is, the cost of land, labor, and other scarce resources, both at the margin and overall. At output OQ_1, distance Q_1E depicts the *marginal cost,* and the area under the supply curve, $OHEQ_1$, depicts the *total cost* of producing output OQ_1.

Hence, amount OQ_1 is just the right amount because any marginal unit of output associated with a lesser amount, such as Q_0, yields a marginal social benefit, *A,* that exceeds the marginal social cost of producing that unit, *D.* So long as a unit's benefit exceeds its cost in this way, additional units of output should be produced, which holds true up to Q_1. Output should not exceed Q_1, however, because any marginal unit associated with a greater amount, such as Q_2, carries a social cost, *B,* that exceeds social benefit, *C.* Thus, if the ideal output is one that maximizes "total benefit − total cost," as guided by society's preferences, Q_1 is that output, where "marginal social benefit = marginal social cost," or MSB = MSC. Net *pluses* occur up to Q_1, as added benefits exceed added costs. Net *minuses* arise thereafter.

Another way of appreciating this result, one that stresses the problem of producing an optimal *mix* of goods when constrained by scarcity, focuses on the P = MC, or price equals marginal cost, condition. Price, as read off the demand curve, indicates the value of the output of productive resources when they are used *here* to provide this commodity, say eggs. Marginal cost, as read off the supply curve, indicates the value of the resources if they were used *elsewhere* to produce other things like wheat, books, records, whatever. After all, the producers of eggs must pay enough for labor, land, energy, and capital to attract them away from those alternative activities. In short, then:

$$\text{price} = \text{value of resources here}$$

$$\text{marginal cost} = \text{value of resources elsewhere}$$

Ideally, *value here should equal value elsewhere,* which is attained when P = MC.

Assume otherwise as a test. If value here exceeded value elsewhere, as *A* exceeds *D* in Figure 2–6 at Q_0, then resources are more valuable here and should therefore be transferred from elsewhere to here, expanding output to Q_1. Competitive markets spur such transfers as profits would be greater here than elsewhere. Conversely, if value elsewhere exceeded value here, as *B* exceeds *C* in Figure 2–6, then resources are worth more elsewhere than here, and output here should be reduced to Q_1 from Q_2, freeing resources for more worthy application elsewhere. Competitive markets foster such transfers by offering greater profit elsewhere than here in such cases. Table 2–1 puts all this in a nutshell.

Technological Efficiency (re How?): The nice answer to "How are goods produced?" is more easily understood because we know that firms in this kind of market will be forced by competition to adopt the most efficient, lowest cost technologies available, and firms will also be compelled to operate at the

TABLE 2–1. Various Resource Allocation Conditions

	Optimal Allocation	Under Allocation	Over Allocation
Market result	P = MC	P > MC	P < MC
General requirement	MSB = MSC	MSB > MSC	MSB < MSC
English translation	value here = value elsewhere	value here > value elsewhere	value here < value elsewhere

low point on their long-run average cost curves. Otherwise, their costs would exceed price and they could not long survive.

Taken together, technical and allocative efficiency achieve what is called **Pareto optimality,** after its formulator Vilfredo Pareto. This ideal is *a situation where no one can be made better off without making someone else worse off.* Stated otherwise, we are *not* at Pareto optimality if Smith's lot can be improved at no loss to anyone else—Jones, Adams, whoever. Ideal markets move society toward Pareto optimality because they entail *exchange.* Whenever *free* and *voluntary* exchange occurs with no adverse third party effects, at least one person is made better off and no one is made worse off. Usually, of course, *both* parties to an exchange benefit. Your trade of $500 for a stereo set makes you *and* the retailer better off. Exchange or market processes can therefore move society from inefficiency toward efficiency.

Equity (re Who?) The foregoing achievements of the perfectly competitive model are indeed marvelous. Strictly speaking, however, the model cannot claim perfection on the ethical criteria of equity—i.e., the question of "who gets the goods and services?" The term "equity" does not have nearly the clarity of "efficiency," but it generally means some "equitable" distribution of income or "equal opportunity." Equity and efficiency *are separable* in the theoretical sense that efficiency can be achieved regardless of whether or not the income distribution is "equitable" or "just." Equity and efficiency *are related* in the sense that the prevailing distribution will substantially influence the kinds of goods included in an efficient mix. Thus a lopsided, unequal distribution of income could yield an efficient mix that includes more Rolls Royces and more caviar than a distribution that is relatively equal. Although theory cannot heighten the attraction of perfect competition by lights of equity, intuition tells us that its absence of excess long-run profits could further ideals of equity.

Technological Change (re What's New?): Theoretically, the perfectly competitive model is less than ideal when it comes to the question of "What's new?" The model is perfectly static, fixed in time, and by definition progressive performance in new products and new processes requires *dynamic* developments.

We shall elaborate on this point shortly when we take up the topic of dynamic competition in earnest. Meanwhile, we shall develop a deeper appreciation for the efficiency and equity achievements of perfect competition if we take a theoretical glimpse of pure monopoly.

B. The Pure Monopoly Model

1. Pure Monopoly Structure and Conduct. The structural conditions for pure monopoly are just the opposite of those for perfect competition. Instead of a large number of relatively small sellers, there is just one. Instead of a standardized product, identical across all sellers, the product may be said to be perfectly differentiated because the monopolist's offering has no close substitutes. Instead

31

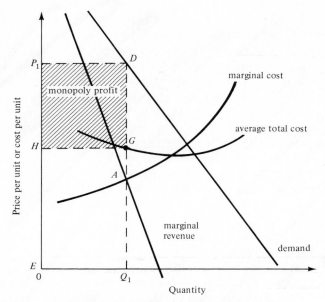

FIGURE 2-7. Monopoly equilibrium solution.

of easy entry for newcomers, <u>entry is blocked in the case of pure monopoly</u> <u>(even though the monopolist may be earning massive excess profits)</u>.

Under these conditions, the demand facing the individual seller and the market-wide demand are one and the same. With conventional cost curves, the resulting profit maximizing price and quantity for a monopolist are shown in Figure 2-7.

As before, the rule of thumb for maximizing profit is marginal cost equals marginal revenue, which occurs at point A with output OQ_1 and price OP_1. Although the MC = MR rule applies here as under perfect competition, the result is markedly different in this case because the downward sloping demand of the monopolist generates a downward sloping marginal revenue curve that lies below the demand curve. Recalling that marginal revenue is the addition to total revenue due to the additional sale of one more unit of output, we may illustrate the relationship between price, quantity, total revenue, and marginal revenue in the simplified schedule of Table 2-2.

Each extra unit sold *adds* to total revenue an amount equal to the price of that unit, but from this the monopolist must *subtract* the price reductions necessary to sustain the sale of all preceding units. Thus in Table 2-2 the marginal revenue of producing the third unit is $6 even though price at that point is $8, because three units generate a total revenue of $24 ($8 × 3), whereas two units generate a total revenue of $18 ($9 × 2), and 24 − 18 = 6. Marginal revenue is lower than price. And, as price declines, marginal revenue declines

TABLE 2–2. Marginal Revenue and Price

P ($)	Q (units)	TR(P × Q) ($)	Marginal Revenue ($)
11	0	0	—
10	1	10	10
9	2	18	8
8	3	24	6
7	4	28	4
6	5	30	2
5	6	30	0
4	7	28	−2

faster. Thus once again we have seen how structure, via its influence on the firm's view of demand, affects conduct.

Economic or excess profit *per unit* in Figure 2–7 is indicated by the distance *DG*. Total dollar excess profit is consequently the area $DGHP_1$. (This assumes once again that ATC includes a normal profit.) Some monopolists may not be able to earn excess profits. Their costs may be high relative to their demand; or their demand may be low relative to their costs. If there were only one movie theater in Ottertail, Minnesota, for instance, it would probably be only a weak monopoly earning only a normal profit. Still, the classic case is one involving excess profit.

2. Pure Monopoly Performance. In traditional theory, monopoly causes poor performance in two main ways, both of which derive from the foregoing profit story. These are illustrated in Figure 2–8, which simplifies matters by assuming constant cost per unit (thereby causing average total cost to match marginal cost). Under perfect competition, price would be P_c, which equals cost and therefore yields no excess profit. The quantity corresponding to P_c is Q_c, which is optimal by previously shown standards, namely $P_c = MC$. In contrast, the monopolist's price is higher at P_m and corresponding quantity is lower at Q_m.

Consumers' surplus under perfect competition would amount to area EBP_c, because the amount consumers would be willing to pay, which is the area under the demand curve, $OEBQ_c$, exceeds the amount they actually pay, OP_cBQ_c, by a value represented by EBP_c. Under pure monopoly, consumers' surplus shrinks to triangle EAP_m. Hence monopoly causes consumers to lose an amount equivalent to P_cP_mAB.

This lost consumers' surplus, P_cP_mAB, may be divided into two kinds of loss. The first part, area ABC, is due to the misallocation of resources that occurs when output falls from Q_c to Q_m. This value, ABC, disappears from the economy completely; it is lost by consumers and not gained by the monopolist. It is the same kind of loss that would occur if earthquakes obliterated our coal reserves, but it is a welfare loss due to *inefficiency*.

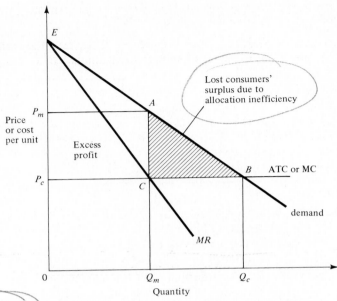

FIGURE 2–8. Monopoly's adverse impact on allocation efficiency and equity.

The second part, area P_cP_mAC, is the excess profit earned by the monopolist at the expense of consumers. This is a *transfer* from consumers to the monopoly's owners, a transfer that may well result in undesirable *inequity*. How markedly the excess profit contributes to an unequal distribution of income depends on the relative financial condition of (1) those who pay the higher price and thereby lose the surplus and (2) those who earn the excess profit and thereby gain the surplus. If those who pay are generally poorer than those who receive, as typically seems to be true, then income distribution is made more unequal by monopoly.

As regards technical efficiency and technological change (the performance questions of How? and What's new?), the theoretical case against monopoly is less clear-cut. For reasons we shall explore extensively later, a monopolist's technical efficiency might be good because of economies of scale, which lower average and marginal cost as size grows. On the other hand, a monopolist's technical efficiency might suffer from slack and sloth—so-called X-inefficiency. Theories concerning a monopolist's progressiveness are equally ambiguous. Invention and innovation can be said to thrive or die under monopoly depending on one's theoretical assumptions. Once again difficulties naturally arise when conclusions concerning dynamics are wrongly extracted from the static, conventional theory of monopoly surveyed to this point.

Having thus come up against the limits of static theory once again, it's time we turned to dynamic theories of competition and monopoly.

34

II. DYNAMIC COMPETITION VERSUS MONOPOLY

Dynamic theories of competition and monopoly are much less refined than traditional theories. They are like scatter-shot as compared to a bullet. One reason for this is that dynamic theories are newer and less fully developed. Another reason is that they attempt to incorporate more realism, as the conditions for either perfect competition or pure monopoly very rarely ever actually occur. Finally, and perhaps most importantly, dynamic theories introduce a time dimension foreign to traditional theories. This introduces the vagaries of indeterminance, a variety of historical circumstances, and the vibrations of changing tastes and technologies, all of which complicate matters immensely.

A. Dynamic Competition

What is happening when ARCO drops credit cards and cuts the price of gasoline? What is happening when Apple Computer introduces a "friendly" new model called Lisa for people who know nothing about computers? These are acts of vigorous competition, yet they spring from contexts that are not perfectly competitive at all. While perusing the brief description of dynamic competition given below, notice that such competition does not rigorously require masses of firms, standardized products, or any of the other conditions of "perfect" competition.

1. Dynamic Competition: Structure. Structurally, theories of dynamic competition often stress two features—industry life cycle and market imperfections. The industry's life cycle, as shown in Figures 2–9 and 2–10, divides into four distinct phases.[1]

- *Introduction,* during which the product is just getting off the ground. The innovator, such as Atari in video games, may enjoy a period of dominance merely by virtue of its great innovative stride. But it faces substantial risk and profits may even be negative.

- *Growth,* during which time the market expands rapidly. Competition takes the form of new entry, new innovations, and new promotions. Market shares are fluid. Profits are typically high.

- *Maturity,* during which time growth subsides as the market reaches relatively large dimensions. Market shares and firm rankings solidify during this phase, and profits may settle at normal levels.

- *Decline,* during which time the market contracts and perhaps even disappears. Competition may center on price level and costs. Exits are prompted by low and falling profits. Decline in one industry may be caused by growth of another, as ice boxes gave way to electric refrigerators.

[1] For elaboration see Michael E. Porter, *Competitive Strategy* (New York: The Free Press, 1980), pp. 156–188.

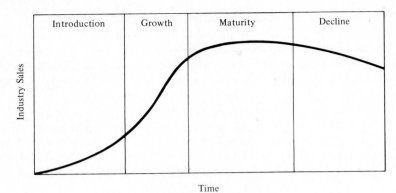

FIGURE 2–9. Industry life cycle over time.

Of course this pattern fits many industries only loosely and others not at all. The duration of the phases varies widely. Some industries skip a phase or two, moving, for example, from growth to decline without pause. Still, the theory yields several broad generalities that cannot be found in traditional, static theory. In particular, the dynamics of the cycle reveal situations where a fewness of firms need not indicate a lack of competition (the "introduction"

Phase	Introduction	Growth	Maturity	Decline
Market Growth	Slow	Rapid	Slow-Level	Negative
Market Size	Small	Medium-expanding	Large	Contracting
Competition	Dominance by innovator, few firms	Entry, many competitors, shifting shares	Solidified shares, product stability	Exits, price competition
Profits	Variable, risky, high to low or negative	High and rising profits	Moderate to low profits	Low and falling profits

FIGURE 2–10. Industry life cycle and competition.

phase) and where high profits may not reflect monopoly power (the "growth" phase). The kind of competition that emerges from "the new commodity, the new technology, the new source of supply, the new type of organization" is according to Joseph Schumpeter, a "process of creative destruction."[2]

As regards **structural imperfections,** the business rivalry that results from

[2] Joseph A. Schumpeter, *Capitalism, Socialism and Democracy* (New York: Harper Torchbook, 1962), p. 84.

dynamic competition is itself a symptom of the absence of perfect competition.[3] For example, whereas the perfectly competitive firm is almost invisibly small, the theory of dynamic competition posits firms large enough to have noteworthy identities and to influence price. For another example, perfect competition assumes that buyers and sellers have perfect information while dynamic competition assumes imperfect information:

> In fact, the entrepreneur's role in society is to discover things which seem to meet such an obvious need that people will think the discoveries were invented by themselves. Or to put the point another way, entrepreneurs act as marriage brokers between that which is possible from a scientific and technological point of view and that which is desirable from an economic point of view.[4]

In the end, the theory of dynamic competition downplays the importance of structure altogether. Its main focus is conduct.

2. Dynamic Competition: Conduct. Dynamic competition could also be called *rivalrous competition,* for it assumes that firms vie with each other in ways not appreciated by the theory of perfect competition. According to J. M. Clark, for instance, dynamic competition "includes initiatory action by a firm, responses by those with whom it deals, and responses to these responses by rival firms, to which one could add the subsequent rejoinders of the initiators."[5] Moreover, these rivalrous actions may involve the entire range of business decision variables—selling prices, advertising promotions, product design, distribution channels, production processes, the lot. Thus a list of conduct characteristics would include the following:

a. Dynamic competition is first and foremost an *activity* of sellers.
b. Dynamic competition arises out of conscious attempts by firms to devise an *overall product offering* which will be perceived by buyers as more attractive.
c. Dynamic competition entials an *independent* striving for patronage whereby firms employ various strategies and counter strategies in efforts to outmaneuver one another over time.
d. As the competitive process unfolds over the long term, active rivalry will result in firms both *creating* and *responding* to new market forces, market trends, and customer tastes and preferences.[6]

---

[3] George W. Stocking and Willard F. Mueller, "The Cellophane Case and the New Competition," *American Economic Review* (March 1955), pp. 29–31.

[4] Burton H. Klein, "Dynamic Competition and Economic Stability," in *Economics and Human Welfare,* edited by M. T. Boskin (New York: Academic Press, 1979), p. 300.

[5] J. M. Clark, "Competition: Static Models and Dynamic Aspects," in *Readings in Industrial Organization and Public Policy,* edited by Heflebower and Stocking (Homewood, Illinois: R. D. Irwin, 1958), p. 251.

[6] Adapted from Arthur A. Thompson, Jr. "Competition as a Strategic Process," *Antitrust Bulletin* (Winter 1980), pp. 789–790.

3. Dynamic Competition: Performance. The theory of dynamic competition does not offer highly refined definitions of allocation efficiency, technical efficiency, and equity, although it does endorse these notions in vague and uncertain terms. More importantly, dynamic competition is said to perform well when (a) customers can choose from a variety of qualities and types of any given product, implying that product differentiation is often better than product standardization; (b) new products and services are developed to better meet the needs of buyers; (c) new production processes emerge to lower costs and improve quality; and (d) these new products and new processes spread rapidly into wide usage, which diffusion will then benefit consumers and workers generally. When reduced to three words, good performance here implies *variety, quality, and progress,* as well as vague notions of efficiency and equity.

B. Monopoly in a Dynamic Context

Perhaps the main conclusion to be drawn from the theory of dynamic competition is that, in the real world, we do not need to achieve the fairyland structural conditions of perfect competition to achieve *effective* competition and many economic benefits. Indeed, some "imperfections" may, after all, be desirable. A few economists press this conclusion to an extreme form, arguing that monopoly power *cannot* be attained or maintained except by firms who win the dynamic competitive race with superior efficiency, outstanding innovativeness, and other forms of good behavior and performance.[7] In this light, monopoly is not a problem. It may even be a solution.

Defenders of dominance notwithstanding, the introduction of dynamics does not do away with the problem of monopoly power. In a dynamic world monopoly power can be attained and maintained by artificial, restrictive means just as readily as by efficient, innovative means. Moreover, such monopoly power may adversely affect performance—stifling technological change, for instance, or fostering inefficiency.

The theories of monopoly in a dynamic context are much more complicated than the static theory outlined earlier. But four main points can be made.

First, a monopolist can often behave strategically, planning and acting to achieve long-run, anti-competitive aims.[8] For example, an established monopolist might build greater production capacity than is needed to meet immediate demand, which excess capacity would then deter the entry of new competitors. Such preemptive capacity would be costly to the established monopolist (and an inefficient use of scarce resources from society's point of view), but the strategy could prove to be highly profitable to the monopolist in the long run, more profitable than allowing competitive entry.[9]

---

[7] Yale Brozen, *Concentration, Mergers, and Public Policy* (New York: Macmillian, 1982).

[8] Steven C. Salop, "Strategic Entry Deterrence," *American Economic Review* (May 1979), pp. 335–338; S. C. Salop and D. T. Scheffman, "Raising Rival's Costs," *American Economic Review* (May 1983), pp. 267–271.

[9] A. Michael Spence, "Entry, Capacity, Investment and Oligopolistic Pricing," *Bell Journal of Economics* (Autumn 1977), pp. 534–544.

Second, the variables that can be used strategically to attain and maintain monopoly power artificially are for the most part the same variables that are used in the course of socially desirable dynamic competition. That is to say, a monopolist can use a number of "weapons" to gain strategic advantages over its rivals or potential entrants. These arms include predatory pricing, preemptive research and development, brand proliferation, product proliferation, and escalated advertising.[10] Each of these create short-run costs but generate long-run gains. Moreover, this list points out the fact that a firm's actions—such as price cutting or advertising—can be either *pro-competitive* (as under the theory of dynamic competition) or *anti-competitive* (as under the theory of dynamic monopoly). The reader is thus duly warned that simple analyses and sweeping generalizations are rare in industrial organization economics.

Third, strategic practices that have monopolistic consequences tend to reverse the causal flows found in the traditional structure-conduct-performance model. In the traditional, static model, market structure causes certain kinds of conduct. Now we see that, conversely, strategic conduct can influence structure. In truth, *simultaneous* causal flows may often be at work in the real world—moving from structure to conduct and from conduct to structure simultaneously. For example, a fewness of sellers may cause intensive advertising while at the same time the intensive advertising may hold down the number of sellers. This obviously complicates analysis and evaluation.

Fourth, dynamics do not necessarily assure good economic performance, especially not in the presence of monopolistic motives and achievements.[11] The emphasis on product differentiation might lead to inefficient wastes—such as too much advertising, too much style change, and too many product varieties. (On the serious side, ask your ophthalmologist about the value of eye drops. On the lighter side, watch the new-product horizon for bulletproof paper towels.) As regards worthwhile technological change, *some* market power may produce favorable results while *too much* might be undesirable.

III. WORKABLE COMPETITION

Where does all this leave us? We have explored the model of perfect competition, discovering some attractive properties that might be useful in evaluating real world industries. In particular, perfect competition yields allocative efficiency,

---

[10] See the papers by Steven Salop, Michael Spence, Richard Craswell, Richard Gilbert, Janusz Ordover, and Robert Willig in *Strategy, Predation, and Antitrust Analysis* (Washington, D.C.: Bureau of Economics, Federal Trade Commission, 1981). See also Richard Schmalensee, "Entry Deterrence in the Ready-to-Eat Breakfast Cereal Industry," *Bell Journal of Economics* (Autumn 1978), pp. 305–327; Marius Schwartz and Earl Thompson, "Entry Patterns Under Decreasing Cost Conditions," Economic Policy Office Discussion Paper, Dept. of Justice (1983); and Oliver Williamson, "Predatory Pricing: A Strategic and Welfare Analysis," *Yale Law Journal* (December 1977), pp. 284–340.

[11] Robin Marris and Dennis Mueller, "The Corporation, Competition, and the Invisible Hand," *Journal of Economic Literature* (March 1980), pp. 32–63.

something that cannot be said of monopoly. Technical efficiency and equity are also apparently served by perfect competition, but less certainly so. Should we then adopt perfect competition as our ideal, pressing public policies to achieve that end? No. We have also learned that the perfectly competitive model is too remote from reality to provide proper guidance and, moreover, it may be downright undesirable. Notions of dynamic competition, which allow for some "imperfections" like product differentiation and which appreciate the importance of technological change, make up for these failings of the perfectly competitive model. Elements of dynamic competition should thus enter any final standard we adopt to evaluate industries. We cannot go so far as to say, however, that dynamics allow a standard so loose as to permit monopoly power that is artificially attained or maintained. Monopolists can use dynamics in their own interest against the public interest.

What finally emerges, then, is the concept of **workable competition,** a set of *operational* norms or standards by which markets may be evaluated. In many ways, workable competition is a first cousin to perfect competition, if not a sibling. Factual *experience,* rather than theory, has shown that, even though the "perfection" of theory is not possible and probably undesirable, vigorous competition in the market place is generally better than no competition—better for political and social ends as well as for economic ends. Thus, borrowing heavily from F. M. Scherer, we conclude this chapter with an outline of some of the criteria of "workability" that have evolved in the literature:[12]

Structural Norms
1. The number of traders should be at least as large as scale economies and industry life cycle permit.
2. There should be no artificial inhibitions on mobility and entry.
3. Where appropriate, there should be moderate and price-sensitive quality differentials in the products offered.
4. Buyers should be well informed about prices, quality, and other relevant data.

Conduct Criteria
5. Some uncertainty should exist in the minds of rivals as to whether price initiatives will be followed.
6. Firms should strive to achieve their goals independently, without collusion.
7. There should be no unfair, exclusionary, predatory, or coercive tactics.
8. Inefficient suppliers and customers should not be shielded permanently.
9. Sales promotion should not be misleading.
10. Persistent, harmful price discrimination should be absent.

[12] F. M. Scherer, *Industrial Market Structure and Economic Performance* (Chicago: Rand McNally, 1970), p. 37. For other reviews of workable competition see S. Sosnick, "A Critique of Concepts of Workable Competition," *Quarterly Journal of Economics,* (August 1958) pp. 380–423; and H. H. Liebhafsky, *American Government and Business* (New York: John Wiley & Sons Inc., 1971), pp. 236–262.

Performance Criteria
11. Firms' production operations should be efficient.
12. Promotional expenses should not be excessive.
13. Profits should be at levels just sufficient to reward investment, efficiency, and innovation.
14. Output levels and the range of qualities should be responsive to consumer demands.
15. Opportunities for introducing technically superior new products and processes should be exploited.
16. Prices should not intensify cyclical instability or inflation.
17. Success should accrue to sellers who best serve consumer wants.

It should be obvious that this approach is basically pragmatic, somewhat rough-and-ready, largely judgmental, certainly "unscientific," and rather imprecise. As H. H. Liebhafsky says, "Such an approach is not satisfactory to anyone who either believes that it is possible to achieve absolute certainty or who is driven into an attempt to achieve it as a matter of his personal emotional make-up."[13] Moreover, value judgments unavoidably enter any application of these criteria. Scherer correctly points out, for instance, that on many of the variables a line must be drawn separating "enough" from "not enough" or "too much." How much uncertainty should exist in the minds of rivals as to whether their price initiatives will be followed? How moderate should quality differentials be? What constitutes misleading sales promotion? How long must price discrimination persist before it becomes persistent? And so on.[14] Moreover, these various criteria need not be given equal weight. And, when some criteria are satisfied but not others, how is one to determine workability? If performance is fairly good but structure is irregular, what then? Some of the values that may influence our judgments on these issues were discussed earlier in Chapter 1. In subsequent chapters we shall discover what specific judgments have been made in the past. We shall also develop a body of information from which the reader may fashion his own informed judgments.

SUMMARY

Table 2–3 outlines the two main theoretical models we have covered—static and dynamic. The traditional static model defines perfect competition in structural terms—i.e., a large number of small sellers producing a standardized product which could easily be produced by new entrants (if high profits attracted them). With price given by market-wide forces of demand and supply, perfectly competitive firms maximize profits by producing where price and marginal revenue equal marginal cost. The resulting overall performance is ideal in terms of allocation and technical efficiency. Given no more than normal long-run profits, it is likely to be good in terms of equity as well.

[13] Liebhafsky, *op. cit.*, p. 261.
[14] Scherer, *op. cit.*, p. 37.

TABLE 2–3. Outline of Main Theories of Competition and Monopoly

Feature	Static Theory	Dynamic Theory
Definition of competition	Atomistic structure with standardized product and easy entry	Centered on rivalrous conduct concerning price, promotion, and product innovation
Competition's benefits	Allocation and technical efficiency plus equity	Technological progress plus some differentiation
Source of monopoly power	Structural conditions	Strategic behavior as well as structural conditions
Monopoly's main drawbacks	Allocation inefficiency and income inequity	Slow technological change and inefficiencies

The traditional static model of monopoly posits structural conditions of an opposite sort—namely, a solitary firm unworried by threats of entry producing a product with no close substitutes. The MC = MR profit rule holds again, but the downward sloping demand curve facing the monopolist causes price to exceed marginal revenue and therefore also to exceed marginal cost. With price greater than marginal cost, allocation inefficiency results. Moreover, the associated excess profits can create inequities.

Dynamic theory introduces some realism, mainly by introducing a time dimension that allows significant volatility and change. Dynamic competition centers on rivalrous conduct concerning such diverse variables as price, product quality, promotion, and innovation. Technological progress is the main benefit claimed for such rivalry. Some product differentiation might also be deemed desirable under certain circumstances. Unfortunately, monopolistic evils lurk in a dynamic world as well as a static world. They can take the form of strategic behavior that hinders entry. Poor innovative performance is another possibility.

When trying to devise a reasonable set of standards to depict desirable structure, conduct, and performance, elements of both theories can be blended into what may be called workable competition. This standard assumes that vigorous competition is good, but shies away from insisting on "perfect" competition. This standard has its vaguenesses and is therefore imperfect. But it also has the attraction of being practical. The characteristics of workable competition are outlined on pages 40 and 41.

42

Part Two: Structure

3

Introduction to Structure

Power tends to corrupt. . . .
—LORD ACTON

In the perfectly competitive market system of Chapter 2, decisions concerning what and how to produce were made by nobody in particular. They were made collectively by the balanced interaction of many faceless sellers and buyers. With decision making thus decentralized, power was also decentralized because "power" in this context is the ability to make and affect decisions. Once we depart from the world of perfect competition, all the key issues concerning market structure relate to power:

1. What is market power?
2. How can market power be measured?
3. What are the sources and causes of market power?
4. How can these sources and causes of power be measured?
5. What policies can be devised to control the distribution of power?

The purpose of this chapter is to provide introductory answers to the first three questions. It serves to preface the more detailed answers to the questions that follow in the next six chapters.

I. WHAT IS MARKET POWER?

Market power *is the ability to influence market price perceptibly.* The key word here is "ability." A buyer or seller may have the ability to influence price but may not actually use that ability. Still, power would be present, just as a boxer's power is always present, outside as well as inside the ring. Stress on ability is important because pricing behavior is not, in and of itself, a feature of market structure. Structure does, however, determine ability.

44

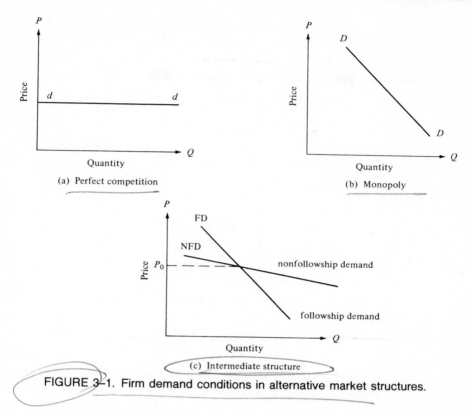

FIGURE 3-1. Firm demand conditions in alternative market structures.

As already indicated in Chapter 2, variations in the features of market structure cause variations in the ways individual sellers view their demand and individual buyers view their supply. Figure 3–1 summarizes individual seller views of demand according to variations in market structure. Figure 3–1(a) depicts the horizontal demand curve of a perfectly competitive seller who has no power to influence price. At the other extreme, 3–1(b) shows a monopolist's demand curve, which is labeled DD because, by definition, this is the market-wide demand curve as well. The monopolist's power is reflected in the wide range of price-options offered by this demand curve.

Between these two extreme cases is an intermediate situation of "rivalry" among a limited number of sellers. Here the firm confronts two demand curves with downward slope, neither of which is the market-wide demand curve. The firm might perceive either one or both (or portions of both) of these demand curves, depending on what assumptions it makes concerning its rivals' behavior. If the firm assumes that its rivals will follow any price change it makes up or down from P_0, which is the going price, then it will consider the "followship demand" curve the applicable demand curve. With rivals matching its every price move, the particular firm cannot gain or lose market share because it will neither take sales away from nor give sales to its rivals through any price

45

change it makes. The downward slope derives entirely from sales variations at the market-wide level, with the individual firm always getting its constant share of market-wide sales. Thus this FD curve could also be called a "constant share" demand curve, and it is a close reflection of the market-wide demand curve.

In contrast, the "nonfollowship demand" curve of Figure 3–1(c) is based on the assumption that rivals in the market do *not* follow the price changes of the firm depicted but instead leave their prices unchanged at P_0. The elasticity of this NFD curve is much greater than the elasticity of the followship curve because, without followship, the firm will win customers away from its rivals when it cuts price below P_0, or lose customers to its rivals when it raises price above P_0. With customers moving amongst firms as well as into and out of the market, the firm's market share will rise with a price cut and fall with a price hike. The NFD curve could therefore also be called a "changing market share curve." A firm confronting this set of demand curves has *some* power over price, but not as much as a monopolist.

II. HOW CAN MARKET POWER BE MEASURED?

The **Rothschild index** is a *theoretical* measure of market power based on a comparison of the slopes of the followship and nonfollowship demand curves.[1] Redrawing these curves in Figure 3–2 and labeling certain points for purposes of computation, we may summarize the Rothschild index as follows:

$$\text{Rothschild index} = \frac{\text{slope of NDF}}{\text{slope of FD}} = \frac{JK/JM}{JL/JM} = \frac{JK}{JL}$$

Under perfect competition the nonfollowship curve would be perfectly horizontal, yielding a ratio of JK/JL equal to zero. On the other hand, a monopolist would observe no difference between the followship and nonfollowship curves. Because the monopolist does not share the market with any rivals, there is no question whether they will or won't follow his price initiatives. When FD and NFD coalesce, the ratio JK/JL equals one. From these two extreme observations it should be clear that intermediate cases range between zero and one, varying directly with market power. In short, the Rothschild index provides one answer to the second question: "How can market power be measured?" Other, more practical, measures derive from the sources and causes of market power.

III. WHAT ARE THE SOURCES AND CAUSES OF MARKET POWER?

The following chapters will focus on three structural characteristics that contribute to market power:

[1] K. W. Rothschild, "The Degree of Monopoly," *Economica* (February 1942), pp. 24–40.

Factors causing market power

1. **Product differentiation:** The greater the degree of product differentiation, the steeper the nonfollowship demand curve and the greater the *JK/JL* ratio. With differentiation, many buyers prefer particular brands for *non-price reasons,* such as style and advertising image. Product differentiation thus produces less price-induced brand switching and more stable market shares in the face of price differentials than would be observed with standardized products.

2. **Market share:** The larger the firm's market share, the closer NFD approaches FD and, consequently, the higher the *JK/JL* ratio. To see this relationship, consider a price cut by a firm with 1% of the market and compare its effect to that of a price cut by a firm with 90% of the market. The small firm will have a highly elastic NFD curve because it can easily double or triple its sales and market share by cutting price. On the other hand, the monster with the 90% share already has so much of the market that, even if it takes the remaining 10% away from its rivals, it won't achieve much of a gain in sales or market share. When measuring the power of a *group* of firms, their market shares may be combined.

3. **Barriers to entry:** The effect of barriers is not directly observable in Figure 3–2 as it stands. Entry is a long-run matter, whereas these curves relate to the short run. However, let FD depict short-run demand, and NFD depict long-run demand (allowing sufficient time for entry to occur); then high barriers to entry will cause NFD to coincide more closely with FD above price P_0, and the *JK/JL* ratio will be greater the more formidable the barriers. In other words, we could look upon new entrants as nonfollowers who eventually come into the market charging price P_0,

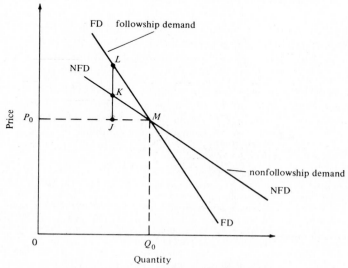

FIGURE 3–2. The Rothschild index.

in the event the established firm boosts price above P_0. Accordingly, the long-run NFD curve will be more elastic under conditions of easy entry than it would be with difficult entry. (Price changes on the downside, below P_0, would relate to ease of rivals' exit rather than entry in this modified view of Figure 3–2.)

As already suggested in Chapter 1, there are numerous other elements of structure that might influence market power—including growth, vertical integration, and diversification. Unfortunately, we have only enough space to touch lightly on these other elements in various spots later. By concentrating on differentiation, market shares, and entry, we follow in the footsteps of Joe Bain, Richard Caves, and Willard Mueller.[2] It should also be stressed that the Rothschild index provides only one answer to the question, "How can market power be measured?" And it is not necessarily the best answer.[3] Its greatest shortcoming is its purely theoretical nature. In practice, it is not possible to estimate the index accurately, so measures of differentiation, market share, and entry barriers are used instead. The index is based solely upon demand factors to the exclusion of supply and cost conditions, which is another weakness. As Edward Chamberlin has remarked, measuring market power is much like measuring one's health: "Some aspects of health can be measured and others cannot. Among the former, we have body temperature, blood pressure, metabolism, weight, etc. But these do not lend themselves to the construction of a single index of health. Similarly, in economics it does not follow that because certain indices are quantitative themselves they can be averaged or in some way reduced to a single index. . . ."[4]

IV. PERFORMANCE MEASURES OF MARKET POWER

Because market power can influence economic performance, economists have devised several measures of market power that refer explicitly to performance. We shall note two such measures—one devised by Abba Lerner, the other by Joe Bain.

The **Lerner index** measures the divergence between price and marginal cost that may result from the exercise of market power:[5]

$$\text{Lerner index} = \frac{\text{price} - \text{marginal cost}}{\text{price}}$$

[2] Joe Bain, *Industrial Organization* (New York: John Wiley & Sons, 1959); R. Caves, *American Industry: Structure, Conduct and Performance* (Englewood Cliffs, N.J.: Prentice-Hall, 1964); W. F. Mueller, *A Primer on Monopoly and Competition* (New York: Random House, 1970).

[3] Other authors of such measures include A. G. Papandreou, "Market Structure and Monopoly Power," *American Economic Review* (September 1949), pp. 883–897, and R. Triffin, *Monopolistic Competition and General Equilibrium Theory* (Cambridge, Mass.: Harvard University Press, 1940).

[4] E. H. Chamberlin, "Measuring the Degree of Monopoly and Concentration," in *Monopoly and Competition and their Regulation,* edited by E. H. Chamberlin (New York: Macmillan, 1954).

[5] A. P. Lerner, "The Concept of Monopoly and the Measurement of Monopoly Power," *Review of Economic Studies* (June 1934), pp. 157–175.

Under perfect competition there is no divergence between price and marginal cost, in which case the Lerner index is zero. With monopoly, however, the divergence can be substantial. Looking back to the monopoly result in Figure 2–7 on page 32, we can see that the Lerner index in that case would be DA/DQ_1. In Figure 2–8 on page 34 the index would be AC/AQ_m. It will be noted that in no case could the index exceed a value of one, so its theoretical range is from zero to one.

One problem with the Lerner index is that a firm's marginal cost usually cannot be estimated. This severely limits its practical application. Another problem rests in the fact that the Lerner index is a measure of actual conduct—a measure of the exercise of power rather than its mere existence. A value of zero, though indicating pure competition, would be observed if a monopolist for some reason chose to keep price low, close to marginal cost, rather than to raise price and maximize profit.

This problem of exercise versus existence also bedevils the **Bain index**, which focuses directly on excess profit.[6] The idea is that competition produces zero excess profit. Hence monopoly power would be revealed by a persistence of positive excess profit—the higher the more the monopoly power.

Estimation of such excess profits, though more practical than estimation of the Lerner index, requires a modification of accounting profit plus an assumption. Accounting profit in total dollars, which may be found in a firm's annual income statement, is

$$\pi_a = R - C - D$$

where $R =$ total revenues
  $C =$ total current costs
  $D =$ depreciation

To obtain excess profit, Bain deducts from accounting profit an assumed (or estimated) "cost" of investors capital, that is

$$\pi_e = R - C - D - iV$$

where $i =$ the rate of return that could be earned on alternative (normal profit) investments
  $V =$ the total value of the owners' investment.

If converted to a percentage rate, the Bain index would be π_e / V.

This discussion does not exhaust the possibilities. However, we must postpone further discussion of performance measures until after we have studied structure in finer detail.

[6] Joe S. Bain, "The Profit Rate as a Measure of Monopoly Power," *Quarterly Journal of Economics,* (February 1941), pp. 271–293.

SUMMARY

Market power is the ability to influence price in the long or short run. Since price is always determined by prevailing supply and demand conditions, at least some control of supply or demand or both is required before such power can be said to exist. Even when the government wants to influence price it must resort to one of these controls, as is illustrated by the government's reliance on rationing tickets to "control" demand when it sets a legal price ceiling below the free-market equilibrium level.

Where do the elements of market structure fit into the picture? They are the means, the elements, or the indices of demand and supply control. Product differentiation may be looked upon as a weak form of demand control. Similarly, a firm with a 70% market share may be said to control 70% of market supply. Also, high barriers to entry give existing firms some degree of control over long-run supply.

Given structure's potential effects on performance, market power may be measured by performance as well as by structure. For the next six chapters, however, we focus on structure.

mkt. structure affects market power

4 Product Differentiation: Theory and Cross-Section Evidence

Go directly to your friendly local monster supermarket. Count the items on the shelves. There are 10,000 of them! And each package is calling out to the housewife . . . Hey, remember me? Remember my advertising, my promises? Remember my company?

—STEPHEN FRANKFURT

Once upon a time, there was a colorless, odorless, and tasteless beverage that was produced by an essentially simple, easily imitated process. The producers of brand "S" couldn't make their brand any more colorless, odorless, or tasteless than other brands of this beverage. But, by advertising heavily and by pricing brand S above the others, they convinced many drinkers that S was the best. In particular, S's advertising stressed the gaiety and modernity of brand S because this theme would appeal to young, affluent adults. As for pricing, the producers of S were so confident that consumers believed price was an index of quality that at one point they actually *raised* the price of S in response to a competitor's price *cut*. The sales of brand S soared.

This sounds like a fairy tale, but it's not. It's the true story of Smirnoff vodka.[1] Indeed, Smirnoff has been so successful with this marketing strategy that during the 1970s it became the number one brand of vodka. Why do we tell the story here? Because it illustrates some of the causes and effects of "product differentiation." Our purpose in this chapter is to explore certain causes and effects of product differentiation, beginning with its effects and ending with its causes. In our study of *effects,* we shall see that, when producers successfully differentiate their products, consumers may choose one brand over rival brands for nonprice reasons. Buyers believe that alternative brands of the same product are not perfect substitutes for each other. Under *causes,* it will be shown that these nonprice reasons for choice may be either real or imaginary, objective or subjective, depending on the various means by which differentiation is achieved. If nonprice differences between brands are real and objective, they are usually the result of manipulations of flavor, quality, warranty, service,

[1] R. D. Buzzell, R. E. M. Nourse, J. B. Matthews, Jr., and T. Levitt, *Marketing: A Contemporary Analysis* (New York: McGraw-Hill, 1972), pp. 10–11.

51

store location, or something similar. If, on the other hand, they are merely imaginary, they are usually created by exhortative advertising, brand name connotation, or superficial variations in packaging.

In particular, it will be shown that some products, like vodka, are highly *differentiable,* whereas others are not. Moreover, certain classes of buyers are more *susceptible* to the influences of differentiation than other classes of buyers. Thus this chapter is primarily concerned with the differentiability of various products and the susceptibility of various buyers. There is no simple relationship between the causes and effects of product differentiation that applies uniformly across all products and purchasers. Exhortative advertising seems to work potently in some cases but not in others. The same holds true for styling, packaging, and other sources of differentiation. Thus, certain prior conditions may strengthen or weaken the cause-and-effect relationship.

I. EFFECTS

A. Changes in Buyer Demand[2]

The key to understanding product differentiation lies in buyer behavior. If buyers act rationally, they will attempt to maximize their material well-being subject to the constraints of limited time and income. To put the matter simply, buyers try to get the most for their time and money. Pursuing this goal, consumers must make decisions at two levels: (1) Which products should be bought—for example, autos, lumber, or hamburgers? (2) Given a choice of product, which brand should be bought—for example, McDonald's versus Burger King? If buyers think (and know for a fact) that all brands and models of a certain product are absolutely identical in their ability to satisfy certain needs, there would be *no* product differentiation. Buyers would maximize their welfare simply by purchasing the lowest priced brand or model. Sellers would be forced to compete solely on the basis of price (assuming they do compete). Competition by advertising or style change would not alter sales; it would only add to costs and subtract from profits. If, in contrast, the product can be successfully differentiated, then buyers can be persuaded by nonprice considerations that they get more for their money by choosing Brand Y over Brand X, or vice-versa. In essence, successful differentiation can either shift the individual seller's demand curve outward, enabling him to sell a larger quantity at a given price, or tilt his demand curve to a steeper slope, enabling him to raise his price without losing many customers. *In short, differentiation gives sellers some power over price.*

Figure 4–1 illustrates the first of these effects. A successful exhortative advertising campaign for Brand Y shifts the demand curve for Y from d_{y1} to d_{y2}, resulting in a greater volume of sales, Q_{y2}, as compared with original sales,

---

[2] Much of this material may be found in E. H. Chamberlin, *The Theory of Monopolistic Competition* (Cambridge: Harvard University Press, 1933).

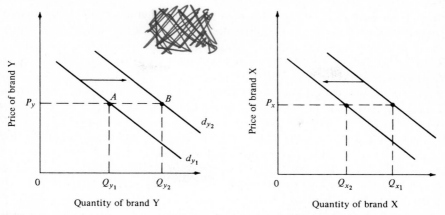

FIGURE 4–1. A shift of sales to Brand Y by means of advertising or differentiation.

Q_{y1}. At constant price P_y, total revenues (price times quantity) rise from OP_yAQ_{y1} to OP_yBQ_{y2}, suggesting increased profits, provided the additional costs of producing and marketing Y are less than the added revenue. Alternatively, price could rise *while quantity is constant*. Assuming Brand X and Brand Y are to some degree substitutes, this favorable shift of tastes to Brand Y will shift the demand curve of Brand X to the left, lowering Brand X revenues. Of course, sellers of Brand X might try to retaliate by changing their promotional pitch or boosting their advertising outlays, but we shall ignore such gamesmanship until later (Chapter 15).

Figure 4–2 illustrates the second possible effect of successful product differentiation. Let curve d_1 depict demand under conditions of little product differentia-

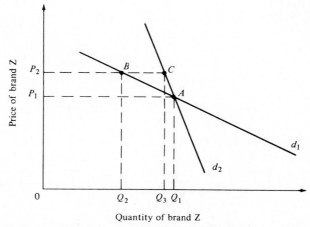

FIGURE 4–2. Reducing elasticity of demand by means of product differentiation.

tion. Then let d_2 depict demand after the introduction of a new advertising theme, which proclaims incessantly that "Brand Z folks would rather fight than switch." If the price of Brand Z had been raised prior to the new campaign from P_1 to P_2, sales would have fallen from Q_1 to Q_2, and total revenues would have dropped from area OP_1AQ_1 to area OP_2BQ_2. But, once most Brand Z buyers are convinced that they would rather fight than switch, the same increase in price would trim sales only slightly, from Q_1 to Q_3, and total sales receipts would actually rise to an amount represented by area OP_2CQ_3. In brief, product differentiation can reduce the price elasticity of demand as well as shift a brand's demand curve outward.

B. The Importance of Knowledge

The extent to which sellers can succeed in achieving these effects, and the means they must employ to do so, depends largely on buyer **knowledge**. Under the ideal circumstances of perfect competition reviewed in Chapter 2, it was assumed that all buyers pursued their goal of welfare optimum with the aid of perfect knowledge. This implies that each buyer

1. Is an expert buyer, readily able to appraise product quality objectively.
2. Has a well-defined set of taste preferences or purchase requirements.
3. Is aware of all purchase alternatives and the terms offered by sellers.
4. Is able to calculate accurately the marginal gains and losses of choosing one combination of commodities over another to obtain the highest possible benefit for any given expenditure.[3]

If all buyers met this description, it would be very difficult for sellers to sell them goods they did not really want, to exaggerate the quality of one brand over another, or to charge outrageous prices for goods that were more cheaply available elsewhere.

It would in short, be impossible *artificially* to shift the demand curve or reduce its elasticity. Product differentiation could still occur under these ideal circumstances, but it would have to be based on genuine, objective, nonprice differences between brands (involving quality, durability, service, convenient location, or the like). By contrast, ignorance and gullibility improve the profitability of seller exhortation, image building, functionless style variation, and related gimmicks that play on the subjective passions and preferences of buyers.

Having linked buyer knowledge to the shape of differentiation activity, let us now take up the question of *what determines buyer knowledge* or the lack thereof. As already suggested, the answer comes in two parts—**buyer character** and **product type.** We can, for the moment, divide all buyers into two broad groups: (1) professional business buyers and (2) household consumers. We can also divide all products and services into two types: (1) search goods and (2) experience goods.

Among buyers, business buyers come about as close to being highly knowl-

---

[3] Tibor Scitovsky, "Some Consequences of the Habit of Judging Quality by Price," *Review of Economic Studies,* Vol. 12, No. 2, pp. 477–485 (1944–1945).

edgeable and fully informed as one could normally expect. Indeed, professional purchasing agents of large firms often specialize in buying such broad categories of goods and services as raw materials, construction, transportation, insurance, heavy machinery, and office supplies. Moreover, they often have the assistance of engineers, scientists, financial wizards, and other experts who conduct tests, arrange credit terms, guide negotiations, and the like—all with an eye to maximizing profits. Perhaps the most important reason for this highly developed expertise is the ability of professional buyers to spread the costs of obtaining this expertise over a large volume of purchases. Thus, their absolute total dollar costs of purchasing may be huge, but on a *per unit* basis these costs will be small. (The aggregate savings gained from avoiding errors is also enormous.)

large co's are more careful buyers thus

On the other hand, we have the typical American consumer, who by comparison is an intellectual weakling. Although not a moron, he or she runs a very small scale operation. Moreover, many if not most of the thousands of decisions consumers make each year are terribly complex, precluding the cultivation of genuine, low-cost per-unit expertise. Their ignorance forces them to rely on an array of homely little **cues,** many of which may not be accurate indicators of product value or quality at all. Studies have shown that consumers may judge the quality of identical hosiery on the basis of scent; the cleaning strength of detergent from suds level and aroma; the mildness of detergent on the basis of color; the thickness of syrup by darkness; the "pickup" of cars by the tension in the spring controlling the accelerator pedal; the quality of beer, floor wax, razor blades, lunch boxes, tennis racquets, and carpeting, on price; the power of kitchen mixers on noise; and the quality of tape recorders on the basis of exaggerated advertising claims.[4] In short, consumers are sensitive to all forms of product differentiation, subjective and objective alike. It is easy to see, then, why sellers of consumer goods account for the lion's share of all money spent on differentiation activities. In contrast, sellers of producers' goods are largely limited to rather objective (and genuine) forms of differentiation. They consequently tend to limit the intensity of their promotional efforts.

typical consumers

perception of quality

Lest we overstate the ignorance and gullibility of the typical consumer, we hasten to add that product type will also determine the degree to which the purchase decision is made by hunch in the fog or by compass in the clear. Nearly all of the products just mentioned, and most of those that are prone to the greatest amount of subjective differentiation, are what may be called **experience goods,** that is, those whose utility can be fully assessed only *after* purchase. To evaluate brands of bottled beer accurately, for example, the con-

experience goods

[4] Donald F. Cox, "The Sorting Rule Model of the Consumer Product Evaluation Process," in *Risk and Information Handling in Consumer Behavior,* edited by D. F. Cox (Boston: Division of Research Graduate School of Business Administration Harvard University, 1967), pp. 324–368; A. G. Bedian, "Consumer Perception of Price as an Indicator of Product Quality," *MSU Business Topics* (Summer 1971), pp. 59–65; A. G. Woodside, "Relation of Price to Perception of Quality of New Products," *Journal of Applied Psychology* (February 1974), pp. 116–118; R. W. Olshavsky and J. A. Miller, "Consumer Expectations, Product Performance and Perceived Product Quality," *Journal of Marketing Research* (February 1972), pp. 19–21; W. B. Cornell, "Price as a Quality Signal," *Economic Inquiry* (April 1978), pp. 302–309.

sumer would obviously have to buy alternative brands in order to experience their taste. The same is true of canned foods, soaps, automobiles, appliances, and related products. It is largely the presence of hidden qualities in these goods that makes them liable to subjective as well as objective differentiations.

A second and contrasting category of commodities may be called **search goods.** In the case of search goods—like fresh fruits and vegetables, raw meat, apparel, shoes, jewelry, and maybe furniture as well—the consumer can judge on the basis of fairly simple inspection *prior* to actual purchase whether a given article is wholesome, handsomely styled, properly fitting, and reasonably priced for the level of quality it represents. At least in these instances, the consumer typically acts in a relatively well-informed manner, being much less sensitive to the blandishments of exhortative advertising, the attractiveness of package coloring, or the image conveyed by brand name.[5]

Goods and services bought by commercial enterprises may also be divided into experience and search categories. The distinguishing characteristic of items in the latter classification is, again, the ability of the buyer to evaluate quality accurately before purchase. Thus, search goods bought by professional buyers include raw materials, basic office supplies (such as pencils and paper), many semifinished articles, steel, and lumber. Although the high-powered capabilities of these buyers may seem to rule out the existence of producers' experience goods, it seems reasonable to place in this category such items as computers, aircraft, complex machinery, and financial services. To the limited extent that business buyers can be swayed by subjective forms of differentiation, these experience goods offer the best scope for such subjective differentiation.

Table 4–1 summarizes these several categorizations. Our division of buyers into two groups—producers and consumers, and our division of all products into two groups—search and experience goods, define four broad market categories. The first division is made vertically, the second division horizontally, yielding a matrix of four cells in Table 4–1. Brief notations within each cell summarize product differentiation in likely form and intensity.

In the case of producer search goods, differentiation centers on variations of size (for example, lumber), shape (for example, steel), composition (for example, metal alloys), terms of sale (for example, credit), and other objective or genuine features. The cost or intensity of differentiation in this case, as measured by differentiation expenditures relative to total sales revenues, is generally low, apparently ranging from 0 to 5% of sales. In brief, the goods of this cell closely approximate the standardized goods of the perfectly competitive model of Chapter 2.

At the opposite extreme are consumer experience goods. To be sure, these goods also vary objectively, but, more important, they are promoted on subjective

---

[5] For elaborations on search and experience goods see R. H. Holton, "Consumer Behavior, Market Imperfections and Public Policy," in *Industrial Organization and Economic Development* edited by J. W. Markham and G. F. Papanek (Boston: Houghton-Mifflin, 1970), pp. 102–115; and Phillip Nelson, "Information and Consumer Behavior," *Journal of Political Economy* (March/April 1970), pp. 311–329.

TABLE 4–1. Differentiation by Broad Market Categories

		Type of Product	
		1. Search	2. Experience
Type of Buyer	1. Producer	Form: Objective Intensity: Low	Form: Mainly objective, some subjective Intensity: Moderate
	2. Consumer	Form: Mainly objective, some subjective Intensity: Moderate	Form: Both objective and subjective Intensity: High

appeals such as exhortative advertising (for example, cigarettes), packaging (for example, perfume), style (for example, autos), and brand image (you name it). Here total marketing costs may run as high as 50% of total sales revenue, although, on average, they appear to be in the neighborhood of 10–15% of total revenues. Accordingly, intensity of marketing effort is said to be "high" for these goods.

Between these two extremes we find producer experience goods and consumer search goods. Differentiation in these cases focuses primarily on objective product features, although subjective appeals undoubtedly influence buyers' decisions too. Marketing expenses for the intermediate goods appear to be more substantial than the skimpy outlays associated with producer search goods but less than those associated with consumer experience goods, which explains the "moderate" designation of Table 4–1.[6]

C. Some Problems and Qualifications

Although this four-part division of products helps in understanding differentiation, it has two possible shortcomings worthy of exploration—irrelevance and oversimplification. A skeptic might argue that these distinctions are meaningless or irrelevant to what really matters most—good industrial conduct and performance. Consider the distinction between search and experience goods as it applies to consumers, for example. If one assumes that consumers act in a cold, calculating manner, with immutable preprogrammed taste preferences, one can demonstrate theoretically that they are no less efficient in their selection of experience goods than in their selection of search goods, despite the abundance of exhortative advertising accompanying experience goods sales. In brief, this theory asserts that consumers randomly sample alternative brands of these products and learn

[6] Detailed cost data on all differentiation efforts are not publicly available. These rough estimates are derived primarily from E. L. Bailey. "Manufacturers' Marketing Costs," *The Conference Board Record* (October 1971), pp. 58–64; and D. Houghton, "Marketing Costs: What Ratio to Sales?" *Printers' Ink* (February 1, 1957), pp. 23–24, 54–55.

from their past purchase experiences which ones they like and which ones they do not like. They then apply this acquired knowledge to more effectual purchasing over time because they accumulate a fund of knowledge comparable to search knowledge. It has even been argued that exhortative advertising *helps* consumers, that they need merely buy the most heavily advertised brand to get the best quality for their money.[7]

Although there may be some truth to this theory, contrary theories and contrary empirical tests abound.[8] There are obvious practical difficulties in keeping up with rapid technological change and in sample purchasing such items as automobiles, refrigerators, and color TVs. Moreover, there is the broader question of whether the "robot model" of consumer behavior is accurate— whether, that is, consumers really *learn to buy what they like* after random sampling. To summarize the opposing position, which supports the preceding division of products, it seems more accurate to say that consumers quite often *learn to like what they buy,* without any random sampling, especially in the case of experience goods.

The literature supporting this latter viewpoint is too vast to review here, but a few summary statements can be made. First, a remarkably large proportion of consumer purchases seem to be made without benefit of any systematic decision making at all—no weighing of options, no sampling, no gathering of information, or the like. Instead, these purchases hinge on such other influences as childhood preferences, habit, attempts to imitate others, exhortative advertising, and random whims.[9] Second, consumers often learn to like what they choose simply because they have made the choice, a behavior that obviously does not jibe with the "robot model" of experience goods sampling. This is due to what is called "cognitive dissonance," and often works even when consumers do weigh their options before purchase. For example, if Smith thinks brands X, Y, and Z are about equally attractive before purchase, his judgement of Y, if selected, will rise after purchase merely because of its selection.[10] Third, the "power of

[7] Phillip Nelson, "Advertising as Information," *Journal of Political Economy* (July/August 1974), pp. 729–754; and P. Nelson, "The Economic Consequences of Advertising," *Journal of Business* (April 1975), pp. 213–241.

[8] For surveys see R. J. Markin, Jr., *Consumer Behavior: A Cognitive Orientation,* (New York: Macmillan Publishing Co., 1974); and T. H. Meyers and W. H. Reynolds, *Consumer Behavior and Marketing Management* (Boston: Houghton Mifflin Co., 1967). For a direct critique of Nelson see Yehuda Kotowitz, "Commentary," in *Issues in Advertising,* edited by D. G. Tuerck (Washington, D.C.: American Enterprise Institute, 1978), pp. 193–198.

[9] Richard W. Olshavsky and Donald H. Granbois, "Consumer Decision Making—Fact or Fiction?" *Journal of Consumer Research* (September 1979), pp. 93–100. On the problems of becoming informed see Hans Thorelli and Sarah Thorelli, *Consumer Information Systems and Consumer Policy* (Cambridge, Mass.: Ballinger Publishing Co., 1977), pp. 18–21.

[10] G. D. Bell, "The Automobile Buyer After Purchase," *Journal of Marketing* (July 1967) pp. 12–16; L. A. Losciuto and R. Perloff, "Influence of Product Preference on Dissonance Reduction," *Journal of Marketing Research* (August 1967), pp. 286–290; R. Mittelstaedt, "A Dissonance Approach to Repeat Purchasing Behavior," *Journal of Marketing Research* (November 1969), pp. 444–446; J. Jacoby and D. B. Kyner, "Brand Loyalty vs. Repeat Purchasing Behavior," *Journal of Marketing Research* (February 1973), pp. 1–9; J. B. Cohen and M. J. Houston, "Cognitive Consequences of Brand Loyalty," *Journal of Marketing Research* (February 1972), pp. 97–99; F. W. Winter, "The Effect of Purchase Characteristics on Post Decision Product Reevaluation,"

suggestion" can apparently be very powerful indeed. If exhortative advertising or some other influence inflates a consumer's pre-purchase attitude toward some brand, bad post-purchase experience does not necessarily deflate that favorable attitude.[11] In sum, many if not most consumers are easily led astray.

What is the importance of these findings to us here? They lend credence to the search–experience goods dichotomy because they indicate a lack of full, objectively applied knowledge in the consumer's purchase of experience goods. In fact, one of the more interesting implications of this dichotomy concerns the relationship between price and product quality. Given the prepurchase evaluation possibilities of search goods, we ought to expect a strong positive correlation between their price level and brand or model quality. For a given product, low quality should sell only at a low price, whereas high quality should justifiably bring a high price. In contrast, the correlation between the price and brand quality of experience goods might be low, since, as we have seen, brands of these commodities are often selected on the basis of unreliable cues and the pull of prior purchase. Such correlations were computed for 35 products by Alfred Oxenfeldt, using Consumer's Union brand evaluation scores and price data. Results for the eight products with highest correlation (maximum possible is +1.0) and the eight products with lowest correlation (lowest possible is −1.0) are presented in Table 4–2. Notice that the eight products having highest correlation are all search goods, whereas seven of the eight products having lowest correlation could be considered experience goods (the single possible exception being men's hosiery).[12] Similar data are not available for producers' goods, but the reader can decide for himself whether producers' goods markets would have a better record than this.

Although these data further indicate that the four-part scheme of Table 4–1 is informative, the scheme does have one major shortcoming: it oversimplifies reality. Many, if not most, products have a blend of search and experience features, precluding any neat, clear-cut assignment to a search or experience

Journal of Marketing Research (May 1974), pp. 164–171; J. L. Ginter, "An Experimental Investigation of Attitude Change and Choice of a New Brand," _Journal of Marketing Research_ (February 1974), pp. 30–40.

[11] Rolph E. Anderson, "Consumer Dissatisfaction: The Effect of Disconfirmed Expectancy on Perceived Product Performance," _Journal of Marketing Research_ (February 1973), pp. 38–44; R. W. Olshavsky and J. A. Miller, "Consumer Expectations, Product Performance, and Perceived Product Quality," _Journal of Marketing Research_ (February 1972), pp. 19–21; and R. L. Oliver, "A Theoretical Reinterpretation of Expectation and Disconfirmation Effects on Postexposure Product Evaluations: Experience in the Field" _Consumer Satisfaction and Complaining Behavior,_ edited by R. L. Day (Bloomington: Indiana University School of Business, 1977), pp. 2–9.

[12] More recent computations of correlations consider only experience goods, apparently because most goods are experience goods. R. T. Morris and C. S. Bronson find a mean correlation of + .29 for a sample of 48 diverse products ("The Chaos of Competition Indicated by Consumer Reports," _Journal of Marketing_ (July 1969), pp. 26–34. Peter Riesz finds a mean correlation of only + .09 for a sample of 40 packaged food products ("Price Quality Correlations for Packaged Food Products", _Journal of Consumer Affairs_ (Winter 1979), pp. 236–247). Among the negatives in these studies are vacuum cleaners (− .66), household detergents (− .28), and frozen pizza (− .44). On consumer efficiency see also E. S. Maynes and T. Assum, "Informationally Imperfect Consumer Markets: Empirical Findings and Policy Implications," _Journal of Consumer Affairs_ (Summer 1982), pp. 62–87.

TABLE 4–2. Coefficients of Rank Correlation Between Brand Quality Score and Brand Price

Product	Number of Brands Tested	Coefficient of Rank Correlation
Top eight products		
Boys' blouses (shirt type)	8	0.82
Men's hats	30	0.76
Women's slips (knitted)	28	0.75
Mechanical pencils	26	0.71
Women's slips (other than knit)	67	0.70
Men's shoes	52	0.70
Diapers, gauze	11	0.57
Children's shoes	8	0.55
Bottom eight products		
Yellow, white, and spice mixes	9	−0.11
Mayonnaise	25	−0.13
Men's hosiery (wool)	9	−0.20
Vacuum cleaners	17	−0.26
Biscuit mixes	10	−0.46
Hot roll mixes	3	−0.50
Waffle mixes	3	−0.50
Gingerbread mixes	6	−0.81

Source: Alfred R. Oxenfeldt, "Consumer Knowledge: Its Measurement and Extent," *Review of Economics and Statistics* (October 1950), p. 310.

good category. Under strict categorization, almost all consumer goods would be experience goods. In addition, numerous product characteristics besides hidden versus observable qualities and buyer type influence differentiability. These other characteristics determine the potency of several specific causes of differentiation—advertising, styling, and packaging. Hence we turn next to these specific causes and these other characteristics.

II. ADVERTISING AS A CAUSE

A. Advertising and the Four-part Classification

The four-part classification of products and buyers predicted that advertising expenditures as a percentage of sales would be lowest for producer search goods and highest for consumer experience goods, with the remaining two classes falling in between. As a beginning to our discussion of advertising, let's look at some numbers that illustrate these relationships. Table 4–3 presents advertising/sales ratios for 24 broadly defined industries, each of which fits fairly neatly into one of the four classes outlined in Table 4–1. Advertising intensity is indeed

TABLE 4–3. Advertising Outlays as a Percentage of Sales By Broad Market Categories, 1981

Producer search goods		Producer experience goods	
Metals-mining	0.5	Engines & turbines	0.7
Crude petroleum	0.1	Farm machinery	1.2
Lumber and wood products	0.4	Electronic computing equip.	1.1
Flat glass	0.2	Semiconductors	1.6
Office furniture	0.9	Industrial meas. instruments	1.7
Iron & steel foundaries	0.2	Data processing services	0.9
Average 0.4%		*Average 1.2%*	
Consumer search goods		**Consumer experience goods**	
Greeting cards	2.2	Books publishing-printing	4.7
Apparel	2.7	Beer	6.9
Footwear	3.0	Soap and detergents	7.1
Meat products	2.1	Radio and TV sets	2.7
Household furniture	1.9	Canned fruits and vegs.	4.2
Retail foodstores	1.1	Hotel-motels	2.6
Average 2.2%		*Average 4.7%*	

Source: *Advertising Age,* August 2, 1982, p. 41.

lowest for the producer search goods of Table 4–3, followed next by producer experience goods. The overall average for all listed producers' goods is 0.8% of sales revenue. In contrast, the overall average for all listed consumers' goods is over four times greater, at 3.5%. Most of this difference is attributable to the consumer experience goods category, which obviously contains the highest outlay ratios in the table.

Comparing all search goods with all experience goods, the averages are 1.3% and 2.95%, respectively. These data do not prove our earlier assertions concerning products and buyers. They are too sketchy to serve as proof. But they are suggestive.

B. Informative Versus Persuasive Advertising

Earlier, when distinguishing subjective and objective forms of product differentiation, we were careful to say that *exhortative* advertising contributed to subjective forms. What other kind is there? The answer is easy. Much advertising is *informative* and may genuinely increase buyer knowledge rather than detract from it or warp it. Indeed, informative advertising may convert experience qualities into search qualities and make consumers more like professional buyers.

The next question is much tougher to answer but unavoidable: How much advertising is beneficially informative and how much is merely persuasive? Defenders of advertising say *all* advertising is informative and none of it is persuasive. Hardboiled critics of advertising say all advertising is persuasive, or at least intended to be such, and none of it is informative. Some say the question cannot be answered because they cannot distinguish between information and persuasion. Finally, some take a middle ground by saying there is no clearcut answer but much of it is informative, providing facts on prices, locations, and availabilities (for example, newspaper classified ads and mail order house catalogs), much of it is purely persuasive (for example, "Coke adds life"), and much of it is a blend of both (for example, the magazine car ad that gives you EPA miles per gallon, an itemization of standard equipment, and a pretty girl sitting in the passenger's seat).

We shall adopt this last view, if only because it seems to be the view held by most folks. In one of the most extensive opinion surveys ever taken, conducted by R. A. Bauer and S. A. Greyser, a large sample of people were asked, first, to press the button on a counter "everytime you see or hear an ad," and, second, to fill out a card for each of these tallied ads that "you consider especially annoying, enjoyable, informative, or offensive." The results indicate that, of the hundreds of ads the average person is exposed to every day, he or she is conscious of only about 76 per day. Of these 76, only 6 of them, or 16%, are sufficiently moving to warrant the completion of a report card. Reactions to the rest were, "So what?" Of the 16% most noteworthy, only 36% (or 5.8% of all tallied ads) were considered "informative" by the respondents.[13]

Of course, the purpose of advertising is not to inform buyers—not in a purely cognitive, unbiased sense anyway. The idea is to sell goods by *influencing* buyers. It will therefore come as no surprise to learn that, when the same survey asked whether "advertising often persuades people to buy things they shouldn't buy," 73% of the respondents agreed. This response corresponds fairly well to earlier polls, taken in 1940 and 1950, that found 80% of those surveyed agreeing that "advertising leads people to buy things they don't need or can't afford."[14]

Although the information quotient for all major media was 36%, the ratings for individual media were quite diverse. The print media, as everyday experience indicates, seem to contain the highest proportions of informative ads, with 59% of especially noteworthy newspaper ads winning this designation in the survey. Magazines were a distant second with 48%, followed by radio with 40% and TV with 31%.[15] Thus, a fuller impression of information content can be gained by considering the distribution of all advertising outlays across the media. These data for 1981 are shown in Table 4–4. The total amount spent during that

---

[13] R. A. Bauer and Stephen A. Greyser, *Advertising in America: The Consumer View* (Boston: Division of Research Graduate School of Business Administration, Harvard University, 1968), pp. 175–183.

[14] *Ibid*, p. 71. See also Helmut Becker, "Advertising Image and Impact," *Journal of Contemporary Business* (Vol. 7, No. 4, 1979), p. 84.

[15] Again, however, these are a very small minority of all counted ads. For an econometric test indicating very little, if any, information content in magazine ads, see L. L. Duetsch, "Some Evidence Concerning the Information Content of Advertising, *American Economist* (Spring 1974), pp. 48–53. On the lack of information in TV advertising see A. Resnik and Bruce Stern, "An Analysis of Information Content in Television Advertising," *Journal of Marketing* (January 1977), pp. 50–53; R. W. Pollay, J. Zaichkowsky, and C. Fryer, "Regulation Hasn't Changed TV Ads Much!," *Journalism Quarterly* (Autumn 1980), pp. 438–446.

TABLE 4–4. United States Advertising Expenditures in 1981 by Media

Medium	Billions of Dollars		Per Cent of Total
Newspapers total	$17.4		28.4
National		2.7	4.4
Local		14.7	24.0
Magazines		3.5	5.8
Farm Publications		0.1	0.2
Television total	12.6		20.6
Network		5.6	9.1
Spot		3.7	6.1
Local		3.3	5.4
Radio		4.2	6.9
Direct mail		8.8	14.3
Business publications		1.8	3.0
Outdoor		0.6	1.1
Miscellaneous		12.1	19.7
Grand Total		61.3	100.0

Source: Reprinted with permission from *Advertising Age* (March 22, 1982), p. 66. Copyright (1982) by Crain Communications, Inc.

year came to over $60 billion, or about 2% of the gross national product. Of this grand total, 37.4% went to newspapers, magazines, and farm and business publications, which entails more information than one who is used to watching TV might suppose. Much direct mail advertising is also fairly rich in information (despite its rude intrusiveness). F. M. Scherer may be on target when he says, "If a horseback generalization must be hazarded, it would be that half of all advertising expenditures cover messages of a primarily informative character, while the other half serve largely to persuade."[16]

Still another way of judging this issue is by product and buyer type. Anyone who has leafed through *Mining Magazine* or *Electrical Review* will conclude that advertising directed toward professional buyers is largely informative. "Because the audience for such advertising is expert," Corwin Edwards explains, "the characteristic advertisement in such publications is of a kind that might persuade an expert: it provides information, avoids garbled treatment of facts, and addresses itself to the reader's intelligence."[17] Alas, this obviously does not hold for most advertising aimed at consumers, but there does seem to be substantial variance across consumer products.

Drawing again from the Bauer–Greyser survey of consumer opinion, the variance across products may be seen in Table 4–5, which includes some data

[16] F. M. Scherer, *Industrial Market Structure and Economic Performance* (Chicago: Rand McNally, 1970), p. 326.

[17] C. D. Edwards, "Advertising and Competition," *Business Horizons* (February 1968), p. 60.

TABLE 4–5. Per Cent of Especially Noteworthy Advertisements Categorized as Being Informative, Enjoyable, Annoying, and Offensive

Industry Classification	Categorization			
	Informative	Enjoyable	Annoying	Offensive
Producer goods				
Agriculture and farming	84	11	5	0
Industrial materials	75	16	9	0
Freight, industrial develop-ment	82	18	0	0
Building materials and equip-ment	64	16	14	6
Consumer-search goods				
Apparel, footwear, accesso-ries	52	25	17	6
Household furnishings	65	23	12	0
Retail and direct-by-mail	62	19	19	0
Horticulture	72	28	0	0
Consumer-experience goods				
Food and food products	31	54	14	1
Toilet goods and toiletries	31	35	31	3
Soaps, cleansers, polishes	28	24	45	3
Smoking materials	8	38	36	18
Confectionary and soft drinks	12	69	17	2
Beer, wine, liquor	5	50	22	23
Automobiles and accessories	48	31	20	1
Drugs and remedies	41	18	36	5

Source: R. A. Bauer and S. A. Greyser, *Advertising in America: The Consumer View* (Boston: Harvard University, 1968), pp. 296–97.

on producers' goods as well as consumers' goods because a number of the consumers surveyed were also producers (that is, businessmen). This table shows, for individual product groups, the distribution of especially noteworthy ads (as explained above) across the four categories of noteworthiness. It is easy to see that respondents were most often impressed by the informative nature of producer goods ads and, to a slightly lesser extent, consumer search goods ads. Moreover, in only a relatively few instances were these ads considered annoying or offensive. By stark contrast, ads promoting most consumer experience goods were apparently not very informative. They often gained noteworthy status on other counts, but these other counts seem more clearly associated with persuasive appeals—that is, enjoyable (attention grabbing) and annoying (repetitious). Indeed, the information content of these ads may be overstated by these data because respondents frequently labeled an ad "informative" on grounds that they "felt they were in the situation," they "wanted to buy the product," or they "used the product," all of which reasons fall outside the realm of what could justifiably be considered informative.[18]

A plausible explanation for this large difference between search goods and experience goods advertising rests on the prepurchase evaluation that can be made of search goods. If the advertised properties of search goods stray too far from their actual properties, consumers are readily able to detect the discrepancies and penalize the promoters with refusals to buy. Advertisers of these products therefore feel constrained to use a more informative approach. They have relatively little use for exaggeration, humor, sex, jingles, plays on insecurity, and cajolery, all of which may be found in the tool boxes of experience goods advertisers.[19] Recalling the advertising expenditures data of Table 4–3, we can postulate a rather interesting conclusion: advertising intensity and information content are *inversely* related. Generally speaking, the greater the dollar outlay relative to product sales, the lower is the information content of the advertising messages.[20] Furthermore, in terms of adequate amounts and efficient applications of buyer knowledge, it seems that advertising is *least* informative where the need for information is greatest (consumer experience goods), whereas it is *most* informative where the need for information is least (producer search goods).[21] This paradox makes it clear that the purpose of advertising is *not* to inform buyers; it is to gain sales by influencing buyers.

C. Advertising and Persuasion

Economists have no theories of how consumers' tastes change or how persuasion works, but most academic social psychologists and many marketing experts earn their daily bread by conjuring up such theories and testing them empirically. Since this is an economics book, we can do little more than touch on these theories and research and refer readers who have an interest in pursuing the subject further to a few surveys of this vast, yet fascinating, literature.[22] Our purpose is to determine the degree to which various products may be differentiated, although we shall now confine our attention to products lying within the broad consumer experience category. As we have seen, subjective differentiation and exhortative advertising are most significant for that group of goods.

---

[18] Bauer and Greyser, *op. cit.*, p. 203.

[19] P. Nelson, "Advertising as Information," *op. cit.*, p. 730.

[20] Alfred Arterburn and John Woodbury, "Advertising, Price Competition and Market Structure," *Southern Economic Journal* (January 1981), pp. 763–775.

[21] See T. Scitovsky, *Welfare and Competition* (Homewood Ill.: Richard D. Irwin, Inc., 1951), Chapter XVIII, for an elaboration of this point.

[22] P. Zimbardo and E. B. Ebbesen, *Influencing Attitudes and Changing Behavior* (Reading, Mass.: Addison-Wesley, 1969); H. C. Triandis, *Attitude and Attitude Change* (New York: John Wiley & Sons, 1971); M. Fishbein and I. Aizen, *Belief, Attitude, Intention and Behavior: An Introduction to Theory and Research* (Reading, Mass.: Addison-Wesley, 1975); R. L. Applbaum and K. W. E. Anatol, *Strategies for Persuasive Communication* (Columbus, Ohio: Chas. E. Merrill Publishing Co., 1974); G. R. Miller and M. Burgoon, *New Techniques of Persuasion* (New York: Harper & Row, 1973); and S. H. Britt, *Psychological Principles of Marketing and Consumer Behavior* (Lexington, Mass.: Lexington Books, 1978).

Before discussing specific subcategories of these products, however, we should clarify our use of the word "persuasion" by reviewing briefly several thoroughly tested, well-established exhortative advertising techniques that are now commonly used to promote most consumer goods:

• There will be more opinion change in the desired direction if the communicator has high credibility than if he has low credibility, where credibility is expertise and trustworthiness. Thus, regarding expertise, race drivers sell oil, singers sell Memorex tape, a washer repairman sells Maytag, and so on.

• Present one side of the argument when the audience is generally friendly, but present both sides or present comparisons when the audience starts out disagreeing with you. Thus, number one selling brands very rarely mention competing products, but Avis is No. 2 to Hertz, so it tries harder; B. F. Goodrich touts its lack of a blimp; and so on.

• A person's opinions and attitudes are strongly influenced by groups to which he belongs and wants to belong. Athletes and entertainers therefore give testimonials for everything under the sun. You drink Pepsi if you want to join the Pepsi generation, and so on.

• Repeating a communication tends to prolong its influence and slight variations of the repetition are advantageous. Thus, how many ways has Miller "Lite" said "It's less filling"? Would you like a dime for every time you've heard that "Coke Is It"?[23]

Of course persuasive techniques are not sure-fire. People are not led around by rings in their noses, at least not most of them nor most of the time. And some consumer experience goods are more promotion prone than others. Among the various product characteristics that determine the effectiveness of exhortative advertising, the following seem particularly important:[24]

1. The degree of interest or "involvement" people have in relation to the product.
2. The presence of powerful emotional buying motives, like health, romance, and safety.

---

[23] This list borrows heavily from Zimbardo and Ebbesen, *op. cit.,* pp. 20–23. See also J. E. Weber and R. W. Hansen, "The Majority Effect and Brand Choice," *Journal of Marketing Research* (August 1972), pp. 320–323; A. G. Sawyer, "The Effects of Repetition of Refutational and Supportive Advertising Appeals," *Journal of Marketing Research* (February 1973), pp. 23–33; J. L. McCullough and T. M. Ostrom "Repetition of Highly Similar Messages and Attitude Change," *Journal of Applied Psychology* (June 1974), pp. 395–397; and Leo Bogart, *Strategy in Advertising* (New York: Harcourt, Brace & World, Inc., 1967). For the most persuasive direct mail techniques see *Fortune,* April 21, 1980, pp. 117, 121. On the role of music see G. J. Gorn, "The Effects of Music in Advertising on Choice Behavior: A Classical Conditioning Approach," *Journal of Marketing* (Winter 1982), pp. 94–101.
[24] One of the earliest such listings is that of Neil Borden, *The Economic Effects of Advertising* (Chicago: Richard D. Irwin Publishers, 1942), pp. 424–428.

3. The perceived risk of getting stuck with a "lemon," especially one that's high-priced.

4. The frequency of purchase and growth of demand.

1. Interest and Involvement. How interested are you in salt? Do you get involved when reading an ad for weed killer? Probably not. On the other hand, what about stereos or cars? When one's interest in a product is high, one is obviously more likely to read magazine ads or pay attention to TV "spots" about the product than otherwise. Hence, because audience attention is a prerequisite to exhortation, high-interest products seem more promotion prone than low-interest products.[25]

A survey designed to test interest and involvement across various products found that the products of greatest interest to men seem to be new cars and pain and tension relievers. In contrast, women seem to be most interested in packaged mixes, canned vegetables, coffee, make-up, and washers. (Women, wives especially, are also more interested in life insurance than are men.)

These differences by sex explain why advertisers try to aim their messages at appropriate segments of the population. When the responses of both sexes are added together, the top two ranked products turn out to be cars and pain and tension relievers.[26] Unfortunately, the products included in the questionnaire were limited to those that are commonly advertised in newspapers, so we do not have involvement scores for products that are heavily advertised in other media such as TV. Nevertheless, it does appear from these data that high interest is positively associated with voluminous advertising.

2. Emotional Connotations. Some products naturally lend themselves to strong emotional appeals like health (drugs, vitamins, toothpaste, for example), sex and romance (perfumes, cosmetics, mouthwash), safety (smoke detectors, tires, shock absorbers), and security (travelers' checks, insurance). The implications of having the opportunity to exploit these appeals should be obvious to the reader, for they make the job of persuasion easier and more profitable. What is probably not so obvious is the subtlety and sophistication with which these opportunities can be exploited.[27] The persuasive power of sex, for instance, does not work equally well across all products. Nor is sex appeal simply a matter of getting a bikini-clad girl into the picture.[28]

---

[25] H. E. Krugman, "The Measurement of Advertising Involvement," *Public Opinion Quarterly* (Winter 1966–67), pp. 583–596.

[26] *A Study of the Opportunity for Exposure to National Newspaper Advertising,* Supervised by the Bureau of Advertising, ANPA, for the Newsprint Information Committee, 1965.

[27] On the use of fear see B. Sternthal and C. S. Craig, "Fear Appeals: Revisited and Revised," *Journal of Consumer Research* (December 1974), pp. 22–34. On the use of sex see Myers and Reynolds, *op. cit.,* pp. 91–93, and Zimbardo and Ebbesen, *op. cit.,* pp. 34–38.

[28] R. N. Kanungo and S. Pang, "Effects of Human Models on Perceived Product Quality," *Journal of Applied Psychology* (April 1973), pp. 172–178; *Wall Street Journal,* November 18, 1980, pp. 1+19.

3. Perceived Risk Inherent in the Purchase. The purchase and consumption of most products involves certain risk—the risk of financial loss from product failure, the risk of embarrassment before the eyes of friends and, still more important, the risk of injury or property damage. Generally speaking, it appears that the persuasive influence of advertising is greatest when perceived risk is low.[29] Advertising tends to work best, therefore, for products that are low in price, low in obvious physical danger, and low in "importance" to the consumer. According to one study, for example, advertising induced twice as much brand switching among household food wraps as it did for ground coffee, and the housewives involved in the study thought that the proper choice of coffee was much more "important" than the proper choice of wrap.[30] As regards price, consumers apparently do not weigh price differences very carefully when prices are low, enabling promoters to induce purchase on nonprice grounds.

4. Purchase Frequency and Sales Growth. High purchase frequency (as with milk, margarine, and bread) implies greater consumer knowledge about the product than low purchase frequency (as with most durables). Moreover, other things being equal, frequently purchased items tend to gobble up large portions of one's budget, provoking greater price consciousness among consumers. For these several reasons, high frequency of purchase is likely to lessen the effectiveness of exhortative advertising and other nonprice promotional efforts.

Going from the extreme of frequently purchased, well-established products to the other of relatively new, never-before-purchased products provides an interesting contrast. Rapidly growing product sales usually stem from a relatively quick accumulation of new users of the product or new uses for the product, or both. Thus, rapid growth provides a fertile field for advertising because advertising may effectively "spread the news," encouraging these conversions and new applications. Of course, intensive advertising may *cause* rapid growth as well as *be caused* by it. Much the same could be said of some of the other factors outlined previously. (Thus, a prime function of advertising is to stimulate interest in products and reduce perceived risk—which implies that high "product interest" and low perceived risk may be as much effects of intensive advertising as they are causes of it.) Still, the important point to be made here is that newness or growth generally improves the persuasive possibilities of advertising, just as do high product interest, strong emotional ties, low risk, low price, and relatively infrequent purchase patterns.

---

[29] J. A. Barach, "Advertising Effectiveness and Risk in the Consumer Decision Process," *Journal of Marketing Research* (August 1969), pp. 314–320; T. Levitt, "Persuasibility of Purchasing Agents and Chemists: Effects of Source, Presentation, Risk, Audience Competence, and Time," in Cox (ed.), *Risk Taking and Information Handling in Consumer Behavior, op. cit.*, pp. 541–558; and L. G. Schiffman "Perceived Risk in New Product Trial by Elderly Consumers," *Journal of Marketing Research* (February 1972), pp. 106–108.

[30] Barach, *op. cit.*

TABLE 4–6. Advertising Outlay of Selected Firms, 1980

Rank in Terms of Dollars Spent	Firm	Main Product Area	Millions of Dollars Spent	Advertising as a Per Cent of Sales
1	Procter & Gamble	Soaps, paper, food	$650	5.7%
2	Sears, Roebuck	Retailing	600	2.4
3	General Foods	Foods	410	6.2
4	Philip Morris	Tobacco, beer	365	3.7
5	Kmart Corp.	Retailing	319	2.2
6	General Motors	Autos	316	0.5
7	R. J. Reynolds Industries	Tobacco, foods	298	2.9
8	Ford Motors	Autos	280	0.8
9	AT&T	Telephones	259	0.5
10	Warner-Lambert	Toiletries, cosmetics	235	6.8
12	PepsiCo	Soft drinks	233	3.9
13	Colgate-Palmolive	Soaps, cleansers	225	9.4
17	Bristol-Myers	Toiletries, cosmetics	196	6.2
19	Esmark	Foods	190	6.4
21	Anheuser-Busch	Beer	181	4.7
31	Gillette	Toiletries, razors	151	6.5
33	Nabisco	Foods	150	5.8
38	Richardson-Vicks	Drugs	134	11.1
41	Chesebrough-Ponds	Toiletries, cosmetics	128	9.3
51	Kellogg Co.	Foods	96	4.4

Source: Reprinted with permission from *Advertising Age,* September 10, 1981, p. 8. Copyright (1981) by Crain Communications Inc.

D. Advertising Data by Company

Taken together, the several factors discussed in the preceding section help to explain why some firms advertise more heavily than others.[31] Table 4–6 shows total dollar outlay and advertising as a percentage of sales for some of the top advertisers in the United States. By both measures of intensity, the

[31] P. W. Farris and R. D. Buzzell, "Why Advertising and Promotional Costs Vary: Some Cross-Sectional Analyses," *Journal of Marketing* (Fall 1979), pp. 112–122; M. M. Metwally, "Product Categories that Advertise Most," *Journal of Advertising Research* (February 1980), pp. 25–31.

leaders are manufacturers of soaps and cleansers, drugs and cosmetics, tobacco, foods, and liquor. Auto firms rank high in total expenditures but low in costs relative to sales. Since the latter measure is economically the more meaningful, autos may be considered moderately advertised, perhaps because of their high-price, high-risk character. (On the other hand, outlay per individual prospective car buyer is substantial.) Although not mentioned in the table, sellers of gum and candy are also among the top.

III. OTHER CAUSES OF DIFFERENTIATION

Data about causes of differentiation other than advertising are not recorded accurately enough to support a detailed discussion of their use or impact. Nevertheless, a few words about these other influences are appropriate.

A. Style and Image

Products and brands are often purchased not only for their functional qualities but for the favorable impression they make (or presumably will make) on other people. Fashion and style serve "as an outward emblem of personal distinction or of membership in some group to which distinction is ascribed."[32] Sociologists call this "reference-group" influence. And it has been observed that: "The conspicuousness of the product is perhaps the most general attribute bearing on its susceptibility to reference group influence: (1) The item must be one that can be seen and identified by others; (2) it must be conspicuous in the sense of standing out and being noticed—i.e., no matter how visible the product is, if everyone owns one, it is not conspicuous in the second sense."[33]

Among the most obvious products fitting the style and image category are clothes, cars and furniture, all of which are subject to style variation. Less obvious are cigarettes, beer, liquor, and magazines. Advertisers of these products are advised to stress the kinds of people who buy the product or brand, "reinforcing and broadening, where possible, the existing stereotypes of users."[34] For less conspicuous products, like laundry soap, canned foods, and weed killer, where "neither product nor brand appear to be associated strongly with group influences, advertising should emphasize the product's attributes, intrinsic qualities, price, and advantages over competing products."

B. Packaging and Brand Name

Packaging affects appearance, convenience in storage or use, shelf-life, waste disposal, safety, brand image, and, consequently, sales. Four examples will suffice:

- The Color Research Institute asked housewives to test a single (identical) detergent packaged in three differently colored boxes—one blue, one brilliant

[32] D. E. Robinson, "The Economics of Fashion Demand," *Quarterly Journal of Economics* (August 1961), p. 380.
[33] S. H. Rewoldt, J. D. Scott, and M. R. Warshaw, *Introduction to Marketing Management* (Homewood, Ill.: R. D. Irwin, Inc., 1973), p. 123.
[34] *Ibid,* p. 125.

yellow, one a mix of blue and yellow. After several weeks the housewives reported that one was too weak (blue), one too strong (yellow), and one was just right (the combination).[35]

• Kraft salad dressing formerly came in cylindrical bottles; however, Wishbone enjoyed great success with its wide-bottom flask bottle, partly because it gave Wishbone more "shelf facings" than Kraft's. Hence, Kraft had to copy.[36]

• In a survey test, consumers were shown two identical items—one packaged, the other not—and were asked to estimate their price. The packaged items were always judged to sell at a higher price than the unpackaged ones.[37]

• Smokers believe that low-tar cigarettes taste stronger if they come in a red pack instead of a white pack.[38]

Needless to say, brand names are also influential, especially for perfumes, cosmetics, drugs, autos, paper products, snack foods, pet foods, and other consumer experience goods. Because thousands of new products are introduced annually, the business of concocting clever new names has become a cottage industry.[39] The perfume "Opium" illustrates that success sometimes rests largely on name alone.[40]

C. Location and Retailing[41]

In retailing we find differentiation in the clerk's friendly smile, the breadth of product selection, the services offered, the availability of credit, and the convenience of store location. Of these, location is often the most important, and its effect depends crucially on the kinds of goods being retailed. Thus one last distinction is needed: that between convenience goods and shopping goods. The distinction is based primarily on frequency of purchase and product price because **convenience goods** are relatively inexpensive items that people buy regularly, such as food, cigarettes, beverages, drugs, and gasoline. **Shopping goods,** on the other hand, are more costly and more intermittently purchased—appliances, stereos, autos, furniture, and apparel, for example. Locating close to consumers has obvious advantages for convenience goods retailers, since consumers value their time and transportation expenses. Convenience may be so important that some retailers (the back-road neighborhood gas station, and the "7–11" store around the corner) may *specialize* in convenience, extracting a price premium from those consumers who particularly favor ease of access.

[35] V. Packard, *The Hidden Persuaders* (New York: David McKay Co., 1957), pp. 16–17.
[36] W. P. Margulies, *Packaging Power* (New York: World Publishing Co., 1970), p. 59.
[37] P. G. Scotese, "The Retail Level," in *Creative Pricing* edited by E. Marting (American Marketing Association: 1968), pp. 110–111.
[38] *Wall Street Journal,* February 29, 1980, p. 10.
[39] *Wall Street Journal,* August 5, 1982, p. 21.
[40] *Wall Street Journal,* February 5, 1980, p. 18.
[41] This section borrows from L. W. Weiss, *Economics and American Industry* (New York: John Wiley & Sons, 1961), pp. 392–394.

Thus, food stores, gas stations, and drug stores dot the landscape here and there; however, shopping goods retailers tend to be clustered closer together in the heart of town, along major thoroughfares, or in large shopping centers. Such clustering enables people who are "in the market" for a new car, stereo, washing machine, or suit of clothes to shop around before they buy, comparing prices, terms, styles, service facilities, and so forth. Moreover, at least *in theory*, such comparison shopping could cause price elasticity of demand for each one of these retailers to exceed that confronting individual convenience goods retailers. In the course of shopping for a "big ticket" item, people could become sufficiently price conscious to suffer a little inconvenience willingly if it produced substantial price savings. In fact, this is not true of a substantial number of consumers. Survey evidence indicates that many consumers visit only one seller for shopping goods as well as for convenience goods. For such major items as new cars, television sets, refrigerators, washing machines, and so on, approximately half of all buyers surveyed said they went to only one store, the one where they made their purchase.[42] This statistic does not necessarily imply that price elasticity at shopping goods retailers is low or that they do not compete in price offerings. All it takes to raise elasticity and encourage price rivalry among retailers is for them to face a measurable, though not necessarily dominant, contingent of price conscious buyers. Still, this statistic does suggest that even shopping goods retailers may have some leeway to use location as a means of differentiating their "product."

Finally, it is important to note that this distinction between convenience goods and shopping goods affects more than just store location. It also affects the retailer's *contribution* to the differentiation of the *specific brands* he sells. In the case of convenience goods, retailers typically offer little or no sales assistance, repair service, or other help. Moreover, the low price and frequent purchase of these goods make "in-store" information search by consumers rather costly relative to the potential benefits. Buyers therefore enter convenience stores "presold," and the retailer's contribution to specific brand differentiation is slight. This places the major burden of building brand image and preselling on the manufacturer.

The contrast in the case of shopping goods is notable. Retailers of these products do offer sales assistance, demonstrations, credit, repair service, delivery service, and so on—each of which greatly affects brand differentiation. Then too, the consumer in this case considers the purchase relatively important and expensive, an attitude that boosts the potential benefits of his or her in-store information search. All this adds up to the retailer of shopping goods having considerably more power over brand differentiation than the retailer of convenience goods has. And manufacturers cannot presell shopping goods as readily as they can convenience goods.

[42] Frederick E. May, "Buying Behavior: Some Research Findings," *Journal of Business* (October 1965), p. 391, and the references therein. See also J. W. Newman and R. Staelin, "Prepurchase Information Seeking for New Cars and Major Household Appliances," *Journal of Marketing Research* (August 1972), pp. 249–257.

These distinctions have been emphasized by Michael Porter, who has also demonstrated their empirical importance.[43] We shall return to Porter's work later. For now, we merely need note that he found manufacturer's average advertising as a percentage sales to be 4.7% for 19 convenience goods industries, and 2.1% for 23 shopping goods industries. This comparison together with the factors discussed earlier, may help to explain why, in Table 4–6, the advertising/sales ratios of auto manufacturers tend to be relatively low.

SUMMARY

A general class of product is differentiated if nonprice considerations influence the brand and model preferences of buyers. The major effects of successful differentiation give sellers some power over price. That is, differentiation can shift the demand curve outward and also reduce price elasticity of demand. This differentiation may be based on objective features such as quality, warranty, service, location, dimension, and flavor. On the other hand, it may also be based on purely subjective buyer preferences, such as those cultivated by exhortative advertising, styling, brand name connotation, and superfluous packaging variation.

Form and strength of differentiation depend heavily on buyer knowledge, which, in turn, depends on buyer and product characteristics. Professional buyers are much more knowledgeable than consumers, so they are much less susceptible to differentiation, especially its subjective forms. Similarly, the subjective differentiability of search goods is limited by the fact that buyers can readily evaluate the quality of search goods prior to purchase. This is not true of experience goods, whose hidden qualities can be thoroughly evaluated only after purchase. Indeed, it appears that, among consumers, certain psychological effects, such as cognitive dissonance, preclude an objective, thoroughgoing evaluation of these goods even after purchase. As a consequence, consumer experience goods are most prone to subjective differentiation and least prone to efficient purchase.

Among the specific causes of differentiation, advertising predominates. Its intensity is subdued and its content most informative when buyer knowledge is well developed, as in the case of producer search goods. At the other extreme, however, we find billions of dollars being spent for the persuasive promotion of consumer experience goods. The effectiveness of such efforts seems to vary across products within the broad category of consumer experience goods, because such effectiveness is largely determined by numerous product characteristics. Among the most important are (1) consumers' "interest" in the product; (2) the emotional connotations associated with the product—for example, health, romance, safety, and security; (3) perceived risk and absolute price; and (4) frequency of purchase and rate of sales growth.

---

[43] Michael E. Porter, "Consumer Behavior, Retailer Power and Market Performance in Consumer Goods Industries," *Review of Economics and Statistics* (November 1974), pp. 419–436.

Finally, we discussed several probable causes of differentiation other than advertising. Detailed data concerning these other causes are not readily available. Nevertheless, it does appear that style variation, packaging, and location often contribute substantially to differentiation. The distinction between convenience goods and shopping goods largely determines the importance of location. The same distinction also affects the potency of manufacturers' advertising.

5

Product Differentiation: Practice and Policy

Ironically, standards have not been completely standardized.
—DAVID HEMENWAY

Two case studies concerning beer and computers occupy the first third of this chapter. The purpose of these case studies is to pump life into the abstract theory and cross-section evidence of the preceding chapter. The main message they convey is simply this: *Trademarks may serve merely to identify the "origin" of goods, but consumers often go further by relying on trademarks to identify a given level of product quality. This reliance often grants sellers some power over price.*

The last two thirds of this chapter review certain policies that affect product differentiation. These policies are related to the case studies and our previous evidence by the following hypothesis: *If quality identifications could be made independent of trademarks, the market power generated by trademarks would weaken and in some instances even die.* To achieve this independent identification, policies would have to make consumers behave more like professional buyers, or make experience goods more like search goods. In short, buyers must be well informed, or readily informed. And, indeed, these are the broad objectives of such policies as the Fair Packaging and Labeling Act, the Truth in Lending Law, and the grade rating and labeling activities of the U.S. Department of Agriculture, all of which are discussed in this chapter.

There are many other policies relating to product differentiation or product quality besides those concerning information disclosure. We should, therefore, distinguish between the policies of immediate concern and those that prohibit deceptive sales promotion. Policies governing deceptive practices, which are discussed in Chapter 16 under "conduct," are generally *pro*scriptive and negative. They *prohibit* certain types of misleading conduct, such as misrepresentation; however, they do not require sellers to make informative pronouncements. In

[handwritten margin note: trademark & brand names signals certain quality level to the consumer]

75

contrast, the disclosure policies of the present chapter are generally *pre*scriptive and positive; they require disclosures.[1]

I. CASE STUDIES

A. Beer

Legend has it that cockroaches are strongly attracted to beer. Indeed, they will even drown in it if given the chance. The author is a believer. He has built ramps to bowls of brew to give roaches the chance, and they took it. Legend also holds that cockroaches favor certain brands of beer, but the author's experiments do not confirm this. Many folks are like cockroaches in that they, too, are attracted to beer. But they, unlike cockroaches, reveal a substantial degree of brand loyalty, loyalty that is expressed even at the expense of burdening their already overburdened budgets.

What makes this loyalty rather interesting—perhaps even astounding—is the fact that most beer drinkers cannot taste any difference between all but a few brands of American beer. This lack of any "genuine" difference among beers has been demonstrated by numerous researchers in a variety of ways, but all of them rely on one basic approach—the "blind" taste test. One of the most comprehensive of these studies was conducted by R. I. Allison and K. P. Uhl.[2] Their test went through two rounds using five well-known national or regional brands of beer on a sample of 326 who drank beer at least three times a week. Round one was designed to answer these questions:

1. Could beer drinkers, in general, distinguish among various beers in a blind test?
2. Could beer drinkers identify "their" brands in a blind test?

For this purpose each participant tested and evaluated (at their leisure) a six-pack of various unlabeled bottled beers, identified only by lettered tags—AB, CD, EF, GH, and IJ.

Possible scoring ranged from zero, which would be "very poor," to 100, which would be "excellent." On average, *all* beers scored within one point of 64, and there was no significant difference between brands. Thus the first answer is clearly "No." Drinkers cannot, in general, distinguish between brands.

The answer to the second question is found in Table 5–1. There the drinkers are segregated into five groups, depending on which of the five brands they claimed was their usual brand, as shown by the left-hand column. The blind ratings of the beers are presented in the body of the table. Thus, for example, drinkers who claimed EF was "their" brand rated EF at 65.0, but gave CD a

---

[1] For a discussion of this categorization scheme see R. H. Leftwich and A. M. Sharp, *Economics of Social Issues* (Dallas: Business Publications, Inc., 1976), Chapter 7.

[2] R. I. Allison and K. P. Uhl, "Influence of Beer Brand Identification on Taste Perception," *Journal of Marketing Research* (August 1964), pp. 36–39. Another example of this genre is S. H. Rewoldt, J. D. Scott, and M. R. Warshaw, *Introduction to Marketing Management* (Homewood, Ill.: Richard D. Irwin, Inc., 1973) Case 2–1. "Falstaff Brewing Corporation," pp. 177–190.

TABLE 5–1. Drinkers' Loyalty to "Their" Brand in Blind Test (Own Brand Rating on the Diagonal)

Brand Drunk Most Often	Taste Test Ratings by Brand Rated					Own Brand Rates Significantly Higher Than All Others?
	AB	CD	EF	GH	IJ	
AB	67.0	62.4*	57.7*	65.0	65.8	No
CD	64.9	65.6	65.4	63.2	63.9	No
EF	68.8	74.5*	65.0	62.5	61.4	No
GH	55.4	59.2	68.7	60.0	71.4*	No
IJ	68.4	60.5*	69.2	62.0	65.6	No

couldn't distinguish among brands

* Brand significantly different from user's own brand.

Source: R. I. Allison and K. P. Uhl, "Influence of Beer Brand Identification on Taste Perception," *Journal of Marketing Research* (August 1964), p. 38. Reprinted by permission of the American Marketing Association.

rating of 74.5. And those who favored a fully dressed GH gave the nude GH a lowly 60.0 rating, which compared quite unfavorably to their rating of the nude IJ. As indicated by the right-hand column of Table 5–1, the answer to question 2 was negative in every case.

Round two was designed to answer one further question:

3. If the labels were left on, how would they infuence the evaluations of various brands?

For this purpose Allison and Uhl picked up the unlabeled empties and gave each drinker a six-pack of labeled beer to taste and rate in the same fashion as in round one. Table 5–2 reveals these results. The first thing to note is that, generally speaking, the labels seem to have improved the taste of all five beers to all drinkers because the numbers in Table 5–2 usually exceed their

TABLE 5–2. Drinkers' Loyalty to "Their" Brand in Label Test (Own Brand Rating on the Diagonal)

Brand Drunk Most Often	Taste Test Ratings by Brand Rated					Own Brand Rates Significantly Higher?
	AB	CD	EF	GH	IJ	
AB	77.3	61.1	62.8	73.4	63.1	Yes
CD	66.3	83.6	67.4	78.3	63.1	Yes
EF	67.3	71.5	82.3	71.9	71.5	Yes
GH	73.1	72.5	77.5	80.0	67.5	Only over IJ
IJ	70.3	69.3	67.2	76.7	73.5	Only over EF

Source: Allison and Uhl, *op. cit.,* p. 39.

corresponding numbers in Table 5–1 by a substantial margin. Note next that this "improvement" is especially evident in the way the drinkers rated their "own" brands, as revealed by a comparison of the diagonal entries of Tables 5–1 and 5–2. Thus AB devotees boosted their rating of AB by 10.3 points once it was labeled, and the other increments were CD, 18.0 points; EF, 17.3; GH, 20.0; and IJ, 7.9. It is not unreasonable to conclude that drinkers generally rated "their" brand above the others when brand image could prompt their taste buds. Statistically significant divergences in this brand-name "improvement" direction are indicated in the right-hand column of Table 5–2. A similar effect was observed by J. D. McConnell, who in a separate test conducted during the late 1960s observed that beer drinkers claimed to taste quality differences among three "brands" where in fact no quality difference existed. In this case the *same* beer was labeled "P," "L," and "M," which labels were said to be priced $0.99, $1.20, and $1.30 per six-pack, respectively. After 2 months of 24 home deliveries to each drinker, the "high-priced" brand outscored the other two on quality by a wide margin. One drinker said of one of the brands he thought was cheap: "I could never finish a bottle."[3]

This is not to say that *all* brands of beer are identical; or that cheap beer is always the best buy. Still, the evidence indicates that brand image is of utmost importance.[4]

B. Computer Systems

On a number of counts the computer industry is truly remarkable. Few other industries have contributed as much to science fiction. Few have grown as rapidly. And few producer goods industries can match computers in strength of product differentiation. Although product differentiation for most consumer goods seems to be based on advertising, differentiation in the computer industry is based primarily on close customer-manufacturer contacts. As Gerald Brock has written, "The user is not purchasing just a machine but a relationship with a manufacturer":

> Manufacturers often promise an undefined amount of help in getting the installation running, which is difficult to value. Most manufacturers have application programs available, either directly through the manufacturer or through a user's group, and plan upgrades of either the hardware or software within the time the user plans to keep a machine installed. The user's expectations about the characteristics and compatibility of the manufacturer's follow-on line of machines have an important influence on selection . . . his beliefs about the reliability and stability of the manufacturer may be as important or even more important than the actual measured performance and price of the machine being considered.[5]

[3] J. D. McConnell: "The Price-Quality Relationship in an Experimental Setting," *Journal of Marketing Research* (August 1968), pp. 300–303.

[4] For a brief review of other taste tests (covering cola drinks and cigarettes as well as beer) the interested reader should consult J. H. Meyers and W. H. Reynolds, *Consumer Behavior and Marketing Management* (Boston: Houghton Mifflin Co., 1967), pp. 16–19.

[5] Gerald W. Brock, *The U.S. Computer Industry: A Study of Market Power* (Cambridge, Mass.: Ballinger Publishing Co., 1975), p. 46.

TABLE 5–3. IBM Disk Customer Loyalty in the Face of
Competitor's Discounts

Competitive Discount (%)	IBM Customers Remaining with IBM		
	Overall (%)	2319A Users (%)	3330 Users (%)
1–5%	97	99	94
6–10	92	95	88
11–15	70	58	64
16–20	46	37	36
Over 20	31	23	22

Source: G. Brock, *The U.S. Computer Industry: A Study of Market Power* (Cambridge, Mass.: Ballinger Publishing Co., 1975) p. 48. Reprinted by permission.

These observations are particularly apropos of the heart of computer installations—the central processing unit, or CPU. These units are complex, costly, delicate—and IBM's special claim to fame. Indeed, IBM's dominance of this aspect of the business led one industry expert to remark that "IBM doesn't have to sell equipment at the same price-performance ratio as its competitors. . . . Most customers won't take the risk of leaving IBM for less than 30% improvement."[6]

The peripheral equipment of computer systems—such as tape drives and disk memories—may be considered much less differentiable. The choice between IBM and competitive "plug compatible" peripheral equipment is relatively straightforward because rivals have successfully copied IBM's specifications and because no substitution of the complete computer system is involved. Still, even in this simplified situation, IBM enjoys an impressive amount of brand loyalty. To measure the intensity of this loyalty, IBM itself conducted a questionnaire survey of its disk customers in the early 1970s, asking them how much lower competitive disk equipment would have to be priced in order for these customers to switch from IBM to a competitor. As may be seen in Table 5–3, IBM would apparently retain 92% of its customers despite competitive discounts of 10%. Furthermore, almost half of IBM's customers were willing to pass up competitive equipment that was priced as much as 20% below IBM's equipment. It seems, then, that IBM's customers and Budweiser's two-legged clientele share at least two things in common—they are human and they tend to be loyal to their chosen brand.

C. A Bit of Theory

It may seem to the reader that these two groups also have in common a good deal of irrationality, but this is not necessarily so. They may merely be

[6] "Itel's Powerful New Computer," *Business Week* (October 25, 1976), p. 74.

uninformed or misinformed. If after being informed that Brand X and Brand Y are virtually identical, the buyer still chooses the more expensive brand, he might then be considered irrational. Of course the key phrase here is "being informed." Consumers are repeatedly "informed" by advertisements that "they may have to pay a little more but they get *so much* more from Brand X." For this reason many people do not believe (or are not persuaded by) truly objective and authoritative information to the contrary, such as that which might be provided by *Consumer Reports* or the government.[7]

Setting this problem aside, we may conclude these case studies and preface our discussion of public policy with a brief explanation of the monetary benefits of correct information and rational action.[8] In essence, benefits arise from *error avoidance.* So much is obvious. Less obvious is the fact that there are two types of errors to be avoided—errors of commission and omission.

An **error of commission** occurs when the buyer makes a purchase on the basis of an excessively favorable prepurchase assessment of the acquired good. In other words, the buyer gets not what he thinks he is getting but something less. The monetary loss of making such an error (or the gain from avoiding same) is illustrated in Figure 5–1 as the shaded area ABC. The demand curve $DACD$ refers to what demand would be like if the good were correctly evaluated, whereas $D'BD'$ depicts an erroneously optimistic level of demand. The latter lies to the right of the former since the uninformed buyer wants to buy more at each possible price than he would if he were fully informed. Thus, given a fixed price equal to OP_0 (or constant marginal costs of supply indicated by P_0AB), the consumer buys an excess equal to the difference between Q_1 and Q_2, that is, $Q_1 - Q_2$. The amount he pays for this excess is the area Q_2ABQ_1, price times the excess quantity. However, the *true value* of the extra units amounts only to Q_2ACQ_1, or the trapezoid below A and C. Thus, the difference between dollar outlay Q_2ABQ_1 and true value Q_2ACQ_1 is ABC, the net loss.

---

[7] An intriguing study of this issue is provided by G. Scherhorn and K. Wieken (S & W) of West Germany. Despite the fact that all heavy duty laundry detergents are pretty much the same, S & W found that seven-eighths of a large sample of German housewives bought expensive detergents because of "preferences resulting from misinformation about quality." Only one eighth had "no preferences for certain brands . . . or brand name detergents in general." Having thus identified the true believers, S & W then sent them a large amount of authoritative but readable "counterinformation," which explained why most detergents were alike and why they were wasting money on the expensive brands. Follow-up interviews disclosed that only 55% of the housewives were "generally convinced by the counterinformation that all detergents tend to meet the same standards of quality," and only "⅓ of the buyers interviewed were ready to buy the detergent which was actually the cheapest." G. Scherhorn and K. Wieken, "On the Effect of Counter-Information on Consumers," in *Human Behavior in Economic Analysis,* edited by B. Strumpel, J. Morgan, and E. Zahn (San Francisco: Jossey-Bass Inc., 1972), pp. 421–431.

[8] This section draws heavily from S. Peltzman, "An Evaluation of Consumer Protection Legislation: The 1962 Drug Amendments," *Journal of Political Economy* (Sept./Oct. 1973) pp. 1049–1091; T. McGuire, R. Nelson, and T. Spavins, "Comment on the Peltzman Paper," *Journal of Political Economy* (June 1975), pp. 655–661; M. R. Darby and E. Karni, "Free Competition and the Optimal Amount of Fraud," *Journal of Law and Economics* (April 1973), pp. 67–88; George Akerlof, "The Market for 'Lemons': Quality Uncertainty and the Market Mechanism," *Quarterly Journal of Economics* (August 1970), pp. 488–500; and R. H. Nelson, "The Economics of Honest Trade Practices," *Journal of Industrial Economics* (June 1976), pp. 281–293.

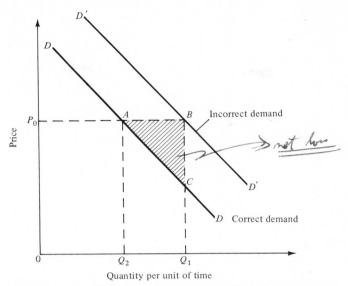

FIGURE 5–1. The monetary loss from an error of commission.

Errors of omission are the opposite. They occur when the buyer buys *less* than he would with full knowledge. The monetary loss from making such an error is illustrated in Figure 5–2 by the area *GHE*. In this case the demand curve *D' GED'* depicts what the demand would be like if the commodity were correctly evaluated, whereas *DHD* represents the erroneously pessimistic demand of buyers who underestimate the value of the product. Given a constant price P_0, a corrective movement from the poorly chosen amount Q_1 to the proper amount Q_2 requires an additional cash outlay equal to area Q_1HEQ_2. But the move yields a greater addition to total benefit, indicated by Q_1GEQ_2. Subtracting the added cost from this added benefit yields a *net* benefit of *HGE*, which in technical jargon is the amount of "consumer's surplus" the consumer misses out on when he errs in the direction of omission. It may now be seen that errors of omission lead to *under*allocations of resources to the particular products or brands, whereas errors of commission lead to *over*allocations to the chosen products or brands. Needless to say, both forms of error are *mis*allocations, and they often represent opposite sides of the same coin. When someone overspends on sugary snacks, for instance, he probably also underspends on nutritious meals.[9]

The next question is: What policies can assist buyers in avoiding these errors? Incredible though it may seem in light of what has been said to this point, one such policy is the issuance and enforcement of **trademarks.** To see this

[9] For concrete evidence see Tyzoon T. Tyebjee, "Affirmative Disclosure of Nutrition Information and Consumers' Food Preferences: A Review," *Journal of Consumer Affairs* (Winter 1979), pp. 206–223; and G. J. Gorn and M. E. Goldberg, "Behavioral Evidence of the Effects of Televised Food Messages on Children," *Journal of Consumer Research* (September 1982), pp. 200–205.

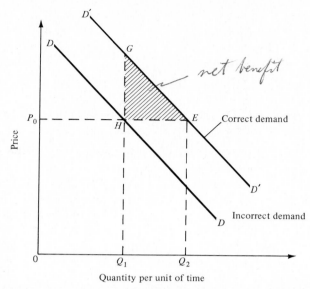

FIGURE 5–2. The monetary loss from an error of omission.

most clearly, the reader might try imagining what the world would be like in the absence of trademarks. Without them how could *Consumer Reports* tell us in March 1981 that Panasonic microwave ovens were better than the Sunbeam brand? Or how could a friend advise us that Levi's trousers are a good buy? How could we be sure that, having been wholly satisfied with an Arrow shirt, we could ever get another one from the same manufacturer? How could we sue the Coca-Cola Company for damages if we found a dead mouse in one of its soda bottles? In other words, it can be argued that, to the extent consumers do learn from experience and to the extent they do learn to buy what they like (rather than like what they buy), trademarks can minimize *repeated* errors merely by identifying good, bad, and mediocre goods and services. Similarly, trademarks are necessary to spreading an individual's or a testing agency's specific knowledge to others. And, finally, in extreme cases of error, individual producers may be held legally as well as economically accountable for their share in any disaster. As Richard Caves and William Murphy have so aptly put it, "By offering the seller's good name as hostage, the trademark provides the buyer with cheap information and assurance about product quality."[10]

---

[10] R. E. Caves and W. F. Murphy II, "Franchising: Firms, Markets, and Intangible Assets," *Southern Economic Journal* (April 1976), pp. 572–586. It may be worth noting that even the Russians use trademarks: "This makes it easy to establish the actual producer of the product in case it is necessary to call him to account for the poor quality of his goods. For this reason it is one of the most effective weapons in the battle for the quality of products . . ." M. I. Goldman, "Product Differentiation and Advertising: Some Lessons From Soviet Experience," *Journal of Political Economy* (August 1960), pp. 346–357. Note too, however, that communists are not always "called to account" in the same manner as capitalists.

Despite these considerable social benefits, the trademark laws as they stand also involve specific *social costs*. Trademark policies are based on the assumption that trademarks serve primarily to identify the *origin* of goods, and that the purposes of such identification are twofold:[11]

1. Protection is furnished the seller from "unfair" competition through the infringement of his mark by an imitator or poacher.
2. Protection is furnished buyers who might be deceived into purchasing the goods of one seller in the belief that the goods are another's.

Unfortunately, this emphasis on origin adds substantially to the social costs of the trademark system without contributing to its social benefits. Benefits derive from the *identification of a given level of quality,* not from the identification of a given origin. Identification of origin on an exclusive, perpetual, and carefully protected basis, as is now practiced, may serve *indirectly* to identify a given level of quality. But it also often facilitates the creation of substantial market power, power that translates into social costs, power achieved by exhortative advertising and other means of questionable social worth. As we shall see more thoroughly later, the available evidence indicates that, when quality guarantees or quality identifications are established independently of trademarks (by professional buyers themselves, by government grade rating and standardization, by consumers search shopping for easily analyzable goods, and so on), monopoly power cannot be based on trademark differentiation and advertising, and burdensome social costs are avoided. The effects of the trademark system are therefore negative when (1) trademarks (and the persuasive advertising promoting them) provide the sole or major source of quality identification for the product *and* (2) grants of exclusive trademark use protect the goodwill (or monopoly) profits that attach to trademarks under such circumstances. Corrective policies should therefore be focused on one or both of the following objectives:

1. Permit trademarks to identify or guarantee quality but remove the rights of exclusivity and perpetuity currently awarded them.
2. Establish quality identifications and guarantees that are *independent* of the trademark system.

With respect to the first, nonexclusive trademark use, Edward Chamberlin once suggested a policy that would permit imitation as long as quality was maintained.[12] Such a policy would, of course, focus the law on identifying quality instead of origin. But this policy is quite radical, and its adoption is unlikely. With respect to the second possible focus of policy, quality identifications and guarantees that are independent of the trademark system, regulations abound. They merit the entire section that follows.

[11] E. W. Kintner and J. L. Lahr, *An Intellectual Property Law Primer* (New York: Macmillan Publishing Co., 1975) p. 250.
[12] Edward H. Chamberlin, *The Theory of Monopolistic Competition,* 8th ed. (Harvard University Press, 1962), p. 273; see also M. L. Greenhut, "Free Entry and the Trade Mark-Trade Name Product," *Southern Economic Journal* (October 1957), pp. 170–181.

II. STANDARDIZATION AND DISCLOSURE

As suggested by the heading "Standardization and Disclosure," information or identification policies other than trademarks may be divided into two categories.[13] And, as suggested by the items listed for each category, the ultimate purpose of these policies is to assist consumers in avoiding errors. They make consumers more like professional buyers and make experience goods more like search goods.

A. Standardization for easier price comparisons
  1. Simplified quantity labeling
  2. Uniform sizes
  3. Price standardization, e.g., "unit" pricing
  4. Warranty standards
B. Quality disclosures
  1. Ingredient disclosure
  2. Open dating of perishables
  3. Specific performance disclosures
  4. Grade rating

Standardization policies typically promote simplification or uniformity or both. The distinction between simplification and uniformity may be seen by an easy example. Suppose ten brick manufacturers were each making the same 50 kinds of brick. Since each producer offered a full range of 50 kinds, each firm's bricks would match those of the others and there would be perfect **uniformity** among sellers. With 50 varieties, however, the situation would not be simple. **Simplification** would be achieved if these firms agreed to cut down the number of their offerings to, say, 12 common types. This would yield a combination of simplification and uniformity—ten firms, each producing the same 12 kinds of brick. Alternatively, simplification could be achieved at the expense of uniformity. If each of the ten brick makers cut back their offerings to four *unique* items, with no one producing the same item, uniformity would disappear. The total, industry-wide variety, however, would have been simplified from 50 down to 40. As far as buyer errors are concerned, uniformity facilitates the comparison of different seller's offerings, whereas simplification may help to keep buyers' minds from boggling.

Quality disclosures are quite different. They sharpen the buyer's awareness of "better" or "worse." For example, all mattress manufacturers may uniformly adhere to a few simple sizes—twin, double, queen, and king. But this says nothing about the range of quality (and some mattresses may feel as if they were made from 50 kinds of brick). Disclosure of ingredients might be helpful in this case, and grade rating would be even more helpful. Policies revealing ingredients and grades may thus be considered quality disclosures.

---

[13] This division and much else in this section owe their origin to David Hemenway, *Industrywide Voluntary Product Standards* (Cambridge, Mass.: Ballinger Publishing Co., 1975).

Before we take a detailed look at specific policies, one more preliminary point needs attention: Why must we rely on the *government* to elevate consumer knowledge and information? What is wrong with relying on free *private* enterprise? If information is a desirable "good," ought not profit opportunities abound for anyone who wants to supply information? The answer to all these questions is, in a word, *imperfections*. The nature of the commodity in question—information—is such that imperfections stand in the way of its optimal provision by private enterprise.

Among the many problems that discourage optimal private provision, two seem paramount. First, sellers of information may face the same problem as the little boy who climbs and shakes the apple tree but gets few of the fallen apples because his buddies on the ground run off with the loot before he can get down. This is "inappropriability," and it often applies to information because information may be spread by means outside the control of the information's original producer—for example, piracy by word of mouth. When a private producer of information is not rewarded in just proportion to the social value of his effort, he extends less effort than is socially optimal. A second and more striking problem arises because buyers of information cannot be truly *well informed* about the information they want to buy. If they were, they would not then need to buy the information.[14] In other words, the seller of information cannot let potential buyers meticulously examine his product prior to sale lest he thereby give it away free. Buyers of information therefore do not know the value of the product they seek (information) until after they buy it. They are consequently vulnerable to errors of commission and omission. Only with objective, outside, nonmarket assistance can they overcome this handicap.

A. Standardization for Easy Price Comparisons

1. Simplified Quantity Labeling. Try this little test on yourself. Which box of detergent is the best buy—25 "jumbo" ounces for 53¢; 1½ pounds for 49¢; or 27½ "full" ounces for 55¢? Prior to the Fair Packaging and Labeling Act of 1966 (FPLA), grocery shoppers took, and failed, real-life tests like this more often than they probably care to remember. In 1965, for instance, a selected sample of 33 married women who were students or wives of students at Eastern Michigan University were asked to pick the most economical package for each of 20 supermarket products. Despite their above-average intelligence and their stimulated attention, these women typically spent 9.14% more on these groceries than they should have.[15] Small wonder they erred, what with the commingling of weight and fluid volumes for the same products; the use of meaningless adjectives, such as "jumbo" and "full"; the frequent appearance of fractional

[14] Kenneth Arrow, "Economic Welfare and the Allocation of Resources for Invention," in *The Rate and Direction of Inventive Activity: Economic and Social Factors* (New York: National Bureau of Economic Research, 1962).

[15] M. P. Friedman, "Consumer Confusion in the Selection of Supermarket Products," *Journal of Applied Psychology* (December 1966), pp. 529–534.

quantity units; and the designation of servings as "small," "medium," and "large," without any common standard of reference.

The Fair Packaging and Labeling Act tidied things up a bit by stipulating:

1. The net quantity be stated in a uniform and prominent location on the package.
2. The net quantity be clearly expressed in a unit of measure appropriate to the product.
3. The net quantity of a "serving" must be stated if servings are mentioned.

This may not seem like much, but FPLA was vigorously opposed by business interests. Some opponents claimed that it was "a power grab based on the fallacious concepts that the consumer is Casper Milquetoast, business is Al Capone, and government is Superman."[16] Their opposition was based on what they apparently thought was a more accurate concept—the housewife as Super-woman. "We suggest," argued the editor of *Food Field Reporter,* "that the housewife . . . should be expected to take the time to divide fractionalized weights into fractionalized prices in order to determine the 'best buy.' "[17] Still others worried about what would happen to the Barbie doll: "Will the package have to say, in compliance with the act's rules, 'One doll, net,' on quantity, and then, on size, '34–21–34'?"[18] Despite such criticism, the FPLA seems to have worked fairly well. The Federal Trade Commission and Food and Drug Administration have encountered problems while enforcing the Act, but nothing insuperable. The problem of what to do with Barbie, for instance, was solved when the Federal Trade Commission declared that she was among the many commodities that were not covered by the Act—toys, chinaware, books, souvenirs, and mouse traps, to name only a few.

2. Uniform Package Sizes. As already suggested, it would be easier for consumers to compare the price per unit of various brands and volumes if sellers adhered to a few common sizes of packaging. Several *nonmandatory* standards emerged from the voluntary sections of FPLA. Dry cereals, for example, are supposed to be packaged in whole ounces only. Jellies and preserves are now supposed to come in sizes of 10, 12, 16, 18, 20, 24, 28, 32, 48, or 64 ounces. However, these voluntary standards do not seem to be very helpful. For more stringent action we must look to state and foreign laws. In the United States, several states have standardized the packaging of bread, butter, margarine, flour, corn meal, and milk. Among foreign countries, Germany, France, England, and Canada have rather extensive mandatory standardization.[19]

---

[16] Michigan Chamber of Commerce, as quoted by R. L. Birmingham, "The Consumer as King: The Economics of Precarious Sovereignty," in *Consumerism,* edited by D. A. Aaker and G. S. Day (New York: Free Press, 1974), p. 186.

[17] A. Q. Mowbray, *The Thumb on the Scale* (New York: J. B. Lippincott Co., 1967), p. 72.

[18] *New York Times,* June 8, 1969.

[19] Committee on Consumer Policy, *Package Standardization, Unit Pricing, Deceptive Packaging* (Paris: Organization for Economic Co-operation and Development, 1975).

3. Price Standardization. Price standardization is an approach still more helpful to consumers than package uniformity and simplification. It may be found in two major forms—unit pricing and truth-in-lending. **Unit pricing** translates all package prices into a price per standard weight or measure, such as 25.3 cents per pound, or 71.4 cents per hundred count. Representing price in this way helps consumers compare prices without superhuman computations. Numerous studies have shown that unit pricing greatly reduces price comparison errors. One such study found that with unit pricing people could pick the least cost item 25% more often than without, and at the same time cut down their shopping time considerably.[20] Extensive national regulations of this type exist only in Germany and Switzerland. In the United States, eleven states have adopted unit-pricing regulations, led by Massachusetts in 1971.[21] Although United States laws thus have restricted application, many grocery stores have voluntarily adopted unit pricing. As a result, it appears that roughly half of all chain-operated supermarkets in the United States and one fourth of all independent supermarkets use unit pricing of some kind.

Of course, retailer adoption and actual consumer use of unit pricing are two different things. Surveys of consumers' use of unit pricing, where it is available, have shown a wide variation of shoppers claiming usage—from 9 to 68%—with an average of only 34%. In accord with the view that the typical shopper is not Superperson, it appears that one reason for this limited reliance on unit pricing is a complete lack of awareness. One study showed that 28% of those not using unit pricing simply didn't know about it. Obviously, limited use also limits the benefits that can be attributed to unit pricing. Thus, one survey estimated that only about 8.8% of observed purchases probably involved the use of unit pricing, and another study concluded that active use saves consumers only about 3% on their grocery bill. Multiplying these two estimates yields an estimated saving of no more than 0.264% on the cost of all purchases. Although this estimate is indeed small, it nevertheless appears to be greater than the costs borne by those retailers who have adopted unit pricing.

Truth-in-lending (TIL) is one form of price standardization that since 1969 has been provided by United States government regulations.[22] However, the scope of these regulations is limited to consumer credit. Before adoption of TIL, numerous studies indicated that only a few people knew how much they actually paid for credit. Two such studies in the 1950s, for instance, indicated that 66–70% of consumers did not have even a vague idea of the annual *percentage rate,* let alone the dollar value, of interest they were paying on their *recent*

---

[20] For a summary of this and other studies see General Accounting Office, *Report to the Congress on Food Labeling: Goals, Shortcomings, and Proposed Changes* (# MWD–75–19) January 1975. This is the main source for this section.

[21] *State Consumer Action: Summary '74,* Office of Consumer Affairs, Department of Health, Education, and Welfare [Pub. No. (OS) 75–116], pp. ix–x.

[22] Material for this topic may be found in *Consumer Credit in the United States,* Report of the National Commission on Consumer Finance (Washington D.C.: U.S. Government Printing Office, 1972) Chapter 10; and *Technical Studies, Vol. I,* of the same Commission, which includes papers by R. P. Shay, M. W. Schober, G. S. Day, and W. K. Brandt.

installment purchases. They almost certainly did not know the interest rates charged by other credit suppliers, information that is, of course, necessary to comparative shopping. Why this vast ignorance? To make a long story short, there was no price standardization in the credit industry. Depending on the method, the price for the same amount of credit might be quoted as being 1%, 7%, 12.83%, or 16%. Indeed, some lenders would not quote *any* rate of charge. They would merely state the number and amount of the monthly payments required.

The purpose of the Truth-in-Lending Law is to let consumers know exactly what the price of credit is and to let them compare the prices of various lenders. Moreover, as argued by the late Senator Paul Douglas: "The benefits of effective competition cannot be realized if the buyers (borrowers) do not have adequate knowledge of the alternatives which are available to them." To achieve these ends the law requires disclosure of two fundamental aspects of credit prices:

1. The *finance charge,* which is the amount of money paid to obtain the credit.
2. The *annual percentage rate,* or **APR**, which provides a simple way of comparing credit prices regardless of the dollar amount charged or the length of time over which payments are made.

From the consumer's viewpoint things are apparently simpler now. Several studies of credit-cost awareness subsequent of TIL have discovered significant improvement in debtor knowledge.

4. Warranty Standardization. The 1975 Magnuson-Moss Warranty-FTC Improvement Act contains a number of requirements for manufacturers regarding standards for written product warranties. For products priced above $15 manufacturers must now specify whether their warranty is "full" or "limited," where:

1. A *full warranty* means that charges for repair or replacement during the warranty period are either minimal or nil.
2. A *limited warranty* limits the seller's obligations, placing more financial responsibility on the consumer.

Moreover, the law holds that the terms and conditions of a written warranty must be stated "in simple and readily understood language." This was in response to consumer complaints that only sober Philadelphia lawyers could understand the language of most product warranties.

Early studies of the impact of this law indicate that its benefits may be rather limited. Apparently, only about 28% of all consumers actually read warranties before making their purchases, so warranty standardization would assist only a minority of consumers in comparative shopping.[23] Moreover, warranties are still very difficult to understand despite the law. Measuring language lucidity

[23] Federal Trade Commission, *Warranties Rules Consumer Baseline Study* (March 2, 1979), p. 129.

by the education level necessary to achieve understanding, one recent study of 125 warranties found that 34% of them were at "college graduate" level and 44% more were at "some college" level. Automobile warranties were found to be especially difficult, generating an average grade level score of 20.2.[24]

It should be noted, however, that the purposes of the Magnuson-Moss Act go well beyond warranty simplification. And in these other respects the Act seems to have been more successful. For instance, there appears to have been some shift from "limited" to "full" warranties, and warranty coverage in terms of duration, scope, and remedies seems to have improved.[25]

B. Quality Disclosures[26]

Critics of the policies mentioned heretofore correctly point out that they simply make price comparisons easier; they do not take into account differences in the *quality* of competing brands or products. Furthermore, some critics assert that these policies cause consumers to *overemphasize* price per unit and *overlook* quality per dollar spent. The latter argument is probably questionable. In any event, the general purpose of the following policies is to help buyers identify quality.

1. Simple Disclosure of Ingredients. The Wool Products Labeling Act of 1939, the Fur Products Labeling Act of 1951, and the Textile Fiber Products Identification Act of 1958 call for the disclosure of ingredients in fur and fiber products. All are enforced by the Federal Trade Commission. Under the first of these, almost all wool products must bear labels showing the percentage of the total fiber weight of "virgin" wool, reprocessed wool, and reused wool. Inclusion of any other fiber must also be identified by generic name (as opposed to trade name) if it exceeds 5% of the total. Similarly, the Fur Act requires fur product labels that disclose the true English name of the animal that grew the fur; the animal's home country if the fur is imported; whether the fur is bleached, dyed, or otherwise artifically colored; and whether it is composed of paws, bellies, scraps, or waste fur. Thus, rabbit cannot be passed off as "Baltic Lion," and sheared muskrat cannot be called "Hudson Seal"—not as long as the FTC's agents stay awake on the job.

Finally, the main purpose of the Textile Act is to reduce confusion that might be caused by the proliferation of manmade chemical fibers and their many trade names. The law requires labels revealing the *generic* names and percentages of all fibers that go into a fabric, except those that constitute less than 5% of the fabric. Thus Dacron, which is a trade name, must be identified as "polyester," its generic name. Over seven hundred other trade names must

[24] F. Kelley Shuptrine and Ellen M. Moore, "Even After the Magnuson-Moss Act of 1975, Warranties Are Not Easy to Understand," *Journal of Consumer Affairs* (Winter 1980), pp. 394–404.

[25] T. Schmitt, L. Kauter, and R. Miller, *Impact Report on the Magnuson-Moss Warranty Act* (Washington, D.C.: Federal Trade Commission, 1980).

[26] For another survey see John A. Miller, "Product Labeling and Government Regulation," *Journal of Contemporary Business* (Vol. 7, No. 4, 1979), pp. 105–121.

be identified as belonging to one of seventeen generic families specified by the FTC. To the extent consumers know the properties of these generic fibers in terms of washing, pressing, dying, and wearing them, the law helps. To the extent consumers do not know, it does not help.

Ingredient labeling regulations for food products has a shorter but more complicated history.[27] Since about 1972 the Food and Drug Administration (FDA) has vigorously expanded its activity in labeling so that detailed disclosures of composition are now required on the labels of most processed food products. The disclosures include:

1. Nutrition information, such as vitamins, minerals, caloric content, carbohydrate content, and protein.
2. Information on cholesterol, fat, and fatty acid composition.
3. Special information on foods intended for infants, nursing mothers, diabetics, the allergic, and the obese.
4. Defining natural and artificial flavors, spices, and colorings.

2. Open Dating. Freshness is obviously an important aspect of the quality of perishable food products. For many years food manufacturers dated their products for inventory control and retailer rotation. Until recently, however, these dates were disguised by codes not known to the public (and often not even known to grocery store managers or clerks). Thus open dating is simply uncoded dating. As of 1980, federal law did not require open dating, but twenty-one states had some form of mandatory open dating with dairy products being the prime target.[28] In addition, many grocery chains have voluntarily adopted it. One problem that remains to be resolved is standardization. "Sell-by" dating is customary, but a confusing variety of other dating methods are also used—"packing date," "expiration date," and so on.

Another form of open dating relates to autos. As of 1975, thirty-seven states had entered the snake pit of used car sales by prohibiting odometer tampering. Thereafter, the federal government also stepped in with passage of the Motor Vehicle Information and Cost Savings Act. This law requires a written, true-mileage disclosure statement at the time of sale for all self-propelled vehicles except those that are over 24 years old or exceed 16,000 pounds. Moreover, the law prohibits disconnecting or resetting the odometer with intent to change the mileage reading or knowingly falsifying the written odometer statement.

3. Specific Performance Disclosures. Beginning with the 1977 models, all new cars sold in the United States have had labels disclosing the estimated number of miles they get per gallon of gas and an estimate of what yearly fuel cost

[27] L. E. Hicks, *Product Labeling and the Law* (New York, AMACOM Division of American Management Associations, 1974).

[28] Congress of the United States, Office of Technology Assessment, *Open Shelf-Life Dating of Food* (Washington, D.C.: August 1979). A study prompting Minnesota's law found that 44% of the baby formula being sold was overage and that since 64% of the store managers could not read a coded date, they could not rotate the stock.

would be if 15,000 miles were traveled per year. Thus, for example, the 1977 Volkswagen Rabbit Diesel, with a 90-cubic-inch engine, was reported to travel 44 miles per gallon and costs $188 in annual fuel expense. By contrast, the 1977 Dodge Royal Monaco with a 440-cubic-inch engine brandished a sticker saying that a standard year's travel in one of them would cost $886, since it averaged only 11 miles per gallon. The Federal Energy Act of 1975 requires these disclosures on the theory that they assist efficiency comparisons and in the hope that car buyers will react to these revelations by shying away from gas guzzlers.

The Federal Energy Act also requires that efficiency ratings appear on major home appliances like refrigerators, freezers, and dishwashers. Administered by the Federal Trade Commission through its rule-making procedures, this program is much more complex than is suggested by the simple energy labels adopted (see Figure 5–3 for a sample).[29] One particularly helpful feature of the label is that it places the appliance on a relative scale, so the shopper need not strain much in making comparisons of energy efficiency. Preliminary study of consumer response to this program indicates its favorable promise.[30]

Another illustration of specific performance disclosure is gasoline octane posting, which has been with us in one form or another since 1973, but only haphazardly enforced. The Federal Trade Commission, which has been the most vigorous advocate of octane-posting; has argued that in the absence of octane-posting, motorists would waste more than $300 million a year by purchasing gasoline with higher octane than they really need. Most people seem to think that higher octane produces greater power. But this is not true. Octane indicates only the anti-knock properties of gasoline. The major brand petroleum companies have persistently opposed octane-posting for fear that it would lead people to recognize that all brands of gasoline of a given octane rating were pretty much alike (which they are).[31]

4. Grade Rating. Disclosures of ingredients, freshness, dimensions, specific performance and the like may guide buyers toward ideal purchasing patterns. But how close to the ideal can these raw data take them? Several recent studies have demonstrated formally what most students already know from informal experience—namely, the information processing capabilities of the human mind are quite limited. Indeed, some evidence even suggests that beyond a certain point additional information may merely confuse and frustrate consumers. Thereafter they no longer move toward their ideal decision, but rather *away* from

---

[29] Federal Trade Commission, Labeling and Advertising of Consumer Appliances (February 1979).

[30] D. L. McNeill and W. L. Wilkie, "Public Policy and Consumer Information: Impact of the New Energy Labels," *Journal of Consumer Research* (June 1979), pp. 1–11.

[31] See *Business Week* (May 31, 1976), p. 21 and F. C. Allvine and J. M. Patterson, *Competition Limited: The Marketing of Gasoline* (Bloomington, Ind.: Indiana University Press, 1972) pp. 24–25. The experience of Germany here is interesting. See Hans and Sarah Thorelli, *Consumer Information Systems and Consumer Policy* (Cambridge, Mass.: Ballinger Publishing Co., 1977), p. 155.

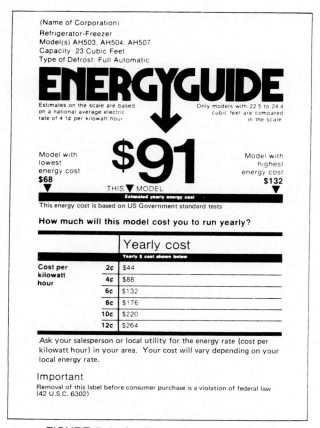

(Name of Corporation)
Refrigerator-Freezer
Model(s) AH503, AH504, AH507
Capacity: 23 Cubic Feet
Type of Defrost: Full Automatic

ENERGYGUIDE

Estimates on the scale are based on a national average electric rate of 4 1¢ per kilowatt hour

Only models with 22 5 to 24 4 cubic feet are compared in the scale

$91

Model with lowest energy cost
$68

Model with highest energy cost
$132

THIS ▼ MODEL

Estimated yearly energy cost

This energy cost is based on US Government standard tests

How much will this model cost you to run yearly?

Cost per kilowatt hour	Yearly cost	
		Yearly $ cost shown below
	2¢	$44
	4¢	$88
	6¢	$132
	8¢	$176
	10¢	$220
	12¢	$264

Ask your salesperson or local utility for the energy rate (cost per kilowatt hour) in your area. Your cost will vary depending on your local energy rate.

Important

Removal of this label before consumer purchase is a violation of federal law (42 U.S.C. 6302)

FIGURE 5–3. Appliance Energy Disclosure

it.[32] Thus grade rating is often recommended as a means of simplifying complex quality information into an ABC format.[33]

The most active federal agency in this respect is the U.S. Department of Agriculture, whose agents grade meat, eggs, butter, poultry, grain, fruits, and vegetables. Beef, for example, is graded "prime," "choice," and "good." This grading is not compulsory. Hence, large brand-name meat packers like Armour, Swift, Morrell, and Wilson are given some elbow room to resist it. They prefer to promote the sale of beef under their own brand names whenever and wherever

[32] J. Jacoby, D. E. Speller, and C. K. Berning, "Brand Choice Behavior as a Function of Information Load: Replication and Extension," *Journal of Consumer Research* (June 1974), pp. 33–42; N. K. Malhotra, A. K. Jain, and S. W. Lagakos, "The Information Overload Controversy: An Alternative Viewpoint," *Journal of Marketing* (Spring 1982), pp. 27–37; N. K. Malhotra, "Information Load and Consumer Decision Making," *Journal of Consumer Research* (March 1982), pp. 419–430.

[33] J. R. Bettman, "Issues in Designing Consumer Information Environments," *Journal of Consumer Research* (December 1975), pp. 169–177.

possible. Among the statistics that reflect past resistance to grading, we find that during the 1950s only 27% of national packer beef was USDA graded, and all but one of the national brand-name packers advocated an end to federal grading. In contrast, the main supporters of the system are independent packers, retail food chains, independent retailers, and consumers. During 1955, for instance, 94% of all beef sold by retail food chains was USDA graded, and 85% of all chains surveyed said they favored compulsory grading or continuation of the present system. These and related data led W. F. Williams, E. K. Bowen, and F. C. Genovese to conclude that:

1. Grade standards have tended to intensify competition.
2. Unbranded packers and wholesalers increased in numbers and volume of meat processed, whereas branded packers declined greatly in number.
3. The system has tended to increase the accuracy, ease, and effectiveness of prices in reflecting value differences at each stage in the marketing system for beef by assisting consumers in the expression of their preferences.[34]

The biggest problem with USDA grade rating is its lack of standardization across products. Top rated apples, peaches, chickens, and some other foods are variously awarded grades of No. 1, Extra No. 1, Fancy, and Grade A. For still other products these grades would indicate second best. Proposed changes would standardize these grade designations, so by the time you read this USDA may have clarified matters considerably.

Auto tires were the subject of an early demonstration of how grading could reduce buyers' erroneous reliance on brand names. Louis Bucklin found that, without grading, consumers tended to overestimate the value of heavily advertised national brands of tires as compared to mildy promoted distributor and local brands, but that with grade rating this bias tended to disappear.[35] Subsequent to that study, and despite sharp objections by major tire manufacturers, a grade rating system was put into effect by the Department of Transportation in 1979 and 1980. Tires are now rated on three characteristics:

1. *Treadwear,* indicated by a numeral such as 90 or 120, with higher numerals indicating higher mileage.
2. *Traction,* where A, B, and C indicate good, fair, and poor traction on wet roads, respectively.
3. *Temperature,* where A indicates the coolest running tire, and B and C rank less well.

Tire manufacturers do their own testing and interpretation under the program, which has led to problems. Although the tests are uniform, they yield

---

[34] Willard F. Williams, E. K. Bowen, and F. C. Genovese, *Economic Effects of U.S. Grades for Beef,* U.S. Department of Agriculture Marketing Research Report No. 298 (Washington D.C., 1959), pp. vii, 158–180. For a more recent discussion see *Business Week,* September 27, 1982, p. 32.

[35] Louis P. Bucklin, "The Uniform Grading System for Tires: Its Effect upon Consumers and Industry Competition," *Antitrust Bulletin* (Winter 1974), pp. 783–801.

TABLE 5–4. Summary of United States Standardization and Disclosure Policies

Policy	Enforcement Agencies*	Products Covered
A. Standardization		
1. Fair Packaging and Labeling Act (1966)	FTC, FDA	Grocery store items, e.g., foods and detergents
2. Size uniformity and simplification	Various state authorities	Bread, margarine, flour, dairy products
3. Unit pricing	Various state authorities	Grocery store items
4. Truth in Lending Act (1969)	FTC, FRB	Consumer credit
5. Warranty standards	FTC	Durables over $15 with written warranty
B. Quality Disclosures		
1. Ingredient labeling:		
Wool Products Labeling Act (1939)	FTC	Wool products
Fur Products Labeling Act (1951)	FTC	Furs
Textile Fiber Identification Act (1958)	FTC	Textiles, apparel, etc.
Food, Drug and Cosmetic Act	FDA	Food products
2. Open dating of perishables	Various state authorities	Grocery perishables
3. Antitampering Odometer Law (1972)	NHTSA	Cars and trucks
4. Performance disclosures		
Fuel efficiency	FEA, FTC	Autos, appliances
Octane rating	FTC, FEA	Gasoline
Tar and nicotine	FTC	Cigarettes
On time performance	ICC	Moving van services
5. Grade rating	USDA	Meat, eggs, butter, etc.
	NHTSA	Tires
	FDA	Suntan oil

* Key: FTC—Federal Trade Commission; FDA—Food and Drug Administration; FRB—Federal Reserve Board of Governors; NHTSA—National Highway Traffic Safety Administration; FEA—Federal Energy Administration; ICC—Interstate Commerce Commission; USDA—U.S. Department of Agriculture.

a range of results. And some companies interpret their results more conservatively than other companies, leading to different grades for very similar test results and different grades for very similarly priced tires.[36] Even so, the system is probably a step in the right direction.

Finally, and most recently, the Food & Drug Administration has launched a rating system for suntan oil based on "sun protection factor" or SPF. Use a #2 SPF oil and you fry. Use a higher numbered oil and you get more protection.[37]

[36] *Wall Street Journal,* December 31, 1980, p. 5.
[37] *Forbes,* June 21, 1982, pp. 80–81.

SUMMARY

Most folks cannot taste any difference between different brands of beer, and computers are bought by expert buyers. Nevertheless, our case studies disclose substantial product differentiation in both industries. This does not necessarily mean that in these instances (and others like them) buyers are irrational. They may merely be uninformed or misinformed. And they may rely heavily on trademarks to guide their purchasing decisions, since in a roundabout way trademarks may often help buyers avoid errors of commission or omission. On the other hand, too heavy a reliance on trademarks and the advertising promoting them may *cause* errors of commission or omission, in which case the owners of prominent trademarks gain at the expense of buyers.

Corrective policies have to focus on one or both of the following objectives: (1) Permit trademarks to identify quality, but remove the rights of ownership exclusivity and perpetuity that presently prevail. (2) Establish quality identifications independent of the trademark system. The first objective lies outside the realm of political possibility. The second has been furthered by two broad classes of policies—standardization (which includes simplified quantity labeling, uniform sizes, and unit pricing) and quality disclosures (which include ingredient labeling, open dating, performance disclosure, and grade rating). These are outlined in Table 5–4.

6

Concentration and Number of Firms: Theory and Cross-Section Evidence

Seller concentration has for a long time received more attention from economists and those concerned with public policy towards industry than any other single characteristic of industrial structure.

—DOUGLAS NEEDHAM

# of firms
size distribution
↓
market power

The number and size distribution of firms are important determinants of market power, just as the height and weight of players are important to the strength of a football team. There are more than a handful of statistical measures of such power. But, which one of these statistics best depicts the population and size distribution of firms in relation to sellers' power over price? Given an answer to this question, how do we define the relevant market to include all the firms that should be included and to exclude all the firms that should be excluded from our statistical calculations? Are Coca-Cola and Budweiser in the same market, for instance?

Turning next to the issue of what *causes* a given number and size distribution of firms, we must ask whether firms get the market shares they deserve. Do General Motors, Ford, and Chrysler, for example, deserve, by their efficiency and quality of product, to account for 70% of all cars sold in the U.S.? Or, did they attain their position merely by acquiring former competitors and hiding behind tariff barriers that inhibited imports? Finally, the federal government has by *policy* broken up large companies, such as Standard Oil of New Jersey (now Exxon) and prohibited numerous attempts at merger, such as Brown Shoe with Kinney, and Clorox with Procter & Gamble. Did these firms deserve what they got? Did they get what they deserved?

These questions highlight the issues taken up in this and the next three chapters. In this chapter, we first discuss various statistical measures of the number and size distribution of firms. Next we review the historic and present conditions of market concentration in the United States. We then consider the causes of those conditions. Finally, we shall move from individual markets to the economy as a whole and consider aggregate concentration.

I. STATISTICAL MEASURES

Several statistical measures of structural power have been devised. Which of these is used in any given instance depends on data availabilities and the immediate purpose. A good measure is one that is easy to calculate, sensitive to major structural changes over time, and indicative of differences in structural power across diverse markets and firms. Above all, *an effective measure must provide fairly accurate predictions of market conduct and performance;* otherwise, it is useless. For this reason, considerations of conduct and performance necessarily intrude in our current discussion. References to a measure's potential weaknesses are most often couched in terms of that measure's lack of predictive force. Still, we shall not lose sight of our present focus, which is primarily structural.

A. The Number of Firms

The most obvious structural measure of market power is the number of sellers. As outlined earlier (in Chapter 1), pure competition and monopolistic competition each require a large number of sellers. Monopoly entails just one seller. In between, oligopoly is characterized by the presence of only a "few" sellers.

In terms of ease of computation and sensitivity to changes over time, this measure has certain advantages. Moreover, the number of sellers is likely to influence behavior because numbers may influence each firm's *expectations regarding the behavior of its rivals.* This influence is most clearly seen in extreme cases. By definition, a firm blessed with monopoly has no rivals, so it may operate in an isolated, independent fashion. At the other extreme, a purely competitive firm has so many rivals that it also acts independently.

Between these extremes, where "few" could mean anything from 2 to 52, numbers retain their relevance. However, their predictive capabilities are reduced. As Douglas Needham explains: "The extent to which the behavior of one firm will influence other firms noticeably may well be related to the number of firms in the market. The smaller the number of sellers, for example, the larger, on average, will be the fractions of a particular market supplied by individual sellers, and any given percentage gain in sales by one seller at the expense of the others results in a more noticeable loss to each of the others and is more likely to invite retaliation. There is, however, no single number of sellers which will in all circumstances distinguish oligopoly market situations from market situations characterized by behavior which is heedless of rival's reactions."[1]

In short, the number of firms is correlated with "the fractions of a particular market supplied by individual sellers." But since these fractions, or divisions, probably influence behavior more directly than mere numbers, it may be better to rely on a measure that actually involves these fractions. Indeed, markets

[1] Douglas Needham, *Economic Analysis and Industrial Structure* (New York: Holt, Rinehart and Winston, Inc., 1969), p. 84.

are often comprised of a "central core" of a few very large firms and a behaviorally inconsequential "fringe" of many small firms. In these instances a raw tally of total numbers may give a false impression of competitive dispersion.

B. The Lorenz Curve and Gini Coefficient

Two measures of fractions are the Lorenz curve and its companion statistic, the Gini coefficient. The absolute number of firms is almost completely suppressed by these measures because they reflect *inequality,* or *relative concentration,* more than anything else.

This may be illustrated with a simple example.[2] Imagine, if you will, four firms in a market with the following percentage shares of market sales (or some other indicator of size, such as assets or employees): firm A, 5%; firm B, 10%; firm C, 15%; and firm D, 70%. The key computations that generate the Lorenz curve are (1) the per cent of market sales, cumulated from the smallest sized firm, and (2) the per cent of the number of firms, cumulated again from the smallest sized firm to the largest. Thus, beginning with A, which is the smallest, 5% of market sales are accounted for by 25% of all firms; 15% of the sales are accounted for by 50% of the firms (A plus B); and so forth. The resulting Lorenz curve is shown in Figure 6–1 as RWVUS.

This Lorenz curve may be compared to the straight diagonal line, *RS*. If each of the four firms had 25% of market sales, the Lorenz curve would match this diagonal line; then 25% of the firms would have 25% of the sales; 50% would have 50%, and so on. Thus, the diagonal indicates an **equal size distribution.** And the more *un*equal the distribution of sales, the greater the divergence between the Lorenz curve and the diagonal. With extreme inequality of shares, the Lorenz curve would look more like a half-open jacknife than the quarter-moon shaped curve of Figure 6–1.

The area between the diagonal and the Lorenz curve, which in the present example equals 2500 percentage points, is often called the **area of concentration.** The **Gini coefficient** summarizes the degree of inequality, since this statistic is the ratio of the area of concentration to the total area under the diagonal. The total area under the diagonal is always 5000, because $\frac{1}{2} \times (100 \times 100) = 5000$. As for the area of concentration, one must add up the areas of the dashed lined triangles and rectangles lying beneath the Lorenz curve, and then subtract the result from 5000. In our present example this is $5000 - 2500 = 2500$. So the Gini coefficient in this case is $2500/5000 = 0.50$.

More generally, it should be clear that, as the Lorenz curve approaches the diagonal, the area of concentration shrinks and the Gini coefficient approaches 0. Conversely, as greater inequality expands the area of concentration, the Gini coefficient approaches a value of 1.

The Lorenz curve and Gini coefficient obviously emphasize the fractions that were ignored by the raw number-of-firms measure. Therefore, they have appeal; however, they also have many drawbacks. The most important of these

[2] Eugene M. Singer, *Antitrust Economics* (Englewood Cliffs, N. J.: Prentice Hall, 1968), p. 141.

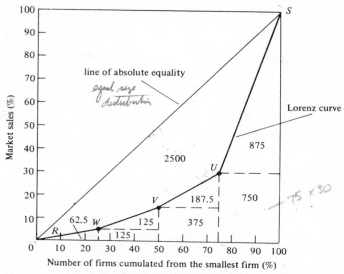

FIGURE 6–1. The Lorenz curve and the Gini coefficient of inequality.

is that they give *too much* emphasis to fractions and percentages, so much, in fact, that they neglect the absolute numbers aspect of structure to an uncalled for and undesirable degree.[3] For example, a Gini coefficient of 0 may give the impression of intense competition, as would be likely in the case of a market comprising 1000 firms, each with 0.1% of total market sales. Yet, a 0 would also derive from the presence of only two firms, each with 50%; or from three firms, each with 33⅓%. And, in neither of these latter instances is the prospect for competition very promising. These absolute numbers are so low that recognized interdependence could very well lead to behavior approaching that of monopoly. Similarly, a decline in the number of sellers in a market could be associated with a *decline* in the Gini coefficient, since it would leave the remaining firms more equal in size if the departing firms were all quite small.[4] The opposite could hold for increases in firm numbers. As a result, changes in structure over time would not be depicted properly.

C. The Concentration Ratio

The concentration ratio combines absolute numbers *and* fractions. It is the per cent of market sales (or some other measure of size, such as assets, employment, or value added) accounted for by an absolute number of the largest firms in the market—for example, the 4 or 8 or 20 largest firms. Because the concentration ratio involves both an absolute number of firms and their size distribution,

[3] M. A. Adelman, "The Measurement of Industrial Concentration," *Review of Economics and Statistics* (November 1951), pp. 269–296.

[4] J. M. Blair, "Statistical Measures of Concentration in Business: Problems of Compiling and Interpretation," *Bulletin of the Oxford University Institute of Statistics* (November 1956), p. 356.

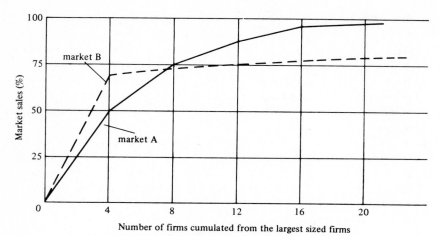

FIGURE 6–2. Concentration curves for two markets.

and because it is also fairly easily constructed, it has become the most readily available and most widely used of all measures of structural power.

Figure 6–2 illustrates two concentration curves and the concentration ratios they generate. The vertical axis is the same as that for the Lorenz curve of Figure 6–1—that is, per cent of total market sales. Its horizontal axis, however, is scaled in terms of the absolute number of firms instead of the per cent of number of firms. Another difference here is that the firms of Figure 6–2 are not cumulated from the smallest first. Instead, cumulation begins with the largest firm at the origin. Thus, the *height* of the curve above a given number of firms is the concentration ratio associated with that number. It is *the percentage of total market sales accounted for by a given number of leading firms.* Thus the four-firm concentration ratio for market A is 50. And the eight-firm concentration ratio for market A is 75.

Among the many virtues of the concentration ratio, two deserve special mention. First, it is the combination of firm numbers *and* size distribution rather than one or the other alone that is most closely connected with behavior. To quote Gideon Rosenbluth, "Economic theory suggests that concentration as defined here is an important determinant of market behavior and market results."[5] Second, concentration ratios are fairly precise and easily understood indexes of market power. As we shall see in the next chapter, they appear in the courtrooms of statistically untrained judges almost as often as they appear in the writings of sophisticated scholars.

This is not to say that the concentration ratio is perfect. Nothing is. Of its many faults, the following three must be counted important:

1. Unlike the Lorenz curve, the concentration ratio describes only one slice of the market's size distribution of firms. It does not summarize conditions

[5] Gideon Rosenbluth, "Measures of Concentration," in *Business Concentration and Price Policy,* edited by G. J. Stigler (Princeton, N. J.: Princeton University Press, 1955), p. 57.

for all firms, only those for the top four or top eight or such. The resulting potential ambiguity is illustrated in Figure 6–2, where market B is more concentrated than market A at the four-firm level, whereas, conversely, market A is more concentrated than market B at the 12-firm level.

2. Even if we settle on one given number of firms as being the best of all possible slices, the concentration ratio provides no information about the size distribution of firms within that slice. Thus in Figure 6–2 we are ignorant of the size distribution of firms 1, 2, 3, and 4.

3. The concentration ratio does not reflect upon other aspects of structure that might be important to behavior, other aspects such as *changes* in the market shares of firms and product differentiation. Other measures have this failing, too, but this fact does not alleviate the problem. Because share changes reflect dynamic competition, an appendix to this chapter covers the subject.

D. The H Index

Many scholars have tried to invent a summary index that would solve these problems.[6] Some progress has been made, but no index attracts universal acclaim, and the concentration ratio remains popular because of its convenience and simplicity. There is a rising star, however, called the H index, so named for its inventors Orris Herfindahl and Albert Hirschman.[7] This summary index is the sum of the squares of the sizes of firms in a market, in which sizes are expressed as a proportion of total market sales (or assets, or employment). In mathematical notation:

$$H \text{ index} = \sum_i \left(\frac{X_i}{T}\right)^2 \qquad (i = 1, 2, 3, \ldots, n)$$

where T represents total market sales, X_i represents the sales of individual firm i, and n is the number of firms in the market. In terms of our earlier example of four firms with 5, 10, 15, and 70% of total market sales:

$$H \text{ index} = (0.05)^2 + (0.10)^2 + (0.15)^2 + (0.70)^2 = 0.525$$

Under pure competition the index would equal 0. Under monopoly it would equal 1. These extremes are perhaps most readily seen by the fact that, if all

---

[6] For clever examples see Janos Horvath, "Suggestion for a Comprehensive Measure of Concentration," *Southern Economic Journal* (April 1970), pp. 446–452. Ann Horowitz and Ira Horowitz, "Entropy, Markov Processes and Competition in the Brewing Industry," *Journal of Industrial Economics* (July 1968), pp. 196–211; Irwin Bernhardt and Kenneth D. Mackenzie, "Measuring Seller Unconcentration, Segmentation, and Product Differentiation," *Western Economic Journal* (December 1968), pp. 395–403; Irvin M. Grossack, "The Concept and Measurement of Permanent Concentration," *Journal of Political Economy* (July 1972), pp. 745–760. For a survey see Leslie Hannah and J. A. Kay, *Concentration in Modern Industry* (London: Macmillan, 1977), pp. 41–63.

[7] A. O. Hirschman, "The Paternity of an Index," *American Economic Review* (September 1964), p. 761. For a recent discussion see William A. Kelly, Jr., "A Generalized Interpretation of the Herfindahl Index," *Southern Economic Journal* (July 1981), pp. 50–57.

firms in the market were of equal size, the Herfindahl-Hirschman H Index would equal $1/n$, which is the inverse of the total number of firms. With n equal to 1, this ratio also equals 1. As the value of n increases, this ratio collapses toward 0.

Because the H index appropriately registers the impact of absolute numbers as well as size inequality, and because the index takes account of all firms in the market simultaneously, it is held in high regard. Another property of the index attractive to some economists is the fact that it gives greater weight to the shares of especially large firms than to those of lesser firms. The squaring in the index does this as reflected in the following comparison: $.6^2 = .36$, whereas $.3^2 + .3^2 = .18$.

The main drawback of the H index is that it requires detailed data on market shares, data often unavailable. The Census Bureau publishes concentration ratios but not H indexes.

II. THE IMPORTANCE OF PROPER MARKET DEFINITION

To this point we have tossed the word "market" around offhandedly. But "market" deserves the same careful handling we would give a stink bomb. This warning applies regardless of whether one is using raw numbers, the Gini coefficient, the concentration ratio, or the H index because market definition determines the total scope of activity against which shares and numbers are computed. Indeed, the predictive accuracy of one's structural measure may depend more heavily on the proper choice of market definitions than on the proper choice of statistical index. All the indexes considered previously correlate well with each other. The rank correlation coefficient between the three-firm concentration ratio and the H index, for example, was found to be $+ 0.98$ for 96 Canadian manufacturing markets.[8] Similar results have turned up in other studies of alternative statistical forms.[9] Thus, if a market has a high four-firm concentration ratio, it will probably also have a high H index, a high Gini coefficient, a high eight-firm concentration ratio, a high 20-firm concentration ratio, and a small number of firms. The same could be said of the choice between sales, assets, value added, and most other units of quantity used for measuring size. Concentration ratios based on these various units of measure are highly correlated.[10] For this reason we shall ignore the debate over alternative units

---

[8] Rosenbluth, *op. cit.*, p. 69.

[9] R. W. Kilpatrick, "The Choice Among Alternative Measures of Industrial Concentration," *Review of Economics and Statistics* (May 1967), pp. 258–260; Christian Marfels, "A Bird's Eye View to Measures of Concentration," *Antitrust Bulletin* (Fall 1975), pp. 485–501.

[10] Rosenbluth, *op. cit.*, pp. 89–92; and John Blair, testimony, *Economic Concentration,* Part 5. Hearings before the Subcommittee on Antitrust and Monopoly of the Committee on the Judiciary, U.S. Senate (1966), pp. 1894–1902. On the other hand Kwoka has shown that, despite high correlations, different measures can yield substantially different explanatory power. Among concentration ratios, the two-firm ratio performs best with his data. See John E. Kwoka, Jr., "Does the Choice of Concentration Measure Really Matter?" *Journal of Industrial Economics* (June 1981), pp. 445–453.

of measure. Broadly speaking, the most commonly used size variable is sales (also referred to as value of shipments).

The problem of market definition centers on the following questions:

1. Does the "market" include those firms that deserve to be in it? That is, *does it include all firms that compete with each other?*
2. Does the "market" exclude those firms that deserve to be out of it? That is, *does it exclude noncompeting firms?*

what defines a mkt?

If a definition fails to include competing firms, the definition is said to be **too narrow,** and the concentration ratio will usually be biased upward. If on the other hand, it fails to exclude *non*competing firms, then it is said to be **too broad,** and the concentration ratio will tend to be biased downward. In the case of either error, the concentration ratio will not predict behavior or performance very well.

This problem of defining the market so as to include competitors while excluding noncompetitors may be further broken into two parts: product delineation and geographic scope.

Product delineation may be illustrated by taking a look at the procedures by which the U.S. Bureau of the Census computes concentration ratios in manufacturing industries. These computations are based on definitions in the federal government's Standard Industrial Classification Code, abbreviated SIC. The SIC refers to markets as industries, and it delineates market breadth with a system of numerical codes. At the broadest level are twenty separate two-digit *major industry groups,* such as "Food and kindred products" (20), "Textile mill products" (22), "Primary metal products" (34), and "Transportation equipment" (37). In turn, each of these two-digit definitions is broken down into narrower three-digit *industry groups,* which are themselves subdivided into still narrower four-digit *industries,* and so on down to the very narrow seven-digit *product.* This progressive subdivision is illustrated in Table 6–1, which displays parts of SIC major industry 20. The sales activities of each firm must be assigned to the different major industry groups, industries, products, and so on. Few firms confine their operations to just one product, or even one industry. Once sales activities are assigned, total sales are computed for each digited market.

TABLE 6–1. Examples Taken from the SIC System

SIC Code	Number of Digits	Designation	Name
20	2	Major industry group	Food and kindred products
203	3	Industry group	Canning, preserving
2037	4	Product group or industry	Frozen fruits and vegetables
20371	5	Product class	Frozen fruits, juices, and ades
2037135	7	Product	Frozen strawberries

Firm shares follow. Concentration ratios are then computed, but only at the four- and five-digit level. Since there are approximately 450 four-digit industries and 1000 five-digit product classes, we can present no more than a small sample of 1977 Census concentration ratios in Table 6–2.

Most research has used ratios for SIC four-digit industries, since they generally represent definitions of about the right amount of detail. Still, the SIC system was not designed primarily for the computation of concentration ratios. The SIC definitions give heavy weight to similarity of production processes (or producer's substitutability) as well as to similarity of product uses (or consumer's substitutability). Although the ideal definition of a market ought to take account of substitution possibilities in *both* production and consumption, the SIC's heavy emphasis on the former yields many four-digit industries that may be considered too broad or too narrow.

Cane sugar refining, 2062, for example, is too narrow because it excludes beet sugar refining (see Table 6–2). Conversely, pharmaceutical preparations, 2834, is too broad because it includes a wide variety of drugs that are not

TABLE 6–2. 1977 Concentration Ratios for Selected Industries

SIC Code	Name	Four-Firm Ratio	Eight-Firm Ratio
37111	Passenger cars (five digit)	99+	100
2067	Chewing gum	93	99
3632	Household refrigerators	82	98
3334	Primary aluminum	76	93
3724	Aircraft engines	74	86
2892	Explosives	64	79
2062	Cane sugar refining	63	90
2822	Synthetic rubber	60	83
3221	Glass containers	54	75
2522	Metal office furniture	47	59
3312	Blast furnaces and steel mills	45	65
3621	Motors and generators	42	55
2211	Weaving mills, cotton	39	58
3143	Men's footwear, except athletic	31	46
3533	Oil field machinery	30	45
2631	Paperboard mills	27	42
2834	Pharmaceutical preparations	24	43
2272	Tufted carpets and rugs	21	35
2421	Sawmills and planing mills	17	23
3544	Special dies, tools, jigs	8	10

Source: U.S. Bureau of the Census, *Census of Manufactures, 1977, Concentration Ratios in Manufacturing,* MC77-SR-9, Washington, D.C., 1981.

close substitutes from the patient's point of view. In Table 6–2 this industry has a four-firm concentration ratio of 24%, but in narrower therapeutic groups we find four-firm ratios such as: anesthetics, 69; antiarthritics, 95; cardiovascular hypotensives, 79; diabetic therapy, 93; and sulfonamides, 79.[11] This discrepancy between broad and narrow definitions in drugs arises because a few firms tend to dominate each therapeutic group but the same firms do not dominate *all* therapeutic groups. When all therapeutic groups are lumped together, the fraction of the "total" business accounted for by any one firm then shrinks.

Another source of error is the exclusion of all imports and exports from Census computations.[12] In particular, significant imports will leave the Census ratio biased upward. The four-firm ratio for passenger cars, for instance, is said to be 99 + in Table 6–2 because there are essentially only four United States producers—General Motors, Ford, Chrysler, and AMC. But in 1982 imports accounted for 27% of all cars sold in the United States. Hence, a more accurate four-firm ratio for that year, with Toyota ranked fourth, would be 77%.

To illustrate the problem of **geographic scope,** we may mention the high transportation costs that prevent petroleum refiners on the east coast from competing with those on the west coast. Refiners do not always operate in more than one region, or all regions. Standard Oil of California, for example, accounts for 16.3% of gasoline sales in Pacific coast states, but 0% in New England and South Atlantic states. The four-firm *national* concentration ratio of 34 in 1973 thus falls below most of the more relevant four-firm *regional* ratios. Sampling a few of these, we see: New England, 41.4; Mid-Atlantic, 41.6; and Pacific, 51.5.[13] Other products experiencing high transportation costs or easy perishability are listed in Table 6–3. In every case the nationwide concentration ratio understates concentration as it is viewed at the more relevant regional or local level.

III. MARKET CONCENTRATION PATTERNS AND TRENDS

Lest this chapter degenerate into a drab parade of procedural issues, we ought now to get down to brass tacks. Just how much concentration is there anyway? And what, if anything, has been the trend over time? A generalized answer to these questions includes the following observations.

A. Manufacturing

In manufacturing, it appears that oligopoly and monopolistic competition predominate. Figure 6–3 shows the distribution of manufacturing shipments

[11] John Vernon, "Concentration, Promotion and Market Share Stability in the Pharmaceutical Industry," *Journal of Industrial Economics* (July 1971), pp. 246–66.

[12] Werner Sichel, "The Foreign Competition Omission in Census Concentration Ratios: An Empirical Evaluation," *Antitrust Bulletin* (Spring 1975), pp. 89–105.

[13] Thomas D. Duchesneau, *Competition in the U.S. Energy Industry* (Cambridge Mass.: Ballinger Publishing Co., 1975), pp. 46–47.

TABLE 6–3. National Versus Regional and Local Markets

SIC Code	Name	National Four-Firm Ratio	Average Regional or Local Four-Firm Ratio
	Regional Market Products		
2095	Roasted coffee	52	71
2791	Typesetting	6	19
2911	Petroleum refining	34	52
3241	Cement, hydraulic	29	55
3446	Architectural metal work	13	37
	Local Market Products		
2024	Ice cream	37	70
2026	Fluid milk	23	57
2051	Bread and related items	23	47
2711	Newspapers	15	73
3251	Brick and structural tile	12	87
3273	Concrete	4	52

Source: David Schwartzman and Joan Bodoff, "Concentration in Regional and Local Industries," *Southern Economic Journal* (January 1971), pp. 343–48.

by four-firm concentration ratio as reported in the *1977 Census of Manufactures*. These are raw data, unadjusted for geographic market definition or other biases, so they reflect only the broad pattern. That pattern includes a relatively low incidence of extreme cases, as only about 6% of manufacturing output came from industries with concentration ratios in either the 0–10% range or the 90–100% range. The vast majority of output came from industries in the 10% to 60% range, and the average concentration ratio is a shade under 40%. Adjustment of these raw data to take account of the biases surveyed above could yield a higher or lower average because judgment would have to guide the adjustments and the biases run positive and negative. For example, William G. Shepherd's adjustment of 1966 Census data caused the average in that year to jump from 39% to 60%, but his manipulation of more recent data apparently produced an opposite shift of direction.[14]

As regards the *trend* in manufacturing markets, let's begin way back in the late 1800s, even though early data are both sketchy and unreliable. It appears that enormous increases in market concentration occurred between 1895 and 1902 as a result of a massive wave of mergers. Then between 1909 and 1947, the pattern is obscured. Some scholars believe, on the one hand, that market concentration declined or stayed the same over the first half of this century.[15]

[14] William G. Shepherd, *Market Power and Economic Welfare* (New York: Random House, 1970), pp. 106–07; and "Causes of Increased Competition in the U.S. Economy, 1939–1980," *Review of Economics and Statistics* (November 1982), p. 619, from which my Figure 6–4 is adapted.

[15] G. Warren Nutter, *The Extent of Enterprise Monopoly in the United States: 1899–1939* (Chicago: University of Chicago Press, 1951), and M. A. Adelman, *op. cit.*

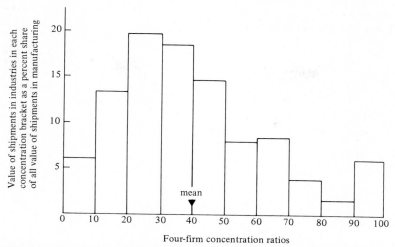

FIGURE 6–3. Concentration pattern in U.S. manufacturing, 1977. Source: Census of Manufactures, 1977, Concentration Ratios in Manufacturing, MC77-SR-9, Washington, D.C., 1981.

On the other hand, Alfred Chandler, Jr., determined that "The percentage of total product value produced by the oligopolists rose from 16% in 1909 to 21% in 1929, and then jumped to 28% at the end of the depression in 1939. Since World War II the figure has remained stable, being 26% in 1947, 25% in 1958, and then up to 27% in 1963."[16] "Oligopoly" in this case is defined as an industry "in which six or fewer firms contributed 50%, or twelve or fewer contributed 75% of the total product value."

Note that differences of opinion can crop up from any number of causes—for example, differing sources of concentration change, such as oligopoly industries getting bigger or big industries getting more oligopolistic. In any event, whatever changes did, in fact, occur over the 1909–1947 period, they were apparently not earthshaking enough to knock you off your chair.

What has happened since 1947? Raw Census data reveal very little change, although estimates by such data are hampered by intermittent changes in the SIC system (changes that abolish some industry codes, merge others, and create new ones for new industries). For the 165 four-digit industries that stayed comparable from 1947 to 1977, average four-firm concentration inched up from 40.4 to 42.3.[17]

However, once the biases in the raw Census data are taken into account, it appears there has been a remarkable shift toward greater competition in manufacturing since the 1950s. Again, problems of definitions and judgment

[16] Alfred D. Chandler, Jr., "The Structure of American Industry in the Twentieth Century: A Historical Overview," *Business History Review* (Autumn 1969), p. 257.

[17] Willard F. Mueller and Richard T. Rogers, "Changes in Market Concentration of Manufacturing Industries, 1974–1977," mimeo, 1982.

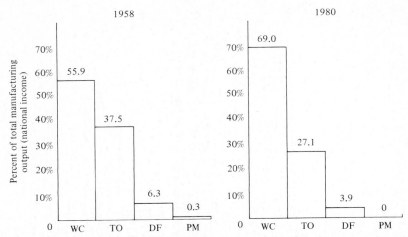

FIGURE 6–4. Trend in competition in U.S. manufacturing, 1959–1980. Source: William G. Shepherd, "Causes of Increased Competition in the U.S. Economy, 1939–1980," *Review of Economics and Statistics* (November 1982), p. 619.

Until 1900 was a shortage of Capital, MKT also small.

muddy the waters here, but the trend seems quite favorable. William G. Shepherd, for instance, has charted changes from 1958 to 1980 according to the following categories of competition:

1. *Pure Monopoly (PM)*: Market share of a single firm at or near 100%, plus blockaded entry, plus evidence of price control.
2. *Dominant Firms (DF)*: A market share of 50% to over 90%, with no close rival, with high entry barriers, with strong price control, and with excess profit.
3. *Tight Oligopoly (TO)*: Four-firm concentration above 60%, with stable market shares; medium or high entry barriers; and a tendency toward cooperation or collusion.
4. *Workable Competition (WC)*: Four-firm concentration below 40%, with unstable market shares and flexible pricing. Low entry barriers, little collusion, and low profit rates.[18]

His results are shown in Figure 6–4, where it may be seen that the share of manufacturing occurring in workably competitive industries (WC) jumped from 55.9% to 69.0% between 1958 and 1980. Correspondingly, all the noncompetitive categories experienced drops.

Shepherd attributes this enormous shift in manufacturing to two primary forces. First, and most important, over a dozen major industries witnessed a flood of new import competition during the 1960s and 1970s as tariff barriers fell and Japan and Europe began flexing their industrial muscles. Imports have

[18] Shepherd "Causes . . .," *op. cit.,* pp. 616–617. Shepherds's term "Effective Competition" has been changed to "Workable Competition" here.

shaken up automobiles, steel, tires, television sets, copy machines, and cameras, to name some of the most important cases. Second, antitrust action has brought competition to numerous other manufacturing industries. Aluminum, telephone equipment, and shoe machinery provide examples.

Overall, then, three phases characterize the trend in concentration in manufacturing. First, during the late 1800s and first decade of the 1900s, concentration shot upward in most major industries, propelled chiefly by mergers. Second, the sketchy record for 1909–1950 indicates relative stability or modest further increases. Finally, raw Census data reveal no change since 1950. But if Shepherd's adjustments for imports and antitrust are correct, we have recently witnessed a dramatic rise in the proportion of output coming from workably competitive industries.

Other sectors of the economy have been measured and studied less intensively than manufacturing, primarily because the Census Bureau does not publish concentration ratios for nonmanufacturing industries. Nevertheless, nonmanufacturing industries are of interest. They account for approximately 75% of our gross national product.

B. Atomistic Industries

Speaking broadly, and beginning at the competitive end of the spectrum, we may note first that, in the United States, market structures are unconcentrated and even atomistic in *agriculture, forestry, fisheries, contract construction,* and *services* (all of which together account for about 20% of gross national product). In the services sector, for instance, it has been very roughly estimated that, on average, local market four-firm concentration for hotel services is 8%; laundries, 13%; eating and drinking establishments, 8%; and automobile repair service establishments, 12%.[19]

As regards trend, agriculture, forestry, and fisheries have always been atomistic. Construction and services have less competitive traditions, but have according to Shepherd moved dramatically in that direction in the last two decades. He claims that workable competition now accounts for about 80% of the output of these sectors, up from 55% in 1958.[20]

Of course, these are just generalizations, and they mask pockets of moderately high concentration in certain localities and in certain unusual lines of product or service (such as farming chinese vegetables, repairing lawn mowers, or servicing cryogenic caskets). Moreover, these generalizations are somewhat misleading in their implication of vigorous rivalry. In many of these fields there is strong product differentiation (as in medical services), official government intervention inhibiting competition (as in agriculture), government ownership of substantial shares of the business or resource (as in forestry), and institutional constraints on competition of various kinds (like union organization of barbers and codes of "ethics" for dentists).

[19] Kenneth D. Boyer, "Informative and Goodwill Advertising," *Review of Economics and Statistics* (November 1974), p. 547. The estimates are for 1963.
[20] Shepherd, "Causes . . .," *op. cit.,* p. 619.

C. Retail Trade

Retail trade also displays some atomistic features and favorable trends, but its oligopolistic tendencies are much more evident than in the sectors just mentioned. By relevant local market definitions, concentration in retailing varies from low to high levels. In 1972, for instance, grocery retailing concentration ranged from 26.3% for four-firms in Charleston, South Carolina, to 81.1% in Cedar Rapids, Iowa. Of the 261 cities with ratios between these bounds, a few are mentioned in Table 6–4.

Table 6–4 also contains selected estimates of local four-firm concentration—that is, multi-city *averages* thereof—for grocery stores, department stores, and several other kinds of retailing. Hence, average local concentration among grocery stores was 52.4% in 1972. The other averages in the table indicate a lower level of concentration in every other branch of retail trade except variety stores, which averaged 55% in 1963. One's overall impression of retailing thus hovers between monopolistic competition and loose-knit oligopoly. On top of this, there are signs that concentration in this sector is on the rise.

TABLE 6–4. Selected Estimates of Local Market Concentration in United States Retailing—1960s and 1970s

Retail Group	Four-Firm Concentration Ratio (%)
Grocery stores (SMSA average)	52.4
Albuquerque, New Mexico	66.3
Boston, Massachusetts	49.0
Chicago, Illinois	57.2
Detroit, Michigan	49.8
Houston, Texas	34.7
San Diego, California	55.2
Washington, D.C.	76.3
Department stores	34.0
Variety stores	55.0
Hardware stores	25.0
Furniture stores	25.0
Drug stores	39.0
Apparel and accessory stores	10.0

Sources: G. E. Grinnell, R. C. Parker, and L. A. Rens, *Grocery Retailing Concentration in Metropolitan Areas, Economic Census Years 1954–72* (FTC Bureau of Economics, 1979), pp. 59–66; Kenneth D. Boyer, "Information and Goodwill Advertising," *Review of Economics and Statistics* (November 1974), p. 547.

TABLE 6–5. National United States Four-Firm Concentration Ratios for Major Fuels and Combined Energy Mining, 1955 and 1970

Industry	Top Four Firms		Top Eight Firms	
	1955	1970	1955	1970
Crude oil	21.2	31.0	35.9	49.1
Natural Gas	18.6	24.4	30.4	39.1
Coal	17.8	30.7	25.4	41.2
Uranium	77.9	55.3	99.1	80.0
Energy ($)	16.1	23.4	27.2	37.8

Note: Natural gas production includes United States and Canada. Uranium concentration is measured at the milling stage.

Source: Joseph Mulholland and Douglas Webbink, *Economic Report on Concentration Levels and Trends in the Energy Sector of the U.S. Economy* (Washington, D.C.: Federal Trade Commission, 1974), p. 148.

D. Mining

Mining brings us another mixed bag. In the life-and-death area of energy mining—which deserves a table all its own and gets it, Table 6–5—we find only moderate levels of concentration on a national market basis. The four-firm ratios for crude oil production, natural gas extraction, and coal mining were 31.0, 24.4, and 30.7% respectively, in 1970. The uranium ratios are twice as high. If one assumes that all these fuels are close substitutes for each other (which is doubtful[21]) then the broader product definition "energy" yields rather low ratios.

Lest these numbers lead the reader to conclude that competition runs rampant in this sector, we should also mention that (1) government intervention produces much ossification, (2) the trend in concentration has been skyward (see Table 6–5), and (3) by narrower, but perhaps more defensible geographic definitions of fuel markets, oligopolistic firms seem to be in control.[22] Furthermore, the energy sector can claim the greatest cartel in all history—the Organization of Petroleum Exporting Countries, or OPEC.

Broad generalizations for other areas of mining are equally difficult. On the one hand we find substantial four-firm control in the United States for gold (79.9), copper (74.8), sulfur (72.0), iron ore (63.9), and lead and zinc

[21] David Schwartzman, "The Cross-Elasticity of Demand and Industry Boundaries: Coal, Oil, Gas, and Uranium," *Antitrust Bulletin* (Fall 1973), pp. 483–507.

[22] See, e.g., John W. Wilson, testimony in *The National Gas Industry*, Hearings before the Subcommittee on Antitrust and Monopoly, Part I, U.S. Senate (1973), pp. 456–504.

(47.0).[23] On the other hand, there are several areas of mining that are fairly atomistic—limestone, common sand and gravel, and phosphate, for example.

E. Finance

Banking, insurance, and other forms of finance are primarily local operations, although some large corporate buyers of these services have the option of easily shifting their accounts and lines of credit across state boundaries, thereby adding an element of nationwide scope. Local concentration in commercial banking tends to be moderate or high. The following 1970 sample of *three-firm* concentration ratios is based on deposits: Atlanta 65.6; Baltimore, 64.2; Chicago, 43.1; Columbus, Ohio, 93.4; Des Moines, 70.6; Indianapolis, 79.9; New York, 48.0; Phoenix, 92.8; Pittsburgh, 80.0; and San Francisco, 77.7.[24] Since by law banks cannot freely operate across state lines, national market three-firm concentration based on deposits is only 9.6%.

Local market concentration in life insurance, which illustrates another area of finance, is not quite as high as in banking. New Jersey is the most concentrated of all state markets, with a four-firm ratio of 56.2% in 1968.[25]

The significance of these several statistics has been shaken by extensive recent deregulation of the banking sector. This deregulation has, for instance, thrown commercial banks and savings and loan institutions into new competition with each other. According to some observers the trend is therefore favorable.

F. Transportation and Public Utilities

Last, but considerably more than least, are several sectors in which deregulation has had an even greater impact. Antitrust policy has also contributed. Air transport, trucking, railroading, and intercity bus services used to be oligopolistic in relevant markets and heavily regulated in cartel-like fashion, but these industries are now substantially free of restraints and in a state of turmoil. Parts of telephone communications, which formerly amounted to pure monopoly, have likewise become more decentralized with technological change, antitrust action, and deregulation. Local electricity and gas retain characteristics of so-called "natural monopoly" that are resistant to such changes, but they now account for only a fraction of the business conducted in these sectors. Figure 6–5 summarizes Shephard's view of these sectors in terms of workable competition (WC), tight oligopoly (TO), dominant firm (DF), and pure monopoly (PM).

[23] J. P. Mulholland and D. W. Webbink, *Concentration Levels and Trends in the Energy Sector of the U. S. Economy* (Washington, D.C.: Federal Trade Commission, 1974), p. 139.
[24] Federal Deposit Insurance Corporation, *Summary of Accounts and Deposits in All Commercial Banks, June 30, 1970* (Washington, D.C.), pp. 18–20.
[25] J. D. Cummins, H. S. Denenberg, and W. C. Scheel, "Concentration in the U.S. Life Insurance Industry," *Journal of Risk and Insurance* (June 1972), pp. 177-199. Concentration in property and casualty insurance is higher and rising. Average state four-firm concentration in 1980 was 43.6% for homeowners insurance and 49.8% for auto liability. John W. Wilson and J. Robert Hunter, *Investment Income and Profitability in Property/Casualty Insurance Ratemaking* (Washington D.C.: J. W. Wilson & Associates, 1983), p. 46. For statewide concentration ratios in consumer finance, see Milton W. Schober and Robert P. Shay, *State and Regional Estimates of the Price and Volume of the Major Types of Consumer Installment Credit in Mid-1971,* Technical Study, Vol. III, National Commission on Consumer Finance (Washington, D.C., 1973), pp. 145-167.

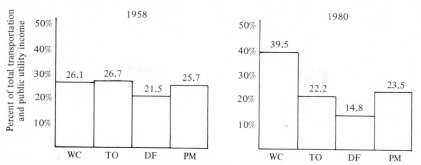

FIGURE 6–5. Trend in competition in transportation and public utilities, 1958–1980. Source: see Fig. 6–4.

G. Conclusion

Where does this cascade of statistics leave us? Is any grand summary possible? Many observers seem to think so, but opinions differ:

> The extent of shared monopoly can modestly be called staggering.
>
> Mark Green[26]

> While there are *some* markets in which the number of competitors is limited, there is not an important national market today (with the possible exception of telephone service) which lacks active competition.
>
> Lee Loevinger[27]

Shepherd's view, which lies between these extremes, is reflected in Figure 6–6.

IV. THE CAUSES OF CONCENTRATION

The next question is what produces concentration? Unfortunately, the answer is complex, so much so that we cannot possibly provide a thorough reply in the remainder of this chapter. All we can do here is outline the various main parts of the answer, refer to subsequent chapters for each item in the outline that is discussed in detail later, and discuss the outline briefly, paying particular attention to those points that are not discussed extensively later on. First the outline:

A. Chance or luck.
B. Technical causes or prior conditions.
   1. Size of the market (Chapter 8, Barriers to Entry)
   2. Economies of scale (Chapter 8, Barriers to Entry)
   3. Scarce resources (Chapter 8, Barriers to Entry)
   4. Market growth rate (Chapter 8, Barriers to Entry)

[26] *The Closed Enterprise System* (New York: Grossman Publishers, 1972), pp. 7–8. (A Nader Study Group Report.)

[27] "The Closed Mind Inquiry—Antitrust Report is Raiders' Nadir," *Antitrust Bulletin* (Fall 1972), p. 758 (emphasis added).

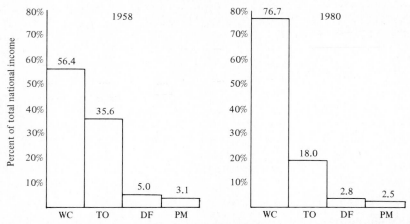

FIGURE 6–6. Trend in competition, summary of U.S. competition, 1958–1980. Source: see Fig. 6–4.

C. Government policy.
  1. Antitrust (Chapter 7, Mergers; Chapter 9, Monopoly; Chapter 14, Restrictive Practices)
  2. Patents, licenses, tariffs, quotas (Chapter 9, Monopoly; Chapter 24, Patent Policy)
  3. Procurement policy
  4. Miscellaneous regulations (Chapter 20, Public Utility Regulation)
D. Business policies (within the context of the foregoing).
  1. Mergers (Chapter 7, Mergers)
  2. Restrictive practices (Chapter 9, Monopoly; Chapters 12, 13, Conduct)
  3. Product differentiation (Chapters 15, 16, Conduct)

Perusal of the outline should reveal why a detailed discussion of all items is inappropriate here. The list is not only long, it contains many items, such as antitrust policy and restrictive practices, that simply do not fit in the present context. Furthermore, many factors, such as economies of scale and scarce resources, transcend in structural importance their contribution to concentration. They influence market power in their own right, independent of their contribution to concentration.

A. Chance or Luck

What do you suppose would happen if you and ten friends got together for an all night gambling session? Assume that each of you brought $50 to fritter away, and that every game played was one of *pure* chance—bingo, perhaps—with all of you having *identical* chances of winning. What do you suppose would be the distribution of money by the break of dawn? Would everyone leave with $50? The laws of probability say "no" (and your own experience

TABLE 6–6. Four-Firm Concentration Ratios Resulting from Simulation Runs of a Stochastic Growth Process

	Four-Firm Concentration Ratio at Year:					
	1	*20*	*40*	*60*	*80*	*100*
Run 1	8.0	19.5	29.3	36.3	40.7	44.9
Run 2	8.0	20.3	21.4	28.1	37.5	41.6
Run 3	8.0	18.8	28.9	44.6	43.1	47.1
Run 4	8.0	20.9	26.7	31.8	41.9	41.0
Run 5	8.0	23.5	33.2	43.8	60.4	60.5
Run 6	8.0	21.3	26.6	29.7	35.8	51.2
Average for 16 runs	8.0	20.4	27.0	33.8	42.1	46.7

Source: Frederick M. Scherer, *Industrial Market Structure and Economic Performance* (Chicago: Rand McNally & Co., 1970), p. 126. Reprinted by permission.

may lead you to agree). A few of you would put together a string of lucky games. A few would lose regularly. The rest would fall in between. The result is such a concentration of winnings (and losings) that two of you would end up with, say, six elevenths or 54.5% of the total $550 in original funds.

Several economists have argued that similar principles apply to firms in markets, that chance explains much concentration.[28] This is best seen by way of a computer simulation experiment conducted by F. M. Scherer. He simulated 16 separate histories of a single market under the following set of assumptions:

1. The market starts the first year with 50 firms, each with $100,000 in sales and a 2% market share. (The four-firm concentration ratio starts then at 8%.)

2. Each firm has *identical chances* for growth, these chances being specified by each firm annually drawing a year's growth from an identical probability distribution.

3. The probability distribution from which these annual growth rates are drawn provides for an *average* annual growth rate of 6%, but a *variance* of growth rates around this average such that the distribution is normal with standard deviation of 16%.

Table 6-6 shows the results of the first six of Scherer's 16 computer runs, together with averages for all 16 simulations on the bottom line. The numbers are four-firm concentration ratios taken at 20 year intervals up to 100 years. Since Lady Luck is at work, the results are not the same for any pair of runs, but the message is clear. Concentration rises rapidly at first, more than doubling in the first 20 years. It rises more slowly thereafter.

[28] P. E. Hart and S. J. Prais, "The Analysis of Business Concentration," *Journal of the Royal Statistical Society,* Series A (Part I, 1956), pp. 150-181; Herbert A. Simon and C. P. Bonini, "The Size Distribution of Business Firms," *American Economic Review* (September 1958), pp. 607-617.

The key to understanding how pure chance could produce these results lies in understanding the following sequence of events: Half of the firms will enjoy better than average growth the first year. Half of that half, or one quarter, will enjoy better than average growth a second year because the same probability distribution applies anew annually to *each segment* of firms and *each firm* regardless of the prior year's experience. Half of that quarter, or one eighth, will enjoy better than average growth in the third year, which means they enjoy three consecutive boom years. Half of that eighth, or one sixteenth, will have better than average growth in the fourth year . . . and so on. In short, the leaders have enjoyed a run of good luck.

The assumptions of this experiment conform to what is called **Gibrat's Law** of proportionate growth. Although real world markets do not conform exactly to these assumptions, there are various forms of evidence that suggest Gibrat's law or something like it is at work.[29] One of the more prominent findings is that, *on average,* the percentage growth of small firms is about the same as that of large firms.[30] This independence of size and growth was implicity assumed for Scherer's experiment.

Still, happenstance cannot be the whole story. It helps to explain why there is always *some* concentration in just about every market, and why the "bad guys" sometimes outstrip the "good." But there is a great deal of *systematic* variation in concentration across markets, something incompatible with pure happenstance. What do we mean by systematic variation? For one thing, similar markets in diverse nations show consistent patterns in degree of concentration. If autos and cigarettes are highly concentrated in the United States, they are likely to be highly concentrated in Britain, France, and Sweden as well. Table 6–7 shows the composite ranking of 17 two-digit industries for 12 European and North American countries, as computed by Frederic Pryor. Averaged over these nations, tobacco and transportation equipment were the most highly concentrated of all manufacturing industries, whereas lumber and furniture were the least concentrated. The concordance coefficient, which indicates the *similarity* of rank orderings across all these 12 nations, was +0.51 and highly significant.[31]

Additionally, when any two nations' rank orders are compared, the correlation coefficient thereby produced is always highly positive.[32] This does *not* mean that the *average level* of market concentration for all industries taken together

[29] See, for example, S. J. Prais, "A New Look at the Growth of Industrial Concentration," *Oxford Economic Papers* (July 1974), pp. 273-288.

[30] Stephen Hymer and Peter Pashigian, "Firm Size and Rate of Growth," *Journal of Political Economy* (December 1962), pp. 556-569; M. Marcus, "A Note of the Determinants of the Growth of Firms and Gibrat's Law," *Canadian Journal of Economics* (November 1969), pp. 587-589.

[31] F. L. Pryor, "An International Comparison of Concentration Ratios," *Review of Economics and Statistics* (May 1972), p. 51.

[32] Besides Pryor see K. D. George and T. S. Ward, *The Structure of Industry in the EEC* (Cambridge, U.K.: Cambridge University Press, 1975), p. 16; Gideon Rosenbluth, *Concentration in Canadian Manufacturing Industries* (Princeton: Princeton University Press, 1957); R. E. Caves and M. Uekusa, *Industrial Organization in Japan* (Washington, D.C.: Brookings Institution, 1976), pp. 19–25; Patricio Meller, "The Pattern of Industrial Concentration in Latin America," *Journal of Industrial Economics* (September 1978), pp. 41–47.

TABLE 6–7. High to Low Concentration Rankings for Two-Digit Industries—United States and Abroad

SIC Code	Industry	12-Country Composite Rank	United States	
			As of 1963	As of 1929
21	Tobacco products	1	1	1
37	Transportation equipment	2	3	6
35	Machinery (except electric)	3	11	9
29	Petroleum and coal products	4	2	3
28	Chemicals	5	6	7
30	Rubber products	6	8	2
36	Electrical equipment	7	5	8
32	Stone, clay and glass	8	7	14
34	Fabricated metal products	9	13	12
33	Primary metals	10	4	4
20	Food and kindred products	11	10	5
26	Paper products	12	12	11
22	Textiles	13	9	10
31	Leather products	14	15	15
23	Apparel	15	14	13
24	Lumber and wood	16	16	16
25	Furniture and fixtures	17	17	17

Sources: Twelve countries: Frederic L. Pryor, "An International Comparison of Concentration Ratios," *Review of Economics and Statistics* (May 1972), p. 135. United States figures: Derived from Alfred D. Chandler, Jr., "The Structure of American Industry in the Twentieth Century: A Historical Overview," *Business History Review* (Autumn 1969), pp. 258–59.

is the same among nations. That is a separate issue. The average height of Pygmies is less than ours, even though their age-height rank ordering correlates with ours. For average market concentration in manufacturing, Pryor finds that, "France, West Germany, and Italy, have weighted concentration ratios somewhat lower than the United States, while . . . Japan, the Netherlands, and the United Kingdom, have weighted concentration ratios only slightly higher than the United States. In only five nations are concentration ratios clearly higher [by about 50%], namely, Belgium, Canada, Sweden, Switzerland, and Yugoslavia."[33]

Table 6–7 also reports the rank order of two-digit industries in the United States as of 1963. These rankings may be compared with the 12-country composite rankings to support our assertion that patterns in degree of concentration are consistent across nations. More important, they may be compared with the rankings of the last column, which are for the United States in 1929. This

[33] F. L. Pryor, *op. cit.*, p. 134. For corroboration concerning the United Kingdom, France, Germany, and Italy, see George and Ward, *op. cit.*, p. 17.

latter comparison reveals a second type of systematic pattern. That is, interindustry differences tend to be stable over long periods of time. Tobacco and transport equipment have perched high atop the list for over a quarter of a century, whereas leather, apparel, lumber, and furniture have invariably roosted on the bottom. We thus have a pattern of persistence at odds with a pattern of pure chance.

B. Technical Causes

A third form of systematic pattern could be claimed if intermarket differences in concentration were closely associated with variations in technological conditions or prior circumstances that could reasonably be expected to affect concentration. In general, such an association does seem to be borne out by research.

Consider first the relationship between market size and concentration. We have already seen how a stringently narrow definition of the market tends to increase measured concentration, whereas an excessively broad definition has the effect of decreasing apparent concentration. Going beyond mere definition to a more substantive association, the same inverse relationship holds between economic market size and concentration, everything else being equal.[34] Large markets, measured by volume of business or buyer population or whatever, seem to have more "room" for a larger number of sellers than small markets. Consequently, large markets have lower concentration ratios than small markets. To take just one example, Table 6–8 reproduces average *two-firm* concentration ratios for commercial banks, categorizing them in terms of four different city sizes and three different types of branching regulation. Note in particular that, for each type of branching policy taken individually, concentration is greatest in areas of smallest population; whereas it is lowest in areas of largest population. In states that permit statewide branching, for instance, the ratio falls from 69.5 to 55.0. An even healthier drop from 68.5 to 42.7% occurs in unit banking states, where each banking firm is limited to only one office. Since branching is banned in these states, additional banking *firms* are almost a necessity for serving the additional demand that goes with additional population.

Economies of scale are another causal factor. They will be discussed at appropriate length in Chapter 8. Suffice it to say here that size of market alone is not enough. The size of *firm* required to achieve all efficiencies (and thereby attain lowest possible cost per unit) is also important. If, for example, low-cost auto production required an output of *at least* 1 million cars per year, then an auto market of 10 million sales per year could be served by ten auto

---

[34] George and Ward, *op. cit.,* pp. 22–23; Caves and Uekusa, *op. cit.,* pp. 22–25; Meller, *op. cit.,* pp. 44–45; F. M. Scherer, A. Beckenstein, E. Kaufer, and R. D. Murphy, *The Economics of Multi-Plant Operation an International Comparisons Study* (Cambridge, Mass.: Harvard University Press, 1975), pp. 221-223; M. D. Intriligator, S. I. Ornstein, R. E. Shrieves, and J. F. Weston, "Determinants of Market Structure," *Southern Economic Journal* (April 1973), pp. 612-625; E. Pagoulatos and R. Sorensen, "A Simultaneous Equation Analysis of Advertising, Concentration, and Profitability," *Southern Economic Journal* (January 1981), pp. 728–741.

TABLE 6–8. Percentage of Total Deposits Held by Largest Two Banking
Organizations in Metropolitan Areas 1968

Population of Standard Metropolitan Statistical Area (SMSA)	Statewide Branching States (%)	Limited Branching States (%)	Unit Branching States (%)
50–100,000	69.5	65.4	68.5
100,000–500,000	68.5	64.4	53.5
500,000–1,000,000	69.1	57.7	47.8
1,000,000 and over	55.0	51.5	42.7

Source: "Recent Changes in the Structure of Commercial Banking," *Federal Reserve Bulletin* (March 1970), p. 207.

makers of efficient scale. If, on the other hand, efficient scale coincided with 5 million units, then there would be "room" for only two low-cost producers, a condition that would obviously aggravate concentration considerably. Stated differently, minimum efficient size and concentration should be positively correlated across markets. Without going into the details now, this association has been found.[35]

A scarcity of resource inputs, such as a scarcity of mineral deposits or uniquely skilled labor, may have a positive effect on concentration similar to the effect of economies of scale. Unfortunately, the data necessary for a cross-section test of this possibility are not available; however, some sketchy case history evidence will be reviewed later.

By contrast, one of the more thoroughly researched hypotheses is that rapid growth in market demand tends to reduce concentration. It would of course be preposterous to suppose that the few leading firms of any market would consciously stand pat while the market grew up rapidly around them, permitting disproportionate expansions of their lesser rivals and a flood of entering newcomers. Still, a hypothesis that rapid growth diminishes concentration must infer some degree of such differential behavior. Accordingly, it has been theorized that leading firms tend to (1) be timid for fear of antitrust prosecution, (2) look more toward diversifying outside the market than merely keeping up within the market, or (3) suffer from the sluggishness that often accompanies large size. However true these possibilities may or may not be, there is substantial evidence indicating that *changes* in concentration *are* inversely associated with

[35] R. E. Caves, J. Khalilzadeh-Shirazi, and M. E. Porter, "Scale Economies in Statistical Analyses of Market Power," *Review of Economics and Statistics* (May 1975), pp. 133–140; Caves and Uekusa, *op. cit.,* pp. 22–25; D. F. Greer, "Advertising and Market Concentration," *Southern Economic Journal* (July 1971), pp. 19–32; and L. W. Weiss, "Optimal Plant Size and the Extent of Suboptimal Capacity," in *Essays on Industrial Organization in Honor of Joe S. Bain,* edited by R. T. Masson and P. D. Qualls (Cambridge, Mass.: Ballinger Publishing Co., 1976), p. 135.

market rate of growth.[36] The association is, however, often weak statistically and of low magnitude. In particular, it has been estimated that a 100-percentage-point increase in market size would usually be necessary to trim four-firm concentration by 2 or 3 percentage points. Slim pickings, indeed.

C. Government Policies

Unlike the foregoing factors, which are largely attributable to Lady Luck or Mother Nature, government policies and business policies are obviously the work of lesser breeds, namely, government officials and businessmen. Among government officials, we find an amazing amount of ambivalence; some would even say schizophrenia. Fritz Machlup neatly summarized the situation when he wrote that "Governments, apparently, have never been able to make up their minds as to which they dislike more, competition or monopoly."[37] On the anti-monopoly side, government has created and mobilized various antitrust laws to dissolve excessive concentrations of market power or to prevent such concentrations from occurring in the first place. On the other side are a host of anticompetitive government policies.[38] These include **tariffs** and **quotas,** restricting the free flow of imports; **licenses,** inhibiting the entry of finance companies, taxi cabs, liquor stores, barbers, beauticians, landscape architects, and various other professionals; **franchises,** granting rights of monopoly to bus lines, athletic stadium concessionaires, water companies, electric and gas companies, and other businesses; and **patents,** awarding 17-year monopolies over the use of new inventions and innovations. The effects of these policies on concentration should be obvious.

The effects of slightly more subtle policies governing commercial bank branching may be seen by referring again to Table 6–8. Local two-bank concentration ratios are more than 10 percentage points higher in statewide branching states than in unit banking states for each size class of city, except the very smallest. Citites in the 50,000–1000,000 population range are usually served by just a few bank offices regardless of branching regulations; hence, the effect in their cases is negligible.

Government procurement policy also has an effect. Briefly stated, the federal government's multibillion dollar purchases of tanks, planes, ships, electronic equipment, and most other durable goods are concentrated among a relatively few supplying firms. In light of the ample concentration caused by factors *unre-*

---

[36] Ralph L. Nelson, *Concentration in the Manufacturing Industries of the United States* (New Haven, Conn.: Yale University Press, 1963), pp. 50–56; W. G. Shepherd, "Trends of Concentration in American Manufacturing Industries, 1947–1958," *Review of Economics and Statistics* (May 1964), pp. 200–212; D. R. Kamerschen, "Market Growth and Industry Concentration," *Journal of the American Statistical Association* (March 1968), pp. 228–241; J. A. Dalton and S. A. Rhoades, "Growth and Product Differentiability as Factors Influencing Changes in Concentration," *Journal of Industrial Economics* (March 1974), pp. 235–240; Richard E. Caves and Michael E. Porter, "The Dynamics of Changing Seller Concentration," *Journal of Industrial Economics* (September 1980), pp. 1–15.

[37] Fritz Machlup, *Political Economy of Monopoly* (Baltimore: The Johns Hopkins University Press, 1952), p. 182.

[38] Walter Adams and Horace M. Gray, *Monopoly in America: The Government as Promoter* (New York: Macmillan Publishing Co., 1955).

TABLE 6–9. Selected Major Mergers Causing High Concentration 1895–1904

Company (or Combine)	Number of Firms Disappearing	Rough Estimate of Market Controlled (%)
U.S. Steel	170	65
U.S. Gypsum	29	80
American Tobacco	162	90
American Smelting & Refining	12	85
DuPont de Nemours	65	85
Diamond Match	38	85
American Can	64	65–75
International Harvester	4	70
National Biscuit (Nabisco)	27	70
Otis Elevator	6	65

Source: Ralph L. Nelson, *Merger Movements in American Industry 1895–1956* (Princeton, N.J.: Princeton University Press, 1959), pp. 161–62.

lated to government procurement, it is not surprising that these purchases should also be concentrated. The government, moreover, obviously has special needs—particularly in the case of complex weapon systems—needs that often force it to show some favoritism toward Gargantuan suppliers. It has nonetheless been argued rather persuasively that the government's expenditures are *more* highly concentrated than these two rationalizations justify.[39] The government's ambivalence thus takes many forms.

D. Business Policies

Table 6–9 offers evidence of the potential and actual effects of business mergers. It not only summarizes the merger history of the ten companies listed but also reflects the history of dozens of other modern-day mammoths that likewise rose to power through combination around the turn of the century. The ten firms of Table 6–9 accounted for the disappearance of 577 formerly independent rivals during this period. The consequences are obvious in the last column of the table, which provides rough estimates of the market shares these combinations acquired. United States antitrust policy currently stands in the way of further merger-built oligopoly. This is not the case in England and West Germany, however, where recent merger activity has contributed substantially to concentration in many major industries.[40]

[39] *Ibid.*, Chapter V; U.S. General Accounting Office, *More Competition in Emergency Defense Procurements Found Possible*, B-171561 (Washington, D.C., March 25, 1971) and *Opportunities for Savings by Increasing Competition in Procurement of Commercial Equipment*, B-164018 (Washington D.C., February 26, 1971).

[40] M. A. Utton, "The Effect of Mergers on Concentration: U. K. Manufacturing Industry, 1954-65," *Journal of Industrial Economics* (November 1971), pp. 42–58; Jürgen Müller, "The Impact of Mergers on Concentration: A Study of Eleven West German Industries," same *Journal* (December 1976), pp. 113-132; Hannah and Kay, *op. cit.*, pp. 64–97.

Less measurable but no less deserving of mention are various business policies that have come to be called "restrictive practices." These include group boycotts, collective rebates, predatory price discrimination, barrier pricing, and exclusive dealing. They generally have no immediate effect on concentration, but over the long haul they can cement existing market power or extend it, as will be shown later when we take up conduct in earnest.

Finally, it appears that under certain circumstances product differentiation may foster concentration. It has been found, for instance, that consumer goods industries experiencing especially high outlays on TV and radio advertising have also experienced especially high increases in concentration over the period 1947–1977. Over the same period concentration tended to fall or remain unchanged in other industries—namely (a) consumer-goods industries experiencing heavy print-media advertising or little advertising generally and (b) producer-goods industries generally.[41] Exactly how the *level* of broadcast advertising could affect *changes* in concentration is not exactly clear, but it is worth recalling from Chapter 4 that TV and radio advertising tends to be "persuasive" whereas print media advertising tends to be "informative" (see page 62). Later we shall explore this area further, paying particular attention to the levels of *both* advertising and concentration or to changes in both (see Chapter 15).

V. AGGREGATE CONCENTRATION

A. Introduction

Let us now broaden our view a bit. Let us leave the lowlands of market concentration and climb into the mountains for a brief look at what is called **aggregate concentration** or **economy-wide concentration**. As these latter names imply, our new viewpoint involves a look at the share of *total* economic activity accounted for by some relatively small groups of enterprises, regardless of their specific markets. Although market and aggregate concentration are in fact related, they are quite different in principle. The many individual markets in the economy could all be highly concentrated. Yet, if the firms in each market were also highly specialized, limiting their activities to just one market, they could then be relatively small and numerous when compared to the economy as a whole. The result: relatively low aggregate concentration despite considerable market concentration. On the other hand, it is possible to have high aggregate concentration together with low market concentration. This would occur if a group of very large firms controlled a dominant portion of total economic activity, but with each firm's individual operations so diversified across a large number of markets that no single operation accounted for a major share of any one market.

[41] W. F. Mueller and R. T. Rogers, "Changes in Market Concentration of Manufacturing Industries, 1947–1977," mimeo (1982). See their paper "The Role of Advertising in Changing Concentration of Manufacturing Industries," *Review of Economics and Statistics* (February 1980), pp. 89–96.

Despite these theoretical possibilities, market and aggregate concentration are closely connected in several ways. First, firms that control large shares of the economy also hold dominant positions in major industries. Exxon and Mobil both rank among the ten largest United States corporations while they hold the lead positions in petroleum production. The same could be said of GM and Ford in automobiles and IBM in computers.

Second, many of the overall leaders are highly diversified. LTV is into steel, aerospace, meat packing, sporting goods, pharmaceuticals, and electronics. ITT, FMC, and Litton are into so many different things that an abridged list for each would mislead you and a complete list would bore you. Thus, many, if not most, of the top 100 are referred to as **conglomerates**.

Finally, aggregate dominance and diversification may augment a firm's power within specific markets. This is especially true of diversification in the form of **vertical integration**, that is, single firm operation at several stages in the production and distribution of a given product. Major petroleum companies, for example, combine crude oil extraction, pipeline transportation, refining, and retail marketing.

B. Trends and Levels

Different definitions of size, different definitions of aggregate scope, and different notions of how many firms constitute a "few" obviously affect the picture. But, generally speaking, aggregate concentration has risen over this century. Figure 6–7 illustrates for four measures: (1) the share of manufacturing, mining, and distributing assets accounted for by the 100 largest such corporations; (2) asset share of the 200 largest manufacturing corporations; (3) manufacturing value added accounted for by the top 200 manufacturers; and (4) the share of deposits held by the 100 leading commercial banks. Thus, for example, 44% of all value added in manufacturing in 1977 can be credited to the 200 largest manufacturing companies, up from a 30% share in 1947. Whether the trends and current levels are alarming or not depends on your value judgments.

Some commentators have argued that there is no cause for alarm in this trend. They claim that although the *share* of the top 100 or so may be rising, the *identity* of the top 100 is constantly changing, implying turnover and competition. There is a grain of truth to this. Our high-altitude vantage point is not Mt. Olympus, so those we see up here do not enjoy eternal life. By raw count, only 21 of the top 100 firms in 1909 remained on the list in 1976. Choice of beginning year is important, however, because 40 new firms entered the top 100 between 1909 and 1919 alone.[42] Since 1919 things have been much more stable, with 51 of that year's top 100 surviving into the 1970s.

What happened to the 49 nonsurvivors of 1919? Only 10 could be considered true failures, exiting by liquidation or suffering a decline in sales. Nine continued to grow and stayed close to the top but were replaced by faster growers. Finally, 30 of the 49 dropouts merged with other large firms, a means of exit that

[42] Robert J. Stonebraker, "Turnover and Mobility among the 100 Largest Firms: An Update," *American Economic Review* (December 1979), pp. 968–973.

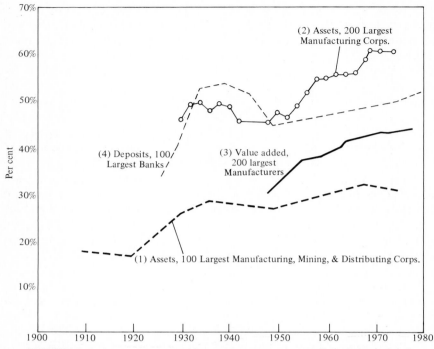

FIGURE 6–7. Long-term trend in aggregate concentration, four series.†

† Sources: Robert J. Stonebraker, "Turnover and Mobility among the 100 Largest Firms: An Update," *American Economic Review* (December 1979), pp. 968–973; Stephan A. Rhoades, "Size and Rank Stability of the 100 Largest Commercial Banks, 1925–1978," *Journal of Economics and Business:* (Vol. 34, #2, 1982), pp. 123–128; *1977 Census of Manufactures: Concentration Ratios in Manufacturing* (U.S. Dept. of Commerce, 1981), p. 9–7; Federal Trade Commission Staff, *Economic Report on Conglomerate Mergers* (1969), p. 173; David Penn, "Aggregate Concentration: A Statistical Note," *Antitrust Bulletin* (Spring 1976), pp. 91–98.

could not be considered "competitive."[43] Not only have truly "competitive" exits been rather rare but their frequency has apparently diminished with time.[44]

To end on a positive note, however, it appears that concentration in the *entire private economy* has not changed much in the last two decades.[45] This conclusion might seem odd in light of the rising concentration in manufacturing and banking shown in Figure 6–7. But concentration in the entire private econ-

[43] Richard C. Edwards, "Stages in Corporate Stability and the Risks of Corporate Failure," *Journal of Economic History* (June 1975), pp. 428-457.
[44] Stonebraker, *op. cit.;* N. Collins and L. Preston, "The Size Structure of the Largest Industrial Firms, 1909–1958," *American Economic Review* (December 1961), pp. 986–1011; S. E. Boyle and J. P. McKenna, "Size Mobility of the 100 and 200 Largest U.S. Manufacturing Corporations: 1911–1964," *Antitrust Bulletin* (Fall 1970), pp. 505-519.
[45] Lawrence J. White, "What has been Happening to Aggregate Concentration in the United States?" *Journal of Industrial Economics* (March 1981), pp. 223–230.

omy is influenced by the relative *size* of the main sectors as well as the trends within those sectors. A major development has been the very rapid growth of a low-concentration sector, namely services, relative to high-concentration sectors, manufacturing in particular.[46]

SUMMARY

Measuring market concentration involves several steps and various options.

First, one or more statistical indexes ought to be selected. A good index should provide good predictions of conduct and performance. It should also be fairly easy to compute. Our survey of possibilities indicates that (1) the absolute number of firms neglected fractional shares, (2) the Gini coefficient neglected absolute numbers, (3) the Herfindahl index registered both numbers and shares in overall summary fashion but was difficult to compile, and (4) the concentration ratio combines numbers and shares while being fairly inexpensive to compile. For the sake of consistency, it is fortunate that all the main indexes yield numbers that correlate well with each other.

Second, a choice must be made of size measure—sales, employment, assets, or something else. We have glossed over this problem. But for our purposes the differences between measures are not crucial.

Third, the market must be defined. Proper definition requires the inclusion of closely competitive offerings and the exclusion of noncompetitive offerings. A definition that is too narrow excludes competitive offerings. One that is too broad includes noncompetitive offerings. These criteria apply to both product breadth and geographic scope.

The data generated from taking these steps indicate a variety of conditions across the economy's many markets and several sectors. In general, four-firm concentration ratios either below 10 or above 90 are relatively rare. Observations in the 20 to 70 range are much more common.

Trends are mixed across sectors, but some interesting recent developments stand out. Manufacturing has become much more competitive since 1960 once imports and antitrust actions are taken into account. Public utilities and transportation have seen a similar transformation because of deregulation and technological change as well as antitrust. Further discussion of the causes of market concentration (or deconcentration) is summarized on pages 113–114.

Aggregate concentration is also of interest. Over 30% of all manufacturing, mining, and distributing corporate assets are accounted for by the 100 largest firms in these areas. Although the trend of this century's previous decades is upward, there are indications that the trend has leveled off. This leveling has occurred for the economy as a whole in part because relatively low-concentration sectors are growing more rapidly than relatively high-concentration sectors.

---

[46] Eli Ginzberg and George J. Vojta, "The Service Sector of the U.S. Economy," *Scientific American* (March 1981), pp. 48–55.

APPENDIX TO CHAPTER 6
Market Share Instability

Market share instability, as opposed to stability, is a measure of dynamic competition because it suggests that firms are actively vying against each other and creating turmoil. The greater the instability, the greater the apparent dynamic competition, but not always. Share instability would *not* signal competitive blessings, for example, if it were due to a rapid rise in concentration and fall in firm numbers. One indication that market share instability is usually associated with competition comes from evidence that collusion fosters stability.[1]

There are several possible measures of market share instability. A market-wide measure is the correlation of firm shares, comparing their values in one year to their values in a later year.[2] A measure specific to an individual firm would take the percentage-point change in share during some time period, and then divide that percentage point change by the beginning share. Adding up such individual changes for all firms in the market would yield a market-wide measure of instability.

What causes market share instability to be high or low? Research reveals a number of interesting findings, including the following.[3]

1. High concentration is associated with low instability, while low concentration is associated with high instability. This inverse relation suggests that high concentration nurtures anticompetitive, collusive behavior.
2. New firm entry into a market increases market share instability, suggesting that entry is a procompetitive force. Because new entry is associated with rapid growth and the early phases of the product life cycle, it appears that rapid growth and youthful product age are also destabilizing forces.
3. Backward vertical integration tends to reduce share instability.
4. If a product is custom-made rather than off-the-shelf, share instability seems to be higher than otherwise.
5. Product differentiation influences instability in ambiguous ways. If measured by the intensity of research and development outlays directed toward new product design and modification, product differentiation appears to destabilize shares. If measured by advertising intensity, product differentiation can be either destabilizing or stabilizing, depending on the circumstances.

---

[1] Jonathan D. Ogur, *Competition and Market Share Instability* (FTC Staff Report, 1976), pp. 30–48.

[2] Michael Gort, "Analysis of Stability and Change in Market Shares," *Journal of Political Economy* (February 1963), pp. 51–63.

[3] *Ibid.*, Ogur, *op. cit.*, R. McGuckin, "Entry, Concentration Change, and Stability of Market Shares," *Southern Economic Journal* (January 1972), pp. 363–370; R. E. Caves and M. E. Porter, "Market Structure, Oligopoly, and Stability of Market Shares," *Journal of Industrial Economics* (June 1978), pp. 289–313.

7

Concentration and Oligopoly: Merger Practice and Policy

The game of picking up companies is open to everybody. All you have to do is have indefatigable drive, a desire to perpetuate yourself or your family in control of an industry, or an unabsorbed appetite for corporate power.

—MESHULAM RIKLIS (who parlayed $25,000 into a $755 million empire fittingly called Rapid-American, Inc.)

Just over three decades have passed since President Truman signed into law the Celler-Kefauver Act of 1950, the most important piece of antitrust legislation of the last half-century. Vigorous enforcement during the Act's first twenty-seven years resulted in 437 merger complaints, challenging 1,406 acquisitions with combined assets exceeding $40 billion.[1]

Yet there is a paradox here. Merger activity has recently reached historic heights. 1929's long-standing record was broken in 1967, when mergers in manufacturing and mining numbered 1,496, thereby exceeding the previous high of 1,245 established in 1929. More recently, in the early 1980s, individual acquisitions of billions of dollars have become common.

This chapter explores this paradox and related matters. We begin with a brief description of various types of mergers and proceed to a historical review of merger activity. An outline of the causes of mergers comes next, followed by a rundown of policy developments under the Celler-Kefauver Act.

I. BACKGROUND

A. Merger Types

The union of two or more direct competitors is called a **horizontal** merger. The combining companies operate in the same market, as is illustrated in Figure 7-1. Bethlehem Steel's acquisition of the Youngstown Sheet and Tube Company in 1957 is an example. A **vertical** merger links companies that operate at different

---

[1] Willard F. Mueller, *The Celler-Kefauver Act: The First 27 Years,* U.S. House of Representatives, Committee on the Judiciary, Subcommittee on Monopolies and Commercial Law (Nov. 7, 1979), pp. 7–8.

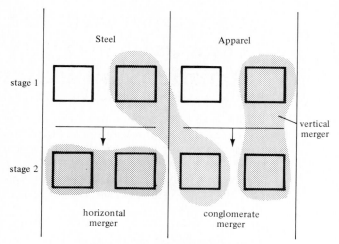

FIGURE 7–1. Types of Mergers

stages of the production-distribution process. This too is illustrated in Figure 7-1, and Bethlehem would provide an example of this type were it to acquire Ford Motors, a big buyer of steel. Broadly speaking, **conglomerate** mergers are all those that are neither horizontal nor vertical. This conglomerate definition covers a lot of ground, however, so the category may be subdivided into three classes: (1) **product extension,** involving producers of two different but related products, such as bleach and detergent; (2) **market extension,** involving firms producing the same product but occupying different geographic markets, for example, dairies in two distant towns; and (3) **pure conglomerate,** involving firms with nothing at all in common, as would be true of a retail grocer and a furniture manufacturer.

B. Some History

A glance at Figure 7–2 reveals why it is customary to speak of three major merger movements in American history. The first movement occurred around the turn of the century. Over the seven-year period 1897–1903, 2,864 mergers were recorded in mining and manufacturing. Measured against our current and more recently set records, this record may not seem like much. However, measured against the economy of 1900 and the resulting market concentration, this first great wave was awesome. Horizontal mergers dominated the scene. Moreover, simultaneous *multiple* mergers, which are now very rare, were an everyday affair. Mergers involving at least five firms accounted for 75% of firm disappearances during this period.[2] This turn-of-the-century merger boom produced such giant companies as U.S. Steel, U.S. Gypsum, International Har-

[2] Ralph L. Nelson, *Merger Movements in American Industry,* 1895–1956 (Princeton, N.J.: Princeton University Press, 1959) p. 29.

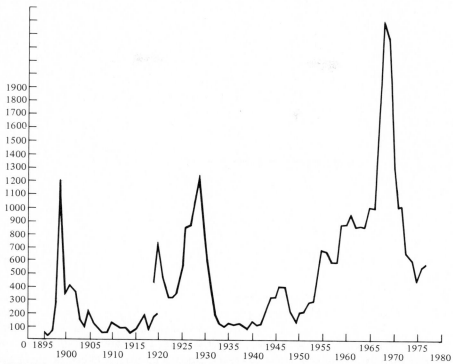

FIGURE 7–2. Number of Manufacturing and Mining Firms Acquired, 1895-1977. (Ralph L. Nelson, *Merger Movements in American Industry,* 1895–1956 (1959), p. 37; Temporary National Economic Committee, *The Structure of American Industry,* Monograph 27 (1941), p. 233; Federal Trade Commission, Bureau of Economics.)

vester, Du Pont, American Tobacco, Pittsburgh Plate Glass, and National Biscuit. Jesse Markham summarized the overall movement neatly when he wrote, "The conversion of approximately 71 important oligopolistic or near-competitive industries into near monopolies by merger between 1890 and 1904 left an imprint on the structure of the American economy that fifty years have not yet erased."[3]

The second major merger wave arose during the Roaring Twenties. From 1925 through 1930, 5,382 mergers were recorded for manufacturing and mining. During the peak year of 1929, ownership shares moved at the feverish pace of more than four mergers per business day. This second movement exceeded the first not only in numbers tallied but also in variety of merger types. Horizontal mergers were again very popular, but vertical, market-extension, and product-extension mergers were also in vogue. It was during this second period that General Foods Corporation put together a string of product-extension acquisitions to become the first big food conglomerate. Its acquisitions included Maxwell

[3] Jesse W. Markham, "Survey of the Evidence and Findings on Mergers," in *Business Concentration and Price Policy* (Princeton, N.J.: Princeton University Press, 1955), p. 180.

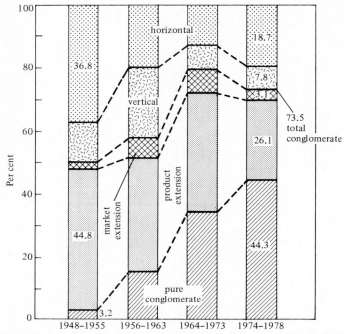

FIGURE 7–3. Distribution of Total Acquired Assets in Large Manufacturing and Mining Mergers, by Type, 1948–1978. (Federal Trade Commission, Bureau of Economics.)

House Coffee, Jello, Baker's Chocolate, Sanka, Birds Eye, and Swans Down Cake Flour. Unlike the first merger movement, these years also witnessed countless mergers in sectors other than manufacturing and mining. At least 2,750 utilities, 1,060 banks, and 10,520 retail stores were swallowed up by acquisition during the twenties.[4]

After two decades of nothing more than a rather meager ripple in the late 1940s, momentum began to build once again in the mid-1950s. Thereafter, the movement swelled incredibly. From 1960 through 1970 the Federal Trade Commission recorded 25,598 mergers. Slightly more than half of these were in manufacturing and mining. The total value of manufacturing and mining assets acquired over this period exceeded $65 billion. This sector's peak year was 1968, when 2,407 firms amounting to more than $13.3 billion were acquired. Putting the matter in relative terms and using an averaging process, we can deduce that, over the period 1953–1968, approximately 21% of all manufacturing and mining assets were acquired.[5]

After a lull in the mid-1970s, the pace quickened again, as shown in Figure

[4] Ibid., pp. 168–69.
[5] Federal Trade Commission, *Economic Report on Corporate Mergers* (Washington, D.C., 1969), p. 666.

7–2. Many of the most spectacular recent acquisitions have been made by oil companies, whose financial coffers have grown fat.

As for merger types, these latest waves have been quite different from those of yesteryear. Horizontal mergers have become much less numerous than conglomerate mergers. Figure 7–3 shows the trend of the last three decades in percentage of *assets* acquired by merger type. As we shall see shortly, much of this trend away from horizontal couplings and toward conglomerate couplings, especially toward pure conglomerates, was due to public policy. The enforcement agencies cracked down rather hard on horizontal mergers whereas they generally ignored conglomerates.

II. REASONS FOR MERGER

When counting the *reasons* for merger, one can get by with only the fingers on one hand, but just barely. In simplest terms, corporate marriage is merely a matter of finding a price that buyers are willing to pay and sellers are willing to accept. Going beyond this truism, however, we encounter complexities. Some motives are constant in the sense that they explain a fairly steady stream of mergers year in and year out. Other motives are more cyclical, a characteristic that helps explain why merger activity heats up and cools down over time. In other words, there are two interrelated issues—underlying cause and timing.

A. Timing of Mergers

Let us consider timing first. Several researchers have found a high positive correlation between the number of mergers per year and the general business cycle.[6] Merger frequency tends to rise and fall as the average level of stock market prices rises and falls.

Exactly why this correlation exists is not entirely clear. Experts speculate that owners of firms expecting eventually to sell out may feel they can get the best deal when stock prices are generally high. Conversely, from the buyers point of view, the basic problem is raising enough cash and securities to make an attractive offer. Hence, acquiring firms may find funds for acquisitions easier and cheaper to come by when stock prices are high.

B. Underlying Causes of Mergers

Underlying causes involve as much intuitive understanding as timing does. They are, however, less mysterious. Sellers and buyers may see things differently while benefiting mutually.[7] *Sellers* appear to have two major reasons for wanting

[6] Nelson, *op. cit.,* pp. 106–26; Markham, *op. cit.,* pp. 146-54; and Willard Mueller, testimony in *Economic Concentration,* Hearings before the Senate Subcommittee on Antitrust and Monopoly, Part 2 (1965), p. 506.

[7] For an excellent discussion of causes see Peter O. Steiner, *Mergers: Motives, Effects, Policies* (Ann Arbor, Mich.: University of Michigan Press, 1975), especially Chapter 2. For a massive empirical study of causes and effects see Dennis C. Mueller, ed., *The Determinants and Effects of Mergers* (Cambridge, Mass.: Oelgeschlager, Gunn & Hain, Publishers, 1980).

to seek out a buyer. First, and most obvious, is the "failing firm" problem. As every used car owner knows, poor performance may prompt a sale. In the case of business enterprises, failure is measured in terms of declining revenues, disappointing profits, recurring losses, and even bankruptcy. Although any such aspect of failure may be an important motive for the sale of a small firm, it could be no more than a very minor motive for most sales of large firms. It has been estimated, for example, that only about 4.8% of all "large" firms bought between 1948 and 1968 were suffering losses before their acquisition, where "large" was defined as having at least $10 million in assets.[8]

A second class of seller's motives relates to individually or family owned firms that are typically small. Merger may be the easiest means for an aging owner-manager to "cash-in" on his lifetime effort and perpetuate the business after his retirement. Some income and estate tax considerations also favor the sale of such firms. Again, however, these seem to be minor factors, mere droplets in the tidal waves of time past.

Of greater importance and keener interest are the *buyers'* motives. After all, the prices buyers pay to former owners typically exceed the book value of the purchased firms' assets and the market value of the former owners' stock holdings. This excess, or "premium," usually varies between 10 and 30%, but may go as high as 50% or more.[9] In early 1977, for example, prospective acquirers of Milgo Electronics were offering to pay $36 a share, whereas the former selling price was only $20 a share. Indeed, buyers may be so aggressive that they occasionally pull a "raid" or "takeover," in which case they succeed in buying a firm whose management opposes the acquisition. Stock owners who sell out against the management's wishes in these instances may not dislike their reluctant managers (although they frequently do); they may merely feel they have received an "offer they cannot refuse." Lest this give the impression that all merger motives are one-sided, we hasten to add that the following list of buyer's motives includes items that could very well be considered "mutual" motives. Buyers and sellers may both benefit if the whole is worth more than the sum of its parts.

1. Monopoly Power. U.S. Steel was apparently worth more than the sum of its 170 parts. Prior to merger in 1901, the total value of the tangible property of the separate firms stood at roughly $700 million. After merger, U.S. Steel estimated its value at close to $1400 million. Why the enormous difference? Market power. After merger, U.S. Steel produced two thirds of all United States semifinished steel and similar percentages of all rails, tin plate, rods, and other

[8] Stanley E. Boyle, "Pre-Merger Growth and Profit Characteristics of Large Conglomerate Mergers in the United States: 1948–1968," *St. Johns Law Review* (Spring 1970, Special Edition), pp. 160–161. See also Robert L. Conn, "The Failing Firm/Industry Doctrines in Conglomerate Mergers," *Journal of Industrial Economics* (March 1976), pp. 181–187.

[9] Steiner, *op. cit.*, p. 179; J. Fred Weston, "Determination of Share Exchange Ratios in Mergers," in *The Corporate Merger*, edited by W. Alberts and J. Segal (Chicago: University of Chicago Press, 1974), pp. 131–138.

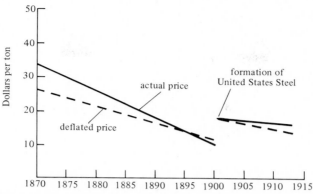

Figure 7–4. Pig Iron Price Trend, Before and After U.S. Steel. (Parsons and Ray, "The United States Steel Consolidation: The Creation of Market Control." *Journal of Law and Economics*, April 1975, p. 186.)

products. The consequences for the price of pig iron are pictured in Figure 7–4, which shows two price trend lines, one deflated by the wholesale price index, the other not. The discontinuous price jump of about 50% in 1901 coincides with the formation of U.S. Steel. This may lead the astute reader to suspect a substantial rise in annual profit rates also, and you would be correct.

U.S. Steel provides just one example. As we have already seen, there were many other huge horizontal mergers at the turn of the century that were probably motivated by the rewards of monopoly. The 70–90% market shares of those days speak fairly plainly for themselves. But a more explicit statement was made by Thomas Edison when he explained the formation of the General Electric Company in this way: "The consolidation of the companies . . . will do away with a competition which has become so sharp that the product of the factories has been worth little more than ordinary hardware."[10]

Whether market power could motivate vertical and conglomerate mergers as well as horizontal mergers is a much debated question. These other forms of merger produce no immediate or obvious increases in market share for the consolidated firm. Nor do they promise added *market* concentration. Hence, theories and empirical tests of possible adverse competitive effects of these mergers must attack the question indirectly.

The major potentially anticompetitive effects of vertical mergers are (1) *foreclosure,* wherein nonintegrated businesses at one level of the production-distribution chain are foreclosed from dealing with suppliers or buyers at other levels because those other suppliers or buyers are owned by vertically integrated rivals, and (2) strengthened *barriers to entry,* which may arise from the foreclosure of potential entrants and the enlarged capital cost requirements associated with

[10] H. C. Passer, *The Electrical Manufacturers; 1875-1900* (Cambridge, Mass.: Harvard University Press, 1953), p. 326.

133

multilevel entry.[11] U.S. Steel provides an example of the barrier effect because the main source of its market power was its aggressive vertical acquisition of most iron ore supplies in North America. Charles Schwab, a prominent steel executive of the day, explained the consequences of U.S. Steel's 75% ore control while testifying in 1911:

> *Mr. Schwab.* I do not believe there will be any great development in iron and steel by new companies, but rather development by the companies now in business.

> *Mr. Chairman.* Now, explain that to us.

> *Mr. Schwab.* For the reason that the possibility of a new company getting at a sufficiently large supply of raw materials would make it exceedingly difficult if not impossible.[12]

As for conglomerate mergers, we can note that the greater size and diversity they gain improves the possibility of *reciprocity.* This is a policy of "I buy from you if you buy from me," and it may tend to foreclose rivals from affected markets. Conglomerate mergers may also eliminate *potential* competitors. In either event, profits might follow from the added power implied. Substantiation or refutation of these and other possible effects is difficult in particular cases and in general. However, several researchers have found that the market shares of firms acquired by conglomerates do not usually grow inordinately after acquisition. They say this shows an absence of adverse competitive effect,[13] implying that most conglomerate mergers could not be motivated by quests for market power.

2. Risk Spreading through Diversification. Suppose you want to get two dozen eggs delivered to your grandmother. Suppose further that she lives in the woods, and the only available delivery service relies on brave but clumsy six-year-old girls attired in red. Experience shows that stumbles over roots and stones make successful egg delivery by any one girl a 50:50 proposition (even apart from the danger of wolves). Your problem then is this: If you want at least *some* of your two dozen eggs to get through, what delivery arrangements should you make? Placing the entire shipment in the hands of one girl means a 0.5 probability that *none* will arrive. However, if you give one dozen to one girl and one dozen to another, there is only one chance in four that no eggs will be delivered because that is the probability of both girls falling down. Similarly, the split shipment offers one chance in four that all eggs will arrive safely.

---

[11] Willard F. Mueller, "Public Policy Toward Vertical Mergers," in *Public Policy Toward Mergers,* edited by F. Weston and S. Peltzman (Pacific Palisades, Calif.: Goodyear, 1969), pp. 150–166.

[12] Parsons and Ray, *op. cit.,* p. 198.

[13] L. G. Goldberg, "Conglomerate Mergers and Concentration Ratios," *Review of Economics and Statistics* (August 1974), pp. 303-309; S. E. Boyle and P. W. Jaynes, *Economic Report on Conglomerate Merger Performance* (Washington D.C.: Federal Trade Commission, 1972), pp. 82–83. But see R. W. Cotterill and W. F. Mueller, "The Impact of Firm Conglomeration on Market Structure: Evidence for the U.S. Food Retailing Industry," *Antitrust Bulletin* (Fall 1980), pp. 557–582.

Two times in every four, one dozen will be broken and one dozen will get through. This example was developed by Roger Sherman to demonstrate the power of diversification in reducing risks.[14] He also demonstrates that still further diversification yields further risk reduction: "The best thing to do is to send 24 girls, each with one egg. The chance that no egg will arrive is then infinitesimally small, and it becomes very probable that about 12 eggs will arrive safely." The obvious moral (don't put all your eggs in one basket) may motivate many vertical and conglomerate mergers.

Diversification, however, is not always favorable; nor is merger the only means of achieving diversification. The conditions required for a positive effect for an acquiring firm are more limited than this simple example suggests.[15] In particular, the variances of the components of a combination must be essentially independent of each other. (The independence of several delivery girls would be severely compromised if they all held hands and thereby tripped over each other.) Failure to meet the conditions necessary for risk reduction may explain why researchers have been unable to find any risk reduction among conglomerate mergers generally.[16] Indeed, the gyrations of some conglomerates, such as LTV and Litton, offer evidence that mergers often augment risk rather than reduce it.

3. Economic Efficiency. The larger size that mergers bring to combinations may yield lower costs of various kinds. These efficiencies may be divided into two broad groups—pecuniary economies and technical economies. **Pecuniary economies** are monetary savings derived from buying inputs more cheaply. Pecuniary gains thus include such things as larger "volume discounts" for the bulk purchase of raw materials or advertising space, lower interest rates on borrowed capital, and greater negotiating strength vis-a-vis labor, tax assessors, and others. In contrast, **technical economies** of scale are "genuine" cost savings. They imply fewer real inputs for a given level of output. Their primary sources are (1) greater specialization of equipment and operators, (2) high speed automation, (3) scaled-up equipment, and (4), in the case of vertical mergers, a refined coordination of effort between several stages of the production process.

Well then, do mergers really produce such economies? Briefly, the general answer is "yes" and "no." It is "yes" if we look only at the justifications businessmen most frequently offer the public for their mergers. It is "no" if we look at the evidence assembled and assessed by most economists studying the question. As Dennis Mueller puts it, the empirical literature draws a surprisingly consistent picture: "Whatever the stated or unstated goals of managers are, the mergers they have consummated have on average not generated extra profits for the

---

[14] Roger Sherman, *The Economics of Industry* (Boston: Little, Brown and Co., 1974), p. 105.

[15] H. Bierman, Jr. and J. L. Thomas, "A Note on Mergers and Risk," *Antitrust Bulletin* (Fall 1974), pp. 523–529.

[16] B. Lev and G. Mandelker, "The Microeconomic Consequences of Corporate Mergers," *Journal of Business* (January 1972), pp. 85–104; Samuel R. Reid, *The New Industrial Order* (New York: McGraw-Hill, 1976), pp. 94–98; R. W. Melicher and D. F. Rush, "The Performance of Conglomerate Firms: Recent Risk and Return Experience," *Journal of Finance* (May 1973), pp. 381–388.

acquiring firms, have not resulted in increased economic efficiency."[17] Thus, although *some* mergers may yield economies, they usually do not.

4. Speculative and Financial Motives. Several influences may raise the price of an acquiring company's stock after a merger or series of mergers, even *without* any increment in market power, or economies of scale, or reduced risk, or enhanced real profit flows, or changes of the real assets under the combined control of the merging companies. Such stock price increases stem from speculation and often feed further speculation. They may stem from the mere *expectation* of real changes, as would be the case if investors expected a merger to capture as much market power as U.S. Steel acquired. Indeed, around the turn of the century many merger "promoters" exploited the expectations of investors by arranging mergers that had little chance of achieving real monopoly power while exaggerating monopoly power's prospects, planting rumors, and pointing to U.S. Steel's success. Once expectations were running wild and the deal was closed, promoters would hasten to sell the stock they obtained as a promotion fee to unsuspecting investor-speculators. These unfortunate folks often "took a bath." Shaw Livermore estimated that 141 of a sample of 328 mergers consummated between 1888 and 1905 were financial failures.[18]

Disclosure regulations have long since discouraged this unscrupulous practice. More recently (and more significantly for our own pocket books) we have the use of what Wall Streeters call "Confederate money" or "P/E magic." This can occur when a conglomerate issues new stock to acquire a firm with a lower price/earnings ratio than its own. When the conglomerate's new stock is exchanged for the stock of the acquired firm, earnings per share of the conglomerate jump, leading investors to buoy the conglomerate's price/earnings ratio, thereby supporting still further acquisitions. Evidence indicates that such price/earnings manipulation played a major role in the merger movement of the sixties.[19] Exactly how major is a matter of opinion. Some experts estimate that its role was the principal reason behind at least 20% of all mergers occurring in 1967.[20]

---

[17] Dennis C. Mueller, "The Effects of Conglomerate Mergers," *Journal of Banking and Finance*, 1 (December 1977), pp. 315–344. In addition to Mueller's citations see G. Meeks, *Disappointing Marriage: A Study of the Gains from Mergers* (Cambridge, U.K.; Cambridge University Press, 1977); and D. W. Colenutt and P. P. O'Donnell, "The Consistency of Monopolies and Mergers Commission Merger Reports," *Antitrust Bullentin* (Spring 1978), pp. 51–82. Indeed, it is interesting that during 1979-1980 many conglomerates developed a "divestiture trend" in hopes of improving their efficiency and profitability. In these two years, for instance, ITT shed 33 companies with combined annual sales exceeding $1 billion. Others unloading baggage included Bendix, GAF, Esmark, and Gulf & Western. For a dissenting view on efficiency, see J. Fred Weston, "Industrial Concentration, Mergers, and Growth: A Summary" in *Mergers and Economic Efficiency*, Vol. 1. (U.S. Department of Commerce, 1980), pp. 38–44.

[18] Shaw Livermore, "The Success of Industrial Mergers," *Quarterly Journal of Economics* (Novermber 1935), pp. 68–96.

[19] Steiner, *op. cit.*, pp. 203–204; Walter J. Mead, "Instantaneous Merger Profit as a Conglomerate Merger Motive," *Western Economic Journal* (December 1969), pp. 295–306.

[20] *Business Week*, March 2, 1968, p. 42.

5. Growth and Personal Aggrandizement. This survey would not be complete without mention of sheer growth and personal aggrandizement as motives. Just how important they are it is impossible to say. The Napoleonic aspirations of acquisitive business leaders cannot be captured by statistics, except insofar as statistics may disprove the importance of other, more publicly professed and more socially acceptable motives, such as economies of scale. You, the reader, are free to judge for yourself. You may draw upon your knowledge of human nature and your reading of whatever biographical material you may wish to look into. Two typical examples you will find are:

- Harold Geneen led ITT in the acquisition of more than 250 companies. A close colleague of his once said, "Three things should be written on Hal Geneen's tombstone—earnings per share, 15% growth per year, and size."[21]

- Charles G. Bluhdorn, who guided Gulf & Western Industries through more than 80 acquisitions in 11 years, had this to say about his company and himself: "No mountain is high enough for us, nothing is impossible. The sky is the limit. . . . I came to this country without a penny, and built a company with 100,000 employees. This is what America is all about . . . to be able to do what I've done is a matter of pride to me and to the country."[22]

To summarize, the motives for merger are many and varied. No one explanation clearly surpasses all others. At any one time, there is a diversity of inducements; over time, trends of intention shift.

III. MERGER POLICY

There are two keys to understanding United States government policy toward mergers. First, the private interests and motives of business managers and stockholders are *not* accorded any weight in such policy. Why? As far as a merger may be socially beneficial, the benefits are usually attainable by means *other* than merger. Economies of scale and diversification, for example, can be achieved by internal expansion as successfully as by merger. In the case of the failing firm or the aging owner-manager in search of a friendly savior, a strict rule denying anticompetitive mergers would probably exclude no more than a few prospective buyers, leaving open the possibility of sale to any number of other

[21] Spoken by Richard H. Griebel, a former ITT executive and president of Lehigh Valley Industries, *Business Week,* May 9, 1970, p. 61. For more on Geneen see Anthony Sampson, *The Sovereign State of ITT* (Fawcett Crest Paperback, 1974).

[22] *Business Week,* July 5, 1969, p. 34. On Victor Posner see *Wall Street Journal,* June 23, 1981, pp. 1, 16; on Russell Chambers see *Wall Street Journal,* December 30, 1982, pp. 1, 12; and on the men involved in the amazing Bendix/Martin Marietta/United Technologies battle of 1982 see *Wall Street Journal,* September 24, 1982, pp. 1, 22. For more solid evidence favoring growth see Alan R. Beckenstein, "Merger Activity and Merger Theories: An Empirical Investigation," *Antitrust Bulletin* (Spring 1979), pp. 105–128.

possible—and more suitable—acquirers. Conversely, for motives that are grounded on purely private gains or socially detrimental pursuits, a strict policy will either be neutral or favorable to the public interest.[23]

The second key was introduced in Chapter 1. Maintenance of competition by structural dispersal of power is a policy objective in and of itself. Many if not most congressmen and judges believe that the growth of large economic groups "could lead only to increasing government control; freedom would corrode and the nation would drift into some form of totalitarianism"[24]

For these several reasons, the law governing most mergers has a structural focus and is designed to curb market power in the early stages (to "nip it in the bud" before it fully blossoms). Indeed, as stated in the preamble to the original Clayton Bill, the purpose of the Clayton Act of 1914 was "to arrest the creation of trusts, conspiracies and monopolies *in their incipiency and before consummation.*" Section 7 of the Clayton Act prohibited potentially anticompetitive mergers—but it had enormous loopholes. These were not plugged until 1950, with passage of the Celler-Kefauver Amendment. The amended statute outlaws mergers

> where in any line of commerce in any section of the country, the effect of such acquisition may be substantially to lessen competition, or tend to create a monopoly.

The Act is enforced by the Justice Department and the Federal Trade Commission. Although hundreds of cases have been decided under the Act, we shall review only a few of the more important ones. Before we do, a brief outline of what to look for may be helpful:

1. The phrase "in any line of commerce" refers to product markets. Major factors affecting the courts' definition of relevant product markets include (a) the product's physical characteristics and uses, (b) unique production facilities, (c) distinct customers, (d) crosselasticity of demand with substitutes, and (e) the absolute price level of possible substitutes.
2. The phrase "in any section of the country" refers to particular geographic markets. Major factors affecting the courts' definition of relevant geographic markets include (a) the costs of transportation, (b) legal restrictions on geographic scope, (c) the extent to which local demand is met by outside supply—for example, little in from outside, and (d) the extent to which local production is shipped to other areas—for example, little out from inside.[25]
3. The phrase "may be . . . to lessen competition" reflects the importance of *probable* adverse effect. In this regard the major factors considered by the courts differ somewhat depending on whether the merger at issue

[23] Derek C. Bok, "Section 7 of the Clayton Act and the Merging of Law and Economics," *Harvard Law Review* (1960), p. 308.

[24] Ibid., p. 235.

[25] K. G. Elzinga and T. F. Hogarty, "The Problem of Georgraphic Market Delineation in Antimerger Suits," *Antitrust Bullentin* (Spring 1973), pp. 45–81. See also Ira Horowitz, "Market Definition in Antitrust Analysis: A Regression Based Approach," *Southern Economic Journal* (July 1981), pp. 1–16.

is horizontal, vertical, or conglomerate. Factors for (a) *horizontal mergers* include the market shares and ranks of the merging firms; concentration in the market; *trends* in market shares and concentration; merger history in the market; declines in the absolute number of firms; and the elimination of a strong, competitively vigorous independent firm. Factors considered for (b) *vertical mergers,* where foreclosure and entry barriers are the potentially adverse effects, include the market shares of the merging firms (each at their respective levels in the production-distribution process); and the trend toward vertical integration in the industry. Factors considered for (c) *conglomerate mergers* include the elimination of a prime potential entrant; the danger of reciprocal buying; and any severe disparity of size between the acquired firm and its competitors.

IV. HORIZONTAL MERGERS

The Bethlehem-Youngstown Case (1958). [26] Bethlehem Steel's acquisition of Youngstown Sheet & Tube in 1957 was the first large merger challenged under the Celler-Kefauver Act. The firms ranked second and sixth nationally among steel producers. Their combined ingot capacity amounted to 21% of total industry capacity. The number one firm, U.S. Steel, had a 30% share at the time, so this merger would have boosted the share of U.S. Steel and Bethlehem taken together from 45 to 50%. In the court's opinion, "This would add substantially to concentration in an already highly concentrated industry and reduce unduly the already limited number of integrated steel companies." The court was also impressed by the fact that, historically, mergers accounted "for the existing high degree of concentration in the industry." Aside from U.S. Steel's origins, "Bethlehem's growth in substantial measure is the result of mergers."

Bethlehem's defense for acquiring Youngstown Sheet & Tube was that the national market was not the relevant geographic market for steel products. It's attorneys urged acceptance of three separate markets within the United States—eastern, midcontinental, and western. Since all Youngstown's plants were located in the midcontinent area whereas all of Bethlehem's plants were either eastern or western, the defense went on to argue that the high costs of steel transportation prevented head-on competition between the merging firms. Moreover, they claimed that the acquisition would bring Bethlehem into the Chicago area, where it could then compete more effectively with U.S. Steel, the dominant force in that area.

The court rejected these arguments. It said that, even though Bethlehem did not have ingot capacity in the midcontinent area, Bethlehem's annual shipments of more than 2 million tons into the area indicated direct competition with Youngstown. Direct rivalry prevailed in other sections of the country as well. Furthermore, the court recognized that market delineation "must be made

[26] *United States v. Bethlehem Steel Corp.,* 168 F. Supp. 576 (1958).

on the basis of where *potentially* they could make sales." In other words, Bethlehem was surely capable of entering the Chicago market by internal expansion instead of by acquisition. As for the argument that the combined companies could better compete with U.S. Steel, the same faulty logic could justify successive mergers until just two or three firms were left in the industry, a situation that could hardly be considered competitive. Thus the merger was enjoined. The benefits of the court's denial were realized for all to see when a few years later Bethlehem *did* build a massive steel plant thirty miles east of Chicago.

The Brown Shoe Case (1962). [27]   Failure to appeal the *Bethlehem* case enabled *Brown Shoe* to achieve the distinction of being the first case to reach the Supreme Court under the Celler-Kefauver Act. In 1955, the date of this merger, Brown was the fourth largest manufacturer of shoes in the United States, accounting for about 4% of total shoe production. Brown was also a big shoe retailer, owning or controlling over 1,230 retail shops. The mate in Brown's merger was Kinney, which likewise engaged in shoe manufacturing and retailing. Retailing was Kinney's *forte,* however, as it was at the time the nation's largest "independent" retail shoe chain, with over 400 stores in more than 270 cities and about 1.2% of all retail shoe sales by dollar volume. The case thus had vertical as well as horizontal aspects. Here we take up the horizontal aspects at retail level, saving the vertical aspects for later.

The Supreme Court decided that relevant product lines could be drawn to distinguish men's, women's, and children's shoes. Defendant Brown wanted still narrower delineations such as "medium-priced" and "low-priced" shoes, but the Court did not agree. As for geographic markets at retail level, the Court decided upon "cities with a population exceeding 10,000 and their environs in which both Brown and Kinney retailed shoes." By this definition, the market shares of the merging companies were enough to arouse the Court's disapproval. For example, the combined share of Brown and Kinney sales of women's shoes exceeded 20% in 32 cities. And in children's shoes, their combined share exceeded 20% in 31 cities. In addition to raw shares, *trends* caught the Court's attention: "We cannot avoid the mandate of Congress that tendencies toward concentration in industry are to be curbed in their incipiency, particularly when those tendencies are being accelerated through giant steps striding across a hundred cities at a time. In the light of the trends in this industry we agree with the Government and the court below that this is an appropriate place at which to call a halt."

The Continental Can Case (1964). [28]   In this case the Supreme Court held illegal a merger between Continental Can, the nation's second largest manufacturer of metal containers, and Hazel-Atlas Glass Company, the nation's third largest producer of glass containers. It was generally agreed that the entire country constituted the geographic market. Thus product market delineation

---

[27] *Brown Shoe Company v. United States,* 370 U.S. 294 (1962).
[28] *United States v. Continental Can Co.,* 378 U.S. 441 (1964).

TABLE 7–1. Percentage of Metal and Glass Container Shipments Accounted for by Continental Can and Hazel-Atlas, 1955

Product Market	Continental Can	Hazel-Atlas	Continental and Hazel-Atlas Combined
Metal containers	33.0	None	33.0
Glass containers	None	9.6	9.6
Metal and glass containers	21.9	3.1	25.0

Source: *U.S.* v. *Continental Can Co.* 378 U.S. 441 (1964).

became the critical issue. Table 7–1 shows the shares of these companies under alternative product market definitions. Continental produced no glass containers, and Hazel-Atlas produced no metal cans. A narrow definition that kept the two products separate would therefore mean no change in market shares as a result of the merger. Conversely, a broad definition combining metal and glass would imply direct competition between the companies and a jump in market share for Continental from 21.9 to 25%. A still broader definition, one including paper and plastic as well as metal and glass, would also place these firms in the same market, but would give them much lower market shares.

A majority of the Court thought that metal and glass containers combined could be considered a proper "line of commerce" for purposes of Section 7:

> Metal has replaced glass and glass has replaced metal as the leading container for some important uses; both are used for other purposes; each is trying to expand its share of the market at the expense of the other; and each is attempting to preempt for itself every use for which its product is physically suitable, even though some such uses have traditionally been regarded as the exclusive domain of the competing industry.

Up to that time this interproduct competition had been especially sharp for packaging beer, soft drinks, and baby food. To a lesser degree it extended to household chemicals and other areas. From recognition of these aspects of competition, it was a small step to a conclusion of merger illegality. The firms were large and highly ranked. Moreover, "the product market embracing the combined metal and glass container industries was dominated by six firms having a total of 70.1% of the business." The Court felt that where "concentration is already great, the importance of preventing even slight increases in concentration . . . is correspondingly great."

The Von's Case (1966). [29] This case is to horizontal mergers what the sixth commandment is to homicide. The acquisition was denied, although neither

[29] *United States v. Von's Grocery Co.,* 384 U.S. 270 (1966).

141

firm involved was really very big and, by usual standards, the market was not highly concentrated. Von's ranked third among retail grocery store chains in the Los Angeles area when in 1960 it acquired Shopping Bag Food Stores, which ranked sixth. Their market shares were, respectively, 4.3 and 3.2%. Hence, their combined sales amounted to 7.5%. This would have boosted the four-firm concentration ratio in the Los Angeles market from 24.4% before merger to 28.8% after. Moreover, 8-firm and 12-firm concentration had been on the rise prior to merger.

These facts might have been moderately damning. But Justice Black chose to neglect them when writing the Supreme Court's majority opinion. He stressed other factors:

> the number of owners operating a single store in the Los Angeles retail grocery market decreased from 5,365 in 1950 to 3,818 in 1961. By 1963, three years after merger, the number of single store owners had dropped still further to 3,590. During roughly the same period from 1953 to 1962 the number of chains with two or more grocery stores increased from 96 to 150. While the grocery business was being concentrated into the hands of fewer and fewer owners, the small companies were continually being absorbed by the larger firms through mergers.

Indeed, Black defines concentration in terms of the *number* of independent firms. He goes on to state that "the basic purpose of the 1950 Celler-Kefauver Bill was to prevent economic concentration in the American economy by keeping a large number of small competitors in business." By this reasoning, a divestiture order was unavoidable.

However laudable these sentiments might be, we may question as a matter of economics whether the massive demise of mom-and-pop grocery stores in Los Angeles was due to mergers like the one denied. Divestiture of Shopping Bag did not resurrect them. They fell by the wayside for reasons of economies of scale, cheap automobile transportation to shopping centers, easy parking in the shopping centers, and the like. Thus the Court seems to have set a stringent legal standard while deferring to a moderate standard of economic proficiency.

The Pabst Case (1966). [30] Both standards carried over into the Pabst case, another denial decided just after the Von's case. In 1958 Pabst was the nation's tenth largest brewer. It acquired Blatz, the eighteenth largest. This merger made Pabst the nation's fifth largest brewer with 4.49% of nationwide sales volume. Thus, in terms of a broad national definition of the market, the ranks and shares involved here were rather low, even lower than those in Von's. Government prosecutors therefore argued acceptance of Wisconsin and a three-state area made up of Wisconsin, Illinois, and Michigan as relevant geographic markets. In Wisconsin, for instance, Blatz had been the largest seller and Pabst had been fourth; after the merger Pabst was first with 23.95% of state sales. The Supreme Court bought the idea of limited state markets without any economic justification:

[30] *United States v. Pabst Brewing Co.*, 384 U.S. 540 (1966).

> The language of [the Act] requires merely that the Government prove the merger has a substantial anticompetitive effect somewhere in the United States—"in *any* section" of the United States. This phrase does not call for the delineation of a "section of the country" by metes and bounds as a surveyor would lay off a plot of ground.

The Court's cavalier treatment of the market definition problem has been strongly criticized.

Recent Developments. In 1968, the Justice Department promulgated a set of "merger guidelines," which specified market share combinations that would "ordinarily" be challenged by the government. Based on cases like *Von's* and *Pabst,* these guidelines were quite strict. For example, a merger of two firms having market shares as low as 10% and 2% in a market where the four-firm concentration ratio exceeded 74% would have violated the 1968 guidelines. This stern stand led some commentators to conclude that horizontal mergers were almost per se illegal.

However, the 1970s and 1980s proved that the law is not that stringent. For example, in grocery retailing the enforcement agencies gave the green light during 1975–76 to three substantial horizontal mergers by large companies—Lucky, Allied, and A & P.[31] Moreover, the government has lost a number of recent cases. Among these, *Pillsbury* (1979) is one of the most interesting. In this case, FTC attorneys challenged a 1976 merger between Pillsbury and Fox Deluxe Foods, both of which produced frozen pizza. Before merger, Pillsbury held 15.4% of the market and Fox accounted for 2.4%. Moreover, there was some trend toward concentration in the market. Nevertheless, the Commission decided *not* to ban the merger on grounds that (1) the merger was not substantially anticompetitive, and (2) Fox owners were exiting from the market and there was a need to preserve exit opportunities for small firms.[32] Explaining the importance of exit opportunities, the FTC argued that the *entry* of new, small firms into the industry would be discouraged if their opportunities to sell out were restricted by law. Thus, maintenance of exit opportunity would, according to the FTC, rebound to make entry easier.

Finally, and most recently, President Reagan's Assistant Attorney General William Baxter rewrote the merger guidelines in 1982 to better reflect the relaxed attitude of the courts. While loosening the merger rules, the new guidelines incorporated two new twists. *First,* they measure structural impact by the *H index,* which involves transformations of market share data. Market shares in percentage form are squared, so that, for example, a share of 10% becomes 100, a share of 2% becomes 4, and their combination of 12% becomes 144. Moreover, instead of measuring market concentration by the sum of the shares of the four leading firms, the *H* index of concentration *squares* the shares of *all* firms and then adds them up. For example, the *H* index for a market of five firms with shares of 35%, 25%, 20%, 15%, and 5%, would be

---

[31] Willard F. Mueller, *The Celler-Kefauver Act . . . op. cit.,* p. 47.
[32] *In the Matter of the Pillsbury Co.,* CCH Para. 21,586 (June 1979), FTC Dkt. 9091.

$$35^2 + 25^2 + 20^2 + 15^2 + 5^2 = 1225 + 625 + 400 + 225 + 25 = 2500$$

This squaring of market shares gives especially large weight to especially large market shares, so it may be a better reflection of anticompetitive impact than market shares plain and simple. The new guidelines permit horizontal mergers in markets having a post-merger H index of 1,000 or less, pose a warning in the 1,000–1,800 range, and threaten serious trouble for any substantial merger in markets with H indexes greater than 1,800.

The *second* new twist in the guidelines is that they incorporate consideration of factors other than market shares and concentration when deciding whether to challenge particular mergers. That is to say, competition may be either less or more intense than is suggested by a given level of concentration. It may be *less* intense if, for example, barriers to entry are particularly high or if extensive joint venture activity inhibits competitive independence. Conversely, competition may be *more* intense if (1) there is *rapid technological change* to stifle collusive understandings and disrupt stodgy strategies, or (2) there is *rapid industry growth,* which creates market turbulence and reduces incentives to collude, or (3) especially *easy entry* to provide potential competition, or (4) substantial *instability of market shares,* something which can signal vigorous competition despite high concentration. Stressing these factors that intensify competition, the new guidelines will permit horizontal mergers that would probably have been challenged under the old guidelines, but they might still maintain a moderately firm stance against horizontal mergers.[33]

Treatment of vertical and conglomerate mergers seems to be easing as well.

V. VERTICAL MERGERS

Short of monopoly, the critical issue in nearly all vertical merger cases is "foreclosure." Before merger, numerous suppliers can compete for each independent user's purchases. After merger, supplier and user are linked by common ownership. Products then typically flow between the merged firms as far as is practicable, and the sales opportunities of other suppliers diminish. If the vertical linkage is trivial, as would be true of a farmer owning a roadside vegetable stand, competition is not affected. If, on the other hand, the foreclosure covers a wide portion of the total market, there may be anticompetitive consequences.

The Brown Shoe Case (1962): Vertical Aspects.[34] Prior to Brown Shoe's acquisition of Kinney in 1955, Brown had acquired a very large number of

---

[33] *Wall Street Journal,* Novermber 16, 1981, p. 2. Statement of Assistant Attorney General Baxter before the Subcommittee on Monopolies and Commercial Law of the Committee on the Judiciary, U.S. Senate, August 26, 1981; David Ranii, "The Antitrust Revolution," *National Law Journal* (Nov. 9, 1981), pp. 1, 18–19. A few cases support Baxter in this. See *U.S. v. General Dynamics,* 415 U.S. 486 (1974); *Kaiser Aluminum & Chemical Corp. v. FTC,* 1981–2 Trade Cases, para. 64, 149 (7th Cir. 1981).

[34] *Brown Shoe Company v. United States,* 370 U.S. 294 (1962).

retail shops. Thus, Kinney was just one in a series of vertical mergers by Brown. In effect, then, Brown was attempting to accumulate captive retail distributors who would buy heavily from Brown's manufacturing arm.

On these vertical aspects the Supreme Court stressed several points. First, since Kinney was the largest independent retail chain, the Court felt that, in this industry, "no merger between a manufacturer and an independent retailer could involve a larger potential market foreclosure." Second, the evidence showed that Brown would use the acquisition "to force Brown shoes into Kinney stores." Third, there was a *trend* toward vertical integration in the industry, a trend in which the acquiring manufacturers had "become increasingly important sources of supply for their acquired outlets," and the "necessary corollary of these trends is the foreclosure of independent manufacturers from markets otherwise open to them." Although Brown's attorneys argued that the shoe industry was composed of a large number of manufacturers and retailers, the Court rejected their arguments on grounds that "remaining vigor cannot immunize a merger if the trend in that industry is toward oligopoly." The Court thus ordered divestiture.

The Cement Cases (1961-1967). Approximately three fourths of all cement is used to produce ready-mixed concrete (cement premixed with sand or other aggregate). Prior to 1960 there was virtually no integration between the cement and ready-mixed concrete industries. By 1966, however, after an outbreak of merger activity, at least 40 ready-mix concrete companies had been acquired by leading cement companies, and several large producers of ready-mixed concrete had begun to make cement. The Federal Trade Commission issued a series of complaints, directed its staff to make an industry-wide investigation, and in January 1967 issued a policy statement challenging vertical mergers in the industry, all of which seems to have reduced acquisition activity appreciably.[35]

In the eyes of the FTC, the relevant geographic markets were regional because 90% of all cement is shipped no more than 160 miles. Within the regional markets four-firm concentration typically exceeded 50%, in part because of economies of scale. Thus it was felt that the vertical merger movement threatened foreclosure in at least some regional markets. Areas particularly affected were Kansas City, Richmond, and Memphis, where more than 30% of all cement produced was consumed by "captive" ready-mix concrete companies. According to the Commission:

> When one or more major ready-mixed concrete firms are tied through ownership to particular cement suppliers, the resulting foreclosure not only may be significant in the short run, but may impose heavy long-run burdens on the disadvantaged cement suppliers who continue selling in markets affected by integration. Acquisitions

[35] Federal Trade Commission, *Economic Report on Mergers and Vertical Integration in the Cement Industry* (Washington, D.C. 1966); Enforcement Policy with Respect to Vertical Mergers in the Cement Industry, January 1967, in Commerce Clearing House, 1971 *Trade Regulation Reports,* #4520.

of leading cement consumers in markets containing comparatively few volume buyers may have the effect of substantially disrupting the competitive situation at the cement level. . . .

In sum, vertical mergers are not likely to be challenged unless there is some *horizontal* problem at one or both of the market levels involved. If the markets are concentrated and the merging firms have substantial shares at their respective levels, the merger's anticompetitive potential could be serious because possible foreclosure is then serious.

VI. CONGLOMERATE MERGERS

The record-breaking merger statistics of the sixties show that the law has been almost inconsequential when it comes to conglomerate acquisitions. If a big conglomerate merger can be twisted into a horizontal or vertical configuration (as happened in the *Continental Can/Hazel-Atlas Glass* case), its chances of legal survival shrink considerably. If, however, it can withstand twisting, its chances of challenge must be somewhere below one in a thousand. In other words, officials are reluctant to apply curbs except where mergers clearly affect *particular markets.*

Thus challenges to **product-extension** and **market-extension** mergers are frequently based on arguments of *potential competition.* Absent its acquisition of the leading bleach company, for instance, a major detergent manufacturer might have entered the bleach market by itself through internal expansion (*de novo*), or by "toehold" acquisition of a small bleach producer, thereby increasing the number of competitors in the bleach market or lessening concentration. Even in the absence of any intended *de novo* entry or toehold acquisition, potential competition might still be worth preserving. If, for example, a western brewer remains at the edge of the eastern market, its presence might constrain the activities of the eastern brewers. They would be less likely to charge excessive prices for their beer. The *Proctor & Gamble* and *Falstaff* cases reviewed below flesh out these examples, and the former illustrates an additional hook on which to hang a challenge—namely, the "entrenchment" or "deep pocket" effect.

Pure conglomerates are less likely to affect specific markets. If *reciprocity* can be shown, as it was in *Consolidated Foods,* the merger may be vulnerable. If the merging parties are truly dominant firms (IBM and GM, say), that too might be vulnerable. But these instances are so rare as to leave pure conglomerates essentially untouchable.

The Proctor & Gamble Case (1967). [36]   Procter & Gamble's 1958 acquisition of Clorox Chemical Co. could be considered a product extension merger. Among other things, Procter was the dominant producer of soaps and detergents, accounting for 54.4% of all packaged detergent sales. Clorox, on the other hand,

---

[36] *Federal Trade Commission v. Procter & Gamble Co.,* 386 U.S. 568 (1967).

was the nation's leading manufacturer of household liquid bleach, with approximately 48.8% of total sales at the time. As these statistics suggest, the markets for detergents and bleach were both highly concentrated. The Supreme Court decided that the merger was illegal, but not wholly or even mainly because of these market shares.

Anticompetitive effects were found in several respects. First, and most obviously, Procter was a prime prospective entrant into the bleach industry. Thus, "the merger would seriously diminish potential competition by eliminating Procter as a potential entrant." Indeed, prior to the acquisition, "Procter was in the course of diversifying into product lines related to its basic detergent-soap-cleanser business," and liquid bleach was a distinct possibility because it is used with detergent.

Second, the Court expressed concern that the merger would confer anticompetitive advantages in the realm of marketing. Although all liquid bleach is chemically identical (5.25% sodium hypochlorite and 94.75% water), it is nevertheless highly differentiated. Clorox spent more than 12% of its sales revenues on advertising, and priced its bleach at a premium relative to unadvertised brands. For its part, Procter was the nation's leading advertiser (and still is).

The Court therefore felt that Procter would unduly strengthen Clorox against other firms in the bleach market by extending to Clorox the same volume discounts on advertising that it received from the advertising media. Moreover, "retailers might be induced to give Clorox preferred shelf space since it would be manufactured by Procter, which also produced a number of other products marketed by retailers." In sum, "the substitution of the powerful acquiring firm for the smaller, but already dominant, firm may substantially reduce the competitive structure of the industry by raising entry barriers and dissuading the smaller firms from aggressively competing."

The Falstaff Case (1973).[37] In 1965, Falstaff Brewing Corp. acquired the Narragansett Brewing Company of New England. Although at the time Falstaff was the fourth largest brewer in the United States, it covered only three fifths of the nation and sold no beer in New England. Thus, Falstaff was extending its market by grabbing Narragansett, which at the time was the largest selling beer in the Northeastern area, holding 20% of the market. The market itself was moderately concentrated, with four firms accounting for 61% of sales in 1965.

The District Court found in favor of Falstaff mainly because Falstaff executives had testified that their company was not a potential competitor in New England. They said they definitely would not enter *de novo*. A majority of the Supreme Court, however, held that this was not enough. They directed the District Court to assess the possibility that Falstaff was *perceived* as a potential entrant *by the brewers already in New England*. With this case, then, the Court accepted a broad interpretation of the potential competition doctrine:

---

[37] *United States v. Falstaff Brewing Corp.*, 410 U.S. 526 (1973).

In developing and applying the doctrine, the Court has recognized that a market extension merger may be unlawful if the target market is substantially concentrated, if the acquiring firm has the characteristics, capabilities, and economic incentive to render it a perceived potential *de novo* entrant, and if the acquiring firm's premerger presence on the fringe of the target market in fact tempered oligopolistic behavior on the part of existing participants in that market. In other words the Court has interpreted Sec. 7 as encompassing what is commonly known as the "wings effect" . . .[38]

On reconsideration the District Court again found Falstaff innocent, ruling that Falstaff was *not* a perceived potential entrant in the New England beer market. It should be noted that similar fates awaited subsequent cases of this type. In banking especially, the government has had little success in arguing the doctrine of perceived potential entry. Thus, the evidence must be pretty solid that the firm at bar is perceived to be a potential entrant for this doctrine to sway the courts toward guilty verdicts.

The Consolidated Foods Case (1965).[39] The Federal Trade Commission found that Consolidated, a large wholesaler and retailer of food products, had violated the law by its purchase of Gentry, Inc., a manufacturer of dehydrated onion and garlic. Reciprocity proved to be the key. Gentry sold its onion and garlic to pickle packers, canners, and other food processors. In turn, many of these processors sold to distributor Consolidated. Once Consolidated acquired Gentry, it asked these processors to buy their needed onion and garlic from Gentry, in light of the fact that Consolidated was buying from them. During the first seven years after merger, Gentry's share of the combined onion and garlic buiness rose from 32% to 35%.

On appeal, the Supreme Court sided with the FTC against Consolidated, saying,

> We do not go so far as to say any acquisition, no mater how small, violates Section 7 if there is a probability of reciprocal buying . . . But where, as here, the acquisition is of a company that commands a substantial share of the market, a finding of probability of reciprocal buying by the Commission . . . should be honored, if there is substantial evidence to support it.

The ITT-Grinnel Case (1970).[40] This case is of interest because the Justice Department tried to argue that a finding of specific anticompetitive effect in specific product and geographic markets was *not* required for illegality. It argued instead that, in the wake of a "trend among large diversified industrial firms to acquire other large corporations," it could be concluded that "anticompetitive consequences will appear in numerous though *undesignated* individual 'lines of commerce.' "

---

[38] *United States v. Marine Bancorporation, Inc.,* 418 U.S. 602 (1974).
[39] *FTC v. Consolidated Foods Corporation,* 380 U.S. 592 (1965).
[40] *United States v. International Telephone and Telegraph Corp.,* 324 F. Supp. 19 (D. Conn. 1970).

The merger at issue was ITT's acquisition of Grinnell, a very large manufacturer of automatic sprinkler devices and related products. Since ITT had been a major participant in the conglomerate merger mania, and since Grinnell was big, this was as good a case as any to test the theory that adding to *aggregate concentration* alone was offensive under the law. But the District Court did not agree, and the Justice Department lost:

> The Court's short answer to this claim . . . is that the legislative history, the statute itself and the controlling decisional law all make it clear beyond a peradventure of a doubt that in a Section 7 case the alleged anticompetitive affects of a merger must be examined in the context of *specific product and geographic markets;* and the determination of such markets is a necessary predicate to a determination of whether there has been a substantial lessening of competition within an area of effective competition. To ask the Court to rule with respect to alleged anticompetitive consequences in *undesignated lines of commerce* is tantamount to asking the Court to engage in judicial legislation. This the Court most emphatically refuses to do.

The District Court opinion was not reviewed by the Supreme Court because the case was settled by consent decree prior to appeal.[41] Thus, the law is still in flux. For the present, though, we have finally bumped into the outer limit of the law. As this limit is limited, conglomerate mergers proceed apace.

The new guidelines for conglomerates reflect this. They merely suggest possible challenges where main potential entrants are eliminated.

VII. REMEDIES AND NOTIFICATION

Judicial statements of legality tell only part of the story. *Remedies* are equally important. For if illegal mergers are allowed to stand, they might just as well be declared legal. The record on this score is blemished because total divestiture to achieve premerger status is by no means always achieved. The data for 1951–1977 prove the point:

> Total divestiture was accomplished in 53 per cent of the completed cases brought by the antitrust agencies. The assets divested represented only 44 per cent of the total assets challenged in all complaints. On the other hand, no divestiture was achieved in 7 per cent of the completed cases. . . . The remaining cases either were dismissed (13 per cent) or achieved only partial divestiture (27 per cent).[42]

Even when divestiture is achieved there may be little remedial improvement if, as is all too common, the divested assets create a nonviable firm or are absorbed by a rival. The latter form of phoney relief is illustrated by the *Continental Can* case discussed earlier. Continental had to sell the Hazel-Atlas Glass Company. But it sold Hazel to the Brockway Glass Company, which was the fourth largest producer of *glass* products in the country. Had Brockway bought

---

[41] For a similar district court opinion see *United States v. Northwest Industries,* 301 F. Supp. 1066 (N.D. Ill. 1969) at 1096.

[42] Willard Mueller, *The Celler-Kefauver Act . . . , op. cit.,* p. 89. This excludes banking cases.

149

Hazel-Atlas in the first place, it would most likely have perpetrated an illegal horizontal merger.[43]

One of the main reasons divestiture is reluctantly and imperfectly imposed is that it is difficult to unscramble the eggs once they are scrambled. Less scrambling occurs when the antitrust agencies are given advance notice of mergers, for then preliminary injunctions can often be obtained preventing the merger's consummation until after completion of legal review. This, in fact, is the purpose of the pre-merger notification provisions of the Hart-Scott-Rodino Act of 1976. Specifically, the Antitrust Division of the Department of Justice and the Federal Trade Commission must receive thirty day notice of acquisitions where one of the parties to the transaction has sales or assets of $100 million or more and the other party has sales or assets of $10 million or more.[44]

VIII. PROPOSED CHANGES IN THE LAW

Table 7–2 confirms the impression conveyed by the previous pages, namely, big horizontal and vertical mergers may be pretty well policed, but big conglomerate mergers, especially the "pure" variety, face no more than token control. Approximately 27.6% of all big horizontal mergers occurring between 1951–1977 were challenged, enough to account for over 62% of all challenges to big mergers. In contrast, only 2.3% of the big conglomerate mergers were challenged, and all but four of these were product or market extension mergers. Only 4 of the 575 pure conglomerates tallied, or 0.7%, sparked formal official reaction.

Some observers have argued that such leniency toward large conglomerates is unwise, that the law should be changed to impede ponderous pure conglomerate acquisitions. Those offering new proposals generally recognize that, in strictly *economic* terms, large conglomeracy is neither clearly good nor uniformly bad. Accordingly, they urge that checks be imposed to preserve "political democracy" and "decentralized decision making."

One such proposal by Senator Edward Kennedy in 1979 would have banned the acquisition of any firm with sales or assets of $2 billion or more by another firm in this size class. For acquisitions above $350 million but below $2 billion this legislation would presume illegality but permit *either* an efficiencies defense *or* a divestiture of old assets equal to those of the new acquisition. In effect, acquisitions *of* Fortune 500 firms *by* Fortune 500 firms would have been greatly discouraged. An alternative proposal by the staff of the Federal Trade Commission at about the same time would permit mergers among the largest firms as

---

[43] For further discussion see Kenneth G. Elzinga, "The Antimerger Law: Pyrrhic Victories?" *Journal of Law and Economics* (April 1969), pp. 43–78.

[44] CCH Trade Reg. Rep. No. 344, Pt. II (July 1978). Actually, the rules are much more complex than this. See the lament of Hugh Latimer, "Premerger Notification," *Regulation* (June 1979), pp. 46–52.

TABLE 7–2. Challenges to Large* Acquisitions in Manufacturing and Mining as Compared to Total Acquisitions, by Type, 1951–1977

Type of Merger	Total Number of Large* Acquisitions	Number of Acquisitions Challenged	Challenged as Per Cent of Total	Per Cent Distribution of Challenges
Horizontal	427	118	27.6%	62.1%
Vertical	236	34	14.4	17.9
Conglomerate	1,669	38	2.3	20.0
Market extension	97	11	11.3	5.8
Product extension	997	23	2.3	12.1
Pure	575	4	.7	2.1
Totals	2,332	190	8.1	100.0

* Large acquisitions are those where the acquired firm had assets of $10 million or more.
Source: Willard F. Mueller, *The Celler-Kefauver Act: The First 27 Years,* U.S. House of Representatives, Committee on the Judiciary, Subcommittee on Monopolies and Commercial Law (Nov. 7, 1979), p. 13.

long as the acquiring firm divests or "spins off" another viable firm of about the same size as the acquired firm within a reasonable time period, say three years.[45]

During the Presidency of Ronald Reagan no such measure could conceivably become law. Perhaps a better approach, one that might stand a better chance of gaining the support of conservatives and liberals alike, would be to change the *tax* system, which encourages corporate growth by acquisition. This encouragement comes in two related ways. First, corporate earnings that are paid out as dividends are taxed twice, once as corporate profits and once as individual income. This encourages the retention of corporate earnings, which can then be used for acquisitions. Second, reinvested retained earnings are eventually taxed because they lead to capital gains when owners sell their stock, but individual capital gains are taxed at a lower rate than dividend income. This likewise encourages earnings retention and growth by acquisition.

Tax reform could take any one of a number of routes, some of which have wide support among economists: (1) tax dividend income and capital gains at the same rate; (2) place an especially high tax on retained corporate earnings; or (3) move to a progressive value added tax.[46] These tax approaches have

[45] For debate of these and other proposals see *Mergers and Economic Concentration,* Hearings, Subcommittee on Antitrust, Monopoly and Business Rights of the Committee on the Judiciary, U.S. Senate, 96th Cong., 1st Sess. (1979).

[46] Milton Friedman, *Capitalism and Freedom* (Chicago: University of Chicago Press, 1962), pp. 130–133; Samuel Loescher, "Limiting Corporate Power," *Journal of Economic Issues* (June 1979), pp. 557–571; Dennis Mueller, "Do We Want a New, Tough Antimerger Law?", *Antitrust Bulletin* (Winter 1979), pp. 807–836. On the practical problems see Charles E. McLure, Jr., *Must Corporate Income be Taxed Twice?* (Washington, D.C.: Brookings Institution, 1979).

the advantage of being "self-administering." Messy problems with imposed spin offs and efficiency defenses would be avoided. Moreover, they would encourage greater use of the external capital market and thereby possibly improve capital market efficiency. Still, the political obstacles to such reforms are very large indeed.

SUMMARY

History reveals an annual stream of mergers that occasionally swells to a flood. Around the turn of the century thousands of multifirm horizontal mergers transformed many manufacturing and mining industries into tight-knit oligopolies and near monopolies. A second major movement during the late 1920s brought further horizontal couplings and introduced extensive vertical and conglomerate activity as well. Most recently, the 1950s and 1960s witnessed the largest merger movement of all. During the 1960s 25,598 mergers were recorded, involving scores of billions of dollars in assets. Most acquisitions were conglomerate in nature, and the most active acquirers were conglomerates.

Generally speaking, merger frequency tends to rise and fall as the average level of stock market prices rises and falls. Thus, the timing of mergers is influenced by financial considerations. In addition, there are several basic underlying stimulants to merger, all of which have played some role in the past, none of which has clearly dominated the scene: (1) The pursuit of market power is most clearly associated with horizontal mergers. The first merger movement provides the best examples of this—including the U.S. Steel merger of 1901. (2) A desire to diversify, and thereby reduce risk, motivates many conglomerate mergers. Although some mergers may further this goal, most apparently do not. (3) Businessmen like to justify their mergers with claims of efficiency or economies of scale. Such claims may occasionally be valid, but the available evidence indicates that these claims are overly optimistic (if that is the right word). (4) Speculation contributed substantially to the merger movement of the sixties. (5) We cannot rule out growth and personal aggrandizement, although these factors are difficult to quantify.

As for policy, most law makers seem to favor structural standards that ignore motives. To the extent that a merger may be socially beneficial, the benefits are usually attainable by other means, such as internal expansion or mutual fund organizations for investments. Errors of denial can thus be fairly easily rectified. However, structural stringency has been achieved only in the case of horizontal mergers and, to a lesser extent, vertical mergers. Conglomerate mergers are largely untouchable under current law, unless they can be pushed or pulled into vertical or horizontal shape by manipulations of "the market's" definition.

The main reason for this disparity is that illegality hinges on a showing of potentially adverse competitive effect in some specific market or markets. This burden of proof is most easily carried in horizontal mergers, where market

152

shares, concentration ratios, and related structural measures readily provide the needed indications. The indicia of potential competitive effect for vertical mergers are similarly structural and only slightly less convenient. However, the harbingers of impact for conglomerates tend to be conduct oriented, thereby defying easy measurement. Substantial absolute size is not itself now subject to serious constraint.

8 Barriers to Entry: Theory and Cross-Section Evidence

An oligopolistic industry may not be oligopolistic for long if every Tom, Dick, and Harry can enter.

—EDWIN MANSFIELD

Copy-cat behavior is generally frowned upon. There are permissible exceptions though. A trial lawyer loves to have judges plagiarize from his "briefs" when they write their opinions because the opinions will then be favorable to the lawyer's clients. An economist likes to see imitation in the form of market entry because entry often brings lower prices, greater product diversity, better quality, and the like. In other words, **entry** is merely a shorthand way of saying that a firm *new to the market* has begun to offer a product or service that is a close *substitute* for the products or services of firms already in the market. The newcomer may be established in another market and may merely ape the sellers already in the market entered. On the other hand, the newcomer could be a spanking-new firm and might do more than merely ape existing sellers. It might offer buyers something special, such as lower prices or faster service. If one of the new offerings is particularly successful in taking business away from established firms, those firms may end up imitating the entrant.

Of course entry does not occur at the drop of a hat. Attempted entry costs money, and there is no assurance that an attempt will prosper. Entry hinges on two conditions—motivation and ability. For **motivation,** the prospects of eventually earning a substantial profit must be good. In **ability,** the potential entrant must be legally and financially capable of making the attempt. Any factor that reduces the motivation or ability of potential entrants despite established firms' excessively high profits may be called a **barrier to entry.** It is the purpose of this chapter to identify, explain, and measure various barriers to entry.

We are interested in barriers to entry for the same reason we were interested in product differentiation and concentration: they are a major source of market power. The concept of barriers is thus useful in explaining conduct and perfor-

154

mance. It also helps to explain variances in observed concentration, because high barriers tend to be associated with high concentration. The concept is useful, moreover, in assessing public policy, for not all barriers are "naturally" or technologically determined; some are artificial and due to human manipulation.

We begin by briefly indentifying and classifying various possible structural barriers. We then reveiw some evidence concerning their prevalence. Finally, we take a penetrating look at each main barrier.

I. AN OVERVIEW OF BARRIERS TO ENTRY

Joe Bain, an early pioneer in research on barriers to entry, defined a barrier as anything conferring advantages on "established sellers in an industry over potential entrant sellers, these advantages being reflected in the extent to which established sellers can persistently raise their prices above a competitive level without attracting new firms to enter the industry."[1] When entry is easy, the advantages of established sellers are slight. When entry is difficult, the advantages of established sellers are great, and barriers may balloon to gargantuan proportions. Following Bain, barriers may be classified into four broad groups: (1) absolute unit cost differences, (2) economies of scale, (3) capital cost requirements, and (4) product differentiation.[2]

A. Absolute Cost Advantage Barriers

The first category of barriers comprises absolute cost advantages of established firms. If for any given level of output, established firms can produce and market their wares at a lower cost per unit than newcomers, then any newcomer takes on the established firms with both hands tied behind its back. Take a look at Figure 8–1. Assuming unit costs go neither up nor down as a function of output, average total costs (ATC) for the entrant are indicated by the uppermost horizontal line of Figure 8–1. The lower ATC line of a typical established firm shows cost advantages at every level of output. If the potential entrant expects his demand curve to be as depicted by the solid, negatively sloped line, then there is no level of output where he can cover his costs with revenues. The prospect's ATC lies above his expected demand at every point. If, on the other hand, the entrant's expected demand curve were more generously located, as suggested by the dashed demand line, or if the entrant's unit costs were lower, then entry would appear profitable. What is likely to raise the potential entrant's unit costs above those of established firms? The entrant may have to pay more for scarce raw materials, ship them greater distances, use inferior production technologies, or pay higher interest rates on borrowed capital.

---

[1] Joe S. Bain, *Barriers to New Competition* (Cambridge, Mass.: Harvard University Press, 1956) p. 3.
[2] *Ibid*, pp. 15–16.

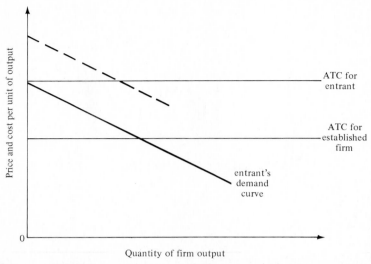

FIGURE 8–1. Absolute cost differences between established firms and potential entrants.

B. Barriers Owing to Economies of Scale

Scalar economies constitute the second general class of barriers. In these instances the unit cost curves confronting potential entrants and established firms are quite similar in elevation and shape. But the *shape* of the curve itself gives established firms an advantage. Figure 8–2 shows the derivation of a long-run unit cost curve for a single plant (or a single-plant firm) that reflects economies of scale. The long-run unit cost curve is best thought of as a *hypothetical* construct that carries real consequences. The potential entrant's engineers could design various possible plants of *identical* output capacity that used *different* production technologies. The resulting short-run unit cost curves might be depicted in Figure 8–2 as *A, B,* and *C* for output Q_1.

Of course it is also possible to hypothesize plants of *differing* output capacity but *identical* technological style. The resulting short-run cost curves in this case could be those labelled *H, J,* and *C* in Figure 8–2. The short-run cost curves of other plants may look like fish scales, but they illustrate the diversity of conceivable designs and capacities. Although the possibilities thus seem rich, only the *lowest* cost possibility would be chosen by rational businessmen for any given level of projected output. For output Q_1 the choice is *A,* for example. Hence, the lower boundary, or "envelope" curve, depicts the long-run average cost curve confronting potential entrants. The curve declines up to output Q_2 because added size brings added efficiency. Beyond Q_2, size confers no additional advantages. Hence Q_2 is often called the **minimum efficient scale (MES).** Beyond Q_3 it is assumed that added size yields *dis*economies, as indicated by a rise in LRAC.

156

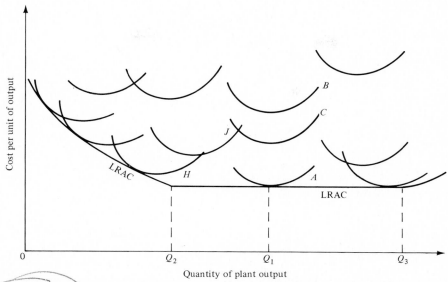

FIGURE 8–2. Derivation of a Long-Run Average Cost (LRAC) curve with economies of scale.

How do scalar economies inhibit entry? The answer is not self-evident. We have already said that given enough money anyone—entrants and established firms alike—could easily build an MES plant. The problem is that existing firms will have *already* built efficient plants. And the added output of an entrant's efficient plant may be so large relative to industry demand that, after entry, product price will fall below the entrant's cost per unit. In other words, there may not be room in the industry for an additional seller when efficient output is large relative to existing output and demand.

For example, assume that DD' is industry demand in Figure 8–3. Assume further that LRAC is the long-run average cost confronting any firm. With two existing firms sharing total industry demand equally, each firm would view its demand as d_2, which is one half of DD' at each possible price. Since d_2 lies above LRAC over a considerable range, each of the two firms could produce and sell at a profit. However, a potential entrant would not have such a favorable view of the situation. If it is assumed that demand would be split evenly three ways in the event of a third firm's entry (a very optimistic assumption for a new entrant to make), each firm's demand would then become d_3, which is one third of DD' at each possible price. But given d_3, there is *no* plant scale that yields a profit to the entrant. There is no point at which LRAC falls below d_3. The result: no third firm entry.

A shift left of LRAC, and a consequentially lower level of MES output, would permit entry. Likewise, a LRAC curve that rose less sharply to the left of MES would also allow entry. But, as it stands, Figure 8–3 looks more like

157

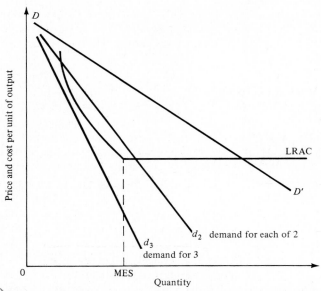

FIGURE 8-3. Economies of scale acting as a barrier to the entry of a third firm.

a bear pit than a welcome mat to third party prospects. Note, too, that a substantial shift outward to the right of the *DD'* line would make room for new entrants. Hence it is cost *relative* to demand that really counts.

Economies of scale may be of two types—pecuniary economies and technical economies. The former are merely monetary savings on the purchase of inputs derived from the greater bargaining power that often goes with greater size. Quantity and volume discounts are of this type. On the other hand, technical economies constitute "real" savings in the sense that fewer of society's scarce resources are used up in the production-distribution process.

C. Capital Cost Barriers

We are now in a position to appreciate capital cost barriers to entry. Minimum efficient scale, MES as defined above, will in part determine the total capital outlay required for efficient entry. Generally speaking, a large MES necessitates a large capital cost outlay. However, since the prices of equipment and construction materials also enter the picture, MES does not always determine the cost. In any event, if the capital costs of efficient entry are appreciably more than what you and your friends can scrape together from your savings, say $1 billion, then capital costs pose a barrier to entry.

This barrier might be classified with the other absolute cost barriers mentioned earlier, since its effect often shows up in higher costs of borrowing, namely, higher interest rates. On the other hand, there are several features of this barrier that distinguish it. For one thing, it is closely connected to scalar elements, whereas other absolute unit cost differences are not. Second, the deterrence of this barrier depends on the nature of the potential entrant as well as the nature of the industry. If the prime potential entrant is already large—a General Motors, say, or an Exxon—then even enormous capital costs pose no problem.

D. Barriers Caused by Product Differentiation

Finally, product differentiation may present a barrier to entry. A newcomer to some industry may face none of the preceding problems but nevertheless find the going tough if the industry has a highly differentiated product. Successful entry would then depend on more than passing tests in production. It would also require mastery of *marketing* problems, for the newcomer would then have to woo customers away from established firms with more than just satisfactory prices. Marketing a differentiated product entails substantial costs—costs of advertising, packaging, style, and so on. And these marketing costs may pose problems for an entrant if they have characteristics similar to those displayed by production cost. That is to say, there may be absolute unit cost disadvantages, economies of scale, or high initial capital costs associated with a newcomer's differentiation effort. Indeed, in theory, "product differentiation" cannot be sharply differentiated as a separate class of barrier. For reasons that will become clear shortly, however, it deserves special treatment.

E. Other Barriers to Entry and a Qualification

Each of the four barriers presented can be considered a structural barrier to entry. Various behavioral or conduct barriers should also be acknowledged. Established firms, for example, may vigorously escalate their advertising outlays when an entrant appears on the horizon. Used thus, advertising poses a problem for the entrant above and beyond any advertising economies of scale or other effects just mentioned. Other behavioral possibilities include collective boycotts, collective aggregated rebates, and predatory pricing. However, behavioral barriers will be taken up later.

In addition, there are various legal barriers to entry. In the extreme, these take the form of licensing, chartering, and franchising regulations administered by local, state, or federal government authorities. Patents also constitute a legal barrier. Discussion of these legal barriers is also postponed, for they fit best in a broad review of regulation and patent policy.

In light of all that's been said, actual entry might seem very rare. It's not for many industries though, partly because of dynamic factors that make entry easier instead of harder. Rapid growth is certainly the most important of these favorable factors, especially if such growth is associated with the early stages of an industry's life cycle, as in semiconductors the last two decades. Rapid growth tends to soften absolute cost disadvantages, counter scale economies, attract capital, and dissolve differentiation barriers.[3]

[3] E. Ralph Biggadike, *Corporate Diversification: Entry, Strategy, and Performance* (Cambridge: Harvard University Press, 1979); D. W. Webbink, "Entry, Price-Cost Margins and Barriers to Entry in 280 4-Digit Industries, 1967–1972," *FTC Working Paper #19,* 1979.

II. EVIDENCE ON THE RELATIVE IMPORTANCE OF BARRIERS IN MANUFACTURING

Before we zero in on some of these barriers and their measurements, it may be helpful to review what little research has been done on the question of which barriers prove the most formidable and most frequently observed. The real trail blazer on this issue was again Bain, who by means of questionnaire surveys and other techniques assessed the prevalence of the four broad types of barriers outlined among 20 major United States manufacturing industries during the late 1940s and early 1950s. Bain concluded from his survey that product differentiation was most important, gaining a "very high" barrier rating in five of his sampled industries and a "substantial" rating in eight. Coming a close second was the capital-cost-requirements barrier, which he rated as "very high" in five industries and "substantial" in five more. Economies of scale were judged to be "very high" barriers in three industries and "substantial" in seven. Finally, absolute cost barriers seemed to be rather inconsequential except in three industries with close connections to mining—steel, copper, and gypsum.[4]

One of the more interesting aspects of Bain's research is that its conclusions are very similar to the results of a survey taken in Japan more than 20 years later. A total of 182 Japanese businessmen were asked to indicate the major "difficulties faced by large public corporations in entering new industries." A summary of their replies is shown in Table 8-1 by the number and percentage of respondents citing each item. (Note that they often cited more than one.) Most often mentioned were two items relating to product differentiation—control of distributive outlets and brand image. At the other extreme is an item that would raise absolute production costs—scarcity of land or water. In between, we find capital requirements. Unfortunately, economies of scale were apparently not included in the survey (although "slow growth of demand" would tend to incorporate scalar effects).

The most comprehensive cross-section statistical study to date is by Dale Orr.[5] Testing the impact of nine different factors on the entry experience of 71 Canadian industries during the mid-1960s, he found that capital requirements, advertising as a per cent of sales, concentration, and size of the industry measured in total sales were all very significant determinants of entry in the expected directions. It is appropriate that intense advertising (which reflects product differentiation) was a significant deterrent to newcomers only in *consumer goods* industries, not in producer goods industries. Although statistical problems prevented a direct test of economies of scale, entry experience was inversely related to capital requirements and concentration—both of which correlate closely with

---

[4] Bain, *op. cit.*, Chapter 6.

[5] Dale Orr, "The Determinants of Entry: A Study of the Canadian Manufacturing Industries," *Review of Economics and Statistics* (February 1974), pp. 58–66. Another valuable study is Robert T. Masson and Joseph Shaanan, "Stochastic-Dynamic Limit Pricing: An Empirical Test," *Review of Economics and Statistics* (August 1982), pp. 413–422, which found product differentiation and scale economies to be important.

TABLE 8–1. Summary of Japanese Survey Concerning Barriers to Entry

Difficulty Cited	Number of Respondents	Per Cent of Respondents
Control of distributive outlets	96	53
Brand image	92	51
Lack of specialized skills (technical or marketing)	80	44
Capital requirements	58	32
Patents and speciality technology	45	25
Low profitability or slow growth of demand	42	23
Scarcity of land or water	29	16

Source: Richard E. Caves and Masu Uekusa, *Industrial Organization in Japan* (Washington, D.C.: The Brookings Institution, 1976), p. 35.

minimum efficient plant size. These results seem to support the hypothesis that substantial economies of scale adversely affect entry. As for the remaining variables tested, Orr found that "research and development intensity and risk are modest barriers to entry, while past profit rates and past industry growth rate had a positive but weak impact on entry."[6]

For our own detailed study of barriers we shall adopt Bain's four broad classifications—absolute costs, economies of scale, capital costs, and product differentiation. Each is treated in turn.

III. ABSOLUTE COST DIFFERENCES

Of all the major barriers, absolute cost differences seem to be the easiest to conceptualize but the hardest to measure systematically across industries. The sources of such differences are diverse and often subtle. The best evidence available tends to be anecdotal and limited to particular industries. Here are a few examples:

1. *Lumber milling:* Established firms owning vast timber lands have an advantage in timber costs over potential entrants. "The original cost of timber to the Weyerhaeuser Company in 1900 was estimated at 10 cents per thousand board feet, whereas the 1959–1962 average out-of-pocket cost of timber purchased from the national forests of the Douglas fir region was about 24 dollars per thousand board feet."[7]

[6] Orr, *op. cit.*, p. 65.
[7] Walter J. Mead, *Competition and Oligopsony in the Douglas Fir Lumber Industry* (Berkeley, Calif.: University of California Press, 1966), pp. 113, 222–23.

2. *Aluminum:* "The entry barriers which are most relevant to the aluminum industry are high capital requirements, availability of high quality, easily accessible bauxite ore, and access to inexpensive sources of electric power."[8]

3. *Petroleum refining in California:* The major refiners own a network of pipelines that crisscross the Los Angeles Basin. Lacking access to those pipelines newly entering refiners must pay the added cost of trucking crude oil to their refineries.[9]

IV. ECONOMIES OF SCALE

A. Sources of Economies of Scale: Plant

In contrast to absolute cost differences, *plant* economies of scale have been thoroughly studied and systematically measured. As a result there is no question that economies of scale do exist. The following lower unit production costs as scale increases.[10]

- *Specialization of labor:* As the number of workers multiplies with plant size, individual workers specialize their activities, thereby becoming more proficient and productive. As a group they can then produce more with less labor time and labor cost.

- *Specialization of machinery:* Small scale operations often must rely on multipurpose machinery and equipment that do many different jobs but no job really well. Large-volume operations permit specialization of equipment, as in the case of iron blast furnaces and cement kilns.

- *Economies of increased dimensions:* Capital equipment in the form of tanks, vessels, and pipelines generate economies because a doubling of their surface area more than doubles their volume capacity. This is often summarized by the 0.6 rule, which states that, if capacity is multiplied by a factor of x, then capital cost is multiplied by $x^{0.6}$. This rule goes a long way toward explaining the evolution of super crude-oil tankers the size of the Empire State building. On long voyages, delivering a barrel of oil in a tanker of more than 100,000 dead weight tons (dwt) capacity costs only one fourth as much as delivery in a 25,000-ton tanker. Above 100,000 dwt, the cost savings taper off; a 250,000 dwt ship is only about 5% more efficient than a 100,000 tonner.

- *Indivisibilities:* There are many costs independent of scale, or fixed, over certain levels of output. When translated into per unit costs (dollars fixed/

---

[8] Council on Wage and Price Stability, *Aluminum Prices 1974–75* (Washington, D.C., 1976) p. 27.

[9] Federal Trade Commission, *Staff Report on the Structure, Conduct and Performance of the Western States Petroleum Industry* (Washington, D.C., 1975), p. 46.

[10] E. A. G. Robinson, *The Structure of Competitive Industry* (Chicago: University of Chicago Press, 1958).

quantity), these fall with added output. Ball bearing production affords an example: "Setting up an automatic screw machine to cut bearing races takes about eight hours. Once ready, the machine produces from 80 to 140 parts per hour. An increase in the total number of parts produced in a batch from, say, 5,000 to 10,000, reduces unit costs by more than 10 percent due to the broader spreading of setup time and skilled labor costs."[11]

• *Massed reserves:* Breakdowns, interruptions, and other contingencies are inevitable. The unit cost of being prepared is probably lower with larger scales. For instance, a plant with 20 identical machines will stock less than 20 times the spare parts that a plant with only one machine would. The firm with 20 machines can safely assume that all its machines are not going to break down simultaneously.

*Dis*economies of scale are obviously another possibility. In their case increased size tends to drive unit costs up rather than down. But theory and empirical evidence related to diseconomies at the plant level are not nearly as refined or as pervasive as those concerning economies. At the multiplant *firm* level there is some positive probability of stretching management too thin or of encountering some other size-related inefficiency.[12] At the individual plant level, however, the chances are slimmer.

Perhaps the only general source of plant diseconomies is outbound transportation. Plant expansion typically implies higher unit transportation costs because a large plant's output must be shipped farther afield than a small plant's output, everything else being equal. Where transportation costs bulk large relative to product value—as is the case for cement, petroleum, and steel—there is a limit to the geographic area that one plant can serve efficiently. This axiom could obviously be translated into a size limit for plants, but for present purposes, this will not be done.

Of course, the effects of various sources of economies, or the lack thereof, differ from industry to industry. They may lead to a relatively small minimum efficient scale, as indicated by MES_a and MES_b in panels (a) and (b) of Figure 8–4. On the other hand, they may lead to a relatively large MES, such as suggested in panel (c) of Figure 8–4. The causes of economies also influence the behavior of costs below MES output. Thus in panels (a) and (b) of Figure 8–4 the two cost curves share the same level of MES. But unit costs of curve (a) rise only slightly at scales less than MES, whereas those of curve (b) rise sharply with diminished scale. By way of example, panel (a) might represent

---

[11] F. M. Scherer, "Economics of Scale and Industrial Concentration," *Industrial Concentration: The New Learning,* edited by H. Goldschmid, H. M. Mann, and J. F. Weston (Boston: Little, Brown, 1974) p. 33.

[12] Dodging diseconomies is the main motive behind the "division" structure of most large corporations. As a 3M executive recently quipped, "We are keenly aware of the disadvantages of large size. We like to say that our success in recent years amounts to multiplication by division." *Wall Street Journal,* February 5, 1982, p. 1. For elaboration see Oliver Williamson, *Markets and Hierarchies: Analysis and Antitrust Implications* (New York: Free Press, 1975), Chapter 8.

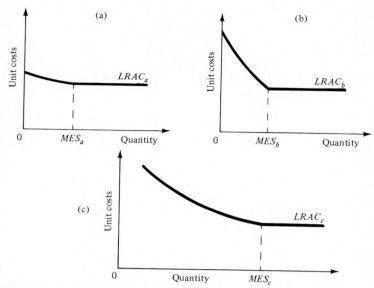

FIGURE 8–4. Alternative configurations of the long-run average cost curve.

the curve confronting beer wholesalers, panel (b) electrical appliance wholesalers, and panel (c) meat and meat products wholesalers.[13]

B. Estimates of Economies

These estimates for wholesale trades are based on what is called "statistical estimation." Two other widely used techniques are the "survivor" and the "engineering" techniques. Each estimation technique has its advantages and disadvantages.[14] However, the engineering approach seems to be regarded by most economists as the most reliable, especially for comprehensive multi-industry comparative studies. By this approach industrial engineers, planning experts, and other industry "insiders" actually responsible for making plant-size decisions are canvassed and questioned about how costs vary with scale and what factors generate economies or diseconomies. The work involved in any large study of this kind is almost preposterous, and for many years Joe Bain was the only researcher to undertake the task. Now his efforts have been supplemented by the work of three scholars—F. M. Scherer, C. F. Pratton, and L. W. Weiss.

Taken together, their studies contain estimates of plant economies of scale for 33 industries as of the late 1960s and early 1970s. The results for 23 of these industries are summarized in columns (1) and (2) of Table 8–2. Some

[13] Louis P. Bucklin, *Competition and Evolution in the Distributive Trades* (Englewood Cliffs, N. J.: Prentice-Hall, 1972) pp. 253–255.

[14] A. A. Walters, "Production and Cost Functions: An Econometric Survey," *Econometrica* (January-April 1963), pp. 39–52; William G. Shepherd, "What Does the Survivor Technique Show About Economies of Scale?" *Southern Economic Journal* (July 1967), pp. 113–122.

TABLE 8–2. Minimum Efficient Scale Plants, Costs of Suboptimal Plants, and Concentration Ratios in United States Manufacturing, Circa 1967

Industry	(1) MES as a Percentage of U.S. 1967 Output	(2) Increase in Unit Cost at ½ MES (%)	(3) "Warranted" Concentration Ratio	(4) Actual Concentration Ratio 1967
Turbogenerators	23.0	not available	92	100
Refrigerators	13.0	4	52	73
Home laundry equipment	11.2	8	45	78
Manmade fiber	11.1	5	44	86
Aircraft (commercial)	10.0	20	40	69
Synthetic rubber	7.2	15	29	61
Cigarettes	6.6	2.2	26	81
Transformers	4.9	7.9	19	65
Paperboard	4.4	8	18	27
Tires and inner tubes	3.8	5	15	70
Blast furnaces and steel	2.7	10	11	48
Detergents	2.4	2.5	10	88
Storage batteries	1.9	4.6	8	61
Petroleum refining	1.8	4.0	7	33
Cement	1.7	13	7	29
Glass containers	1.5	11	6	60
Ball and roller bearings	1.4	8	6	54
Paints, varnishes	1.4	4.4	6	22
Beer	1.1	10	4	40
Flour mills	0.7	3	3	30
Machine tools	0.3	5	1	21
Cotton textiles	0.2	5	1	36
Shoes	0.2	1.5	1	26

Source: F. M. Scherer, A. Beckenstein, E. Kaufer, and R. D. Murphy, *The Economics of Multi-Plant Operation* (Cambridge, Mass.: Harvard University Press, 1975), Chapter 3; C. F. Pratton, *Economies of Scale in Manufacturing Industries* (New York: Cambridge University Press, 1971); L. W. Weiss, "Optimal Plant Size and the Extent of Suboptimal Capacity," in *Essays on Industrial Organization in Honor of Joe S. Bain*, edited by R. T. Masson and P. D. Qualls (Cambridge, Mass.: Ballinger Publishing Co., 1976), pp. 123–41.

industries were studied by more than one of these researchers: in such cases the numbers reported in Table 8–2 are average or consensus figures.

To simplify interindustry comparison, the estimated MES of each industry in column (1) is expressed as a percentage of total United States output in 1967. In addition, the industries are arrayed from highest MES to lowest. At one extreme, efficient turbogenerator production required a plant size that would account for 23% of total United States output. At the other extreme, efficient shoe production could be achieved with a plant that was so small relative to total industry output as to account for only 0.2% of production.

Column (2) shows how sharply the unit cost curve rises at scales less than MES. It shows the percentage increase in unit costs that would occur by moving from a full MES plant to one just half the size (in a few cases it is one third MES, which was Scherer's standard). It is rather interesting to note that high levels of MES, such as those observed for manmade fibers and cigarettes, are not always—or even usually—associated with high rates of cost increase at suboptimal scales. In other words, the figures of columns (1) and (2) do not correlate closely.

When the figures of column (1) are multiplied by a factor of 4, the result is column (3). This result is a rough indication of what the national four-firm concentration ratio would be like in each industry if each firm among the top four had a level of output matching MES. In other words, column (3) could be considered the degree of concentration "warranted" by economies of scale at the plant level. These figures may be compared with those of column (4), which are the actual four-firm concentration ratios of these industries in 1967. It is easy to see that columns (3) and (4) are correlated; with high values typically at the top and low values at the bottom. In a few instances actual and warranted concentration nearly coincide. Aside from these few instances, however, actual concentration is much higher than it would be if each leading firm operated one MES plant. As Scherer concludes, "nationwide oligopoly and high seller concentration cannot be viewed primarily as the inevitable consequence of production scale economies at the plant level."[15]

Now Scherer's is an *extremely* important conclusion. It indicates that policies aimed at the attainment and maintenance of competitive market structures are *not* hopelessly at odds with the cost conditions underlying most industries,[16] that most industries need *not* be dominated by only a few giants in order to be efficient. (It carries political and social implications as well.) Still, the conclusion must be qualified in two respects—geographic market definition and multiplant economies.

C. Geographic Market Definition

First, the minimum efficient market share estimates of Table 8–2 are based on the assumption that the relevant market for every industry is nationwide. This assumption is often inappropriate. Indeed, 13 of the industries listed in Table 8–2 could be considered at least partly regional on the basis of their transportation costs. Notable among them are cement, petroleum, glass containers, and steel, all of which have transportation costs exceeding 5% of product value on a typical haul. Weiss estimates, for example, that there are approximately 24 separate regional cement markets in the United States.[17] Cement's

[15] F. M. Scherer, *op. cit.,* p. 28.

[16] C. Kaysen and D. Turner, *Antitrust Policy* (Cambridge, Mass.: Harvard University Press, 1965), p. 6.

[17] L. W. Weiss, "The Geographic Scope of Markets in Manufacturing," *Review of Economics and Statistics* (August 1972), pp. 245–266.

MES, compared to the average regional market, produces a market share of 40% for one plant instead of 1.7% as suggested by Table 8–2.

This is an extreme case, but it hits the nail on the head. When the other regional industries of Table 8–2 are adjusted in like manner, their "warranted" four-firm concentration ratios rise substantially. The average concentration ratio of column (3) as it stands is 19.6%. After adjustment for regional markets, the average jumps to 35.7%. Instead of having four industries with warranted concentration greater than 40, adjustment yields a total of eight. A "relevant market" qualification is thus justified. Having said as much, we should also note that these particular data overstate the qualification that would be necessary if this sample of industries were truly representative. The sample is biased in the direction of more regional market fragmentation than would be found for all manufacturing industries. Whereas 57% of the industries listed in Table 8–2 are regional, only about 33% of all United States four-digit industries could be so classified.

D. Multiplant Economies

Our second qualification also pushes in the direction of greater warranted four-firm concentration than Table 8–2 suggests. This qualification, however, has nothing to do with breadth of relevant market definition. It has to do instead with the implicit assumption that just one plant is sufficient for a firm to gain all possible economies. In cases where substantial additional economies could be achieved from *multiplant* operations, the warranted national concentration ratios of column (3) could be increased (without affecting regional ratios). One problem with the continued use of the word "warranted" in this connection is that many multiplant economies tend to be purely pecuniary as opposed to real. The word "warranted" was not warped when applied to single plants because most economies in the case of single plants constitute genuine social savings. But pecuniary economies cannot claim social benefits. In any event, this area of multiplant economies has been more thoroughly and expertly explored by Scherer's team than by anyone else, so we shall press his findings into sevice here.

Scherer's results cover 12 industries, as shown in Table 8–3. Column (1) summarizes the main sources of multiplant economies. Column (2) gives Scherer's estimate of MES plant size. Column (3) shows the estimated number of MES plants that a firm needs to exploit all major multiplant economies of scale. When the plant shares of column (2) are multiplied by the number of plants in column (3), the result is the estimated national market share of an efficient *firm* in column (4). These estimates range from a high of 20% for refrigerators to a low of 1% for fabric weaving. They do indeed indicate a greater level of warranted concentration than was suggested by our consideration of single plant economies alone (ignoring for the moment the fact that pecuniary economies may not be "warranted"). The minimum market share for an efficient shoe producer would be 1% instead of 0.2%; for an efficient bottle producer, 4–6% instead of 1.5%; and so on.

TABLE 8–3. Summary of Main Sources of Multi-Plant Economies and Firm Size Required to Experience Not More Than Slight Price/Cost Handicaps (12 Industries)

Industry	(1) Major Sources of Possible Multiplant Economies	(2) Estimated MES Plant Market Share (%)	(3) Number of MES Plants Needed to Have Not More Than Slight Disadvantage	(4) Share of U.S. Market Required in 1967 (%)	(5) Average Market Share per U.S. Big Three Member Firm (%)
Beer	Advertising, massed reserves	3.4	3–4	10–14	13
Cigarettes	Advertising, massed reserves	6.6	1–2	6–12	23
Fabric weaving	Market access, capital	0.2	3–6	1	10
Paints	Vertical ties, research	1.4	1	1.4	9
Petrol refining	Advertising, vertical ties, capital	1.9	2–3	4–6	8
Shoes	Advertising, massed reserves	0.2	3–6	1	6
Glass bottles	Capital, research	1.5	3–4	4–6	22
Cement	Capital	1.7	1	2	7
Steel	Capital	2.6	1	3	14
Bearings	Market access, research	1.4	3–5	4–7	14
Refrigerators	Market access	14.1	4–8 (multiproduct)	14–20	21
Storage batteries	Market access, massed reserves	1.9	1	2	18

Source: F. M. Scherer, A. Beckenstein, E. Kaufer, and R. D. Murphy. *The Economics of Multi-Plant Operation: An International Comparison* (Cambridge, Mass.: Harvard University Press, 1975), pp. 94, 334–336.

Still, despite this accounting for multiplant economies, warranted concentration remains low in most industries. Compared with the average national market shares of big-three member firms reported in column (5) of Table 8–3, the efficient market shares of column (4) are quite small. The only exceptions are beer, refrigerators, and, perhaps, petroleum refining. To the extent that these estimates are valid, "national market seller concentration appears in most industries to be much higher than it needs to be for leading firms to take advantage of all but slight residual multiplant scale economies."[18]

E. Summary

In sum, neither of these two major qualifications—regional market definition and multiplant economies—severely damages our earlier conclusion. Each has been significant in the experience of several industries, implying in these instances the presence of formidable barriers and the inevitability of substantial market concentration. Yet economies of scale appear to pose no more than a moderate barrier to entry for the majority of United States manufacturing industries, and they "warrant" no more than moderate concentration. This optimistic conclusion cannot be equally applicable to countries having sparser populations and lower levels of income than the United States. Minimum efficient scales would gobble up larger percentage chunks of their smaller economic markets. Even abroad, however, economies of scale probably generate less concentration than many people seem to think.[19]

V. CAPITAL COSTS

The significance of capital costs may be inferred from column (1) of Table 8–3. Evidence abounds that small firms pay a higher price for their capital funds than larger firms do. The questions remaining are the following: What are the sources of this cost differential? Does it reflect real economies or just pecuniary advantages? As luck would have it, the answers are mixed because the differential

---

[18] F. M. Scherer, A. Beckenstein, E. Kaufer, and R. D. Murphy, *The Economics of Multi-Plant Operation* (Cambridge, Mass.: Harvard Univ. Press, 1975), p. 339. See *Business Week*, February 26, 1979, pp. 128–132, for a very interesting story on how MetPath successfully acted on the knowledge that there were plant economies but no multiplant economies in its industry, clinical lab testing, worth $12 billion annually.

[19] The view that observed concentration cannot, in general, be justified by real economies is not held by all economists. John McGee claims that "the *existing* structure of industry is the *efficient* structure." ("Efficiency and Economies of Size," in *Industrial Concentration: the New Learning, op. cit.,* p. 93; and John McGee, *In Defense of Industrial Concentration,* New York: Praeger, 1971). There are two problems with this extreme position, however. First, it is based on the premise that firms get big *only* by virtue of their efficiency, which is not true. As we have seen, efficiency may often produce bigness, but bigness is also the result of other factors, such as luck and mergers (O. E. Williamson, "Dominant Firms . . . Considerations," *Harvard Law Review,* June 1972, pp. 1512–22). Second, McGee's argument verges on tautology. He asserts that markets are "biased toward efficiency . . ." and "market results *are* evidence of efficiency." In other words, he claims that we know big firms are better simply because they are big! On this shortcoming see Joseph Brodley, "Massive Size, Classical Economics, and the Search for Humanistic Value," *Stanford Law Review* (June 1972), pp. 1155-1178.

is a product of at least three factors—transaction costs, risk, and loan market imperfections.

A. Transaction Costs

The effect of transaction costs may be appreciated in a personal analogy. When you borrow money from a bank to buy a car, there are certain fixed costs associated with the transaction. These include the bank's costs of reviewing your application, checking-out your credit record, posting your loan on the books, and processing your payments. For the most part, the absolute dollar value of these costs does not vary with the size of your loan. In cost *per dollar borrowed*, therefore, these costs fall as loan size increases, permitting lower interest rates on larger loans.

Multiply this example by the sum you would like to win in a lottery and you have some idea of the situation confronting small businesses requiring small loans. Indeed, the principle applies to equity stock issues as well as loans. This probably explains, at least in part, why average common stock flotation costs "for a cross section of manufacturing corporation issues during the early 1950s ranged from 20 percent of the funds raised for issues totaling less than $500,000 through 10 percent for issues in the $2–5 million bracket to 5.5 percent for issues between $20 million and $50 million."[20] Savings of transactions costs obviously qualify as "real" social savings.

B. Risk

As regards risk, small companies seem to suffer greater fluctuations in their sales and profits than big companies. The higher risks of default that small firms present lenders and investors must be compensated by higher interest rates on loans and bonds or by a price premium on equity stock issues. In the case of bonds, for example, W. B. Hickman found that relatively small firms did default more often than large corporations. Consequently, interest rates paid were inversely related to firm size. However, Hickman also found a large "fudge" factor that worked to the disadvantage of small firms. He found that *even after adjustment* for default losses, the relation of interest rates to size was inverted. In other words, small companies apparently pay a risk premium that exceeds the actual risk of default.[21] Whether reduction of this superfluous surcharge could be counted as a real economy for a large firm is questionable.

C. Loan Market Imperfections

Perhaps the clearest cases of pecuniary economies in this context are those associated with market "imperfections." Suppose that competition among banks for the extension of business loans is imperfect in the following ways: Locally and regionally bank concentration is high, but nationally bank concentration

---

[20] Scherer, Beckenstein, Kaufer, and Murphy, *op. cit.*, pp. 284-285. See also S. H. Archer and L. G. Faerber, "Firm Size and the Cost of Externally Secured Equity Capital," *Journal of Finance* (March 1966), pp. 69–83.

[21] W. B. Hickman, *Corporate Bond Quality and Investor Experience* (Princeton, N. J.: Princeton University Press, 1958).

is low because banks cannot engage in interstate branching. Suppose also that small borrowers are pretty much confined to dealing with the banks in their own local area, whereas huge borrowers such as GM, GE, and GT & E are sufficiently well known, sufficiently diverse in their operations, and sufficiently big to take their business of borrowing anywhere they fancy. Under these suppositions, you would expect banks to exploit their local market power over small firms by charging them high rates of interest. But, in the big-league nationwide market, you would expect competition to keep interest charges at a minimum.

Abundant evidence confirms these suppositions. Numerous cross-section studies have shown that business loan interest rates rise with local bank concentration, but only on loans to small businesses, not on those to big businesses.[22] One study concluded that "The level of market concentration has a statistically significant impact on rates paid by firms with assets up to at least $5 million."[23]

On top of all this, a small firm may have difficulty raising capital at any price, even if the firm has proved itself successful. Such is the story behind Atari Inc., which was founded by Nolan Bushnell not long after he graduated from the University of Utah in 1968. Atari introduced the world to "Pong," "Gran Trak 10," and other now famous video games. Bushnell first put $250 of his own savings into his company. Then he guided it through an enormous spurt of growth, but he could not raise enough capital to keep up with his market. "Unable to meet the demand stimulated by Pong's success, Atari watched licensees and competitors walk off with most of the spoils. 'We sold fewer games of the Pong type than anybody else,' Bushnell says, 'because we didn't have the cash to produce what the market demanded.' "[24] He finally sold out for $15 million to Warner Communications, Inc., a giant conglomerate rich in cash. *Business Week* summarized the situation: "When a small company invades a big market, success can be almost as hard to cope with financially as failure."[24]

VI. PRODUCT DIFFERENTIATION (AGAIN)

A blend of barrier concepts is involved in product differentiation. We first consider advertising and then turn to other forms of differentiation.

A. Advertising

Advertising may stymie new entrants with a triple whammy: (1) it can raise the absolute costs of doing business due to "carry-overs"; (2) it may entail

---

[22] Fine examples include F. R. Edwards, "Concentration in Banking and Its Effect on Business Loan Rates," *Review of Economics and Statistics* (August 1964), pp. 294–300; Paul A. Meyer, "Price Discrimination, Regional Loan Rates, and the Structure of the Banking Industry," *Journal of Finance* (March 1967), pp. 37–48.

[23] Donald Jacobs, *Business Loan Costs and Bank Market Structure* (New York: Columbia University Press, 1971), p. 57.

[24] *Business Week,* November 15, 1976, p. 120.

economies of scale; and (3) it may add substantially to the capital costs of entry.[25] Economists do not argue that advertising always or inevitably has these effects. Rather, they argue that it *can* have these effects under certain circumstances. Our job now is to delineate these circumstances.

▪ *The Carry-Over Effect*. One of the main characteristics of advertising that may give established firms an advantage over entrants is its "lagged" or "carry-over" effect. January's advertising brings in September sales, and the lag may even last for years. There are several reasons for this extension of advertising effect:[26]

- Continued brand loyalty, though probably maintained by customer satisfaction, may have its origin in the persuasiveness of a single, long-forgotten ad.

- It may take a series of ads to break through the sales resistance of buyers. The last ad triggering the purchase cannot get all the credit.

- The potential customer, persuaded though he may be, may not be "in the market" for the product until later. This is particularly true of durables, such as tires and appliances.

Thus if the annual advertising outlay of each established firm in a market is $10 million, and if all the firms enjoy an equal volume of sales, it is not enough for a new entrant to spend his $10 million on advertising. He will *not* gain sales equal to the established firms during his first year in business, even if his product offering is identical to that of established firms in every other particular—price, quality, availability, and so forth. He is confronted by the aggregation of entrenchment. Only *some* of the sales of the established firms during the new firm's entry year are generated by their $10 million outlay of that year. The additional sales of each are attributable to advertising outlays of *previous* years.

If the advertising outlays of established firms have a carry-over effect of 0.4 (that is, an annual decay rate of 0.6), each established firm enjoys sales from its $10 million spent in the year *prior* to entry worth the equivalent of $4 million in advertising outlays the year *after* entry (0.4 × $10 million). From advertising *two* years previously each gains sales worth $1.6 million in terms of what it would cost them in current advertising dollars (0.4 × 0.4 × $10 million). Adding other prior years, this may be summarized in an equation:

$$\text{established firm's advertising value per year} = \underbrace{\$10m}_{\text{current}} + \underbrace{\$4m + \$1.6m + \$0.64m + \$0.256m + \cdots}_{\text{carry-over}}$$

[25] William S. Comanor and Thomas A. Wilson, "Advertising Market Structure and Performance," *Review of Economics and Statistics* (November 1967), pp. 425–426; Comanor and Wilson, *Advertising and Market Power* (Cambridge, Mass.: Harvard University Press, 1974), Chapter 4; Comanor and Wilson, "Advertising and Competition: A Survey," *Journal of Economic Literture* (June 1979), pp. 453–476.

[26] K. S. Palda, *The Measurement of Cumulative Advertising Effects* (Englewood Cliffs N.J.: Prentice-Hall, 1964), p. 9.

In other words, the entrant would have to spend approximately $16.67 million during its first year in the market in order to match the advertising potency of each established firm—$10 million to match their current year's outlay plus $6.67 million to make up for lost time and counter established firm carry-over. Another way of looking at this phenomenon is to consider that, even if the established firms happened to spend nothing whatever on advertising during the entrant's first year, the entrant would have to spend $6.67 million on advertising just to pull even with them in the battle for customers. Thus the entrant's advertising costs per unit of sale will, in at least the first year, exceed those of established firms at every level of possible output.

Of course this is a simplified example. The 0.4 carry-over is only illustrative. Actual estimates of carry-over vary, depending on the commodity and the firm in question, and the lag structure assumed is only one of a number possible. Still, the main point is adequately represented, and significant carry-over effects have been found for a wide variety of products.[27] Moreover, empirical evidence has linked greater carry-over with higher barriers to entry.[28]

Economies of Scale. As for economies of scale in advertising, it would be a pretty good bet that they are present whenever we observe an inverse relationship between market share and firm advertising outlays relative to sales, while leading firms are gaining market share or holding steady. To illustrate, these were the advertising outlays *per car sold* for United States auto manufacturers over the period 1954–1957: GM, $26.56; Ford, $27.22; Chrysler, $47.76; Studebaker–Packard, $64.04; and American Motors, $57.89.[29] Despite the relatively low outlays per car, leading firms GM and Ford thrived. Contrary-wise, the relatively enormous outlays of Studebaker–Packard failed to keep it alive. Another example comes from breakfast cereals. In 1964 selling and advertising expenses of the largest four firms were 14.9% of sales, for the next four 17.7%, and for all others 19.8%.[30] Despite the relatively low expenditures of the top four, their combined market share was on the rise at the time. Or take liquor. Case sales of the leading brand in the early 1960s exceeded case sales of the next leading brand by more than 300%, while its advertising expenditure per

---

[27] See Jean Jacques Lambin, *Advertising, Competition and Market Conduct in Oligopoly over Time* (Amsterdam: North-Holland Publishing Company, 1976), pp. 94–96; and Darral G. Clarke, "Econometric Measurement of the Duration of Advertising Effect on Sales," *Journal of Marketing Research* (November 1976), pp. 345-357.

[28] Randall S. Brown, "Estimating Advantages to Large Scale Advertising," *Review of Economics and Statistics* (August 1978), pp. 428–437; Sharon Oster, "Intraindustry Structure and the Ease of Strategic Change," *Review of Economics and Statistics* (August 1982), pp. 376–383; Takeo Nakao, "Profit Rates and Market Shares of Leading Industrial Firms in Japan," *Journal of Industrial Economics* (June 1979), pp. 371–383. For theories of the effect see John M. Vernon, *Market Structure and Industrial Performance* (Boston: Allyn and Bacon, Inc., 1972), pp. 93–98; and Roger Folsom and D. F. Greer, "Advertising and Brand Loyalty as Barriers to Entry," *Symposium on Advertising and the Food System* (Madison: University of Wisconsin Press, 1983).

[29] L. W. Weiss, *Economics and American Industry* (New York: John Wiley & Sons, 1961). p. 342. For more detailed data see Charles E. Edwards, *Dynamics of the United States Automobile Industry* (Columbia, S.C.: University of South Carolina Press, 1965), p. 219.

[30] National Commission on Food Marketing, *Studies of Organization and Competition in Grocery Manufacturing,* Study No. 6 (Washington, D.C.: U.S.G.P.O., 1966), p. 206.

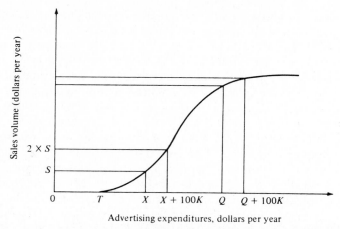

FIGURE 8–5. Sales volume as a function of advertising outlay, holding other factors constant.

case was only half as great.[31] Economies of scale here are obvious; however, they are *not* obvious for all products at all times.[32] In many instances they are either completely absent or not strong enough to make much difference.

Whether such economies arise depends on how sales respond to various levels of advertising outlay. Consider Figure 8–5, which depicts sales volume (on the vertical axis) as a function of the firm's advertising expenditures (on the horizontal axis), holding other elements such as price and rival firm advertising constant. At very low levels of advertising outlay, below threshold T, advertising has little or no effect on sales. Because we are presently interested in the experience of entering firms, the OT range assumes no positive sales at all. (For an established firm the entire function would have to be shifted upward to reflect the fact that even with zero current outlays there would be some positive level of sales attributable to carry-over.) Explanations as to why such a threshold may be present are many and varied, depending on the product and market:[33]

- It may be impossible to buy key forms of advertising below certain minimum quantities. For instance, the smallest amount of national television advertising possible could not be bought with pocket change. The time and

---

[31] James M. Ferguson, "Advertising and Liquor," *Journal of Business* (October 1967), pp. 414–434.

[32] R. Schmalensee, *On the Economics of Advertising* (Amsterdam: North-Holland Press, 1972); J. L. Simon and G. H. Crain, "The Advertising Ratio and Economies of Scale," *Journal of Advertising Research* (September 1966), pp. 37–43; J. M. Ferguson, *Advertising and Competition; Theory, Measurement, Fact* (Cambridge, Mass.: Ballinger, 1974) Chapter 4; D. Greer, "Product Differentiation and Concentration in the Brewing Industry," *Journal of Industrial Economics* (July 1971), pp. 19–32.

[33] R. D. Buzzell, R. E. M. Nourse, J. B. Matthews, Jr., and T. Levitt, *Marketing: A Contemporary Analysis* (New York: McGraw-Hill, 1972) pp. 533-534.

production costs of putting even a 10-second "spot" on the air are substantial. (A 30-second ad during the 1983 Super Bowl cost $400,000.)

- There may be a "psychological threshold" in the minds of potential buyers that may be broken only by some minimum volume of promotion.

- There may be a minimum volume of promotion needed to induce retailers and wholesalers to carry the manufacturer's product line.

Beyond threshold T, the sales response function enters a range of increasing returns. Here, increasing amounts of promotion yield *more* that proportionate increases in sales revenues. An addition of $100,000 in expenditure to outlay X does not double total outlay but it does double sales volume from S to $2 \times S$ on the vertical axis. The reasons sales may climb at an increasing rate are similar to those underlying the threshold effect. A firm can gain efficiency in this range by hiring marketing specialists (instead of having their shipping clerks dabble in ad design), by allocating its money among the various media more and more efficiently, by exploiting a "band wagon" promotional pitch, by gaining discounts in its purchase of advertising messages; and by other means.[34]

It is the combination of threshold and increasing returns effects that is relevant to economies of scale. Over this range (roughly 0 to $X + 100K$ in Figure 8–5) advertising costs *as a percentage of sales* start out very high and then fall as absolute (total dollar) advertising outlay increases. This is not the end of the story, however. The presence of a threshold and increasing returns is commonly observed.[35] But, if these effects do not extend into very large levels of absolute outlay, then all economies could easily be exploited by rather small firms and new entrants. And beyond this small-firm range of economies, diminishing returns set in. Additional advertising outlays will eventually stimulate *less* than proportionate increases in sales revenues, as shown by Q and $Q + 100K$ in Figure 8–5. The reason for this diminishing stimulation is fairly obvious:

> Once salesmen have called on all the prospective customers with high purchase potential, they must turn to less and less promising prospects. Once advertising messages have reached the primary audiences with sufficient frequency, additional messages must be directed to audiences with lower and lower levels of response.[36]

---

[34] An example of discounts is provided by the Hearst Corporation (owner of *Cosmopolitan, Good Housekeeping,* and other magazines). In 1976 it offered discounts to advertisers who bought space in any three of its magazines according to the following schedule: 12 pages, 5% off; 15 pages, 6%; 18 pages, 7%; 21 pages, 8%; 24 pages, 9%. (*Wall Street Journal,* November 14, 1975, p. 3). See also *Business Week,* November 24, 1980, p. 52; *Wall Street Journal,* July 8, 1982, p. 6.

[35] Buzzell, *et. al., op. cit.,* pp. 533–34; A. G. Rao and P. B. Miller, "Advertising/Sales Response Functions," *Journal of Advertising Research* (April 1975), pp. 7–15; J. J. Lambin, *op. cit.,* pp. 127–130; Brown, *op. cit.;* M. M. Metwally, "Sales Response to Advertising of Eight Australian Products," *Journal of Advertising Research* (October 1980), pp. 59–64. For a dissenting view see Julian L. Simon and Johan Arndt, "The Shape of the Advertising Response Function," *Journal of Advertising Research* (August 1980), pp. 11–28. They stack the deck, however, by considering irrelevant studies.

[36] Buzzell, *et. al., op. cit.,* p. 534.

Indeed, beyond $Q + 100K$, advertising may reach a point of complete saturation, where further promotion adds nothing at all to sales.

In sum, economies of scale are substantial only where the threshold effect and increasing returns operate over a large range. This is reflected in the following *Business Week* quote concerning entry into the cosmetics industry:

> "The real challenge is simply gaining distribution," says market researcher Solomon Dutka . . . "to have sales volume and to be a factor in this business, you must have distribution. Yet to gain distribution, you must have sales volume or the big store groups won't bother with you. So when somebody tries to get into this business . . . they have to create volume artificially"—meaning the use of heavy and costly advertising and promotion.[37]

Unfortunately, no one can accurately estimate the range of threshold effect and increasing returns for particular industries. Moreover, experts do not agree on what causes short or long ranges. One study finds some evidence that economies of scale are most prevalent in industries with high advertising/sales ratios, but this is not wholly supported by other evidence.[38] The present author's pet theory is that economies loom largest in consumer goods industries experiencing frequent style changes (autos and cosmetics), or new titles and editions (books and records), or rapid brand multiplication (breakfast cereals and cigarettes).[39] The turbulent and continual changes endemic to these industries force successful firms to cross the threshold level of advertising outlay recurrently, not just once-and-for-all. The expense of each crossing may be thought of as a "fixed" expense of doing business (unrelated to the level of output) because sales are not a function of advertising until after the threshold is crossed. Given high "fixed" promotional expenses in these industries, the largest firms will have the lowest advertising costs *per unit of sales* because they will be able to spread these costs over a larger volume of sales than smaller firms.

Advertising Increases Capital Cost of Entry. Finally, if economies of scale or goodwill carry-overs exist in advertising, the need to obtain substantial funds for advertising will increase the capital requirements for new entry well beyond those needed for physical plant and equipment. As W. Comanor and T. Wilson point out, "this investment in market penetration will involve a particularly risky use of funds since it does not generally create tangible assets which can be resold in the event of failure."[40]

To end on a more positive note, we should mention that advertising can *assist* entry as well as curtail it. How better could a newcomer call attention

---

[37] *Business Week*, November 29, 1976, p. 44.

[38] Comanor and Wilson, *op. cit.* (1974), p. 214. Compare Simon and Crain, *op. cit.*, p. 41. A major weakness of the Simon-Crain study, however, is its failure to separate consumer and producer goods.

[39] D. Greer, "Some Case History Evidence on the Advertising-Concentration Relationship," *The Antitrust Bulletin* (Summer 1972), pp. 320–324. See also Richard Schmalensee, "Entry Deterrence in the Ready-to-Eat Breakfast Cereal Industry," *Bell Journal of Economics* (Autumn 1978), pp. 305–327.

[40] Comanor and Wilson, *op. cit.* (1967), p. 426.

to his new offering than by advertising vigorously? This procompetitive possibility is fully explored in Chapter 15. For now, no more need be said except that the procompetitive effect can easily be outweighed by the anticompetitive, barrier effects outlined previously. Empirical verification of a net procompetitive effect is limited to consumer search good and consumer search services, such as retailing. Where retailer advertising as a percentage of sales is high, profits tend to be low, indicating intense competition.[41] Conversely, experience goods industries demonstrate just the opposite: high advertising is associated with high profits, as one would expect if advertising constituted a barrier to entry.[42] In short, it appears that advertising builds the highest barriers in consumer experience goods industries. In other industries (consumer search goods and perhaps producer goods), it may on balance be neutral or even beneficial to entry and competition.

B. Other Product Differentiation Barriers

The first thing to acknowledge with respect to other forms of differentiation is that they too may harbor economies of scale. In the medical equipment and supplies industry, where salesmen's salaries and expenses account for most promotional expenses, small firms incur selling costs per sales dollar twice as high as those of large firms.[43] Style change in the auto industry provides another example. Economists have shown that the costs of special tools and dies may decline with increasing firm size.[44]

Aside from scaler effects, however, there are a number of factors in this area that may favor established firms still further. If the product is one for which consumers switch brands frequently or commonly buy more than one brand, then brand proliferation by existing firms may reduce a newcomer's expected sales.[45] Assume for the sake of illustration that the newcomer's brand would be the fourth in an industry in which three existing firms supply one brand apiece. The newcomer would get 25% of all the random brand switchers his first year. Now let's switch assumptions. Assume that each of the three existing firms has five brands, yielding a total of 15 existing brands. Then the newcomer entering with one brand would get only one sixteenth, or 6.25%,

[41] Kenneth D. Boyer, "Information and Goodwill Advertising," *Review of Economics and Statistics* (November 1974), pp. 541–548.

[42] We shall explore these studies in detail later. Three key ones, however, are M. E. Porter, "Consumer Behavior, Retailer Power and Market Performance in Consumer Goods Industries," *Review of Economics and Statistics* (November 1974), pp. 419–436; Robert J. Stonebraker, "Corporate Profits and the Risk of Entry," *Review of Economics and Statistics* (February 1976), pp. 33–39; Emilio Pagoulatos and Robert Sorensen, "A Simultaneous Equation Analysis of Advertising, Concentration and Profitability," *Southern Economic Journal* (January 1981), pp. 728–741.

[43] R. D. Peterson and C. R. MacPhee, *Economic Organization in Medical Equipment and Supply* (Lexington, Mass.: Lexington Books, 1973), pp. 58–59.

[44] J. A. Menge, "Style Change Costs as a Market Weapon," *Quarterly Journal of Economics* (November 1962), pp. 632–47; Lawrence White, *The Automobile Industry Since 1945* (Cambridge, Mass.: Harvard University Press, 1971), pp. 39–41.

[45] R. G. Lipsey, G. R. Sparks, P. O. Steiner, *Economics,* 2nd ed. (New York: Harper & Row, 1976), p. 300; Steven R. Cox, "Consumer Information and Competition in the Synthetic Detergent Industry," *Nebraska Journal of Economics and Business* (Summer 1976), pp. 41–58.

of the random switchers.[46] Still another type of barrier arose among grocery retailers in connection with trading stamps. During the 1960s, when trading stamps were in vogue, the largest retail food chains enjoyed, in the use of trading stamps, exclusive advantages that could not be topped by smaller retailers.[47]

Finally, economic theory and evidence are converging on a conclusion that "pioneering" brands have an important advantage over subsequent "me too" brands. This could be called *first-mover advantage* or differentiation by experience.[48] Thus Miller "Lite" has held its lead in light beer despite the strenuous efforts of imitators. "Tareyton" broke new ground with a charcoal filter and has held its ground since. "Bayer" aspirin has yet to be unhorsed in aspirins. And so on. Even though an imitation brand may advertise vigorously to win converts, such information and persuasion as the advertising contains may not readily substitute for the experience consumers have with the pioneering brand:

> First entry allows a brand to exploit or shape a growing yet amorphous transition in consumer tastes. First entry also allows the brand to set product standards and levels of consumer satisfaction which consumers then come to expect as a minimum from follow-on brands.[49]

SUMMARY

We can execute a neat exit from this chapter on entry by reiterating just a few key points:

1. Anything giving established firms substantial advantages over potential entrant firms constitutes a barrier to entry.
2. Because barriers are a source of market power, they will be useful in explaining conduct and performance.
3. Virtually all structural barriers to entry can be classified into four factor groups: absolute unit cost differences, economies of scale, capital costs, and product differentiation. Product differentiation is a blend of the first three factors.

---

[46] Of course, the firm could enter with five brands instead of one, in which case it would boost its chances with any switcher back up to 25%. However, this would require the crossing of five Figure 8–4 type thresholds instead of one, leaving it at a disadvantage.

[47] Federal Trade Commission, *Economic Report on the Structure and Competitive Behavior of Food Retailing* (Washington, D.C.: U.S.G.P.O., 1966), pp. 242–244.

[48] Ronald S. Bond and David F. Lean, *Sales Promotion and Product Differentiation in Two Prescription Drug Markets* (Washington D.C.: FTC Staff Report, 1977); Ira T. Whitten, *Brand Performance in the Cigarette Industry and the Advantage of Early Entry 1913-74* (Washington, D.C.: FTC Staff Report, 1979); Richard Schmalensee, "Product Differentiation Advantages of Pioneering Brands," *American Economic Review* (June 1982), pp. 349–365.

[49] Whitten, *op. cit.,* p. 4.

4. Absolute cost differences raise the entrant's costs of doing business (at every level of output) compared to the costs for established firms.

5. Economies of scale cause unit costs to fall with added size of plant or firm. If minimum efficient scale is large relative to total industry output, there will be little "room" in the industry for a large number of plants and firms, thus occasioning substantial barriers and fostering high concentration.

6. The capital costs of entry may be great, in which case new entrants will have difficulty raising funds at costs comparable to those of large established firms. To some degree this cost differential reflects real economies, for example, transaction costs. The differential is also caused by capital market imperfections, in which case it largely reflects pecuniary economies.

7. Empirical studies of entry barriers disclose a particularly potent effect for product differentiation in consumer experience goods industries. This is not so true of producer and consumer search goods, at least as regards advertising. Still, the influence of other forms of differentiation may often be significant even in these instances.

8. (Behavioral and legal barriers have been saved for later treatment.)

Barriers to Entry, Concentration and Monopoly: Practice and Policy

In this society of ours, we depend on diffusion of power as the best means of achieving political democracy. . . . If we fail the danger is clear to anyone who has studied history—particularly that of the Axis powers prior to World War II.

—SENATOR PHILIP A. HART

Practically everything about monopolization is big. The companies are big. The cases are big. The stakes are big. And chapters written about it are big.

We begin by exploring the wording of the Sherman Act and its rule of reason interpretation. Next we trace the history of monopolization law through three eras—(1) 1890–1940, the era of dastardly deeds, (2) 1945–1970, the era of *Alcoa,* and (3) 1970–present, an era of refinement and retreat. The issue of entry enters repeatedly.

I. THE SHERMAN ACT: SECTION 2

The Sherman Act was passed in 1890 in response to public outcries that something ought to be done about the large "trusts" that were beginning to flourish at that time. The first big trust was Standard Oil, formed in 1882. It was followed quickly by the Whiskey Trust, the Sugar Trust, the Lead Trust, and the Cotton Oil Trust. Senator Sherman exclaimed that without federal action the country would soon have "a trust for every production and a master to fix the price for every necessity of life." Hence, his Sherman Act.

Broadly speaking, the Act contains two main sections outlawing (1) collusive restraints of trade and (2) monopolization. The first refers to collective conduct such as price fixing and is governed by a "per se" rule. We postpone treatment of restraints of trade until Chapter 12, where we treat them in depth.

A. The Rule of Reason

Section 2 of the Sherman Act declares that:

Every person who shall monopolize, or attempt to monopolize, or combine or conspire with any other person or persons, to monopolize any part of the trade or commerce among the several States, or with foreign nations, shall be deemed guilty of a felony . . . .

Although Section 2 covers those who "combine or conspire" to monopolize, it is primarily concerned with single firm activities and structural conditions. Having said that, we must ask: Why the word "monopolize"? Why not "monopoly"? What is the test of monopolization? How large a market share is required? What is meant by a "part of the trade or commerce"?

Simple summary answers to these questions might seem feasible. The Sherman Act is, after all, approaching its hundredth anniversary, and several hundred cases have been brought by the Justice Department under Section 2. Most issues, it would seem, should be settled now. Unfortunately, they are not. Judicial personnel, economic knowledge, political philosophies, and business practices change over time, much as fashion changes. Even more significant, the wording of the statute was left vague enough to invoke extensive judgment.

A Sherman Act Section 2 violation is not as clear-cut as shoplifting or murder. Monopolizers cannot be caught in the act. They are never really caught at all. They are accused and judged by a "rule of reason." The result is drawn-out deliberations. Trials of three years are not unheard of, and in one case more than 1,200 witnesses testified.

Illegal monopolization is not established without proof of two factors: (1) substantial market power, and (2) intent. As Justice William Douglas wrote in the *Grinnell* case, the offense of monopoly "has two elements: (1) the possession of monopoly power in the relevant market and (2) willful acquisition or maintenance of that power . . . ."[1] Reason is exercised to establish both elements. In appraising monopoly **power,** the courts have considered barriers to entry of various kinds—including patents, pecuniary and real economies of scale, product differentiation, absolute capital costs, and several conduct-related barriers. Profits, too, have come under review. The one index of monopoly power consistently receiving greatest attention, however, is the market share of the accused. In this interpretation, reason must be called upon to answer two key questions: What is the relevant market? What market share is sufficient to establish unlawful power?

B. Market Definition: Power Question 1

Section 2 refers to "any part of the trade or commerce," a phrase now taken to mean "relevant market." As we now know, markets do not have bright-line boundaries as do nations or continents. As a result, many factors influence market determination:[2]

1. The physical characteristics of the products.
2. The end uses of the products.

---

[1] *U.S.* v. *Grinnell Corporation,* 384 U.S. 563 (1966).

[2] For an overview see Alvin M. Stein and Barry J. Brett, "Market Definition and Market Power In Antitrust Cases—An Empirical Primer on When, Why and How," *New York Law School Law Review* 24 (1979), pp. 639–676.

3. The cross-elasticity of demand between products.
4. The absolute level of various sellers' costs.
5. The absolute level of product prices, apart from consideration of cross-elasticities.
6. The geographic extent of the market.

The diversity of judgments the relevant market has provoked may be illustrated by two contrasting cases.

In *Du Pont* (1956) a majority of the Supreme Court defined the market broadly to include *all* flexible packaging materials (cellophane, foil, pliofilm, polyethylene, and so on) instead of merely cellophane, which Du Pont dominated.[3] The decisive argument for the Court's majority was cross-elasticity of demand, as may be seen from the opinion:

> If a slight decrease in the price of cellophane causes a considerable number of customers of other flexible wrappings to switch to cellophane, it would be an indication that a high cross-elasticity of demand exists between them; that the products compete in the same market. The court below held that the "great sensitivity of customers in the flexible packaging markets to price or quality changes" prevented DuPont from possessing monopoly control over price. . . . We conclude that cellophane's interchangeability with other materials mentioned suffices to make it a part of this flexible packaging material market.

Although Du Pont produced 75% of all cellophane sold in the United States, this amounted to only 14% of all "flexible packaging." Hence the broad definition made a big difference, and Du Pont won acquittal.

Three dissenting justices had doubts. They felt that cellophane was virtually unique. Cellophane's price, in particular, had been two to seven times higher than that of many comparable materials between 1924 and 1950. Yet during this period "cellophane enjoyed phenomenal growth," *more* growth than could be expected "if close substitutes were available at from one seventh to one half cellophane's price." Furthermore, they thought cross elasticity was low, not high. The price of cellophane fell substantially while other prices remained unchanged. Indeed, "during the period 1933–1946 the prices for glassine and waxed paper actually increased in the face of a 21% decline in the price of cellophane." If substantial "shifts of business" due to "price sensitivity" had in fact occurred, producers of these rival materials would have had to follow cellophane's price down lest they lose sales.[4]

Ten years later, in the *Grinnell* case (1966) a majority of the Court spoke as the minority did in *Du Pont*. They defined the market narrowly to include only "accredited central station protective services" (whereby a client's property is wired for burglaries and fires, signals of which are then sent electronically

---

[3] *U.S.* v. *E.I. duPont de Nemours Company,* 351 U.S. 377 (1956).

[4] For an economic critique see, G. W. Stocking and W. F. Mueller, "The Cellophane Case and the New Competition," *American Economic Review* (March 1955), pp. 29–63. Note that when a monopolist raises price and thereby moves up its demand curve, elasticity will rise. Therefore high elasticity might signal the presence of monopoly instead of its absence.

to a continuously manned central station accredited by insurance underwriters). Other means of property protection were excluded from the relevant market for various reasons:[5]

> Watchmen service is far more costly and less reliable. Systems that set off an audible alarm at the site of a fire or burglary are cheaper but often less reliable. They may be inoperable without anyone's knowing it . . . . Proprietary systems that a customer purchases and operates are available, but they can be used only by a very large business or by government. . . . And, as noted, insurance companies generally allow a greater reduction in premiums for accredited central station service than for other types of protection.

Because Grinnell had 87% of the market as defined, the Court could not let it off the hook like an undersized trout. Grinnell suffered some dismemberment.

C. Market Share: Power Question 2

The cases cited indicate that a market share of 14% does not amount to illegal monopoly but 87% does. What about the area in between? What market share makes an illegal "monopoly"? In two major cases the Supreme Court ruled that 64% of the farm machinery industry and 50% of the steel industry did not amount to monopoly. An influential appeals court judge, Learned Hand, once expressed the opinion that, while any percentage over 90 "is enough to constitute a monopoly; it is doubtful whether sixty or sixty-four per cent would be enough; and certainly thirty-three per cent is not."[6] For these several reasons the consensus seems to hold that market shares below 60% lie snugly beneath the Court's reach. And even 70 or 75% may manage to escape its grasp.

D. Intent

Actually, there is even more uncertainty than the above figures suggest. The issue of **intent** is also important. Generally speaking, there is a trade-off between the market share and the degree of intent the prosecuting attorneys must prove to win a guilty verdict. A clearcut case of 95% market share would probably run afoul of the law with relatively little proof of intent. Conversely, intent would gain importance when a market share of less than 60% was involved.

Indeed, Section 2 forbids mere *attempts* to monopolize as well as monopolization itself. Although the scope of this offense is much disputed and unclear, it seems safe to say that the requirements for proving a charge of "attempt" are now much more rigorous with respect to intent than they are in cases of pure monopolization. Traditionally, proof of an attempt to monopolize requires two elements: (1) a *specific intent* to monopolize and (2) a *dangerous probability of success.*[7] The requirement of specific intent—such as would be shown by clearly anticompetitive acts like blatant predatory pricing, coercive refusals to

---

[5] *U.S.* v. *Grinnell Corporation et al.,* 384 U.S. 563 (1966).

[6] *U.S.* v. *Aluminum Company of America,* 148 F. 2d 416 (1945), 424.

[7] Lawrence Sullivan, *Handbook of the Law of Antitrust* (St. Paul, Minn.: West Publishing Co., 1977), pp. 134–140.

183

deal, and sabotage—arises because in this context the monopolization is not actually achieved. Without indications of specific intent, a court could not be sure that monopolization was what the defendant had in mind. Moving beyond attempts to situations where monopoly has been achieved, only "general" intent need be proved because any specific intent is then largely manifest in the end result.[8]

Use of the word "monopolize" in the Sherman Act (rather than "monopoly") implies that simple possession of a large market share is not itself frowned upon. An illegality requires more: some positive drive, some "intent" to seize and exert power in the market. Only a moment's reflection reveals the wisdom of this policy. What of the innovator whose creativity establishes a whole new industry, occupied at first by just his firm? What of the last surviving firm in a dying industry? What of the superefficient firm that underprices everyone else through genuine economies of scale or some natural advantages of location? What of a large market share gained purely by competitive skill? To pounce on these monopolies would have to be regarded as cruel (since they are actually "innocent"), stupid (since it would be punishing good performance), and irrational (since no efficient structural remedy, such as dissolution, could ensue). Thus a finding of intent to monopolize is essential, even though it may not be easy.

In Section 2 cases a monopolist's intent emerges from its particular acts or its general course of action. With this statement we come to the point where, for pedagogical purposes, three more or less distinct eras of Section 2 interpretation may be distinguished depending on what the courts have required of plaintiffs to prove intent.

- *1890–1940:* In the early days, the Supreme Court usually held that an offensive degree of intent could be established only with evidence of abusive acts. This could be called the era of leniency because "well-behaved" monopolists with as much as 90% of the market were welcomed if not cherished.

- *1945–1970:* The *Alcoa* case of 1945 set a very stringent standard, excusing monopolists only when power was "thrust upon" them, as if by accident. Little was needed to show offensive intent because "no monopolist monopolizes unconscious of what he is doing."[9]

- *1970–Present:* Most recently the pendulum has swung back toward leniency. A string of lower court decisions gives monopolists spacious room for aggressive, if not abusive, conduct. Still, this era's record is mixed because the Supreme Court has not spoken.

We take up each era successively.

---

[8] The "dangerous probability" requirement has stirred controversy of late because some lower courts have recently held that near monopoly or a high probability of actual monopolization are necessary to a finding of dangerous probability. See especially *U.S.* v. *Empire Gas Co.* 537 F.2d 296 (8th Cir. 1976), *cert. denied,* 429 U.S. 1122 (1977).

[9] *U.S.* v. *Aluminum Company of America,* 148 F. 2d 416 (1945).

II. THE EARLY DAYS: 1890–1940

A. An Overview

Before *Alcoa,* the Supreme Court usually held that an offensive degree of intent could be established only with evidence of abusive, predatory, or criminal acts. The types of conduct that qualified included the following: (1) predatory pricing, that is, cutting prices below costs on certain products or in certain regions and subsidizing the resulting losses with profits made elsewhere; (2) predatory promotional spending or predatory pricing on "fighting brands" or "bogus independent" firms or upon new facilities or new products; (3) physical violence to competitors, their customers, or their products; (4) exaction of special advantages from suppliers, such as "railroad rebates"; (5) misuse of patents, copyrights, or trademarks; and (6) preclusion of competitive opportunities by refusals to sell, exclusive dealing arrangements, or anticompetitive tie-in sales.

For the most part, this list of "predatory tactics" is derived from the major early cases listed in Table 9–1. The first five cases mentioned there ended in convictions. The last five mentioned ended in acquittals. Notice from the center column that the market shares of the convicted monopolizers are not markedly greater than those of the acquitted firms, although in the latter group there are two with only 50% of industry sales. The big difference lies in the next column, where a "Yes" indicates that obviously predatory tactics were used by the defendant and a "No" indicates a fairly clean slate in this regard. With but one exception, those guilty of dirty tricks were also found guilty of monopolizing. Conversely, the "good" trusts managed to get off. The obvious implication

TABLE 9–1. Major Section 2 Cases, 1911 to 1927

	Industry	Percentage of the Industry (%)	Predatory Tactics Present?	Date of Final Judgment
I. Unlawful monopolies				
Standard Oil of N.J.	Petroleum	85–90	Yes	1911
American Tobacco Co.	Tobacco products	76–97	Yes	1911
E. I. Du Pont	Explosives	64–100	Yes	1911
Eastman Kodak Co.	Photo equipment	75–80	Yes	1915
Corn Products Refining Co.	Glucose	53	Yes	1916
II. Cases of acquittal				
United Shoe Machinery Co.	Shoe machinery	90	No	1917
American Can Co.	Packers' cans	50	Yes	1916
Quaker Oats Co.	Rolled oats cereal	75	No	1916
U.S. Steel Corp.	Steel	50	No	1920
International Harvester Co.	Harvesters	64	No	1927

Source: Milton Handler, *Trade Regulation,* 3rd ed. (New York: Foundation Press, 1960), pp. 378–79.

must be qualified by the example of several railroad cases. Between 1904 and 1922, the Supreme Court decided against three railroad combinations that did not employ predatory practices to gain substantial market shares.[10] Even so, we can buttress the message of Table 9–1 by consulting the Court's opinions.

B. Standard Oil of New Jersey (1911)

Standard Oil (now Exxon) was the most notorious monopoly of its time. First organized in Ohio in 1870, by 1872 it had acquired all but a few of the three dozen refineries in Cleveland. Additionally, it had garnered complete control of the pipe lines running from oil fields to refineries in Cleveland, Pittsburgh, Philadelphia, New York, and New Jersey. Further transportation advantages were gained from the railroads through preferential rates and large rebates. From this strategic footing Standard Oil was able to force competitors to join the combination or be driven out of business. As a result, the combine grew to control 90% of the petroleum industry, a dominance that produced enormous profits. Under legal attack from authorities in Ohio, the company was reorganized in 1899 as Standard Oil of New Jersey, a holding company. The new combine continued to exact preferential treatment from railroads and to cut crude oil supplies to competing refiners. Business espionage, local price warfare, and the operation of bogus independents were also Standard tactics. As the Supreme Court said, "The pathway of the combination . . . is strewn with the wrecks resulting from crushing out, without regard to law, the individual rights of others."[11]

In writing the Supreme Court's opinion, Chief Justice White emphasized intent, contrasting the tainted history of Standard Oil with what he called "normal methods of industrial development." Thus, by implication, the Court acknowledged that power alone was not enough, that monopoly in the concrete was condoned absent the willful drive. In applying this interpretation of Section 2 to the facts of Standard Oil, White said that the combine's merging and acquiring alone gave rise to a "prima-facie presumption of intent." He went on, however, to state that this prima-facie presumption was "made conclusive" by considering the rapacious conduct of the New Jersey corporation.

In sum, White gave birth to an infantile form of the rule of reason as we know it today. He found himself "irresistibly driven to the conclusion that the very genius for commercial development and organization which it would seem was manifested from the beginning soon begot an intent and purpose to exclude others . . . by acts and dealings wholly inconsistent with . . . normal methods." Given its context, White's "rule of reason" came to mean that a monopolist would not be forced to walk the plank unless he had *behaved unreasonably*.

---

[10] Northern Securities Co. (1904), Union Pacific (1912), and Southern Pacific (1922).

[11] *Standard Oil Company of New Jersey* v. *U.S.*, 221 U.S. 1 (1911). John McGee has argued that Standard's predatory pricing was less than alleged, even nonexistent, "Predatory Price Cutting: The Standard Oil (N.J.) Case," *Journal of Law & Economics* (October 1958), pp. 137–169. But his account has been questioned by F. M. Scherer, *Industrial Market Structure and Economic Performance* (Chicago: Rand McNally, 1970), pp. 274–276.

Dissolution of the combine followed, yielding thirty-four separate companies. Historically, these offspring tended to be regionally and vertically specialized— e.g., Standard Oil of California (now Chevron), Standard Oil of New York (Mobil), Standard Oil of Indiana (American), and Standard Oil of New Jersey (Exxon).[12] With time, they spread into each other's territory to compete.

C. American Tobacco (1911)

The story in tobacco is similar to that in oil except that advertising and promotion were big weapons.[13] The story centers on James Duke, whose power play started in cigarettes, then spread to other branches of the trade. By 1885 Duke had secured 11–18% of total cigarette sales for his company through an arduous promotional effort. He then escalated ad and promotional outlays to nearly 20% of sales, thereby forcing a five-firm merger in 1889 and acquiring 80% control of all cigarette sales. His American Tobacco Company grew still further until he held 93% of the market in 1899. Coincident with this final gathering of power, cigarette profits swelled to 56% of sales in 1899.

With these stupendous profits Duke launched massive predatory campaigns to capture other tobacco markets, which were at the time bigger than cigarettes. One measure of this effort is the American Tobacco Company's annual advertising and selling cost as a percentage of sales at crest levels in the target markets— 28.9% for plug and twist, 24.4% for smoking tobacco, 31.7% for fine-cut chewing, and 49.9% for cigars. Duke even went so far as to introduce deliberately unprofitable "fighting brands," one of which was appropriately called "Battle Ax." Losses ensued; mergers followed; and after the entire industry (except for cigars) was under American's thumb, advertising receded substantially to such relatively peaceful neighborhoods as 4 and 10% of sales.

Just before the Supreme Court's ruling against American in 1911 the combine controlled the following shares: smoking tobacco, 76.2%; chewing tobacco, 84.4%; cigarettes, 86.1%; snuff, 96.5%. Stressing the crude behavior of the combine, the Court found American's acts unreasonable. Dissolution ensued, creating oligopoly in place of monopoly.[14] Competition improved, but not markedly.

D. United States Steel (1920)

A chain of mergers occurred around the turn of the century, eliminating the independence of 170 steel companies and culminating in the formation of U.S. Steel Corporation in 1901. When formed, this behemoth accounted for 66% of all American steel production. Its market power is evident in the fact that U.S. Steel's capitalization was double the market value of the stock of its constituent companies. Still, the Corporation's market share dwindled a bit by

---

[12] Others included Atlantic Refining, Conoco, Marathon, Std. of Kentucky, Std. of Louisiana, and Std. of Nebraska.

[13] For a summary see D. F. Greer, "Some Case History Evidence on the Advertising-Concentration Relationship," *Antitrust Bulletin* (Summer 1975), pp. 311–315.

[14] *U.S.* v. *American Tobacco Co.*, 221 U.S. 106 (1911).

187

1911, when, flush with success in *Standard Oil* and *American Tobacco,* the Justice Department filed suit. Its share fell further, and in 1920 U.S. Steel won acquittal.

In acquitting United States Steel the Court held that the corporation's 50% market share (at the time of the case) did not amount to excessive power, and, even if it had amounted to excessive power, the corporation had not abused it: "It resorted to none of the brutalities or tyrannies that the cases illustrate of other combinations." The corporation "did not oppress or coerce its competitors . . . it did not undersell its competitors in some localities by reducing its prices there below those maintained elsewhere, or require its customers to enter into contracts limiting their purchases or restricting them in resale prices; it did not obtain customers by secret rebates . . . there was no evidence that it attempted to crush its competitors or drive them out of the market . . ." In short: "The corporation is undoubtedly of impressive size. . . . But the law does not make mere size an offense, or the existence of unexerted power an offense. It, we repeat, requires overt acts. . . ."[15] U.S. Steel was indeed a combination formed by *merger.* But merger was not then considered evidence of intent even though it is obviously an "overt act."

Allowing monopoly by merger was no mere oversight, for in a stinging dissent Justice Day reminds the majority that the Sherman Act expressly bans "combinations" and goes on to argue that the "contention must be rejected that the [U.S. Steel] combination was an inevitable evolution of industrial tendencies compelling union of endeavor." Nevertheless, the view that abusive "overt acts" were required to prove intent prevailed in this and other opinions of the day.

III. THE *ALCOA* ERA: 1945–1970

A. An Overview

Although the *U.S. Steel* interpretation may not have gutted Section 2, it certainly bloodied it a bit. Section 2 lay incapacitated until 1945, when the *Alcoa* decision brought recuperation.[16] In essence, *Alcoa* lengthened the list of intent indications beyond predatory and abusive tactics. According to *Alcoa,* unlawful intent can almost be assumed unless the defendant is a "passive beneficiary" of monopoly power or has had monopoly power "thrust upon" him. To *any* extent the monopolist reaches out to grasp or strives actively to hold his dominant position, he is denied the right to claim that he has no unlawful intent. This hard line is softened by other language in the opinion that exempts monopoly gained by "superior skill, foresight and industry." Subsequent cases changed the wording to permit monopoly grounded on "a superior product, business acumen or historic accident."[17] But the *Alcoa* interpretation remained fairly well intact for nearly three decades.

[15] *U.S.* v. *United States Steel Corporation,* 251 U.S.417 (1920).
[16] *U.S.* v. *Aluminum Company of America,* 148 F. 2d 416 (2d Cir. 1945).
[17] *U.S.* v. *Grinnell Corp.,* 384 U.S. 563 (1966).

B. Alcoa (1945)[18] *read again*

The Aluminum Company of America provides many interesting economic lessons as well as legal lessons. For more than half a century it dominated all four stages of the United States aluminum industry: (1) bauxite ore mining, (2) conversion of bauxite into aluminum oxide or alumina, (3) electrolytic reduction of alumina into aluminum ingots, and (4) fabrication of aluminum products, such as cable, foil, pots and pans, sheets, and extrusions. Alcoa's dominance derived mainly from various barriers to entry:

Patents. Until 1886, the processes for extracting pure aluminum were so costly that it was a precious metal like gold or platinum. In that year, just after graduating from Oberlin College, Charles Hall discovered electrolytic reduction of alumina into aluminum. His discovery was later duplicated by C. S. Bradley. Alcoa acquired the rights to both their patents, and thereby excluded potential entrants legally until 1909.

Resources Controlled. Resource limitations also barred entry. Alcoa integrated backwards into bauxite mining and electric power, the two key resources for producing aluminum. Although these resources were too plentiful to be fully preempted by a single firm, Alcoa vigorously acquired, developed, and built the lowest cost sources of each.

Economies of Scale. As if all that were not enough, economies of scale constituted an additional barrier. Of the several stages of the production process, the second stage—conversion of bauxite into alumina—yielded the greatest efficiencies from increased size. Until 1938 there was only *one* alumina plant in the entire United States. The unit costs of a 500,000-ton per year plant embodying 1940 technology were 10–20% below the unit costs of a 100,000-ton plant. And it was not until 1942 that United States consumption of alumina topped 500,000 tons. The dire implications for entry into alumina production during that era should be obvious. Economies were not nearly so pronounced for reduction and fabrication (there being four smelting plants in the United States during the 1930s and a goodly number of fabricators).

Nonetheless the barriers associated with alumina spilled over into these other stages because Alcoa was *vertically integrated.* However efficient a producer of ingot or fabricated products might be, he was ultimately dependent on Alcoa for his raw materials and simultaneously competing with Alcoa as a seller. This put independents in a precarious position. Alcoa could control the independents' costs *and* selling price. Were Alcoa unkind enough to raise its price of ingot and lower its price of foil, say, the foil fabricators would be in a bind. The "price squeeze" would pinch the margin between their costs and selling price. Just such a squeeze was alleged in 1926 and 1927, when Alcoa reduced

---

[18] Primary sources for this section are L. W. Weiss, *Economics and American Industry* (New York: John Wiley & Sons, 1961), Chapter 5; Merton J. Peck, *Competition in the Aluminum Industry: 1945–1958* (Cambridge, Mass.: Harvard University Press, 1961).

the margin between ingot and certain types of aluminum sheet from 16 cents to 7 cents a pound and then kept it there until 1932. Two independent rollers of sheet initiated an antitrust suit that was settled out of court.

The Antitrust Suit. The government lost its antitrust suit at the district court level in 1941 after a three-year trial. The district judge relied heavily on the *U.S. Steel* case of 1920. He felt that mere size, unaccompanied by dastardly deeds, did not violate Section 2. The Supreme Court could not hear the Justice Department's appeal because four Court Justices disqualified themselves on grounds of prior participation in the case, leaving less than a quorum. However, the New York Circuit Court of Appeals was designated court of last resort for the case. That three-judge panel, acting under the leadership of Judge Learned Hand, decided against Alcoa, thereby reversing the lower court and boldly overturning precedent.[19]

On the question of market power, the Circuit Court determined that Alcoa controlled over 90% of primary aluminum sales in the United States, the other 10% being accounted for by imports.[20] "That percentage," Hand said, "is enough to constitute a monopoly." On the issue of intent, the Court *rejected* the notion that evil acts must be in evidence. Lacking substantial judicial precedent for this position, the Court looked to congressional intent:

> [Congress] did not condone "good trusts" and condemn "bad" ones; it forbade all. Moreover, in so doing it was not necessarily actuated by economic motives alone. It is possible, because of its indirect social or moral effect, to prefer a system of small producers . . . to one in which the great mass of those engaged must accept the direction of a few.

By this interpretation a monopolist could escape only if its monopoly had been "thrust upon it," only if "superior skill, foresight and industry" were the basis for its success. Was this true of Alcoa? The Court thought not, emphasizing conditions of entry:

> It would completely misconstrue "Alcoa's" position in 1940 to hold that it was the passive beneficiary of a monopoly. . . . This increase and this continued undisturbed control did not fall undesigned into "Alcoa's" lap. . . . There were at least one or two abortive attempts to enter the industry, but "Alcoa" effectively anticipated and forestalled all competition. . . . It was not inevitable that it should always anticipate increases in the demand for ingot and be prepared to supply them. Nothing compelled it to keep doubling and redoubling its capacity before others entered the field.

Assistance to Entrants. Today, partly as a result of this decision, Alcoa accounts for less than one third of all United States aluminum ingot capacity.

---

[19] *U.S.* v. *Aluminum Company of America,* 148 F.2d 416 (1945).

[20] Market definition was a key issue here. (1) If "the market" *included* scrap as well as primary aluminum and *excluded* the ingot Alcoa retained for its own use, then its share would have been only 33%. (2) If "the market" *included* scrap as well as primary aluminum and *included* Alcoa's total ingot production, then its share would have been 64%. (3) The 90% figure derives from *excluding* scrap and *including* Alcoa's total production.

The government did not bring this about by breaking Alcoa into fragments. Instead, it encouraged and subsidized new entry into the industry. After World War II, the government's war plants were sold at bargain-basement prices to Reynolds and Kaiser (two former fabricators). This move alone reduced Alcoa's market share to 50%. Later, during the Cold and Korean Wars of the 1950s, the government aided the entry of Anaconda, Harvey (now owned by Martin Marietta), and Ormet. These firms were the beneficiaries of rapid amortization certificates, government-guaranteed construction loans, long-term contracts to supply the government's stockpile of aluminum, and cut-rate government electricity. Changing economic conditions also helped. The demand for aluminum in the United States has increased 3,000% since 1940 and 1,000% since 1950. Simultaneously, costs as a function of plant size have not altered appreciably. As a consequence, economies of scale have shrunk to the point at which a minimum efficient scale alumina plant would account for only about 8% of total United States capacity, and a minimum efficient scale ingot plant would account for only about 3%. These developments enabled still further entry during the 1960s and 1970s.

C. United Shoe Machinery (1953)

U.S. v. *United Shoe Machinery* was tried in 1953, was decided against United Shoe, and was affirmed per curiam by the Supreme Court in 1954.[21] United was found to supply somewhere between 75 and 85% of the machines used in boot and shoe manufacturing. Moreover, it was the only machinery producer offering a full line of equipment. United had many sources of market power, but the following are especially noteworthy:

1. Like Alcoa, United held patents covering the fundamentals of shoe machinery manufacture at the turn of the century. These basic patents were long expired by the 1950s, and with some effort competitors could "invent around" United's later patents. Still, at the time of the suit, United held 2,675 patents, some of which it acquired and some of which impeded entry.

2. A logical strategy for a new entrant would have been to start with one or two machine types and then branch out into a more complete line. Indeed, this was the approach of United's major rival, Compo, which specialized in "cementing" machines. United's answer to the challenge, however, was a discriminatory price policy that fixed a lower rate of return where competition was of major significance and a higher rate of return where competition was weak or nonexistent.

3. There was some weak evidence of economies of scale. Economies were suggested by the fact that United had only one manufacturing plant. The evidence is weak, however, because the plant was essentially a large

---

[21] *U.S.* v. *United Shoe Machinery Corp.*, 110 F. Supp. 295 (D. Mass. 1953), aff'd per curiam, 347 U.S. 521 (1954). See also Carl Kaysen, *United States* v. *United Shoe Machinery Corporation* (Cambridge, Mass.: Harvard University Press, 1956).

"job shop" with a wide variety of products and small orders. Mass production techniques were not involved.

4. Finally, United never sold its machines; it only leased them. This policy precluded competition from a second-hand market. Furthermore, the terms of the leases restricted entry into new machinery production. Ten years was the standard lease duration. If a lessee wished to return a machine before the end of his ten-year term, he paid a penalty that tapered down from a substantial amount in the early years to a small amount in the later years. If he was returning the machine for replacement, he paid a lower penalty if he took another United machine than if he switched to a rival manufacturer's machine. Moreover, service was tied in. No separate charges were made for repairs and maintenance, with the result that a newly entering firm had to build a service organization as well as manufacturing and marketing capabilities.

On the basis of these facts, the court ruled against United, saying that the "defendant has, and exercises, such overwhelming strength in the shoe machinery market that it controls that market." What is more, "this strength excludes some potential, and limits some actual, competition." Regarding intent, the court conceded that "United's power does not rest on predatory practices." However, United's lease-only system, its restrictive lease clauses, its price discrimination, and its acquisition of patents

> are not practices which can be properly described as the inevitable consequences of ability, natural forces, or law. They represent something more. . . . They are contracts, arrangements, and policies which, instead of encouraging competition based on pure merit, further the dominance of a particular firm. In this sense they are *unnatural* barriers . . . [italics added].

The court ordered United to sell as well as lease its machines, to modify the terms of its leases, and to divest itself of some assets.

Among other cases of the *Alcoa* era, *Grinnell* (1966) is notable for saying that monopolization based on "superior product, business acumen, or historic accident" would not be illegal. Grinnell Corp. did not pass the test.[22]

IV. 1970–PRESENT: REFINEMENT AND RETREAT

The ground work for a hard line against dominant firms was laid with the *Alcoa* era, but there was little follow-through. United Shoe and a few others suffered some dismemberment then. But the government seemed to be ignoring

---

[22] *U.S.* v. *Grinnell Corporation*, 384 U.S. 563 (1966). The case apparently stimulated competition substantially. See Don E. Waldman, *Antitrust Action and Market Structure* (Lexington, Mass.: Lexington Books, 1978), pp. 49–57. Waldman has also shown that government action against du Pont during the 1950s stimulated competition in the cellophane industry by stimulating new entry, even though the government lost the case in court. "The du Pont Cellophane Case Revisited," *Antitrust Bulletin* (Winter 1980), pp. 805–830.

real giants like GM and IBM. At least two factors could explain the timidity of officialdom—(1) inadequate resources and (2) inadequate legal clout.

The *first* is easiest to explain because it is easy to imagine the immense resources consumed by a "big case." Dozens of years, scores of lawyers, millions of dollars, thousands of documents, hundreds of witnesses, hordes of motions, and countless other items drain plaintiffs and defendants in these cases. To bring a decent case against a genuine giant the Antitrust Division of the Department of Justice would have to be revamped, reorganized, and refinanced. Estimates of the social benefit/cost ratios of big cases are generally favorable—for instance, Standard Oil, 67; American Tobacco, 21; Alcoa 19; and United Shoe Machinery 5.[23] But inertia curbs commitment.

The *second* problem, inadequate legal clout, arose from gaps in the law. Up to this point we have mentioned the law's firm grasp of two rather polar conditions, outright cartelization and obvious monopolization. There is a space between, however, one that eludes antitrust treatment. That space is occupied by tight-knit oligopolies. If four fairly equal-sized firms control an industry, for example, they may skirt Section 1 with tacit collusion while at the same time ducking Section 2 because none of them individually has more than 30% of the business. Many of the nation's behemoth's fall into this category—very big absolutely but not really big relative to a relevant market. This could be called the **structural gap.**

An additional gap in the law applied even for firms with very large market shares, namely, uncertainty as to what kinds of conduct would indicate intent. What, specifically, could pass innocently for "a superior product, business acumen, or historic accident"? It was clear that blatantly predatory practices, major mergers, and restrictive licensing would not pass. It was equally clear that dominance built on significant innovation or economies of scale would pass. But what of the middle ground? What about aggressive expansion of capacity, voluminous advertising, trivial new product proliferation, and deep but above cost price cutting? Their uncertain implications for intent opened a **conduct gap.** The uncertainty stemmed from the difficulty of trying to curb monopoly without squashing business incentive. *Alcoa* was not much help on this score, as seen by the inconsistency in two of Judge Hand's statements—(1) Congress "did not condone 'good trusts' and condemn 'bad' ones; it forbade all;" and yet (2) "The successful competitor, having been urged to compete, must not be turned upon when he wins." This tension, a circuit court has recently complained, "makes the cryptic *Alcoa* opinion a litigant's wishing well, into which, it sometimes seems, one may peer and find nearly anything he wishes."[24]

Against this background, the 1970s opened auspiciously for proponents of vigorous antitrust policy. The authorities launched several "big" cases against IBM, Xerox, and AT&T. Enforcement resources grew rapidly. And attempts to close the structural and conduct gaps in stringent fashion were embodied

---

[23] William G. Shepherd, *The Treatment of Market Power* (New York: Columbia University Press, 1975), Chapter 7 and Appendix 3.
[24] *Berkey Photo* v. *Eastman Kodak Co.,* 603 F2d 263 (2d Cir. 1979).

STRUCTURE

in new legislative proposals for industrial deconcentration and in innovative cases against "shared monopolies." The temper of the times was captured in a lengthy *Business Week* special report on the "mounting political pressure to toughen antitrust enforcement." The report concluded that "Business almost certainly faces even tougher antitrust enforcement and possibly even a new antitrust law aimed at breaking up the corporate giants in the country's basic industries."[25]

The ominous storm blew over by the early 1980s, however, producing little more than light rain. The light rain came in the form of consent settlements in the *Xerox* and *AT&T* cases, settlements that were momentous to Xerox and AT&T but not really important to resolution of either the structural gap or the conduct gap (as these were rather special cases). The structural gap cleanly escaped closure when the proposed legislation died in Congress and the "shared" monopoly cases died in the Federal Trade Commission. The conduct gap narrowed in the direction of greater, not lesser, *leniency* for dominant firms when the case against IBM was dropped by the Justice Department in January 1982, the groundwork for the abandonment being laid by a string of circuit court decisions favorable to aggressive dominant firms—in particular, *Berkey Photo*, v. *Eastman Kodak Company* (1979), and *California Computer Products* v. *IBM* (1979)—and by the installment of a conservative, William Baxter, in the office of Assistant Attorney General for Antitrust. To outline our coverage of these developments:

A. Shades of a Tougher Stance; *Xerox* and *AT&T*
B. Continuation of a Structural Gap
  1. Unpassed Legislation
  2. "Shared" Monopoly Dies on the Vine
C. Closing the Conduct Gap
  1. *Berkey* v. *Kodak* (1979)
  2. *Calcomp* v. *IBM* (1979)
  3. *U.S.* v. *IBM* (dismissed 1982)

A. Shades of a Tougher Stance: Xerox and AT&T

Xerox. Two "big" government cases provide the most dramatic signs of a stimulated Section 2 during this current era. In 1973 the Federal Trade Commission charged Xerox with monopolizing the copier industry, alleging that Xerox controlled 95% of the plain-paper copier business and 86% of the total office-copier market. The allegations of offensive conduct paralleled those of *United Shoe Machinery*. That is, Xerox's licensing, pricing, and patent policies were said to exclude competition artificially. Xerox responded by negotiating a settlement in 1975, one that provided for (1) licensing patents on reasonable royalties, (2) supplying "knowhow" to competitors, (3) modifying price policies, and (4)

[25] "Is John Sherman's Antitrust Obsolete?" *Business Week*, March 23, 1974, pp. 47–56. See also *Business Week*, December 13, 1976, pp. 52–59.

194

selling as well as leasing copy machines. The consent decree has been denounced for being ineffectual, but it may have helped the entry of Savin, IBM, and others—entries that jolted the industry with new competition.[26]

AT&T. The American Telephone & Telegraph case was launched by the Justice Department in 1974. Admitting that AT&T's monopoly of most telephone service could be justified by "natural" economies of scale, the Justice Department claimed that AT&T should not be allowed to extend that monopoly power into contiguous fields where economies were significantly less consequential—equipment manufacturing in particular. Thus the government sought to split AT&T into portions representing regulated "natural" monopoly activities and *non*regulated, potentially competitive activities. Such a split would prevent AT&T from using its monopoly power in regulated markets to subsidize its operation in unregulated markets, hurting competition in the latter. The suit was settled in early 1982 by a consent decree that will cause AT&T to shed its regulated regional phone service utility companies, leaving a unit comprised of AT&T Long Lines, Bell Laboratories, American Bell, and Western Electric. This case is unique however. It portends little for firms untouched by public utility regulation.[27]

B. Continuation of the Structural Gap

1. Congressional Action (or Inaction). The problems of (1) immune oligopolies, (2) conduct uncertainties, and (3) mammouth cases might all be alleviated if the law shifted toward a more purely structural orientation, one essentially eliminating the intent requirement. A number of such proposals have been made, each presenting essentially the same thrust—namely, dissolution of an industry's leading firms should follow almost automatically once it is found that some high concentration threshold has been crossed for a substantial duration. Defenses against dismemberment are usually allowed by such proposals, but they are limited to proofs that the concentration was grounded on either economies of scale in production or valid patents.[28]

The Industrial Reorganization Act proposed by the late Senator Philip Hart in 1973 provides an example. Under this scheme, the rule of reason would be curtailed. There would be a *presumption* of monopoly power whenever one or more of the following criteria were met:[29]

---

[26] Don E. Waldman, "Economic Benefits in the *IBM, AT&T,* and *Xerox* cases: Government Antitrust in the 70's," *Antitrust Law and Economics Review* (No. 2, 1980), pp. 75–92.

[27] *Wall Street Journal,* January 11, 1982, pp. 1, 4; January 12, 1982, p. 3; January 21, 1982, pp. 1, 21.

[28] See, e.g., *The Report of the Task Force on Antitrust Policy* (for President Johnson), reprinted in *The Journal of Reprints for Antitrust Law & Economics* (Winter 1969), Part 1, pp. 633–826.

[29] *The Industrial Reorganization Act, Hearings* before the U.S. Senate Subcommittee on Antitrust and Monopoly of the Committee on the Judiciary, Part I (1973). See also National Commission for the Review of the Antitrust Laws and Procedures, *Report to the President and the Attorney General* (Washington, D.C., January 1979), pp. 151–163.

1. Four or fewer firms accounted for half or more of an industry's sales in a single year.
2. There has been no substantial price competition for three consecutive years among two or more firms within the industry.
3. A company's average rate of return (after taxes) exceeds 15% of its net worth for each of five consecutive years.

However, a company running afoul of one of these criteria would not face automatic fragmentation. A special commission would review the case, at which time the company could defend itself by showing that its power was due "solely to the ownership of valid patents, lawfully acquired and lawfully used," *or* that its divestiture would "result in a loss of substantial economies." Predictably, this proposed legislation touched off bitter controversy, and it is doubtful whether such a stringent measure can ever pass. Its benefits are too vague to many observers, and its business opponents are too powerful in the halls of Congress.

2. "Shared Monopoly." Not waiting for Congress to plug the structural gap, the FTC filed suit in 1972 charging three large breakfast cereal producers with "shared monopoly."[30] Kellogg, General Mills, and General Foods collectively account for 81% of the ready-to-eat cereal market. But individually, the largest (Kellogg) controls no more than 45%. The accusations bringing these firms together under one suit were legal novelties:

1. *Brand proliferation.* The companies introduced 150 brands between 1950 and 1970, advertising them heavily and artificially differentiating them, thereby feigning competition and discouraging new entry.
2. *Control shelf space.* They crowded competitors off grocers' shelves with their countless brands and marketing clout.
3. *Forbearance.* They minimized price competition by tacit mutual agreement not to challenge each other's price increases and by limiting coupons, premiums, and cents-off deals.

The remedies sought involved more than dissolution. They included the forced licensing to other companies of any new brands developed by Kellogg, General Mills, and General Foods.

The companies won, though. In January 1982 the FTC decided to let stand the trial judge's ruling that the case should be dismissed. As one commissioner put it, the FTC should not restructure oligopolies "without a clear supportive signal from the Congress."[31] Thus it may be doubted that the structural gap will ever be closed by innovative judicial interpretations of existing statutes.

C. Narrowing the Conduct Gap with Leniency

If anything, judicial interpretation has recently turned in a lenient, rather than a stringent direction. In particular, the lower courts recently exonerated

[30] *In the Matter of Kellogg Co., et al.,* Docket #8883, Complaint, April 26, 1972.
[31] *Wall Street Journal,* January 18, 1982, p. 6.

Kodak and IBM of monopolization in major private suits. These courts found that many allegedly exclusionary practices merely reflected these firms' "superior product, business acumen," or "skill, foresight, and industry"—not the willful maintenance of monopoly power. As one commentator put it, these cases give a monopolist "greater freedom to fight off its competitors." And in so doing, "they invite comparison with the earliest Section 2 cases," which required "overt acts" for proof of intent.[32]

1. Kodak (1979).[33] Kodak lords over the photography industry, dominating the manufacture of still cameras, film, and paper used to print color pictures. During the late 60s and early 70s its shares of these markets ranged from 64 to 94%. In photofinishing, however, it held about 10%.

Berkey is primarily a photofinisher, but between 1966 and 1978 it competed with Kodak in still cameras. Disappointed with its lack of success in still cameras, Berkey sued Kodak for monopolizing the camera and film markets. A jury favored Berkey, but the circuit court of appeals reversed, and the Supreme Court let the reversal stand.

Berkey's claims concerning Kodak's massive dominance were never questioned. As the court put it, "If a finding of monopoly power were all that were necessary to complete a violation of Section 2, our task in this case would be considerably lightened." Berkey's claims concerning intent were severely questioned, however. These claims centered on Kodak's introduction in 1972 of its 110 compact camera *system.* The word "system" needs stress because it was more than just a new camera, it included entirely new film (Kodacolor II), film format, and photofinishing. Kodak decided upon its package approach rather haltingly, in large part because of uncertainties as to the adequacy of its old film and the performance capabilities of its new film. Berkey challenged the introduction of the 110 system using essentially three arguments:

> *first,* that because Kodak set *de facto* standards for the photography industry, it had a special duty to refrain from surprise innovations and was required to make adequate predisclosure to enable rivals to stay competitive with it; *second,* that the introduction of Kodacolor II as part of the 110 system was not technically necessary for the new camera and was instead a use of Kodak's monopoly power in film to gain a competitive advantage in cameras; and *finally,* that limiting Kodacolor II to the 110 format unlawfully foreclosed competition by other manufacturers in existing formats.[34]

While rejecting Berkey's arguments the circuit court explicitly rejected *Alcoa's* "thrust upon" standard. Kodak, the court said, may "compete aggressively," even to the point of using its *combined* film and camera capabilities to bolster its faltering camera sales. An integrated business does not "offend

---

[32] John A. Maher, "Draining the *ALCOA* 'Wishing Well.' The Section 2 Conduct Requirement after *Kodak* and *Calcomp,*" *Fordham Law Review* (December 1979), pp. 294–295.

[33] *Berkey Photo, Inc.* v. *Eastman Kodak Company* 603 F.2d 263 (2d Cir. 1979), cert. denied 444 U.S. 1093 (1980).

[34] Maher, *op. cit.,* pp. 312–313 (emphasis added).

the Sherman Act whenever one of its departments benefits from association with a division possessing a monopoly in its own market."

2. Calcomp (1979).[35] In 1969 and 1970 IBM began to suffer substantial competition from new "plug compatible" peripherals manufacturers, or PCMs. By May 1971 the PCMs had 14.5% of IBM's disk-drive market and 13.7% of its tape-drive market. Moreover, these shares would have been about 20% by 1976 had IBM not done something. But IBM did do something. On May 27, 1971, it introduced long-term leases coupled with price reductions of 20–35% on equipment vulnerable to such competition.

Within 48 hours PCM company stock-prices began a nose dive (Telex down 14%, Memorex down 15%, Marshall Laboratories down 18%), and within the year following, PCM equipment orders were off 44% from the previous year, despite deep defensive price cuts by the PCM companies. They lost money for the next 2 years. For its part, IBM made up its lost revenues by increasing prices in other product lines—central processing units, card equipment, and maintenance services—just two months after the May reductions. These increases varied from 4 to 8% on equipment, and some maintenance charges rose 25%.

This and related episodes sparked a rash of PCM suits charging IBM with monopolization of peripherals markets.[36] CalComp's suit was typical, and all of CalComp's allegations of IBM wrongdoing were rejected by the circuit court. *First,* IBM's price cuts on peripherals were allegedly predatory. But this claim was rejected because CalComp failed to prove that IBM's prices were below cost. *Second,* CalComp argued that IBM's recoupment with price increases on other products was an unlawful use of IBM's power in the main frame market. This claim also lost its wheels, however, because *complete* recoupment had not been shown and because rising costs may have justified those price increases (suspicious timing notwithstanding). *Third,* CalComp contended that IBM had coupled its price reductions with unnecessary and artificial changes in its peripheral equipment design, which changes were specifically aimed at crippling the PCMs. Rejecting this contention, the court noted that the new models were not completely lacking in advantages over the old, so they offered similar performance at reduced prices. In language reminiscent of *U.S. Steel,* the court concluded that IBM's conduct was not "*unreasonably* restrictive of competition."

Summary. Kodak and *CalComp* thus closed a good deal of the conduct gap by providing cover for a monopolist's "hard competition." Berkey's instructions seem especially solid. Monopolists may innovate significantly improved products without disclosure of trade secrets or provision of other aids to rivals. Monopolists need not restrain their research and development efforts. Further-

[35] *California Computer Products, Inc., et al.* v. *International Business Machines,* 613 F.2d 727 (9th Cir. 1979).

[36] *Telex Corp.* v. *IBM,* 510 F.2d 894 (10 Cir. 1975), *Memorex Corp.* v. *IBM,* 636 F.2d 1188 (9th Cir. 1980), *Transamerica Computer Co.* v. *IBM,* 481 F. Supp. 965 (1979).

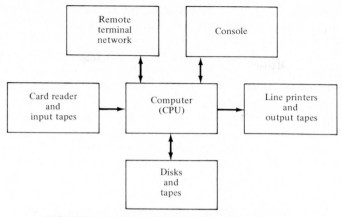

FIGURE 9–1. Overview of a Computer System.

more, diversified monopolists may exploit benefits of association among their various divisions insofar as those benefits are based on "more efficient production, greater ability to develop complementary products, reduced transaction costs," and so forth: (*not* including coercive acts like tying).

The clear teaching from *Calcomp* is that a monopolist may fend off rivals with price cuts so long as its prices remain profitable—that is, remain above average total cost. Beyond this, *CalComp's* lessons become muddled and even questionable. In particular, the Ninth Circuit Court gave its opinion on a very important issue that was not presented in the facts of *CalComp* when it said that *even deeper* price reductions "down to the point of marginal cost [or average variable cost] are consistent with competition on the merits." This is a reiteration of what the same circuit said in an earlier case,[37] but this position has been rejected by other courts[38] and the Supreme Court has yet to lend its official approval. Thus the question of just how deep a monopolist may innocently reduce its prices remains open.

In any event, *Berkey* and *CalComp* paved the way for Reagan's Assistant Attorney General Baxter, who withdrew the government's big case against IBM even though it had been prosecuted for 13 years under four presidents previous to Reagan and was just months away from a district court opinion. This withdrawal was historic.

3. IBM (Dismissed 1982).[39]   As shown in Figure 9–1, a computer system has numerous components, much as a stereo system has. IBM, Sperry Rand,

---

[37] *Janich Brothers* v. *American Distilling Co.,* 570 F. 2d 848 (9th Cir. 1978) *cert. denied* 439 U.S. 829 (1978).

[38] *Transamerica Computer Co.* v. *IBM Corp.,* CCH, para. 62,989 (D.C. N.Ca., October 1979), and *O. Hommel Company* v. *Ferro Corp.,* CCH, para. 62,720 (D.C. W.Pa., June 1979). Indeed, the 9th Circuit itself recently backed off: *William Inglis & Sons Baking Co.* v. *ITT Continental,* 668 F.2d.1014 (9th Cir. 1982).

[39] *U.S.* v. *International Business Machines Corp.,* 69 CIV 200, So. Dist. of N.Y.

and the other big companies are called **systems suppliers,** for they produce and market a full line of "hardware" equipment together with "software" programs and services to run their systems. A second sector is made up of **plug-compatible** or **peripherals** manufacturers. They produce printers, tape drives, disc drives and other individual items of peripheral equipment that can be plugged into the central system. Third, there are a host of service bureaus, consulting groups, programmers, and leasing firms that deal primarily in services rather than manufacturing. They are often lumped together as **software houses.** Finally, the newest segment of the industry sells **minicomputers.** These are small, relatively low-cost computers. Responsibility for development of these devices rests not with the huge systems suppliers but with smaller firms like Data General, Hewlett-Packard, and Apple.

IBM's Market Share.[40] Before Baxter, the Justice Department contended that the market should be defined narrowly to include "general purpose" computers and peripheral products compatible with IBM equipment—systems suppliers, essentially. Moreover, the Department measured market shares in terms of the lease value of computers *installed*—that is, the rental value of all general purpose systems in use whether leased or purchased. By this reckoning, IBM's annual market share ranged between 68 and 75 per cent over the period 1964–1972.

In contrast, IBM argued the market should include practically everything having to do with computers. Inclusion of all electronic data processing businesses reduced IBM's market share to 33 per cent. Moreover, this 33 per cent figure threw together all annual revenues from sales and rentals. It was not based on installed equipment.

IBM's Intent. IBM contended that, even if the 68 to 75% figures were accurate, its power derived from superior skill, foresight, and industry. But the historical record is far from clear on this point.

From 1924 IBM has supplied a broad line of business machines. Its early forte was punch card tabulating equipment. In 1935, IBM had under lease 85.7% of all tabulating machines, 86.1% of all sorting machines, and 82% of all punch card installations then used in the United States. IBM did not fully appreciate the computer's potential until 1951, when one of IBM's best customers, the U.S. Census Bureau, accepted delivery of the world's first commercial computer from Univac, a division of Remington Rand (now Sperry Rand). At the time, IBM held 90% of the punch card tabulating machine market, and Remington Rand accounted for the remaining 10%. Hence, IBM rightly viewed Univac I as a threat to its existence.

Shortly after IBM entered the computer field (delivering its first machine in 1953), two other business machine manufacturers joined IBM and Sperry Rand—National Cash Register (NCR) and Burroughs. As it turned out, prior business-machine experience was a crucial determinant of success in computers.

[40] For brief discussion see Leonard W. Weiss, "The Structure-Conduct-Performance Paradigm and Antitrust," *Univ. of Pennsylvania Law Review* (April 1979), pp. 1124–1130.

IBM's big advantage lay in its accumulation of tabulating machine customers who had vast amounts of data already coded on punch cards, plus a natural interest in any means of rapidly processing them. IBM catered to this group by designing its computers to read their cards. IBM had more than just good contacts; it had a good reputation. During 1956, "IBM shipped 85.2% of the value of new systems, and Remington Rand only 9.7%—approximately the same relative shares as then existing in the tabulating machine market."[41]

IBM's "lag-behind-then-recover-quickly" pattern of behavior became almost commonplace thereafter. Remington Rand and RCA were the first to introduce transistorized computers. Philco introduced the first large-scale solid state system. Data General was the first with medium-scale integration and complete semiconductor memories. Honeywell and Burroughs were the most innovative with operating systems and compilers. General Electric developed time sharing. And so on. Attempted entry often motivated these efforts. What is more, these efforts nibbled away much of IBM's early market share, but IBM always managed a rebound by duplication. By contrast, many of these innovators are no longer producing computers.

Several barriers to entry into the general purpose field protected IBM from those innovative would-be competitors. In economies of scale, a 10% share of the market or thereabouts seems to have been necessary to achieve full production efficiency. In product differentiation, two interrelated factors fostered fairly intense brand loyalty when it came to complete systems—(1) buyer ignorance, and (2) a lack of standardization.[42] Finally, capital requirements for new entry amounted to about $1 billion, a princely sum.

Specific Charges. On intent, the Justice Department levied a number of specific charges. It alleged that IBM tried to maintain control and to inhibit entry deliberately through a wide variety of questionable marketing, financial, and technical maneuvers. These included:

- "Bundling," whereby IBM quoted a *single* price for hardware, software, and related support. (IBM unbundled in 1970, after the suit.)

- "Fighting machines," whereby IBM introduced selected computers with inordinately low prices in those sectors of the industry where its competitors appeared to be on the verge of success.

- "Paper machines," whereby IBM tried to dissuade computer users from acquiring or leasing Control Data's 6600 (an advanced, truly remarkable machine) by announcing that IBM would soon have a comparable and perhaps even superior product, when in fact IBM had no such thing.

After reviewing the evidence amassed against IBM, Assistant Attorney General Baxter was not convinced, so he withdrew the suit in January 1982. He

---

[41] Gerald Brock, *The U.S. Computer Industry: A Study of Market Power* (Cambridge, Mass.: Ballinger Publishing Co., 1975), p. 13.
[42] Ibid., p. 47, 51.

said that several of the acts attributed to IBM "may have occurred." But he said the most persuasive instances took place outside the market covered by the lawsuit. He did not think IBM had committed any "serious business improprieties," so the case was "without merit" and the government's chances of winning were "only one in ten thousand."[43]

Several days later Judge Edelstein, who had presided over six years of trial only to be denied the chance to decide the case, was quoted as saying that Mr. Baxter suffered from "myopia and misunderstanding of the antitrust laws and this case specifically." "Even one with a prodigious intellect," Edelstein said, "couldn't be expected to come up with a reasoned evaluation" of the case in the four or five months Mr. Baxter spent studying it.[44]

An interesting irony is that IBM's dismissal and AT&T's consent decree were announced on the same day, January 8, 1982. Thus although IBM may have been let off the hook, AT&T may one day become IBM's most vigorous foe.

In short, the structural approach grounded on *Alcoa* thus seems forsaken if not forgotten. Illegal monopoly will apparently not be found without proof of *palpably anticompetitive conduct,* a conduct approach reminiscent of *U.S. Steel.* The structural approach could be faulted for possibly punishing some meritorious winners of the competitive battle, thereby casting a wet blanket on incentives.[45] On the other hand, the conduct approach of *Berkey, CalComp,* and Mr. Baxter might yield more artificial monopoly power than is desirable.

During the *Alcoa* era a large dominant firm could not do the same things as a smaller rival—e.g., vary price sharply depending on competitive conditions, aggressively build plants to meet anticipated demand, license instead of sell goods, or accumulate acquired patents. Though "normal" or "reasonable" for a small firm, such tactics could not be used by a dominant firm to maintain dominance—i.e., drive smaller rivals from the field. Now there is apparently greater freedom for a "monopoly" to defend its position.

SUMMARY

The Sherman Act outlaws monopolization. Establishing a violation requires proof of two elements: (1) substantial market power, and (2) intent. Reason, estimation, and hunch make appraisal of these elements uncertain. Hence we find very big cases in this area. Just about everything is considered except the rainfall in Indianapolis.

---

[43] *Wall Street Journal,* January 11, 1982, pp. 1, 6; January 26, 1982, p. 10. On the evidence "outside" the market see Russell W. Pittman, "Predatory Investment: *U.S.* v. *IBM,*" Economic Policy Office Discussion Paper, U.S. Department of Justice Antitrust Division, EPO 82–5 (1982), which shows that IBM did indeed engage in predatory practices against CDC in the scientific computer field.

[44] *Wall Street Journal,* January 26, 1982, p. 10.

[45] Defenders of the structural approach point out, however, that power meritoriously gained cannot justify an award of perpetual power. Patents, for instance, last only 17 years.

When attempting to examine market power, the courts consider barriers to entry of various kinds and profits. The item receiving greatest attention, however, is market share. Broad definitions of the market tend to favor defendants; narrow definitions favor the prosecutors. Which way the court will turn in any particular case is often unpredictable. Once a market definition is established, percentage points become all important. The consensus is that a market share well below 60% lies beneath the reach of the law (unless abusive practices are present), whereas shares above 80% make Justice Department attorneys look good in court.

On the issue of intent, interpretations may be divided into three periods. (1) Before *Alcoa* in 1945, intent could be demonstrated only by evidence of predatory, exclusionary, or unfair acts. The rule of reason essentially meant condemnation of unreasonable behavior. (2) After *Alcoa* and until recently, intent could be demonstrated by evidence that a dominant firm's actions were not "honestly industrial," not "passive," not reflective of "superior skill," "superior product," "business acumen," or "historic accident." This reading of Section 2 left monopolists room to maneuver, but not much. (3) The period since about 1970 reveals conflicting strains and ambiguity, mainly because of a *structural gap,* which left tight-knit oligopoly or "shared monopoly" largely untouched, and a *conduct gap,* which left unclear the status of conduct that was neither so bad as to be clearly abusive nor so good as to be plainly passive. Contributing to the muddle is a basic tension in the law as inherited from *Alcoa,* a tension created by a willingness to condone monopoly (pure and simple) and a simultaneous desire to condemn monopolization (tainted and crude).

Thus the early portion of the current period witnessed efforts to confirm and even extend *Alcoa.* Big cases were brought against Xerox, AT&T, and IBM. The FTC instituted shared monopoly proceedings against the cereal oligopolists. In addition, "presumptive rules" were proposed, whereby defendants would have to prove their innocence if they transgressed some previously specified criteria, such as having more than 40% of the market for three years running. Such legislation would have closed the structural gap by reaching oligopolists and closed the conduct gap by limiting what dominant firms could do without demonstrating intent.

Most recently, however, these rumblings have been silenced. *Xerox* and *AT&T* were settled by stringent consent decrees. But the shared monopoly proceedings and legislative proposals came to naught, leaving the structural gap untouched. Moreover, the conduct gap has been largely closed in the lenient direction with substantial movement away from *Alcoa* toward *U.S. Steel. Kodak* and *CalComp* led the way. Baxter's withdrawal of *IBM* capped the trend. Whether these developments take us too far in condoning monopolization is a much debated question.

Part Three: Conduct

10 Introduction to Conduct: Profit Maximization (?)

*Would you tell me, please, which way
I ought to go from here? asked Alice.
That depends a good deal on where
you want to go to, said the Cat.*

—LEWIS CARROLL

Passage into Part III signals that our journey is now well underway. Conduct comes next, which means that this chapter must ponder theories of firm motivation in general and profit maximization in particular. Structure alone does not determine conduct. The *combination* of structural conditions and firm motivation determines conduct. According to traditional theory, profit maximization motivates all firms in *all* market settings. It is the diversity of structures that produces diverse conduct from this universal motivation. If a monopolist charges a higher price than a group of purely competitive firms would, it is not because the monopolist is a profit maximizer and the competitive firms are philanthropists. Theoretically, all firms are out to make as much money as they can. The monopolist charges more simply because he faces less competition.

If, contrary to conventional theory, firm motivation varied as much as structure varies, conduct would be less predictable. Economists would have to step aside in favor of psychologists (or other motivation experts). Unfortunately for economists, variance in structure itself probably promotes some variances in motivation. Owners of purely competitive firms are *compelled* to toe the profit maximizing line lest they go bankrupt. On the other hand, monopolistic and oligopolistic firms may have sufficient market power that their owners and managers need not scratch for every penny of possible profit. Such firms have the option of enjoying the "easy life," of coasting along with only "satisfactory" or "reasonable" earnings. As an executive of U.S. Steel once claimed, "U.S. Steel has never tried to price to maximum profit. . . ."[1]

This relation between structural and motivational variances, as well as related factors, has sparked controversy. Like a ravenous bookworm the controversy

---

[1] A. D. H. Kaplan, J. B. Dirlam, and R. F. Lanzillotti, *Pricing in Big Business* (Washington, D.C.: Brookings Institution, 1958), p. 23.

206

has consumed thousands of pages of scholarly journals and dozens of books. Some economists stick to conventional theory. Some advocate alternative possible motivations, such as sales maximization or growth maximization. Some argue that firms are not motivated to maximize anything. They say, without respect for the English language, that firms are merely "satisficers." This brief catalog of positions on firm motivation provides an outline for this chapter.

I. PROFIT MAXIMIZING—TRADITIONAL THEORY

The hypothesis of firm profit maximization rests on three essential assumptions concerning the people who own and operate "the firm"; (1) single-minded purpose; (2) rational or forced choice of objective; and (3) the adherence to operational rules of optimality.

A. Single-Minded Purpose

The first of these assumptions infers that no matter how big and diverse the firm happens to be, all its owners and employees work as one to achieve its objective. Warehousemen may have the hoarding instincts of squirrels. Salesmen may simply want to sell, sell, sell, even at give-away prices. And the typical junior executive may yearn to romance his or her secretary. However, traditional theory holds that while on the job these dedicated souls either set aside their personal obsessions or bend them to benefit the enterprise. All work as a team. No one is ever at cross purposes.

B. Rationality

What objectives do the efforts of these single-minded individuals further? Since control of a capitalistic firm rests with its owners, and since the owners are rewarded by profits, the traditional assumption of rationality implies a goal of profit maximization. Whether the owner fits the legendary image of the economic entrepreneur or the more common mold of the average upper-crust stockholder, he has committed his capital to conditions of uncertainty. The reward for subjecting his capital to some risk of loss is profit. It is only natural, then, for firms to try to maximize profits. Or so it is assumed.

C. Operational Rules

"Profit maximization" is meaningless unless it can be translated into an operational objective. Left in vague form, the objective does not specifically indicate precisely what businessmen must do in their daily affairs to achieve it. Many operational rules are possible (such as "no one ever went broke underestimating the taste of the American public"). However, as outlined in Chapter 2, traditional economic theory offers a rather technical rule: *Expand production and promotion as long as added revenues exceed added costs; cut back whenever the resulting reductions in costs exceed the reductions in revenues.* In short, operate where marginal revenue equals marginal cost—or, symbolically, MR = MC.

This rule stems from the standard definition of total profit, which is the difference between total revenue and total cost, that is, TP = TR − TC. We know by now that demand is the crucial determinant of the firm's marginal revenue function. In turn, market structure is a crucial determinant of demand as viewed by the typical firm in the market. Thus, in traditional theory, structure influences conduct through its influence on the marginal revenue portion of the firm's profit maximizing computation.

D. Criticism of Traditional Theory

If traditional theory is vulnerable to criticism, it must be vulnerable in one or more of these three underlying assumptions. In fact, virtually all criticism may be gathered under three broad labels designating focuses of attack: (1) realism in process, (2) managerialism, and (3) behavioralism. These classifications of criticism are outlined in Table 10–1 according to the degree in which each school of criticism accepts (yes) or rejects (no) the three basic assumptions of traditional theory itemized on the left-hand side.

"Realism in process" thus identifies a form of criticism that generally accepts the assumptions of single-mindedness and rational choice but rejects the notion that MR = MC is an adequate operational objective for businessmen. Conversely, "managerialism" identifies the position of analysts who are not much bothered by the problem of operational feasibility. However, they seriously doubt that the typical firm is run for the single-minded pursuit of the owners' interests. They argue that in most large corporations the owners (stockholders) and managers (president, vice-presidents, and so on) are *not* the same people and they are *not* driven by the same objectives. Since *managers* are allegedly the ones primarily in control, they can pursue objectives in *their* self interest rather than the owners'. This split obliterates the assumption of single-mindedness (or redirects it), and opens the door to goals other than profit maximization.

TABLE 10–1. Outline of Three Main Schools of Criticism According to Their Acceptance (YES) or Rejection (NO) of Traditional Theory's Key Assumptions

Traditional Theory's Assumption	Classification of Criticism		
	Realism in Process	Managerialism	Behavioralism
Single-mindedness	Yes	No	No
Rational profit maximization	Yes	No	No
Operational feasibility	No	Yes	No
Overall acceptance of profit maximization?	No	No	No

Finally, there is a third group of critics called the "behavioralists." They deny that profit maximization is typical of American business for reasons that blend realism in process and managerialism. They stress the complexity of business organizations. They note a diversity of motives among salesmen, production workers, warehousemen, and others in the firm besides those of owners and managers. As for goals, they believe that humans engage in "satisficing" rather than maximizing behavior and that human rules of daily operation reflect this.

The remainder of this chapter is divided into three parts, one for each class of criticism. One important thread of thought to which we shall return repeatedly is this: Pricing policy and cost experience are two largely *separable* issues in this question of profit maximizing. On the whole, a firm is more likely to *price* its wares in conformity with profit maximizing precepts than to manage its *costs* in the miserly, tight-fisted fashion that profit maximization implies. Assume that we (1) drew the name of a *Fortune* 500 firm from a random hat, (2) sent out a team of economists, accountants, and engineers to assess its behavior, and (3) recommended any steps that would move it in the direction of profit maximization. Chances are that our experts would come up with some sound recommendations for cutting costs. On the other hand, the chances of their coming up with price policy changes are slimmer.

The reason for this asymmetry is simple. The main burden of most price policy adjustments would be carried by persons *outside* the firm—by customers if it is a price increase or by competitors if it is a price decrease. Hence sound price adjustments are likely to have been made *already by the firm*. The main burden of any cost adjustments, on the other hand, would be borne by persons *inside* the firm—by folks who would lose their jobs or would have to work harder. Hence, profitable adjustments in this area are *not* likely to have already been made. It is here we would probably find flab.[2]

II. REALISM IN PROCESS

The basic thrust of the realism in process criticism is that the simple rule MR = MC is *non*operational. Businessmen cannot maximize profits by this rule alone, even if they wanted to. Among the many pertinent questions left at least partially unanswered by this rule are the following:

1. *What costs and revenues are supposed to be included in this calculation over what time period?* An accountant's view of "costs" differs from an economist's view, as is illustrated by their differing treatments of "depreciation" and "normal profit." Moreover, the economist's "short run" and "long run" do not correspond to the accountant's "calendar quarter" and "fiscal year." Their decisions on the content of calculations will differ. On top of all this, many decisions are nonmarginal from anyone's viewpoint (for example, acquiring a large subsidiary or bribing a Senator).

[2] D. C. Hague stresses this point in *Pricing in Business* (London: George Allen & Unwin, 1971), pp. 83–84.

The MR = MC rule allegedly collapses under the weight of these big decisions.

In defense of traditional theory, it ought to be acknowledged that experts in managerial economics have unravelled many of these knotty problems.[3] They have shown that wide application of marginal concepts is by no means impossible. Moreover, as far as the time problem is concerned, profit maximization is now commonly translated into maximization of the discounted present value of the firm. This approach converts future earnings into a present value form that blends the short and long run.

2. *How can risk be properly accounted for?* Even assuming the businessman knows the probabilities associated with the various possible outcomes of his decisions, there is no universally acceptable way of identifying the profit maximizing course of action whenever substantial risk is involved. Scherer explains the situation with the aid of a problem:

> Imagine a decision-maker weighing two alternative policies, one offering a best-guess profit expectation of $1 million with a 10 percent chance of bankrupting the firm (whose net worth is currently $4 million), the other an expected profit of $2 million with a 30 percent chance of disaster. Which is the rational choice?[4]

Application of sophisticated expected-value criteria cannot yield the "right" answer. The answer requires extensive information on the attitudes of the firm's owners toward increases in wealth versus total loss of their equity, *plus* some technique for properly aggregating these attitudes. Achieving world peace would be easier.

3. *What is the profit maximizing course of action when uncertainty prevails?* In the preceding problem it was assumed that the 10 and 30% probabilities for bankruptcy were *known* to be the true probabilities. Hence, it was purely a case of "risk." As with the toss of a coin, the ultimate outcome was unknown, but the probabilities were certain. When the decision-maker knows *neither* the ultimate outcome *nor* the probabilities of the possible outcomes, he knows about as much as a blind man in a dark room looking for a black cat that may not be there. Economists dryly say he is "uncertain." Accordingly, they have dryly devised a number of techniques to assist rational (cold-blooded) decision making in this situation (including "maximax," "maximin," and "regret hedging").[5] But none of these really qualifies as profit maximizing.

Defenders of orthodoxy argue that full knowledge is not necessary, that an earnest effort and an "intuitive understanding" are all that are required.

---

[3] See, e.g., Ralph Turvey, "Marginal Cost," *Economic Journal* (June 1969), pp. 282–298; and E. F. Brigham and J. L. Pappas, *Managerial Economics* (Hinsdale, Ill.: Dryden Press, 1976).

[4] F. M. Scherer, *Industrial Market Structure and Economic Performance* (Chicago: Rand McNally, 1970), p. 28.

[5] For a popular account see Shlomo Maital, *Minds, Markets, and Money* (New York: Basic Books, 1982). On the technical side G. Loomes and R. Sugden, "Regret Theory," *Economic Journal* (December 1982), pp. 805–824.

Fritz Machlup, for example, uses the analogy of one driver passing another on a two-lane country road, which motorists do all the time without the aid of sophisticated physics and differential calculus. He summarizes his argument by stressing the uses of *subjective* knowledge:

> It should hardly be necessary to mention that all the relevant magnitudes involved—costs, revenue, profit—are subjective—that is, perceived or fancied by the men whose decisions or actions are to be explained rather than "objective" . . . . Marginal analysis of the firm should not be understood to imply anything but subjective estimates, guesses and hunches.[6]

The critics remain unmoved by this analysis, however. They claim that Machlup's argument rests on a tautology—that "maximization" becomes meaningless if it is allowed that anything businessmen happen to do is considered maximizing. Even if Machlup's theory is interpreted to mean that businessmen merely *try* to—rather than actually do—maximize profits, uncertainty critics would reply that this has little value as a description, prescription, or prediction of business behavior.[7]

(Interestingly, Machlup's defense of orthodoxy has received some rather unorthodox support from research on executive extrasensory perception. In one test of precognition, a number of business executives were divided into two groups "according to whether they had at least doubled their company's profits over the last five years or not." The profit makers "all scored above chance" in predicting a computer's random numbers. "One executive who had not doubled his company's profits had an average score but all others in his group scored below average [that is, below chance]."[8] Not being one to stick my neck out, I register my reservations by putting this entire paragraph between parentheses.)

III. MANAGERIALISM (OR REALISM IN MOTIVATION)

There are two parts to this line of criticism:

1. Managers, not owners, are in control of our main corporations.
2. The managers do not want to maximize profits; they cast their eyes on other ends.

A. Control by Managers

To understand the first point we must look behind the standard pyramid of corporate structure that, as in Figure 10–1, places owners at the top. In *theory,* the stockholders elect a board of directors to represent their views.

---

[6] Fritz Machlup, "Marginal Analysis and Empirical Research," *American Economic Review* (September 1946), pp. 521–522.

[7] Joseph McGuire, *Theories of Business Behavior* (Englewood Cliffs, N.J.: Prentice-Hall, 1964), p. 83.

[8] *New York Times,* August 31, 1969.

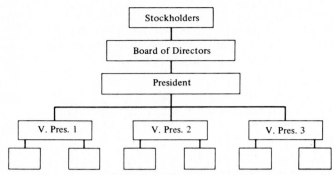

FIGURE 10–1. Standard corporate organization structure.

The board meets only infrequently, and it does not make daily decisions. However, the board hires and fires managing officers according to how well they serve the owners' interests. Hence, power corresponds to placement in the pyramid.

In *practice,* only stockholders or *proxyholders* who attend the annual meeting of owners can cast votes in the election of directors. The emphasis here is on proxyholders because the stockholders of most major corporations are too numerous, too apathetic, too timid, and too far-flung geographically to attend the annual meetings. Hence the usual election procedure is for *management* to nominate a slate of candidates and then ask the stockholders for proxies, that is, permission to use the stockholders' votes on behalf of this slate of candidates. Ninety-nine percent of the time a majority of stockholders sign over their proxies to management. In short, the managers select and control the board. Indeed, managers *themselves* hold a majority of seats on the boards of many major corporations. "The board of directors becomes, in effect, a rubber-stamping body routinely approving the decisions and recommendations of management rather than an independent watchdog with a vigilant eye to the interests and desires of the corporation's owners."[9]

The extent and trend of management control over corporations in the United States is illustrated in Table 10–2. The data refer to the top 200 corporations in 1929 and 1974. It is easy to see that among these firms management control predominates and is on the rise. In 1929, 40.5% of the top 200 qualified for the management-control category, more than any other group. By 1974 this percentage reached 82.5%. The only remaining bastion of stockholder control is so-called "minority control," in which no single owner or close-knit group of owners holds more than a majority of outstanding shares, but a big chunk of the voting stock is in the hands of an influential individual, family, or group of business associates.

[9] Robert Larner, *Management Control and the Large Corporation* (New York: Dunellen, 1970), p. 3.

TABLE 10–2. Summary According to Type of Ultimate Control of the 200 Largest Nonfinancial United States Corporations, 1974 and 1929

Type of Control	Number of Corporations		Proportion of Companies	
	1929	1974	1929	1974
Management control	81	165	40.5%	82.5%
Minority control	65	29	32.5	14.5
Private or majority ownership	19	3	9.5	1.5
Other (e.g., legal device)	35	3	17.5	1.5
Total	200	200	100%	100%

Source: Edward S. Herman, *Corporate Control, Corporate Power* (Cambridge: Cambridge University Press, 1981), pp. 58–64.

Of course, owners retain the option of buying and selling stock, no matter how diverse or detached they may be. Furthermore, such buying and selling conceivably offers a means of rewarding and punishing management. If it does, stockholders are not irredeemably "poor cousins in the corporate family, ignored by a management which, if not feathering its own nest with bonuses and stock options, is yielding to the greater pressure of unions, customers, and government."[10] Rather, stockholders are catered to and pampered as a source of capital, even though most capital is raised from other sources. Economists who hold this view argue that the equity investor is not so unlikely a source of capital as to suffer anyone to treat him highhandedly. Unfortunately, this argument is often exaggerated. Such indirect stock-market control cannot be stringent. At best, share trading is a long leash. After analyzing this form of control in some detail, Oliver Williamson concluded that "individually and collectively, capital market controls experience weaknesses sufficient to warrant much of the expressed concern over the separation of ownership from control in the large corporation."[11]

B. Theories of Managerial Motives

So much for the first introductory proposition. Managers typically *do* sit in the driver's seat. What of the second proposition? Do manager's really turn the steering wheel in directions other than that of profit maximization? The

[10] Shorey Peterson, "Corporate Control and Capitalism," *Quarterly Journal of Economics* (February 1965), pp. 3, 20–21.
[11] Oliver Williamson, *Corporate Control and Business Behavior* (Englewood Cliffs, N.J.: Prentice-Hall, 1970), p. 104. Empirical support for this position is provided by B. Hindley, "Separation of Ownership and Control in the Modern Corporation," *Journal of Law and Economics* (April 1970), pp. 185–210. On the other hand see J. R. Davies and D. A. Kuehn, "An Investigation into the Effectiveness of a Capital Market Sanction on Poor Performance," in *Welfare Aspects of Industrial Markets* edited by A. P. Jacquemin and H. W. de Jong (Leiden: Martinus Nijhoff, 1977), pp. 329–344.

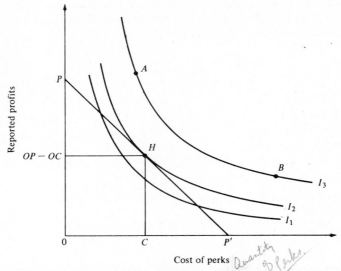

FIGURE 10–2. Managerial trade-off between company profits and executive perks.

answer is "yes," "no," "maybe," and "sometimes," depending on whom you consult. Those who say "yes" argue that (1) managers lack the incentive to steer toward profit because their incomes are not directly linked to profit levels, or (2) if there is close linkage, managers are moved by *non*monetary motives. Those who say "no" argue that (1) managerial remuneration *is* atuned to profit performance, and (2) managers respond accordingly. Those who say "maybe" or "sometimes" stress that it is difficult to generalize. They point out that corporations and managers come in many different sizes, shapes, colors, and qualities. They correctly maintain that no single theory is equally applicable to the corner grocer and Alcoa. With these views in mind, let's look into several theories of "managerial enterprise" and then survey the available evidence.

1. Managerial Utility. Oliver Williamson's theories of managerial utility assume that for tax and other reasons managers are interested in executive jets, liberal expense accounts, and other emoluments or perquisites as well as personal income and company profits.[12] Let the horizontal axis of Figure 10–2 indicate the monetary value of "perks" and the vertical axis indicate profits. Each curve, I_1, I_2, and I_3, represents a given level of manager satisfaction realized from various combinations of perks and profits. I_1 is the lowest level of satisfaction depicted, and I_3 is the highest. Managers are *indifferent* as between any two points on a given I curve, such as A and B on I_3; that is, all points on I_3 yield the same degree of reward. Accordingly, these are called **indifference curves.**

[12] O. E. Williamson, *The Economics of Discretionary Behavior: Managerial Objectives in a Theory of the Firm* (Chicago: Markham Publishing Co., 1967).

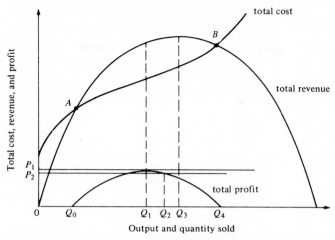

FIGURE 10–3. Sales revenue maximization, subject to minimum profit constraint.

Managers would obviously like the very generous volumes of perks and profits that lie in the region northeast of I_3, but they are restrained by realities. Point P on the vertical axis represents the *maximum* level of profits the company can earn. Perks at that point are zero, but it defines the extent to which perks are possible. Since $1 worth of increased perks must reduce profits by $1, movement to the right from P reduces profits along the line PP', which has a negative slope of 1. At point H on PP' the value of perks is OC. Hence the corresponding level for profit is OP minus OC, or $OP - OC$, as indicated on the vertical axis. In other words, line PP' is a perks/profits **possibilities curve**. Any point *in*side the triangle POP' is possible. Any point *out*side is not. Managers maximize their satisfaction by choosing that combination of possible perks and profits landing them on their highest indifference curve. In this case it is I_2 at point H.

Notice that, according to this model, managers select the *same* price and output policies as a simple profit maximizer. If they did not, the PP' line would be closer to the origin, meaning reduced overall managerial satisfaction on an indifference curve such as I_1. However, internal costs will be higher in this model than in the simple profit maximizing model because perks don't grow on trees.

2. Sales Maximization. Figure 10–3 presents the basic sales revenue maximization model developed by W. J. Baumol.[13] The horizontal axis measures output and quantity sold. The vertical axis depicts total dollar cost, revenue, and profit. Assuming the firm faces a linear negatively sloped demand curve (such as that facing the monopolist on page 32), total revenue will look like a McDonald's

[13] W. J. Baumol, *Business Behavior, Value and Growth* (New York: Macmillan Publishing Co., 1959).

215

golden arch. Subtracting total cost from total revenue yields total profit, which is zero at two quantities (Q_0 and Q_4), corresponding to the intersection of total cost and total revenue at points A and B. Profit maximizing output would be OQ_1, with profit equal to OP_1. Sales revenue maximization would require greater output at Q_3. Note that profits are lower at Q_3 than Q_1. Moreover, although it is not shown here, Q_3 implies a lower product price than the profit maximizing solution Q_1.

If managers were operating under a minimum profit constraint that was *above* the profit level associated with absolute revenue maximization, they would be forced to raise price, reduce output, and move in the direction of profit maximization. One such profit floor might be OP_2 in Figure 10–3, in which case quantity would be Q_2 instead of Q_3. Why a minimum profit constraint? One is probably necessary to satisfy the neglected but not totally forgotten stock holders. Although these are the most often cited conclusions for this model it should be noted that the assumption of monopoly limits its generality. It has been argued that under oligopoly there is no substantial behavioral difference between profit and sales maximization.[14]

3. Maximizing Growth or Present Value of Revenue.[15] We mentioned growth motivations earlier when discussing mergers. Here we shall focus on simple theories of "internal" growth maximization, which follow neatly from the preceding analysis. We begin by announcing three important principles:

1. Growth of sales requires expansions of capacity and, consequently, adequate capital to finance expansion. Maximum profits can supply the needed funds either directly through retained earnings or indirectly by attracting the capital of additional equity investors and bond buyers. In theory, growth rate maximization often corresponds exactly to profit maximization; in fact, numerous statistical studies demonstrate a close positive association between growth rate and profit.[16]

2. Growth *rate* is only one possible measure of growth. Another is the *present value of the firm's future stream of sales revenues.* This is the sum of each future years' expected sales revenue, discounted by an appropriate percentage rate to account for the fact that each dollar obtained five or ten years from now is worth less than each dollar obtained in

[14] W. G. Shepherd, "On Sales Maximizing and Oligopoly Behavior," *Economica* (November 1962), pp. 420–424; B. D. Mabry, "Sales Maximization vs. Profit Maximization: Are they Inconsistent?" *Western Economic Journal* (March 1968), pp. 154–160. Moreover, risk lowers Q below the standard result, so revenue maximization in the face of risk could yield a Q that matches the Q of orthodox theory. Stephen M. Miller and Anthony A. Romeo, "Alternative Goals and Uncertainty in the Theory of the Firm," *Southern Economic Journal* (July 1979), pp. 189–205.

[15] On growth maximization see Robin Marris, *The Economic Theory of Managerial Capitalism* (New York: Free Press, 1964); John Williamson, "Profit Growth and Sales Maximization," *Economica* (February 1966), pp. 1–16; for a simpler treatment, K. Heidensohn and N. Robinson, *Business Behavior* (New York: Wiley & Sons, 1974), Chapter 8.

[16] J. L. Eatwell, "Growth Profitability and Size: The Empirical Evidence," in *The Corporate Economy,* edited by R. Marris and A. Wood (Cambridge, Mass.: Harvard University Press, 1971), pp. 409–418.

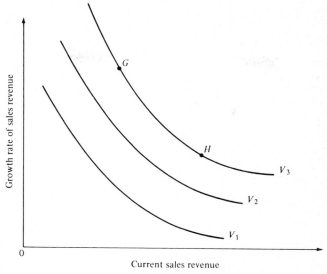

FIGURE 10–4. Relationship between the present value of future sales (Vs), growth rate of sales, and current sales.

the current year. In other words, an added dollar's worth of sales in the current period is actually "worth" more to the firm in terms of present value than is an added dollar's worth of sales in any subsequent period. This principle may be seen in Figure 10–4. Each curve, V_1, V_2, and V_3, indicates a *given present* value of sales revenue, with V_1 being the lowest and V_3 the highest present values explicitly depicted. Any two points on a single curve, such as G and H on V_3, represent the *same* present value. The negative slope of these curves indicates that a given present value can be achieved *either* by high current sales revenues and low growth (low future revenues), *or* by low current sales revenues and high growth, *or* by some combination in between. To appreciate this, note that the horizontal axis is *current sales* revenue and the vertical axis is the *growth rate* of sales. These V curves may be called **given-present-value** lines.

3. Once again we may take account of the owners' interest by specifying a minimum profit constraint below which profits ought not fall.

These three principles are combined in Figure 10–5, which itself is a modified combination of Figures 10–3 and 10–4. Figure 10–3 has been rotated clockwise 90 degrees and placed underneath Figure 10–4. Thus, all axes move positively. Output is measured on the lowest axis; current sales revenue, costs, and profit are measured on the horizontal axis; and the growth rate of sales revenue is measured vertically upward. The first principle may be seen in the close correspondence between the growth rate curve in the upper half of Figure 10–5

217

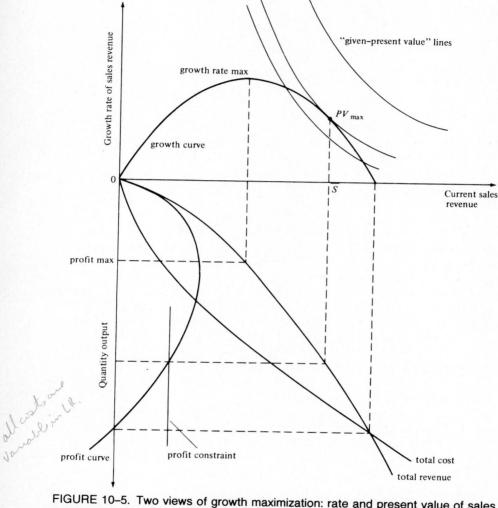

FIGURE 10–5. Two views of growth maximization: rate and present value of sales. Source: Douglas Needham, Economic Analysis and Industrial Structure (New York: Holt, Rinehart and Winston, 1969), p. 9.

and the profit curve in the lower half. When profit is zero, growth rate is zero. When profit is at its maximum level, growth rate too reaches a maximum because profits are needed to finance growth. It should be clear, then, that under present assumptions, the price, quantity, and cost behavior of the growth *rate* maximizer matches that of the profit maximizer.

218

The second principle is embodied in the given-present-value lines V_1, V_2, and V_3 carried over from Figure 10–4. If "growth" is taken to mean present value of future sales rather than *rate* of expansion, the higher the V_i the better. However, the growth rate curve defines those combinations of growth rate and current sales revenue that are within the realm of *possibility*. No point on V_3 is possible. A number of points on V_1 are possible. Maximum present value is attained at "*PV* max" on V_2. Because the given-present-value lines slope down from left to right, it follows that *PV* max will occur at a point to the right of "growth rate max." Furthermore, this *PV* max solution implies that a present-value maximizer will behave pretty much like a sales maximizer. That is to say, the present-value maximizing firm will have a lower price, a lower rate of profit, and a higher volume of current period sales than a profit maximizer. If the sales maximizer and present-value maximizer were operating under the same profit constraint, that profit constraint would be depicted as in Figure 10–5. This of course takes account of principle three.

As in the simple sales maximization model, these theories of growth maximization ignore the problem of oligopolistic interdependence. This is undoubtedly their greatest weakness because oligopoly is typical of American industry.

Avoidance of Risk and Uncertainty. Avoidance of risk and uncertainty should not be regarded as a goal in itself. Nevertheless, recent theoretical and empirical work has established that many firms, especially managerially controlled firms, strive to avoid risk and uncertainty.[17] Hence avoidance of risk could be considered an important secondary or supplementary objective to those already discussed. Introduction of this element increases the complexity of the theorizing and alters the conclusions reached by simpler models.

C. Empirical Findings on Manager's Motives

What do you suppose would happen if you went around and asked the executives of the 500 largest corporations what their objectives were? Would they give you straight answers? It would be nice if they did, but highly unlikely. Although no stigma attaches to profits *generally* (we are after all a capitalist society), most folks seem to regard fat profits and giant firms a suspicious combination. Mindful of their public image, corporate executives are usually not going to blab about any undying effort they may make to maximize profit. On the contrary, their alertness to public relations would tend to produce claims of "reasonable profits," "progress," and "healthy growth." Existing advertising campaigns trumpeting these purposes predict the answers you would probably hear to your question. But the influences of image-consciousness constitute only

[17] J. K. Galbraith, *The New Industrial State* (Boston: Houghton Mifflin, 1967), Chapters 3 and 7; R. E. Caves, "Uncertainty, Market Structure and Performance: Galbraith as Conventional Wisdom," in *Industrial Organization and Economic Development,* edited by J. W. Markham and G. F. Papanek (Boston: Houghton Mifflin Co., 1970); R. Schramm and R. Sherman, "Profit Risk Management and the Theory of the Firm," *Southern Economic Journal* (January 1974), pp. 353–363; and K. J. Boudreaux, "Managerialism and Risk-Return Performance," *Southern Economic Journal* (January 1973), pp. 366–372.

one problem standing in the way of fully satisfactory tests of these theories. Others include (1) poor data, (2) an enormous number of variables affecting the outcomes in question, (3) limited differences in the conclusions of various theories, (4) the fact that much observed behavior can be explained by more than one theory, and (5) the quirkiness of individual corporate conduct. Nevertheless, a few testable hypotheses emerge from the theories, and economists have attempted to test them.

Are managers' incomes more closely associated with profits, sales, or growth? Snap judgement might lead you to conclude that most managers steer in the direction of sales maximization. Everyone knows that the presidents of IBM and GM make more money than the president of your local pizza parlor, even when all three firms earn 20% on investment. In this sense raw size does determine executive remuneration, suggesting perhaps that size guides executive action. Promotion from pizza to computers would call for a hefty raise. Even so, an accurate test of the relation between managers' incomes and profit, sales, or growth would require an explanation of what happens to the manager's income *within* a given firm (or what kind of performance would *cause* the manager's interfirm promotion). The best of the appropriate studies have reached the following conclusion: Managers' monetary rewards are more closely and more positively associated with *profit* performance than either sales volume or growth rate, although these latter factors do have an effect.[18] As profits go up, measured in terms of absolute dollars or percentage return on capital invested, so do executives' salaries, bonuses, stock options, and the price of their ownership shares. These particular studies do not show that managers actually maximize profits.[19] Reaping and sowing are two different things. Still, the research does tend to bolster traditional theory.

Are managers moved by nonmonetary rewards? Human nature tells us that they are and so does some empirical evidence. Williamson finds that executive compensation is positively associated with "staff" personnel and other emolument expenditures. He has also assembled a number of case studies showing "excessive" emoluments.[20] Corroborating these results, several statistical studies of the banking industry show that managerial control boosts occupancy, equipment, furniture, and personnel expenses, especially when such management con-

---

[18] Robert Masson, "Executive Motivations, Earnings, and Consequent Equity Performance," *Journal of Political Economy* (November 1971), pp. 1278–1292; R. J. Larner, *op. cit.,* pp. 33–61; W. G. Lewellen and B. Huntsman, "Managerial Pay and Corporate Performance," *American Economic Review* (September 1970), pp. 710–720; G. K. Yarrow, "Executive Compensation and the Objectives of the Firm," in *Market Structure and Corporate Behavior,* edited by K. Cowling (London: Gray-Mills Publishing Co., 1972), pp. 149–173; Samuel Baker, "Executive Incomes, Profits and Revenues: A Comment," *Southern Economic Journal* (April 1969), pp. 379–383; and G. Meeks and G. Whittington, "Directors Pay, Growth, and Profitability," *Journal of Industrial Economics* (Sept. 1975), pp. 1–14.

[19] Moreover, some managers are grossly overpaid. *After retiring* as chairman of ITT, Harold Geneen won a $1.7 million "consulting agreement" with ITT, plus "supplementary" pension payments of $112,384 annually, plus his regular pension of $130,713, plus office space, staff, security, and transportation "assistance." *Wall Street Journal,* April 3, 1980, p. 26.

[20] O. E. Williamson, *op. cit.* (1967), pp. 85–135.

trol is accompanied by market power.[21] (Of course business lore's most famous executive hedonist is Hugh Hefner, whose flamboyant life style at the expense of Playboy Enterprises Inc. once caused company auditors to bill him $796,413 on behalf of stockholders.[22])

More comprehensively, R. A. Gordon offers evidence and argument that managers are moved by "the urge for power, the desire for prestige and the related impulse of emulation, the creative urge, the propensity to identify oneself with a group and the related feeling of group loyalty, the desire for security, the urge for adventure and for 'playing the game' for its own sake, and the desire to serve others."[23] These findings are not necessarily inconsistent with profit maximizing on the price side, but they do suggest cost side conduct that is less than frugal.

Can anything be concluded from direct observation of price and output behavior? In a broad sense we shall be exploring empirical evidence of this sort throughout most of the remainder of this book. We shall observe many earmarks of extensive profit maximization, including price discrimination, positive associations between price level and concentration, and positive associations between profits and market power. However, this evidence does not explicitly refute sales or growth maximizing because these latter theories include allowance for profit constraints. If these profit constraints varied in accordance with market structure, the broad empirical findings just mentioned could emerge despite the adoption of sales or growth maximization objectives. Thus, several economists have attempted rather specific tests of these theories, particularly sales revenue maximization. Virtually all of those testing the sales objective have concluded that it is not the goal adopted by most firms. Rather, firms seem to favor some form of profit or growth maximization.[24] For example, one implication of sales revenue maximization is that firms would attempt to increase sales if their actual profits exceeded their minimum profit constraint. M. Hall's search for such behavior turned out negative: he found no strong positive relationship between sales volume and estimated departures from the profit constraint.

Tests of the growth maximization hypothesis are more difficult to devise,

---

[21] Cynthia Glassman and Stephen A. Rhoades, "Owner vs. Manager Control Effects on Bank Performance," *Review of Economics and Statistics* (May 1980), pp. 263–270; T. H. Hannan and F. Mavinga, "Expense Preference and Managerial Control: The Case of the Banking Firm," *Bell Journal of Economics* (Autumn 1980), pp. 671–682; and James A. Verbrugge and John S. Jahera, Jr., "Expense-Preference Behavior in the Savings and Loan Industry," *Journal of Money, Credit, and Banking* (November 1981), pp. 465–476.

[22] *Wall Street Journal,* April 4, 1980, p. 4.

[23] R. A. Gordon, *Business Leadership in the Large Corporation* (Berkeley: University of California Press, 1966), pp. 305–316.

[24] M. Hall, "Sales Revenue Maximization: An Empirical Examination," *Journal of Industrial Economics* (April 1967), pp. 143–156; B. D. Mabry and D. L. Siders, "An Empirical Test of the Sales Maximization Hypothesis," *Southern Economic Journal* (January 1967), pp. 367–377; Samuel Baker, "An Empirical Test of the Sales Maximization Hypothesis," *Industrial Organization Review,* Vol. 1, No. 1 (1973), pp. 56–66; J. W. Elliot, "A Comparison of Models of Marketing Investment in the Firm," *Quarterly Review of Economics and Business* (Spring 1971), pp. 53–70. An interesting exception is C. L. Lackman and J. L. Craycroft, "Sales Maximization and Oligopoly: A Case Study," *Journal of Industrial Economics* (December 1974), pp. 81–95.

partly because of the similarity between growth *rate* and profit maximization. Nevertheless, Dennis Mueller has argued that a modified version of the growth hypothesis is consistent with the behavior of a substantial number of firms.[25] He argues, in particular, that managers are probably pushing growth beyond the rate desired by stockholders if stockholders want more of the firm's profit paid out in dividends (and less profit retained for internal investment) than the managers are willing to provide. Interestingly enough, he finds that *mature* firms in relatively slow growth industries, such as those in steel and foods, are the ones that most frequently display excessive profit retention. Rapidly growing young firms in dynamic industries like electronics are, by this standard, *not* the ones guilty of sacrificing profits for growth, despite the fact that they are among the fastest growers in the economy. (Things are not always what they seem.) In addition, Mueller's study underscores the fact that no *one* objective guides all firms.

When manager controlled firms and owner controlled firms are placed side by side and compared, do any differences appear? The "box scores" for tests of this question are presented in Table 10–3, which classifies the names of researchers in this area according to their findings. One's immediate impression is that their findings vary widely. Proponents and opponents of "managerialism" have each had their innings. The results vary because each researcher uses his own blend of sample, time period, and statistical technique, but a few tentative conclusions are possible. First, the "profit rate" column shows that *no* empirical study has found manager controlled firms earning higher average rates of profit than owner controlled firms, whereas eleven have found managerial rates to be generally lower (as usually predicted by "managerial" theories), and eight have found no significant difference. Among those finding "no difference" are several that do find managerial profits somewhat lower on average than owner controlled profits, but not "significantly" so. It appears, on balance, that owner controlled firms probably have an edge in profit performance, but nothing outstanding.

This broad summary conceals two noteworthy refinements. First, one would expect very little difference in profit rates among firms facing intense competition. Profit maximizing for them is a matter of survival, not of type of control. Conversely, greater differences are likely among firms with substantial market power. For them, managerial discretion comes into play. In other words, managerial discretion ought to depend on the presence of monopoly power. Palmer explored this possibility and found very little difference in profit rates where monopoly power was "low": 9.98% for manager control versus 10.59% for owner control. On the other hand, where monopoly power was "high," he found a significant difference: 11.41% for manager control versus 14.77% for owner control.[26] The second refinement concerns the way profits are measured.

[25] Dennis C. Mueller, "A Life Cycle Theory of the Firm," *Journal of Industrial Economics* (July 1972), pp. 199–219.
[26] See also Y. Amihud and J. Kamin, "Revenue vs. Profit Maximization: Differences in Behavior by the Type of Control and by Market Power," *Southern Economic Journal* (January 1979), pp. 838–846.

TABLE 10–3. Summary of Tests for Differences in Firm Performance by Type of Control

Direction of Managerial Divergence	Performance Measure			
	Profit Rate	Growth Rate	Variance in Profit	Retention Rate
Higher	—	—	Palmer, Stano	Williamson
Lower	Monsen et al., Palmer, Radice, Larner, Shelton, Boudreaux, Both-well, Stano, McEachern, Steer, Glassman	Radice, Steer	Boudreaux, McEachern, Herman	Kamerschen, Herman
No difference	Qualls, Hindley, Sorenson, Holl, Kamerschen, Kania, Thonet, Herman	Sorenson, Holl, Kania, Thonet, Herman	Larner, Holl, Kania, Thonet	Sorenson, Holl, Kania

Sources: Boudreaux, *Southern Economic Journal* (1973), pp. 366–72; Hindley, *Journal of Law and Economics* (1970), pp. 185–221; Holl, *Journal of Industrial Economics* (1975), pp. 257–71; Kamerschen, *American Economic Review* (1968), pp. 432–47; Kamerschen, *Quarterly Journal of Economics* (1970), pp. 668–73; Larner, *Management Control and the Large Corporation* (New York: Dunnellen, 1970), pp. 25–32; Monsen, et al., *Quarterly Journal of Economics* (1968), pp. 435–51; Palmer, *Bell Journal of Economics* (1973), pp. 293–303; Palmer, *Western Economic Journal* (1973), pp. 228–31 (see also March 1975 issue); Qualls, *Essays on Industrial Organization* (1976), pp. 89–104; Radice, *Economics Journal* (1971), pp. 547–62; Shelton, *American Economics Review* (1967), pp. 1252–58; Sorenson, *Southern Economic Journal* (1974), pp. 145–48; Williamson, *Economics of Discretionary Behavior,* (Chicago: Markham Publishing Co., 1967), pp. 135–38; Kania and McKean, *Kyklos* (1976), pp. 272–90; Mario Stano, *Bell Journal of Economics* (1976), pp. 672–679; Steer and Cable, *Journal of Industrial Economics* (1978), pp. 13–30; Bothwell, *Journal of Industrial Economics* (1980), pp. 303–311; Thonet and Poensgen, *Journal of Industrial Economics* (1979), pp. 23–37; McEachern, *Managerial Control and Performance* (Lexington, Mass.: D. C. Heath, 1975); Herman, *Corporate Control, Corporate Power* (Cambridge: Cambridge Univ. Press, 1981); Glassman and Rhoades, *Review of Economics and Statistics* (1980), pp. 263–270.

When profits are measured as a percentage of *sales,* control does not seem to have as much effect as when profits are measured as a percentage of stockholders' *equity.* This leads David Qualls to argue that control causes very little difference in price and output policy, the two key variables in our subsequent discussions of conduct.[27]

Under growth rate, variance in profit (risk), and the rate at which profit earnings are retained (rather than paid-out), Table 10–3 discloses fewer studies and an even greater spread of results, rendering conclusions for these measures all the more tentative. Still, this writer tends to side with those who find *no*

[27] If profit as a percent of sales is *P/S,* and profit as a percent of equity is *P/E,* then control can affect one but not the other if control affects *E/S.* For more evidence of this point see J. Mingo, "Managerial Motives, Market Structures and the Performance of Holding Company Banks," *Economic Inquiry* (September 1976), pp. 411–424.

significant difference between manager and owner controlled firms in these three categories. Once again, the two types of control seem so similar that we need not be greatly concerned with the influence "managerialism" may have on motivation.

Are the empirical answers to all the foregoing questions consistent? Broadly speaking, "yes." The fact that managers' compensation is generally tied to profits leads one to expect that profit performance will not vary markedly by type of control, which is the case. On the other hand, the discoveries concerning perks and emoluments touch a responsive chord in anyone who can imagine himself in the expensive shoes of a senior executive fairly free from the reins of influential owners. For this and other reasons, we should expect some indication that profits of managerially controlled firms are less than those of owner controlled firms, which is also the case, especially where monopoly power is present. By the same token, there are indications that monopoly power and management control permit an attitude toward costs more lackadaisical than otherwise. Finally, these several inferences are consistent with conclusions emerging from direct tests of the sales revenue maximization hypothesis. These tests reveal that, as a general policy, most firms do not strive after short-term sales, heedless of the consequences for profits.

IV. BEHAVIORALISM AND "SATISFICING"

A. The Behavioralist View

Although the empirical studies just reviewed typically give primacy to profits (or profitable pricing behavior), they do not prove conclusively that profit maximization is in fact the sole objective of most businesses. General Motors' executives might shoot for and attain profits equalling 20% of stockholders' equity. This is well above the average for all manufacturers, and the executives might be generously rewarded for the achievement. However, might they be capable of attaining 30% if they *really* tried? No one really knows for sure, but it is this kind of possibility that leaves room for those holding "behavioralist" views. Behavioralists attack all three basic assumptions of the traditional position—single-mindedness, maximizing rationality, and operational rules of thumb.[28]

 Against single-mindedness, behavioralists argue that "the firm" cannot have goals. Only individuals have goals. And, although a few executives at the top may be rewarded for the firm's profit performance, their benefits may not encourage the tens of thousands of other workers scattered throughout the typical large corporation. Buried in the organization's countless nooks and crannies are specialists in production scheduling, sales, repair service, transportation, engineering, materials procurement, personnel, safety, insurance, tax, finance, accounting, payroll, warehousing, research and development, environmental pro-

---

[28] R. M. Cyert and J. G. March, *A Behavioral Theory of the Firm* (Englewood Cliffs, N.J.: Prentice-Hall, Inc., 1963); Herbert A. Simon, "Rational Decision Making in Business Organizations," *American Economic Review* (September 1979), pp. 493–513.

tection, and so on ad infinitum. To believe that all segments of all echelons can march in lock-step fashion after profits strains credulity. We are not talking about the cells of a cheetah's body or a bee colony; we are talking about imperfect and willful human beings. Assembly line foremen may find make-work jobs for surplus workers in order to be "one of the boys." Scientists may pursue projects of personal intrinsic interest but of poor profit potential. Environmental engineers may be more dedicated to preserving the foliage than to preserving the discounted present value of the firm. Behavioralists point out that "policy side-payments" are often inescapable to keep some semblance of a "coalition of coalitions." For example, "in order to get the vice-president of marketing to stay within the organization, it may be necessary to commit resources to research on new products."[29] The ramifications involve political bargaining, not just economic computing.

In place of maximizing rationality the behavioralists postulate "organizational slack" and "satisficing." Slack takes many forms they say:

> prices are set lower than necessary to maintain adequate income from customers; wages in excess of those required to maintain labor are paid; executives are provided with services and personal luxuries in excess of those required to keep them; subunits are permitted to grow without real concern for the relation between additional payments and additional revenues; public services are provided in excess of those required.[30]

Satisficing is a corollary. Whereas a "maximizer" tries to find the course of action that brings him as close as possible to some objective (often a lofty objective), a "satisficer" does not. He sets *minimum* levels of performance in several variables below which he does not want to fall. To explain the matter by analogy, suppose the proverbial haystack has more than one needle hidden in it. Whereas the maximizer would search until he believed he had found the sharpest needle in the haystack, the satisficer would stop when he found one "sharp enough" for his immediate purpose.[31] Once such a minimum aspiration level is achieved, the satisficer coasts.

As far as operational rules of thumb are concerned, the behavioralists reject the notion of MR = MC and put a wide variety of rules in its place: (1) standard percentage markups above cost for pricing, (2) smoothing of production scheduling; (3) maintenance of some minimum inventory as a percentage of sales; (4) percentage market share goals and salesmens' quotas; (5) minimum profit measured in an absolute dollar amount or percentage return on investment. Specific examples of these goals might be a 40% markup for pricing, a market share of 20%, capacity utilization running at 90%, and a 10% return on investment. Whenever one of these minimum aspiration levels is not achieved, behavioralists assume that nonroutine problem solving activities will be instituted to find a

---

[29] K. J. Cohen and R. M. Cyert, *Theory of the Firm* (Englewood Cliffs, N.J.: Prentice-Hall, Inc., 1965), p. 331.

[30] *Ibid.*, p. 333.

[31] J. C. March and H. A. Simon, *Organizations* (New York: John Wiley & Sons, Inc., 1958), p. 141.

"satisfactory" solution. There may be inconsistencies among the objectives, and various efforts at problem solving may proceed in isolation from each other; but complete consistency and coordination are beyond the capability of human beings (acting individually or as a group).

Behavioralists advance these thoughts largely on the basis of realism. They do not believe that business action can be deduced from theoretical postulates of firm maximization of any variable. They emphasize *observation* of how businessmen act every day, hoping that perhaps this observation may eventually, through induction, yield some generalizations.

B. Problems and Evidence

As you should by now expect, traditionalists espousing profit maximization and managerialists do not agree with these tenets of behavioralism. Traditionalists and managerialists criticize behavioralism on several grounds, three of which may be taken up here.[32]

In the first place, behavioralism is said to suffer from the "fallacy of misplaced concreteness" or "hyperfactualism." A theory is supposed to be like a road map of New York State. It is a simplified, condensed, somewhat inaccurate view of reality. Nevertheless the map shows the best route from Ithaca to Buffalo without detailing every pothole and traffic light. Thus, the theory of profit maximizing may not be capable of predicting in 1977 the exact price of a full-sized 1981 Buick Electra (or even whether Electras will be offered in 1981), but it does suggest an increase in price in the event of a severe fuel consumption tax. Moreover, one need not know the details of GM's internal clashes and divergence of opinions to make this prediction. Some defenders of the profit maximization assumption go so far as to say that it need not be descriptively realistic *at all,* so long as firms behave "as if" they are maximizing profits.[33] This, however, is an extreme view, which itself is fallacious.

A second line of criticism questions the status of behavioralism as a theory, claiming that to a great extent behavioralism is more "framework" than "theory":

> Frameworks outline the components of a set of phenomena that must be taken into account when efforts to explain the phenomena are undertaken. In themselves, however, they are not explanatory. . . .[34]

Thus, behavioralists may list a number of possible goals, a variety of actors, certain bargaining strategies, and several colorful experiences. But without hypotheses, which are subject to disproof, their list is just a list (like a grocery list). Behavioralists might even observe that a 40% markup is the basic price

[32] F. Machlup, "Theories of the Firm: Marginalist, Behavioral, Managerial," *American Economic Review* (March 1967), pp. 1–33; R. Marris, *op. cit.,* pp. 266–77; W. J. Baumol and Maco Stewart, "On the Behavioral Theory of the Firm," in *The Corporate Economy,* edited by R. Marris and A. Wood (Cambridge, Mass.: Harvard University Press, 1971), pp. 118–143.

[33] M. Friedman, "The Methodology of Positive Economics," in *Essays in Positive Economics* (Chicago: University of Chicago Press, 1953).

[34] N. A. McDonald and J. N. Rasenau, "Political Theory as an Academic Field and Intellectual Activity," in *Political Science: Advance of the Discipline,* edited by M. D. Irish (Englewood Cliffs, N.J.: Prentice Hall, 1968), p. 44.

policy in the lingerie department of a department store, and thereby predict the *exact* retail price of 99% of all garments sold, knowing only the garments' wholesale cost. Yet this is not the application of a theory. It does not explain *why* the action occurs or *what* might cause the markup to increase or fall substantially. Behavioralism merely predicts that a firm will behave in a certain fashion because past experience of what firms do indicates that a certain course of action is probable. "Such predictions are often *ad hoc* in nature and applicable only to a given situation."[35]

Finally, and perhaps most important, the minimum "aspiration levels" that guide behavioralist managers may actually be "maximizing levels." If the managers of GM state that their profit goal is "no less" than 20% return on invested capital, their phrase "no less" seems to suggest that they are satisficers. On the other hand, 20% might in fact be the best they can do, in which case they would actually be maximizers. How could such a coincidence of "aspiration" and "optimization" come about? One possibility is that initial aspiration levels may be set rather low. Once it becomes apparent that reaching a low aspiration level is as easy as jumping over a three-foot high bar, the aspiration level may be raised. Subsequent adjustments could follow the familiar sequential pattern of a high-jump bar during a track meet. It is set at ever higher notches until missed. A jumper who is "satisfied" with seven foot one inch might be pretty close to his best.

This last problem makes empirical verification of satisficing, as opposed to maximizing, difficult, especially with respect to pricing policy. The difficulty, perhaps even futility, is illustrated by the analysis of an extensive research project headed by D. C. Hague of the University of Manchester in England. The results appear in a book entitled *Pricing in Business,*[36] which upon casual reading seems to provide resounding support for behavioralism. Of the 13 firms studied in depth (by interviews, attendance at meetings, perusal of documents, and so on), only five are said to be profit maximizers; the other eight are judged to be profit satisficers. What is the basis for this division? Hague's primary criterion was each company's *non*operational objective as revealed in the course of interviews with top management. He branded firms as satisficers upon hearing such catch-phrase objectives as "to return a satisfactory reward on overall company operations;" "the broad aim is to obtain a given percentage return on investment;" and "to maintain adequate growth while maintaining profitability so far as this is possible."

Reliance on interviews and nonoperational objectives casts doubt on the resulting assessments of motivation. Hague himself supplies enough additional information about a number of his satisficers to allow us to substantiate these doubts. Take for example the case of "Basic Foods" (not the company's real name). On page 71 of *Pricing in Business* we are told that "Pricing decisions were made to meet a combination of marketing (i.e., sales volume and market

[35] J. V. Koch, *Industrial Organization and Prices* (Englewood Cliffs, N.J.: Prentice-Hall 1974), p. 43.
[36] D. C. Hague, *Pricing in Business* (London: George Allen & Unwin, 1971).

share) and financial (i.e., sales value and profit) objectives," thereby making Basic Foods a satisficer. Yet, on page 237 we are told that any "final" price change recommendations for Basic Foods were likely to be ones "that gave the best long-run increase in profit, as compared with the no-change case."

Several other questionable classifications lead me to believe that maximizers actually outnumber satisficers in Hague's sample. His study thus illustrates our earlier reservations about interview research. Still, there is much truth to behavioralism. And at one point Hague succinctly states much of that truth when he admits that "firms that are satisficers when taking decisions about production, inventories, employment, etc., may become maximizers when they set prices" because they "are forcing those outside the firm to bear the burden of change."[37] What is more, pricing seems to be the province of top drawer executives, many of whom apparently have a monetary stake in policies that improve profits.[38]

SUMMARY

A reasonably correct understanding of firm motivation is essential to a reasonably correct understanding of firm conduct in the market place. According to traditional theory, all firms maximize profits. Conduct differs across firms solely because of differences in the structure of the markets the firms happen to occupy. In monopoly markets, profit maximization often implies a "high" price. In purely competitive markets it implies a "low" price.

The postulate of profit maximization rests on three basic assumptions—single-mindedness, rational maximizing, and operational feasibility. The first of these postulates holds that, despite much diversity, all people associated with "the firm" work together toward a single objective. The second assumption specifies that this objective is profit maximization. Profit is the owner's reward, and, because owners control the traditional firm, profit maximization is both natural and rational. The third assumption rules out any real-world difficulties in following the simple MR = MC recipe.

Attacks on traditional theory have chewed away at the validity of these assumptions. Early on, the critics were most bothered by the *non*operational nature of the MR = MC calculus. Perhaps their most enduring blow in this respect was to point out that rigorous profit maximization is either meaningless or impossible in the face of risk and uncertainty. A second school of criticism, managerialism, has attacked the notion of a single-minded firm and displaced profit as the firm's sole object. Arguing that managers control the largest modern corporations, managerialists have devised such theories as managerial utility,

[37] *Ibid.* p. 83. The best research on managerialism suggests much the same thing. See Cynthia A. Glassman and Stephen A. Rhoades, "Owner vs. Manager Control Effects on Bank Performance," *Review of Economics and Statistics* (May 1980), pp. 263–270, where lower managerial profits appear to be caused by higher costs.

[38] Hague presents evidence on this point (pp. 200–243). See also D. Tuson, "Pricing: Whose Responsibility?" in *Creative Pricing*, edited by E. Marting (American Management Association, 1968), pp. 39–48.

sales maximization subject to minimum profit constraint, growth rate maximization, and maximization of the discounted present value of sales revenues. However, empirical tests of the observable implications of these managerial theories have done no more than tarnish the traditional theory, except on the cost side, and then primarily under conditions of market power. Where competition does not keep costs in check, profit maximization has been rather bruised and battered by the tests.

Finally, the behavioralists attack every one of traditional theory's assumptions. They argue that "the firm" can only be multiminded in light of its complexity and internal diversity. They claim that satisficing makes more sense and is more frequently observed than maximizing. They also deny that profit maximization can be an operational objective. Although common sense and a rudimentary knowledge of the modern bureaucratic corporation tell us that these claims carry much truth, it is difficult to test the extent of this truth empirically. Satisficing behavior is often similar to profit maximizing, especially in price policy.

In short, this chapter reads like a ride on an old-time merry-go-round. We repeatedly rode away from the golden ring of profit maximization. Yet somehow we kept coming back to it. After several speedy inspections from different angles, it appears that the ring might be made of brass or tin rather than gold. Nonetheless, those running our major business firms seem to have their eyes on it too. Most of them are also reaching for it with different degrees of effort. As one of the first and foremost critics of traditional theory concedes, "basically profits and profit expectations continue to guide decision-making in the giant as well as the small enterprise."[39]

APPENDIX:
Perks, Growth, and Itel Corp.

Figure 10–2 assumed that perks ate up profit. Figure 10–5 suggested that excessive current sales (or short-term size) could reduce future growth by ravaging the profits that would fuel future growth. Are these claims accurate? The amazing story of Itel Corporation says "Yes."

Fathered in 1967 by an aggressive president, Itel grew at an astonishing pace during the 1970s to become a very large diversified financial-services company that specialized in leasing computers, shipping containers, railroad cars, and other transportation equipment. From 1976 to 1978, its assets more than doubled to reach $1.3 billion. During 1978 alone, its employee roster jumped from 4,000 to 6,400.[1] The price of the company's stock soared to $39 from $18 during six months of 1978, a year of $47 million profits.

But the bubble burst in 1979. Losses in that year were $433.3 million. Stock price plummeted 79% to $5. Employment fell to 1,000 by early 1980. And

[39] R. A. Gordon, *op. cit.,* p. 336.
[1] *Forbes,* May 28, 1979, p. 39.

shortly thereafter Itel filed for protection under Chapter 11 of the federal Bankruptcy Act.[2]

What happened? Excessive perks for one thing. "From its leased Mercedes automobiles to its sumptuous office suites replete with Oriental carpets, designer furniture and views of San Francisco Bay, Itel's ambiance was calculated to impress."[3] The company's headquarters became famous for its beautiful secretaries. In 1979, some 1,300 employees and their spouses were treated to an extravagant month-long holiday in Acapulco, Mexico, which cost the company about $3 million. And so on.

Explosive growth also contributed. According to the *Wall Street Journal,*

interviews with former insiders, competitors, analysts and Itel's sober new management team depict a company that rose and fell in a climate of overweening ambition and runaway growth plans. Propelled by an aggressive and overpaid marketing machine, Itel's expansion ran on, heedless of bad news in the market and almost unchecked by any controls until it was too late, these sources say.

"Growth junkies," snipes one former insider. "Go-go boys."[4]

[2] *San Jose Mercury,* July 25, 1982, pp. 1F–2F.
[3] *Wall Street Journal,* February 22, 1980, p. 1.
[4] *Ibid.,* p. 1.

11 Price and Production Behavior in the Short Run: Theory and Cross-Section Evidence

. . . true oligopoly is interdependence plus uncertainty.

—DONALD DEWEY

Of the several aspects of conduct mentioned previously, none have received greater attention from economists and businessmen than price and production policies. It is proper then that we take these up before other forms of conduct. We begin with *short-run* price and production policies in this chapter and the next. *Long-run* aspects come later.

The principal short-run issues include price rivalry among "existing" sellers, price behavior during slumps in demand, supply control over the business cycle to stabilize price, and price fixing. Considering the long run, our scope will broaden to include not only existing competitors, but also potential and past competitors. That is to say, we shall consider how pricing influences the birth and death of firms.

Within the short-run context we have already presented simple theories of price determination under perfect competition and monopoly. The present chapter will focus on behavior associated with structural conditions that lie between those extremes—namely, oligopoly and monopolistic competition. The first section discusses interdependence, which is a prime determinant of how firms in these settings view their demand curves. The second section introduces complications and uncertainties, particularly those associated with cyclical swings of demand. Next we review several pricing mechanisms used to cope with these complications and uncertainties. The concluding section is devoted to cross-section empirical evidence of short-run price behavior.

I. INTERDEPENDENCE

A. The Cournot Model

Well over a century ago, Augustin Cournot demonstrated the importance of interdependence in oligopoly with a clever theoretical model.[1] He assumed the following:

- There are two sellers (we call them **J** and **K**).

- The product is homogeneous, spring water to be exact.

- Each seller has zero marginal costs.

- Finally, and very importantly, he assumed that each seller in selecting his output level would believe that his rival's level of output would not change. This belief holds despite the fact that each rival's output does change as the theory unfolds. Hence sellers do not learn by experience and their actions center on quantity instead of price.

Cournot's model is illustrated in Figure 11–1, where $D'D$ indicates market wide demand. We begin with firm **J**, who is the first to sell and who therefore assumes that **K**'s present output will remain at zero. **J** maximizes profit by producing 1,000 units, which is determined by equating $D'D$'s marginal revenue R_0 with marginal cost, which is zero. Firm **K** now starts selling. By assumption, **K** believes that **J** will continue to produce 1,000 units. Hence **K** perceives its demand curve to be HD, which when shifted to the price axis becomes $E'E$. The marginal revenue curve associated with **K**'s demand $E'E$ is R_1, so firm **K** maximizes its profit by selling 500 units (where marginal revenue meets marginal cost).

With **K**'s output set at 500, **J**'s original output of 1,000 is no longer best for **J**, however. If **J** assumes that **K**'s output will remain at 500, it will now view its demand as $F'F$, which is demand when 500 units are subtracted from $D'D$. Seeing $F'F$ as its demand, **J** then maximizes profit by equating marginal revenue R_2 with marginal cost at 750 units. Once **J** is set at 750, it is then **K**'s turn to react once more, triggering further rounds of action-reaction that are not shown in Figure 11–1.

Although these further rounds are not shown, it should be apparent from what has happened already that **J** and **K** are converging toward a common level of output. The first output pairs were 1,000 (**J**) and 0 (**K**), followed by 750 (**J**) and 500 (**K**). In the end, they each wind up with outputs of 666⅔ units, which when combined yield 1,333⅓ units total output and price P, as shown in Figure 11–1.

Under perfect competition, output would be higher at 2,000 units and price would be lower at zero. Pure monopoly, on the other hand, would place output at 1,000 and price at E'. Thus Cournot's model yields an equilibrium that is

---

[1] A. Cournot, *Researches into the Mathematical Principles of the Theory of Wealth* (New York: Macmillan, 1897), first published in Paris in 1838.

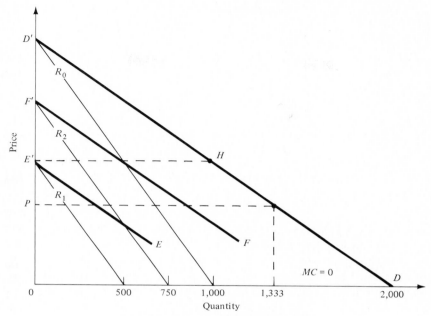

FIGURE 11–1. The Cournot Model.

"in between" these structural extremes. Moreover, if we introduced additional firms into the model, moving from duopoly to triopoly to still more populous forms of oligopoly, market output and price would move in the direction of the perfect competition results.

The assumptions of Cournot's model are very unrealistic. Yet these implications of the model are not too misleading, in large part because they derive from seller interdependence. Turning to more modern theories we shall see that interdependence remains, but the focus is mainly on *price* behavior instead of quantity behavior.

B. Modern Theory: Two Demands

The interdependence of oligopolists and monopolistically competitive firms is reflected in the demand curves they confront. Whereas a pure monopolist sees the market-wide demand curve and the purely competitive firm sees a perfectly elastic demand curve, those in between may view *two* demand curves. Two curves are necessary to account for the possible reactions of rivals—followship or nonfollowship—given a change in the firm's price. The **followship** demand curve applies if a change in price is aped by rivals. A price reduction under followship conditions will gain added sales for the firm but not at the expense of rivals because they will have lowered prices too. The sales come from added *market-wide* sales, which, if distributed among all rivals according to their pre-existing market shares, would leave each firm's market share unchanged.

233

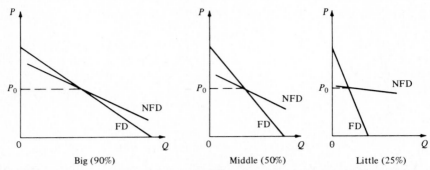

FIGURE 11-2. Followship (FD) and nonfollowship (NFD) demand curves for various sized firms.

Conversely, a price increase curtails a firm's sales in proportion to the market's loss of sales, provided all firms act uniformly on the increase. The followship curve could therefore also be called a **constant market share** demand curve.

As indicated by the FD curves in Figure 11-2, followship demand varies depending on firm size. Each panel of Figure 11-2 assumes the *same* market-wide demand. But FD for the "Big" firm is drawn on the assumption of a 90% market share; that for "Middle" assumes a 50% market share; and "Little" assumes a 25% market share. The firms could not all be in the same market, but each FD is a reflection of the market-wide demand underlying the illustrations. This may be appreciated by noting that the elasticity of each FD curve at price P_0 is the same, and each such elasticity in turn matches market-wide elasticity. Price P_0 divides each FD curve into upper and lower portions. Elasticity is the same at P_0 because the length of the upper portion *relative* to the lower portion is the same in each case.

Although the followship curves are identical in elasticity, such is not true of the **nonfollowship** demand curves labeled NFD. They do vary in elasticity across firms within a given market because the assumption underlying their construction—that rivals do *not* match price changes—yields substantially different quantity results depending on firm size. Big firm's NFD will have an elasticity very similar to its FD though slightly higher. An unfollowed price cut below P_0 would cause customers to switch to Big. But the most Big could gain from competitors would be an additional 10 percentage points of market share, since at price P_0 Big already enjoys 90%. Comparing 10 to 90 implies a low elasticity for Big's NF curve. At the other extreme, an unfollowed price cut of similar magnitude on the part of Little could easily double Little's sales volume, implying that Little's nonfollowship demand curve at P_0 is highly elastic. Putting two and two together we may conclude that: the smaller the firm relative to its market, the greater the divergence between its followship and nonfollowship demand curves and between their elasticities. Since product differentiation also influences demand, a related conclusion holds that the more differentiated the firm's product is, the less the divergence will be. Or the more standardized

234

the product, the greater the divergence between FD and NFD and their elasticities.

As structure affects a firm's demand elasticities in this fashion, it will also affect the firm's opportunities for earning sales revenues and thereby its price behavior. The linkage between demand elasticity and total revenue is summarized in the two-part diagram of Figure 11–3. The horizontal axis of both parts is quantity. The vertical axis of the upper part is price; that of the lower part is total revenue. Because total revenue is price times quantity, the *area* under the demand curve at any point equals the vertical *distance* under the total revenue curve of the lower part. At point *H,* for example, total revenue is *OJHK,* and this corresponds to *GF* using the total dollars vertical scale of the total revenue diagram. It should be clear, then, that a price reduction will increase total revenue if demand is elastic, as it is in the *AH* range and below to E = 1. But a price reduction will decrease total revenue if demand is inelastic,

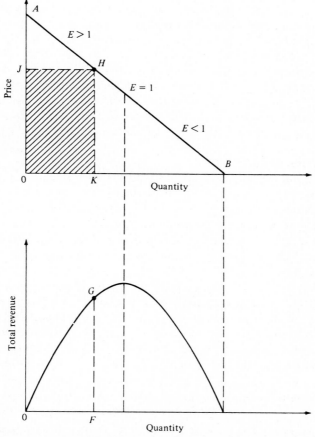

FIGURE 11–3. Relationship between demand elasticity and total revenue.

as it is between E = 1 and B. Conversely, a price increase will boost the firm's total revenue if demand is inelastic but trim total revenue if demand is elastic.[2]

These relationships tell us a great deal about which of the three firms of Figure 11-2 has the most to gain from a trip down its nonfollowship demand curve via price cuts below P_0. Little has the most elastic NFD; hence, it would gain the most, assuming that it could in fact move down its NFD. Conversely, Big has the least to gain from such behavior. We can therefore surmise that relatively small firms are more likely to cut prices and bestow bargains than big firms. Turning the issue around, we may ask which firm is most likely to gain from a price *increase*. Big is the most likely gainer in this case. We can expect, therefore, to find relatively large firms most frequently cast in the role of upside price leader.

These deductions are fair and proper, but they are nevertheless a bit premature. We have not considered two important factors that may affect their accuracy: (1) Costs are as important as revenues in determining behavior, for costs as well as revenues determine profits. (2) Just as we mortals cannot be in two places at one time, so too the firm cannot be on more than one demand curve at any one time (except where the curves intersect). A price cut will take it down either NFD *or* FD, not both. A price increase is an either/or journey in the opposite direction. Because the elasticities of NFD and FD differ, we must discover *which* curve the firm regards as its *actual* demand curve under various circumstances. The firm's view of its terrain determines what steps the firm takes, if it takes any at all. We shall demonstrate the significance of these additional considerations by exploring two classical models of firm conduct— "monopolistic competition" and the "kinky demand curve" of oligopoly.

C. Monopolistic Competition

Assume, as did the originator of this model, Edward Chamberlin,[3] that *all* firms in the market are small, smaller even than Little of Figure 11-2. Assume further that each firm has a negatively sloped, though highly elastic, nonfollowship demand curve because each has a differentiated product. These assumptions yield a model of short-sighted price cutting. In other words, the interdependence of the firms goes *unrecognized* in this case, with the result that price competition predominates.

Figure 11-4 depicts the situation as viewed by a typical small firm. We begin with all firms charging price P_1. The typical firm is earning excess total profits equal to the difference between P_1 and average total cost (ATC) directly below point A *times* the quantity produced (assuming that the average total cost curve includes a normal profit as a cost). Though adequate, the firm's profit could be increased if it cut price to P_2 without being followed by rivals.

---

[2] In early 1980 IBM raised prices on its 4300 series equipment. *Business Week* reported that, as a result, IBM's revenue would increase by about $1 billion because, "No one expects the higher prices to reduce demand." (January 28, 1980, p. 84).

[3] Edward Chamberlin, *The Theory of Monopolistic Competition,* 8th ed. (Cambridge, Mass.: Harvard University Press, 1962).

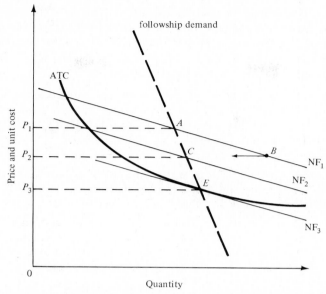

FIGURE 11–4. Short-sighted price cutting under monopolistic competition.

In that event, it would move down its nonfollowship demand curve NF_1 to a point such as B. Notice the very high elasticity of NF_1. Quantity nearly doubles. So this ploy yields a substantial increase in total revenue, while declining unit costs (ATC) keep total costs from rising by as much. However, the profit gains last only as long as rivals fail to follow, because these gains are procured at their expense. Their demand curves will have shifted to the left, leaving them with fewer customers, higher costs, and lower profits. To regain their former market shares, these rivals cut their prices to P_2 as well, an action that shifts the firm of Figure 11–4 from point B to point C. After cut and countercut, the result is a movement down the followship demand curve from A to C and to a new nonfollowship curve NF_2. As the firm of Figure 11–4 is typical of all firms in the market, this descent carries all other firms with it. If our typical firm is short sighted enough to try the same stunt again, the others will naturally follow and further downward shifts will ensue. Equilibrium is reached at point E, at which point any further price cutting takes the firm below average total cost. Here, theory posits a truce.

Of course the key to this scenario is the inability of the small firm to see beyond its first step down the nonfollowship curve. The firm does not consider the inelastic followship curve relevant. The temptations of NF's high elasticity are too great. The firm feels it is too small to have an impact on others in the market. The consequence is price competition. The pattern may be illustrated with an example taken from grocery retailing, which in certain cities might qualify as monopolistically competitive. In 1975 and 1976 price wars broke

237

out in several cities, despite the fact that industry executives unanimously decried them, saying that "price wars always hurt profits and rarely change market shares among the combatants—the supposed goal." Except for consumers, who obviously benefit, "everybody fights harder and everybody loses."[4] Here is the story of one of the bloodiest battles of this period:

> The Chicago price war, undoubtedly one of the longest and costliest in supermarket history, began abruptly. On a Saturday afternoon in April . . ., the manager of a Jewel Food Store heard from a visitor that a nearby Dominick's store was changing a lot of prices. Unusual for a Saturday, the manager thought. He sent an employee to check.
>
> The employee found Dominick's aisles swarming with stock boys repricing merchandise. *And all the prices were being reduced.* Within minutes, Jewel employees throughout the area were scouting Dominick's stores. Their reports were startling. . . . Dominick's was slashing prices as much as 15% on "hundreds and hundreds" of items.
>
> On Tuesday, Jewel's response was ready. Jewel was cutting prices on 3,327 items from 2% to 30%. On Friday, National Tea announced it was reducing prices. . . . Other competitors jumped in quickly.
>
> Mr. DiMatteo [the manager of Dominick's] says he thought he could batter the competition. So he ordered the price cuts. . . . However, "the competition jumped in a lot faster than I thought they would," he concedes, "I thought we'd be alone for a while."[5]

Although the followship demand curve was not wholly invisible to Mr. DiMatteo, it was certainly obscure and broken as depicted in Figure 11–4. As for the ultimate effects on market share, "Progressive Grocer, a trade magazine, found that 95% of the Chicago shoppers it questioned at one point during the price war said they were going to the same store as they had before the battle broke out."[5]

D. The Kinky Demand Curve of Oligopoly

Fewer firms in the market, with larger market shares, convert conditions to **oligopoly**, and the interdependence becomes *recognized.*[6] One way of demonstrating this conversion is the theory of "kinked demand." Let P_0 in Figure 11–5 represent the going market price. Q_0 is then the firm's output, and K indicates the firm's position on its demand curves. Given these conditions, what action is best for the firm? Is it likely to slash price, boost it, or leave it unchanged? If the firm thinks its prices below P_0 will be followed, then *below* point K the followship demand curve alone is relevant. The NF demand curve thus disappears below K. Conversely, if the firm is doubtful that its price increases

---

[4] "Supermarket Scrap," *Wall Street Journal,* July 19, 1976.

[5] *Ibid.*

[6] R. L. Hall and C. J. Hitch, "Price Theory and Business Behavior," *Oxford Economic Papers* (May 1939), pp. 12–45; P. M. Sweezy, "Demand Under Conditions of Oligopoly," *Journal of Political Economy* (August 1939), pp. 568–573.

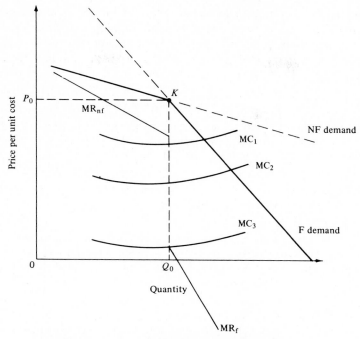

FIGURE 11–5. The kinked demand oligopoly model.

will be followed, then above K only the NF demand curve is applicable, and the F curve does the vanishing act.

Now, a split personality may be fine for anyone with too many friends, but schizophrenic demand curves such as these put the firm in a straightjacket. Costs aside, it should be clear that a price cut below P_0 would substantially diminish total revenue because the F curve below K is inelastic. Moreover, things are just as bad the other way around. A price increase above P_0 would reduce total revenue substantially because NF above K is highly elastic. With total revenue falling from a step in either direction, the best strategy is to stand pat.

Furthermore, this rigidity of price may not be compromised by cost considerations. If the firm is operating under the MR = MC rule of profit maximization, marginal costs can vary over a spacious range without causing price to flutter from its P_0 perch because the marginal revenue curve is discontinuous. The discontinuity arises because the marginal revenue applicable to price increases is MR_{nf}, which is derived from the *nonfollowship* demand curve above K, whereas the marginal revenue applicable to price reductions is MR_f, which is derived from the *followship* demand curve below point K. Marginal cost is shown to vary from MC_1 to MC_3, but it always remains equal to marginal revenue.

Perhaps the most striking example of this situation was uncovered by Bjarke

Fog in the course of interviewing business people in 139 Danish firms about their pricing policies. He came across a leather tannery that charged a higher price for dyed shoe leather than it did for black shoe leather, even though the costs of making the former were lower than the costs of making the latter. It seems that the price differential originated in 1890, when cost differences did warrant the price differential. When asked why the price differential continued long after costs had changed, the firm's manager replied:

> Perhaps we ought to raise the price of black leather somewhat and lower the price of dyed leather to a corresponding degree, but we dare not do so. The fact is that we shall then run the risk of being unable to sell black leather shoes, whereas our competitors will also reduce their prices for dyed shoes.[7]

In sum, kinked demand theory yields two basic predictions: (1) Oligopolists will refrain from price cutting when their followship demand curves are inelastic; and (2), except in rapid inflation, oligopoly prices will tend to be rigid, despite moderate changes in costs. Although both predictions are consistent with the opinions of businessmen and much of their observed behavior, the model suffers several serious limitations.[8] In many respects it is a model of rigidity that, as presented above, is itself too rigid.

E. Criticisms and Modifications to the Kinky Model

Consider first the matter of moderate increases in costs. The theory is most applicable when the costs of an *individual* oligopolist rise but those of others in the market remain unchanged. A firm confronted with unique cost increments has no reason to expect that a price increase on its part will be followed by its less troubled rivals. But what about cost increases that confront *all* rivals simultaneously? A hike in the cost of steel to automakers, for example? Or a 15% rise in labor costs due to a newly signed collective bargaining contract? The oligopolist who attempts to initiate price increases to cover these costs is not really sticking his neck out very far. Followship is likely. Thus, the business press is riddled with news accounts of oligopolists raising prices after such across-the-board cost increases. Oligopolists have even been accused of predicating price increases on the mere *expectation* of future cost increases.

A second limitation is suggested by the first. Kinked demand theory may partly explain the rigidity of an *existing* price level, but it does not explain how prices reached that level in the first place. In other words, it is an instructive but *incomplete* theory of oligopolistic price behavior. Besides uniform cost increases, it ignores the possibility of price leadership and cartelization. It yields no solid predictions as to whether prices will be higher in concentrated markets

---

[7] B. Fog, *Industrial Pricing Policies* (Amsterdam: North-Holland Publishing Co., 1960), p. 130.

[8] For a critique see G. J. Stigler, "The Kinky Oligopoly Demand Curve and Rigid Prices," *Journal of Political Economy* (October 1947), pp. 432–449. For critiques of Stigler see C. W. Efroymson, "The Kinked Oligopoly Curve Reconsidered," *Quarterly Journal of Economics* (February 1955), pp. 119–136; R. B. Heflebower, "Full Costs, Cost Changes, and Prices," in *Business Concentration and Price Policy* (Princeton: Princeton University Press, 1955), pp. 361–392; J. M. Clark, *Competition as a Dynamic Process* (Washington, D.C.: Brookings Institution, 1961), pp. 287–289.

as compared with unconcentrated ones. And it does not tell us whether profits will be greater where barriers to entry prevail.

These criticisms may be expanded into a third and somewhat different shortcoming of the theory. In its simple form, the theory imparts an impression of interfirm uniformity that is often unrealistic. A cursory reading of the theory conjures up notions of a market in which all firms are exactly the same size and weight (say, ten firms each with one tenth of the market), all offer identical products, and all charge exactly the same price. Such an image must be rejected, however. Everyone knows that oligopolists usually differ in size, products, and prices—even within the same narrow market definition.

A very large and efficient firm may act as price leader, for instance. Because leadership implies followship, such a firm would usually see only the followship demand curve, upside and down. No kink would be visible, as the kink is created by a combination of nonfollowship and followship curves. Historically, General Motors has usually served as such a leader in the auto industry. The qualification "usually" is needed because GM's price increases have occasionally not been followed during severe slumps in demand, and Japanese producers have recently given GM some stiff competition. At the other size extreme, a very small firm, such as AMC in the auto industry, would not see any kink if its price moves were never followed.

The most likely candidates for the kinky demand are therefore an industry's medium-sized firms, like Ford or Chrysler. They are big enough to usually be followed on the down side, too big to be ignored even by GM. Yet they are not qualified by size, efficiency, or historical reputation to be assured that their price increases will usually be honored by imitation.[9]

Diversity of size is not the only threat to the kinked demand curve. Diversity of prices may also obscure the kink. In turn, price diversity may be due to differences in firm size and product differentiation. The diversity will have a pattern to it if the industry's firms are clustered in strategic groups. A *strategic group* is a group of firms pursuing a similar strategy in terms of such things as advertising intensity, product quality, price policy, geographic scope, and breadth of product line.[10] In detergents, for example, Procter & Gamble, Colgate, and Lever Brothers follow a high price, intensive advertising, consumer oriented strategy. Less well-known firms sell under the private labels of retail chains and accordingly follow a low price, no advertising strategy. Still other firms specialize in bulk, industrial detergents.

The diversity of prices and strategic groups in many real-world markets is illustrated by Table 11–1, which presents data on retail gasoline prices in Washington, D.C., by brand, as of late 1969. The first column reports the number of stations selling each brand, except that independents are lumped in one cate-

[9] L. J. White, *The Automobile Industry Since 1945* (Cambridge, Mass.: Harvard University Press, 1971), pp. 111–35; S. E. Boyle and T. F. Hogarty, "Pricing Behavior in the American Automobile Industry, 1957–71," *Journal of Industrial Economics* (December 1975), pp. 81–95.

[10] Richard E. Caves and Michael E. Porter, "From Entry Barriers to Mobility Barriers," *Quarterly Journal of Economics* (May 1977), pp. 241–261; Michael E. Porter, *Competitive Strategy* (New York: Free Press, 1980), pp. 126–155.

TABLE 11–1. Price Levels of Gasoline Stations Located in Washington D.C.—Fall 1969

Brand	Number of Stations Surveyed	Total Stations (Market Share) (%)	Brand's Stations	
			Pricing above Reference (%)	Pricing below Reference (%)
Exxon	144	20.7	36.8	14.6
American	90	12.9	20.0	15.6
Shell	73	10.5	15.1	13.7
Texaco	66	9.5	9.1	36.4
Sunoco	61	8.8	4.9	16.4
Gulf	59	8.5	10.2	23.4
Mobil	50	7.2	4.0	54.0
Sinclair	32	4.6	9.4	53.1
Citgo	28	4.0	7.1	42.9
Atlantic	26	3.7	0	84.6
Scott	15	2.2	0	100.0
Phillips	14	2.0	0	50.0
Hess	9	1.3	0	100.0
Independents	30	4.3	0	100.0
Total	697	100.0		

Source: F. C. Allvine and J. M. Patterson, *Competition, Ltd.: The Marketing of Gasoline* (Bloomington: University of Indiana Press, 1972), p. 13.

gory at the bottom. The second column converts these numbers of stations into estimates of market share. Thus, Exxon's 144 stations comprise 20.7% of all stations. In addition, the brands are arrayed from largest market share to smallest. Pricing is conveniently summarized by reporting the percentage of each brand's stations pricing above and below the reference price for regular gas in the market. For example, 53 Exxon stations, or 36.8% of Exxon's total, priced above reference. The "reference price" (which at that time was a mere 35.9 cents) is a kind of base or modal price that guides the actions of most gasoline retailers, especially the so-called "major brands." The majors are of course familiar to every driver and television viewer. They stress service, saturation of locations, credit cards, advertising, tires, batteries, accessories, clean restrooms, gasoline additives, and other nonprice forms of competition. As Table 11–1 suggests, they also have the lion's share of the business. They may be contrasted with the independents, which generally offer spartan accommodations, abbreviated service, very little advertising, and "competitive" prices. (Quite often they also carry quaint names like Hi-Rev, Rotten Robby's, and Stinker).

Our earlier discussions of product differentiation led to expectations of the majors charging higher prices than the independents, and Table 11-1 bears out those expectations. The vast majority of major brand stations priced at or above reference. *All* independents priced below reference (by at least 4 cents a gallon or 11%). Moreover, theories concerning nonfollowship elasticity and monopolistic competition suggest that firms with small market shares are more likely to charge lower prices than firms with large market shares. This, too, is borne out by these data. As one reads down Table 11-1, the percentage of stations pricing above reference dwindles as the percentage of stations pricing below reference grows. It should also be mentioned that this generalization holds not only for majors within a given market, but also for a *given* major operating in *various* markets. Exxon, for instance, had the largest market share and highest prices in Washington, D.C. Yet at the same time in San Francisco, Exxon ranked ninth with only 3.8% of the market. There, 87.4% of its stations were pricing *below* reference. In other words, majors often behave like independents, at least with respect to price, when their market share is like that of independents.[11]

As for kinks, they are somewhat ill-defined and variable across firms and geographic markets, but they are not destroyed by price differentials. A price differential may not cause continual shifting of market share in favor of the low priced brand because of product differentiation. In the gasoline industry it is "customary" for independents to price a few cents below dominant majors. At that point the independents could very well see a kink. Cuts below the customary differential tend to be followed by the majors.

One final limitation of the simple model is that prices may be rigid for reasons other than kinked demand.[12] Consider first the cost of changing prices. It may be high enough to inhibit frequent alterations, especially when price lists are voluminous and complex. What's more, buyers of certain products may prefer a stable price, even though it may on average be higher than a fluctuating price. A molder of plastic houseware products enunciated this point somewhat incoherently when he upbraided his suppliers at a trade convention:

> When you producers were selling polyethylene to us molders at the stable price of 41 cents a pound, my company made much more money than we do now, when price is much lower but bounces up and down with every deal. Why? Simply because I didn't have to spend all my time rushing around to see if I could make as good a deal as the next guy—and never be quite sure.[13]

---

[11] The pattern of small-share-low-price is common to many industries, in large part apparently because of the elasticity differences outlined in Figure 11-2. Kodak has 90% of the film market in the U.S. and sets prices high, while Fuji, with only about 10%, prices 5% to 10% below Kodak. In Japan, it's the reverse. Kodak has a 12% share there and prices below Fuji, which holds 70% of the market. (*Forbes,* November 22, 1982, pp. 55–56.) Gillette and Bic alternate roles in U.S. markets for disposable razors, pens, and lighters. (*Fortune,* February 25, 1980, pp. 148–150.)

[12] Stigler, *op. cit.;* T. Scitovsky, *Welfare and Competition* (Chicago: Richard Irwin, 1951), Chapter XII.

[13] E. Marting, *Creative Pricing* (American Management Association, 1968), p. 37. For sellers' views see A. A. Fitzpatrick, *Pricing Methods of Industry* (Boulder, Colorado: Pruett Press, 1964), p. 67; *Wall Street Journal,* December 15, 1982, p. 1 (on auto sales).

Finally, the last factor worth mentioning helps to introduce our next section. Many changes of condition that would normally provoke price changes under pure competition do not do so under oligopoly because they are considered *temporary* changes, which, if responded to, might prove unsettling. Swings in the business cycle are the most important of these. Since frequent price revisions can shake up even the coziest nest of oligopolists and jostle them into occasional price wars, oligopolists tend to favor stable prices. As we shall see more clearly, recognized interdependence often leads to tacit collusion, cartelization, and other forms of pricing cooperation. But cooperation can be a delicate thing. And fluctuating prices may camouflage "chiseling" and provoke serious "misunderstandings"—two factors corrosive to cooperation.[14]

II. CYCLICAL COMPLICATIONS AND UNCERTAINTIES

On June 14, 1977, St. Joe Minerals Corporation announced a massive cutback in zinc refinery output from 95% to 65% capacity utilization. Why the cut? To keep price from falling. As the company's spokesman put it, "We're hoping production restraint . . . will be sufficient to prevent further cuts and allow zinc price to move back toward a more healthy level."[15] At about the same time, *Business Week* was explaining to its readers why prices on paper goods had held fairly steady during 1975 despite the worst decline in paper demand in 40 years: "Instead of running their mills flat-out in good times and bad, paper company managers now try generally to cut production instead of prices when demand weakens."[16] These are two examples of a very important and fundamental rule of economics: if prices are to be controlled in either the short or long run, one must control demand or supply, or both. In the case of oligopolists coping with cyclical swings in demand, the only option usually open is supply control. Cyclical swings in demand are either inherent in the product[17] or a result of economy-wide difficulties. Both causes are beyond the control of individual firms.

A. A Bit of Theory

The principle is illustrated in Figure 11–6.[18] It depicts demand and unit costs for two firms. The underlying conditions are the same for each, except

[14] In light of the fact that the kinky demand curve has genuine but *limited* relevance, it is not surprising that sweeping tests of its existence *in general* come up empty handed. See Walter J. Primeaux, Jr. and Mickey C. Smith, "Pricing Patterns and the Kinky Demand Curve," *Journal of Law & Economics* (April 1976), pp. 189–199.

[15] *Wall Street Journal,* June 15, 1977.

[16] *Business Week,* May 2, 1977, p. 55.

[17] A curious example of this is textiles. For many decades this industry experienced a mysterious and never fully explained cycle of high demand in odd-numbered years and low demand in even-numbered years. J. W. Markham. *Competition in the Rayon Industry* (Cambridge: Harvard University Press, 1952), pp. 112–115.

[18] For a similar discussion see R. Sherman, *The Economics of Industry* (Boston: Little, Brown and Co., 1974), pp. 148–150; Markham, *op. cit.;* and Robert E. Smith, "A Theory for the Administered Price Phenomenon," *Journal of Economic Issues* (June 1979), pp. 629–645.

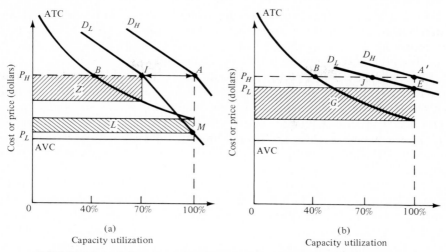

FIGURE 11–6. Price and quantity responses to fluctuations in demand.

that 11–6(a) assumes a kinked demand whereas 11–6(b) assumes an elastic demand. The horizontal axis in each case is capacity use, which is simply an alternative way of expressing quantity. The vertical axis measures price and costs per unit of output. For simplicity, average variable costs (AVC) are assumed to be the same for each unit of output up to full capacity. (They are still "variable" in the sense that total dollar costs rise with added output.) When fixed costs per unit are added to AVC, the result is total unit costs, ATC (which in this case do not include a normal profit). Thus at price P_H the break-even point for each form is at point B, which corresponds to 40% capacity utilization. Demand is shown to fluctuate cyclically between a high level, D_H, and a low level, D_L.

Looking first at Figure 11–6(a), we can compare the implications of adjusting to slack demand by cutting price, as opposed to cutting quantity, when demand is price *in*elastic (which is typical below the kink in the short run). For demand D_H,the firm is at point A. Capacity utilization is 100%, and profit with price P_H is lucrative. As demand shifts back to D_L, full capacity can be maintained only by cutting price from P_H to P_L, moving the firm from A to M. However, unit costs exceed price at that point, yielding losses indicated by shaded area L. The firm would continue to produce in the short run, despite the loss, because it is covering its variable costs, AVC, and part of its fixed cost. In short, absorbing the slack by a move from A to M is distasteful to the firm (but not to its customers). Had the firm been able to maintain price at P_H by cutting back capacity use to 70%, it would be at point I. Even though this tactic boosts unit costs substantially, they are still less than P_H at I. Hence, total profits are indicated by shaded area Z. From the firm's viewpoint, the superiority of this A to I supply adjustment is quite plain. Profits are not only maintained

245

over phases of the cycle, they are more stable over numerous cycles. Why, then, would any firm want to end up at M, as many often do? Although they do not want to, they may be *forced* to by price competition, which brings us to Figure 11–6(b).

Quantity curtailment plus price maintenance are the preferred combination only under the right circumstances—of which inelastic demand is the most important. If on the other hand short-run demand is very responsive to small price shadings, as is assumed in Figure 11–6(b), quantity maintenance, coupled with price cutting, would be the more profitable combination. In 11–6(b) demand shifts by the *same* magnitude as in 11–6(a). A constant price P_H begets 70% capacity use in both cases. Point J in 11–6(b) corresponds to point I in 11–6(a). Thus the profit consequences of maintaining price in 11–6(b) are the same—that is, total profit at J would equal area Z. Area Z may be compared to area G in 11–6(b) to see the greater rewards bestowed by cutting price to P_L and moving from J to E. Area G clearly exceeds area Z. Adjustment A' to E is superior to A' to J.

The only remaining question is *when* does each model apply? As already suggested, the inelasticity of Figure 11–6(a) seems typical of medium and large firms in most oligopolistic industries because their followship curves reflect market-wide demand, which itself is typically inelastic in the short run—especially in producer goods industries such as steel, zinc, aluminum, paper, and chemicals. These oligopolists will try to avoid price cuts in periods of declining demand, recognizing the likelihood of their detection and imitation by competitors, with a resulting loss of profits by all. Figure 11–6(b) on the other hand seems typical of (1) the small firms in these same oligopoly industries, (2) the small firms *wholly populating* monopolistically competitive markets, and (3) the few large oligopolists who just happen to be in markets with highly elastic short-run demands.

To small firms in monopolistically competitive industries, the high elasticity of Figure 11–6(b) is a tempting illusion of nonfollowship. The consequences of their price cutting copy those of Figure 11–4 seen earlier. Their price competition magnetically draws them down the followship curve to points like M in Figure 11–6(a). On the other hand, these elastic curves may *not* be illusory to the small firms that play in the yards of large oligopolists. If the large firms in an oligopolistic industy are intent on maintaining price for reasons defined in Figure 11–6(a), their smaller rivals may correctly see nonfollowship curves of the Figure 11–6(b) variety. At the very least, those who play at the knees of big oligopolists would be strongly tempted to test just how real their nonfollowship curves really were. Several predictions concerning the cyclical variability of prices and quantities naturally follow:

1. Within oligopolies, small "fringe" firms are more likely than large firms to be the sole price cutters or to lead the industry in a general round of price shading when demand flags.

2. Within oligopolies, the large firms are more likely than small firms to cut output in the face of slack demand.

3. Price stability and quantity variability should be associated with concentrated oligopolies—as opposed to unconcentrated oligopolies, monopolistic competition, or pure competition.

Although considerations of demand elasticity have led us to these hypotheses, cost considerations would bolster them, especially the first two. For various reasons the short-run cost curves of smaller firms are often higher and steeper in slope than the cost curves of large firms. The implications of this for price and output policy may be seen by mentally lifting the ATC curve of Figure 11–6 (b) a little higher than it is, then giving it a slight clockwise twist. The break-even point shifts to the right. The firm then would want all the more to maintain full capacity utilization.[19]

B. The Evidence

Evidence for the first two hypotheses comes mainly from *intra*industry experiences. The third hypothesis receives its greatest support from systematic *inter*industry statistical studies. Hence, we postpone our empirical exploration of the third hypothesis, and turn directly to the first two.

For small-firm price cutting during slumps we have space for only a few stories:

• During the 15 months prior to January, 1975, the U.S. sank into a very severe recession; U.S. auto sales plunged 25% from mediocre 1973 levels; and the industry cut back capacity use close to 50%. Price reductions were resisted. Indeed, GM led price increases averaging $1,000 per car. Then that January, Chrysler, the smallest of the big three, broke the ice by cutting price as much as $400 per car under its "Car Clearance Carnival" rebate program. For a while GM and Ford did not join the carnival: "It will be late in January before anybody really knows what's happening," said a Ford executive. Chrysler was sufficiently successful, however, that the Big Two and AMC soon followed.[20]

• The rebates lasted only six weeks. Thereafter, general recovery lifted *big* car sales substantially but *small* car sales only moderately. This created particular problems for "tiny" AMC. Hence, in November, 1976, AMC cut prices on Gremlins and Pacers by $253, or roughtly 7%. AMC said it was hoping this would boost its sales 30%, which implies a high nonfollowship elasticity estimate of 4.3. Unfortunately for AMC, GM followed with a $200 rebate program for three of its small car models that were also in excess supply.[21]

---

[19] This point is stressed by Markham, *op. cit.,* pp. 150–157.

[20] *Business Week* and *Wall Street Journal,* various issues. Benefits to consumers were in the neighborhood of $100 million.

[21] *Wall Street Journal,* Nov. 5, 1976 and Nov. 17, 1976.

• The president of a small rayon company once summarized price cutting in that industry with these words: ". . . when demand is not so great and there are large stocks on hand, some of the smaller producers, ourselves included, must of necessity be a little under the price of Viscose and Dupont. . . ."[22]

• In 1960–1961, capacity use in the steam turbine generator industry dropped to 60%. Allis-Chalmers, the industry's smallest producer, led a "dramatic plunge in price levels."[23]

• During the massive recession of 1981–1982, the airline industry fought intermittent price wars. One-way coach fares between New York and California, for example, plunged from $478 to $99. Relatively small carriers such as World Airways, Air Florida, Capitol International, and Continental Airlines triggered the discounting. The big guys had to follow, but they occasionally signalled for truce by attempting to lead fare increases. United Airlines said, "We didn't start it. We want to stop it."[24]

That should give you the idea. Many similar illustrations of the second hypothesis are available,[25] but one clear case will suffice. Column 1 of Table 11–2 presents the rated capacity of United States aluminum ingot producers in December 1974, expressed as a percentage of total industry capacity. These percentages would be market shares if all firms were producing at full capacity. The industry was not operating at full capacity during the first half of 1975, however, because of the severe recession. Thus, the second column of Table 11–2 reports each individual firm's percentage rate of capacity utilization in May 1975. It is not difficult to see that size and capacity utilization are *inversely* related. As the source of these data explains:

The three smallest firms operated at full capacity for the year 1975. These are remarkably high levels . . . considering that the impact of the recession on the aluminum industry was the worst in magnitude since the Great Depression. The explanation for this disparity in capacity utilization across firms of different size appears to be that the smaller firms used small discounts from list price to operate at full capacity levels, while the majors were holding prices at list. The larger firms chose to hold price and cut back production. . . .[26]

Although these experiences indicate that concentration helps secure short-run supply control (and thereby price control), concentration is not a conclusive or even a necessary condition. **Linear cost curves**, such as those used in drawing

[22] Markham, *op. cit.*, p. 75.

[23] R. G. M. Sultan, *Pricing in the Electric Oligopoly, Vol. I* (Cambridge, Mass.: Harvard University Press, 1974), pp. 151, 211.

[24] *Wall Street Journal*, October 19, 1981, p. 6; April 28, 1982, pp. 1, 24.

[25] For examples see Markham, *op. cit.*, p. 136–138; *Business Week*, October 28, 1972, pp. 39–40, and December 14, 1974, p. 27; D. O. Parsons and E. J. Ray, "The United States Steel Consolidation: The Creation of Market Control," *Journal of Law and Economics* (April 1975), pp. 214–215.

[26] Council on Wage and Price Stability, Staff Report, *Aluminum Prices* 1974–75 (Washington, D.C., U.S.G.P.O., 1976), p. 121. See also *Business Week*, Nov. 17, 1975, pp. 151–153.

TABLE 11–2. Distribution of Aluminum Capacity and
Capacity Utilization, 1975

Company	(1) Per Cent of U.S. Capacity (Dec. 1974)	(2) Per Cent Capacity Utilization Rate (May 1975)
Alcoa	32.0	74
Reynolds	19.8	67
Kaiser	14.7	73
Conalco	7.0	66
Anaconda	6.1	77
Howmet	4.4	85
Martin Marietta	4.2	80
Revere	4.0	62
National-South- wire	3.7	100
Alumax	2.7	99
Noranda	1.4	100

Source: Council on Wage and Price Stability, Staff Report, *Aluminum Prices 1974–75* (Washington, D.C., 1976), p. 122.

Figure 11–6 are also helpful. If, for reasons of plant design or inherent technology, unit costs were to rise steeply on either side of 98% capacity utilization, the utilization rate would be much less flexible.[27]

Durability of product aids as well. Style change, organic decay, whatever shortens product life span: perishables tend to be marked down quickly if they are not moving briskly into the hands of consumers. Durability permits an alternating current of inventory accumulation and discharge that cushions the shock of abrupt swings in demand, thereby smoothing out the rough linkage between consumer's pantry and manufacturer's plant.[28] Indeed, the aluminum ingot industry usually relies more heavily on inventory variation than production variation because ingots are more than durable; they are cheaply storable. A measure of these ingot qualities is that the majors used to maintain two pounds of fabrication capacity for every one pound of ingot capacity.[29]

For related reasons, **vertical integration** also helps supply control, although in its case the linkage secured may run from the consumer all the way back

[27] G. Stigler, "Production and Distribution in the Short Run," *Journal of Political Economy* (June 1939), pp. 305–327. For examples of "go" or "no go" facilities, see J. M. Blair, *Economic Concentration* (New York: Harcourt Brace Jovanovich, 1972), p. 282; Andrew Likierman, "Pricing Policy in the Texturising Industry, 1958–71," *Journal of Industrial Economics* (September 1981), pp. 25–38.

[28] F. M. Scherer, *Industrial Market Structure and Economic Performance* (Chicago: Rand McNally, 1970), pp. 149–156.

[29] M. J. Peck, *Competition in the Aluminum Industry 1945–1958* (Cambridge, Mass.: Harvard University Press, 1961), Chapter 6.

to the mineral pit, as in petroleum and steel.[30] An example of a *lack* of vertical integration contributing to price combat arose recently in the paper linerboard industry. It started in January 1977, when a nonintegrated company, Great Northern Nekoosa, slashed prices from $215 a ton to $195 a ton:

> Most of the other major producers have integrated operations that produce both linerboard and the finished box. But Great Northern sells all its linerboard on the open market. Mr. Bellis said, "It is fine for the integrated producers to say don't cut price when half the time they're taking it out of one pocket and putting it into another." He added: "If we hadn't cut prices our customers would have deserted us."[31]

Finally, and perhaps most important, there are a variety of **pricing mechanisms** or **rules of thumb**, that, when either imposed or voluntarily adopted, contribute to price stability by providing guidance, uniformity, or centralization to what might otherwise tend to be a rather diffuse, chaotic, even competitive pricing process. These mechanisms or rules of thumb serve purposes other than cyclical price stabilization. Indeed, they are vital to daily decision making and they foster industry discipline in good times as well as bad. Therefore, they warrant special attention.

III. PRICING MECHANISMS AND RULES OF THUMB

One thing to remember while reviewing these pricing mechanisms and rules of thumb is that their incidence and effectiveness varies according to market structure. Their usage is not randomly distributed; their impact is not always trenchant. Incidentally, their names are not exactly catchy either; cost-plus pricing, target-profit pricing, price leadership, cartelization, and government tampering.

A. Cost-plus and Target-profit Pricing[32]

Cost-plus or "full-cost" pricing usually involves estimating the average variable costs of producing and distributing the product, adding a charge for overhead, and then adding a percentage markup for profits. In retailing, adding a common percentage markup to the wholesale cost of goods sold is quite common. Target-profit pricing is a variant of cost-plus pricing with an important application in manufacturing. It was originally devised by GM executives to achieve a target rate of profit while maintaining price and flexing output. The technique is illustrated in Figure 11–7, which may be considered a total-dollars version of Figure 11–6(a).

[30] M. G. de Chazeau and A. E. Kahn, *Integration and Competition in the Petroleum Industry* (New Haven, Conn.: Yale University Press, 1959), Chapter 17; W. Adams and J. B. Dirlam, "Steel Imports and Vertical Oligopoly Power," *American Economic Review* (September 1964), pp. 626–655.

[31] *Wall Street Journal,* February 4, 1977.

[32] For details see Kent B. Monroe, *Pricing: Making Profitable Decisions* (New York: McGraw-Hill, 1979), pp. 51–102.

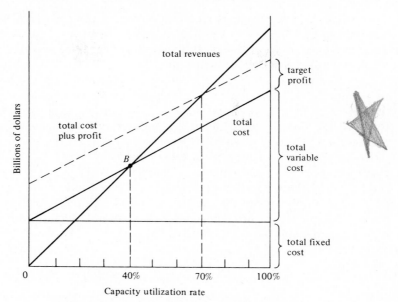

FIGURE 11–7. Target profit pricing model.

Target profit is defined as a certain percentage of investment, not sales. Hence, the technique is not simply a matter of wedging a nice profit percentage into price. Multiplying the target of, say, 40% before taxes times total investment yields a "hoped-for" dollar target profit. When this target profit is added to total cost, the result is the top broken line of Figure 11–7. Notice that target profit does not vary with output, but total costs do. Since target-dollar profit does not vary with output, the apparent implication is that the firm will have to *raise* price in recessions and *cut* price in booms. But such actions would drive customers away just when they are most needed and attract them when already abundant. The trick is to set price in such a way that the firm earns its target *on average* over the cycle while holding price fairly constant.

The firm achieves this balance by calculating cost and profit per unit on the basis of **standard volume**, or average output, which in Figure 11–7 is 70% of capacity. Thus, for example, if GM's standard volume is 5 million cars and its pretax target profit $5 billion, profit per standard volume car would be set at $1000 ($5 billion/5 million cars). If hypothetical overhead is $10 billion, fixed cost per standard volume car is then $2000 ($10 billion/5 million cars). With variable costs of $2500 per car, price comes to $5500 ($1000 + $2000 + $2500); and this price will determine the slope of the total revenue line in Figure 11–7. Of course, this example abstracts from the realities of many model lines, occasional rebate programs, and escalating costs of production over time.[33]

[33] *Wall Street Journal,* October 23, 1981, pp. 1, 25.

CONDUCT

But the idea is clear. In good years, with production above standard volume, realized profit will exceed target profit, as total revenues in Figure 11–7 exceed total cost plus target profit. In slack years, the opposite holds. On average, the target will be grazed if not hit squarely.

Interview surveys and case studies reveal widespread use of these various techniques. R. L. Hall and C. J. Hitch canvassed 38 firms and determined that 30 of them followed some form of cost-plus or target pricing.[34] Fog's study of 138 Danish firms turned up evidence that the most usual method among them could be considered "flexible full-cost pricing."[35] A. Silberston concludes his review of British pricing studies by saying that "full cost can be given a mark of beta query plus."[36] Finally, A. D. H. Kaplan, J. B. Dirlam, and R. F. Lanzillotti interviewed officials in 20 large United States corporations, ten of which were apparently using target-profit techniques. Besides GM, the ten included such renowned companies as U.S. Steel, DuPont, General Electric, Alcoa, International Harvester, and Union Carbide.[37] However, few of these firms had targets as high as GM's 20% after taxes. In fact, one aimed for only 8%.

These several studies touched off a heated debate over whether firms maximized profits. In light of our last chapter, we shall not pursue this question here other than to note that target-profit and cost-plus pricing are not necessarily inconsistent with profit maximization, especially in the long run. As A. E. Kahn has observed, one should not confuse *procedures* with *goals*.[38] Some may use the target procedure to shoot for only 8%, but that may be the best they can do. One thing all successful target pricers share in common is a substantial ability to control supply in the short run.

B. Price Leadership

Many of the firms not classified as target or cost-plus pricers in the studies cited previously could be considered followers of larger "price leaders" who do employ such techniques. "The development of price leadership in large-scale industry," according to some experts, "has roots in the earlier experience of violent price fluctuation and cut-throat competition, which culminated in consoli-

[34] Hall and Hitch, *op. cit.*
[35] Fog, *op. cit.*, p. 217. This description also fits A. A. Fitzpatrick's finding for glass containers, paint, and furniture. *Pricing Methods of Industry* (Boulder, Colorado: Pruett Press, 1964).
[36] A. Silberston, "Price Behavior of Firms," *Economic Journal* (September 1970), p. 545.
[37] A. D. H. Kaplan, J. B. Dirlam, and R. F. Lanzillotti, *Pricing in Big Business* (Washington, D.C.: Brookings Institution, 1958); and R. F. Lanzillotti, "Pricing Objectives of Large Companies," *American Economic Review* (December 1958), pp. 921–940. An executive of U.S. Steel once explained their policy as follows: "If customers don't buy their steel [in a slump] there isn't too much you can do about it . . . I doubt that you would go out and buy two new cars instead of one if steel prices were cut. . . . Over the long pull, American steel mills have operated at about 75 percent average capacity. If you operate at 90 percent over a stretch, you've then got to figure on a stretch at 60 percent of capacity. Basically you must be able to make adequate profits at the average." G. J. McManus, *The Inside Story of Steel Wages and Prices 1959–1967* (Philadelphia: Chilton Book Co., 1967), p. 63.
[38] A. E. Kahn, "Pricing Objectives of Large Companies: Comment," *American Economic Review* (September 1959), pp. 670–678.

TABLE 11–3. Outline of Three Broad Types of Price Leadership

Characteristic	Dominant Firm Leadership	Collusive Price Leadership	Barometric Price Leadership
Concentration ratio	Very high one-firm ratio	Medium to high four-firm ratio	Low four-firm ratio
Leader's Qualification	Immense relative size and efficiency	Size, age, custom, efficiency	Forecasting ability, sensitivity
Cost across firms	Diverse	Roughly similar	Diverse
Changes in who leads?	Never	Occasionally	Often
Disciplinary problems	Never	Sometimes	Frequently
Followship lags	Never	Temporary	Leader "lags"
Examples	Aluminum (until recently), computers	Steel, cigarettes	Gasoline, turbines

dation of competitors, as in steel, copper, oil production, tin cans, and farm equipment. Such experience has generated a distinct predisposition on the part of managements to avoid price changes except through periodic, well-considered, and well-publicized alterations in recognized *base* prices."[39] Under a diversity of structural conditions, price leadership takes many forms, but compressing them into three broad types will simplify the situation. These types are dominant-firm leadership, collusive leadership, and barometric leadership.[40] Table 11–3 summarizes the salient characteristics of each type.

1. Dominant-Firm Leadership. Dominant-firm price leadership is a giant/pygmy situation. One firm controls 50–95% of the market. Awed by its immense size and efficiency, the smaller firms willingly, if sheepishly, accept its leadership. Because unit costs of the fringe firms typically exceed those of the dominant firm materially, the small fry refrain from cutting prices below those set by the leader. Moreover, they virtually always follow the leader's up-side price changes without hesitation. This means that the leader's disciplinary problems are few and far between. It also indicates that fringe firms probably prefer a

[39] Kaplan, Dirlam, and Lanzillotti, *op. cit.,* p. 271.
[40] J. W. Markham, "The Nature and Significance of Price Leadership," *American Economic Review* (December 1951), pp. 891–905; Scherer, *op. cit.,* pp. 164–173.

higher level of price than the leader usually sets for the market. As with the other summary descriptions of Table 11–3, the illustration posits generalities that do not fit any particular industry perfectly, but there are a few examples that fit the dominant firm mold fairly well. Not surprisingly, many examples come from the annals of Section 2 Sherman Act prosecutions—United Shoe Machinery, IBM, and Alcoa. In the case of Alcoa, we refer to the period of 1946–1965, during which time Alcoa did face some domestic competition but was still quite dominant. In those years Reynolds and Kaiser repeatedly expressed their preferences for prices higher than those Alcoa selected.[41] Of late, Alcoa's dominance has waned, as was implied by our earlier discussion of Table 11–2.

2. Collusive Price Leadership. This might better describe aluminum nowadays. Typifying this category are medium-to-high four-firm concentration ratios; a leader whose relatively large size (say, 20–30% of the market) and ancient lineage signify qualities befitting an industrial chieftain; a cost structure across firms that is uniform enough to generate fairly harmonious notions about what the industry's price level should be; widespread agreement among the oligopolists over long periods of time as to who their leader should be; few disciplinary problems with "chiselers"; and lags in followership short enough to save the leader from repeated embarrassment.

The cigarette industry provides a classic example from the era when non-filtered regulars were all you could buy.[42] After the Sherman Act dissolution of American Tobacco in 1911, the industry came to be divided primarily between Reynolds, American, and Liggett & Myers. The popularity of "Camels" gave Reynolds a 40% share of the market by 1920, top spot, and rights to leadership. Between 1923 and 1941, American and Liggett & Myers stuck to Reynolds' prices like a Marlboro tattoo. There were eight list price changes during the period. Reynolds led six of them, five up and one down, with the others following usually not more than a day behind. The two Reynolds did *not* lead were price *cuts* initiated by American in 1933 that were necessitated by remarkable circumstances.

The circumstances were these: As the nation slid into the Great Depression and the prices of leaf tobacco and other cigarette materials were falling along with commodity prices in general, R. J. Reynolds led two bold increases in the wholesale price of cigarettes—7% in October 1929 and another 7% in June 1931. Consequently, retail prices of popular brands wound up at 15 cents. Now this may not seem like much by today's inflated standards, but it was enough to give the three companies profits that exceeded 30% of net sales less tax. At the time of the last of these 7% increases the so-called "10-cent" brands accounted for less than 1% of the total market. For obvious reasons,

[41] M. J. Peck, *op. cit.,* Chapter 4.
[42] William Nicholls, *Price Policies in the Cigarette Industry* (Nashville, Tenn.: Vanderbilt University Press, 1951); R. B. Tennant, *The American Cigarette Industry* (New Haven, Conn.: Yale University Press, 1950).

however, their sales thereafter skyrocketed to account eventually for more than 20% of the market in the final two months of 1932. Upon feeling this slap, the three large companies retaliated. American led a 12% wholesale price cut on January 3, 1933, then initiated a second cut of 8% one month later, bringing the retail prices of the three companies down to 10 and 11 cents. This knocked the 10-cent brands' market share back to 7% almost immediately. After about a year the three large companies slowly began to raise their prices again. The renewed escalation enabled the 10-cent brands to regain a bit of their lost ground but never to recoup it completely.

From 1901 until 1962 U.S. Steel served as leader in steel, thus providing another example of collusive leadership. Even in 1939, after U.S. Steel's market share had dwindled to less than 40%, the president of one of its larger rivals said that the "pace is set, if that is a good word, by the Steel Corporation."[43] During the first 15 years after World War II, U.S. Steel led the industry in 11 of its 12 price increases. But then in April 1962 U.S. Steel fell from grace. Just five days after signing a modest wage settlement with the steelworkers' union that could not have increased the industry's unit labor costs, U.S. Steel announced a price increase of $6 a ton that was quickly followed by all but a few other producers.

Only four months earlier President Kennedy had introduced his wage-price "guidepost" program, designed to stem inflation. He also had a hand in the union's wage restraint. Thus Kennedy could not ignore big Steel's brassiness. He publicly castigated the industry's executives, calling them "irresponsible." (Privately, he called them "S.O.B's" and "bastards."[44]) This helped Inland and Kaiser Steel to decide a few days later that they would not follow U.S. Steel's lead. Whereupon first Bethlehem, then U.S. Steel, and then the others rescinded their increases.

Now there is no clearly identifiable leader in steel. U.S. Steel's market share has shriveled to about 20% and vigorous new competition comes from imports and so-called "minimills."[45] Indeed, structural and behavioral changes have been so great that the industry has drifted toward barometric price leadership.[46]

3. Barometric Price Leadership. Under barometric price leadership, conditions are substantially competitive. Use of the word "leadership" in this case may even be misleading. The leader is often no more than the first firm to announce formal revisions in *list* or *book* prices to reflect prevailing *realized* or *transactions* prices. In other words, the leader's main qualification in this case is his acute sensitivity to market pressures. The barometric leader "commands adherence

[43] L. W. Weiss, *Economics and American Industry* (New York: John Wiley & Sons, 1961), p. 293.

[44] A. M. Schlesinger, Jr., *A Thousand Days* (Boston: Houghton Mifflin Co., 1965), p. 531.

[45] Walter Adams and Hans Mueller, "The Steel Industry," *The Structure of American Industry*, (New York: MacMillan, 1982), pp. 73–135.

[46] Such a transformation recently occurred in the British oil industry. R. M. Grant, "Pricing Behavior in the UK Wholesale Market for Petrol 1970–80," *Journal of Industrial Economics* (March 1982), pp. 271–292.

of rivals to his price only because, and to the extent that, his price reflects market conditions with tolerable promptness."[47] If the firm actually does lead, it should be a good forecaster of the imminent trend, especially on the up side. International Paper Company illustrates the consequences of up-side error. Its unsuccessful attempt to lead an increase in late 1976 cost it 100,000 tons of production, 1.4 percentage points off its 12.7% market share, and a bundle of profits.[48] Other indices that ironclad coordination is lacking under barometric leadership include a diversity of cost levels across firms, frequent changes in the identity of the leader, bigger disciplinary problems than are found under dominant firm and collusive leadership, and substantial lags in followship should the leader act more as a forecaster than as an announcer of prevailing reality.

Barometric leaders usually occupy unconcentrated industries as well, but not always. This last fact underscores the lack of precision in these three categories of leadership. For example, during the 1950s the steam turbine electric generator market was highly concentrated. General Electric (GE) (with a 60% share), Westinghouse (with 30%), and Allis-Chalmers (with 10%) accounted for all United States production. Moreover, in book prices, GE was the undisputed leader. GE's price book was the Sears' catalog of the industry, and the others copied it to the letter.[49] Still, in *transactions* prices, GE appears to have been only a barometric leader. This is shown in Figure 11–8, which charts an index of the industry's transactions prices together with GE's transactions prices *relative* to those of its rivals. Notice that GE's transactions prices were slightly *below* its rivals' prices during periods of high demand and rising industry prices. Conversely, GE's transactions prices were slightly *above* its rivals' prices during periods of slack demand and falling industry prices. A partial explanation for this behavior was GE's desire to maintain a 60% market share while serving as leader. During slumps GE's share would diminish as rivals priced beneath it. During booms its share would be restored as rivals eagerly took advantage of the opportunity to advance their prices while GE acted in a more leisurely way.

C. Cartelization

Another feature to notice in Figure 11–8 is the sharp rise in turbine generator prices after 1954, a rise that is followed by an equally sharp fall after 1959. During the years in between, GE, Westinghouse, and Allis-Chalmers conspired to fix prices—that is, they operated a loose-knit cartel. All in all, the price fixing extended to 19 other electrical equipment products, to 26 other firms, and, in these broader respects, to many years before 1955. This is a fascinating bit of evidence drawn from a much larger topic than we can treat now. Hence the next chapter is devoted entirely to cartelization. Here we may note in passing that securing a uniformity of behavior among otherwise competitive firms is the essence of cartelization. Cooperation is refined, formalized, and often pursued

[47] Stigler, *op. cit.* (1947), pp. 445–446.
[48] *Business Week,* May 2, 1977, p. 54.
[49] Sultan, *op. cit.,* pp. 213–214.

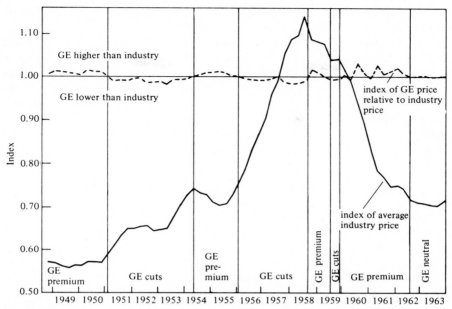

FIGURE 11–8. GE and industry prices of turbine electricity generators. Source: Ralph G. M. Sultan, *Pricing in the Electrical Oligopoly,* Vol. 1 (Boston: Division of Research, Graduate School of Business Administration, Harvard University, 1974), p. 282.

with vigor. When cartelization is applied to pricing, the results can include less variation across firms, greater stability over time, and, as suggested in Figure 11–8, higher absolute levels of price. It will be shown in the next chapter that structural conditions affect the ease with which cartel agreements can be privately devised. As you might guess, fewness of firms and high market concentration are conducive to cartel conduct.

D. Government Intervention

With minor exceptions *private* cartelization is illegal in the United States. Cartelization nevertheless permeates many industries. Sanctioned and supervised by various governmental bodies, it has spread under the cover of more euphemistic names such as "parity price supports," "marketing agreements," "oil prorationing," "collective bargaining," and "regulation." The list could easily be expanded to include various forms of cartelization affecting United States foreign trade. In many instances, the government was pushed into these policies at the insistence of politically powerful commercial groups. These groups believed that supply control and price stability would be of dramatic benefit to them. They also perceived the possibility of gaining higher *absolute* prices, profits, and incomes as well, but they were not in a position to attain these several objectives without the government's help. Generally speaking, their industries and markets were *too* competitively structured to secure these ends by price

257

leadership or similar informal cooperation (or even secret, illegal cartelization). Thus, stripped to its essentials, the government's agricultural price support program attempts to curtail production and keep "surplus" commodities off the market during periods of slack demand or inadvertently abundant production. When demand expands or nature withholds, land is allowed back into production, excess inventories are disgorged, and so forth. Of course in this industry the business cycle causes only a fraction of the demand curves' volatility. Foreign demand for our exports dances to the cruel tune of foreign droughts, freezes, floods, blights, and pestilent hordes. Forms of government cartelization other than those in agriculture will be taken up in later chapters.

IV. CROSS-SECTION STATISTICAL EVIDENCE[50]

We are finally ready for the evidence concerning *inter*industry differences in cyclical price behavior. Figure 11–9 restates the main hypothesis. Its horizontal axis measures positive and negative percentage changes in quantity, whereas its vertical axis indicates positive and negative percentage changes in price. Instances in which competitive industries have displayed almost perfect vertical movement along the vertical axis exist. In these cases quantity has remained fairly constant, while price has absorbed the cyclical swing. Conversely, there are also instances of highly concentrated industries moving horizontally along the $+\Delta Q - \Delta Q$ axis, displaying very little change in price for enormous variations in quantity.[51]

Although these are the extreme patterns our earlier theory may have suggested, the theory was deliberately oversimplified. A more realistic but still abstract view of the matter is depicted by the diagonal lines of Figure 11–9. The solid lines going through the origin show prices in unconcentrated industries (low CR) rising more during booms and falling more during slumps than prices in highly concentrated industries (high CR). So oligopolistic prices might not be absolutely "rigid"—merely "sticky," or, more precisely, "relatively sticky" as compared to competitive prices. The dashed lines of Fig. 11–9 indicate that this hypothesis could still hold during broad-based secular inflation. In other words, both diagonals going through the origin have equal parts of plus and minus price change for an overall average of zero net change. Regrettably, we have of late experienced *general* inflation, with prices typically going up faster or slower but almost always going up. The dashed diagonals thus indicate the same degree of stickiness and variability amidst secular inflation as the solid diagonals do with no net inflation.

The first evidence confirming the presence of relatively inflexible prices among

[50] Other surveys of the statistical evidence that have influenced this section are A. E. Kahn, "Market Power Inflation: A Conceptual Overview," in *The Roots of Inflation* (New York: Burt Franklin & Co., 1975); R. E. Beals, "Concentrated Industries, Administered Prices, and Inflation: A Survey of Recent Empirical Research," Report to the Council of Wage and Price Stability (processed June 17, 1975); F. M. Scherer, *op. cit.*, Chapters 12, 13.

[51] F. C. Mills, *Price-Quantity Interactions in Business Cycles* (New York: National Bureau of Economic Research, 1946), pp. 29, 46–47.

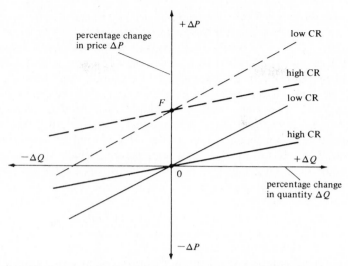

FIGURE 11–9. Price movements relative to quantity movements and concentration.

oligopolistic industries was presented by Gardner C. Means in 1935.[52] He called them "administered prices," and the name has stuck. Since that time Means has presented further positive evidence for subsequent periods. Unfortunately, he has been overselective in his choice of industries and time periods; overzealous in propounding his views; and occasionally inconsistent in his interpretations. As a consequence, he has stirred up a string of formidable critics.[53] A blow-by-blow account of the debates is unnecessary. The lessons to be learned may be stated simply: (1) There are many factors, such as costs, that are much more important than concentration in determining price changes, and (2) prices vary widely across industries for reasons too complex to pin down easily.

This is not to say, however, that concentration has no influence or that its influence is trivial. The weight of accumulated evidence now seems to rest on the side of Means (although it is not as impressive as Means would like to think). David Qualls computed year-to-year price change variance of 30 four-digit industries for which wholesale price data were available over the period 1957–1970. He then divided his sample into two groups, depending on whether the industry's four-firm concentration ratio was greater or less than 50%. Comparing the two groups, he found that average variance in the unconcentrated industries greatly exceeded average variance in the highly concentrated industries, 39.0% to 6.2%.[54]

[52] *Industrial Prices and their Relative Inflexibility,* " Senate Doc. 13, 74th Congress, First Session, 1935.
[53] See, e.g., G. J. Stigler, "Industrial Prices as Administered by Dr. Means," *American Economic Review* (September 1973), pp. 717–721; J. F. Weston, S. Lustgarten, and N. Grottke, "The Administered-Price Thesis Denied: Note," *American Economic Review* (March 1974), pp. 232–234.
[54] P. D. Qualls, "Price Stability in Concentrated Industries," *Southern Economic Journal* (October 1975), pp. 294–298.

259

Philip Cagan's comprehensive study of pricing during our post World War II recessions also lends support to the pattern of Figure 11–9.[55] He used wholesale price indexes for over 1,000 narrowly defined industries that he divided into three concentration categories—high, medium, and low. In all five recessions studied up through 1970, average prices in the high concentration category decreased *less* than those in the low concentration category. Moreover, Cagan found a shift over time that would correspond to a shift of the solid diagonals of Figure 11–9 up toward the dashed diagonals. Thus, during the 1969–1970 recession, only the low concentration category experienced any decline in average price levels. Prices in the medium and high groups actually increased.

Instead of examining raw prices, some researchers have explored changes in prices *less* variable costs, otherwise known as **price-cost gross margins.** The foregoing findings with respect to price fluctuations do not rule out the possibility that gross margins might behave independently of market power. On the other hand, our earlier theories suggest that margins, like prices, should be more flexible in competitive industries than in oligopolies. That is, they should compress more during slumps and expand more during booms, everything else being equal. Evidence on this point also goes as far back as the Great Depression. Once again it must be acknowledged that the evidence has been less than crystal clear and that conflicts of opinion have abounded. Still, the bulk of the best evidence seems to show an inverse relationship between concentration and margin flexibility. During cyclical *up*swings, margins tend to rise in competitive industries relative to those in oligopolistic industries; during *down*swings, the opposite occurs.[56]

These several findings concerning prices and gross margins in the United States receive independent corroboration from other studies. First, these patterns have been observed abroad in Canada and Japan.[57] They are supported also by United States and United Kingdom studies of a different genre. Tests of

[55] P. Cagan, "Changes in the Recession Behavior of Wholesale Prices in the 1920's and Post-World War II," *Explorations in Economic Research NBER* (Winter 1975), pp. 54–104. See also A. S. Eichner, "A Theory of the Determination of the Mark-up Under Oligopoly," *Economic Journal* (December 1973), p. 1187; and L. W. Weiss, "Stigler, Kindahl, and Means on Administered Prices," *American Economic Review* (September 1977), pp. 610–619.

[56] A. C. Neal, *Industrial Concentration and Price Inflexibility* (Washington, D.C.: American Council on Public Affairs, 1942); L. W. Weiss, "Business Pricing Policies and Inflation Reconsidered," *Journal of Political Economy* (April 1966), pp. 177–187; P. Cagan, "Inflation and Market Structure," *Explorations in Economic Research* (Spring 1975), pp. 203–216; J. A. Dalton, "Administered Inflation and Business Pricing: Another Look," *Review of Economics and Statistics* (November 1973), pp. 516–519; H. N. Ross, "The Determination of Industrial Price Flexibility," *Industrial Organization Review* (No. 3, 1975), pp. 115–129; H. J. Sherman, *Profits in the United States* (Ithaca, N.Y.: Cornell University Press, 1968), Chapters 6 and 7. For contrary evidence see P. D. Qualls, "Market Structure and Cyclical Flexibility of Price-Cost Margins," *Journal of Business* (April 1979), pp. 305–325.

[57] W. Sellekaerts and Richard Lesage, "A Reformulation and Empirical Verification of the Administered Prices Inflation Hypothesis: The Canadian Case," *Southern Economic Journal* (January 1973), pp. 345–360; K. Dennis, "Market Power and the Behavior of Industrial Prices," *Essays on Price Changes in Canada* (Ottawa: Prices and Incomes Commission, 1973), pp. 53–91; R. E. Caves and M. Uekusa, *Industrial Organization in Japan* (Washington, D.C.: Brookings Institution, 1976), p. 97; J. J. McRae and F. Tapon, "A New Test of the Administered Pricing Hypothesis with Canadian Data," *Journal of Business* (July 1979), pp. 409–427.

the relationship between market power and the temporal variance of profits as a per cent of assets or stockholders equity disclose an inverse association between concentration and profit variance.[58] Then too there appears to be a consistent and significant positive relationship between *employment* variability and seller concentration.[59]

In short, the evidence does not refute the foregoing theories, and your patience with this chapter has not gone for naught. Unfortunately, the behavior observed does wear on the patience of our aggregate economic policy makers. Historically, their main weapon against price inflation has been the occasional curtailment of aggregate demand by means of fiscal and monetary restraint. The idea is that reduced demand reduces prices. But to the extent that market power inhibits price reductions, application of this policy does little more than increase unemployment. Arthur Burns, former chief of United States money supply operations, has often expressed his frustrations. He once said that "Improved policies of managing aggregate demand, important though they may be, will not of themselves suffice to assure prosperity without inflation. Structural reforms are also needed."[60]

SUMMARY

Between August 1982 and February 1983 the wholesale price of gasoline fell about 16 cents a gallon. Reflecting their lower costs, gasoline retailers cut their price to motorists by about 14 cents a gallon. In contrast, the wholesale price of home heating oil fell about 15 cents a gallon during the same months, but the reduction was *not* passed on to consumers by heating oil retailers. Why the big difference? "One reason," according to the *Wall Street Journal,* "is that the gasoline business is more competitive than the heating oil business."[61]

Cournot would understand this contrast if he were still alive. Fortunately, his theory of interdependence is still alive to help us understand the contrast. His theory has been improved upon, however.

[58] J. Samuels and D. Smyth, "Profits, Variability of Profits, and Firm Size," *Economica* (May 1968), pp. 127–139; F. R. Edwards and A. A. Heggestad, "Uncertainty, Market Structure, and Performance," *Quarterly Journal of Economics* (August 1973), pp. 456–473. The last one complements F. R. Edwards, "Concentration in Banking and Its Effect on Business Loan Rates," *Review of Economics and Statistics* (August 1964), pp. 294–300, where it is shown that bank concentration and interest rate flexibility are inversely related.

[59] D. S. Smith, "Concentration and Employment Fluctuations," *Western Economic Journal* (September 1971), pp. 267–277; H. Demsetz, "Where is the New Industrial State?" *Economic Inquiry* (March 1974), pp. 1–12; Robert M. Feinberg, "Market Structure and Employment Instability," *Review of Economics and Statistics* (November 1979), pp. 497–505. On a closely related point see Raymond S. Hartman, "Some Evidence on Differential Inventory Behavior in Competitive and Noncompetitive Market Settings," *Quarterly Review of Economics and Business* (Summer 1980), pp. 11–27.

[60] Arthur Burns, *Industrial Reorganization Act Hearings,* U.S. Senate Subcommittee on Antitrust and Monopoly, Part 1 (1973), p. 47.

[61] *Wall Street Journal,* February 18, 1983, p. 19. For a similar contrast in behavior on a much broader scale see Peter M. Holmes, *Industrial Pricing Behavior and Devaluation* (London: Macmillan, 1978).

CONDUCT

Analysis of short-run price and production policy under oligopoly and monopolistic competition now centers on the firm's twofold demand curves. These curves' price elasticities, shapes, visibilities, and shifts tell most of the story. The followship curve reflects market-wide demand and is typically rather inelastic. Conversely, the nonfollowship demand curve reflects switches of market share. The smaller the firm and the more standardized the product, therefore, the more price elastic the nonfollowship curve is. Under monopolistic competition all firms face highly elastic nonfollowship demand curves. The phoney promises these curves give price cutters of increased total revenue are too alluring to resist. Abundant small firm populations also keep interdependence unrecognized and followship demand curves invisible. The result is price competition.

Under oligopoly, with its fewer and larger firms, interdependence is recognized. Kinked demand theory explains why price cuts are resisted. To large firms the nonfollowship demand curve is less elastic and therefore less alluring than to small firms. Even more important, only the followship demand curve is visible on the down side. On the up side, only strong dominant price leaders see the followship demand curve. The theory's major implication is rigid prices, or, when amended by certain realities such as inflation, *relatively* rigid prices (especially on the down side).

This implication holds even in the face of fluctuating demand. Supply control facilitates the maintenance of prices and profits within a given cycle, plus greater stability across numerous cycles. Comparatively large firms (with relatively inelastic demand curves) appreciate this quality of supply control the most. The elastic nonfollowship demand curves of smaller firms often entice them into secret discounting or thinly veiled price cutting when demand is slack. Intraindustry experiences repeatedly demonstrate the different views large and small firms have of the same market.

Short-run stability, guidance, coordination, and uniformity are furthered by various "mechanisms" or pricing procedures. The most important of these are cost-plus pricing, target-profit pricing, price leadership, and cartelization. These techniques tend to be most highly refined, most consistently adhered to, and most commonly observed in markets displaying stronger as opposed to lesser market power. Those in markets of lesser market power must rely on government intervention, usually in some form of cartelization, to secure the discipline that cyclical supply control requires.

Finally, cross-section evidence is not altogether solid. Still, it seems to show relatively inflexible prices and gross margins in industries bearing ossified structures as compared to those displaying more competitive characteristics. Interindustry studies of profits and employment corroborate this inference.

12 Price and Production Behavior: Cartel Practice and Policy

Between 1969 and 1973 I saw the retail price of a loaf of bread in Phoenix go from 35¢ to 69¢. At least 15% of that increase could be traced to our conspiracy. There's no question that price-fixing is a cost factor for the consumer.

—Confession of DONALD PHILLIPS, former vice-president of Baird's Bread Co.

In a word, the subject of this chapter is cartelization. Broadly defined, a **cartel** *is an explicit arrangement among, or on behalf of, enterprises in the same line of business that is designed to limit competition among them.*[1] The concept includes price-fixing, explicit collusion, and conspiracy. It might involve no more than a sociable discussion of prices over cocktails, or it might be so complex as to involve sales quotas, customer allocations, weekly meetings, enforcement committees, penalty formulas, and kangaroo courts. There are buyer cartels and seller cartels. They may be open or secret, governmental or private, legal or illegal, local or international.

Cartels fit within the short-run context of the preceding chapter for many reasons. When privately devised, they are often short-lived. Their purpose, moreover, is frequently (if not usually) price stabilization rather than flagrant price escalation. Then too, their popularity among businessmen seems to vary inversely with the business cycle. But the fit is very imperfect. Cartels, it must be emphatically acknowledged, are not always "short-run" phenomena. As suggested by this chapter's opening quote, cartels may last for years. The British/Indian ocean liner shipping "conference" celebrated its *centennial* anniversary in 1975. The electrical equipment price fixing conspiracy operated intermittently for over 20 years.

Cartels may also raise prices and profits sharply. Some recent evidence indicates that a sample of large United States firms involved in illegal price fixing had *lower* profits than other large firms, thus suggesting a short-run "preventive"

---

[1] G. W. Stocking and M. W. Watkins, *Cartels or Competition* (New York: Twentieth Century Fund, 1948), p. 3.

purpose to their activity.[2] But there are also numerous instances of prices increasing from 30 to 60%, even hundreds of per cents, under cartels.[3] The most famous cartel of all time—the Organization of Petroleum Exporting Countries, or OPEC—gained global notoriety by quadrupling the price of crude oil in 1973 and then tacking on price increases at fairly regular intervals during the decade thereafter.

In short, "the typical purpose and effect of cartelization is to set prices higher than would prevail under competition, to reduce them as seldom as possible, and to raise them further whenever the opportunity permits."[4] Attainment of these ends often requires restrictions extending beyond price and output. Advertising, product quality, and other variables have felt the grasp of concerted business practices. Unavoidably, then, this chapter is more than just an elaboration of the preceding chapter's short-run pricing subjects. It introduces the long-run subjects of the next chapter and other aspects of conduct as well.

We begin by surveying United States government policy. A study of structural conditions favorable to cartelization follows. We then review the electrical equipment cases and conclude with an extended discussion of the crude petroleum industry and OPEC.

I. UNITED STATES GOVERNMENT POLICY

A. Per Se Violation

"Every contract, combination . . . or conspiracy, in restraint of trade or commerce among the several States, or with foreign nations, is hereby declared to be illegal." So reads Section 1 of the Sherman Act of 1890. It is the backbone of United States antitrust policy. There are numerous exemptions (regulated industries, export cartels, and milk among them), but this is the basic policy applying to most interstate commerce. As enforced, the law is rather empty of economic content, for violation is a *per se* offense. That is to say, explicit (albeit secret) collusion to fix prices, allocate territories, or otherwise rig the market is illegal *regardless* of the reasonableness or unreasonableness of the economic consequences. The only proof required is proof that conspiracy actually occurred. Indeed, mere *attempts* to fix prices are punishable. This dictum contrasts markedly with the "rule of reason" approach to monopolization cases.

Stringent interpretation of the law dates back to 1897, when the Supreme

---

[2] P. Asch and J. J. Seneca, "Is Collusion Profitable?" *Review of Economics and Statistics* (February 1976), pp. 1–12. But see on the other hand Robert M. Feinberg, "Antitrust Enforcement and Subsequent Price Behavior," *Review of Economics and Statistics* (November 1980), pp. 609–612.

[3] See, e.g., W. B. Erickson, "Price Fixing Conspiracies: Their Long-term Impact," *Journal of Industrial Economics* (March 1976), pp. 189–202; and W. F. Mueller, "Effects of Antitrust Enforcement in the Retail Food Industry," *Antitrust Law & Economics Review* (Winter 1968–69), pp. 86–87.

[4] Corwin D. Edwards, *Economic and Political Aspects of International Cartels* (Washington, D.C.: Subcommittee on War Mobilization of the Committee on Military Affairs, U.S. Senate, 1944), p. 13.

Court decided *U.S. v. Trans-Missouri Freight Association.* The Court's most explicit early expression of the *per se* doctrine is found in its 1927 opinion *U.S. v. Trenton Potteries.* Twenty three corporations producing 82% of the vitreous pottery fixtures (bathroom bowls, tubs, and so on) in the United States were accused of conspiring to fix prices and limit production. The Court rejected their argument that the "reasonableness" of their prices should be considered, saying that

> The aim and result of every price-fixing agreement, if effective, is the elimination of one form of competition. The power to fix prices, whether reasonably exercised or not, involves power to control the market and to fix arbitrary and unreasonable prices. The reasonable price fixed today may through economic and business changes become the unreasonable price of tomorrow. Once established, it may be maintained unchanged because of the absence of competition secured by the agreement for a price reasonable when fixed. Agreements which create such potential power may well be held to be *in themselves* unreasonable or unlawful restraints. . . .[5]

This rigorous standard of illegality might lead you to think that businessmen strenuously shun complicity in conspiracies for fear of being caught. Alas, life is not so simple. Well over a thousand civil and criminal prosecutions have been brought under Section 1 and many more will surely follow. Of late, the Justice Department has launched an average of 20 criminal cases a year. With bathroom bowls still fresh on our minds, we should mention that since *Trenton Potteries* in 1927, members of the vitreous plumbing fixture industry have twice been caught and found guilty of further price fixing (a most unsanitary record). The latest conspiracy, in the 1960s, came to light when Internal Revenue Service agents stumbled onto three tape recordings of price-fixing meetings stashed in the abandoned desk of a man they were investigating for income tax evasion. The 15 firms involved include American Standard, Borg-Warner, and Kohler Company. Estimates of impact indicate that prices were lifted roughly 7% on $1 billion worth of business. "Price fixing rather than competition has been a way of life in the industry," commented an industry official who testified as a key government witness.[6] Unfortunately, this example is not unique. Recidivism is quite common in antitrust.

B. Remedies

A major contributor to the problem of widespread and repeated offenses has been the prevalence of kid-glove penalties. Until very recently, criminal violations were merely misdemeanors; fines could be measured in peanuts ($50,000 at most); suspended sentences were fashionable; jailings were extremely rare and brief; and many civil cases were brought. In short, crime paid. Donald Phillips, the confessed price-fixer we quoted at the outset, put it this way: "When you're doing $30 million a year and stand to gain $3 million by fixing prices, a $30,000 fine doesn't mean much. Face it," he said, "most of us would be

---

[5] *United States v. Trenton Potteries,* 273 U.S. 392 (1927), p. 397. (Emphasis added).
[6] See *Washington Post,* June 6, 1971; and *Fortune,* December, 1969.

265

willing to spend 30 days in jail to make a few extra million dollars. Maybe if I were facing a year or more, I would think twice."[7]

Some trend toward more deterrent penalties has developed. Of the 54 persons who went to prison for price fixing and other pure antitrust violations between the passage of the Sherman Act in 1890 and January 1977, most of them served time after 1959. In addition, the Act was amended in 1974 to make criminal violation a *felony,* punishable by as much as 3 years in prison, with fines as high as $100,000 for individuals and $1 million for corporations.

Violators not only face these criminal sanctions, they may be sued by their victimized buyers for *three times* the financial loss suffered from the conspiracy. In the plumbing fixture case, treble damages were reckoned at $210 million, but out-of-court settlements with the victimized plaintiffs brought actual payments down to $28 million. In broader terms, the popularity of treble damage suits has burgeoned since 1960. At one time recently they were running at a rate of more than 2,000 suits per year, largely because the electrical equipment conspiracies had an immense scope. Since 1960, total damages collected by electric-cartel victims (plus the enviable fees collected by their lawyers) probably exceed $500 million.[8]

C. "Reserved Cities," "Dancing Partners," and "Poker"

Given a punitive per se rule, the key remaining question is *what* constitutes "price-fixing" or "collusive restraint." Businessmen have demonstrated skill when it comes to colluding. Their artistry may be divided into two broad categories—(1) cases with clear evidence of anticompetitive collusion, and (2) cases offering no more than circumstantial evidence. This section covers the first category. Subsequent sections handle the second.

For sheer simplicity of obvious evidence, no collusive technique tops the *single sales agency,* whereby producers refuse to sell directly to their customers and instead sell through a common central agency that sets price for all participants.[9] Equally obvious would be a short, written *contract* specifying minimum prices. Only a bit more complicated, is the *market allocation* approach, whereby each cartel member is assigned exclusive access to certain geographic areas or customers.

The classic *Addyston Pipe & Steel* case of 1899 provides a good example of this last tactic. Six manufacturers of cast iron pipe, including Addyston, entered into agreement that, among other things, assigned certain southern and central United States cities to individual members of the cartel. These "reserved cities" were the exclusive province of the designated member. The price at which pipe was sold in each reserved city was determined jointly by the cartel,

[7] *Business Week,* June 2, 1975, p. 48.
[8] For more on penalties see K. G. Elzinga and W. Breit, *The Antitrust Penalties: A Study in Law and Economics* (New Haven, Conn.: Yale University Press, 1976).
[9] To a large degree, this form governs the international diamond industry headed by De Beers. Even the USSR sells through De Beers. For fascinating accounts see Edward Jay Epstein, *The Rise and Fall of Diamonds* (New York: Simon & Schuster, 1982); *Fortune,* September 6, 1982, pp. 42–53; and *Business Week,* June 1, 1981, pp. 104–105.

the member to whom the business was assigned paying a fixed bonus into the cartel's profit sharing pool. In order to give appearances of continued competition other members submitted fictitious bids to customers in reserved cities, "fictitious" because these bids were always at prices higher than those charged by the designated member.[10]

Some forms of agreement involve no direct communications concerning price. Nevertheless, Justice Department lawyers have been able to ferret out many such offenses. One of their most celebrated victories was *U.S. v. Socony-Vacuum* (now called Mobil) in 1940. The defendants were major integrated oil companies accounting for 83% of all gasoline sales in the midwestern states. They instituted a "dancing partner" program in the midwest, under which each major agreed to buy the "surplus" gasoline of some particular independent refinery. "Surplus" was gasoline that could not be disposed of except at "distressed" prices. The independents were small and lacked spacious storage facilities. They consequently sold their "surpluses" at whatever discounted price they could get.

The defendant majors were not accused of direct price fixing. Indeed, their surplus purchases from "partners" were at prices determined by the force of competition in the other sales made by all refiners. The essence of the accusation was that removal of excess supply from the market *indirectly* propped up the price. To be sure, the defendants argued that their activities did not constitute price fixing. They were even so bold as to argue before the Court that their innocence was confirmed by their buying most heavily when prices were *falling* and lightly when prices were *rising*. But of course this is exactly the way an indirect method of price support should work. And the Court was not fooled:

> That price-fixing includes more than the mere establishment of uniform prices is clearly evident from the Trenton Potteries case itself . . . purchases at or under the market are one species of price-fixing. In this [oil] case, the result was to place a floor under the market—a floor which served the function of increasing the stability and firmness of market prices. . . . Under the Sherman Act a combination formed for the purpose and with the effect of raising, depressing, fixing, pegging, or stabilizing the price of a commodity in interstate or foreign commerce is illegal *per se*.[11]

A string of related cases recently in the news involves *bid rigging* among highway construction contractors in the South. In 1979, executives of five of Nashville's largest paving companies met at a hotel for what was supposed to be a poker game. In fact, the poker was just a cover. They met to rig the bids on three local highway projects. Nine months later one of the poker players pleaded guilty to price fixing, and, in exchange for a light sentence, divulged extensive information about the industry's bid rigging in general. The game then became dominoes, as the Justice Department's investigations soon led to indictments against 57 corporations and 80 of their officers in at least six southern states.[12]

---

[10] *Addyston Pipe and Steel Company v. U.S.,* 175 U.S. 211 (1899).
[11] *United States v. Socony-Vacuum Oil Co.,* 310 U.S. 150 (1940).
[12] "Highway Robbery?", *Wall Street Journal,* May 29, 1981, pp. 1, 25.

CONDUCT

D. Trade Associations

Notwithstanding the Court's strong per se stance, not all collective activity is forbidden. Competitors are still free to form, and to take active part in, trade associations. These associations raise problems, however. Because "education" is a prime purpose of trade associations, it is quite common for them to collect and disseminate information on a wide variety of subjects, prices included. Moreover, trade association meetings are conducive to talk of prices. As a former assistant manager for a textile firm said: "I don't know what people would do at a trade association meeting if not discuss prices. They aren't going to talk just about labor contracts and new technology."[13] Fortunately for the consumer, trade association cover cannot immunize outright conspiracies from prosecution. In truth, approximately 30% of all cases brought by the government involve trade associations.

Still, the "information" activities of trade associations do pose ticklish problems for drawing the legal line between what does and what does not constitute price fixing. On the one hand, it can be argued that enhanced knowledge on the part of industry members lessens market imperfections, thereby fostering more effective competition. On the other hand, too much knowledge may inhibit price competition. Recall from the previous chapter that price cutters often attempt to *conceal* their discounts in order to forestall followship. They know that their down-side nonfollowship demand curves may disappear when exposed to the full light of day, leaving them only the inelastic, unattractive, and unprofitable followship demand curve to contend with.

Illegal information activities are illustrated by the *American Column and Lumber* case of 1921.[14] The hardwood flooring trade association involved required each of 365 participants to submit six reports to its secretary: (1) a daily report of all actual sales: (2) a daily shipping report, with exact copies of the invoices; (3) a monthly production report; (4) a monthly stock report; (5) current price lists; and (6) inspection reports. In turn, the trade association secretary supplied detailed reports to the firms from this information. The exchange was supplemented by monthly meetings where, among other things, speakers urged cartel-like cooperation with exhortations such as, "If there is *no increase in production,* particularly in oak, there is going to be good business," and *"No man is safe in increasing production."*

The Supreme Court decided this was "not the conduct of competitors." In subsequent cases the Court has frowned upon trade association programs involving elaborate standardization of the conditions surrounding sales, reports of future prices, and requirements that members must adhere to their reported prices. As regards *permissible* trade association activities, programs appear to be lawful "when they limit price reports to past transactions, preserve the ano-

[13] *Business Week,* June 2, 1975, p. 48. See also Jeffrey Sonnenfeld and Paul R. Lawrence, "Why Do Companies Succumb to Price Fixing?", *Harvard Business Review* (July-August 1978), pp. 145–157.

[14] *American Column and Lumber Co. et. al. v. United States,* 257 U.S. 377 (1921).

268

nymity of individual traders, make data available to buyers as well as sellers, and permit departure from the prices that are filed."[15]

E. Conscious Parallelism

We saw in the last chapter that cartelization was only one of a number of suppressors of price competition. Recognized interdependence produces cartels, but it also produces kinked demand curves, price leadership, and uniform cost-plus pricing, all of which—*despite the absence of any explicit agreement*—may yield behavior that closely resembles cartel behavior (namely, high and stable prices). Stated differently, "economic theory has suggested that this kind of noncompetitive behavior might well arise in an 'oligopoly' situation . . . without overt communication or agreement, but solely through a rational calculation by each seller of what the consequences of his price decision would be, taking into account the probable or virtually certain reactions of his competitors."[16] Such oligopolistic uniformity of behavior has been called **tacit collusion** or **conscious parallelism.**

How have the courts handled this problem? Does mere conscious parallelism fall within the meaning of "contract, combination, . . . , or conspiracy," which are specified by the Sherman Act? In short, is it illegal? The simplified answer that we must limit ourselves to here comes in two installments. First, *in and of itself,* conscious parallelism is *not* illegal. It does not provide conclusive circumstantial evidence of conspiracy. The Supreme Court's clearest statement to this effect is found in the *Theatre Enterprises* case of 1954:

> this Court has never held that proof of parallel business behavior conclusively establishes agreement or, phrased differently, that such behavior itself constitutes a Sherman Act offense . . . "conscious parallelism" has not yet read conspiracy out of the Sherman Act entirely.[17]

Second, and on the other hand, consciously parallel behavior may well indicate an unlawful conspiracy or agreement *when viewed in conjunction with additional facts.* These additional facts may be subdivided into two categories

1. Additional independent evidence of a more formal agreement, as illustrated by the following:[18]
   (a) Identical sealed bidding on nonstandard items (for example, large turbine generators).

[15] C. Wilcox, *Public Policies Toward Business,* 3rd ed. (Homewood, Ill.: Richard Irwin, 1966), p. 129.

[16] D. F. Turner, "The Definition of Agreement Under the Sherman Act: Conscious Parallelism and Refusals to Deal," *Harvard Law Review* (February 1962), p. 661. For elaboration see *The Journal of Reprints for Antitrust Law and Economics,* Vol. XIII (1982), No. 2.

[17] *Theatre Enterprises, Inc. v. Paramount Film Distributing Corp.,* 346 U.S. 537 (1954). See also *United States v. National Malleable & Steel Castings Co.,* 1957 Trade Cases, para. 68,890 (N. D. Ohio, 1957), *affirmed per curiam,* 358 U.S. 38 (1959).

[18] Turner, *op. cit.,* and R. A. Posner, *Antitrust Law, An Economic Perspective* (Chicago: University of Chicago Press, 1976), pp. 62–70.

    (b) Basing-point pricing systems, whereby all sellers quote identical delivered prices to any given buyer despite substantial transportation costs and widely differing delivery distances.

    (c) Elaborate exchanges of information, such as those encountered in trade association cases.

    (d) Unnatural product standardization or false denials of interfirm quality differences.

    (e) Simultaneous and substantial price increases (coupled with output reductions) unexplained by any increase in cost.

2. Additional independent evidence that the conduct is restrictive or *exclusionary,* such as

    (a) Parallel buying up of scarce raw materials that are not, in fact, used.

    (b) Parallel and predatory price cutting.

    (c) Crosslicensing of patents.

The *American Tobacco* case of 1946 discussed earlier on pages 254–255 is illustrative.[19] Unlawful conspiracy was found in that case, even though there was no evidence of meetings in smoke-filled rooms or other rendezvous. Parallel pricing behavior (based on Reynold's leadership) was placed in the context of additional facts. In particular, (1) prices were raised despite cost reductions and a massive depression; (2) the three largest companies bought up cheap tobacco they did not use but the "10-cent" brands would have used; and (3) the three largest companies cut prices only after the "10-cent" brands won a healthy market share. The Court declared that "No formal agreement is necessary to constitute an unlawful conspiracy." In this case, conspiracy was proved "from the evidence of the action taken in concert" and from "other circumstances."

F. Basing-point Pricing

Of all the "plus" factors listed, perhaps the one in greatest need of further explanation is the item (b) in group 1—basing-point pricing systems. A simple example of this is the old "Pittsburgh Plus" single basing-point system of the steel industry. Until 1924 all steel producers, regardless of their mill locations, quoted prices as if they were shipping from Pittsburgh. A steel company located in Gary, Indiana, when quoting a price to a buyer located in nearby Chicago, would add to the factory price the railroad freight cost from Pittsburgh to Chicago, rather than the slight freight cost from Gary to Chicago. The excess transportation charge pinned on the buyer was called "phantom freight."

Conversely, if the Gary plant was quoting a price to a buyer in New York, it would add to the factory price the freight cost from Pittsburgh to New York, rather than the larger and truer freight cost from Gary to New York. This undercharging of New York buyers meant that the seller had to "absorb freight." The mills located at the "base," in Pittsburgh, neither charged phantom freight nor absorbed freight on *any sale.* Their transport charges matched their transport

[19] *American Tobacco Co. v. United States,* 328 U.S. 781 (1946).

costs. But sellers at all other locations dealt shamelessly in fictitious transport figures. When they were located closer to the buyer than the Pittsburgh mills, they quoted phantom freight. When they were located farther from the buyer than the Pittsburgh mills, they absorbed freight.

The system is illustrated in Figure 12–1, where horizontal distance represents geographic distance (with Chicago, Pittsburgh, and New York located west to east) and vertical distance represents seller's cost—manufacturing cost first (which does not differ with location) and transportation cost second (which goes up with distance travelled). Thus the transportation cost of mill M_1 shipping to buyer B_1 is zero, but to buyer B_2 it is yx and to buyer B_3 it is vz. Under "Pittsburgh Plus," the double shafted line emanating from Pittsburgh would be the delivered price line for *all* sellers. Price x would be quoted to buyer B_2 by M_2 and M_3 as well as M_1, even though the transport costs of M_2 and M_3 would be quite different, as indicated by the single solid and broken lines, respectively. Delivered price to buyer B_1 would be u. To buyer B_3 it would be z. When M_2 charges buyer B_2 price x, it is charging phantom freight equal to xy. When M_2 charges buyer B_3 price z, it must absorb the wz portion of total freight cost wv.

The Pittsburgh Plus system achieved one particularly important result. As a given *buyer* saw it, *all sellers* were quoting exactly the same price to him. This did not mean that all buyers were quoted the same price, as buyers close to the base saw low identical quotes and buyers distant from the base saw high identical quotes. Yet each buyer saw but one price. The single base system of Pittsburgh Plus was abandoned under pressure from the FTC in 1924. Yet this uniform result still held after the steel industry converted to a *multiple* basing-point system by introducing Gary and Birmingham as additional bases. The base closest to the buyer then provided the key to all quotes.

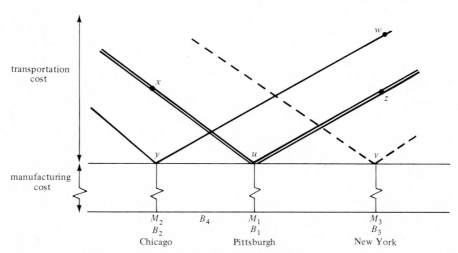

FIGURE 12–1. The Pittsburgh Plus Basing-Point System

Why would the sellers want to quote identical prices to each buyer? To facilitate collusion and effective price leadership. These systems simplify the pricing of colluding firms. They nullify any interfirm cost advantages attributable to geographic location. They enable the leader to lead with ease from the base. They permit price discrimination as when in Figure 12–1 seller M_2 charges a high price x to low cost buyer B_2 while charging a low price of u to high cost buyer B_1. They have also been attacked on these grounds as indicative or supportive of restrictive agreements.

Attacks against basing-point pricing in steel, cement, and corn oil were carried out in the late 1940s with the aid of evidence indicating artificially contrived support.[20] The circulation of uniform railroad rate books, the policing of shipments to prevent destination diversion or truck hauling, the creation of fictitious railrates to places not served by railroads, the complete absence of f.o.b. pricing—all these and other facets of the systems revealed that they were not innocently natural competitive developments but rather conspiracies. Moreover, the products involved—steel, cement, and corn syrup—indicated that such systems are especially pertinent to homogenous, bulky commodities with relatively high transportation costs. In steel, for instance, transportation averages 10% of buyers' total cost.

Official attention to basing-point pricing rekindled during the late 1970s when the plywood industry was caught in a scheme that was simultaneously simple and complex.[21] Prior to 1963 all construction plywood was produced from Douglas fir in the Pacific Northwest. The South had abundant yellow pine timber, but the peculiar resins and pitch of yellow pine prevented its bonding into a durable sandwich board. Development of a new glue solved this problem, giving birth to a southern pine plywood industry. This southern branch grew prodigiously from one producer in 1963 to twenty-five in 1973, nurtured in part by freight cost advantages vis-a-vis the northwest industry. Southern plywood could be delivered in Chicago, for example, at half the transport cost of northwestern plywood, a potential saving of 10% to plywood purchasers off their total delivered price. Yet the full potential of this saving was not realized by buyers because the southern mills priced their plywood as if it had been shipped from a fictitious base mill in Portland, Oregon, discounting slightly so as to make southern pine plywood a bit more attractive price-wise. Georgia-Pacific initiated the system when it expanded beyond the northwest into the South but declined to offer f.o.b. mill prices at its southern mills for buyers desirous of providing their own transportation (although G-P did offer f.o.b.

[20] *Corn Products Refining Company* v. *Federal Trade Commission,* 324 U.S. 726 (1945); *FTC* v. *Cement Institute,* 333 U.S. 683 (1948); *Triangle Conduit and Cable Co.* v. *FTC,* 168 F. 2d 175 (7th Cir. 1948). In *Cement* price uniformity was strikingly illustrated when each of eleven companies, bidding for a 6,000 barrel government order in 1936, submitted sealed bids of $3.286854 per barrel.
[21] For details see Samuel M. Loescher, "Economic Collusion, Civil Conspiracy, and Treble Damage Deterrents: The Sherman Act Breakthrough with Southern Plywood," *The Quarterly Review of Economics and Business* (Winter 1980), pp. 6–35.

prices from its northwest mills). Subsequent southern producers, even those without northwest mills, followed Georgia-Pacific's lead, to the financial disappointment of southern and eastern plywood purchasers. Complexities arose, however, because the system was not, strictly speaking, a Portland-base-price-plus-freight system. Moreover, plywood prices vary sharply with variations in construction demand and vary somewhat between producers, giving appearances of some competition. Nevertheless, upon trial and deliberation, the Federal Trade Commission concluded that the industry's pricing system illegally restrained price competition and maintained an undue amount of phantom freight for southern producers.[22]

G. Summary

To summarize the overall legal situation, we may call upon a panel of experts, the Supreme Court:

> [P]rice fixing is contrary to the policy of competition under the Sherman Act . . . its illegality does not depend on a showing of its unreasonableness, since it is conclusively presumed to be unreasonable. It makes no difference whether the motives of the participants are good or evil; whether the price fixing is accomplished by express contract or by some more subtle means; whether the participants possess market control; whether the amount of interstate commerce affected is large or small; or whether the effect of the agreement is to raise or decrease prices.[23]

II. DETERMINANTS OF CARTELS AND THEIR POTENCY

A pet theory of anti-antitrusters is that cartels cannot "really" get off the ground. Or if they do, their life is "short and turbulent." In a related vein, a few economists believe that collusive behavior is unrelated to such important structural features as concentration and the number of firms in the market.

The aim of the present section is to show that these views are wrong. They stem from preconceived notions and an empirical literature replete with instances of cartel collapse. This literature is useful, but it gets more respect than it deserves. As George Stigler remarks, "This literature is biased: conspiracies that are successful in avoiding an amount of price-cutting which leads to collapse of the agreement are less likely to be reported or detected."[24] Thus, many cartels endure, even as many fall apart. The feasibility, incidence, and endurance of collusion are all largely determined by structural and technological conditions.[25]

---

[22] *In the Matter of Boise Cascade Corp. et al.,* 91 FTC 1 (1978). The FTC ruling was later overturned on appeal, but a private case held up. *Wall Street Journal,* September 9, 1981, p. 48.

[23] *United States v. McKesson & Robbins, Inc.,* 351 U.S. 305 (1956), pp. 309–310.

[24] G. J. Stigler, "A Theory of Oligopoly," *Journal of Political Economy* (February 1964), p. 46.

[25] *Ibid;* Posner, *op. cit.,* pp. 47–61; P. Asch, "Collusive Olipology," J. M. Kuhlman, "Nature and Significance of Price Fixing Rings," and W. B. Erickson, "Economics of Price Fixing," all in *Antitrust Law & Economic Review* (Spring 1969), pp. 53–122.

A. Feasibility and Necessity

Before considering specific conditions, we must make a few preliminary observations. Perhaps the most important thing to keep in mind is that the purpose of all collusion is to maximize joint profits, for only if firms act together can they price and produce like a monopolist. Furthermore, common sense tells us that cartelization occurs only when it is both *feasible* and *necessary* to achieving the objective of joint-profit maximization. If cartelization were not feasible, it surely would not occur. If it were not necessary to achieving the objective, it would likewise not occur, especially if it is illegal and heavily penalized.

The trick, then, is to recognize that "feasibility" and "necessity" are determined by structure. In particular, they vary *inversely* with structure. This relationship is most readily seen through two extreme but simple circumstances, both of which would preclude cartelization. First, where there are hundreds of small firms selling a standardized product (for example, wheat), cartelization is absolutely *necessary* to achieving joint maximization but it is *im*possible to bring off privately (without government approval and imposition). Recognized interdependence is too remote. The incentives for price cutting are too great. Private enforcement of an agreement is too costly in manpower and money. And, if collusion is illegal, detection by the antitrust authorities would be too easy. The result is *no* cartel (unless the government wants to use its police power to establish one). Second, moving to the opposite extreme, imagine a market occupied by just two sellers of a simple standardized product (for example, aluminum ingots). In this case, a private cartel is quite *feasible* but wholly *un*necessary to achieving the joint-profit maximization objective. Recognized interdependence is unavoidable. The incentives for price cutting are virtually nil. The opportunity for simple price leadership is clearly open. The chances that "conscious parallelism" will yield a monopoly outcome are very good. And, if explicit collusion is illegal, the wisdom of private cartelization in this case is questionable to say the least. Again the result is *no* cartel. Tacit collusion prevails instead.

To repeat, only when cartelization is both *feasible* and *necessary* to achieving the profit objective are we likely to find it, given a hostile legal environment. When structural conditions are highly unfavorable, necessity and impossibility combine to produce competition. When structural conditions are highly favorable, possibility and a lack of necessity combine to produce *tacit* collusion. In between, necessity and feasibility blend, and cartelization is likely to occur.

B. Effect of Number of Firms

With respect to numbers of firms, these considerations of likelihood lead us to expect that cartel occurrence is least common in markets with either a very large or a very small number of firms. Some intermediate range of "fewness" seems most conducive, since it offers a combination of necessity and feasibility. The present author and Art Fraas tested this expectation by (1) compiling a useable sample of 606 illegal price-fixing conspiracies from the records of all

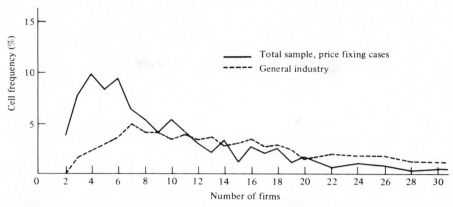

FIGURE 12-2. Frequency distribution of numbers of firms involved in price fixing.

Section 1 prosecutions dispatched between 1910 and 1973; (2) counting the number of firms involved in each of these cases; and (3) computing a frequency distribution for these cases based on the number of firms.[26]

The resulting frequency distribution is shown in Figure 12-2 by the solid line. The vertical axis there is percentage frequency of each number of firms, as given on the horizontal axis. (Note that no fewer than two firms can conspire.) For example, in roughly 10% of all the sampled cases of cartelization, four firms were party to the illegal conspiracy. If by contrast 50% of the sampled cases involved four firms and 50% involved five, the distribution would look like a limbless tree, 50 percentage points tall, rooted at 4 and 5 on the horizontal axis. But this is obviously an improbable vegetable. Rather, the distribution bears out expectation. It has a roughly arched, positive-negative configuration. The positively sloped portion of the distribution (beginning with two firms and rising) seems to reflect a trade-off between tacit and express collusion, with the incidence of explicit collusion rising and the incidence of tacit collusion falling as the number of firms in the explicit conspiracies (and in the market)[27] rises. On the other hand, the negatively sloped portion of the price fixing distribution (beginning at about six firms) probably reflects a region of trade-off between express collusion and competitive independence. As the number of firms rises over this range, express collusion becomes less and less feasible.

[26] Arthur G. Fraas and D. F. Greer, "Market Structure and Price Collusion: An Empirical Analysis," *Journal of Industrial Economics* (September 1977), pp. 21–44. For related studies see G. A. Hay and D. Kelley, "An Empirical Survey of Price Fixing Conspiracies," *Journal of Law and Economics* (April 1974), pp. 13–38; and A. Phillips, "An Econometric Study of Price-Fixing Market Structure and Performance in British Industry in the Early 1950s" in *Market Structure and Corporate Behavior,* edited by K. Cowling (London: Gray-Mills Publishers, 1972), pp. 177–192.

[27] Hay and Kelley (*op. cit.*) report data on the number of firms in each of 34 conspiracies and the total number of firms in each of the 34 markets involved. The simple correlation between the two is .96.

This plot may be compared to the dotted line distribution of Figure 12–2. It represents all industries generally, not just instances of price fixing. Data for 1,569 narrowly defined manufacturing markets of fairly uniform geographic scope underly the distribution. A comparison of the two distributions indicates that a low number of firms is indeed conducive to collusion. The general industry distribution is spread out, whereas the price-fixing distribution is bunched toward the low numbers end.

We now have our first hint as to why many cartels are feeble and fragile while others are strong and durable. If the behavioral trade-off is between tacit collusion and cartelization—that is, if a cartel is set up because tacit collusion is not working well for profit achievement—then the cartel is probably built upon a fairly solid structural foundation. Its prospects appear promising. On the other hand, if the behavioral trade-off is between cartelization and competition—that is, if the cartel amounts to a last gasp effort to pull the industry from the pit of vigorous competition—then the cartel's life expectancy and potential effectiveness naturally seem dim. One implication is that fewness of firms and cartel effectiveness go hand in hand. Unfortunately, no accurate data are available to test this notion systematically. Still, the circumstantial evidence seems favorable to it.[28] One problem with any test of such a proposition is that many factors *other* than firm numbers have an influence. Even as few as two firms might compete wholeheartedly given the right surrounding circumstances.

C. Other Structural Factors

The theoretical influence of other structural factors is outlined in Table 12–1. The format of the table is illustrated by inclusion of the number of firms in the market as the first condition listed. From left to right across the three columns, the number of firms mentioned rises from "very few" to "many." This pattern accords with the column headings that indicate a declining feasibility but a rising necessity of cartelization for joint-profit maximization as one reads from left to right.

Concentration. The second condition listed is concentration. The theory behind the table's specifications for this variable should be obvious because concentration is inversely correlated with the number of firms in markets and in conspiracies.[29] High to moderate four-firm concentration would seem to be most conducive to cartelization, as indicated in column (2). Extremely high concentration would of course foster tacit collusion, and vice-versa for competition. Moreover, George Hay and Dan Kelley found that concentration and cartel stability

[28] Fritz Voigt, "German Experience with Cartels and their Control during Pre-War and Post-War Periods," in *Competition, Cartels, and their Regulation,* edited by J. P. Miller (Amsterdam: North-Holland Publishing Co., 1962), p. 171; G. W. Stocking and M. W. Watkins, *Monopoly and Free Enterprise* (New York: Twentieth Century Fund, 1951), p. 112. On the other hand, see R. A. Posner, "A Statistical Study of Antitrust Enforcement," *Journal of Law and Economics* (October 1970), p. 402.

[29] Using Hay and Kelley data again (*op. cit.*), the correlation between concentration and the number of conspirators is −0.69.

TABLE 12–1. Outline of Conditions Affecting the Incidence of Cartelization: Graded on the Basis of Feasibility and Necessity

Market Condition or Characteristic	(1) Feasibility: Excellent Need: Unnecessary (Tacit Collusion)	(2) Feasibility: Good Need: Helpful (Cartel)	(3) Feasibility: Poor Need: Essential (Competition)
Number of firms	Very few (2–5)	Several (5–25)	Many (30+)
Concentration ratio	Very high	High-medium	Low
Type of product	Standardized	Slightly different	Differentiated
Rate of technological change	None	Slow-moderate	Rapid
Frequency (and size) of sales	Frequent (small)	Often (medium)	Lumpy (large)
Opportunity for secret deals	None	Some	Great
Rate of growth	Slow	Medium	Rapid
Elasticity of demand	Low (less 0.5)	Medium	High (2)
Production costs across firms	Identical	Similar	Diverse

are positively associated. For their sample of 65 cases "the preponderance of conspiracies lasting ten or more years were in markets with high degrees of concentration."[30]

Firm numbers and concentration are listed first because they seem to be the most important variables mentioned. The other variables can be influential, however, as fewness of firms and high concentration are not sufficient in themselves to assure tacit collusion (although they appear to be essential to such a result). The other variables affect feasibility and necessity for the same basic reasons that numbers and concentration do. They affect the ease of reaching an agreement, the incentive to "cheat" or "double-cross" one's co-conspirators, and the ease of detecting double-crossers.

Type of Product and Technological Change.[31] Type of product and rate of technological change are alike in their influences. Product differentiation or rapid change inject complexities that make it hard to reach an agreement in the first place. These complexities, moreover, make detection of double-crossers

---

[30] Hay and Kelley, *op. cit.,* p. 26.
[31] Sonnenfeld and Lawrence, *op. cit.,* pp. 148–149; R. E. Caves and M. E. Porter, "Market Structure, Oligopoly, and Stability of Market Shares," *Journal of Industrial Economics* (June 1978), pp. 289–313.

more difficult. Price cuts may be shrouded in the folds of product variations.[32] Double-crossing itself can take forms other than price cutting—namely, escalations in advertising or styling or research or some other nonprice variable. In light of these possibilities, it is not surprising that many cartels attempt to standardize their product, restrict advertising, and regulate technological change, for standardization and stagnation are most conducive to cooperation.

Type of Sale and Opportunity for Secret Dealing. If sales move in large lots over intermittent time intervals, then each sales transaction produces a particular and important surge in the seller's revenue stream. The pay-off to any given instance of price shading in this situation can be very lucrative. Temptations to cheat may therefore tug strongly here. This intermittent sales factor, plus healthy doses of rapid technological change and product differentiation, help to explain why the market for commercial airliners is intensely competitive despite its dominance by just two firms—Boeing and McDonnel-Douglas. Infrequent orders of multimillion dollar denominations tend to knock airliner prices into tail spins. As S. L. Carroll observed, "If any collusion, market sharing or market splitting has occurred among the airframe companies, it has been well hidden indeed. . . . The lumpy and discrete nature of orders makes competitive concessions quite tempting."[33] Conversely, an even flow of *frequent* and *small-sized* sales is most accommodating to colluders.

Much the same could be said of opportunities for secret dealing. Where these opportunities are slight, agreements are easy to police and the incentive to double-cross is considerably reduced. Conversely, a prevalence of secrecy enables price discounting under the table, which improves the down-side viability of the seductively elastic nonfollowship demand curve.

Rate of Growth and Elasticity of Demand. A rapid rate of growth in industry demand can upset the best laid plans for several reasons. Perhaps the most important is that the gains to be had from collusion then appear less attractive to potential participants. This may explain why cartels are often called children of depressions. Rapid growth may also confound policing and enforcement efforts. With new customers flocking to the market and old ones expanding their buying, it is difficult to measure market shares and to detect diversions of business that may be caused by double-crossing. Conversely, shares can be pinpointed and diversions due to price shading can be more easily discovered under stable conditions.

Elasticity of demand enters the picture for related reasons. As Hay and Kelley put it, "The more inelastic is industry demand, the greater are the poten-

---

[32] During the late 1970s, members of the European Economic Community's steel cartel cheated by adding "bonus" tonnage to deliveries and by deliberately "delivering late," which "tardiness" then permitted them to pay buyers a fine, i.e., discount. Kent Jones, "Forgetfulness of Things Past: Europe and the Steel Cartel," *The World Economy* (May 1979), p. 150.

[33] Sidney L. Carroll, "The Market for Commercial Airliners," in *Regulating the Product Quality and Variety,* edited by R. Caves and M. Roberts (Cambridge, Mass.: Ballinger, 1975), pp. 150, 163. See also John Newhouse, *The Sporty Game* (New York: Knopf, 1982).

tial rewards to the price fixers. Concomitantly the smaller will be the sacrifice in terms of capacity utilization."[34]

Production Costs. Finally, it should be obvious why production costs might influence collusion. Widely divergent costs across firms would breed divergent opinions concerning what price should prevail, threatening the success of negotiations. An efficient way of coping with divergent costs is to close down inefficient plants and firms; then devise a profit pooling arrangement whereby the benched third stringers are rewarded for their idleness. But, of course, this also raises difficulties. No one likes being a third stringer, and the compensation fringe firms may therefore request of the first stringers might seem "unreasonably" high. Moreover, such a plan would be more readily detectable by antitrust prosecutors. When discussing costs and cartels F. M. Scherer has also stressed the unsettling impact of uneven cost *changes* across firms: "The more rapidly producers' cost functions are altered through technological innovation, and the more unevenly these changes are diffused throughout the industry, the more likely conflict in pricing action is."[35] He cites an example drawn from an industry previously mentioned: "In the sanitary pottery fixtures industry, conflicts attendant to the introduction of tunnel kilns (replacing more costly beehive oven processes) were in part responsible for the failure of producers to eliminate widespread price-cutting despite repeated attempts to reach collusive agreements."[35]

The Importance of Each Factor. The relative importance of these numerous conditions is difficult to test empirically. Aside from the obvious problems of measuring them and uncovering observations of them (cartelization is after all secretive), their effects in real life are not nearly so neat and straightforward as our simple outline in Table 12-1 implies. The conditions may interact on behavior. Various combinations may be particularly potent or weak. In short, the factors do not willingly submit themselves to systematic analysis. For example, Table 12-1 says that rapid technological change nourishes spirited competition. But, if most other factors favor tacit collusion, rapid technological change may merely force cartelization upon the industry, something which can hardly be considered spirited competition. For another example, Table 12-1 suggests that ten firms are too plentiful to permit effective tacit collusion. But no one would strain himself imagining a ten-firm industry in which nearly all the other conditions point in the direction of tacit collusion—with the result that tacit collusion consequently prevails.

Empirical work is also hampered by the fact the cartels differ in *design.* Two industries might have virtually identical structural conditions. Yet one industry might be successfully cartelized and the other not, despite very serious attempts in the latter case to smother competition. A researcher observing the two industries might well conclude erroneously that some obscure and irrelevant

---

[34] Hay and Kelley, *op. cit.,* p. 15.

[35] F. M. Scherer, *Industrial Market Structure and Economic Performance* (Chicago: Rand McNally 1970), p. 192.

structural difference caused the disparity. However, the true explanation might rest instead on the particular design of the successful cartel.[36] Its penalty system, policing technique, and allocation mechanism might be works of art, with unique and seemingly unimportant details that make them masterpieces (if that is not too noble a word).

Notwithstanding the difficulties, there are many case studies that provide crude evidenciary support for the assertions of Table 12–1.[37] Further support may be found in a statistical analysis of the 606 cases of illegal price fixing mentioned earlier.[38]

D. Summary

In short, evidence indicates that the structural conditions most favorable to tacit cooperation are a relatively small number of rival firms in a market setting relatively free of complications. Moreover, a variety of regimental or disciplinary devices facilitates tacit or explicit collusion under more adverse structural conditions. To state these results somewhat differently: evidence suggests that, as the number of firms in the market or the complexity of structural conditions increases, conspirators must resort to arrangements of increasingly elaborate design or efficiency to achieve their joint profit-maximizing objectives. Indeed, this finding probably explains why many elaborately formal cartels are eventually undermined by double-crossing, bickering, and dissolution. Elaborate cartels probably arise most often where structural conditions are more favorable to *competition* than to collusion. However, to conclude from this that cartels are nearly always short-lived and feeble would be wrong. In the region of trade-off between tacit and express collusion, at least, cartels probably yield stable and substantial gains for their organizers (as well as losses for their customers).

III. THE ELECTRICAL EQUIPMENT CASES[39]

The electric equipment cases are to American price fixing what Watergate is to American political corruption. The collusive activity began some time in the 1920s or 1930s (it was so long ago no one seems to know exactly when). At first it was a rather casual adjunct to the industry's trade association activities, involving just a few products. By the 1950s, however, conspiracy had spread

---

[36] Jones, *op. cit.*, gives a good example.

[37] F. Voight, *op. cit.*; Stocking and Watkins, *op. cit.*: H. C. Passer, *The Electrical Manufacturers: 1875–1900* (Cambridge, Mass.: Harvard University Press, 1953); G. B. Richardson, "The Pricing of Heavy Electrical Equipment: Competition or Agreement?" *Bulletin of the Oxford University Institute of Economics and Statistics* (1966), pp. 73–92; S. M. Loescher, *Imperfect Collusion in the Cement Industry* (Cambridge, Mass.: Harvard University Press, 1959); Jones, *op. cit.*; Sonnenfeld and Lawrence, *op. cit.*

[38] Fraas and Greer, *op. cit.*

[39] This section draws from R. G. M. Sultan, *Pricing in the Electrical Oligopoly, Vol. 1* (Cambridge Mass.: Harvard University Press, 1974); C. C. Walton and F. W. Cleveland, Jr., *Corporations on Trial: The Electric Cases* (Belmont, Calif.: Wadsworth, 1964); and R. A. Smith, *Corporations in Crisis* (Garden City, N.Y.: Anchor Books, 1966), Chapters 5 and 6.

TABLE 12–2. Extent and Coverage of the Electrical Equipment Price Fixing Conspiracies

Product	Annual (1959) Dollar Sales ($ millions)	Number of Firms Indicted	Share of Market (%)
Turbine generators	$400*	3 (6)*	95 (100)
Industrial control equipment	262*	9*	75*
Power transformers	210	6	100
Power switchgear assemblies	125	5 (8)*	100
Circuit breakers	75	5	100
Power switching equipment	35*	8 (15)*	90–95*
Condensers	32	7	75–85
Distribution transformers	220	8	96
Low-voltage distribution equip.	200*	6 (10)*	95*
Meters	71	3	100
Insulators	28	8	100
Power capacitors	24	6	100
Instrumental transformers	16*	3 (4)*	95*
Network transformers	15	6	90
Low-voltage power circuit breakers	9	3 (5)*	100
Isolated phase bus	7.6	4	100
Navy and marine switchgear	7	3	80
Open-fuse cutouts	6	8	75
Bushings	6	4	100
Lightning arresters	16	7	100

* Includes companies named as co-conspirators but not indicted.
Source: Adapted from *Corporations on Trial: The Electric Cases* by Clarence C. Walton and Frederick W. Cleveland, Jr., © 1964 by Wadsworth Publishing Company, Inc., Belmont, California 94002. Reprinted by permission of the publisher.

to every corner of the trade. Table 12–2 gives some idea of the vast scope of the price fixing and of the structure of the markets involved. Roughly $7 billion of business was involved. The products ranged from $2 insulators to multimillion dollar turbine generators. The average number of firms participating in each market was 6.6. Several of the larger participants—such as General Electric, Westinghouse, Allis Chalmers, McGraw-Edison, and I-T-E Circuit Breaker—operated and conspired in many of the markets. Smaller firms—like Moloney Electric and Wagner—were more specialized. In all, 29 firms and 44 individuals were indicted during 1960 for criminal conspiracies in 20 separate product lines.

Table 12–2 gives the impression that high concentration and a paucity of firms might have permitted tacit collusion in four or five of these markets. But conditions not revealed in the table provided substantial competitive pull, thereby abetting explicit collusion. First, many of these products were not standardized but custom-made and differentiable. Various collusive steps were taken to standardize product quality, especially in the early years. Second, many items of equipment were sold in big chunks, which amplified the incentive to cut prices to gain business. Even within given product lines, large orders received larger discounts off "book" price than small orders. A third factor was the volatility of the business cycle in the electrical apparatus field. These goods are durable capital equipment and experience fluctuations in demand far beyond those encountered by most other industries. Slack demand seems to have caused much price cutting, even when the conspiracies were in high gear. Finally, technological change was fairly brisk during the decades involved.

Collusive procedures and experiences varied from product to product, from sealed-bid sales to off-the-shelf transactions, and from higher to lower levels of management. One common thread, however, was the atmosphere of skullduggery surrounding all the conspiracies. Code names, pay-phone communications, plain envelope mailings, destruction of evidence, clandestine meetings in out-of-the-way places, faked expense account records, and secret market allocations all entered the plot. Perhaps the most sensational technique devised was the "phase of the moon" system developed for sealed-bid switchgear sales:

> This system was intended to fix automatically the price each conspirator would quote, with a rotation of the low price among competitors to create the illusion of random competition. The contemplated range of bid prices was modest. According to the "moon sheet," which was in effect from December 5, 1958 through April 10, 1959, position would be rotated among the five major competitors every two weeks.[40]

Disclosure of the system inspired some jokester in General Electric to rewrite the words to the then popular song "Moonglow." Sung to the same tune, the first verse went like this: "It must have been Moonglow/Way up in the blue/ It must have been Moonglow/That brought that bid to you."[41]

Despite all the shenanigans, it is not clear that the conspirators were able to raise or stabilize prices appreciably in all product lines. Double-crossing was fairly commonplace. A "white sale" drove prices down to 60% of book in 1955. Many participants have made self-serving claims that their efforts failed, and it can be argued that supply and demand remained important determinants of price level.[42] On the other hand, a federal trial judge was persuaded by the evidence that prices of turbine generators would have been 21% lower were it not for the conspiracy. In addition, solid evidence indicates a substantial price impact in circuit breakers and insulators plus some indirect overall effect via stabilization of market shares.[43] In any event, economic consequences were

[40] Sultan, op. cit., p. 39.
[41] J. G. Fuller, The Gentlemen Conspirators (New York: Grove Press, 1962), p. 66.
[42] Sultan is the industry's best defender, op. cit.
[43] Ibid., pp. 85, 210, 273; David F. Lean, Jonathan D. Ogur, and Robert P. Rogers, Competition and Collusion in Electrical Equipment Markets: An Economic Assessment (Federal Trade Commission Staff Report, July 1982); Bruce T. Allen, "More on the Turbine Market," Industrial Organization Review (Vol. 7, 1979), pp. 61–72.

relevant only to the treble damage suits, which yielded $400 million or there-abouts. The government's criminal suits were settled under the *per se* rule, with seven executives serving brief stints in the slammer and with fines totaling $1,954,000, the bulk of which was paid by the companies.[44]

IV. THE OIL INDUSTRY AND OPEC[45]

A. Introduction

Of the oil industry's several sectors—crude extraction, transportation, refin-ing, and marketing—crude extraction (hereafter called "crude") is the most interesting to us here. Both in the United States and abroad that sector has spawned some rather remarkable cartels or "near" cartels. At the same time competition has not been altogether absent. For most of its history, the crude industry seems to have been caught in the region of trade-off between cartelization and competition. Calouste Gulbenkian, a pioneer of Iraqui oil development, may have said it best when he quipped, "Oilmen are like cats; you can never tell from the sound of them whether they are fighting or making love."

This turbulent blend should lead anyone who has followed the discussion this far to anticipate at least two aspects of the oil story: (1) many oil cartels have been less than love-ins, and (2) the most enduring and significant cartels have been encouraged, supported, and run by government agencies (exempted thereby, or beyond the reach of the Sherman Act). The crude industry's habit of falling under collectivized or centralized control—either private or official—has led many observers to argue that "socially acceptable operation of the indus-try *necessarily requires* either government regulation of output or the domination of the industry by firms large enough to exercise a strong control over total output and to keep competition, especially price competition, within very narrow limits."[46]

---

[44] An electrical equipment cartel currently operates outside the reach of U.S. law in international markets. For details see Barbara Epstein and Richard Newfarmer, *International Electrical Associa-tion: A Continuing Cartel,* Report, U.S. House of Representatives, Committee on Interstate and Foreign Commerce (June 1980).

[45] Main sources for this section are M. G. de Chazeau and A. E. Kahn, *Integration and Competition in the Petroleum Industry* (New Haven, Conn.: Yale University Press, 1959); M. A. Adelman, *The World Petroleum Market* (Baltimore: Johns Hopkins University Press, 1972); J. M. Blair, *The Control of Oil* (New York: Pantheon Books, 1976); N. H. Jacoby, *Multinational Oil* (New York: Macmillan Publishing Co., 1974); R. Engler, *The Brotherhood of Oil* (Chicago: University of Chicago Press, 1977); Anthony Sampson, *The Seven Sisters* (New York: Viking Press, 1975); U.S. Senate, Subcommittee on Multinational Corporations of the Committee on Foreign Relations, *Report on Multinational Oil Corporations and U.S. Foreign Policy* (U.S. G.P.O., 1975); U.S. Senate, Subcommittee on Antitrust and Monopoly of the Committee on the Judiciary, *Hearings on Government Intervention in the Market Mechanism: Petroleum,* parts 1–5, 91st Congress, First and Second Sessions (1969, 1970); Walter Measday, "The Petroleum Industry" in *The Structure of American Industry,* edited by W. Adams (New York: Macmillan Publishing Co., 1977); E. T. Penrose, *The Large International Firm in Developing Countries* (Cambridge, Mass.: The MIT Press, 1968); S. L. McDonald, *Petroleum Conservation in the United States* (Baltimore: Johns Hopkins Press, 1971).

[46] Penrose, *op. cit.,* p. 165.

In short, the belief of such observers in a "natural" need for centralization rests on the assumption that the industry is inherently unstable, so unstable as to bring forth booms and busts unless somehow "regulated." The industry is said to be less self-adjusting than most: "hectic prosperity is followed all too swiftly by complete collapse, and redress can be hoped for only from the efforts of 'eveners' adjusters, and organizers."

Not all experts hold this view; many refute it. Although we cannot pursue the debate here, there seems to be enough truth to the instability argument to give industry leaders and governments an excuse to play the part of "eveners, adjusters, and organizers." (Of course governments have also been spurred to action by the strategic military and economic importance of oil.) Our discussion of these cartelization efforts is split between the domestic United States and foreign markets.

B. United States Domestic Crude Oil

Figure 12–3 reveals that prior to 1934 the price of domestic crude oil was highly unstable. The solid line shows peaks and valleys in price level of alpine proportions in those years. Moreover, the high frequency of change—as indicated by the dashed line—was equally unsettling. The data traced there actually understate the true volatility because they refer to a representative *posted* price, not to actual *transactions* prices, which fluctuated even more wildly. For example, discovery of the immense East Texas Field in 1930 and the country's simultaneous slide into depression combined to press down the posted price shown in Figure 12–3 to 61 cents a barrel in 1933, but some transaction prices fell to the amazingly low figure of 10 cents a barrel. This instability may be attributed to a "law of capture" as well as to inelasticities and shifts of supply and demand. Under the "law of capture" crude oil belonged to whomever got it out first. Couple this law with (1) fragmented property ownership over a given oil reser-

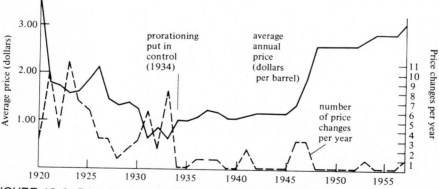

FIGURE 12–3. Price level and changes for U.S. crude oil, Oklahoma 36° gravity. Source: M. G. deChazeau and A. E. Kahn, *Integration and Competition in the Petroleum Industry,* (New Haven: Yale University Press, 1959),pp. 138, 148–9.

voir, (2) the fluid nature of the stuff, plus (3) generous amounts of greed, and you have a mad rush to drain the reservoir. The goal of each owner was simply (and crudely): "get it out while the getting's good." The results were:

- Appalling *physical waste* because of reckless damage of the reservoir's natural drive pressures and loss of oil by evaporation in makeshift open-air storage vats.

- Enormous *"economic waste"* because of extraction and consumption of crude oil when its value was low and excessive investment in drilling.

- Added *instability* of prices and producer incomes.

Broad-based private cartelization was impossible, given the thousands of producers. Hence, during the depths of greatest difficulty in the early 1930s, remedial steps were taken by state and federal authorities that eventually led to a table-like structure of price support resting on four legs: (1) demand prorationing, (2) the Connally "Hot" Oil Act, (3) the Interstate Oil Compact, and (4) import quotas.

State Controls. **Demand prorationing** was a system of flexible production control first instituted by state authorities in Oklahoma and Texas, later emulated in Louisiana, Kansas, and New Mexico (thus including the states most bountifully blessed with oil). Its effects on prices may be seen in Figure 12–3, where after 1934 prices are much less volatile than before. Moreover, those changes that do occur thereafter are almost always increases.

Operation of the system is illustrated in Figure 12–4. In essence, supply was restricted or expanded to whatever level was necessary for price to be at

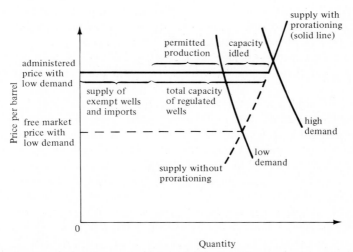

FIGURE 12–4. Restriction of supply under demand prorating, lifting prices to "administered level" above free market level.

or above the "administered price" level. The supply curve looked like an L lying down. This configuration means that supply was perfectly price elastic up to full capacity use (at the corner of the L). Thereafter, the supply curve that prevailed in the absence of prorationing took over. Not all wells were subject to regulation, the main exemptions being "discovery" wells and inefficient "strippers," the latter being wells physically incapable of producing more than a few barrels a day. Moreover, state authorities had no control over imports into the United States. Hence, exempt and import supplies were subtracted from projected demand before determining the output allowed from the regulated wells. In short, the fraction of allowed capacity utilization was reckoned monthly by the following formula:

$$\text{fraction of capacity utilization for regulated wells} = \frac{\text{demand} - (\text{exempts} + \text{imports})}{\text{total capacity of regulated wells}}$$

Allowable utilization therefore decreased with decreased demand or increased imports, exempt capacity, and total regulated capacity. In Figure 12–4 the fraction for "low demand" is about 0.7, whereas that for "high demand" is 1.0. Competitive drilling was limited indirectly through regulations defining what constituted "total capacity" for each producer. These definitions embodied well spacing formulas, which for many years were faulty in not eliminating law-of-capture competitive drilling completely.

Federal Controls. As for the three other legs of price support, all were federal measures. The Connally "Hot" Oil Act of 1935 prohibited the interstate shipment of crude oil (or products refined from crude oil) produced in excess of the state allowables. Without this law, state officials doing the prorationing were handicapped. Cheating was easy. The year 1935 also saw passage of the Interstate Oil Compact Commission Act, providing a forum for the prorationing agencies of producing states. There they could collude and coordinate their "conservation" efforts lest they compete with each other at the state level for ever larger shares of national output. Finally, mandatory import quotas came much later, beginning in 1959.

During the early years of prorationing, restrictions on imports were not needed. The United States dominated world oil in those days, being the richest in then-known reserves, the most productive, and the largest exporter. As late as 1949 the United States accounted for 36% of the world's reserves and 55% of its production. Until World War II, moreover, all international shipments of crude were priced according to a "Houston-plus" single basing-point system. Thereafter, United States fortunes began three decades of decline. Development of superabundant and cheap mideastern supplies threatened the United States industry. A new basing point was established in the Persian Gulf, and United States prices rose relative to those of the new base. As this price differential widened, United States imports multiplied several times over, gushing in at a rate of 18.3% of total United States crude consumption by 1958, the year before mandatory quotas.

The consequences for United States production were enormous. In that year capacity utilization of Texas's regulated wells was only 33%, down from 100% utilization in 1948. Imports were not the sole cause of this, however. Ample exemptions from prorationing in states with prorationing, an absence of prorationing in less nicely endowed and more costly crude-producing states (such as Mississippi, Colorado, Wyoming, and Montana, which in 1958 were producing at 86 to 100% of capacity), some unchecked competitive drilling in several states, and tax incentives that encouraged needless drilling everywhere also contributed to the problem. These several factors raised United States costs, precluding a painless price cut to meet the foreign competition. Indeed, the price of Texan crude was actually *increased* at the behest of producers, once in mid-1953, then again in January 1957.

Bloated by high costs (which pinched consumers $2.15 billion a year) but flush with political clout (owing to campaign contributions and bribes as well as popular votes), the industry escaped threat when the federal government set quotas to limit imports (quotas of sufficient magnitude that they cost consumers an additional $7 to $8 billion a year). "National defense" was proclaimed the reason. The regrettable influence of factors other than imports may be seen by the fact that later, in 1964, after the quota program was in full swing, regulated wells in Texas were held to only 28% of their full capacity. Those in Louisiana and Oklahoma were also working only 32% and 28% of the time. Finally, the effect of prorationing can be seen by comparing the price developments in states with and without prorationing; the latter generally maintained full capacity utilization. Prices in *non*prorationing states were from one to *nine times* more variable than prices in prorationing states over the period 1948–1967.[47]

As this is written (1983), prorationing allowables are pegged at 100%, and they have been since 1972. Import quotas have been discontinued since 1973. The Connally "Hot" Oil Act and Interstate Compact Commission Act are still on the books but superfluous. The first sign of change occurred without popular notice in 1969; ominously, United States productive capacity began to decline. At current rates of consumption the United States will probably run very short of crude petroleum within our lifetimes. Another sign of exhaustion is a trend toward higher concentration in reserve ownership and production. The eight largest firms accounted for 36% of United States crude production in 1955, but 54% in 1973.

C. The International Crude Oil Market

Inside the United States, the last three decades have seen some decline in government cartelization plus some increase in private centralization, but opposite trends have occurred in the international sphere. Prior to about 1950 the

[47] McDonald, *op. cit.*, pp. 190–191.

foreign sector was rife with the cartel handiwork of the major companies, the eldest of the Seven Sisters in particular. Between 1950 and 1970 the power of the Seven Sisters diminished. And finally, since 1970, OPEC, a cartel comprised of the *governments* of 13 of the world's leading crude exporting countries, has taken command.

Before 1950. The **Seven Sisters** are Exxon, BP (British Petroleum), Shell, Gulf, Texaco, Socal (Standard of California), and Mobil. They came by their collective name because, like mortal sisters, they fought and competed with each other while preserving a family affinity.[48]

> The problem of deciding whether the operation of the industry in any period is best described in terms of an "international petroleum cartel" or of the rivalries among the firms engaged in it, is precisely the problem of deciding how much weight to give to the competitive as contrasted to the co-operative elements, and it must be admitted that the latter often seemed to be predominant.[49]

The Seven Sisters stood virtually (but not virtuously) alone in foreign trade prior to 1950. They controlled crude prices and output in the producing countries through cartel arrangements among themselves and by concession agreements with foreign producing country governments. Under "concessions" these govern-ments ceded to the oil companies authority to engage in the exploration and exploitation of certain territories, which in the early days amounted to entire countries. In exchange, the companies paid royalties and taxes on oil extracted.

We shall skip over the "Red Line" and "As Is" agreements, two cartels of the pre-World War II era instigated by Exxon, Shell, and BP. Instead, we shall focus on the postwar origins of Aramco, which brought Socal, Texaco, Exxon, and Mobil together in what eventually proved to be the richest concession of all—Saudi Arabia. Strictly speaking Aramco was a joint-venture, not a cartel, but it typifies the cooperative arrangements that replaced the prewar cartels and formed the basis for intercompany cooperation during the 1950s and 1960s. Moreover, it neatly illustrates the competitive-cooperative behavior of the Sisters.

Here is the story.[50] As of 1947 the Saudi Arabian concession was entirely in the hands of Socal and Texaco, two newcomers to the international scene of the times, who had developed it from scratch beginning in 1936. They operated Aramco through a joint-venture called "Caltex." More important, their exclusive ownership of those enormous oil reserves made the industry more competitive by threatening the market power of the then more well-established international majors—Exxon, Mobil, and BP:

> By 1947, Caltex had tripled its market share both East and West of Suez. With 33¢ a barrel production costs, Caltex could market Arabian crude for as little as 90¢ a barrel while the older international majors were selling for $1.30 and up. . . . Exxon and Mobil rightly concluded that their longterm market prospects in

---

[48] Sampson, *op. cit.,* p. 59.
[49] Penrose, *op. cit.,* p. 150.
[50] Distilled from *Report on Multinational Oil Corps., op. cit.,* Chapters II and IV.

Europe were unfavorable if they failed to get a share of the vast low-cost reserves of [Aramco].

Exxon and Mobil launched a two-part plan: (1) buy into Caltex's Aramco, and (2) once in, secure a 50% price increase for Aramco's crude. As Exxon and Mobil saw it, there were only two main obstacles to their scheme. First, if Caltex discovered their true intentions, the deal would collapse. Part two of the plan was therefore kept secret pending completion of part one. The second obstacle concerned antitrust. Mobil's chief attorney explained the problem in a confidential memo:

> The arrangement would place practical control of crude reserves in the Eastern Hemisphere in the hands of seven companies. . . . I cannot believe that a comparatively few companies for any great length of time are going to be permitted to control world oil resources without some sort of regulation.

As it turned out, he was wrong. The deal went through without antitrust opposition, Exxon buying 30% and Mobil buying 10% leaving Caltex 60%. When drawing up the papers, Exxon and Mobil were able to insert technical language, which went unnoticed by Caltex, to facilitate the price increase part of their plan. Hence, "No sooner had the Aramco merger contracts been signed than a major fight erupted between Caltex and Exxon/Mobil over the price of Arabian Oil." The fight was bitter. Caltex felt cheated. But Exxon and Mobil pressed hard. A Mobil representative even turned sarcastic. "I hope and trust," he said, "our Texas friends will . . . turn to Webster's and look up the definition of 'partnership.' I am quite sure it does not define it as 'a combination of people welshing on their original agreement because it temporarily does not suit their own self-interest.'" In the end Exxon and Mobil won. Aramco's price jumped 40% to $1.43.

From 1950 to 1973. Table 12–3 outlines the shifting balance of power from 1950 to 1973, a period of "recognized interdependence" rather than cartelization. As of 1950, OPEC had not yet been formed. The Seven Sisters lorded over all with 88% of all foreign production and a seamless web of joint-ventures (such as Aramco) binding them together. However, as the first two lines of Table 12–3 indicate, their power thereafter declined. Among the many "independent" companies entering the foreign market during the 1950s and 1960s were Amerada-Hess, ARCO, Citgo, Getty, Occidental, Phillips, Marathon, and Sun.

The added competition was one major cause of foreign market price reductions during the 1950s. A second factor pulling prices down was the United States import quota program of the late 1950s. It sealed off the world's most oil-thirsty market and diverted foreign supplies elsewhere. A third cause of price depression grew with an enormous increase in Russian oil exports.

These several developments combined to lower transactions prices first, then posted prices. By 1959, some discounts off the posted price of $2.08 ran as high as 40¢. To the oil companies the "posted" price was essentially fictional. However, the posted price was not fictional to oil-producing country govern-

CONDUCT

TABLE 12–3. Outline of the Shift of Power from the Seven Sisters to OPEC, 1950–1973

Index of Power	Year			
	1950	1960	1970	1972/3
A. Power of the 7 sisters				
1. Market share abroad (%)	88	72	71	71
2. Strength of collusive agreements	Joint-ventures	Independents arrive	Independents a problem	Disarray
3. U.S. production as per cent of world (%)	54	36	23	21
4. Spare capacity (U.S. imports per cent of consumption) (%)	9	13	23	36
B. Power of OPEC				
1. "Free" world production (%)	(No OPEC)	45	61	65
2. Knowledge	—	Poor	Good	Very good
3. Unity of interest	—	Weak	Moderate	Strong
4. Boldness	—	Meek	Pushy	Brassy
5. Strength of demand (oil as per cent of total world energy) (%)	—	36	44	46

ments, for their revenues were keyed to that price. Hence, when the majors unilaterally reduced posted prices in 1959 and 1960 to better reflect transactions prices, Saudi Arabia, Iran, Iraq, Kuwait, and Venezuela threw tantrums. More important, they responded by forming OPEC to make their views felt and protect their interests.

Turning to the bottom half of Table 12–3, we see that at first, in 1960, OPEC was not much to look at. Accounting for less than half of "free" world production, OPEC lacked full knowledge of the trade, solidarity, and boldness. OPEC's only real achievement in its early years was to prevent further cuts in posted prices. With time, and with the addition of Indonesia, Nigeria, Libya, Algeria, Qatar, United Arab Emirates, Gabon, and Ecuador to its membership, OPEC grew powerful in measurable and unmeasurable ways. Its shares of world production and exports burgeoned, while the world's dependency on oil reached addictive dimensions.

In such intangibles as knowledge, solidarity, and boldness, changes occurred that can only be touched upon here. For example, one of OPEC's first acts was to commission an independent research study of the profits the Sisters were earning on their investments in the Middle East and Venezuela. They found that "between 1956 and 1960, the rate of return on net assets was 71 per cent in Iran, 62 per cent in Iraq, 14 per cent in Qatar, 61 per cent in Saudi Arabia, and 20 per cent in Venezuela."[51] (These amazing profits are partly explained by the fact that unit costs amounted to no more than about 25¢ a barrel in the Middle East.)

The eagerness of newly entering independents to bid high for concessions taught other lessons. For example, oil reserves were more rapidly developed by granting a number of concessions instead of just one and by encouraging independent entry. Still other lessons were learned when reports of the Sister's pre-1950 cartel activities were made public. As one Kuwaiti said; "OPEC couldn't have happened without the oil cartel. We just took a leaf from the oil companies' book. The victim had learned the lesson."[52] Capping these lessons, OPEC members expanded their experience by gaining increased control of their concessions.

Things came to a head in October 1973. United States demand had far outstripped its domestic supplies, forcing abandonment of import quotas and 100% capacity use in prorationing states. Moreover, European consumption reached an all-time high. In fact, for the first time in more than 14 years the transactions price of oil rose *above* the posted price, which was $3.01 a barrel. In sum, events could not have put OPEC in a more powerful position. Then war broke out between Israel and the Arabs. A partial oil embargo followed, lifting the auction prices of crude oil as high as $17 a barrel, way above the $3 posted price. With a hop and a skip, OPEC lifted the posted price. Hopping first to $5.11, then skipping to $11.65 within a few months time, OPEC shocked the U.S. and the world.

OPEC Since 1973. For most of the rest of the 1970s OPEC managed things in an orderly fashion. The cartel's price continued to rise by small steps—5% here, 10% there. Output varied to support price. And just as Texas carried the main burden of supply control in the United States, Saudi Arabia served as the main "evener and adjuster" in OPEC. Its role was based on its vast oil reserves. Its philosophy was explained by its oil minister, Sheik Zaki Yamani: "Usually any cartel will break up, because the stronger members will not hold up the market to protect the weaker members. But with OPEC, the strong members do not have an interest to lower the price and sell more."[53] The cartel's success during this period yielded hundreds of billions of dollars in profits, some of which was spent by OPEC countries to nationalize the oil assets they contained, thereby ending the concessions of the oil companies.

Thereafter, however, the cartel fell into disarray, partly because of revolution in Iran and war between Iraq and Iran. Prices doubled during 1979, but not uniformly, with the result that for a while member prices ranged from over

---

[51] Mana Saeed Al-Otaiba, *OPEC and the Petroleum Industry* (New York: Wiley & Sons, 1975), p. 109.

[52] Sampson, *op. cit.*, p. 162.

[53] *Ibid.*, p. 295. For further details on OPEC see *OPEC: Twenty Years and Beyond,* edited by Ragaei El Mallakh (Boulder, Colorado: Westview Press, 1982) and Ian Seymour, *OPEC Instrument of Change* (New York: St. Martin's Press, 1981).

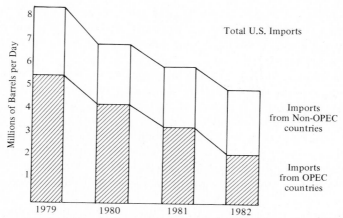

FIGURE 12–5. U.S. crude oil and petroleum product imports, 1972–1982. Source: *Monthly Energy Review* (December 1982).

$35 per barrel to less than $30. Order was restored temporarily with posted prices eventually clustering around $34 a barrel in 1981. The order was only temporary, however, because 1979's price escalations aggravated two forces that had been building for some time:

- First, the output of *non*-OPEC oil burgeoned as the high prices fostered discovery and development. The new oil came from Mexico, the North Sea, and elsewhere.

- Second, the world's demand for oil plummeted as conservation efforts took hold and the world fell into a deep recession. Oil consumption of major western countries dropped 20% between 1979 and 1982.

Figure 12–5 shows the results of these forces from a U.S. perspective. Our imports from OPEC tumbled.

In response to these developments, OPEC cut production from 31.1 million barrels a day in 1979 to 18.5 in 1982. The cut was massive enough to spark sharp disputes within OPEC as to who should curb output the most, but not massive enough to prevent tremendous downward pressure on prices. What began as price shading in 1982 turned into rampant discounting in 1983, with prices dropping from well above to well below $30 a barrel. As these words are written, it is not clear where this slide will end. One sign that prices may sink into the low twenties is a change in Sheik Yamani's attitude. In February 1983 he was no longer saying that the "strong would support the weak." Rather, he was shouting that Saudi Arabia wasn't going to "take any more" of the price discounting by other OPEC countries. Such discounting had pulled Saudi output down to little more than three million barrels a day from the ten million barrels a day produced in 1981.[54]

[54] *Wall Street Journal,* February 23, 1983, p. 3.

SUMMARY

When successful, cartels stifle competition. They restrict and regulate output, thereby raising and stabilizing price. United States antitrust law generally forbids such "restraints of trade" on a *per se* basis. Violators face civil or criminal prosecution (or both), regardless of the reasonableness of their intentions or the success of their efforts. Given a *per se* rule, the key question then becomes: What constitutes a "contract, combination . . . or conspiracy, in restraint of trade," as specified by Section 1 of the Sherman Act? Certain fairly obvious activities clearly come within reach of these words, activities such as market allocations, explicit price fixing, and single sales agencies. In addition, prosecutors have tracked down, and courts have found guilty, some more devious undertakings, including concerted purchases of "distressed" surpluses and certain trade association information schemes. Plain and simple "conscious parallelism" lies beyond the clutches of the law. But "conscious parallelism" has been found in violation when coupled with either (1) additional circumstantial evidence of conspiracy (for example, basing-point pricing), or (2) concerted activities of an exclusionary or predatory nature.

Public records of prosecuted conspiracies and other evidence enable limited study of the incidence and endurance of private cartels. Conceptually, the ground most fertile for cartelization lies between the spacious acreage where competition thrives and the narrow plots where tacit collusion grows. Thus private cartelization requires that the number of firms in the market be few, but not "too" few. Likewise, concentration must be high but not "too" high. And so on. Other conditions favorable to private collusion, either tacit or explicit, comprise a standardized product, slow growth, slow technological change, smoothly flowing sales, little opportunity for secret deals, low elasticity of demand, and uniform production costs among competitors. Of course cartels can be established by the government even in market environments harsh on private cartelization.

Our case studies of electrical equipment and crude oil illustrate these points. Scarcity of firms and high concentration in some sectors of the former industry might have permitted tacit collusion were it not for large and "lumpy" sales, some product differentiation, and fairly rapid technological change. Confronted with these impediments to tacit collusion, formal cartelization seemed the only means of securing stability and better profits. In the case of crude oil, the domestic and foreign industries present different pictures. Stateside, a diffuse market structure and an unsteady record of price and output led to a form of government cartelization that was particularly important from 1933 to 1973. Dwindling domestic supplies and unquenchable demand have since set the control machinery on "idle." Abroad, the Seven Sisters alternated between cartelization and competition, the former predominating prior to 1950, the latter breaking through more and more regularly with the entry of vigorous independents between 1950 and 1973. Since 1973, the Organization of Petroleum Exporting Countries, or OPEC, has established itself as the greatest and wealthiest cartel of all time. Ever-present undercurrents of competition may eventually sink OPEC, but for now it is only floundering.

13 Price and Production Strategy in the Long Run: Theory and Cross-Section Evidence

Count the day lost
whose descending sun
Sees prices shot to hell
and business done for fun.

—BUSINESSMAN'S LAMENT

Like the anatomy of an insect, our prior discussion of short-run price and output behavior can be reduced to three segments:

1. *Objectives* (stability and avoidance of falling profits)
2. *Conditions* affecting achievement of these objectives (number of firms, concentration, lumpiness of sales, and so on)
3. *Mechanisms* used for or arising from interdependence (cartelization, kinky demand, price leadership, and so on)

The issues in this chapter's long-run analysis may be similarly segmented for purposes of comparison. As for firm *objectives,* long-run profit maximization heads the list. Other objectives—such as long-run supply control or market share maintenance—can be considered derivatives or translations of this main objective. *Conditions* affecting the achievement of long-run profits include many factors from our short-run analysis, namely, the number of firms, concentration, product differentiation, and technological change. But two additional conditions distinguish long-run analysis—the condition of entry and long-run price elasticity of demand. Finally, we may list *mechanisms* in order of their treatment hereafter:

1. Entry limit pricing
2. "Open" pricing
3. Price discrimination
4. Predatory pricing
5. Tying arrangements
6. Exclusive dealing

These items deserve special notice not only because they have a long-run use in exploiting a given degree of market power but because they may affect market

294

power itself. That is, they may influence the life and death of rivals as well as observed prices, outputs, and profits. We therefore acknowledge that structure-to-conduct is not the only possible direction of causal flow. Conduct may determine structure as well, providing a feedback effect. Still another way of contrasting the present long-run and the more limited short-run contexts involves the scope of recognized interdependence. In the short run, recognized interdependence extends only to *existing* rivals. In the long run, recognized interdependence enlarges to include *potentials*—the potential entry of a new rival or the potential demise of an old rival.

We start with a review of some cross-section evidence. We next discuss the six mechanisms listed.

I. STRUCTURAL CONDITIONS AND SOME EVIDENCE

Contrary to custom, we shall begin rather than end this chapter with cross-section empirical evidence. The approach enables us to emphasize at the outset the importance of structural conditions to what follows. Without this emphasis, structure could easily get buried under all the curve bending yet to come. Moreover, most of the available cross-section evidence relates indirectly, as opposed to directly, to the details of these long-run theoretical models.

An army of theories probes the long-run implications of numbers of firms and levels of concentration. These theories date from Cournot's work in 1838 to the latest issues of scholarly journals and differ in assumptions, complexity, and reality. They drift into and out of theoretical fashion. And, although they do not pinpoint what constitutes a competitive structure, they almost invariably indicate the same general tendency:

> As the number of firms in the market shrinks and as concentration rises, price competition usually lessens to the point of encouraging increased prices and restrainted output in the long run.

These price and output effects are of course not ends in themselves. They are steps taken by businesses to secure higher profits. Hence a corollary hypothesis holds that fewness and concentration favor (but do not assure) excessively high long-run profits.

We shall see later (in Chapter 19) that evidence concerning the profit corollary is easy to come by. More than 100 cross-section statistical studies have confirmed, more or less strongly, a positive association between concentration and profits. However, statistical tests of the price-concentration relationship are not so easy because prices usually cannot be compared across markets. Profit rates may be standardized as a percentage of assets or stockholders equity, but prices cannot be so standardized. Thus, the profit rates of panty-hose knitters, steel rollers, auto assemblers, and candle dippers may be meaningfully arrayed for tests of competitive effect. But their prices are obviously not of the same species. Any array would be awry.

CONDUCT

Statistical tests of the price-concentration hypothesis are therefore relatively few—numbering only 20 or so. The only such tests possible are *intra*industry, *inter*market, and cross sectional. That is to say, they compare prices of a *given* product or services in diverse geographic markets at one point in time. Products and services so studied include life insurance, bank checking accounts, auto loans, business loans, newspaper advertising space, bread, beer, and drug and grocery retailing.[1] Note that most of these are services because the approach requires relatively narrow geographic markets. Note also that we have already reported the research results concerning business loans (in Chapter 8). Those results agree with the others—prices and concentration *are* positively related. The result for commercial bank new auto loans may be seen by comparing the average interest rate on a standardized auto loan in the ten states having the highest and the ten states having the lowest bank concentration as of 1971. The former was 10.7% annual interest, the latter 9.9%.[2]

[1] J. D. Cummins, H. S. Denenberg, and W. C. Scheel, "Concentration in the U.S. Life Insurance Industry," *Journal of Risk and Insurance* (June 1972), pp. 177–199; John H. Landon, "The Relation of Market Concentration and Advertising Rates: The Newspaper Industry," *Antitrust Bulletin* (Spring 1971), pp. 53–100; B. M. Owen, "Newspaper and Television Station Joint Ownership," *Antitrust Bulletin* (Winter 1973), pp. 787–807; F. R. Edwards, "Concentration in Banking and its Effect on Business Loan Rates," *Review of Economics and Statistics* (August 1964), pp. 294–300; P. A. Meyer, "Price Discrimination, Regional Loan Rates, and the Structure of the Banking Industry," *Journal of Finance* (March 1967), pp. 37–48; D. Jacobs, *Business Loan Costs and Bank Market Structure* (New York: Columbia University Press, 1971); F. W. Bell and N. B. Murphy, "Impact of Market Structure on the Price of a Commercial Bank Service," *Review of Economics and Statistics* (May 1969), pp. 210–213; George Kaufman, "Bank Structure and Performance: the Evidence from Iowa," *Southern Economic Journal* (April 1966), pp. 429–439; A. A. Heggestad and J. J. Mingo, "Prices, Nonprices, and Concentration in Commercial Banking," *Journal of Money, Credit and Banking* (February 1976), pp. 107–117; F. R. Edwards, "The Banking Competition Controversy," *National Banking Review* (September 1965), pp. 1–34; Douglas F. Greer and Robert P. Shay, *An Econometric Analysis of Consumer Credit Markets in the United States*, Technical Study Vol. IV, National Commission on Consumer Finance (Washington, D.C., 1973), Chapter 2 and 4; H. W. de Jong, "Industrial Structure and the Price Problem: Experience in the European Economic Community," in *The Roots of Inflation*, edited by G. C. Means et al. (New York: Burt Franklin & Co., 1975), pp. 199–209; *Prescription Drug Price Disclosures*, Staff Report to the Federal Trade Commission (processed, 1975), part III; pp. 41–44; Almarin Phillips, "Evidence on Concentration in Banking Markets and Interest Rates," *Federal Reserve Bulletin* (June 1967) pp. 916–926; R. C. Aspinwall, "Market Structure and Commercial Bank Mortgage Interest Rates," *Southern Economic Journal* (April 1970) pp. 376–384; S. A. Rhoades, "Does the Market Matter in Banking?" Research Papers in Banking and Financial Economics (Washington, D.C., Federal Reserve Board, 1977); C. C. Slater, *Baking in America: Market Organization and Competition* (Evanston, Northwestern University Press, 1956), pp. 254–257; H. P. Marvel, "Competition and Price Levels in the Retail Gasoline Market," *Review of Economics and Statistics* (May 1978), pp. 252–258; R. Kessel, "A Study of the Effects of Competition in the Tax-Exempt Bond Market," *Journal of Political Economy* (July 1971), pp. 706–738; M. L. Marlow, "Bank Structure and Mortgage Rates," *Journal of Economics and Business* (No. 2, 1982), pp. 135–142; D. B. Graddy and R. Kyle, III, "The Simultaneity of Bank Decision-making, Market Structure, and Bank Performance," *Journal of Finance* (March 1979), pp. 1–18. S. A. Rhoades and R. D. Rutz, "The Impact of Bank Holding Companies," *Journal of Economics and Business* (No. 4, 1982), pp. 355–365; D. Hester, "Customer Relationships and Terms of Loans," *Journal of Money, Credit, and Banking* (August 1979), pp. 349–357.
[2] *Consumer Credit in the United States*, Report of the National Commission on Consumer Finance (December 1972), pp. 118–119.

One of the best studies of this type, concerning grocery retailing in 1974, was conducted by a team of University of Wisconsin economists. They compiled observations of the weighted average price to consumers of a "grocery basket" comprised of 94 comparable grocery products. Cross-section observations for several retail chains operating in 35 United States cities were included in the analysis.

The statistical upshot is summarized in Table 13–1. Row numerals indicate representative values of "relative firm market share," which is the individual retailer's market share in a single city divided by that city's four-firm concentration ratio, expressed as a percentage. For example, a top-ranked retailer with 15% market share in a market where the next three largest retailers enjoy 5% each would have a "relative" market share of 50%, because 15/(15 + 5 + 5 + 5) = 0.5.

The column headings indicate four representative values of four-firm concentration (40, 50, 60, and 70), each with two types of summary results. The dollar figures are estimates of "grocery basket" prices to consumers, holding all variables not mentioned in the table constant. The figures in parentheses show the percentage difference between each price and $90.95, which is the price when concentration is 40 and relative market share is 10 (the first cell in the upper left-hand corner of the table). Thus, for any given level of relative market share, it appears that grocery prices rise as concentration increases from 40 to 70. Price across the first row goes from $90.95 to $95.78, a leap of 5.3%. Across the bottom row, price jumps from $94.18 to $99.01, this last figure being 8.9% greater than the first cell's $90.95. At first glance these findings seem to conflict with our earlier stories of price wars in grocery retailing. However, they do not. City markets *vary* in structure, some being more competitive than others. Table 13–1 spans the range of possibilities.

A scan down the columns of Table 13–1 conveys the impression that a large relative market share also lifts prices. In light of our earlier discussion of gasoline retailing (page 242), these particular results should not strike you as a bolt from the blue. Translating the combined results for concentration and relative firm market share into even more arresting numbers, the Wisconsin team estimated that, nationwide, "monopoly overcharges" in the industry were in the neighborhood of $662 million during 1974, with great variations across cities.[3]

It almost goes without saying that the group also found a significant positive association between profits and these two measures of market power. However, we shall not pursue the profit issue now except to note that these results for prices and those from similar studies are essential to a proper interpretation

[3] B. W. Marion, W. F. Mueller, R. W. Cotterill, F. E. Geithman, and J. R. Schmelzer, *The Profit and Price Performance of Leading Food Chains 1970–74*, A Study for the Joint Economic Committee, U.S. Congress, 95th Congress, First Session (1977), p. 4. See also R. M. Lamm, "Prices and Concentration in the Food Retailing Industry," *Journal of Industrial Economics* (September 1981), pp. 67–78.

TABLE 13–1. Estimated Prices of Grocery Baskets for Different Combinations of Relative Market Share and Four-Firm Concentration, October 1974

Relative Firm Market Share	Four-Firm Concentration Ratio							
	40		50		60		70	
	Price ($)	Difference (%)	Price ($)	Difference (%)	Price ($)	Difference (%)	Price ($)	Difference (%)
10	90.95	(0)	91.84	(1.0)	93.64	(3.0)	95.78	(5.3)
25	91.65	(0.8)	92.54	(1.8)	94.34	(3.7)	96.48	(6.1)
40	93.16	(2.4)	94.05	(3.4)	95.85	(5.4)	97.99	(7.7)
55	94.18	(3.6)	95.07	(4.5)	96.87	(6.5)	99.01	(8.9)

Source: B. W. Marion, W. F. Mueller, R. W. Cotterill, F. E. Geithman, and J. R. Schmelzer, *The Profit and Price Performance of Leading Food Chains 1970–74*, A Study for the Joint Economic Committee, U.S. Congress, 95th Congress, First Session (1977), p. 66.

TABLE 13–2. Comparison of Average Prices in Countries With and Without Patent Protection for Drug Products, Spring 1959

Product (Producer)	Price in Countries with Product Patents ($)	Price in Countries without Product Patents ($)
Meticorten (Schering)	21.55	15.10
Miltown (Carter-American Cyanamid)	3.31	2.52
Diabinese (Pfizer)	4.87	4.82
Penicillin V (Eli Lilly)	13.80	10.97
Chloromycetin (Parke, Davis)	4.08	3.46
Aureomycin (American Cyanamid)	5.53	4.71
Achromycin (American Cyanamid)	5.68	4.68

Source: U.S. Senate, Subcommittee on Antitrust and Monopoly of the Committee on the Judiciary, *Administered Prices Drugs, Report*, 87th Congress, First Session, (1961), p. 109.

of the many profit studies reviewed later. Without these price studies we could never be certain that the observed positive association between profits and concentration (or profits and market share) was indeed due to "market power." A skeptic could argue that the cause of the positive profit association was not market power pushing up prices, but rather some *nonprice* profit-enhancing variable like productivity or efficiency, which could be positively but unmeasurably associated with concentration. In other words, profit studies substantially outnumber price studies, but the latter carry as much weight as the former in condemning excessive market power.

As we have seen, high concentration and high barriers to entry typically go hand in hand. We may assume, then, that these concentration-price studies reflect some positive price influence from substantial barriers to entry. More direct evidence of the barriers effect is available in Table 13–2, where patents serve as the entry barrier in question. This table's data come from a study sponsored by the Senate Subcommittee on Antitrust and Monopoly, which explored the effect of patent protection on drug prices. A survey was taken of prices in 18 countries—7 with patents for drug products and 11 without. Two columns of manufacturers' prices are presented in Table 13–2: those "with" and those "without." Both prices in each pair of average prices are derived from a *single* multinational company, apply to a *single* brand-name product and refer to *identical* dosages. All that changes is country group. As can be seen, prices tend to be higher in countries with drug product patents than in those without. The greatest differential is 42.7% for Meticorten. The smallest is 1% for Diabinese. Thus, high barriers to entry apparently also boost prices.[4]

[4] For related findings see H. D. Walker, *Market Power and Price Levels in the Ethical Drug Industry* (Bloomington, Ind.: Indiana University Press, 1971), Chapters 6, 7.

Cross-section price studies concerning other structural variables are equally informative. Figure 13–1 presents further findings in the drug market that reflect the combined effects of numbers of firms, product differentiation, and buyer power. Each of the 44 dots represents a major drug purchase by the U.S. Military Medical Supply Agency during 1959 and early 1960. Two characteristics of each sale are plotted there: (1) the number of firms bidding on the supply contract, as shown on the horizontal axis, and (2) the lowest price at which MMSA was able to buy the drug, which is expressed as a percentage of the price charged to retail druggists for the same product sold under brand name. The scatter diagram shows that *all* sales to the government's MMSA were priced below sales to retail druggists. The discount may be explained partly by the larger lot sizes of these sales and partly by the fact that product differentiation is much more prevalent in the general commercial sector than in the government sector. Moreover, the diagram plainly shows an inverse relationship between MMSA prices and the number of bidders.

Finally, it should be observed that power on the *buyer's* side of the market may influence price level. As if turnabout were truly fair play, conventional theory holds that concentration on the buyer's side may yield sufficient "monopsony" or "oligopsony" power to *reduce* seller's prices. Some of the bargain prices enjoyed by the government in Figure 13–1 probably reflect this buyer power. Government is a *big* buyer. In other areas, cross-section statistical studies

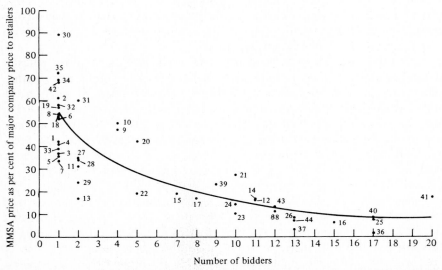

FIGURE 13–1. MMSA drug procurement: relationship of number of bidders to MMSA price expressed as percent of commercial price, 1959 and early 1960. Source: U.S. Senate, Subcommittee on Antitrust and Monopoly of the Committee on the Judiciary, Administered Prices of Drugs: Report. 87th Congress, 1st Session (1961), p. 95.

of raw materials and labor supplies have shown that, indeed, monopsony or oligopsony power often does depress prices.[5]

II. ENTRY LIMIT PRICING

A. The Theory

Barriers to entry are crucial to any discussion of long-run price strategy, for without them excessive prices and profits could not endure. The theory of "limit pricing" reflects this nicely: sellers in concentrated markets will set prices high enough to make excess profits but not so high as to attract new entry. Three assumptions underlie the theory:[6]

1. Established sellers and potential entrants seek maximum profits over the long run.
2. Established sellers think potential entrants will expect them to maintain their outputs in the event of new entry, letting price fall with the entrant's added output.
3. Established sellers have no difficulty colluding to determine and set the entry-limiting price.

The first postulate explicitly recognizes that anticipated profitability guides both classes of decision makers—entrants and established firms. Potential entrants calculate prospective profits from expected post-entry demand and cost conditions. In turn, the entrant's post-entry demand and cost conditions depend on the post-entry behavior of established sellers. The dependency is most readily seen with respect to post-entry demand. In essence, the more the established firms produce after the new firm's entry, the lower the entrant's demand will be at any given price. Figure 13–2 depicts this with a set of three demand curves. The long, uppermost curve is market-wide demand. The two shorter and lower curves represent the *entrant's* post-entry demand given two specific levels of post-entry output by *established* firms—Q_1 and Q_2. Given post-entry output Q_1, the entrant's demand curve is that segment of the market's demand curve extending southeast of point *A*. Given Q_2, the entrant's demand curve is that segment of the market's demand curve to the right of point *B*. These segments are shifted to the vertical axis to accord with the entrant's view of them.

---

[5] W. J. Mead, *Competition and Oligopsony in the Douglas Fir Lumber Industry* (Berkeley, Calif.: University of California Press, 1966), Chapters 11 and 12; J. H. Landon, "The Effect of Product-Market Concentration on Wage Levels: An Intra-industry Approach," *Industrial and Labor Relations Review* (January 1970), pp. 237–247; James L. Smith, "Risk Aversion and Bidding Behavior for Offshore Petroleum Leases," *Journal of Industrial Economics* (March 1982), pp. 251–269.

[6] D. K. Osborne, "On the Rationality of Limit Pricing," *Journal of Industrial Economics* (September 1973), pp. 71–80; J. S. Bain, *Barriers to New Competition* (Cambridge, Mass.: Harvard University Press, 1956); P. Sylos-Labini, *Oligopoly and Technical Progress* (Cambridge, Mass.: Harvard Univerity Press, 1962); D. Needham, "Entry Barriers and Non-price Aspects of Firms' Behavior," *Journal of Industrial Economics* (September 1976), pp. 29–43; F. Modigliani, "New Developments on the Oligopoly Front," *Journal of Political Economy* (June 1958), pp. 215–232.

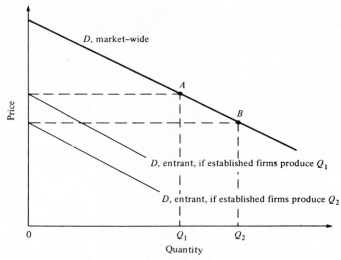

FIGURE 13–2. Derivation of post-entry demand facing a potential entrant.

These entrant demands are merely illustrative. Others are obviously possible. And the theory would now come to a grinding halt without further specification as to what the post-entry output of established firms will be. This then is where assumption 2 comes in. It is essential to much existing theory and is often called the "Sylos postulate" in honor of an entry theorist, P. Sylos-Labini, who relied heavily upon it. Given the Sylos postulate, the potential entrant must contend with a demand curve derived from that segment of the market-wide demand curve extending to the right of the *pre-entry* quantity produced by existing firms. In other words, established firm output is assumed to be fixed in the event of entry. We shall explore the reality of this assumption shortly. Present acceptance of it permits immediate consideration of the cost side of the potential entrant's profit calculations. For given the Sylos postulate demand curve, the potential entrant need only compare his cost conditions to this demand in order to reach a yes or no decision on entry.

Most entry barriers may be categorized as either (1) absolute cost differences between established firms and potential entrants, or (2) economies of scale. Figure 13–3 illustrates the first of these possibilities. It is like Figure 13–2, except that average total costs (ATC) have been added in simplified form for both the entrant and established firms. As depicted, the potential entrant, compared to established firms, suffers an absolute cost disadvantage at every level of output. Distance xz indicates the extent of disadvantage per unit of output.

Now, if established firms set price at P_{max} in hopes of maximizing their short-run profits, they would be inviting entry. Given the Sylos postulate, the entrant's post-entry demand curve would then be D_1, which exceeds the entrant's unit cost (ATC, entrant) over a substantial range. Entry would be profitable

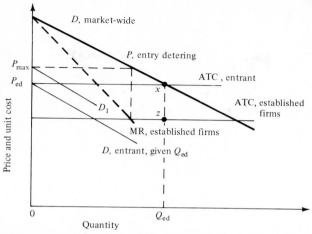

FIGURE 13–3. Entry limit pricing with absolute cost differences.

for the newcomer. Entry would also cut price and profit of established firms, however, so they may attempt to prevent the entry. The key question is what pre-entry combination of price and quantity will block the newcomer? According to assumption 3, the established firms know the answer and act together to implement the impediment. Price P_{ed} corresponds to output Q_{ed}, and, given the Sylos postulate, the combination will deter the entry. With Q_{ed}, the entrant's post-entry demand curve falls below D_1. More important, it falls below the entrant's unit costs at every level of output, preventing the entrant from earning any post-entry profit. In other words, P_{ed} is the highest price the established firms can charge without attracting entry. If the extent to which industry price can exceed average cost of the established firms is used to measure the height of entry barriers, then distance xz is the barrier premium in this case.

Barriers attributable to economies of scale add complexities to the theory because the barrier premium will then be a function of (1) the size of the market, (2) the elasticity of market-wide demand at any given price, (3) the scale at which economies of scale are exhausted, and (4) the rate of decline in the unit cost curve when moving from zero output to minimum efficient output. At least two diagrams are called for in this case—Figures 13–4(a) and 13–4(b). Their solid-line average total cost curves (ATC) display identical economies up to a minimum efficient scale (MES). Furthermore, it is now assumed that existing firms and potential entrants confront the *same* ATC curves. Thus, everyone is equally efficient or inefficient at a given level of output.

Figure 13–4(a), then, illustrates the effect of differing elasticities of demand. When the solid-line market-wide demand applies, P_{ed} and Q_{ed} are the entry deterring price and output. The resulting entrant's demand of D_{ent} is insufficient to cover cost at any output. And vw is the barrier premium associated with this particular solution. Note, however, that demand is inelastic at point v. In

303

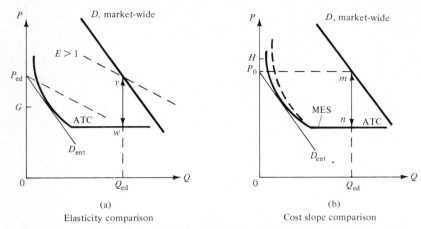

(a)
Elasticity comparison

(b)
Cost slope comparison

FIGURE 13–4. Maximum price-cost premiums with economies of scale.

contrast, the dashed demand curve of lesser slope is elastic. Were it applicable, P_{ed} and Q_{ed} would no longer deter entry because the entrant's dashed demand curve would then exceed extrant's cost. Given the Sylos postulate, established firms must cut price to G and expand output beyond Q_{ed} to deter entry in this instance. As a result, their barrier premium would shrink to less than one half the value of vw. Conversely, if we imagined a *lower* elasticity than that displayed by the solid line demand at v, entry deterring price would be higher than P_{ed} and the premium would be greater than vw.

Turning to Figure 13–4(b), we see that for a given level of minimum efficient scale, MES, the barrier premium will be greater the more rapidly unit cost rises at less than MES scale. Entry deterring price associated with the solid unit cost curve is P_0, and the resulting barrier premium is mn. A more rapid ascent of unit costs, as indicated by the dashed curve, would permit an even higher pre-entry price at point H plus a correspondingly larger barrier premium. Conversely, a flatter, less sharply rising unit cost curve would force the entry deterring price and barrier premium below P_0 and mn.

The reader should be able to see the similar effects ensuing from a shift right or a shift left of the MES, holding everything else about the cost curve constant (that is, its height and shape). The reader should also be able to work out the effects of market size, which may be accounted for by shifts of the market-wide demand curve. Lest your efforts go sour, however, we shall include the implications of such moves in the following summary of limit pricing theory: Entry deterring price and barrier premium will be higher (1) the greater the absolute cost disadvantage of potential entrants, (2) the lower the market-wide elasticity of demand at any price, (3) the sharper the increase in entrant's unit costs below minimum efficient scale output, (4) the larger the level of output at minimum efficient scale, and (5) the smaller the absolute size of the market.

B. Critique of the Theory

However neat and tidy these conclusions may seem, they can be misleading. The theory underlying them is too tightly bound and gagged by assumptions to give us any more than a very vague prediction of actual behavior. Our brief critique below will center on the Sylos postulate of identical pre- and post-entry established-firm output.

Can the pre-entry conduct of established firms be predicted? . . . No. The thinking of potential *entrants* is fairly straightforward. Their behavior depends on their expectations of post-entry established-firm reaction. But the theory is not based on entrant behavior. It is primarily grounded upon a very delicate balance of established-firm mental reasoning that may or may not be true. Established firms are presumed to *think* that potential entrants *think* not in terms of post-entry reactions but rather in terms of *pre-entry* policy. To be sure, pre-entry policy may signal something about post-entry reaction, but the meaning of such signals is not chiseled in granite on Wall Street. Moreover, the gap between signal senders and receivers is large, and the number of parties involved great enough to foul up communications. Indeed, the signal the theory postulates seems unrealistic. Established firms set price at the blocking point *and keep it there indefinitely.* A more realistic theory might have established firms reducing price when entry is imminent and raising it when the threat has subsided. Take, for example, Shop-Rite's attempted entry into the Washington, D.C., grocery retailing market in 1967:

> This chain came into the Washington market by opening three stores. It has since closed two of them. *Just prior* to this chain's entry into the Washington market, the stores of two leading Washington area chains [Safeway and Giant] located near the stores of the new entrant cut their prices substantially below those charged in the rest of the metropolitan area. In doing so, these stores operated on abnormally low margins and . . . sustained substantial losses.[7]

Thus, contrary to the theory, established firms are often capable of identifying specific entry threats as they arise, especially where substantial plant and equipment purchases must precede entry. Moreover, established firms might deliberately maintain excess capacity, which capacity could be used to increase output and depress price at the appearance of an entrant on the horizon. This approach is not always optimal, but J. Wenders has shown that, when it is profitable, it invalidates the Sylos postulate.[8]

Can the post-entry conduct of established firms be predicted? . . . No. Theorists who rely heavily on the Sylos postulate like to argue that a constant output policy is plausible because it is most unfavorable to entrants. As we have just

[7] Federal Trade Commission, *Economic Report on Food Chain Selling Practices in the District of Columbia and San Francisco* (Washington, D.C., 1969), pp. 4, 23. For a related example see J. B. Dirlam and A. E. Kahn, *Fair Competition* (Ithaca, N.Y.: Cornell University Press, 1954), pp. 213–214.

[8] J. T. Wenders, "Excess Capacity as a Barrier to Entry," *Journal of Industrial Economics* (November 1971), pp. 14–19. See also A. M. Spence, "Entry, Capacity, Investment, and Oligopolistic Pricing," *Bell Journal of Economics* (Autumn 1977), pp. 534–544.

seen, however, this conclusion is unwarranted. Post-entry reactions of established firms can be much more nasty than this. On the other hand, they can also be rather accommodating. Established firms often cut back output to make room for entrants. Established firms are not necessarily moved to this action by the spirit of benevolence; it may be better for their profits to see that price is maintained. Several examples are provided by the large electrical equipment manufacturers, who, during the great price-fixing conspiracies, allocated market shares of certain product lines to smaller rivals that had not produced in those submarkets before. To accommodate the entrants, General Electric and Westinghouse had to give up some of their market shares.[9] In short, the post-entry behavior of established firms is largely unpredictable.

Can potential entrant conduct be predicted?. . . No. Entry will not necessarily occur even if price is maintained well above the so-called "entry deterring" level. Potential entrants know that it is post-entry price that counts, and nightmares of bloody post-entry price wars may keep them out. Conversely, entry may very well occur despite the diligent efforts of established firms to keep pre-entry price below the probable unit costs of potential entrants. Inexperienced entrants may be overly optimistic about their cost prospects or about the mood of existing sellers. (After all, a pessimist is just an experienced optimist.) In sum, the theory provides predictions about the behavior of potential entrants that seem no more solid than those concerning established firms.

Does limit pricing theory explain maximum long-run price level? . . . No. Despite appearances, it can be argued that the theory does not really explain maximum long-run price level.[10] The theory predicts a price level low enough to ward off entry, and presents this prediction as the more plausible of two possible options—(1) an especially high price, such as P_M in Figure 13-5, that invites entry, and (2) a lower entry-deterring price, such as P_E in Figure 13-5. Because theory chooses the lower of these two options, P_E, it appears that this conduct establishes the *utmost* long-run price. But there really is no such price option in the *long run.* Under either option, price will end up at the *same* level. If price is initially set high enough to attract entry, then a multiplication of competitors will drive price down until it equals the entry-deterring price P_E (at which point entry stops). If price is initially set at entry-deterring level, P_E, it obviously ends at the entry-deterring level. The only long-run difference in these two options is the number of firms eventually in the market and the likely level of concentration, with the first distinction obviously yielding the more competitive structure of the two. Since the high initial price option yields a more competitive structure, a further unwinding of the theory might produce predictions concerning different long-run price levels, but only indirectly. That is to say, the more competitive of the two structures might foster a relatively lower price level in the long run, a level *below* entry-deterring price

[9] C. C. Walton and F. W. Cleveland, Jr., *Corporations on Trial: The Electric Cases* (Belmont, Calif.: Wadsworth, 1964), p. 52.
[10] D. K. Osborne, "The Role of Entry in Oligopoly Theory," *Journal of Political Economy* (August 1964), pp. 396–402.

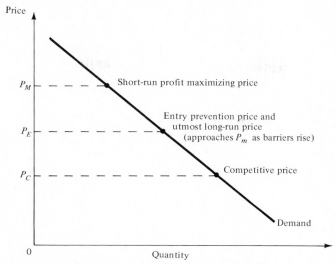

FIGURE 13–5. Alternative price levels and the theory of limit pricing.

near P_C in Figure 13–5. Aside from this possibility, however, the theory of limit pricing conduct is more important from the standpoint of *concentration* than of price.

Notice: we are *not* saying that barriers to entry themselves are unimportant to price level. We are saying that, in theory, barriers to entry *alone* explain *utmost possible* long-run price (and the higher the barriers, the higher this maximum long-run price P_E will be relative to the purely competitive price P_C). Simple price setting does not determine that maximum. We are also saying that pricing conduct can, and does, affect *actual* long-run price level, but only through two channels: (1) As already suggested, conduct together with concentration will determine *where* observed price actually lies between utmost long-run (entry-deterring) price P_E and purely competitive price P_C. (2) Conduct other than simple price setting may affect the height of barriers to entry, thereby *indirectly* affecting utmost long-run price.

III. OPEN PRICING

A. Theory

Disenchantment with limit pricing theory has led many theorists to devise models of "open pricing." Early theories of open pricing stressed the notion that established firms might actually earn higher profits by pricing high and inducing entry than by holding prices down. By open pricing, established firms deliberately give up part of the market to newcomers; however, they earn hefty profits in the short run before entries divide demand. Of course established firm profits will fall as entry proceeds; their market share will shrink and market

307

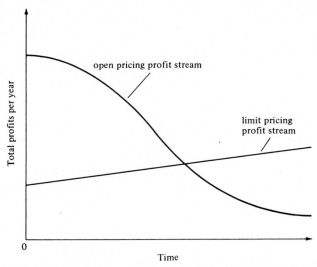

FIGURE 13–6. Profit streams of established firms under two price strategies.

price will fall. This profit trend is shown by the declining curve in Figure 13–6. Lucrative early profits turn into skimpy profits with time. By contrast, the profit stream associated with a limit pricing strategy is fairly steady over time and may actually rise slightly if the market is growing. This too is shown in Figure 13–6.

Although the limit pricing profit stream is below the open pricing profit stream at the start, it eventually supersedes the latter. This raises a pertinent question: Is open pricing therefore a model of *short-run* profit maximizing and limit pricing a model of *long-run* profit maximizing? Despite your eyeball's affirmative answer, your mind should be telling you "No, both models are similar in that both assume *long-run* profit maximization as the goal of established firms." Both models can be put on the same footing for long-run comparison by (1) properly *discounting* each profit stream to reduce the value of distant and therefore less useful dollar revenues, (2) adding up the discounted values in each resulting series, and (3) thereby converting the profit stream to *present values.* Given a common objective of long-run profit maximization, the strategy yielding the highest present discounted value will be chosen.

Advocates of the open pricing model argue that "the present value of a series of declining profits . . . may exceed the present value of a perpetual profit rate. . . ."[11] Not surprisingly, advocates of the limit price model think the opposite. Actually, recent theorists have refined and elaborated this basic issue until it is now inaccurate to regard it as a stark either-or matter. Their models do not speak in terms of open pricing's flood of entry versus a drought induced by limit pricing. Theorists who continue to assume that established

[11] G. J. Stigler, *The Theory of Price* (New York: Macmillan Publishing Co., 1952), p. 234.

firms control the entry spigot try to determine what *intermediate and varying rate* of entry will maximize the present value of established firm profits under diverse assumptions.[12]

B. Empirical Evidence on "Open" and "Limit" Pricing

Empirical tests of these various hypotheses are extremely difficult. Attempts tend to crack up on many of the same rocks endangering empirical explorations of whether firms try to maximize profits. Business intentions hide beneath brain folds, and observable outcomes may not correspond with intentions. Nevertheless, a few pieces of empirical evidence are available, and they indicate a mixed pattern. Open pricing, limit pricing, and intermediate pricing all appear.

Prominent examples that appear to fit the open pricing mold include the steel, corn-product, and copper markets. U.S. Steel's early high price policy and continued loss of market share received earlier mention. But one does not have to look far for equally valid examples of what appear to be limit pricing. During the first half of this century Alcoa reported no more than moderate profits despite its considerable power. Similarly, General Foods Corporation is said to price its specialty products at low to moderate levels in "full realization that a high price will restrict the volume and . . . speed up the process of developing competition."[13] Another example from the food industry is Campbell Soup, which "has steadfastly refused to raise prices far enough above costs to reap a short-term deluge of profits, thereby discouraging any real competition."[14]

Some firms have switched from limit pricing to open pricing as circumstances changed. For example, Du Pont, United Shoe Machinery, and Kodak apparently employed limit pricing during the first half of this century to help maintain monopoly power in cellophane, shoe machinery, and film processing. But they switched to open pricing after antitrust actions induced them to encourage entry.[15]

Finally, there are examples of single firms demonstrating *both* theories at the *same time* in different markets. One is Xerox. It appears to have engaged in limit pricing for its very high-volume market (serving customers making more than 100,000 copies per machine per month); simultaneously it used open pricing in the low-volume market (below 5000 copies per machine per month). In the middle volume range, Xerox followed an "in between" policy. Who threatened entry? Patents prevented any "dry process" entry in the early years of Xerox's success. But electrofax technology was developed at about the same

---

[12] D. W. Gaskins, "Dynamic Limit Pricing: Optimal Pricing Under Threat of Entry," *Journal of Economic Theory* (September 1971), pp. 306–322; D. P. Baron, "Limit Pricing, Potential Entry, and Barriers to Entry," *American Economic Review* (September 1973), pp. 666–674; M. Kamien and N. Schwartz, "Limit Pricing and Uncertain Entry," *Econometrica* (May 1971), pp. 441–454.

[13] A. D. H. Kaplan, J. B. Dirlam, and R. F. Lanzillotti, *Pricing in Big Business* (Washington, D.C.: Brookings Institution, 1958), p. 216.

[14] T. Horst, *At Home Abroad* (Cambridge, Mass.: Ballinger Co., 1974), p. 16.

[15] Don E. Waldman, *Antitrust Action and Market Structure* (Lexington, Mass.: Lexington Books, 1978), pp. 41–49, 146–149; Waldman, "The du Pont Cellophane Case Revisited," *Antitrust Bulletin* (Winter 1980), pp. 805–830.

time and was liberally licensed to all comers by RCA. Thus the impact of Xerox's pricing policies may be gauged in terms of electrofax firm entry into these submarkets up through 1967. Limit pricing held entry down to just three firms. Open pricing brought in twenty-five. In between, ten newcomers entered the middle volume segment of the copy machine market.[16]

Several cross-section statistical studies have sought more general conclusions than these individual examples provide. Like the individual examples, these statistical studies yield mixed results. Yet the mixed results seem to reveal an interesting pattern. First, in terms of Figure 13–5, relatively few firms raise price to the very high short-run profit maximizing level of P_M, and these few are typically protected by very high barriers to entry, so that entry deterring price P_E is pretty close to P_M in these cases. Stated differently, extreme instances of "open" pricing seem rare. Second, extreme instances of "limit" pricing seem equally rare. In terms of Figure 13–5, most firms with discretionary pricing power choose to price somewhat above P_E rather than below, thereby inducing *some* entry but preventing floods of newcomers. Thus, actual price typically lies somewhere between P_M and P_E, falling further below P_M as P_E falls further below P_M toward P_C when entry is easy.[17]

In sum, theories of an intermediate sort—those hypothesizing that firms maximize the present value of their profit stream by allowing an *intermediate and varying rate* of entry—have received support. As a result:

> High market shares *are* usually eroded over time. The average decay process is strong enough to abate monopoly positions in the course of 20 to 30 years. Yet this rate is exceedingly moderate.[18]

Still, there are exceptions where entry is barred for many decades or gushes in rather rapidly and expansively. The exceptions include cases where entry is fended off not so much by persistently moderate prices and profits as it is by sharp below-cost price cuts, quick advertising escalations, and other predatory tactics.

One last generalization is particularly heartwarming and therefore worthy of mention. Fresh entry of material significance is usually followed by price reductions.[19]

---

[16] E. A. Blackstone, "Limit Pricing and Entry in the Copying Machine Industry," *Quarterly Review of Economics & Business* (Winter 1972), pp. 57–65.

[17] Robert T. Masson and Joseph Shaanan, "Stochastic-Dynamic Limiting Pricing: An Empirical Test," *Review of Economics and Statistics* (August 1982), pp. 413–422.

[18] W. G. Shepherd, *The Treatment of Market Power* (New York: Columbia University Press, 1975), pp. 113–129.

[19] Between 1971 and 1982 the retail price of soft contact lenses fell from $400 to $100 largely because Bausch & Lomb's monopoly withered following the entry of nearly 30 competitors. *Wall Street Journal*, November 24, 1982, pp. 27, 33; *Fortune*, July 27, 1981, pp. 56–60; *Business Week*, November 17, 1980, pp. 173–184. Other cases are too numerous to list, but a few interesting instances should be cited: W. H. Martin, "Public Policy and Increased Competition in the Synthetic Ammonia Industry," *Quarterly Journal of Economics* (August 1959), pp. 373–392; Elizabeth Marting (ed.), *Creative Pricing* (American Management Association, 1968), p. 30; "A Painful Headache for Bristol-Myers?" *Business Week*, October 6, 1975, pp. 78, 80; M. N. Harris "Entry and Long-Term Trends in Industry Performance," *Antitrust Bulletin* (Summer 1976), pp. 295–314.

IV. PRICE DISCRIMINATION

Like a pesky housefly, price discrimination unavoidably invaded the foregoing discussion. Safeway and Giant Foods used it to repulse Shop-Rite's entry into Washington, D.C. The large multinational drug companies used it with results shown in Table 13-2. Most every enterprise and market provides examples. For *price discrimination occurs whenever a seller sells the same commodity or service at more than one price,* for example, Meticorten at $21.55 and $15.10. Moreover, even if the sale items are not exactly the same, price discrimination is said to occur if the seller sells very similar products at different price/cost ratios. IBM, for instance, used to rent two disk-drive systems that differed only slightly in cost and model number (the 2314 and 2319) but immensely in price ($1455 a month versus $1000). The broad definition includes cases in which costs differ and identical prices are charged, and cases involving high prices on low-cost sales coupled with low prices on high-cost sales (as frequently occurred under the single basing point system discussed in Chapter 12).

A. Essential Conditions

Three conditions are essential for price discrimination: (1) The seller must have some *market power.* A purely competitive firm does not have sufficient control over price to engage in discrimination. (2) The seller must confront buyers who have *differing price elasticities of demand.* These elasticity differences among classes of buyers may be due to differences in income level, differences in "needs," differences in the availability of substitutes, differences in use of the product, and so on. Without different elasticities, buyers would not willingly pay different prices. To practice price discrimination, of course, the seller must be able to identify these different demands. (3) These various buyer elements must be kept *separate.* Without separation, low-price customers could resell their purchases to the high-price customers, subverting the seller's ability to identify and segregate the different demands. A grisly example of the importance of market separation was furnished during the early 1940s by Röhm & Haas, in connection with its sale of methyl methacrylate plastic. General industrial users were charged 85 cents a pound, whereas dental laboratories and dentists who used the plastic for making dentures were charged 45 *dollars* a pound. After many dental buyers discovered the difference, "bootlegging" or, more technically, arbitrage became a problem. To stifle bootlegging the company considered poisoning the industrial plastic. The Food and Drug Administration would have then unwittingly enforced separation of the markets for Röhm & Haas. To quote from Company correspondence:

> A millionth of one percent of arsenic or lead might cause them [the FDA] to confiscate every bootleg unit in the country. There ought to be a trace of something that would make them rear up.[20]

[20] Corwin D. Edwards, *Economic and Political Aspects of International Cartels,* U.S. Senate, Subcommittee on War Mobilization of the Committee on Military Affairs, 78th Congress, Second Session (1944), p. 19.

Röhm & Haas eventually rejected the idea, but it did start rumors that the industrial material had been adulterated.

B. Analysis of Price Discrimination

Theoretically, price discrimination is usually analyzed in three categories—first degree, second degree, and third degree.

First Degree Discrimination. This is perfect discrimination. Each and every unit sold goes for the very highest price above cost it can fetch. Each and every buyer pays as much as he is willing to pay for the quantity he wants. Figure 13–7 compares first degree price discrimination with single, uniform pricing. With a single price of *OB, OQ* units would be purchased, yielding total revenues equal to *OBCQ,* which is price times quantity. Given constant total unit costs of *OB,* including a normal profit, the seller earns no more than a normal profit. Buyers willingly pay *OBCQ.* Indeed, by definition of the demand curve, they would actually be willing to pay *OBCQ plus* the shaded area *ABC,* or *OACQ.* The difference between what they actually pay and what they are willing to pay is called "consumers' surplus," which in this case is *OACQ − OBCQ,* or *ABC.* Under first degree price discrimination, sellers are able to extract this consumers' surplus as well as the *OBCQ* revenue obtained from the single price. Seller's total revenue then equals the entire area under the demand curve between *A* and *C,* and profits bulge.

For obvious reasons, such perfect discrimination is extremely difficult in the real world and is never achieved in practice. However, Xerox may have

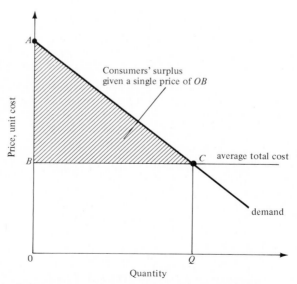

FIGURE 13–7. First degree price discrimination.

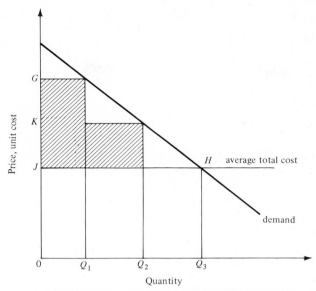

FIGURE 13–8. Second degree price discrimination.

come pretty close to perfection, at least during the 1960s.[21] The company did not at first sell its 914 copy machines. It *leased* them and *metered* the intensity of their use, charging $25 per month plus 3.5 cents per copy. Low intensity users paid little; high intensity users paid a lot. In this way price was tailored to each individual customer's willingness to pay and elasticity of demand. Was this profitable? Absolutely!

> The estimated cost of producing the original 914 copier was approximately $2500. Some users, because of the large number of copies they make on their leased Xerox machines, have paid Xerox an *annual rental* of more than $20,000 per machine or—assuming at least a five-year machine life—a total "purchase price" of more than $100,000 for each such machine.[22]

The key to the system was the meter. Most sellers cannot practice first degree discrimination because they cannot measure the depth of each buyer's desire and ability to pay. In addition, leasing kept buyers separate from each other. Had Xerox *sold* its machines at widely differing prices, bootleggers would not have gone begging.

Second Degree Discrimination. Second degree price discrimination is illus- trated in Figure 13–8. Demand is partitioned into three blocks. Quantity OQ_1, is sold at price OG. Quantity Q_2-Q_1 is sold at price OK. And finally, quantity

[21] E. A. Blackstone, "The Copying-Machine Industry: Innovations, Patents, and Pricing," *Antitrust Law and Economics Review* (Fall 1972), pp. 105–122.
[22] *Ibid.*, p. 112.

313

Q_3-Q_2 is sold at price OJ. Total revenues obtained are $OJHQ_3$ plus the shaded area. In other words, this system is like first degree discrimination only less refined. Much less consumers' surplus is extracted. Standard examples include "quantity discounts" and "block rate" pricing of electricity and gas. Xerox used such a scheme during the late 1960s for its copier-duplicators (not its 914s). Its charges were 4¢ each for the first three copies from the same original, 2¢ each for the fourth through the tenth copies, and 1¢ each for every copy above 10. (This too was profitable. Overall, Xerox earned 21–30% after-tax return on net worth during the period 1962–1970.)

Third Degree Discrimination. This is depicted in Figure 13–9. The negatively sloped demand curves indicate monopoly power. Differences in their angles of descent and intercepts indicate differing elasticities of demand at each possible price, with the result that buyers in market X have the relatively more elastic demand. Total unit cost (ATC) is the same in both markets because the product is basically the same. Moreover, ATC is again assumed to be constant. This means that ATC and marginal cost (MC) are identical. Following the conventional profit maximizing formula of MR = MC, we find that P_x and Q_x are the optimal combination in market X, whereas P_y and Q_y are the optimal combination in market Y. Shading again indicates excess profits. Notice that price in the relatively elastic market, P_x, is substantially below price in the relatively inelastic market, P_y. Indeed, nothing would be sold in market X at price P_y. Notice also that if these markets could not be kept separate, their demands, their elasticities, and of course their buyers, too, would blend, leaving only one market for the seller instead of two.

Third degree discrimination is considerably more widespread than second degree and much more so than first degree. Examples abound. The auto industry alone provides many interesting illustrations:

1. Fleet buyers have frequently been able to buy new cars at unit prices considerably below those paid by individual consumers.

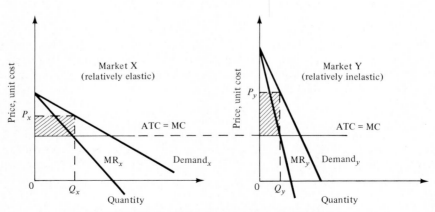

FIGURE 13–9. Third degree price discrimination.

2. Manufacturers' markups vary across model lines. In the past, big luxury line cars carried the greatest spread between wholesale price and direct manufacturing cost. Ford, for example, charged the following markups as a percent of manufacturer's price in 1966: Ford "Custom" two-door sedan, 6.7%; "Galaxie 500" sedan, 13.4%; and "LTD" two-door hardtop, 21.1%.[23] More recently, relative elasticities of demand seem to have shifted with the skyrocketing popularity of small cars as compared to big cars, and the auto manufacturers have modified the size of these profit margins accordingly. GM took the lead in 1980 by *lowering* the price of its luxury cars 2.4% while *raising* the price of its subcompacts 10.1%.[24]

3. Manufacturers charge a much higher profit markup on repair parts than on parts in the form of fully assembled new vehicles. Two key factors help to explain the difference: (a) parts generally have a very low price elasticity of demand, and (b) assemblers may try to use parts sales to "meter" each consumer's intensity of auto use.[25]

4. When selling repair parts, the Big Three vehicle manufacturers have apparently discriminated against their own dealers. Rough estimates from the late 1960s indicate that independent warehouse distributors paid about 30% less for assembler brand parts than what franchised dealers paid.[26] Independent wholesalers enjoyed bargain prices because, to some degree, they could turn to alternative parts suppliers. In fact, only about 40% of all parts moving through independent channels at that time came from vehicle producers; the other 60% came from independent parts manufacturers. By contrast, franchised dealers were "persuaded" to buy at least 75% of their parts from the vehicle manufacturers. Instruments of producer persuasion included threat of franchise cancellation, delayed shipment of new vehicles at the beginning of the new model year, and so on. The dealers' burden is lightened somewhat by the manufacturers' efforts to "persuade" consumers through advertising and warrantee stipulations that "factory authorized service" is the only kind of service they should get. GM's massive "Mr. Goodwrench" campaign is a good example of this.

5. Finally, discrimination occurs in dealers' showrooms, as cars are one of the few (legal) commodities still available to consumers at negotiated and therefore variable prices. No more than about 40% of all buyers pay full "sticker" price. Those not paying sticker, dicker. And some dicker better than others.

Other common examples of third degree price discrimination relate to firms selling in several product lines, with differing degrees of market power across

[23] U.S. Senate, Select Committee on Small Business, *Hearings on Planning, Regulation, and Competition: Automobile Industry—1968,* 90th Congress, Second Session (1968), pp. 273–321.
[24] *Business Week,* September 22, 1980, pp. 78–88.
[25] R. W. Crandall, "Vertical Integration and the Market for Repair Parts in the U.S. Auto Industry," *Journal of Industrial Economics* (June 1968), pp. 212–234.
[26] R. W. Crandall, "The Decline of the Franchised Dealer in the Automobile Repair Market," *Journal of Business* (January 1970), pp. 22–23.

those product lines. In accord with the empirical findings reviewed earlier, intra-firm price/cost ratios tend to be positively associated with the firm's market power across products.[27]

C. Social Effects

Actually, the catch-as-catch-can price discrimination of auto showrooms fits none of the theoretical models just outlined. Other real-life forms also fail to fit, such as discrimination associated with basing-point pricing, or with secret "off-list" discounting during recessions, or with predatory pricing. Even so, the social desirability of all forms of price discrimination may be judged by three criteria—income distribution effects, efficiency effects, and competitive effects. The first two of these criteria will be fully explored in Part IV when we come to performance. However, it should be recognized now that blanket labels of "good" or "bad" are inappropriate.

With respect to income distribution, for instance, price discrimination quite clearly adds to profits at the expense of consumers. Since this may contribute added inequality to society's unequal distribution of income, many would say that is bad. On the other hand, profit-enhancing price discrimination may occasionally make the difference between profit and loss, in which case the very existence of the enterprise in question depends on its ability to discriminate. Suppose, for example, that some small town could not attract the services of a physician unless it allowed him to charge the rich higher prices than the poor, there not being much income from that particular practice under a flat fee system. The profit-enhancing properties of discrimination in this instance would be good. Good and bad competitive effects can also be found. It is these competitive consequences that we shall develop more fully now and in the next chapter, beginning with predatory pricing.

V. PREDATORY PRICING

A. Definition

There are two elements common to all phenomena called "predatory pricing." First, predatory pricing involves temporary price cuts, not for purposes of enlarging demand but rather for purposes of eventually restricting supply. Once the predator is in a position to restrict supply (either by himself or with the cooperation of others), price is then increased. Since "predation" usually requires price to be cut at least below total unit cost, and since the eventual increase carries price well above total unit cost, the stream of profits generated by this ploy is the opposite of that generated by open pricing, as depicted in Figure 13–6. That is to say, losses lead profits. Predatory pricing would make no sense if

[27] For examples see Kaplan, Dirlam, and Lanzillotti, *op. cit.*, pp. 72–74; and C. Kaysen, *United States v. United Shoe Machinery Corporation* (Cambridge, Mass.: Harvard University Press, 1956), pp. 74–77, 125–134; M. J. Peck, *Competition in the Aluminum Industry 1945–1958* (Cambridge, Mass.: Harvard University Press, 1961), Chapter V.

the losses incurred during the predatory campaign were not rewarded by profits after the campaign is over.

The second element of predatory pricing is the predator's "staying power" or "deep pocket," which must be greater or deeper than that of the rivals who are to be preyed upon. As with Nature's great predator *Felis leo,* large absolute size is an advantage. "If such a concern finds itself matching expenditures or losses, dollar for dollar, with a substantially smaller firm, the length of its purse assures it of victory."[28] As with Nature's other ferocious predator, *Homo sapiens,* versatility and guile also help. The business counterparts of these advantages are diversification and price discrimination. Thus, business predation typically involves selling at a loss in one geographic area or in one product line while selling at a profit, perhaps even a substantial profit, elsewhere.

In short, these two elements of predatory pricing relegate the beast to the family tree of "limit pricing" and "price discrimination." Let us now consider the three specific forms it takes: (1) driving competitors from the field, (2) disciplining uncooperative competitors, and (3) hindering entry. These are simply three roads to the broad objective of eventually restricting supply.[29]

B. Driving Competitors Out

Use of predatory pricing to drive competitors out is obviously what gives the practice its name:

> The most extreme form of predatory pricing takes place when a seller holds price below the level of its rivals' costs (and perhaps also its own) for protracted periods, until the rivals either close down operations altogether or sell out on favorable terms. The predator's motivation is to secure a monopoly position once rivals have been driven from the arena, enjoying long-run profits higher than they would be if the rivals were permitted to survive.[30]

Of the two forms of victim liquidation, *bankruptcy* and *merger,* the one more favorable to the profit positions of both predator and prey is merger. Unless the victimized rival is very weak to begin with, or unless the predator applies nonprice harassments such as sabotage or patent infringement suits, a price war to the finish can be very expensive for both combatants. As Lester Telser

[28] Corwin D. Edwards, "Conglomerate Bigness as a Source of Power," in *Business Concentration and Price Policy* (Princeton, N.J.: Princeton University Press, 1955), p. 334.

[29] What follows is a distillation of a rather lengthy debate between those who argue that predatory pricing of any kind is essentially irrational and nonexistent versus those who take a less skeptical view. Among the former group are J. S. McGee, "Predatory Price Cutting: The Standard Oil (N.J.) Case," *Journal of Law & Economics* (October 1958), pp. 137–169; L. G. Telser, "Cutthroat Competition and the Long Purse," *Journal of Law & Economics* (October 1966), pp. 259–277; R. O. Zerbe, "The American Sugar Refinery Company 1887–1914: The Story of a Monopoly," *Journal of Law & Economics* (October 1969), pp. 339–375; and R. H. Koller II, "On the Definition of Predatory Pricing," *Antitrust Bulletin* (Summer 1975), pp. 329–337. On the other side are R. C. Brooks, Jr., "Injury to Competition Under the Robinson-Patman Act," *University of Pennsylvania Law Review* (April 1961), pp. 777–832; F. M. Scherer, *Industrial Market Structure and Economic Performance* (Chicago: Rand McNally, 1970), pp. 273–278; and B. S. Yamey, "Predatory Price Cutting: Notes and Comments," *Journal of Law & Economics* (April 1972), pp. 129–142.

[30] Scherer, *op cit.,* p. 273.

puts its, "Since both firms can benefit by agreeing on a merger price, and both stand to lose by sales below cost, one would think that rational men would prefer merger."[31]

Indeed, the attractions of merger may be great enough to make price cutting of any kind seem superfluous. But merger is often illegal, and selective and controlled price cutting can serve several purposes even when merger is legal and the ultimate goal. The price the predator must pay to acquire rivals will be lower according to the vigor of the warfare or the *threat* of warfare. If mere threat can cause victims to sell out cheaply, so much the better. But a threat is hollow unless occasionally carried out. Another purpose served by combining predatory pricing and merger, as opposed to simply buying up rivals, is that such a policy discourages entry. A predation-free policy of merger at attractive prices to those selling out would stimulate the entry of new firms, thereby foiling plans for eventual monopolization. Case histories of firms that have used predatory pricing to gain monopoly power seem to bear out this reasoning. As mentioned in Chapter 9, most of the interesting examples occurred around the turn of the century, and antitrust has made even uninteresting examples now rather rare. Tobacco, sugar, oil, and business machines are among the industries with interesting skeletons in their closets.[32]

C. Disciplining Uncooperative Competitors

In October 1953, after a costly union wage settlement had substantially increased the labor costs of brewing beer, Anheuser-Busch (AB) attempted to lead a general price increase everywhere except Wisconsin and Missouri. However, several local and regional brewers failed to follow. According to AB's president, August A. Busch, Jr., that was the first time he could remember when, after the large brewers increased their prices, all locals and regionals did not increase their prices also. In an apparent attempt to punish selected mavericks, AB cut its price in the St. Louis market from $2.93 a case to $2.35 a case, thereby eliminating the price "premium" AB maintained between itself and "inferior" regional brands such as Falstaff. Although failure to follow had not actually occurred inside St. Louis (because there had been no attempt by AB to raise prices there), the maverick St. Louis brewers, Falstaff among them, sold beer *outside* St. Louis where price increases *were* attempted and ignored. Perhaps AB feared that its punitive motive would have been obvious to antitrust authorities had it cut prices in, say, Illinois, where an up-and-down sequence would have stuck out like a sore thumb. In any event, motive may be inferred from President Busch's later testimony that AB might not have "done anything" if these regional rivals had also raised their prices in October 1953. AB's price cut in St. Louis lasted 13 months, during the course of which its market share

---

[31] Telser, *op. cit.*, p. 265.

[32] Besides the preceding references see U.S. Bureau of Corporations, *Report of the Commissioner of Corporations on the Tobacco Industry* (Washington, D.C., 1909, 1915), Parts I, II, and III; A. S. Eichner, *The Emergence of Oligopoly* (Baltimore: Johns Hopkins Press, 1969); William Rodgers, *Think: A Biography of the Watsons and IBM* (New York: Stein and Day, 1969), Chapters 2, 3, 4.

there jumped from 12.5% to 39.3%, a *tripling* at the expense of the mavericks. Then, in February 1955, AB announced a 20% price increase. Not wanting to make the same mistake twice, the battered regionals followed.[33]

In sum, this is an example of predatory pricing for disciplinary purposes. It has both the main elements of predation—deep, temporary price cuts plus an imbalance of power. But the objective is not one of driving rivals from the market. Other examples could be drawn from gasoline retailing, grocery retailing, cement, building materials, and sugar.[34]

D. Predatory Pricing to Deter Entry

The price of 1,000 5 mg. Valium tablets to Canadian hospitals in 1969 was $42.70. Shortly thereafter it fell to *zero,* as Hoffmann-LaRoche Limited (Roche), who held a monopoly on diazepam (Valium's generic name), tried to fend off the entry of Vivol, Horner Company's brand of diazepam.[35] Roche thought its monopoly was worth preserving because Valium, a tranquilizer, had become very profitably the most heavily prescribed drug in Canada after oral contraceptives. Horner's attempted entry followed on the heels of a change in Canadian patent law, which brought the compulsory licensing of drug patents. The battle centered on the hospital market rather than the retail market because the hospital market was the easiest door by which to enter. Once a product gained a foothold there, hospital doctors and interns would also prescribe it in their private practice.

Knowing of Horner's plans to launch Vivol in early 1970, Roche officials decided in late 1969 that an extended giveaway of Valium would be wise:

> It is our feeling that this tactic will not only abort Horner's efforts but serve as a warning to [other drug manufacturers] who seem to be showing an interest in this product.

In May 1970, after Horner's first shipments to hospitals, Roche personnel agreed that "the pipeline would be kept filled" by giving away Valium. So in June, Roche began giving Valium away free to hospitals, a program that lasted one year and dispensed a total of 82 million pills, the market price of which would have been about $2,600,000.

---

[33] R. C. Brooks, Jr., offers a good brief account of these events, U.S. Congress, House of Representatives *Hearings on Small Business and the Robinson-Putman Act,* Vol. 2, 91st Congress, (1970), pp. 721–738. It should be admitted that this interpretation is not universally accepted among economists. For example, Koller claims there was no predation in the AB case ["The Myth of Predatory Pricing: An Empirical Study," *Antitrust Law and Economics Review* (Summer 1971), pp. 105–123].

[34] Federal Trade Commission, *Economic Report On the Structure and Competitive Behavior of Food Retailing* (January 1966), pp. 121–142; *Federal Trade Commission v. Cement Institute, et. al.,* 333 U.S. 683 (1948); C. D. Edwards, *Maintaining Competition* (New York: McGraw-Hill Book Co., 1964), pp. 169–170; A. S. Eichner, *op. cit.,* pp. 243–246; F. C. Allvine and J. M. Patterson, *Competition, Ltd.: The Marketing of Gasoline* (Bloomington, Ind.: Indiana University Press, 1972), Chapters 5–7.

[35] What follows comes from "Reason for Judgment in Her Majesty the Queen v. Hoffmann-LaRoche Limited," Released on February 5, 1980, mimeo, Supreme Court of Ontario.

Horner, as you might well guess, did not make much headway in the hospital market during Roche's giveaway. Indeed, it may be that some of Horner's personnel began taking their Vivol tranquilizers to stay calm. Still, Roche's strategy was not completely successful because Horner enjoyed surprising success in the non-hospital market, selling over $12,000,000 worth of Vivol between 1970 and 1974.

Our earlier Shop-Rite example would also fit under predatory pricing to deter entry. But a summary is now in order, not further examples.[36] Predatory pricing may thus affect market structure as much as limit pricing and open pricing, especially in its starkest forms. When used to discipline mavericks, its structural effects are slight but its price-level effects can be substantial. Because predatory pricing inflicts injury on the predator as well as the prey, it is much less common than merger or cartelization, two techniques that often substitute for predatory pricing.[37]

VI. TYING AND EXCLUSIVE DEALING

Earlier we said that conduct other than simple price setting may affect the height of barriers to entry. Terms and conditions of sale such as tying and exclusive dealing occasionally have this influence. Under **tying arrangements** the seller allows the buyer to buy one line of the seller's goods *only* if the buyer also buys other goods as well. For instance, if Xerox required users of its machines to buy copy paper from Xerox, that would be tying. **Exclusive dealing** is closely related. A seller, usually a manufacturer, gives the buyer, who is usually a wholesaler or retailer, access to the seller's line of goods only if the buyer agrees to handle no goods from any of the seller's rivals. In other words, exclusive dealing binds a buyer to make *all* his purchases from a particular seller. It differs from tying in that (1) it may cover a considerable range of goods, and (2) it limits buyers to a single source of supply. For a hypothetical example, General Electric might require its appliance wholesalers to carry only General Electric appliances, thereby excluding Westinghouse, Whirlpool, and others from the wholesaler.

Tying and exclusive dealing are treated extensively in the next chapter for they are the focus of much antitrust policy. We mention them here because they may be used to further price discrimination or hamper entry.

[36] But if you want more see G. W. Brock, *The U.S. Computer Industry: A Study of Market Power* (Cambridge, Mass.: Ballinger, 1975), pp. 109–134; and U.S. Senate, Subcommittee on Antitrust and Monopoly, *Hearings on the Industrial Reorganization Act* Part 7, "The Computer Industry," 93rd Congress Second Session (1974), pp. 5637–5794. For a summary of recent predatory pricing in gypsum see *Recent Efforts to Amend or Repeal The Robinson-Patman Act,* Hearings before the Ad Hoc Subcommittee on Antitrust . . . and Related Matters of the Committee on Small Business, U.S. Congress, House, 94th Congress Second Session (1975–76), Part 1, pp. 514–520; Part 2, pp. 36–57. The gypsum case illustrates "discipline" as well as entry "deterence."

[37] Predation by cost increase is often more effective than predation by price reduction, partly because the predator need not then suffer substantially. See Steven C. Salop and David T. Scheffman, "Raising Rivals' Costs," *American Economic Review* (May 1983), pp. 267–271.

320

SUMMARY

The principal objective assumed for this chapter's analysis is long-run profit maximization. Given favorable structural conditions concerning the number of firms, concentration, condition of entry, product differentiation, and long-run elasticity of demand, pursuit of this objective may lead to higher prices and lower output than would prevail under pure competition. These effects are most readily seen in intraindustry, intermarket, cross-section statistical studies that reveal a positive association between prices and high concentration, fewness of sellers, product differentiation, and high barriers to entry. For buyers, "monopsony" power appears to reduce prices paid.

Mechanisms provide some crucial linkage here. Objectives and structural conditions alone do not produce these price and output effects directly. Given the profit objective, conditions may permit limit pricing, open pricing, price discrimination, predatory pricing, tying, and exclusive dealing. Substantial barriers and high concentration, for instance, are prerequisites to limit pricing. In turn, these mechanisms may be used either to exploit or expand market power, or both. When used to enhance market power—that is, to increase concentration or hamper entry—we have a case of reverse causal flow. Whereas the conventional model posits structure causing conduct, here we find instances of conduct altering structure. Later chapters will see even greater attention paid to this possibility.

14 Price and Production Strategy in the Long Run: Public Policy

That the Robinson-Patman Act . . . is the most controversial of our antitrust laws may be the understatement of the century.

—FREDERICK ROWE

There are many things in life that can be either good or bad depending on the circumstances—wealth and wine, for instance. The same applies to price discrimination, tying, and exclusive dealing. Under some circumstances, these practices increase competition. At times they lessen competition. It is this good/bad dichotomy that makes public policy in this area a delicate exercise. Indeed, public policy itself can be procompetitive or anticompetitive. And when public policy attempts to govern such dichotomous practices it may do more harm than good. Policy cannot easily extract pure essence of good when treating acts of uncertain and variable virtue.

The purpose of this chapter is to review and assess public policy governing price discrimination, tying, and exclusive dealing (there being no policies concerning "limit" or "open" pricing). The statute law in these areas began in 1914 with Sections 2 and 3 of the Clayton Act. Section 2, concerning price discrimination, was greatly altered by the Robinson-Patman Amendment of 1936. Now, more than a thousand enforcement actions later, we confront a large body of case law that requires summary consideration. Controversy sparked by price discrimination policy also receives attention. A discussion of Section 3 of the Clayton Act, concerning tying and exclusive dealing, concludes the chapter.

I. PRICE DISCRIMINATION

The Clayton Act's original Section 2 outlawed only flagrantly predatory price discrimination. Its limited scope, plus several loopholes, yielded few prosecutions. As mentioned in the previous chapter, predatory pricing is rare, especially when illegal. While this law lay idle, chain stores revolutionized grocery, drug, and department store merchandising. Small, single-shop, "mom-and-pop" stores suffered and, during the Great Depression, began dropping like blighted apples. The outcries of their owners caused the Federal Trade Commission (FTC) to study and report. Although the FTC's report found much virtue in chain stores, it also found that "a most substantial part of the chains' ability to undersell independents" could be attributed to the chains' ability to buy goods from manufacturers more cheaply than independents could. The chains' **oligopsony** buying power "forced" manufacturers to discriminate in favor of chains. Moreover, their large size enabled chains to buy directly from manufacturers, thereby sidestepping independent brokers, wholesalers, jobbers, and other middlemen as well as underselling independent retailers. So Congress went to bat for small business. In the words of Congressman Patman in 1935:

> The day of the independent merchant is gone unless something is done and done quickly. He cannot possibly survive under that system. So we have reached the cross road; we must either turn the food . . . business of this country . . . over to a few corporate chains, or we have got to pass laws that will give the people, who built this country in time of peace and who saved it in time of war, an opportunity to exist. . . .[1]

In short, the purpose of the Robinson-Patman Act of 1936 went well beyond the traditional antitrust purpose of maintaining competition. It injected two new objectives: *protection* of small business and maintenance of *"fair"* or "equitable" price relationships between buyers who compete with each other as sellers.

A. Subsection 2(a) of Robinson-Patman

The aims of protection and equity lurk beneath the tortured language of all six main subsections in the Act, especially 2(a). Subsection 2(a) prohibits a seller from charging different prices to different purchasers of "goods of like grade and quality" where the effect "may be substantially"

1. "to lessen competition or tend to create a monopoly in any line of commerce," or
2. "to injure, destroy, or prevent competition with any person" (or company)
   (a) "who either grants or"
   (b) "knowingly receives" the benefit of the discrimination, or
   (c) "with customers of either of them."

Thus, there are two definitions of **illegal competitive effect:** (1) a *broad* definition, that refers to substantial lessening of competition in the *market as a whole,* and (2) a *narrow* definition that refers to injury to *particular competitors.* The broad definition reflects the traditional antitrust aim of maintaining competition, and its language matches that applying to mergers. In contrast, it is the narrow definition that reflects the aims of protection, equity, and fairness.

[1] Hearings Before the House Committee on the Judiciary on *Bills to Amend the Clayton Act,* 74th Congress First Session (1935), pp. 5–6.

Either of these two forms of competitive damage may occur in

(a) the seller's market, which is called **primary level injury**
(b) the buyers' market, which is called **secondary level injury**
(c) the market containing customers of the buyers, which is called **tertiary level injury.**

If, for example, a manufacturer cuts price to one wholesaler but not to others, it might damage competition among manufacturers (primary level), or among wholesalers (secondary level), or among retailers who buy from the wholesalers (tertiary level). If it were a matter of direct sales to retailers, then retailers would be the buyers of the discriminating seller, and they would then be considered "secondary" level. If this sounds confusing to you, you are not alone, as indicated by itemization of the first common criticism of the act.

Common Criticism 1: The act is "a roughly hewn, unfinished block of legislative phraseology," a "masterpiece of obscurity," a source of "crystal clear confusion."[2]

Compounding the confusion, several types of price discrimination have been found injurious to competition. Some of these were merely alluded to in the previous chapter. They are (1) volume or quantity discounts, (2) territorial price discrimination, and (3) functional discounts. These are outlined in Table 14–1, together with indications of the level at which they are said to damage competition and the specified breadths of injury typically used in the past by the FTC and appellate courts when enforcing the statute. The dashes in the table identify combinations of level and type that are rarely if ever attacked under the law. These blank combinations are eligible for illegality, but the authorities tend to ignore them. The bottom row of Table 14–1 shows the defenses discriminators of each type occasionally used to fend off FTC attorneys. These defenses—"cost" and "good faith"—are explicitly recognized by the Robinson–Patman Act:

- *Cost defense:* "nothing herein . . . shall prevent differentials which make only due allowance for differences in the cost of manufacture, sale, or delivery resulting from [differing methods of sale or delivery]."

- *Good faith defense,* Subsection 2(b): "nothing herein . . . shall prevent a seller rebutting the prima-facie case . . . by showing that his lower price . . . was made in good faith to meet an equally low price of a competitor . . ."

Unfortunately, these defenses do not offer much protection in practice. The cost defense has fallen into disuse because the FTC and appellate courts have been very stingy in allowing its application. They require elaborate proofs and reject justifications based on reallocations of overhead costs. The meeting competition in good faith defense is disallowed if the price reduction is excessively

[2] "Eine Kleine Juristische Schlummergeschichte," *Harvard Law Review,* (March 1966), p. 922.

TABLE 14–1. Summary Outline of Injury Definition Applied, Given the Basic Types of Discrimination Found to be Illegal and Market Level of Reference

| | Type of Price Discrimination | | |
Level of Injury	Volume or Quantity Discounts	Territorial Price Discrimination	Functional Discounts
Primary level	Broad or narrow	Broad or narrow	—
Secondary level	Narrow	Narrow	Narrow
Tertiary level	—	—	Narrow
Main line of possible defense	Cost	Good faith	Cost or good faith

aggressive (gaining business rather than merely keeping it); if it continues after lower prices of competitors are known to have been raised; or if there is a lack of precise knowledge concerning competitors' prices. Moreover, the firm may not meet competition if it has reason to believe that the price being met is itself unlawful. In light of their rare use, these defenses do not deserve detailed treatment here.

Common Criticism 2: By amendment or reinterpretation, the defenses open to discriminators ought to be liberalized.

Before delving into the case law concerning the act, we may note in its language two major anomalies. First, despite its origins, the statute's fire is focused not on the power or conduct of oligopsonistic *buyers* but rather on the conduct of *sellers*. As Corwin Edwards observes:

> The avowed purpose of the Congress was to use the law of price discrimination to curb the buying power of chain stores and other large buyers. However, the means to be employed consisted primarily in forbidding sellers, the presumed victims of that buying power, from granting the concessions that were exacted from them. . . . If the statute was an effort to protect competition from the pressure of powerful buyers on weak sellers, it was anomalous to provide that protection primarily by action against weak sellers who succumbed to the pressure. Such a process bears some resemblance to an effort to stamp out mugging by making it an offense to permit oneself to be mugged.[3]

Our roster of antitrust defendants has so far been dominated by giants like IBM and Alcoa. The roster of Robinson-Patman defendants, however, introduces a population largely composed of midgets such as Samuel H. Moss, Inc., and Fruitvale Canning Company. The possibility that this oblique approach on sellers might backfire is illustrated by the *Jens Risom* case of 1967, in the office furniture

---

[3] Corwin D. Edwards, *The Price Discrimination Law* (Washington, D.C.: Brookings Institution, 1959), p. 63.

field. Furniture manufacturers such as Risom sold to retailers at a discount off list price amounting to as much as 50%, whereas their sales to interior decorators, who competed with the retailers, were at no more than 40% discount. As a result of the FTC's order ending the discrimination, Risom and some other manufacturers eliminated interior decorators as direct buying customers. These decorators thereafter had to buy furniture for their clients through retailers. Thus, although the intent of the FTC's order was to place decorators on an equal competitive footing with retailers, decorators ended up at the mercy of the retailers with whom they competed. Subsequent to the order, several decorators reported that their clients' costs had increased—one giving estimates of increases ranging from 10 to 20%, depending on which retailer supplied the decorator's clients with furniture.[4]

A second notable quirk concerns the statute's definition of price discrimination. Price differences unjustified by cost differences are "discriminatory," but cost differences unaccompanied by price differences are not. In other words, the economic definition of discrimination—differing price/cost ratios, even if prices are identical—is rejected by the statute in favor of a definition that hinges almost entirely on price differences alone. The consequences of this approach are illustrated by the *Binney & Smith* case. Binney & Smith, Co., was found by the FTC to have sold school supplies at a uniform price to both jobbers, who are middlemen, and large retail chains. This price uniformity, though obviously injurious to jobbers, was not questioned by the FTC.[5]

Common Criticism 3: Even accepting the act's purposes as proper, the statute is ill-conceived. Indeed, many proponents of protection and fairness are disappointed with it.

Before discussing the types of discrimination listed in Table 14–1, we should first specify the kinds of evidence that indicate "broad" or "narrow" injury, the two designations comprising the body of Table 14–1. **Broad** (or **marketwide**) **injury** to competition is indicated by substantial reductions in the number of competitors in the market, elevated barriers to entry, a lack of competitive behavior in pricing, or foreclosure of substantial parts of the market to existing competitors. **Narrow** (or **competitor**) **injury** is indicated by simple price differences among customers, or a price difference coupled with diversion of business from the disadvantaged buyer toward the favored buyer, or diversions away from a nondiscriminating seller toward a discriminating seller. Injuries embraced by this narrow definition are clearly more personal than those embraced by the broad definition. That is, the discrimination appears to cripple a *single* firm or particular *class* of firms. Obviously, the broad definition coincides more nearly with a purely economic definition of competition, while the narrow definition coincides with some notions of fairness.

[4] *Recent Efforts to Amend or Repeal the Robinson-Patman Act*, Part 1, Hearings before the Ad Hoc Subcommittee on Antitrust . . . and Related Matters of the Committee on Small Business, U.S. Congress, House, 94th Congress, First Session (1975), pp. 282–312.
[5] Edwards, *op. cit.*, p. 311.

To search out the extent to which the FTC relies on these two options, R. Brooks studied the records of 73 subsection 2(a) cases that were actually tried (rather than settled by consent degree) between 1936 and 1969. He found evidence of broad injury in only one third of the cases (with some trend away from strictly narrow injury during the 1960s).[6] A quick glance at Table 14–1 also reveals that narrow evidence of injury is more commonly used by the FTC, especially when judging injury at secondary and tertiary levels. At primary level, broad injury has been found only in cases concerning volume or quantity discounts and territorial price discrimination.

Volume and Quantity Discounts. These are first cousins to second degree price discrimination. Quantity discounts are based on the amount purchased in a *single* transaction, with large quantities lowering price. Volume discounts are based on *cumulative* purchases, involving numerous transactions, during some stated period of time, such as one year. Of the two, volume discounts are least likely to be cost-justifiable and more anticompetitive in the broad sense. For these reasons the FTC has attacked volume discounts much more vigorously than it has quantity discounts. At primary level, volume discounts can heighten barriers to entry or foreclose small sellers from substantial segments of the market.[7]

Although such discounts may have genuine anticompetitive effects at primary (seller's) level, very few cases have actually been argued on these grounds. The rarity may be due to a dearth of situations causing broad injury at primary level. Then again, it may also be a consequence of the fact that, under the act, volume and quantity discounts are more easily prosecuted on grounds of narrow injury at the secondary or buyer level. Recall that a major purpose of the act was to make such prosecutions as these easier.

The classic case here is *Morton Salt,* decided by the Supreme Court in 1948. Morton sold its table salt at $1.60 a case in less-than-carload lots, at $1.50 a case for carload lots, and at still lower prices of $1.40 and $1.35 for annual volumes exceeding 5,000 and 50,000 cases, respectively. In defense of these prices, Morton claimed that they were equally available to all, that salt was just one tiny item in grocers' inventories, and that therefore competitive injury could not arise. Rejecting these arguments the Court concluded as follows:

> The legislative history of the Robinson-Patman Act makes it abundantly clear that Congress considered it to be an evil that a large buyer could secure a competitive advantage over a small buyer solely because of the large buyer's quantity purchasing ability. . . . Here the Commission found what would appear to be obvious, that the competitive opportunities of certain merchants were injured when they had to pay [Morton] substantially more for their goods than their competitors had to pay. . . . That [Morton's] quantity discounts did result in price differentials between

---

[6] R. C. Brooks, Jr., Testimony, *Small Business and the Robinson-Patman Act,* Hearings before the Special Subcommittee on Small Business and the Robinson-Patman Act of the Select Committee on Small Business, U.S. Congress, House, 91st Congress, Second Session (1970), Vol. 2, p. 657.

[7] R. C. Brooks, Jr. "Volume Discounts as Barriers to Entry and Access," *Journal of Political Economy* (February 1961), p. 65.

competing purchasers sufficient to influence their resale price of salt was shown by the evidence. . . . Congress intended to protect a merchant from competitive injury attributable to discriminatory prices on any or all goods sold in interstate commerce, whether the particular goods constituted a major or minor portion of his stock. . . . [In] enacting the Robinson-Patman Act Congress was especially concerned with protecting small business. . . .[8]

This narrow, numerical interpretation of injury was later carried to such extremes that during the 1950s the FTC inferred injury despite evidence that "the beneficiaries of the discrimination were small and weak," and despite "unanimous statements by the disfavored customers that they were not injured."[9] Since then, this hard line has softened somewhat, but a fairly stringent interpretation of secondary line injury still prevails.

Critics of this policy argue that although individual *competitors* may suffer, *competition* may not. Such discrimination in favor of large buyers is said to "introduce flexibility into the distributive system, helping to compress traditional markups, and prevent or disrupt a rigid stratification of functions."[10] Moreover, a large buyer "which does indeed make possible cost savings on the part of its suppliers may yet, in facing impure markets, have to coerce suppliers into giving it the concessions which its greater efficiency justifies."[10] In short, price discrimination may increase price flexibility and rivalry at primary and secondary levels; it may also contribute to efficiency. Even so, enhanced competition is not automatic. Price concessions are not always passed on to consumers or spread throughout the market. Moreover, loss of even a few competitors diminishes competition where there are only a few to begin with. The ultimate effect depends heavily on the circumstances. Hence controversy will continue.[11]

Territorial Price Discrimination. This type of discrimination takes two forms: (1) selective geographic price cutting and (2) fictional freight charges imposed under basing-point pricing systems. Both received earlier mention. The former has produced many illegal primary line injuries, whereas the later has been charged with injuring competition at secondary level. As indicated in Table 14–1, neither can be defended by cost justifications. Because geographic price cutting includes "predatory pricing," several primary line cases of this sort cast a good light on the Robinson-Patman Act. In fact, they give the FTC its finest hours of enforcement.[12] These cases contain poignant examples of genuine

---

[8] *Federal Trade Commission v. Morton Salt Co.,* 334 U.S. 37 (1948).

[9] Edwards, *op. cit.,* p. 533, referring to Standard Motor Products (Docket No. 5721), and Moog Industries (Docket No. 5723).

[10] J. B. Dirlam and A. E. Kahn, *Fair Competition* (Ithaca, N.Y.: Cornell University Press, 1954), pp. 204–205.

[11] For a good discussion of the circumstances see *ibid,* Chapters 7 and 8. See also L. S. Keyes, "Price Discrimination in Law and Economics," *Southern Economic Journal* (April 1961), pp. 320–328.

[12] *E. B. Muller & Co. v. FTC,* 142 F. 2d 511 (6th Cir. 1944); *Maryland Baking Co. v. FTC,* 243 F. 2d 716 (4th Cir. 1957); *Forster Mfg. Co. v. FTC,* 335 F. 2d 47 (1st Cir. 1964). Among private cases see *Volasco Prods. Co. v. Lloyd A. Fry Roofing Co.,* 346 F. 2d 661 (6th Cir. 1965); *Moore v. Mead's Fine Bread Co.,* 348 U.S. 115 (1954); and *Continental Baking Co. v. Old Homestead Bread Co.,* 476 F. 2d 97 (10th Cir. 1973).

broad injury to competition; they also contain striking evidence of predatory intent. Some excerpts from business correspondence follow:

> "So by continuing our efforts and putting a crimp into him wherever possible, we may ultimately curb this competition if we should not succeed in eliminating it entirely."

> "Don't try to follow me. If you do, we will put you out of business."

The latter message was no idle threat; ensuing below-cost prices ultimately throttled the smaller competitor.[13]

Still, geographic price discrimination may also be procompetitive. It may be used for promotional purposes; for entering new geographic markets; or for further penetrating established markets to spread overhead costs. When used for these laudable purposes, it is usually less systematic than the "sharp-shooting" associated with predation. Nevertheless, procompetitive territorial pricing has occasionally been attacked by the FTC. In the *Page Dairy* case, for instance, the FTC myopically went after a firm whose unsystematic price discrimination was actually undermining its competitors' efforts at cartelization:

> From the trial record it appears that before the complaint against Page Dairy, other dairies had made an unsuccessful effort to draw it into agreement to fix prices. . . . It is a reasonable inference that the competitors of the company brought its prices to the Commission's attention, not because the local discrimination was unusual, but because Page Dairy was a price-cutter and would not co-operate with other dairies.

> The Commission's order in 1953 required Page Dairy to cease selling to any buyer at a lower price than to any other buyer where it was in competition with any other seller. The immediate effect of the order was a price increase by Page Dairy, as a result of which various dairies that had been troubled by price competition of the company felt that their problems had been met.[14]

The line between geographic price cutting that is predatory or destructive of competition and that which promotes or expands competition is obviously difficult to draw. "But," according to the critics, "one thing is certain: it cannot be drawn merely at the point where a price reduction diverts trade from a competitor."[15]

Common Criticism 4: As interpreted, the law stifles genuine price competition, thereby raising and stiffening price levels.

Returning to the bright side of the coin, the FTC put the Robinson-Patman Act to good use in attacking collusive basing-point price systems in the *Corn*

---

[13] *Forster Manufacturing Co., op. cit.*

[14] Edwards, *op. cit.,* pp. 443–444. For a related example see William K. Jones, Testimony, *Small Business and the Robinson-Patman Act,* Hearings before Special Subcommittee on Small Business of the Select Committee on Small Business, House, 91st Congress, First Session (1969), Vol. 1, p. 109.

[15] Philip Elman, "The Robinson-Patman Act and Antitrust Policy: A Time for Reappraisal," *Washington Law Review,* Vol. 42 (1966), p. 13.

Products Refining case of 1945 and others.[16] As we have seen, basing-point systems are price-fixing mechanisms, but the FTC's initial assault was based on narrow secondary line injury under Subsection 2(a). (Later, in *Cement Institute,*[17] a restraint of trade approach was applied.) The defendant in *Corn Products* produced glucose in Chicago and Kansas City plants, but maintained Chicago as a single basing point. Thus, both plants sold only at delivered prices computed as if all shipments originated in Chicago. Kansas City candy manufacturers who bought glucose from the Kansas City plant were charged phantom freight, as if the sweetening had come all the way from Chicago. After hearing the case on appeal, the Supreme Court accepted the FTC's finding that the candy manufacturers located in Kansas City competed with those in Chicago. The Court also bought the idea that, though small, the price differentials on glucose would affect the candy makers' costs and final prices. The cost differences were said to be "enough to divert business from one manufacturer to another." Consequently, narrow competitive injury was adjudged at the secondary or buyer level (between candy manufacturers), and the price system was banned.

Functional Discounts. As indicated by Table 14–1, primary level injury is not usually associated with functional discounts, but findings of narrow injury at secondary and tertiary levels have been frequent. By definition, functional discounts are determined not by amounts purchased or buyer location but rather by the functional characteristics of buyers. Functions in the "traditional" distribution network are well known: Producers sell to wholesalers, who sell at a higher price to jobbers, who in turn sell at a higher price to retailers, who finally sell at a still higher price to consumers. Other functional differences may be based on other buyer classifications, such as government versus private.

The problem of illegal price discrimination arises when people of different functions compete. Most commonly, "traditional" channels get jumbled, as when resale competition crops up between resellers in different classifications, or when a producer sells at various levels in the distribution network to someone's disadvantage. In other words, discrimination between buyers who are *not* in competition with each other is *not* a violation. The FTC has never ruled against a functional discount *per se;* somebody down the line must be disadvantaged relative to his competitors.

For example, if a producer charges a lower price to its direct-buying retailers than to its independent wholesalers, competition may be injured at the *retail* level between its direct buyers and the *customers* of the independent wholesalers. In *Tri-Valley Packing Association v. FTC,* a processor of canned fruits and vegetables sold its canned goods at lower prices to certain retail chains with buying agencies in San Francisco than it charged retailers and wholesalers who did not have buying agencies in San Francisco. The FTC and appellate court found violation of Subsection 2(a) because the direct buying retailers had an

---

[16] *Corn Products Refining Company v. FTC,* 324 U.S. 726 (1945).
[17] *FTC v. Cement Institute,* 333 U.S. 683 (1948).

advantage over their competitors who had to buy from the higher paying wholesalers.[18]

A different problem arises when a buyer performs a dual role, say wholesaling *and* retailing, in which case he may get a large wholesaler's discount that gives him a competitive advantage when reselling as a retailer but not when reselling as a wholesaler.[19] Critics point out that compliance with the Robinson-Patman Act in these instances often raises a serious inconsistency. Compliance implies that the producer must control the prices at which his independent middlemen resell. But such control involves the producer in "resale price maintenance," or vertical price fixing, which is generally illegal under Section 1 of the Sherman Act.[20]

Common Criticism 5: Compliance with the price discrimination law in this and other respects is inconsistent with other antitrust policies.

An Overview. Critical analyses of the Robinson-Patman Act suggest that procompetitive discriminations may be distinguished from anticompetitive discriminations by whether they are perpetrated by firms with small or large market shares. *Systematic, large-firm discriminations tend to be anticompetitive, whereas unsystematic, small-firm discriminations tend to be competitive.* But there are exceptions.

The criticism may give the added impression that enforcement zealous enough to crush many small-firm discriminations must have also stamped out large-firm discriminations altogether. But this inference would be fallacious. Discrimination can take many forms not reached by the law. A powerful seller may favor particular buyers by making uniform price reductions upon that part of his product line most important to those particular buyers. Moreover, a powerful seller can sometimes refuse to sell to those he disfavors. Similarly, a powerful buyer, deprived of discriminatory price concessions, can nevertheless obtain substantial advantages in acquiring goods:

> It can (a) take a seller's entire output ·at a low price; (b) obtain low prices from sellers who are meeting some other seller's lawful competition; (c) buy goods cheaply abroad; (d) obtain low prices upon goods so differentiated from what bears higher prices that the prohibition of the law is inapplicable; (e) obtain goods of premium quality without paying a premium price; (f) buy large amounts under long-term contract when prices are unusually low; or (g) produce goods for itself.[21]

For these many reasons, chain stores have thrived despite the law. The shrewd reader may think up other avenues of evasion. Brokerage payments and preferential promotional services or allowances cannot be among them, however. Dis-

---

[18] *Tri-Valley Packing Ass'n v. FTC,* 329 F. 2d 694 (9th Cir. 1964).

[19] *FTC v. Standard Oil Co.,* 355 U.S. 396 (1958) and 340 U.S. 231 (1951); *Mueller Company v. FTC,* 323 F. 2d 44 (7th Cir., 1963).

[20] Edwards, *op. cit.,* p. 312.

[21] Corwin D. Edwards, "Control of the Single Firm: Its Place in Antitrust Policy," *Law & Contemporary Problems* (Summer 1965), p. 477.

crimination via these routes is foreclosed by Subsections 2(c), (d), and (e) of the Robinson-Patman Act, each of which warrants a few words.

B. Subsections 2(c), (d), and (e)

As may be seen from Table 14–2, these portions of the Robinson-Patman Act are *not* simple extensions of Subsection 2(a) governing seller's price differences. Whereas some kind of probable competitive injury must be shown under 2(a), such is not the case for (c), (d), and (e). Furthermore, whereas 2(a) discriminators may defend themselves by cost justifications or demonstrations of meeting competition in good faith, those running afoul of Subsections 2(c), (d), and (e) may not, except for (d) and (e) with respect to good faith. In other words, these additional provisions of the act specify what could be considered *per se* violations.

Subsection 2(c), the **brokerage provision,** outlaws payment or receipt of brokerage fees that cross the sales transaction from seller to buyer. It also prohibits any compensation *in lieu* of brokerage. Brokers (whose job it is to match up buyers and sellers without ever taking title to the goods) are quite active in the grocery game plus a few other distributive trades. Subsection 2(c) was aimed primarily at a practice in the food industry by which chain stores large enough to buy direct, without benefit of brokers, got price reductions equivalent to the brokerage fees that sellers would have otherwise paid. In practice, however, this provision outlawed *all* brokerage commissions, large or small, except those paid to a truly independent broker. At times, 2(c)'s rigorous application has harpooned marketing arrangements that helped small concerns. In the *Biddle* case, for instance, Biddle sold market-information services to 2,400 grocery buyers—placing their orders with sellers, collecting brokerage from sellers, and then passing some brokerage on to the buyers in the form of reduced information fees.[22] This practice was declared illegal, however, as were others equally beneficial to small independents.[23] The courts held that "The seller may not pay the buyer brokerage on the latter's purchases for his own account" (period). The Supreme Court's *Broch* opinion of 1960[24] has since introduced a modicum of flexibility into brokerage cases, but a modicum is not a magnum.

Subsection 2(d) makes it unlawful for a seller to make any **payment to a buyer** in consideration of the buyer's promotion of the seller's goods, unless similar payments are made available on "proportionately equal terms" to *all* competing buyers. Subsection 2(e) makes it unlawful for the seller himself to **provide promotional services** to or through a buyer unless he provides opportunity for such services on "proportionately equal terms" to *all* other competing buyers.

For example, if Revlon were to provide Macy's, Bullock's, and Sears with in-store demonstrators of Revlon cosmetics, or if they *paid* these large retailers

---

[22] *Biddle Purchasing Co., v. FTC,* 96 F. 2d 687 (1938).

[23] See, e.g., *Quality Bakers v. FTC,* 114 F. 2d 393 (1940); and *Southgate Brokerage Co. v. FTC* 150 F. 2d 607 (1945).

[24] *FTC v. Henry Broch & Co.,* 363 U.S. 166 (1960).

TABLE 14–2. Comparative Outline of Subsections 2(a), (c), (d), (e), and (f), of the Robinson-Patman Act

Subsection	(1) Competitive Injury Required?	(2) Cost Defense Available?	(3) Good Faith Defense Available?	(4) Violator is Buyer or Seller?
2(a) General	1. Yes	2. Yes	3. Yes	4. Seller
2(c) Brokerage	1. No	2. No	3. No	4. Both
2(d) Promotional pay	1. No	2. No	3. Yes	4. Seller
2(e) Services	1. No	2. No	3. Yes	4. Seller
2(f) Buyer inducement	Buyer liability for knowingly inducing violation of one of the above			

to conduct these demonstrations, then Revlon would have to make equal-proportionate opportunities of some kind open to all retailers who compete with Macy's, Bullock's, and Sears in cosmetics. You may ask proportionate to what? And in what way? Does that mean that Revlon must circulate a midget giving one-shot, 15-minute demonstrations amongst independent corner drug stores for every fully developed model it sets up in Macy's for a week-end visit?

The FTC and the courts have chopped through a thick jungle of questions such as these during the past 40 years. And, in order to guide the ordinary, time-pressed businessman through the treacherous path so cleared, the FTC has kindly drawn-up a long "Guide for Advertising Allowances and other Merchandising Payments and Services" that attempts to clarify the case law for laymen. Among other things, it states that a seller's burden under the law is heavier than mere selection of the appropriate allowances or services. He must (1) know which customers compete with each other, (2) notify each competing buyer that these aids are available, and (3) police the destination of any payments to make sure they are properly spent.[25] Although the general economic effect of these regulations is unclear, a multitude of small merchants seems to support them on grounds of fairness and equity. Interviews with apparel merchants, after intensive FTC activity concerning 2(d), turned up the following typical response: "It cleaned up the problem of individually negotiated advertising allowances which was inherently unfair to the small guy."[26] Although most economists do not ridicule such sentiments, they tend to be skeptical, even cynical.

Common Criticism 6: Subsections 2(c), (d) and (e) should not pose per se violations. Discriminations of any kind should be subjected to tests of competitive injury and be allowed liberal cost and good faith defenses.

[25] P. Areeda, *Antitrust Analysis* (Boston: Little, Brown and Co., 1974), p. 951–960.
[26] *Recent Efforts . . . , op. cit.,* p. 346.

333

C. Subsection 2(f), Buyer Inducement

Subsection 2(f) makes it unlawful for any buyer "knowingly to induce or receive a discrimination in price which is prohibited by this Section." Here Congress finally addressed the problem it was really most worked up about—the big buyer who pressures his suppliers for discriminatory concessions. However, this subsection has been used more sparingly than a spare tire because the Supreme Court has made it difficult for the FTC to apply. The FTC's attorneys have the burden of proving (1) that an illegally injurious discrimination occurred, (2) that it was not cost justified, and (3) that the buyer *knew* it was not cost justified.

Ordinary 2(a) cases require no more of the FTC's attorneys than item (1). In 2(a) cases the burden of proof regarding costs naturally rests with the discriminator who wants to defend himself, and buyer knowledge is irrelevant. This absence of items (2) and (3) makes "kid stuff" of typical 2(a) prosecutions. But according to the Supreme Court's view of 2(f), a buyer cannot be expected to know the details of his supplier's cost, and a buyer may therefore be unaware that the bargain prices he pays are illegal.[27] Off hand, this ruling might make any such prosecutions seem impossible, since wily buyers might evade offenses by maintaining a state of carefully contrived ignorance. But prosecution is merely difficult. The Court has said that buyer knowledge of unjustified discounts may be inferred "where his experience in the trade should make it clear that a difference in price exceeds a difference in cost."[28]

D. Declining Robinson-Patman Enforcement

On the one side we have seen corrective action appropriate to antitrust policy. On the other side we have seen official applications of dubious merit—attacks on harmless trade practices, protective interventions where injury was slight, and even anticompetitive proceedings. The controversy between those seeing Dr. Jekyll and those seeing Mr. Hyde reached a particularly high pitch during the late 1960s and early 1970s. Two task forces on antitrust policy appointed by two successive presidents (Johnson and Nixon), plus a blue-ribbon committee appointed by the American Bar Association, severely criticized the act and the FTC's enforcement of it. Later, President Ford's people in the Justice Department proposed radical modifications in the statute. Central to this and similar proposals is abolition of the narrow-injury test, but some critics have urged *complete abolition* of the Robinson-Patman Act. In response to these developments, Congress held three sets of hearings,[29] but no new legislation

---

[27] *Automatic Canteen Co., v. FTC,* 346 U.S. 61. See also *Great Atlantic & Pacific Tea Co. v. Federal Trade Commission,* 440 U.S. 69 (1979).

[28] C. Wilcox and W. G. Shepherd, *Public Policies Toward Business* (Homewood, Ill.: R.D. Irwing, 1975), pp. 183–184.

[29] *Recent Efforts to Amend or Repeal. . . , op. cit.,* Parts 1, 2, and 3; *Small Business and the Robinson-Patman Act, op. cit.,* 3 volumes; *Price Discrimination Legislation*—1969, Hearings before the Subcommittee on Antitrust and Monopoly of the Committee on the Judiciary, U.S. Senate, 91st Congress First Session (1969).

came of them, primarily because small-business trade associations mobilized to thwart reform. Small business merchants seem to revere the current law with religious fervor, despite the fact that it has often been used to their disadvantage. "Please don't let the Robinson-Patman Act die," they plead. "All small businesses need it to survive."[30] Admittedly, the act's principal achievements lie in the realms of protection and fairness (though not necessarily fairness to consumers).

For its part, the FTC seems to have responded to the criticism by drastically altering its enforcement policies. In 1961 the FTC issued 105 complaints and 90 orders under the act; in 1971 it issued just 12 complaints and 15 orders; and between 1976 and 1982 the FTC averaged only 1 complaint and 1 order per year.[31] As a former Commissioner put it, "Robinson-Patman is being slowly anesthetized."[32]

Aside from official enforcement, private suits are also possible and quite common. In truth, a private treble damage suit, *Utah Pie Co. v. Continental Baking Co.,*[32] was the fuse that ignited much of the recent debate. The Utah Pie Company, a small Salt Lake City purveyor of frozen pies, sued three formidable pie opponents—Continental, Carnation, and .Pet—for injuriously cutting prices below cost in Salt Lake City while maintaining prices elsewhere. In 1967, the Supreme Court held that the three national firms had violated Subsection 2(a) despite the fact that Utah Pie had enjoyed the largest share of the local market and had maintained profits throughout the price war. According to one critic, the Supreme Court used subsection 2(a) "to strike directly at price competition itself."[33]

Before leaving price discrimination and turning to tying and exclusive dealing, we should note the following oversimplified contrast. To the extent that price discrimination is anticompetitive, it works through *price* differentials that favor big firms over small firms. To the extent tying and exclusive dealing are anticompetitive, they work through *cost* differentials that favor big firms over small firms. Imagine, for example, that final good G has two "components," G_1 and G_2. G_1 might be film, and G_2 film developing. Or G_1 might be personal computers and G_2 retail dealership services which are necessary for the demonstration, sale, and servicing of personal computers. If a dominant firm could gain control over *both* G_1 and G_2 through tying or exclusive dealing, then rivals could be forced to supply *both* G_1 and G_2, something that might raise rivals' *costs* relative to those of the dominant firm (especially if the dominant firm has somehow

---

[30] *Recent Efforts to Amend or Repeal. . , op. cit.,* Part 3, p. 207.

[31] *Federal Antitrust Enforcement and Small Business,* Hearings before the Committee on Small Business, U.S. Senate, 97th Congress, 2nd Session (1982), pp. 178–179.

[32] "Robinson-Patman is not Dead—Merely Dormant," address by Paul Rand Dixon, May 21, 1975 (mimeo).

[32] *Utah Pie Co. v. Continental Baking Co.,* 386 U.S. 685 (1967).

[33] W. S. Bowman, "Restraint of Trade by the Supreme Court: The Utah Pie Case," *Yale Law Journal* (November 1967), p. 70.

garnered the lowest cost sources of G_1 or G_2 or both). With rivals weakened, competition might also be weakened.[34]

II. TYING

Season tickets, book club memberships, and the razors that come packaged with blades all have one thing in common: they are tie-in sales, where the sale of one item is tied to the sale of another. These particular ties are innocuous, since one has the option of making separate purchases at reasonable prices. But policy problems arise when the customer is *required* to buy a second product in order to get the one he wants. Under Section 3 of the Clayton Act, such required tie-in sales are prohibited where the effect "may be to substantially lessen competition or tend to create a monopoly." Tying is also occasionally attacked under Section 1 of the Sherman Act as a restraint of trade. These prohibitions suggest that tying may bolster barriers to entry or enable a monopolist controlling the tying (or principal) good to extend his monopoly power into the market for the tied (or second) good. Both are real possibilities. Although policy is complicated by the fact that tying serves other purposes that may not be anticompetitive, these other purposes are not necessarily *pro*competitive. Hence, this area is not plagued by bitter controversy. Four purposes of tying deserve mention.

A. Economies or Conveniences

Shirts sold with buttons, autos with tires, and pencils with erasers illustrate combinations more efficiently manufactured and distributed than constituent parts. These ties are so close that we think of each as being one product, the parts of which come in fixed proportions, such as seven buttons to a shirt. Since consumers would probably have to pay more for the privilege of buying separate parts, these ties are economically "natural."

B. Goodwill

A manufacturer of a delicate machine that consumes, dispenses, or processes materials may tie machine and materials together, thereby denying machine users the option of purchasing materials from independent sources. IBM, for example, used to require that IBM punch cards be used in its key punch, card sorting, and other processing equipment. Defending itself against antitrust prosecution, IBM claimed that the tie-in was necessary to protect its reputation, that use of just anybody's cards would clog its machines and tarnish its industrial honor. The Supreme Court rejected IBM's goodwill defense because there was

---

[34] Still, tying and exclusive dealing are not always anticompetitive. Steven Salop and David Scheffman, "Raising Rivals' Costs," *American Economic Review* (May 1983), pp 267–271; Marius Schwartz and David Eisenstadt, "Vertical Restraints," Antitrust Division Economic Policy Office Discussion Paper (December 2, 1982).

ample evidence that other manufacturers' cards met high standards of quality.[35] However, in other cases, some not involving machines and materials, this justification might be valid.

C. Price Discrimination[36]

In the previous chapter we saw how Xerox practiced price discrimination by leasing and metering the use of its copy machines. A machine's "consumption" of materials, such as paper, ink, staples, or film, may also, like a meter, measure intensity of use. Thus, when meters are impractical, easily tampered with, or prohibitively expensive, manufacturers of machines may try to sell or lease their machines at a low rate and tie-in the sale of materials priced well above cost. In this way, customers with intense demands would pay more than marginal users. Moreover, profits would be greater than those obtained without such price discrimination, especially if the producer has monopoly power in the machine's market. Notice that this tie-in may merely *exploit* more fully some already existing monopoly power. It does not necessarily entail an *extension* of market power into the tied good's market. For example, even in the absence of antitrust policy, Xerox could not monopolize the paper industry by tying copy paper to its machines because very little paper is used for that specific purpose.

D. Anticompetitive "Leverage"

Under certain conditions, however, a firm with monopoly control over the typing product may be able to extend its power by tying. One key condition is that the tying and tied goods be complements, such as bread and butter:

> Assume that a seller with a complete monopoly on bread ties sales of his brand of butter to the bread, where butter was formerly sold in a perfectly competitive market. If there is no use for butter except to spread on bread, the tie-in will lead to a complete monopoly in the butter market. In any event, the bread monopolist will achieve some degree of monopoly power in the butter market. But as he raises the price of his butter, the amount of bread he can sell at what used to be the best monopoly price will fall. The amount of leverage he can exert depends upon the elasticity of the demand curve for butter and the magnitude of the shifts in the demand curve for bread caused by increases in the price of butter.[37]

The lower the elasticity and the smaller the shifts, the greater the leverage.

E. The Law

When enforcing the law, the Department of Justice, the FTC, and the federal courts give little weight to any but this last motive. In the Supreme Court's

[35] *International Business Machines v. U.S.*, 298 U.S. 131 (1936).
[36] M. L. Burstein, "A Theory of Full-Line Forcing," *Northwestern University Law Review* (March-April, 1960), pp. 62–95.
[37] W. L. Baldwin and David McFarland, "Tying Arrangements in Law and Economics," *Antitrust Bulletin* (September–October 1963), p. 769. Tying's anticompetitive effect need not be limited to exclusion. It may, for instance, aid cartel discipline. See F. J. Cummins and W. E. Ruhter, "The *Northern Pacific* Case," *Journal of Law and Economics* (October 1979), pp. 329–350.

view, "Tying agreements serve hardly any purpose beyond the suppression of competition."[38] Still, tying is governed mainly by a rule of reason. Thus it is best to summarize by saying that violations will be found when the answers to *all* the following questions are "yes":

1. Are two products (or services) involved?
2. Does the seller possess sufficient economic power in the market of the tying product?
3. Is there substantial commerce in the tied goods?
4. Are defenses of "reasonableness" absent?

Of these questions, the first and third rarely raise thorny problems. The first is needed merely to prevent single products, like shirts with buttons, from being considered two products. The third is easily answered because "substantial commerce" seems to mean to the Court anything over a million dollars worth of business.

As regards "sufficient economic power" in the tying good, question (2), the Supreme Court has found a variety of conditions providing yes answers: (a) a large market share or "market dominance" in the tying good, (b) patents, copyrights, or trademarks for the tying good, (c) high barriers to entry in the tying-good market, and (4) uniqueness or "special desirability" of the tying good.

For example, a landmark case in patents is *International Salt* of 1947.[39] International had a "limited" patent monopoly over salt dispensing machines used in food processing. Users of the machines had to buy their salt from International or find other machines. International argued that preservation of goodwill required the tie-in, that only its own salt was of sufficient purity to provide top-quality dispensing. The Supreme Court rejected this assertion, observing that no evidence had been presented to show "that the machine is allergic to salt of equal quality produced by anyone except International." Moreover, the presence of the patents caused the Court to dispense some salty *per se* references, such as, "it is unreasonable, *per se,* to foreclose competitors from any substantial market."

Requisite power based on copyrights and uniqueness is illustrated by *U.S. v. Loew's, Inc.* (1962), which involved "block-booking." When selling motion pictures to television stations, Loew's had "conditioned the license or sale of one or more feature films upon the acceptance by the station of a package or block containing one or more unwanted or inferior films." Put bluntly, the practice could tie *Gone With the Wind* and *Getting Gertie's Garter.* On the question of economic power, the Supreme Court decided that each film "was in itself a unique product"; that feature films "were not fungible"; that "since each defendant by reason of its copyright had a 'monopolistic' position as to

[38] *Standard Oil of California et. al., v. U.S.,* 337 U.S. 293 (1949).
[39] *International Salt Co. v. U.S.,* 332 U.S. 392 (1947).

338

each tying product, 'sufficient economic power' to impose an appreciabale restraint on free competition in the tied product was present."[40]

Finally, the fourth question concerning reasonable defenses has on occasion been answered in favor of defendants. In particular, goodwill defenses have been used successfully on several occasions.[41]

III. EXCLUSIVE DEALING

Under an exclusive dealing agreement, the buyer obtains the seller's product on condition that he will not deal in the products of the seller's rivals. The buyer, say an appliance wholesaler, agrees to secure his total requirements of a particular product, kitchen appliances, from one supplier, say General Electric. Such an arrangement may carry anticompetitive effects, especially when used by a seller or a group of sellers with a large market share:

> Once a large or dominant supplier in a market obtains for his exclusive use a correspondingly large share of available outlets on a lower level of distribution, he has probably imposed prohibitive cost disadvantages on existing or potential rivals, since they are likely to have to create new outlets in order to participate in the market. The same is true where a group of suppliers collectively (if not collusively) obtain exclusive obligations from dealers—and thus produce an aggregate foreclosure.[42]

Such arrangements advance the supplier's interests not only because they have a possible exclusionary effect but because they also assure that distributors will devote their undivided energy to the supplier's products, something particularly important where personal sales, repair service, and promotion are required. Moreover, the arrangement offers the possibility of more predictable sales.[43]

From the buyer's or distributor's point of view, there are a number of reasons for accepting exclusive dealing:

• Supplies may be more certain and steady, especially in times of shortage.

• Specialization entails lower inventories than would be required with several brands of the same product.

• If exclusive dealing is rejected, the buyer may no longer be a buyer (that is, the seller "forces" acceptance).

• Acceptance may be conceded in exchange for a commitment from the seller that protects the buyer-dealer from competition of other buyer-dealers

[40] *U.S. v. Loew's, Inc.*, 371 U.S. 38 (1962).
[41] *U.S. v. Jerrold Electronics Corp.*, 365 U.S. 567 (1961), and *Dehydrating Process Co., v. A. O. Smith Corp.*, 292 F. 2d 653 (1st Cir.) *cert. denied*, 368 U.S. 931 (1961).
[42] D. N. Thompson, *Franchise Operations and Antitrust* (Lexington, Mass.: Heath Lexington Books, 1971), p. 59.
[43] For additional rationales see Schwartz and Eisenstadt, *op. cit.*, pp. 91–95; Howard P. Marvel, "Exclusive Dealing," *Journal of Law and Economics* (April 1982), pp. 1–25.

handling the same brand (for example, territorial assignments or limits on the number of dealerships).

According to Section 3 of the Clayton Act and the Supreme Court's interpretation of it, exclusive dealing is not *per se* illegal. Hence, the Court considers economic conditions and purposes when determining illegalities. Two main factors are the seller's market share and the prevalence of the practice among all sellers. Beyond this, uncertainty is rife, as illustrated by the Supreme Court's decisions in *Standard Stations* (1948) and *Tampa Electric* (1961). At issue in the former case were contracts obligating 5,937 Standard service stations to take their full gasoline requirements and in some instances tires, batteries, and accessories as well, from Standard Oil Company of California. In addition, all other major suppliers used similar contracts. The Supreme Court *refused* to consider economic justification for the contracts and chose a test centering on the "quantitative substantiality" of the restraint. Stressing the fact that Standard's contracts covered 6.7% of the market and the fact that sales of $58 million were involved, the Court found a violation of Section 3 because the contracts "foreclosed competition in a substantial share of the line of commerce affected."[44] District and circuit courts thereafter applied the quantitative substantiality test until 1961.

In the *Tampa Electric* opinion of 1961, the Supreme Court said it *would* consider economic justifications for exclusive dealing. However, it is still uncertain just how important economic justifications will eventually become because the contract at issue in *Tampa* involved only 1% of the market, and, according to the Court, it would probably have gotten by the substantiality test anyway:

> There is here neither a seller with a dominant position in the market . . . nor myriad outlets with substantial sales volume, coupled with an industry-wide practice of relying upon exclusive contracts . . . nor a plainly restrictive tying arrangement. . . . On the contrary, we seem to have only that type of contract which may well be of economic advantage to buyers as well as to sellers.[45]

At this point the reader may be wondering why, if all but the most measly of such contracts are banned, any kid on Main Street can observe extensive exclusive dealing in the retailing of gasoline, autos, tires, fast-foods, and other products. The answer comes in two parts. First, vertical ownership and integration lie behind some of those observations, in which case the absence of a truly independent dealer precludes the possibility of exclusive dealing. Second, much *tacit* exclusive dealing occurs.[46] This latter phenomenon is on all fours with tacit price fixing. Tacit "understandings" are not illegal; only explicit ones

---

[44] *Standard Oil of California and Standard Stations, Inc. v. U.S.,* 337 U.S. 293 (1949).

[45] *Tampa Electric Co. v. Nashville Coal Co., et. al.,* 365 U.S. 320 (1961). See also Derek C. Bok, "The Tampa Electric Case and the Problem of Exclusive Arrangement," *The Supreme Court Review* (1961), pp. 267–332.

[46] Thompson, *op. cit.,* Chapter 4. See also A. R. Oxenfelt, *Marketing Practices in the TV Set Industry* (New York: Columbia University Press, 1964), p. 123; and L. P. Bucklin, *Competition and Evolution in the Distributive Trades* (Englewood Cliffs, N.J.: Prentice-Hall, 1972), pp. 272–275.

are. And a powerful manufacturer may be able to impose tacit exclusive dealing by refusing to sell to those who cannot or do not take the manufacturer's hint that this is what he wants. *Collective* refusals to sell are essentially *per se* illegal.[47] So are refusals whose *clear* purpose it is to secure cooperation in an illegal scheme.[48] But, beyond these narrow boundaries, the right of refusal to sell poses an ever-present punitive threat.

Much the same could be said, in terms of both law and business practice, about another form of exclusive dealing—namely, assignment of exclusive territories. The buyer or distributor in this case receives the exclusive right to handle the seller's product in a given geographic market. Such agreements obviously curtail *intra*brand competition among distributors. But they may also bolster *inter*brand competition under certain circumstances.[49]

SUMMARY

The Robinson–Patman Act has been called the "Magna Carta" of small business. Others have named it "Typhoid Mary." Ever since it amended Section 2 of the Clayton Act in 1936, it has stirred controversy. Perhaps *any* law governing price discrimination would be controversial. Price discrimination always entails a high price somewhere and a low price somewhere else. Those who see evil in price discrimination tend to see the high price more readily than the low price. Those who see goodness in price discrimination seem to have reverse viewing capabilities. In addition to viewer attitudes, circumstances make a difference.

In any event, the Robinson–Patman Act outlaws price differences where the effect may be broad or narrow competitive injury at any one of three levels—primary, secondary, or tertiary—unless the difference can be defended on grounds of "cost justification" or "good faith" price mimicry. Three major classes of price discrimination have been found to violate these standards at least occasionally: (1) volume or quantity discounts, (2) territorial discrimination, and (3) functional discounts. The first two are particularly prone to true anticompetitive effects, and a number of these cases cast the FTC in good light. On the other hand, attacks against all three have produced instances of ill-advised enforcement.

Subsections 2(c), (d), and (e) prohibit any discrimination that takes the form of brokerage payments, discounts in lieu of brokerage, payments for promotion or other services, and direct provision of promotion or other service. These are generally *per se* prohibitions because potential competitive injury need not be shown and, for the most part, these practices cannot be defended on grounds

---

[47] *Klor's, Inc. v. Broadway-Hale Stores, Inc.*, 359 U.S. 207 (1959).

[48] C. H. Fulda, "Individual Refusals to Deal: When does Single-Firm Conduct Become Vertical Restraint?" *Law and Contemporary Problems* (Summer 1965), pp. 590–606.

[49] Thompson, *op. cit.*, Chapter 7. *Continental TV, Inc., et al. v. GTE Sylvania Inc.*, 433 U.S. 36 (1977).

of cost or good faith. Finally, Subsection 2(f) addresses the problem that Congress was most concerned about, for it bans knowing inducement or receipt of an unlawfully discriminatory price. Despite the efforts of Congress and the FTC, the Act has apparently not stemmed the advance of chain stores. Chains have found ways around the law. In addition, the FTC has recently eased up on the Act's enforcement.

Section 3 of the Clayton Act outlaws tying and exclusive dealing where the effect "may be to substantially lessen competition or tend to create a monopoly." The key legal test of tying is whether the firm has monopoly power in the tying good market, and, if so, whether a substantial volume of business is accounted for by the tied good. Even where power and substantiality indicate a violation, the tie-in may escape illegality, at least temporarily, on grounds that it protects goodwill. The illegality of exclusive dealing hinges mainly on the market power of the seller and the prevalence of the practice in the relevant market. The extent to which competitively innocuous economic justifications can save otherwise illegal exclusive dealing is uncertain. Be that as it may, it appears that many anticompetitive exclusive dealing arrangements escape the law's embrace because they are tacit rather than explicit.

15

Product Differentiation Conduct: Theory and Evidence

Tell Miller to come right along, but tell them to bring lots of money . . .

—AUGUST A. BUSCH III, chief executive,
Anheuser-Busch Inc. (in response to
Miller's threatened dethronement of the
"King of Beers," late 1970s)

What is the relationship between concentration and advertising? To what extent does product differentiation contribute to market power? How do business rivals wield advertising as a weapon of competition? These are some of the grand mysteries of industrial organization economics, and over the past two decades research has rapidly piled up clues to their solution. The job of this chapter is to sift through these clues and reach some tentative conclusions.

The scene is set by Figure 15–1. The double-shafted arrows indicate causal connections we have already explored. Of those connections, the most important for our present purposes is that between product differentiability and advertising, style, and other forms of product differentiation. It was shown in Chapter 4 that advertising intensity corresponds positively to product differentiability. In particular, advertising as a percentage of sales tends to be higher for consumer goods as compared with producer goods; for "experience" goods as opposed to "search" goods; for nondurable "convenience" goods as compared with durable "shopping" goods; for goods susceptible to promotion by strong emotional appeal; and so forth. Much the same was said of other forms of product differentiation, though less rigidly. Variations in packaging, flavor, style, and the like are not uniformly profitable across all products.

Nothing said in this chapter will alter those conclusions. They provide a base upon which we now build. For the time being, we shall stuff producer goods into the nearest closet and consider only consumer goods. We shall also assume a condition of *ceteris paribus* or "other things being equal" throughout most of this chapter's analysis. That is to say, we shall take differentiability as "given" or "already accounted for" when postulating various swellings and contractions of differentiation effort.

The numbered, single shafted arrows of Figure 15–1 indicate causal connec-

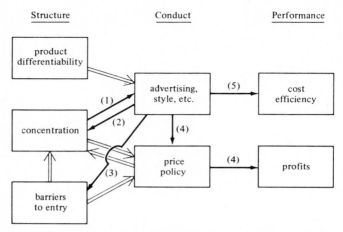

FIGURE 15–1. Product differentiation issues in the context of structure, conduct, and performance.

tions discussed in this chapter. Their numbers specify sequence of treatment. After a few preliminary remarks about profit maximizing theory, we consider

1. Concentration as a cause of advertising intensity.
2. Advertising as a cause of concentration.
3. Advertising as a barrier to entry.
4. Advertising's influence on prices and profits.
5. The cost efficiency implications of advertising activity.

Advertising is emphasized throughout because data for other forms of differentiation effort are deficient. Still, these other forms will not be completely ignored. The sketchy evidence concerning them is intriguing.

I. PROFIT MAXIMIZATION AND OVERVIEW

A. Simple Theory

Advertising can be profitable because it can enlarge sales volume or permit price increases. But advertising costs money, and its potency as a generator of revenues during a single year is limited. Hence, each firm confronts the question of how much should be spent on advertising to maximize profits. A simplified theoretical answer assumes (1) a short-run time horizon with no lagged effects to advertising, (2) constant advertising outlays on the part of all rival firms, (3) constant product quality, and (4) full knowledge of certain elasticities. Under these conditions the firm's profit maximizing advertising-to-sales ratio would be[1]

---

[1] Robert Dorfman and Peter Steiner, "Optimal Advertising and Optimal Quality," *American Economic Review* (December 1954), pp. 826–836.

$$\frac{A}{S} = \frac{\dfrac{\%\Delta \text{ in } Q}{\%\Delta \text{ in } A}}{\dfrac{\%\Delta \text{ in } Q}{\%\Delta \text{ in } P}}$$

where A/S is advertising outlay relative to sales revenue, Q is quantity of product sold, P is price, Δ is change, $(\% \Delta \text{ in } Q)/(\% \Delta \text{ in } A)$ is advertising elasticity of demand, and $(\% \Delta \text{ in } Q)/(\% \Delta \text{ in } P)$ is price elasticity of demand. Lurking beneath this maximization equation is the familiar rule of MR = MC, but you must realize that this equation gives a simplified view of the impact of market structure on advertising intensity.

Consider first the upper term on the right-hand side, namely, advertising elasticity of demand, $(\% \Delta \text{ in } Q)/(\% \Delta \text{ in } A)$. This is a measure of sales response to advertising, and it is largely determined by product differentiability. The greater the advertising elasticity, the greater the sales responsiveness. Hence the greater the advertising elasticity, the greater the firm's A/S, everything else being equal.

So much, of course, is not really new. What is new concerns the lower term on the right-hand side, that is, *price* elasticity of demand $(\% \Delta \text{ in } Q)/(\% \Delta \text{ in } P)$. This term's placement indicates an inverse relationship between the firm's advertising intensity, A/S, and the firm's price elasticity of demand (holding advertising elasticity constant). The greater the price elasticity, the lower the firm's ad outlay relative to sales. Conversely, the lower the price elasticity, the greater the ad effort. Because a firm's price elasticity of demand is a function of its market share, this discovery leads to a simple theory connecting concentration to ad intensity at market-wide levels. As a firm's market share rises, its demand curve becomes more and more like market-wide demand and thereby becomes less and less elastic. Hence, rising market share might be associated with rising A/S for the market as a whole. And rising market concentration might likewise be associated with rising A/S.

The gist of the theory is most clearly seen in the extreme case of purely competitive firms selling a perfectly standardized product in a market of very low concentration. With $(\% \Delta \text{ in } Q)/(\% \Delta \text{ in } P)$ being infinitely high for each firm, A/S will be zero. Or, in terms of real world inquiry: Do wheat farmers advertise? (Do hermits fraternize?).

This reasoning, unqualified, yields a "linear hypothesis," with advertising intensity and market concentration positively related throughout their range, as depicted in Figure 15–2. A few economists believe this to be the true relationship between advertising and concentration.[2] They bolster their belief with causality theories reaching well beyond matters of elasticity. Some of these theories will be taken up later. We do not pursue them now, however, because the linear hypothesis is plagued by various problems. Although there is some evi-

---

[2] E.g., H. M. Mann, J. A. Henning, and J. W. Meehan, Jr., "Advertising and Concentration: An Empirical Investigation," *Journal of Industrial Economics* (November 1967), pp. 34–45.

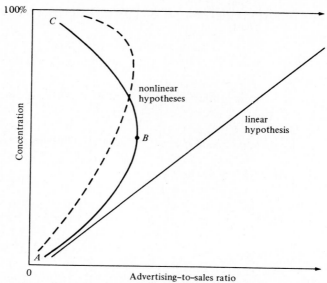

FIGURE 15–2. Hypothetical relations between advertising intensity and concentration.

dence supporting the positive linear hypothesis,[3] there is also much evidence to the contrary.[4] Differing samples and differing perspectives have produced these differing results, thereby igniting controversy. All in all, this author is convinced that the linear hypothesis sits on thin ice.

B. Problems and Complexities[5]

The main problem with the linear hypothesis as presented is that its underlying assumptions are unrealistic. For one thing, advertising *has* lagged effects, so the assumption of a short-term time horizon is myopic. For another, the theory assumes that business executives have accurate estimates of the effect of advertising and price variation on sales volume. To credit most executives with such insight would be fanciful. Estimates are clouded by a vast array of

[3] *Ibid.;* S. I. Ornstein, J. F. Weston, M. D. Intriligator, and R. E. Shrieves, "Determinants of Market Structure," *Southern Economic Journal* (April 1973), pp. 612–625; R. M. Bradburd, "Advertising and Market Concentration: A Re-examination," *Southern Economic Journal* (October 1980), pp. 531–539; R. W. Ward and R. M. Behr, "Revisiting the Advertising-Concentration Issue," *American Journal of Agricultural Economics* (February 1980), pp. 113–117.

[4] Leading papers are L. G. Telser, "Advertising and Competition," *Journal of Political Economy* (December 1964), pp. 537–562; and R. B. Ekelund, Jr., and W. P. Gramm, "Advertising and Concentration: Some New Evidence," *Antitrust Bulletin* (Summer 1970), pp. 243–249. For reviews of these and other papers see James M. Ferguson, *Advertising and Competition: Theory, Measurement, Fact* (Cambridge, Mass.: Ballinger, 1974), Chapter 5; and Richard A. Miller, "Advertising and Competition: Some Neglected Aspects," *Antitrust Bulletin* (Summer 1972), pp. 467–478.

[5] For details see K. Cowling, J. Cable, M. Kelly, and Tony McGuinness, *Advertising and Economic Behavior* (London: Macmillan, 1975).

other variables affecting sales volume, such as general economic trends, tastes, and competitive activity.

Mention of competitive activity raises a third and more significant shortcoming in the simple theory, namely, the theory's unrealistic assumption of constant rival firm advertising. What one firm does will often affect the behavior of others, in advertising as well as price strategy. This reciprocal dependency is illustrated by the estimate that, on average, a 1% increase in advertising by one cigarette company provokes a 1.12% increase in the advertising of its competitors.[6] Similarly, a statistical study of 60 firms showed that the most important determinant of each firm's advertising outlay was the A/S ratio of the industry it occupied.[7]

There are other problems as well, and, on the whole, a "nonlinear" hypothesis is theoretically and empirically more tenable, at least in this author's eyes. Two versions of the nonlinear hypothesis are depicted in Figure 15–2—the line labeled ABC and the dashed line. In contrast to the linear hypothesis, it is assumed that concentration and advertising intensity are positively related only up to a point, after which point, in the region of high concentration, the relationship becomes negative. The implication is that advertising as a percentage of sales will *not* be highest where concentration is highest but rather where concentration is moderately high, such as at point B. Cross-section statistical tests of the nonlinear hypothesis using four-digit industries suggest that A/S reaches a maximum where four-firm concentration is from 36 to 72%.[8] Other estimates peg the maximum at still higher levels of concentration, as suggested by the dashed line in Figure 15–2.[9] What is more, intensities of differentiation effort *other* than advertising seem to follow a nonlinear pattern. Such is true, for instance, of "product proliferation" when measured by the birth rate of new flavors (e.g., honey-nut corn flakes), new formulas (e.g., diet soda), new brands (e.g., "Barclay" cigarettes), and the like.[10]

There is a catch, however. This depiction of behavior raises the possibility that *two* directions of causality prevail, not one: advertising-to-concentration as well as concentration-to-advertising. Thus, the next several sections cover

[6] H. G. Grabowski and D. C. Mueller, "Imitative Advertising in the Cigarette Industry," *Antitrust Bulletin* (Summer 1971), pp. 257–292.

[7] D. C. Mueller, "The Firm's Decision Process: As Econometric Investigation," *Quarterly Journal of Economics* (February 1967), pp. 58–87.

[8] Allyn D. Strickland and Leonard W. Weiss, "Advertising, Concentration, and Price-Cost Margins," *Journal of Political Economy* (October 1976), pp. 1109–1121; Stephen Martin, "Entry Barriers, Concentration, and Profits," *Southern Economic Journal* (October 1979), pp. 471–488.

[9] Cowling, Cable, Kelly, McGuinness, *op. cit.;* Stephen Martin, "Advertising, Concentration, and Profitability," *Bell Journal of Economics* (Autumn 1979), pp. 639–647.

[10] John M. Connor, "Food Product Proliferation: A Market Structure Analysis," *American Journal of Agricultural Economics* (November 1981), pp. 607–617. See also F. F. Esposito and Louis Esposito, "Excess Capacity and Market Structure," *Review of Economics and Statistics* (May 1974), pp. 188–194; F. T. Knickerbocker, *Oligopolistic Reaction and Multinational Enterprise* (Cambridge, Mass.: Harvard University Press, 1973), Chapters 3 and 4; and John T. Scott, "Nonprice Competition in Banking Markets," *Southern Economic Journal* (January 1978), pp. 594–605. See also Chapter 23 in this book.

theories and evidence surrounding the nonlinear hypothesis.[11] The material is too bulky to be swallowed whole, so it is sliced into the following pieces:

1. Concentration as a cause of advertising
   (a) Positive range
   (b) Negative range
2. Advertising as a cause of concentration
   (a) Positive range
   (b) Negative range

II. CONCENTRATION AS A CAUSE OF ADVERTISING

A. Positive Range (Concentration as a Cause)

What was said previously about elasticities and advertising could obviously be reapplied here as one explanation for a positive relation between concentration and advertising where concentration is low to moderate. That is, rising concentration reduces individual firm price elasticity of demand, thereby boosting A/S at firm and industry levels.

In addition, there may be a trade-off between price and nonprice competition as concentration rises. At low levels of concentration, price competition seems preeminent. Firm survival and expansion depend mainly upon efficiency and price shading. However, at moderate levels of concentration firms begin to appreciate the financial dangers and futility of price rivalry. In this range of concentration firms may therefore shift their emphasis from price to *non*price competition. Indeed, if tacit or explicit collusion in price is easier to achieve than collusion in nonprice factors, price combat may well lapse while advertising warfare rages. Collusion over price policy is likely to be easier than collusion over nonprice policy because price double-crossing is often more readily detectable and more quickly countered than *non*price double-crossing. Whereas price policy is often clearly definable and highly visible, nonprice policy usually entails a myriad of subtle dimensions, lags, and complexities. Thus, even though equal advertising outlays might be mutually agreed upon, media mix, message content, timing, and other important factors remain variable and potentially corrosive to collusion.

Unrestrained nonprice rivalry may be more rousingly described in *game-theory* terms, using an example developed by Willard Manning and Bruce Owen

---

[11] Principal sources are *ibid;* Strickland and Weiss, *op. cit.;* D. F. Greer, "Advertising and Market Concentration," *Southern Economic Journal* (July 1971), pp. 19–32; D. F. Greer, "Some Case History Evidence on the Advertising-Concentration Relationship," *Antitrust Bulletin* (Summer 1973), pp. 307–332; John Cable, "Market Structure, Advertising Policy and Intermarket Differences in Advertising Intensity," in *Market Structure and Corporate Behavior,* edited by K. Cowling (London: Gray-Mills, 1972), pp. 105–124; C. J. Sutton, "Advertising, Concentration, and Competition," *Economic Journal* (March 1974), pp. 56–69; N. Kaldor and R. Silverman, *A Statistical Analysis of Advertising Expenditure and of the Revenue of the Press* (Cambridge, U. K.: Cambridge University Press, 1948), pp. 34–35; R. E. Caves, M. E. Porter, A. M. Spence, and J. T. Scott, *Competition in the Open Economy* (Cambridge: Harvard University Press, 1980).

TABLE 15–1. Network Payoff Matrix

			Network 2 (*in italics*)			
			Low Input Level		*High Input Level*	
Network 1	Low Input Level	A	50	*50*	A	0	*100*
		C	25	*25*	C	25	*50*
		π	25	*25*	π	−25	*50*
	High Input Level	A	100	*0*	A	50	*50*
		C	50	*25*	C	50	*50*
		π	50	*−25*	π	0	*0*

compare *compare*

A = Audience in dollars of advertising revenues
C = Cost of programming effort in dollars
π = A − C = profit in dollars

to analyze nonprice competition in television networking.[12] It seems that ABC, NBC, and CBS do not compete with each other in the prices they charge advertisers or the rates they pay to their affiliated local stations (who receive a percentage cut of the networks' ad revenues as reward and inducement for airing the networks' programs). On the other hand, the networks do compete rather strenuously in "programming" because (1) popular programming attracts viewers, (2) advertisers "buy" viewers from the networks on the basis of viewer ratings, and (3) each rating point represents more than $40 million in additional network revenues over the course of a season. A game-theory model is particularly appropriate to this case because the networks vie with each other in the context of what they assume is a *given* overall viewing audience. That is to say, the networks think total audience size is determined by factors beyond their control, such as age composition of the population and the number of women working outside the home (which affects daytime audience size). The networks are, in effect, dogs fighting over the same bone (the collective viewer's head).

Assume for simplicity two networks, two levels of programming input, and a total audience worth 100 units of advertising revenue. The situation is then captured in Table 15–1, which is a four-cornered "pay-off" matrix. Each corner has six numbers labeled A, C, and π: where A is audience measured in advertising revenues, C is cost of programming, and π is A minus C, or dollar profit from networking. The three numbers to the left in each group belong to Network 1. Those on the right, in italics, belong to Network 2. Note that each pair of A's always adds up to 100, in accord with our assumption that total audience size is exogenously fixed. The distribution of the 100 between the two networks,

[12] Willard G. Manning and Bruce M. Owen, "Television Rivalry and Network Power," *Public Policy* (Winter 1976), pp. 33–57.

however, is determined by the relative intensity of their programming effort. When *both* are "low" or *both* are "high," there is a 50:50 split. When one is "low" and the other is "high," the latter garners all the bones. In turn, "low" and "high" levels of expense are assumed to be 25 and 50, respectively. The crucial question is, then, what level of programming will the networks pursue? The answer is found in the profit figures and network strategies.

Let's look first at Network 1. If Network 1 assumes that Network 2 will adopt a "low" effort for next season, then the profits Network 1 compares are those circled on the left-hand side—that is, 25 if it opts for a "low" effort versus 50 if it opts for a "high" effort. Network 1 would obviously choose "high" effort under this assumption. However, what if Network 1 assumes a "high" level of effort on the part of its arch rival? The answer is the same. In this case Network 1 compares −25, which its "low" effort would bring, and 0, which its "high" effort would bring. Although the 0 profit is unsavory, it is better than a loss of −25. Hence once again a "high" effort is chosen.

Now, what about Network 2? Which option will it pursue? Its profits (and losses) are in italics, and, since the pay-off matrix is symmetrical, it too chooses the "high" level option. If it assumes a "low" for Network 1, it compares *25* and *50*. If it assumes a "high" for Network 1, it compares *−25* and *0*. The latter pay-offs are preferable in each case. So Network 2 likewise pursues the "high" option. With both 1 and 2 pursuing a "high," they "overdose". Outlays for programming are excessive, and profits are miserably zero. Only collusive agreement to follow a "low" policy can cheer them, yielding profits of 25 and *25*. However, it would be dangerous for one rival to initiate a de-escalation, and tacit collusive agreement may be difficult.

This type of rivalry game is called the "prisoner's dilemma." Such game theories have been devised for price policy, but most real world applications relate to nonprice competition.[13] Rivalry in real world TV networking has typically not been intense enough to produce losses. Restraint and positive profit have been achieved by various "rules of thumb" applied at various times, such as for a series, 26 weeks of new episodes and 26 weeks of reruns.[14] Even so, restraint has been less than perfect, and network profits could benefit by more explicit and extensive collusion (if, that is, the antitrust laws were scrapped). A similar, pertinent example of excessive advertising in oligopolistic manufacturing is drawn from cigarettes. Julian Simon calculates that a $2.2 million reduction in cigarette advertising in 1961 would have led to only a $1.25 million decline in total sales revenue.[15]

---

[13] John McDonald, *The Game of Business* (Garden City, N.Y.: Doubleday, 1975).

[14] Rerun rules are easy to police and profitable. Reruns cost 20% of the original, yet they deliver 60% of the original's audience levels and ad revenues. During the late 1970s ABC shook things up a bit, however, by abandoning old rerun formulas and adopting a "living schedule." The resulting outbreak of competition led to frenzied programming rivalry and jittery financial forecasts. *Wall Street Journal,* October 4, 1977, p. 40; and November 30, 1977, p. 1.

[15] Julian Simon, "The Effect of the Competitive Structure Upon Expenditures for Advertising," *Quarterly Journal of Economics* (November 1967), p. 621.

B. Negative Range (Concentration as a Cause)

When concentration reaches really lofty heights, a negative relation (such as in the BC range of Figure 15–2) may be expected for at least two reasons. The higher industry price levels implied by ever higher concentration raise the industry's price elasticity of demand. And, according to the profit maximizing formula outlined earlier, rising price elasticity should shrink the industry's advertising to sales ratio. More obviously, ever higher concentration makes tacit or explicit collusion in nonprice activities more and more feasible.

An especially interesting example of the collusive aspect of concentration concerns advertising in the British soap industry.[16] At the turn of the century a loose oligopoly prevailed with the largest firm, Lever Brothers, holding a 20% market share. Advertising competition throbbed painfully. So in 1906 William Lever openly tried to organize a cartel, arguing that some "measures must be adopted by the leading soap-makers in conference to allay the fierce competition which has arisen amongst them, to terminate the frenzied competitive advertising which was daily becoming more intolerable. . . ." But the newspapers would have none of this. After receiving their first advertising contract cancellations, they editorially attacked the "Soap Trust" with such fervor that it soon had to be disbanded. Lever slowly alleviated his frustration, however, by acquiring one competitor after another until in 1920 he could claim control of 71% of the industry. Advertising appropriations declined concurrently. Other examples of express collusion cover a wide variety of products and a diversity of nonprice activities, including trading stamps, coupon offers, product quality, and product style, as well as advertising.[17]

Just as rising concentration should eventually reduce nonprice competition, so, too, falling concentration in this region should increase it. Falling concentration reduces the ability of oligopolists to hold differentiation outlays down to joint profit maximizing levels. Deteriorating collusion is important in this respect, but there are other factors as well. Examples of such inverse relations abound in both time-series and cross-section forms:

- In 1911, when tobacco was chewed as often as smoked, an antitrust decree fractured the monopolistic American Tobacco Company into several successor companies. Comparing A/S during the 2 years preceding the decree with A/S during the 2 years following, we find that A/S *rose* 32% for navy plug tobacco, 15% for flat plug, 148% for plug-cut smoking, 41%

---

[16] See Greer, *op. cit.* (1973), pp. 318–319.

[17] *Government Intervention in the Market Mechanism, The Petroleum Industry, Part 1,* Hearings before the Subcommittee on Antitrust and Monopoly, U.S. Senate, 91st Congress, First Session (1969), pp. 569–570; L. P. Bucklin, *Competition and Evolution in the Distributive Trades* (Englewood Cliffs, N.J.: Prentice-Hall, 1972), p. 131; T. A. Murphy and Y. K. Ng, "Oligopolistic Interdependence and the Revenue Maximization Hypothesis," *Journal of Industrial Economics* (March 1974), pp. 229–230; Corwin D. Edwards, *Cartelization in Western Europe* (Washington, D.C.: Bureau of Intelligence and Research, U.S. Department of State, 1964), pp. 10, 14; and C. L. Pass, "Coupon Trading— An Aspect of Non-price Competition in the U. K. Cigarette Industry," *Yorkshire Bulletin of Economic and Social Research* (November 1967), pp. 124–136.

for long-cut smoking, 81% for granulated smoking, and 93% for domestic blend cigarettes.[18]

• Cross-section evidence on advertising in the drug industry is shown in Figure 15–3. The observations are supplied by John Vernon, who found an inverse relationship between concentration and advertising intensity. The beginnings of a nonlinear form are evident as well.[19]

• For a sample of 40 highly concentrated city banking markets, Lawrence White found a very robust inverse relationship between commercial bank concentration and the intensity of *branching activity*. He estimated there were 47.5% more banking offices in the least, as compared with the most, concentrated market in his sample (everything else being equal).[20]

• In another cross-section study of local banking markets, which are generally highly concentrated, Arnold Heggestad and John Mingo found inverse relationships for a wide assortment of nonprice variables, including extraordinary banking hours and the availability of trust services and overdraft privileges.[21]

To summarize, concentration of intermediate orders seems most conducive to vigorous nonprice competition. Concentration of either high or low extremities seems least conducive.

III. ADVERTISING AS A CAUSE OF CONCENTRATION

A. Positive Range (Advertising as a Cause)

There are three ways in which advertising may foster high degrees of concentration. First is the existence of economies of scale to advertising. As stated earlier in Chapter 8 the incidence of such economies varies across industries. Where such economies do prevail, they contribute to concentration, but only up to the point of their exhaustion.

Second, and aside from scalar effects, one or several of the largest firms in an industry might consistently maintain greater advertising outlays relative to sales than smaller firms maintain. The big spenders could possess larger financial

---

[18] Greer, *op cit.* (1973), p. 327.

[19] John M. Vernon, "Concentration, Promotion, and Market Share Stability in the Pharmaceutical Industry," *Journal of Industrial Economics* (July 1971), pp. 246–266. See also J. J. Lambin, *Advertising, Competition and Market Conduct in Oligopoly Over Time* (Amsterdam: North Holland Publishing Co., 1976), p. 135, Table 6.23, lines 4 and 6; W. J. Primeaux, Jr., "An Assessment of the Effect of Competition on Advertising Intensity," *Economic Inquiry* (October 1981), pp. 613–625.

[20] Lawerence J. White, "Price Regulation and Quality Rivalry In a Profit-maximizing Model," *Journal of Money, Credit and Banking* (February 1976), pp. 97–106. The most and least concentrated markets in his sample had Herfindahl indexes of 0.48 and 0.15, respectively. In terms of number-equivalence this is two and seven firms.

[21] A. A. Heggestad and J. J. Mingo, "Prices, Nonprices, and Concentration in Selected Banking Markets," *Bank Structure and Competition* (Chicago: Federal Reserve Bank of Chicago, 1974), pp. 69–95.

resources, greater foresight, or predatory designs. A striking instance of predatory advertising occurred in the tobacco industry around the turn of the century, before the antitrust action of 1911.[22] The story centers on James Duke, whose power play started in cigarettes, then spread to other branches of the trade. By 1885 Duke had secured 11–18% of total cigarette sales for his company through an arduous promotional effort. He then escalated ad outlays to nearly 20% of sales, thereby forcing a five-firm merger in 1889 and acquiring 80% control of all cigarette sales. His American Tobacco Company grew still further until he held 93% of the market in 1899. Coincident with this final gathering of power, cigarette ad expense as a per cent of sales fell to 11% in 1894, then to 0.5% in 1899. And cigarette profits swelled to 56% of sales in 1899.

With these stupendous profits Duke was able to launch massive predatory campaigns to capture other tobacco markets. One measure of this effort is the American Tobacco Company's annual advertising and selling cost as a percentage of sales at crest levels in the target markets—28.9% for plug and twist, 24.4% for smoking tobacco, 31.7% for fine-cut chewing, and 49.9% for cigars. Duke even went so far as to introduce deliberately unprofitable "fighting brands," one of which was appropriately called "Battle Ax." Losses ensued; mergers followed; and after the entire industry (except for cigars) was under American's thumb, advertising receded substantially to such relatively peaceful neighborhoods as 4 and 10% of sales. Thus the episode traces a full nonlinear course (*ABC* in Figure 15–2), illustrating more than mere predation.

A third positive force of advertising on concentration is similar to predation in that it produces an escalation of outlays; it is different in that no single firm plays the role of "heavy." How might innocent escalation come about? There are any number of possibilities. Some firms, large or small, might have outstanding success in their advertising campaigns or might establish initially favorable A/S ratios, thereby inadvertently or advertently enjoying unusually rapid growth at the expense of rivals. But, after suffering losses in market share, most of the rivals attempt to emulate these successful companies through increased advertising outlays. Then everyone is off to the races. Competitive rounds of escalation could continue, resulting in cost-price squeezes, losses, bankruptcies, mergers, and ever higher concentration. Prisoners' dilemma game theory is obviously applicable here.

Fantastic as this scenario may seem, the beer industry played it just recently.[23] The traces are sketched in Figure 15–3 in terms of five-firm concentration ratio and advertising as a percentage of sales. (The concentration ratio is based on national sales, thereby understating the "true" level of concentration, which would be based on regional, not national, markets. You may compensate, however, by mentally shifting the Figure 15–3 curve up a bit.) Beginning in 1947, concentration was low to moderate, and advertising was just slightly above 3% of sales revenue. Promotion expense rose rapidly thereafter, as one firm

[22] Greer, *op. cit.* (1973), pp. 311–315.
[23] D. F. Greer, "Product Differentiation and Concentration in the Brewing Industry," *Journal of Industrial Economics* (July 1971), pp. 201–219.

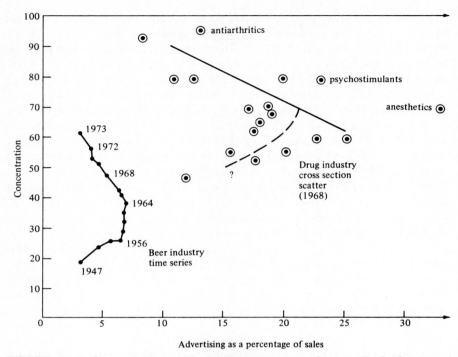

FIGURE 15–3. Concentration and advertising intensity. Source: D. F. Greer and J. M. Vernon in *Journal of Industrial Economics,* July 1971, updated.

after another leap-frogged ad outlays relative to sales. The process was apparently aggravated by the advent of TV advertising, a decline in tavern sales, the rise of package sales, the geographic expansion of many brewers, and a massive labor strike that closed down Schlitz, Pabst, and Miller for over 2 months in 1953. By the early 1960s, advertising relative to sales was hovering near the 7% level. (And expenditures for packaging differentiation had also burgeoned.[24])As a result, profits wilted. Profits after taxes as a per cent of equity fell from 19% in 1947 to 6% in 1960 and 1961. *All firms,* big and small alike, were pulled down financially, as if by quicksand. Most of those effectually engulfed were small, however, suggesting that economies of scale may have been at work as well.[25] In 1947 there were 404 brewing companies, in 1974 only 58. Many disappeared by merger (distress sales). Others simply folded. As concentration continued to climb, advertising activity eventually subsided and profits recovered.

The sources underlying Figure 15–3 show this subsidence of advertising during the early 1970s. But they are not current enough to show the advertising

[24] Kenneth Fraundorf, "The Social Costs of Packaging Competition in the Beer and Soft Drink Industries," *Antitrust Bulletin* (Winter 1975), pp. 803–831.
[25] On the other hand, the fact that profits of *all* firms suffered indicates that economies of scale were not the sole cause.

354

scuffle touched off by Miller in the late 1970s. Miller has had remarkable success in gaining market share by spending on advertising three times as much per barrel as the other brewers (its parent company, Philip Morris, subsidized the early losses of this strategy), and by "segmenting" the market with different buyer images for each of its labels—"Miller High Life," "Lite," and "Löwenbräu." Between 1972 and 1982, Miller quintupled its market share from 4% to 23% and punched its way into second place behind Anheuser-Busch. Miller's rivals retaliated vigorously, or, as William Coors put it, the industry went "berserk with advertising expenditures." Ad outlays as a percent of sales in 1981 approached the peak level of 1964, so the outburst alters the neat nonlinear pattern of Figure 15-3, but probably only temporarily (as the concentration trend continues).[26] Advertising wars are like price wars: they can erupt and subside almost any time.

B. Negative Range (Advertising as Cause)

In the range of inverse relationship, advertising may push up concentration as long as advertising outlays exceed the industry (or monopoly) optimum level. The heavy cost burden, particularly in the region of most intensive nonprice competition, may provoke mergers and failures, as just illustrated in the case of beer.

A still more interesting possibility entails rising advertising as a cause of *decreasing* concentration, where concentration is initially very high. Most obviously, advertising may assist new entry. In fact, entry can sometimes be accomplished through little or nothing more than an ingenious or lavishly financed advertising campaign. It can also be achieved through product differentiation generally, in which advertising plays only a part. Even if technological innovation or price discounting rather than advertising or differentiation are the means of a newcomer's entry into a highly concentrated market, his eventual success could be endangered if he did not vigorously promote his sales. In any event, it is not likely that entry will dent concentration appreciably or durably unless the entrant spends considerably more on advertising relative to sales than established firms spend. This expenditure in turn hoists the market-wide A/S ratio. Thus, in a study of 34 new brands of grocery and drug products that were successful enough to gain 2–39% market shares within 2 years after introduction, James Peckham found the entrants had advertised much more intensively than established firms. On average, the entrants' share of total industry advertising exceeded their share of total sales by 70%.[27] And these were not just "me too" products.

---

[26] D. Greer, "The Causes of Concentration in the U.S. Brewing Industry," *Quarterly Review of Economics and Business* (Winter 1981), pp. 87–106; *Advertising Age*, August 2, 1982, p. 41; *Beverage Industry*, September 24, 1982; C. M. L. Kelton and W. D. Kelton, "Advertising and Intraindustry Brand Shift in the U.S. Brewing Industry," *Journal of Industrial Economics* (March 1982), pp. 293–303.

[27] James O. Peckham, "Can We Relate Advertising Dollars to Market Share Objectives?" in *How Much to Spend for Advertising?* edited by M. A. McNiven (National Association of Advertisers, 1969), pp. 23–30.

Pepsi-Cola provides a good example. During the 1930s Coca Cola enjoyed 60% of all soft drink sales and Pepsi-Cola was languishing in receivership. Pepsi was successfully revived after some modification of its flavor and an exuberant ad campaign financed at a cost per case nearly three times greater than Coke's cost per case. By 1940 Pepsi had 10% of the market to Coke's 53%. Pepsi's market share continued to grow and Coke's continued to wither as long as Pepsi held a substantial edge in ad cost per case. By the early 1960s, Pepsi held about 20% to Coke's 38%. At that point their shares began to stabilize. Coke had by then escalated its ad outlays per case to match those of Pepsi more closely, and it has since yielded little further ground.[28] The result is less power for Coke and the Pepsi generation of a threefold increase in industry ad cost per case. (And you thought "the Pepsi generation" was an age group.) Notice that this example illustrates more than the entrant's contribution to a rising industry A/S ratio. Coke's reaction to Pepsi's entry illustrates a *second* source of rising A/S. Established firms are not likely to stand idly by and watch their market shares evaporate. They retaliate, counter punch, throw "empties," whatever. This observation brings us once again to entry barriers.

To recap briefly before continuing, an escalation in advertising may cause concentration to rise or fall; which alternative results usually depends on the initial level of concentration.

IV. ADVERTISING AS ENTRY BARRIER

Earlier, in Chapter 8, we considered the possibility that product differentiation could pose a barrier to entry. That discussion, however, was mainly confined to *static* barriers, such as the barrier implied by large economies of scale. Here we acknowledge a *dynamic* advertising barrier. When Coke suffered insults at the hands of Pepsi, its response was slow and moderate. But such is not always the case. Established firms may lash out at newcomers, uncoiling massive barrages of advertising, promotion, and other nonprice artillery. Here are a few examples:

• Between 1900 and 1902 a tremendous jump in the popularity of Turkish tobacco cigarettes trimmed 16 percentage points off the American Tobacco Company's 93% market share. The Company rushed its own Turkish brands to market and jacked up its cigarette ad outlay from 0.5 to 20.3% of sales.[29]

• In 1961 a new firm entered the Australian soap market, which was then essentially split between two dominant firms. The two old-timers inflated their ad outlays 45 and 100% within a year.[30]

[28] By 1981 Pepsi's share inched up to 24% and Coke's slipped to 36%. *Wall Street Journal,* May 24, 1982, p. 21.
[29] Greer, *op. cit.,* p. 326.
[30] M. A. Alemson and H. T. Burley, "Demand and Entry into an Oligopoly Market: A Case Study," *Journal of Industrial Economics* (December 1974), pp. 109–124.

- In 1980 Procter & Gamble launched "High Point" instant decaffeinated coffee, challenging General Foods' "Sanka," the age-old leading brand. In response, promotional spending on "Sanka" soared seven-fold to an annualized rate of $90 million.[31]

In short, product differentiation may pose a barrier to entry for reasons other than those mentioned in Chapter 8—lagged carry-over, economies of scale, and static capital costs. Moreover, these examples help to explain the emphasis businessmen give to product differentiation when voicing their opinions on barriers.

V. ADVERTISING, PRICES, AND PROFITS

Given the flip-flop nature of our preceding remarks, you might suspect that advertising can either increase or decrease prices and profits. You would be right. One of the main factors determining whether it is an increase or a decrease is the *source level* in the stream of production and distribution. *Manufacturers'* advertising frequently *raises* prices and profits for manufacturers as it builds brand loyalties and market power. Conversely, *retailer's* advertising frequently *lowers* prices and profits among retailers because at that level advertising tends to be informative, procompetitive, and effective at creating efficiencies.

A. Manufacturers' Advertising, Prices, and Profits

Although manufacturers' advertising frequently raises prices and profits, such is not always the case. Table 15–2 attempts an oversimplified summary by distinguishing two realms: one in which advertising displays anticompetitive traits and one in which it acts neutrally or perhaps even procompetitively. On the anticompetitive side, where intensive advertising tends to raise prices, profits, and entry barriers, we find experience goods whose qualities cannot be assessed before purchase, especially nondurable "convenience" goods of this type, such as soap, aspirin, soft drinks, breakfast cereals, and many other low-priced grocery and drug items. (Beer fits this category, too, so the rising ad costs and falling profits in that industry during the 1950s may be considered a transitory, disequilibrium development.) Exhortative TV advertising typifies their promotion, building relatively strong (and mindless) brand allegiances among consumers. On the neutral or procompetitive side, where advertising intensity is less closely associated with price and profit levels, we find search goods whose qualities can readily be assessed before purchase, and what may be called "big-ticket," durable shopping goods, like furniture and appliances. Compared to the anticompetitive realm, advertising for these goods tends to be more informative and

---

[31] *Business Week*, January 26, 1981, p. 65. For further examples see *Federal Trade Commission v. Procter & Gamble Co.*, 63 F.T.C. 1465, at p. 1518; Greer, *op. cit.* (1973); Alan Bevan, "The U.K. Potato Crisp Industry, 1960–72: A Study of New Competition," *Journal of Industrial Economics* (June 1974), pp. 281–297, and R. W. Shaw and C. J. Sutton, *Industry and Competition* (London: Macmillan, 1976), p. 42.

TABLE 15–2. Summary of the Effects of Advertising on Prices, Profits, and Barriers to Entry in Manufacturing: Two Broad Classes of Goods

Nature of Division	Anticompetitive Realm, Advertising **raises** Prices, Profits, and Barriers	Neutral or Procompetitive Realm, Advertising has **no effect** on or **lowers** Prices, Profits, and Barriers
Type of *product*	Experience goods, nondurable convenience goods (e.g., soap, beer, soft drinks)	Search goods, durable shopping goods* (e.g., furniture, appliances, autos)
Type of *advertising* (chief message and media)	Exhortative, broadcasting media (TV especially)	Informative, print media some exhortation
Type of *consumer* effect	Brand loyalty, reduced price elasticity of demand	Mixed effects, but brand switching and increased price elasticity

* Note: Nonprice activities other than advertising (for example, styling) may have anticompetitive effects for these products.

more reliant on print media—newspapers and magazines in particular. Also, the retailers of these goods play a key part with demonstrations, credit, repair services, and the like. The economic consequences are in the end more favorable for consumers.

This is an oversimplified summary because most products carry some characteristics from both realms, as a continuum, not a gap, bridges the two sides. Moreover, there are some obvious exceptions, such as cigarettes and liquor, which belong in the anticompetitive first realm but which by law cannot be advertised on television. Still, the broad classification helps to reveal the basic pattern that emerges from a wide range of evidence.

Formal statistical analyses have confirmed the message of Table 15–2 in several ways:

- A study of advertising-profit correlations found (1) a significant *positive* correlation of 0.78 for *nondurable experience* goods, (2) a significant *negative* correlation of $-.65$ for *durable experience* goods, and (3) a nonsignificant *negative* correlation of -0.02 for *search* goods such as clothing, hats, and furniture.[32]

- A more sophisticated statistical study discovered: (1) A strong *positive* association between advertising intensity and profits for nondurable *"convenience"* goods. The author's explanation was that these goods are "presold"

[32] Phillip Nelson, "The Economic Consequences of Advertising," *Journal of Business* (April 1975), p. 237.

and inexpensive, so manufacturers have tremendous influence over brand choice and persuasive advertising is especially effective. (2) *No* association between advertising intensity and profits for durable *"shopping"* goods. Author's explanation: Manufacturers' exhortative advertising is of little influence here because of hefty product prices, heavy retailer influence, and an emphasis on other forms of differentiation.[33]

• When advertising expenditures on television, magazines, and local newspapers are analyzed separately, it appears that *television* advertising has the most potent *positive* impact on profits, especially for convenience goods. Local newspaper advertising is at the opposite pole, with a mild inverse (procompetitive) association.[34]

• The frequency with which advertisers disclose price in their ads probably measures two things: the intensity of price competition and the level of information content in their advertising. A very interesting study of magazine advertising found that (1) in *convenience* goods industries, high overall ad outlays are associated with a *lack* of price competition and information content, while (2) in *shopping* goods industries, high overall ad outlays seem to *stimulate* price competition and information disclosure.[35]

More concretely, the positive relationship between advertising and price for many products is shown in price differences between "distributor" (or private label) brands and "advertised manufacturer" brands. Table 15–3 shows the retail prices and market shares of these two types of brands for seven food products, as estimated by the National Commission on Food Marketing. In every instance, price of the advertised brand exceeds average price of the distributors' brands, by a low of 5% for canned peaches to a high of 32% for frozen orange juice. On average, these advertised brands are 21% more costly to consumers than the distributors' brands. A similar study of British markets found price differences of 18%, 16%, and 29% for instant coffee, margarine, and toothpaste.[36] To conduct your own research, make a quick visit to the nearest Safeway, A & P, or other large chain. (For really whopping price differences, check out the drug and detergent shelves.)

---

[33] Michael E. Porter, "Consumer Behavior, Retailer Power and Market Performance in Consumer Goods Industries," *Review of Economics and Statistics* (November 1974), pp. 419–436.

[34] Michael E. Porter, "Interbrand Choice, Media Mix and Market Performance," *American Economic Review* (May 1976), pp. 398–406.

[35] Alfred Arterburn and John Woodbury, "Advertising, Price Competition, and Market Structure," *Southern Economic Journal* (January 1981), pp. 763–775. Further pertinent findings are in P. W. Farris and D. J. Reibstein, "How Prices, Ad Expenditures, and Profits are Linked," *Harvard Business Review* (November 1979), pp. 173–184 (Exhibit IV); E. Pagoulatos and R. Sorensen, "A Simultaneous Equation Analysis of Advertising, Concentration and Profitability," *Southern Economic Journal* (January 1981), pp. 728–741; Blake Imel, Michael R. Behr, and Peter G. Helmberger, *Market Structure and Performance* (Lexington, Mass.: Lexington Books, 1972); J. J. Lambin, *Advertising, Competition, and Market Conduct in Oligopoly Over Time* (Amsterdam: North-Holland Publishing Co., 1976).

[36] David Morris, "Some Aspects of Large-Scale Advertising," *Journal of Industrial Economics* (December 1975), pp. 119–130. See also Stephen Nickell and David Metcalf, "Monopolistic Industries and Monopoly Profits," *Economica Journal* (June 1978), pp. 254–268.

CONDUCT

TABLE 15–3. Relative Prices and Sales of Distributors' and Manufacturers' Brands, 1966

	Average Retail Price per Case		Percentage of Sales Accounted for by	
Product	Distributors' Brands ($)	Advertised Brands* ($)	Distributors' Brands (%)	Advertised Brands (%)
Frozen orange juice	8.74	11.57	79	20
Frozen green beans	4.94	6.42	77	21
Canned green peas	4.76	5.54	29	60
Canned peaches	6.24	6.54	47	53
Catsup	4.46	5.51	28	70
Tuna fish	12.72	15.46	31	63
Evaporated milk	6.52	7.49	45	54

* These data are for a typical advertised brand. All others are averages.
Source: National Commission on Food Marketing, *Special Studies in Food Marketing,* Technical Study 10 (Washington, D.C., 1966), pp. 66, 70–71.

At this point the defenders of advertising cry, "Foul! These are unfair comparisons! As any fool can plainly see, heavily advertised, higher priced brands are of higher quality than those cheap brands." Indeed, some defenders claim that people get *more* for their money by buying advertised brands, inflated prices notwithstanding. Well, what about this quality claim? Is it the "real thing"? As you might guess, rigorous research into this question is very difficult to conduct. Nevertheless, a few bits of reliable evidence are available, and they yield a tentative, two-part answer: (1) On the whole, advertising intensity is apparently *not* positively associated with product quality, but (2) there is sufficient variance across products to include many instances where a correspondence between advertising intensity and quality is indeed the case. (Whether the occasional quality premium *fully* justifies the associated price premium is, however, another issue.) Consider the following:

1. One of the most notorious instances of price difference concerns prescription drugs, where unadvertised "generic" products are dirt-cheap compared to advertised brand names—for example, for reserpine $1.10 versus $39.50, for meprobamate $4.90 versus $68.21, tetracycline $8.75 versus $52.02, and penicillin G $1.75 versus $10.04 (in 1972). Yet drug quality is very closely regulated by the U.S. Food and Drug Administration, and no notable quality differences between "generic" and "brand" named drugs has been found despite extensive testing.[37]

[37] Milton Silverman and Philip R. Lee, *Pills, Profits and Politics* (Berkeley, Calif.: University of California Press, 1974), pp. 138–189, 334; *Drug Product Selection,* Staff Report to the Federal Trade Commission (January 1979), pp. 51–53, 236–256.

2. H. J. Rotfeld and K. B. Rotzoll studied 12 product classes, including drain cleaner, laundry detergent, cooking oil, peanut butter, cat food, and toothpaste. They correlated quality rank (as determined by *Consumer Reports* and *Consumers Bulletin*) with brand advertising intensity (as measured by absolute dollars spent on national media) for each product. They concluded that quality and advertising intensity were *not* positively related when comparing only nationally advertised brands. *But*, when comparing nationally advertised brands with "local," nonnationally advertised brands, they found the quality of the former generally surpassing that of the latter. Results were thus "mixed."[38]

3. As for distributor versus manufacturer brands, many come off the *same* assembly line to the *same* technical specifications. They differ only in label and perhaps "trim." Thus, more than half of all tires sold in the United States under distributor labels are produced by Goodyear, Firestone, Goodrich, Uniroyal, and General. And according to the editor of *Modern Tire Dealer Magazine*, "there is no noticeable quality difference among nationally advertised tires, the associate brands made by the smaller companies, and private-label brands made by both."[39]

It appears, then, that the quality argument has many weak spots. However, defenders of advertising have a further argument debunking the notion that advertising inordinately raises prices and profits. This is the "subjectivist" argument. This holds that advertising adds a "value" not in the product, for which the consumer may rightfully wish to pay extra. The housewife pays more for the highly advertised brand, thinking that she thereby gets more for her money. Since she *thinks* she is getting more, she *must* be getting more, or so it is argued. Perhaps the "security" of the advertised brand warms her heart. Perhaps she feels that her family will love her more for using a familiar brand. In other words, advertising sells hope, confidence, elation, and faith with each unit of canned milk, detergent, soda, aspirin, and drain cleaner. The problem with this argument is that it is tautological.[40] By *definition*, the consumer is *always* right and rational, even if he or she continues to pay extra after being informed that to do so is foolish. *By definition*, higher prices are *always* justified by higher "quality." But arguments by definition are dead-end streets.

In sum, advertising by manufacturers lifts prices, profits, and barriers to entry over a wide range of consumer products—in particular, nondurable experi-

[38] H. J. Rotfeld and K. B. Rotzoll, "Advertising and Product Quality: Are Heavily Advertised Products Better?" *Journal of Consumer Affairs* (Summer 1976), pp. 33–47.

[39] *Washington Post*, April 20, 1975, pp. M1, M3. On TV sets see *Washington Post*, June 8, 1975, pp. F1, F8. Principal TV suppliers for Sears, Wards, and J. C. Penney have been General Electric, Sanyo, Panasonic, RCA, and Admiral. For both tires and TVs, private label prices apparently average 8–10% less than manufacturer label prices. On the quality of private label canning as in Table 15–3, see National Commission on Food Marketing, *Fruit and Vegetable Industry*, Study No. 4 (June 1966), p. 191.

[40] William Breit and K. G. Elzinga, "Product Differentiation and Institutionalism: New Shadows on an Old Terrain," *Journal of Economic Issues* (December 1974), pp. 813–826; Paul W. Farris and Mark S. Albion, "Reply," *Journal of Marketing* (Winter 1982), pp. 106–107 (indeed, for an interesting comparison between reality and theory read pages 94–105 in the same journal).

ence goods or "convenience" goods. Though such adverse effects are sometimes observed for other products, the record is mixed, occasionally being favorable.

B. Retailers' Advertising, Prices, and Profits

The impact of retailer advertising is quite different than manufacturer advertising. At retail level it generally seems to foster *lower* prices and *lower* profit margins (and perhaps *easier* entry too).

Lee Benham, for instance, examined retail prices of eyeglasses in states that legally restricted merchant advertising and retail prices in states that had few or no restrictions on advertising. Comparing the most and least restrictive states, he discovered a $20 difference in average prices in 1963. Where advertising was prohibited, the price of eyeglasses averaged $37.48. Conversely, where advertising was wholly unrestricted, prices averaged $17.98.[41] Moreover, Benham surveyed several large "commercial" retailers, such as Sears, asking which states they felt were the most and least difficult to enter with respect to eyeglass merchandising. According to Benham, "The states ranked as most difficult were classified as 'restrictive,' those ranked least difficult were classified as 'nonrestrictive,' and the remaining states were classified as 'other.' "[42]

Similarly, John Cady analyzed prescription drug retail prices for the effects of state restrictions on retail drug *price* advertising. Comparing the retail prices of 10 representative prescription drugs across states, he found that restrictions on price advertising *raised* prices an average of 4.3%, with the highest differential being 9.1% for one sampled product.[43]

Broad statistical studies corroborate these. Kenneth Boyer, for instance, analyzed two separate subsamples, one of which was retail and service enterprises (such as grocers, drugstores, auto dealers, laundries, and hotels). He compared their behavior with that of consumer goods manufacturers generally. He discovered:

1. A strong *positive* correlation between advertising intensity and profits for *manufacturers* (as usual, when all consumer goods are included).
2. A weak *negative* correlation between advertising intensity and profits in *retail and service trades.*[44]

Why these favorable results for retail advertising? There seem to be several related reasons. First, retailing tends to be a "search" service—that is, consumers

[41] Lee Benham, "The Effect of Advertising on the Price of Eyeglasses," *Journal of Law & Economics* (October 1972), pp. 337–352.

[42] L. Benham and A. Benham, "Regulating Through the Professions: A Perspective on Information Control," *Journal of Law & Economics* (October 1975), pp. 426–427.

[43] John F. Cady, "An Estimate of the Price Effects of Restrictions on Drug Price Advertising," *Economic Inquiry* (December 1976), pp. 493–510. See also W. Luksetich and H. Lofgreen, "Price Advertising and Liquor Prices," *Industrial Organization Review,* Vol. 4, No. 1 (1976), pp. 13–25. See also Alex Maurizi and Thom Kelly, *Prices and Consumer Information* (Washington D.C.: American Enterprise Institute, 1978), p. 40; Amihai Glazer, "Advertising, Information, and Prices—A Case Study," *Economic Inquiry* (October 1981), pp. 661–671.

[44] Kenneth D. Boyer, "Information and Goodwill Advertising," *Review of Economics and Statistics* (November 1974), pp. 541–548.

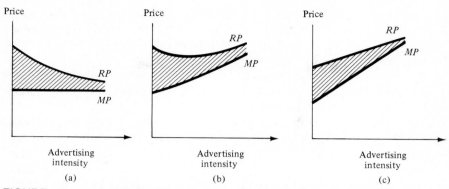

FIGURE 15–4. Advertising and price level. RP = retailer's price to consumer; MP = manufacturer's price to retailer. Shaded area denotes retailer's markup margin.

have powers of prepurchase assessment, and price receives great emphasis. This is particularly true of drug and eyeglass retailing, where the beneficial effects of advertising are most thoroughly documented. Once a doctor prescribes the drugs or glasses needed, the question of where to buy them can be answered by fairly simple search, a search focusing mainly on price. Availabilities and convenient location also carry weight; hence, they too receive attention in retailer advertising.

Second, as suggested by the first point, retailer advertising tends to be informative, just like search good advertising. Information on price heightens price competition, which in turn encourages retailer efficiency:

> In general, large-volume low-price sellers are dependent upon drawing consumers from a wide area and consequently need to inform their potential customers of the advantages of coming to them. If advertising is prohibited, they may not be able to generate the necessary sales to maintain the low price.[45]

C. Manufacturers and Retailers Together

A simplified summary of our findings for manufacturers and retailers taken together is shown in Figure 15–4, where RP is the retailer's price to consumers, MP is the manufacturer's price to retailers, and the shaded area indicates the retailer's markup over cost of goods sold. If it is assumed that greater advertising intensity at retail level usually reduces retailers' markups, then the vertical distance between MP and RP will shrink as indicated by all three shaded areas in Figure 15–4. What happens to price to consumers then depends largely on what happens to price at manufacturer's level: (a) Consumers' price falls with greater advertising intensity in panel (a) where manufacturers' advertising is neutral, as appears to be the case for search goods and shopping goods. (b) Consumers' price falls and then rises if as in panel (b) retailers' markup at first falls *more* rapidly and then falls *less* rapidly in comparison to the rising

---

[45] Benham, *op. cit.*, p. 339.

manufacturers' price MP. This ambiguous collection of possible consumer prices might hold for many consumer convenience goods. (c) Finally, other consumer convenience goods seem to fit the pattern of panel (c), with consumers' price rising steadily.

It's this author's guess, for example, that video games and refrigerators fit class (a); many prepared foods and candies probably illustrate class (b), with different products occupying different positions; finally, soft drinks, breakfast cereals, aspirin, detergents, beer, cigarettes, and liquor appear to be among the occupants of class (c). Relationships between advertising and profits may follow analogous patterns.[46]

VI. IS ADVERTISING EXCESSIVE?

The last item on our agenda alludes to the possibility that advertising may be burning up more scarce productive resources than is socially optimal. Early debate of this issue tended to lump all advertising together and assume an "either-or" answer—either it was excessive or it was not. More recently the debate has entered a new and more refined phase, pushed by the discoveries outlined in the preceding discussion and by the work of William Comanor and Thomas Wilson, whose theories cast fresh light in this old corner.[47]

To appreciate the current view, we must recognize that there are *two* demand curves for advertising messages—one generated by advertisers who seek to make sales and one representing the desires of consumers seeking information. Of course, these demands may vary from one market to another, and the type of messages demanded by the sellers may be quite different from the type of messages demanded by consumers. If we grant that social welfare is measured by the extent to which consumers' demands are met, "excessive" advertising may be measured by the extent to which the sellers' demand for messages in any given market exceeds the consumers' demand for messages in that market.

Although real world measurement of this potential divergence is impossible, a few educated guesses are feasible. First, as we have seen, interbrand rivalries may rocket advertising intensity to stratospheric levels, especially in the middle range of market concentration. It seems safe to say that such cross-cancelling "competitive" advertising is excessive from the social point of view. Indeed, it is excessive from the sellers' point of view as well as the consumers' because the sellers' hyperactive demand for messages stems from a "prisoners' dilemma," and escape via collusion would presumably curtail this demand.[48]

[46] Much of this overall view is due to Robert L. Steiner, who also recognizes possible interactions between manufacturers and retailers. See e.g., his "Marketing Productivity in Consumer Good's Industries—A Vertical Perspective," *Journal of Marketing* (January 1978), pp. 60–70.

[47] W. S. Comanor and T. A. Wilson, *Advertising and Market Power* (Cambridge, Mass.: Harvard University Press, 1974), pp. 16–21.

[48] For specific evidence of excess advertising see Lambin, *op. cit.,* Henry G. Grabowski, "The Effects of Advertising on Intraindustry Shifts in Demand," *NBER Explorations in Economic Research* (Winter-Spring 1977–1978), pp. 375–401; Jeffry M. Netter, "Excessive Advertising: An Empirical Analysis," *Journal of Industrial Economics* (June 1982), pp. 361–373.

A second broad class of excesses probably occurs where intensive advertising permits firms to raise prices, reap supernormal profits, and bar entry. Under such conditions (outlined in Figure 15–4), sellers' demand for messages is likely to far outdistance that of consumers. "It is in such markets," Comanor and Wilson explain, "that one can infer that advertising is clearly excessive from a social standpoint, since those benefits to the firm that are not benefits to consumers accrue precisely because of the anticompetitive effects of the advertising."[49]

Finally, it is not preposterous to suppose that markets thick with exhortative advertising also inflict excesses detrimental to the social interest. Such markets are substantially the same as those just mentioned, but they deserve this slightly different acknowledgement because the message demands of sellers and consumers may differ in *quality* as well as *quantity*. Consumers would probably prefer a maximum of information and a minimum of exhortation in the messages they demand of the media. (Consumers' demand, if known, would indicate their willingness to pay money for the ads.) Conversely, sellers often find it profitable to maximize exhortation and minimize information, even to the point of lying. Thus, wherever persuasion predominates there is again a big gap between the two demands and an indication that society's scarce resources are being squandered.

In markets *other* than those identified, advertising quantity and quality should be more nearly optimal. Although this is not a happy ending, it is at least a mitigating circumstance.

SUMMARY

The foregoing discussion went well beyond what is usually considered "conduct." Profits and cost efficiencies are not yet fully fair game, since they are more comprehensively treated later under "performance." Still, limited consideration of them is appropriate here, and it certainly cannot be claimed that we have ignored conduct.

Having discussed the close connection between product differentiability and nonprice activities earlier, we focus in this chapter on the relationship between concentration and advertising. The causal flow between these latter variables is two-way; just about everyone agrees on that. There is less agreement concerning the nature and form of the relationship. Of the several competing theories, the "nonlinear" hypothesis is preferred here. It holds that peak nonprice activity occurs where concentration is neither extremely high nor especially low but rather somewhere in the middle or upper-middle region. As for causality, the nutshell view of the present author is this:

Concentration as a cause: (1) Firm level price elasticities fall with rising concentration, thereby initially boosting industry A/S. However, as concentra-

---

[49] Much the same might be said of product proliferation in some industries. See F. M. Scherer, "The Welfare Economics of Product Variety: An Application to the Ready-to-Eat Cereals Industry," *Journal of Industrial Economics* (December 1979), pp. 113–134.

tion reaches very high levels, price level is likely to rise, which, in turn, increases price elasticity and lowers A/S. (2) At moderate concentration, price competition wanes while nonprice competition rages. With greater market power, however, collusive understandings may hold even nonprice competition in check.

Advertising as a cause: Economies of scale to advertising, predation, and inadvertent ad warfare are three ways by which this causal flow may operate in low to moderate ranges of concentration. Indeed, whenever nonprice costs are significantly excessive from the industry-wide standpoint, there is pressure for coalescence. In the range of negative relationship, advertising may assist entry, and this added A/S may reduce concentration. Of course the prospect of retaliation always poses a barrier to entry, too. So advertising is not unambiguously pro-entry.

This last observation is reflected in the discussion of prices and profits. Persistent advertising of promiscuous intensity is positively associated with prices and profits, but only under certain circumstances. These are outlined in Table 15–2 and Figure 15–4.

Finally, there seems to be a number of markets where advertising is unsatisfactory on a scale of social optimality (or cost efficiency). These markets may be grouped in three not necessarily exclusive classes: (1) those in the throes of white-hot nonprice rivalry of the prisoner's dilemma type, (2) those in which advertising makes a major contribution to market power, and (3) those saturated with persuasive, exhortative advertising.

16 Product Differentiation Policy: Unfair and Deceptive Practices

If there is a dividing line between liberty and license, it is where freedom of speech is no longer respected as a procedure of truth and becomes the unrestricted right to exploit ignorance and to incite the passions of people.

—WALTER LIPPMANN

This chapter is stunning, dazzling, thrilling, tremulous with passion, and even haunting. The chapter is, in short, a blockbuster.

These are lies, of course. But can you think of a better way to herald a discussion of deceptive practices? The statute under review here is Section 5 of the Federal Trade Commission Act (as amended by the Wheeler-Lea Act of 1938), which states that *"Unfair methods of competition in commerce, and unfair or deceptive acts or practices in commerce, are declared unlawful."* Since passage of the FTC Act in 1914, more than 3,300 cases of deception have been prosecuted by the FTC.

Before delving into the details of what is prohibited by Section 5 of the FTC Act, it would be wise to note briefly what is *not* prohibited or controlled. The law does not protect the public from inane, absurd, tasteless, and boringly repetitive advertising. Likewise, United States policy places no limits on levels of dollar outlay. Outlay limits have occasionally been imposed in Europe, but not in the United States. Finally, "puffing" is permitted, even though, strictly speaking, much of it is mendacious.[1] Thus, our senses are pelted by such exaggerations as

Budweiser is the King of beers.

Zenith Chromacolor is the biggest breakthrough in color TV.

State Farm is all you need to know about insurance.

Our survey of what is illegal comes in five parts and focuses primarily on advertising: (1) the criteria applied to determine deception; (2) specific examples

[1] I. L. Preston, *The Great American Blow-Up* (Madison, Wis.: University of Wisconsin Press, 1975).

of advertising that have collided with the criteria; (3) FTC procedures; (4) remedies applied to cleanup; and (5) miscellaneous unfair practices.

I. WHAT IS "DECEPTIVE"?

A. Truth, Falsity, and Deception

Innocent souls tend to think in simple terms: truth should be legal, falsity illegal. But this rule would be impractical, the controversies over truth being what they are. A better rule, the one actually applied by law, centers on the *deception* of potential buyers: "that which is not deceptive is legal, and that which is deceptive is illegal." This rule is different because falsity and deception are *not* necessarily the same. Although most false claims are deceptive, a claim may be false but not deceptive. Conversely, although most true claims are not deceptive, some true claims may be deceptive. These divergences arise because of the gap between any message's sender and receiver. Whereas truth and falsity hinge upon the literal content of the message sent, deception depends upon what goes on in the minds of folks receiving the message—that is, the potential buyers.

Take for example Exxon's promise to put a tiger in your tank. The claim is patently false. There is no tiger. Yet you are not deceived and neither is anyone else. So the FTC does not flinch.

Examples of literal truth that actually deceive are equally easy to come by. In 1971 the FTC found deception in nonfalse television ads showing Hot Wheels and Johnny Lightning toy racers speeding over their tracks. To the TV viewer, the racers seemed to move like bullets. But this was merely a "special effect," which was achieved by filming the racers at close range from clever angles. The representation was technically accurate but nevertheless misleading.[2] Many further examples relate to "half-true" advertisments that, although literally true, leave an overall impression that is quite incorrect.[3]

Who Is Deceived? Given that deception lies in the mind of the observer rather than in the body of the advertisement, the next question is who among observers is to be protected? If one gullible person is misled, does that constitute illegal deception? What about 3%, or 15%, of the population? When reviewing a case in 1927 the Supreme Court held that Section 5 was "made to protect the trusting as well as the suspicious." Accordingly, the FTC and the appellate courts have adopted a fairly stringent standard, one that protects the ignorant, the unthinking, and the trusting as well as the suspicious and hard headed.[4] The authorities have decided, for example, that a hair coloring could not claim

---

[2] *Mattel,* 79 FTC 667 (1971); *Topper* 79 FTC 681 (1971).

[3] *P. Lorillard Co.* v. *FTC,* 186 F. 2d 52 (4th Cir. 1950).

[4] *Charles of the Ritz Dist. Corp.* v. *FTC,* 143 F. 2d 676 (2d Cir. 1944). See also Ira M. Millstein, "The Federal Trade Commission and False Advertising," *Columbia Law Review* (March 1964), pp. 457–465.

that it colored hair "permanently." The FTC is especially protective of the ignorant, unthinking, and trusting when it comes to claims of safety or health. Were an advertiser to intimate falsely that cleaning solvent "X" was nonflammable, he would ignite a blast of official rebuke.

Still, the authorities have not gone so far as to protect the "foolish or feeble minded." They permit obvious spoofs, such as love-starved girls feverishly attacking a defenseless boy (who uses Hai Karate recklessly), and a rampaging bull that is released merely by uncorking a malt liquor (Schlitz). Moreover, as already noted, the authorities permit generous amounts of puffery, not to mention "minor" sleight of hand and tongue.

B. Intent and Capacity

Prior to the FTC Act, misrepresentation and deception could be successfully prosecuted only with great difficulty. The common law was rigged in favor of the con artist because conviction could be obtained only if the injured buyer could prove in court that

1. He understood the seller's claim to convey a fact (not a puff).
2. He had relied upon the claim.
3. He was justified (and not just stupid) in relying on the claim.
4. He had suffered financial or other injury by so relying on the claim.
5. Most difficult of all, the seller *knowingly intended* to deceive him (the buyer).

In brief, conviction required a showing of *actual* deception in the mind of the buyer and *deliberate* intent in the mind of the seller. Common law cases were consequently very rare. Perhaps the only justification for this approach was the fact that sellers could suffer harsh penalties if convicted.

The FTC Act changed all this. No component of this maze of proofs now has to be shown to exist by the FTC in order for it to reach a guilty verdict. The Commission's decision hinges solely on whether or not a sales claim possesses the *capacity or tendency to deceive.* Proof of intent is not required. The Commission attacks the ad, not the advertiser. Likewise, proof of actual deception is not required. The Commission may examine an advertisement and determine on the basis of its own expertise whether there is a *potential* for deception. The Commission need not poll consumers, nor hear from complaining witnesses.[5] Even if suspected deceivers defend themselves by providing a parade of witnesses who say they have not been misled, the FTC can still find a violation.[6]

Despite the power of the FTC to rely upon its own expertise, it has nevertheless tended in recent years to supplement its own intuitive understanding with consumers' testimony, public opinion polls, and outside experts. Whereas prior to 1955, 92% of all FTC cases were decided solely on the basis of Commission expertise, between 1955 and 1973 no more than 57% of all cases were so decided.

[5] *Montgomery Ward & Co.* v. *FTC* 379 F. 2d 666 (7th Cir. 1967).
[6] *Double Eagle Lubricants, Inc.* v. *FTC,* 360 F. 2d 268 (10 Cir. 1965).

And over the years 1970–1973, only 36% of all cases were so decided.[7] Greater reliance on outside experts' and consumers' views may be due to the Commission's recent attempts to stem more subtle forms of deception and to counter criticisms that its traditional methods were too presumptive, too shoddy, and too arbitrary.

Given the FTC's fairly free hand, what of punishment and remedy? Does a guilty verdict bring fines, damage payments, and jailings, as could happen under pre-FTC common law? . . . No. As we shall see later when we discuss remedies, lenient standards of offense are coupled with lenient measures of penalty. Reprimands plus orders of "cease and desist" are, in the main, what face the two-faced (except in certain cases where the consumer's physical well-being is at stake[8]). As Ivan Preston puts it, the present "strategy is one of prevention rather than punishment and remedy. The goal is to give maximum aid to consumers at the sacrifice of less than maximum punishment to offenders, rather than the opposite."[9]

What of Competitive Effects? The original FTC Act made no specific mention of deception. It simply said: "Unfair methods of competition in commerce are hereby declared unlawful." As a result, early FTC assaults on deception were grounded on the theory that deceivers gain unfair competitive advantages over their more honest rivals. This approach was only partially successful and severely limited. After 1929, when the FTC moved against the blatantly fake claims of Raladam Company (that its "desiccated thyroid" obesity cure was completely safe and effective), these limits materialized. Reviewing the case in 1931, the Supreme Court ruled in favor of Raladam, saying that the FTC must prove competition "to have been injured, or to be clearly threatened with injury," in order to find a violation.[10] Injury to *consumers,* or potential injury to *consumers,* did not count. To rectify this shortcoming, Congress passed the Wheeler-Lea Amendment in 1938. The Amendment removed the FTC's obligation to demonstrate injury to competition by outlawing "deceptive acts or practices" as well as "unfair methods of competition." It was this legislation, then, that made "capacity and tendency to deceive" the sole criteria. (Actually, it is deceptive for me to say that "capacity and tendency" are the *sole* criteria. A misleading claim is not illegal unless it is "material," that is, affects the consumer's decision. Thus we all know Joe Namath is fibbing when, in the midst of plugging Hamilton Beach popcorn poppers, he leeringly tells us that his favorite off-the-field pleasure is making popcorn. But this misrepresentation is "immaterial.")

---

[7] M. T. Brandt and I. L. Preston, "The Federal Trade Commission's Use of Evidence to Determine Deception," *Journal of Marketing* (January 1977), pp. 54–62.

[8] In Section 14 of the FTC Act, Congress provided criminal penalties in certain cases of deception involving food, drugs, or cosmetic devices: "Any person . . . who violates any provision of Section 12 (a) shall, if the use of the commodity advertised may be injurious to health . . . , or if such violation is with intent to defraud or mislead, be guilty of a misdemeanor." Criminal prosecutions under this section are not brought by the FTC but may be recommended by the FTC to the Justice Department.

[9] Preston, *op. cit.,* p. 136.

[10] *FTC* v. *Raladam Co.,* 258 U.S. 643 (1931).

II. EXAMPLES OF DECEPTION

There is a rich variety of illegal deceptions. Unfortunately, we have space for only a few broad classes:[11] (1) claims of composition, (2) claims of function or efficacy, (3) endorsements, and (4) mock-ups.

A. Claims of Composition

The Fair Packaging and Labeling Act, and similar acts governing textiles, furs, and woolens, now regulate ingredient claims for many products. Those claims not so covered are subject to a host of FTC precedents under Section 5. Naked lies, such as calling pine wood "walnut," are out. Many more slippery representations are now explicitly defined by the FTC. Here is a sampling:

"Down" indicates feathers of any aquatic bird and therefore excludes chicken feathers.

"Linoleum" designates a product composed of oxidized oil and gums mixed "intimately" with ground cork or wood flour.

"Vanilla" unqualified, describes only that which is obtained from the vanilla bean.

In 1977, General Motors found itself confronting more than one hundred private suits for deceptively using Chevrolet engines in its Oldsmobiles. There was nothing wrong with the Chevy engines. Indeed, GM had mixed engines amongst its models for years. The problem arose because GM's advertising for the Olds "Rocket V-8" had been particularly effective. As the *Wall Street Journal* explained it, "GM's advertising for years has stressed the purported merits of individual models, including the superiority of Oldsmobile's Rocket engine." But now, customers "find there is little difference in the engines involved" and they therefore feel deceived. GM has been forced to compensate upset customers for what it calls a "breakdown in communications." ("It just didn't occur to us," GM's chairman said, that "people were interested in where the engines were built.") More interesting, GM has now changed its advertising. Instead of plugging the supposed merits of any given engine, it is advertising its "great family of engines."[12]

B. Claims of Function or Efficacy

During the late 1960s, Firestone advertised that its "Super Sports Wide Oval" tires were

built lower, wider. Nearly two inches wider than regular tires. To corner better, run cooler, stop 25% quicker.

When sued by the FTC, Firestone presented evidence that cars with these tires traveling 15 miles per hour *did* stop 25% quicker than those with ordinary

---

[11] For more complete surveys see E. W. Kintner, *A Primer on the Law of Deceptive Practices* (New York: Macmillan Publishing Co., 1971), and G. J. Alexander, *Honesty and Competition* (Syracuse, N.Y.: Syracuse University Press, 1967).

[12] "Bizarre Backfire," *Wall Street Journal,* July 27, 1977, p. 1.

width tires. However, the tests were done on very low-friction surfaces, equivalent in slickness to glare ice or waxed linoleum. Thus "Wide Ovals" might enable some poor soul who crashes through the end of his garage to stop short of the kitchen refrigerator. But slippery surfaces and slow speeds are obviously not typical of United States highway conditions. Hence the FTC decided that Firestone's ads were deceptive.[13]

Deceptive claims of efficacy or function may even run afoul of the law when they are less explicit, when, that is, they enter the realm of innuendo and suggestion. Indeed, it could be argued that this is an area where puffery is rather limited. Thus, a drug treatment for delayed menstruation was said to violate the law for advertising with such phrases as "at last—it CAN BE SOLD" and "Don't Risk Disaster," which falsely implied the product induced abortion.[14] Another example concerns "Vivarin," a simple but costly tablet containing caffeine and sugar in amounts roughly equivalent to those in a half-cup of sweetened coffee. The offending ad, which ran in 1971, had a middle-aged woman speaking as if she had just discovered a sure-fire aphrodisiac:

> One day it dawned on me that I was boring my husband to death. It wasn't that I didn't love Jim, but often by the time he came home at night I was feeling dull, tired and drowsy. [Then I began taking Vivarin.] All of a sudden Jim was coming home to a more exciting woman, me. We talked to each other a lot more. . . . And after dinner I was wide-awake enough to do a little more than just look at television. And the other day—it wasn't even my birthday—Jim sent me flowers with a note. The note began: "To my new wife. . . ."[15]

More mundane but equally misleading in the judgment of the FTC was a "Wonder Bread" campaign of the 1960s, which, among other things, included compelling TV commercials showing bread-eating children growing from infancy to adolescence before the viewer's very eyes while a narrator intoned that since Wonder Bread was "enriched," it "Helps build strong bodies 12 ways." The FTC charged that the ads deceptively represented Wonder Bread as an "extraordinary food for producing dramatic growth in children."[16]

C. Endorsements

Mention of endorsements brings to mind athletes like Joe Namath, Billy Jean King, Jack Nicklaus, and O. J. Simpson. These are certainly very important people in advertising, and the FTC has several rules of thumb governing star testimonials. Thus, for example, an endorser must be a "bona fide" user of the product unless such would be clearly inappropriate (as was true of Joe Namath's peddling pantyhose). Moreover, the Commission urges that ex-users not be represented as current users, although this is obviously difficult to enforce.

[13] *Firestone Tire and Rubber Co.,* 81 FTC 398 (1972).
[14] *Doris Savitch v. FTC, 218 F. 2d 817 (2d Cir. 1955).*
[15] *Advertising of Proprietary Medicines, Hearings,* U.S. Senate, Subcommittee on Monopoly of the Select Committee on Small Business, 92nd Congress, First Session (1971), Part 1, pp. 24, 229.
[16] *ITT Continental Baking Co.,* 83 FTC 865 (1973).

But celebrity endorsements are not the only kind, or even the most important kind. There are "lay" endorsements, "expert" endorsements, "institutional" endorsements, "cartoon character" endorsements, and more, all of which have at one time or another reached the FTC's attention. The flavor of the Commission's thinking in these and related matters may be tasted by quoting Section 255.3, Example 5, from the FTC's "Guides Concerning Use of Endorsements and Testimonials in Advertising":

> An association of professional athletes states in an advertisement that it has "selected" a particular brand of beverages as its "official breakfast drink." [The] association would be regarded as expert in the field of nutrition for purposes of this section, because consumers would expect it to rely upon the selection of nutritious foods as part of its business needs. Consequently, the association's endorsement must be based upon an expert evaluation of the nutritional value of the endorsed beverage [rather than upon the endorsement fee]. Furthermore, . . . use of the words "selected" and "official" in this endorsement imply that it was given only after direct comparisons had been performed among competing brands. Hence, the advertisement would be deceptive unless the association has in fact performed such comparisons . . . and the results . . . conform to the net impression created by the advertisement.[17]

D. Mock-ups

When filming TV commercials, technicians often substitute whipped potatoes for ice cream, soap suds for beer foam, and wine for coffee. The "real thing" melts under the hot lights, or fades, or looks murky on TV screens. Such artificial alterations and substitutions for purposes of picture enhancement are called **mock-ups.** Although these mock-ups are obviously innocuous (indeed, they may often reduce deception rather than produce it), advertisers have not confined their "doctoring" to innocent, nondeceptive, and prudent dimensions:[18]

• When Libby-Owens-Ford Glass Company wanted to demonstrate the superiority of its automobile safety glass, it smeared a competing brand with streaks of vaseline to create distortion, then photographed it at oblique camera angles to enhance the effect. The distortionless marvels of the company's own glass were "shown" by taking photographs with the windows rolled down.

• Carter Products promoted its Rise shaving cream with a mock-up that was equally unfair to poor old Brand X. A man was shown shaving with an "ordinary" lather, which dried out quickly after application. He then switched to Rise and demonstrated how it fulfilled its slogan, "Stays Moist and Creamy." Unbeknownst to the TV audience, the substance he used on the first try was not a competing brand nor a shaving cream at all. It

---

[17] *Code of Federal Regulations,* Vol. 16, "Commercial Practices," p. 347.
[18] Quoting from Preston, *op. cit.,* pp. 235, 243. The cases referred to are *Libby-Owens-Ford* v. *FTC,* 352 F. 2d 415 (6th Cir. 1965), and *Carter Products* v. *FTC,* 323 F. 2d 523 (5th Cir., 1963).

was a preparation specially designed to come out of the aerosol can in a big attractive fluff and then disappear almost immediately.

In 1965, the Supreme Court voiced its opinion of such behavior in *Colgate-Palmolive Co.* v. *FTC.*[19] The TV commercial in question purported to show that Colgate's Rapid Shave shaving cream was potent enough to allow one to shave sandpaper with an ordinary blade razor. The ad's action and words went together: "apply . . . soak . . . and off in a stroke." But it was a hoax. What appeared to be sandpaper was actually loose grains of sand sprinkled on plexiglas. And the soak was a 2-second pause. Curious consumers who tried real sandpaper informed the FTC that it couldn't be done. So the Commission asked Colgate to come clean. In its defense, Colgate claimed that you *could* shave sandpaper with very small grains of sand, soaked for over an hour. It said the mock-up was necessary because such fine grain sandpaper looked like plain paper on TV, and the true soak could not be captured in a few seconds. Indeed, Colgate felt so adamant about defending its ad that it fought the FTC all the way to the Supreme Court. The key questions addressed by the Court were as follows:[20]

1. Were undisclosed mock-ups of *mere appearance* acceptable? That is, could whipped potatoes stand-in for ice cream? The Court said yes.
2. Were undisclosed mock-ups demonstrating *un*true performance acceptable? That is, could Rapid Shave be "shown" shaving the ribs off a washboard? The Court said no, clearly not.
3. Were undisclosed mock-ups demonstrating *true* performance acceptable? That is, assuming Rapid\ Shave *could* easily shave any sandpaper, was an undisclosed mock-up of this acceptable? The Court again said no. When the appearance is *central* to the commercial, and the clear implication is that we are seeing something real when, in fact, we are not, then the mock-up is illegal unless disclosed by saying "simulated" or something similar. Of course, if the real performance is possible and a real performance is shown, there is no problem.

Absolute truth is thus not required. Inconsequential mock-ups for appearance's sake are permitted without an admission of fakery to the audience. Simulations are also allowed with disclosure. But mock-ups that materially deceive cannot be defended. Now, given your newly acquired knowledge of the law, let's test it. How would you react if you were an FTC Commissioner and you caught Campbell's Soup Company putting marbles in the bottom of its televised bowls of soup, thereby making the vegetables and other solid parts of the soup appear attractively and abundantly above the surface? Is this mere appearance? Or is it a material deception? (Your test is not a mock-up test. The case actually came up in 1970. For the FTC's answer see footnote 21.)

[19] *Colgate-Palmolive Co.,* v. *FTC,* 380 U.S. 374 (1965).
[20] Preston, *op. cit.,* p. 238.
[21] Consent settlement, *Campbell's Soup,* 77 FTC 664 (1970). The FTC thought this was deceptive.

III. FEDERAL TRADE COMMISSION PROCEDURES[22]

When attacking problems of deception (or other problems within its jurisdiction), the FTC may proceed in one of three ways: (1) complaint plus prosecution, (2) guides, or (3) trade regulation rules.

A. Complaint Plus Prosecution

This is a case-by-case approach in the sense that a particular ad or ad campaign is assailed. The complete chain of formal process is as follows: The advertiser is issued a "complaint"; his case is tried before an "administrative law judge"; the judge renders an "initial decision"; the initial decision is reviewed by the full FTC; the Commission's decision may then be appealed by the "respondent" to federal courts of appeal on questions of law, perhaps even ending up like the *Colgate-Palmolive* case in the lap of the Supreme Court. This procedure may be cut short at the outset by consent settlement, in which instance a remedy is reached without formal trial.

B. Guides

Whereas such case-by-case proceedings are ad hoc, piecemeal, and particular, industry guides and trade regulation rules are broader, more general, and less judicial. Their more sweeping scope often improves the efficiency and efficacy of enforcement. Industry guides are distillations of case law, usually promulgated without formal hearings. They are issued to summarize and clarify case law for the benefit of the individuals regulated. These guides are nonbinding; they do not directly affect case-by-case procedure.

In short, industry guides are merely an expression of the FTC's view as to what is and what is not legal. There are guides for advertising fallout shelters, advertising shell homes, advertising fuel economy for new autos, advertising guarantees, and many others—a number of which are not directly related to advertising at all.

C. Trade Regulation Rules

These are, in contrast to guides, much more serious. Like legislation, they embody the full force of law. Respondents may be prosecuted for violating the rule itself, rather than for violating the vague prohibitions of Section 5. Rules ease the burden of proof borne by the FTC's prosecuting attorneys because, once a transgression is detected, the respondent's only defense is to prove that the rule does not apply to his case. Since trade regulation rules carry so much

---

[22] Much of this and the next section is based upon M. J. Trebilcock, A. Duggan, L. Robinson, H. Wilton-Siegel, and C. Massee, *A Study on Consumer Misleading and Unfair Trade Practices,* Vol. 1 (Ottawa: Information Canada, 1976), Chapter III; U.S. Congress, House, *Oversight Hearings into the Federal Trade Commission—Bureau of Consumer Protection, Hearings,* Committee on Government Operations, 94th Congress, Second Session (1976); and G. G. Udell and P. J. Fischer, "The FTC Improvement Act," *Journal of Marketing* (April 1977), pp. 81–85.

force, the Commission formulates them by following an elaborate set of procedures.[23]

Since these rule-making procedures were first established in 1962, more than 20 rules have been enacted. The first few were simple, even trivial, governing such matters as size labeling of sleeping bags and use of the word "leak-proof" for dry-cell batteries. More recently, the FTC has grown confident. Rules now govern door-to-door sales, grocery store stocking of sale merchandise, gasoline octane disclosure, mailorder merchandise, and warranty disclosure.[24]

The Magnuson-Moss Federal Trade Commission Improvement Act of 1975 greatly strengthened the FTC's authority to issue trade regulation rules. The FTC's efforts prior to 1975 were challenged by litigation, but Section 202 of the Act of 1975 gave the FTC express authority to devise rules defining specific acts or practices as unfair or deceptive. The first rule issued under the Act was the "Eyeglass Rule," of 1978, which among other things prohibits restraints on the advertising of optometrists. Such restraints (many imposed by state regulation) were found to *increase* the price of eyeglasses to consumers.[25]

On the other hand, as we shall see in a moment, the Federal Trade Commission Improvements Act of *1980* weakened FTC authority.

IV. REMEDIES

The product of these and other procedures is a variety of remedies designed to quash current violations, discourage future violations, and, in rare instances, erase the ill effects of past violations. The remedies include cease and desist orders, affirmative disclosure, and corrective advertising.

A. Cease and Desist Orders

The traditional, and in most instances of trial settlement the *only,* remedy applied is an order to cease and desist. This simply prohibits the offender from engaging further in practices that have been found unlawful or in closely similar practices. Thus Firestone was ordered to stop advertising that its tires could stop 25% quicker; and Colgate was ordered to cease "shaving" sand off plexiglass amidst ballyhoo about sandpaper. By themselves, such orders are of course little more than slaps on the wrist. No penalties are levied. Penalties may be imposed only if the errant behavior persists *after* the order is issued. (Under the FTC Improvement Act of 1975, the Commission may ask a federal court to impose civil penalties of up to $10,000 per day of violation against those who breach its cease and desist orders.) But since penalties do not apply to original violations, it is often argued that advertisers are not significantly deterred from dealing in deception.

---

[23] Trebilcock, et al., *op. cit.,* pp. 153–54.

[24] Leaf through *Code of Federal Regulations,* Title 16.

[25] In re FTC Trade Regulation Rule, Advertising of Opthalmic Goods and Services, *Trade Regulation Rep.* No. 335 (June 1978).

In support of the argument, it has been estimated that *one third* of the members of the Pharmaceutical Manufacturers Association have at one time or another engaged in illegally deceptive advertising.[26] Moreover, recidivism is common. Once one deceptive campaign is stopped, another with different deceptions may be launched. Firestone's 25% quicker claim, for instance, was Firestone's third violation in 15 years.

B. Affirmative Disclosure

This remedy is especially appropriate for two particular types of deception—misrepresentation by silence and exaggerated claims of brand uniqueness. To check the problem of deceptive silence, an affirmative disclosure order prohibits the advertiser from making certain claims unless he discloses at the same time facts that are considered necessary to negate any deceptive inferences otherwise induced by silence. Perhaps the most familiar example of affirmative disclosure is the FTC's requirement that cigarette advertisers disclose the dangers inherent to smoking: "Warning: The Surgeon General Has Determined That Cigarette Smoking Is Dangerous to Your Health." Another noteworthy example concerns Geritol, which ran into trouble for representing its iron tonic as a cure for tiredness, loss of strength, wan appearance, and associated afflictions. The Commission's order for affirmative disclosure specified that if Geritol was going to sell its tonic as a cure for tiredness, it then had to disclose the fact that there is really very little connection between tiredness and iron deficiency, and that the vast majority of people who are tired are not tired because of iron deficiency.

C. Corrective Advertising

Whereas affirmative disclosure may prevent the *continuance* of misleading claims into the future, the purpose of corrective advertising is to wipe out any *lingering ill effects of* deception. What do we mean by lingering ill effects? There are several possibilities. From a purely economic point of view, deceptive advertising continues to generate sales even after it has stopped because of the "lagged effect" of advertising. So long as the ill-gotten gains in sales continue, the deception will return a profit and the deceiver's more truthful competitors will suffer a disadvantage. Moreover, deceptive claims may be dangerous to consumer welfare where issues of health and safety are involved. If some people continue to believe their tires stop 25% quicker, even after this claim is taken out of circulation, there is a problem of lingering ill effect. Accordingly, the typical corrective advertising order comes in two parts:

1. Cease and desist making the deceptive claim.
2. Cease and desist *all* advertising of the product in question unless a specified portion of that advertising contains, for a specified time period, a statement of the fact that prior claims were deceptive.

[26] R. Burack, "Introduction to the Handbook of Prescription Drugs," in *Consumerism,* edited by Aaker and Day (New York: Free Press, 1974), p. 257. The regulations referred to here are actually those of the FDA, not the FTC, but they are similar.

377

Until 1977, the legal status of corrective advertising was shaky. Although the remedy was imposed in several pre-1977 consent settlements, the FTC did not apply it in a contested case and the appellate courts did not pass on its legality until the *Listerine* litigation. Listerine, presently the nation's largest selling mouthwash (with about 40% of the market), was for decades promoted as a cold preventative as well. From 1938 to late 1972 Listerine labels declared that the stuff "KILLS GERMS BY MILLIONS ON CONTACT . . . For General Oral Hygiene, Bad Breath, Colds and resultant Sore Throats." Moreover, countless TV commercials showed mothers extolling the medicinal virtues of gargling with Listerine twice a day. "I think," they would crow, "we've cut down on colds, and those we do catch, don't seem to last as long."

Although the makers of Listerine deny that their ads ever suggested that Listerine would prevent colds, millions of folks got that message. The company's own polls showed that nearly two out of every three shoppers thought Listerine was a help for colds. Medical experts testifying at the FTC trial thought otherwise. Except for some temporary relief from sore throat irritation more easily achieved by gargling with warm salt water, Listerine was, in the experts' eyes, worthless. Believing the experts and taking into account the magnitude, duration, and prevalence of this particular deception, a unanimous Commission ordered the company to include the following statement in a portion of its future ads: "Contrary to prior advertising, Listerine will not help prevent colds or sore throats or lessen their severity."

Arguing that this order infringed their rights of free speech and exceeded FTC authority, the makers of Listerine (Warner-Lambert) appealed to high federal court. In its opinion of August 1977, the Court of Appeals generally favored the FTC's side of the case. Unlike the FTC, however, the Court thought a "softer" correction would do. It said the words "contrary to prior advertising" should be dropped from the correction because they would serve only to "humiliate" the company. Warner-Lambert remained disgruntled, appealed to the Supreme Court, and lost. Corrective advertising should thus become a well-established, if seldom used, FTC remedy.[27]

Having reviewed remedies, you can now more fully appreciate our earlier assertions concerning lenient treatment of offenders. Although even the harshest of these measures may seem rather light, it can be argued that none should be heavier as long as the burden of proof borne by prosecutors is rather light.

V. MISCELLANEOUS UNFAIR PRACTICES

The FTC's enforcement of Section 5 extends considerably beyond "advertising" and "deception." Misleading claims may be dispersed toe-to-toe, just as easily as over the airwaves or on the printed page. Furthermore, our emphasis on deception should not obscure the fact that many practices are banned for being

[27] *Wall Street Journal,* August 3, 1977 and December 19, 1975; "Back on the Warpath Against Deceptive Ads," *Business Week* (April 19, 1976) pp. 148–151.

"unfair," even if not deceptive. In the abstract, the FTC has said that "unfair" cannot be narrowly defined, that a number of factors would influence its judgment—such as, whether the questioned act or practice is immoral, unethical, oppressive, unscrupulous, or financially injurious to buyers. In the concrete, the FTC frowns upon:

1. *Bait and switch,* in which the seller lures the buyer into the store with some kind of "bait," like a sale price for a cheap model, then "switches" the buyer to something else.
2. *Merchandise substitution,* like the sale of 1980 model trucks as 1981 model trucks.
3. *Silent warranties,* where a manufacturer follows a secret policy of extending warranties to some but not all customers.

The last of these arose when in the late 1970s the FTC accused auto makers of waging so-called "secret warranty" campaigns as a means of paying for repairs to troublesome cars on an individual basis (for individuals who were troublesome in their complaints), without formally notifying the general public. Ford's alleged campaign was especially massive, involving more than 6 million Ford cars and trucks produced between 1974 and 1978 that were susceptible to premature engine wear and cracked blocks. Under a consent order in 1980, Ford agreed to (1) notify affected car owners by mail whenever it offers extended warranty coverage; (2) offer customers "technical service bulletins" describing in plain English the existence of any engine or transmission problems that could cost over $125 to repair; and (3) set up a toll-free 800 telephone number for owners to use in requesting service bulletins. FTC action to end Ford's secrecy prior to this order reportedly saved consumers more than $30 million in repairs.[28]

Other recent FTC efforts to eradicate unfairnesses sparked stormy protests from the affected industries. A proposed trade regulation rule to restrict advertising aimed at young children, particularly TV advertising of sugared cereals and candy, provoked shrill opposition from cereal and candy manufacturers, TV networks, grocers, and others in the business community. They derided the FTC for brazenly becoming a "National Nanny." They maintained that, as easy as it might be to sell candy to a baby (or, more accurately, to the baby's parents through the baby's prompted appeals), it was not "unfair."

Equally controversial was a proposed rule regulating funeral parlors. After lengthy and costly study, the FTC's staff accumulated substantial evidence indicating that funeral homes frequently if not regularly took financial advantage of bereaved survivors. They apparently did this by (1) refusing to provide adequate price information, (2) embalming without permission, (3) needlessly requiring a casket for cremation, (4) harrassing "discount" funeral homes, (5) misrepresenting local health requirements, (6) refusing to display inexpensive caskets, (7) disparaging customers who showed a concern for funeral costs (which now average over $2,000) and by other means.[29]

[28] *Wall Street Journal,* February 22, 1980, p. 12.
[29] *Funeral Industry Practices,* Final Staff Report to the Federal Trade Commission, June 1978.

Waging an intense lobbying campaign against the FTC, the Commission's business foes succeeded in securing congressional passage of the Federal Trade Commission Improvements Act of 1980. The Senate version of this bill would have terminated the FTC's investigation of children's advertising while the House bill would have killed the funeral proceedings. The final version did not go this far, but some shackles were imposed.

For example, the final bill trimmed the scope of any FTC rule regulating funeral home practices. As of this writing (1982) the FTC's revised funeral industry proposals would merely:

- Require the availability of price lists, including price quotations over the telephone.

- Prohibit funeral directors from saying that a deceased person must be embalmed (unless local law requires embalming).

- Prohibit claims that a casket is required for cremation.

This legislation of 1980 and the furor surrounding it have had repercussions not reflected in the law itself. The FTC grew weak in the knees, aborting the development of new trade regulation rules that were not fueling the controversy. Robert Reich, director of FTC policy planning, may have put it best when he said, "Big Brother Consumer Protection is dead."[30] The irony of this turn of events is that, just a few years before the FTC Improvements Act of 1980, the FTC was being lambasted with criticism that it was *not* doing enough for consumer protection. Indeed, it was this criticism that eventually resulted in the proconsumerist FTC Improvements Act of 1975.

SUMMARY

In April, 1972, the American Association of Advertising Agencies released the results of a poll of some 9,000 students from 177 universities and colleges. The students took a dim view of advertising. Fifty-three percent told the AAAA that they considered advertising believable only "some of the time."[31] Was their skepticism unfounded?

Section 5 of the Federal Trade Commission Act (as amended by the Wheeler-Lea Act of 1938) bans "Unfair methods of competition in commerce, and unfair or deceptive acts or practices in commerce. . . ." The key criterion for determining violation by deception is whether a claim has the capacity and tendency to deceive. Truth and falsity are relevant but not conclusive, for true claims may deceive and false claims may not. As deception lies in the mind of the observer, some standard must be set as to who will be protected from deception. United States authorities supposedly protect the ignorant, the hasty, and the

---

[30] "Slowing Down the FTC," *Wall Street Journal,* July 30, 1979. See also Michael Pertschuk, *Revolt Against Regulation* (Berkeley: University of California Press, 1982).
[31] *Business Week,* June 10, 1972, p. 48.

trusting as well as those less easily deceived. Still, the authorities have not gone so far as to protect the pathologically credulous and feeble minded. Likewise they allow abundant amounts of "puffery."

Of the many specific types of deception that have collided with this criterion, four were presented—those concerning (1) claims of composition, (2) claims of function or efficacy, (3) endorsements, and (4) mock-ups. A never ending chain of cases under Section 5 has, over the years, outlined certain standards or rules in each of these areas. With respect to mock-ups, for instance, the Colgate Rapid Shave case is a particularly important link in the law. The Supreme Court reaffirmed what advertisers already believed—that undisclosed mock-ups of mere appearance were acceptable, and that undisclosed mock-ups demonstrating *un*true performance were unacceptable. The Court broke new ground also by ruling that undisclosed mock-ups demonstrating *true* performance were unacceptable insofar as the demonstration was central to the commercial. Ever since, the word "simulated" has appeared frequently on TV.

The FTC relies on three main procedures and four principal remedies to enforce the Act. The procedures are (1) complaint plus prosecution or consent decree, (2) advisory guides, and (3) compulsory trade regulation rules. The first is a case-by-case approach. The latter two are broader in scope, reaching entire industries or complete categories of deceptive acts.

The principal remedies are (1) cease and desist orders, (2) affirmative disclosure, and (3) corrective advertising. The first is the traditional mainstay.

Finally, the FTC's zealous efforts to curb "unfairnesses" during the late 1970s sparked angry charges from industry that it was being overbearingly unfair to business. The agency's staff was developing some of the most far-reaching proposals on record just at the time deregulation generally was coming into vogue. The result was the FTC Improvements Act of 1980, which directly curbed existing FTC activities and indirectly dampened the agency's ardor.

17 Multimarket Strategies

"In the past we have been characterized as a company that was not absolutely committed to any activity."

—CARL N. GRAF (President, W.R. Grace & Co.)

Coca Cola makes movies and makes moves around the world. Esmark counts Swift hams and Playtex girdles among its many products. Mobil Oil operates abroad and owns Montgomery Ward. ITT seems to be into practically everything every place—bread, books, insurance, telephones, radios, and so on. Until recently, Beatrice Foods could boast of 435 divisions and 9,000 products ranging from yogurt to toilet seats.

To this point, our analysis of conduct has focused on single markets or industries. However, the typical large corporation is not so confined. Its operations span many markets and industries, extending to everything under the sun. Multimarket spread includes **vertical integration** (that is, operation at several stages of the production process), **conglomeracy** (that is, diversity of all kinds), and **multinationalism** (that is, foreign as well as domestic operation).

This chapter surveys these three multimarket forms—the reasons for each and the conduct associated with each. We may introduce them by noting that multimarket forms typically result from a firm's long-run *strategic planning*. As P. F. Drucker has remarked, strategic planning relates to "size and complexity, diversity and diversification, growth, change and innovation."[1] Moreover, firms within a given industry can often be divided into different *strategic groups* depending on whether or not they have multimarket connections. Earlier we encountered strategic divisions based on product differentiation—e.g., private-label brands versus advertised brands. Now we encounter behavioral differences based on different degrees and different kinds of multimarket spread.

---

[1] P. F. Drucker, *Management: Tasks, Responsibilities, Practices* (London: Heinemann, 1974), p. 603.

I. VERTICAL INTEGRATION

A. Advantages to the Firm

Exxon explores for crude oil, extracts it, transports it to refineries, refines it into gasoline and other products, then finally ships and sells these products to ultimate consumers like you and me. Exxon is thus vertically integrated because it combines under single ownership several stages of the production-distribution process.

The economic advantages of vertical integration include the following:

1. *Technical efficiency:* Vertical integration may cut production costs for technical reasons. Integrated production of steel, for instance, enables the metal to remain hot from blast furnace to carbon burn-off to rolling and drawing. Costly reheating at each stage is eliminated.
2. *Transaction cost savings:* Vertical integration may reduce or eliminate the buying and selling costs that two separate firms would incur. IBM's semiconductor division need not "market" its integrated circuits and IBM's computer division need not "shop" for integrated circuits because these IBM divisions complement each other internally.
3. *Research and development:* It may improve the productivity of research and development efforts. Since vertical integration puts producers in closer touch with ultimate buyers, innovation may be better tailored to demand. Coordination of R & D among diverse component suppliers is also less of a problem. These factors explain much vertical integration in the electronics industry.
4. *Facilitate entry:* Vertical integration may be the best way to achieve new entry. When a firm expands backward to preceding stages or forward to succeeding stages, it is entering new markets. If achieved without merger, this can stir competition. Thus, nearly all significant entry into aluminum ingot production since 1940 has been achieved by such fabricators as Reynolds and Kaiser integrating backward.

These several advantages might benefit consumers as well as the firms pursuing vertical integration. This is true even when vertical integration may be viewed merely as a marketing ploy, as when, for example, Xerox launched its string of retail stores in 1980 to push small copiers, personal computers, typewriters, and other business machines suitable for small businesses.

Vertical integration has its drawbacks, however, so not every company finds it profitable. The factors that make it profitable *vary* across industries and across companies. But research on the profitability of vertical integration yields one fairly solid conclusion: big firms, with relatively large market shares, tend to find vertical integration much more profitable than small firms.[2] Exactly why

---

[2] Robert D. Buzzell, "Is Vertical Integration Profitable?" *Harvard Business Review* (January 1983), pp. 92–102.

this is so is not clear. A partial explanation may be, however, that large firms can use vertical integration in anticompetitive ways whereas small firms cannot. These anticompetitive possibilities, which we turn to next, include collusion and vertical cross-subsidy (or "price squeeze").

B. Vertical Integration and Collusion

Figure 17–1 illustrates four integrated and four independent firms operating three stages of a production process—crude materials, C, manufacturing, M, and retailing, R. The first two stages are linked by vertical integration, whereas manufacturing and retailing are free of ownership connections. Quite clearly, the singular ties of vertical integration suggest order, whereas the many trade ties of independence look like the work of a mad spider.

The implications for competitive conduct should be obvious. The independence of retailers tends to undermine any collusion among the manufacturers because (1) the retailers may compete among themselves, eroding prices at retail level and drawing manufacturers into price rivalry; (2) retailers may maintain final prices, but manufacturers might still have an incentive to offer the retailers secret price concessions to induce them to shift their buying patterns. An absence of vertical integration, moreover, tends to undermine collusion among the retailers themselves, because cartel-like agreements at the retail level are then complicated by the need to cover buying as well as selling practices. In short, thoroughgoing, effective cartelization of the industry as drawn in Figure 17–1 would require agreement among eight firms (1, 2, 3, 4, a, b, c, d). Complete vertical integration throughout would cut the number of agreeing parties to four. (For the acme of chaos, complete independence everywhere would raise the number of firms to 12.) Since fewness of firms simplifies collusive agreement, vertical integration may do likewise.

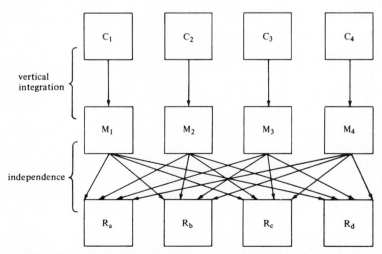

FIGURE 17–1. Vertical integration versus vertical independence.

Once agreement is reached, vertical integration also eases the problem of enforcement. This is explained by William Adams:

> One reason for such increased adherence to the collusive scheme is the heightened probability that cheating in any one market is more likely to be detected when all participating firms interact in the same economically related markets. As a result, if those colluding in one market find that a colleague has enhanced his market position in other economically related markets they share, they are less likely than otherwise to ascribe the result to chance, and will retaliate accordingly.[3]

Examples of vertical integration's contribution to tacit or explicit collusion include light bulbs,[4] petroleum,[5] steel,[6] textiles,[7] and drugs.[8] Moreover, statistical analysis shows that vertical integration seems to foster market share stability within an industry, something which also suggests a contribution to collusion.[9]

C. Vertical Cross-Subsidization

A multimarket firm can divert income from one market to another. It can subsidize losses in one market with profits from another; it can make investments in production, advertising, and research in one market, drawing the necessary resources from others. This capability gives a multimarket firm "exceptional leeway in market policy and exceptional possibility of imposing its will upon its more specialized rivals."[10]

The most commonly alleged form of vertical cross-subsidization is the so-called "price squeeze." The classic example occurred in aluminum, when Alcoa had a monopoly on ingots prior to 1940. Alcoa did two things with its ingots. Some it rolled and fabricated internally; others it sold to independent rollers and fabricators, such as Reynolds, who at the time had no ingot capacity. Survival of these independents obviously depended on prices at two levels: (1) the price they paid for ingots and (2) the price at which they sold their sheets and fabrications.

Alcoa clearly controlled the price of ingots. Alcoa was also big enough in downstream markets to influence the price of sheets and fabrications. Hence,

---

[3] William J. Adams, "Market Structure and Corporate Power: The Horizontal Dominance Hypothesis Reconsidered," *Columbia Law Review* (November 1974), p. 1284.

[4] Lester G. Telser, "Why Should Manufacturers Want Fair Trade," *Journal of Law & Economics* (October 1960), pp. 96–104.

[5] M. A. Adelman, "World Oil and the Theory of Industrial Organization," *Industrial Organization and Economic Development,* edited by J. W. Markham and G. F. Papanek (New York: Houghton Mifflin, 1970), p. 145. See also M. G. de Chazeau and A. E. Kahn, *Integration and Competition in the Petroleum Industry* (New Haven, Conn.: Yale University Press, 1959), pp. 428–449.

[6] W. Adams and J. B. Dirlam, "Steel Imports and Vertical Oligopoly Power," *American Economic Review* (September 1964), pp. 626–655.

[7] Irwin M. Stelzer, "The Cotton Textile Industry," in *The Structure of American Industry,* 3rd ed., edited by W. Adams (New York: Macmillan, 1961), pp. 42–73.

[8] Peter M. Costello, "The Tetracycline Conspiracy," *Antitrust Law & Economics Review* (Summer 1968), pp. 13–44.

[9] R. E. Caves and M. E. Porter, "Market Structure, Oligopoly, and Stability of Market Shares," *Journal of Industrial Economics* (June 1978), pp. 289–313.

[10] C. D. Edwards, *Economic Concentration,* Part 1, Hearings before the Subcommittee on Antitrust and Monopoly, U.S. Senate, 88th Congress, Second Session (1964), p. 43.

CONDUCT

Alcoa could, and allegedly did, raise the price of ingots and use the proceeds to lower the price of sheets and fabrications. This pinched the independents. With their ingot costs rising and their final fabrication prices falling, their profits were disappearing. Alcoa, for its part, presumably suffered losses at fabrication stage, but these could be covered by its ingot profits.[11]

In sum, vertical integration may be either a boon or a bane, depending on the circumstances.[12]

II. CONGLOMERATES

A. The Benefits of Conglomeration

The benefits claimed for conglomerate diversification are much less substantial than those that can be attributed to vertical integration. They include:[13]

1. *Reduced instability and uncertainty:* If a firm draws its profits from a number of products experiencing different cyclical peaks and valleys, it can smooth its profit flows. Moreover, a firm's stability might be improved if it deals in products that vary by stage of product life cycle. Products in "decline" can be counterbalanced by those experiencing rapid "growth".
2. *Efficiency:* According to some commentators, conglomeracy enables the exploitation of "synergy" or managerial economies. A beer company may thus branch out into snack foods, as Anheuser-Busch has done, because these products may be distributed and perhaps marketed together.
3. *New entry:* Conglomerate expansion is a source of new entry, provided it is achieved by internal expansion or "toe hold" acquisition. Exxon's effort to enter the office machinery industry illustrates this possibility.

Realization of these several benefits depends partly on the size and diversity that a firm has already achieved. That is to say, the magnitude and chaotic diversity of the country's twenty leading conglomerates seem to be way beyond the levels of size and diversity that could reasonably be justified by these several rationales. Indeed, many huge conglomerates seem to be admitting this when they engage in extensive self dismemberment. Recent divestiture programs ex-

---

[11] *U.S. v. Aluminum Company of America,* 148 F. 2nd 416 (2nd Cir., 1945) and 91 F. Supp. 333 (S.D.N.Y., 1950). More recently see *Greyhound Computer v. International Business Machines,* 559 F. 2d 488 (1977), pp. 498–505. It may be argued that Alcoa was not trying to injure its rival fabricators, but rather was trying to use vertical integration as a means of achieving price discrimination. Martin K. Perry, "Forward Integration by Alcoa: 1888–1930," *Journal of Industrial Economics* (September 1980), pp. 37–53.

[12] This may also be shown by the "pure theory" of vertical integration, which we ignore as being a bit too esoteric. Using assorted assumptions concerning fixed or variable factor proportions, contracting costs, pure competition, and pure monopoly, it may be demonstrated theoretically that vertical integration raises, lowers, or leaves unchanged the price of the "final" product. See G. Hay, "An Economic Analysis of Vertical Integration," *Industrial Organization Review,* Vol. 1, No. 3 (1973), pp. 188–198, F. Warren-Boulton, "Vertical Control with Variable Proportions," *Journal of Political Economy* (July 1974), pp. 783–802.

[13] C. J. Sutton, *Economics and Corporate Strategy* (Cambridge: Cambridge University Press, 1980), pp. 51–76.

ceeding one billion dollars in sales or assets have been adopted by ITT, W. R. Grace, Beatrice Foods, and Gulf & Western. (Moreover, heavy costs may be incurred instead of benefits. Shortly after American Can bought Sam Goody Inc., a record store chain, Goody and its officers were indicted for racketeering, interstate shipment of stolen property, and dealing in counterfeit recordings. The record business has thus given American Can a record headache.[14])

As for the anticompetitive possibilities of immense conglomeracy, they include mutual forebearance, reciprocity, and cross-subsidization.

B. Conglomerates and Forbearance

Mutual forbearance among conglomerates is similar to tacit collusion among firms in the same market. Rather than compete vigorously by invading each other's bailiwicks, conglomerates may follow a strategy of "live and let live." As the size and diversification of conglomerates expand, they meet each other in more and more markets, they become more fully aware of each other's special concerns, and they grow to appreciate their mutual interests.

What motivates this? Conglomeracy raises the possibility of massive retaliatory attack in one market as punishment for competitive transgressions in another market. Corwin Edwards outlines the implications:

> A large concern usually must show a regard for the strength of other large concerns by circumspection in its dealings with them, whereas such caution is usually unnecessary in dealing with small enterprises. The interests of great enterprises are likely to touch at many points, and it would be possible for each to mobilize at any one of these points a considerable aggregate of resources. The anticipated gain to such a concern from unmitigated competitive attack upon another large enterprise at one point of contact is likely to be slight as compared with the possible loss from retaliatory action by that enterprise at many other points of contact.[15]

Circumspection finds expression in much business lore. ITT has in the past been so diligent about avoiding the wrath of IBM that a highly paid man was hired by ITT to do nothing more than stop ITT's companies from moving into computers.[16] Less dramatic but no less revealing is the case of National Bank of Commerce of Seattle, which turned down large prospective customers in western Washington on grounds that "our bank did not wish to fish in the Old National's fishing hole. . . ."[17]

Perhaps the most interesting example of conglomerate confrontation, threatened retaliation, and eventual accommodation involved Consolidated Food Corporation and National Tea Corporation in 1965. Consolidated was a grocery *retailer* and *manufacturer,* whose credits in this latter capacity include Sarah Lee frozen foods. National Tea was at the time the fourth ranked grocery *retailer*

[14] *Business Week,* March 24, 1980, pp. 130–132.
[15] Corwin D. Edwards, "Conglomerate Bigness as a Source of Power," in *Business Concentration and Price Policy* (Princeton, N.J.: Princeton University Press, 1955), p. 335.
[16] Anthony Sampson, *The Sovereign State of ITT* (Greenwich, Conn.: Fawcett, 1974), p. 103.
[17] From company correspondence, government's exhibit, *U.S. v. Marine Bancorporation, Inc.,* 94 S.Ct. 2856 (1974).

in the United States and, as such, it purchased Sarah Lee cakes plus other items from the manufacturing divisions of Consolidated for resale in its stores. In other words, Consolidated was one of National's manufacturing suppliers and also one of its retail competitors.

The confrontation occurred in Chicago, where Consolidated had seven stores against National's 237. In an attempt to expand its rather measly market share there, Consolidated initiated a "miracle prices" campaign, announcing in double-page ads that it had "smashed" price levels "on over 5,000 items." The miracle prices menaced National Tea's profits. So, shortly after Consolidated conjured its prices down, National Tea's president warned Consolidated that "there will be fewer of your lines on our shelves." Making good its threat, National apparently ordered no Sarah Lee bakery items for a week and told its store managers to sweep Sarah Lee from their shelves. Consolidated got the message. It made its miracle prices disappear. It eventually went so far as to sell off all its Chicago stores, thereby making *itself* disappear as a retailer in National's biggest market.[18]

Rigorous statistical studies of the importance of mutual forbearance are virtually impossible because the necessary data rarely exist. Nevertheless, two such studies have demonstrated the significance of such behavior in banking and manufacturing. The study for banking, by Arnold Heggestad and Steve Rhoades, is easiest to describe because the conglomeracy in that case was based on geographic spread. Because commercial banking is primarily a local market activity, and because many banks operate in more than one local market, the following inquiry was pursued: Is competitive intensity within a given local market determined solely by the *internal* structural conditions in that market, such as concentration and barriers to entry, or is it also determined by the frequency with which the firms in that market confront each other on the *outside*, in other local markets? Using a variety of measures for "competitive intensity"— including market share turbulence, price levels, and profit rates—Heggestad and Rhoades found that frequent outside contact *does* make a significant difference in the direction of mutual forbearance. In particular, if the firms in a local market have *no* competitive encounters in other markets, that local market tends to be vigorously competitive (other things equal). Conversely, if the firms in a local market encounter each other extensively and frequently elsewhere, then competition in that local market tends to be muted, puny, and lethargic. Hence, Heggestad and Rhoades conclude that "multimarket meetings do adversely affect the degree of competition within markets."[19]

---

[18] Federal Trade Commission, *Economic Report on the Structure and Competitive Behavior of Food Retailing* (1966), pp. 145–146. For other examples see Federal Trade Commission, *Economic Report on Corporate Mergers* (1969), pp. 458–471; and F. M. Scherer, A. Beckenstein, E. Kaufer, and R. D. Murphy, *The Economics of Multi-Plant Operation* (Cambridge, Mass.: Harvard University Press, 1975), pp. 137, 165, 314.

[19] Arnold A. Heggestad and Stephen A. Rhoades, "Multi-Market Interdependence and Local Market Competition," *Review of Economics and Statistics* (November 1978), pp. 523–532; and "Multi-Market Interdependence in Banking: a Further Analysis," (mimeo, 1978). The manufacturing study is John T. Scott, "Multimarket Contact and Economic Performance," *Review of Economics and Statistics* (August 1982), pp. 368–375.

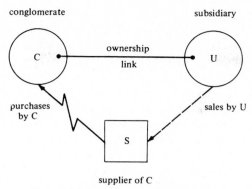

conglomerate
subsidiary

FIGURE 17–2. Reciprocity.

C. Reciprocity in Conglomerates

Simply stated, **reciprocal buying** is "the use by a firm of its buying power to promote its sales."[20] "I'll buy from you if you'll buy from me," expresses the philosophy. As old as barter and often as trifling, reciprocity may nevertheless have anticompetitive consequences when used by giant firms.

Conglomeracy is an important factor because diversification is often associated with reciprocity. In Figure 17–2, for instance, conglomerate C owns subsidiary U. Firm S is a supplier to C and also a potential buyer of U's product. Thus C can coax S into buying from its subsidiary U by pointing out to S the fact that C and U are essentially the same company and that C is a big buyer of S's goods. Conglomeracy plays its part because C and U would not be linked without it.

To what extent is reciprocity actually practiced? Survey evidence from the early 1960s indicates that, at least in the past, the practice was quite popular. When asked, "Is reciprocity a factor in buyer-seller relations in your company?", 100% of all sampled purchasing agents in chemicals, petroleum, and iron and steel answered "yes." Purchasing agents from services and consumer goods industries reported significantly less reliance on reciprocity, but well over one third of them admitted that it was "a factor" in their trade relations.

In addition, the same sample survey reveals that large firms practiced reciprocity to a greater extent than small firms; 78% of the purchasing agents in firms with annual sales exceeding $50 million reported reliance on reciprocity, whereas only 48% of those in firms with annual sales less than $10 million gave affirmative reports.[21] A separate but less reliable study of the same period suggests that reciprocity was also positively associated with diversification. Firms with their fingers in many pies appear to have relied on it more heavily than

[20] G. W. Stocking and W. F. Mueller, "Business Reciprocity and the Size of Firms," *Journal of Business* (April 1957), p. 75.
[21] F.T.C., *Merger Report, op. cit.,* pp. 332–336.

did more specialized, less diversified firms.[22] The findings for size and diversification dovetail because firm size and diversification are positively correlated.

Reciprocity may now be on the decline, however. Questionnaire surveys from the 1970s reveal substantially lower reported rates of practice. For example, fewer than 20% of the large firms responding to a recent Harvard University survey gave any indication of reciprocal dealings.[23] Whether this remarkable drop in affirmative response betokens a genuine and dramatic change in business practice is impossible to say. Nevertheless, between 1963 and 1971 the antitrust authorities criticized reciprocity as being anticompetitive and cracked down with a string of hostile suits that were supported in federal courts by trial or consent settlement. Although reciprocity is not now *per se* illegal, these major events may have produced a genuine reduction in its usage. Then again, events may have merely driven reciprocity underground, with the result that fewer firms are willing to admit that they engage in it, even though business continues "as usual." Actually, the downturn in survey statistics probably reflects some unknown blend of both business policy and public pronouncement.[24]

Because reciprocity can be quite innocuous, the picture of its competitive effects is cloudy. Even so, the antitrust authorities' hostility toward the practice is not altogether unwarranted. Any attempt here to sort out the circumstances of harmless and harmful reciprocity would involve tortuous reasoning.[25] We shall therefore simply stress its offensive potentials.

Once again the key to understanding anticompetitive effects is a recognition that competition in one market may not depend solely on conditions inside that market. Conditions outside, in other markets, may have decisive impact. In the case of reciprocity, competition among sellers and potential sellers in one market (that in which U sells in Figure 17–2) is affected by the monopsony buying power of a firm in another market (that in which C buys in Figure 17–2). Note that the monopsony buying power *might* be exploited entirely within the confines of the market where it lodges. The firm with buying power, C, might negotiate preferential price discounts from its supplier S, or might insist that supplier S throw some extra goods into the bargain. If the monopsony power were so confined, there would then be no adverse competitive consequences in any other market. However, there are some good reasons why the monopsonist might prefer to exploit its monopsony power via reciprocity, thereby entangling other markets where (in the form of U) it acts as a *seller* instead of a buyer:

1. Supplier S may not be able or willing to offer special price discounts to the big buyer because to do so might (a) put pressure on the supplier

[22] Bruce T. Allen, "Industrial Reciprocity: A Statistical Analysis," *Journal of Law & Economics* (October 1975), pp. 507–520.

[23] J. W. Markham, *Conglomerate Enterprise and Public Policy* (Cambridge, Mass.: Harvard University Press, 1973), pp. 77–82.

[24] F. R. Finney, "Reciprocity: Gone But Not Forgotten," *Journal of Marketing* (January 1978), pp. 54–59.

[25] Peter O. Steiner, *Mergers: Motives, Effects, Policies* (Ann Arbor, Mich.: University of Michigan Press, 1975), pp. 218–254.

to reduce prices to *all* buyers, (b) violate the Robinson-Patman price discrimination act, or (c) violate some official price regulations.

2. Conglomerate buyer C may not have true monopsony power in the sense of not buying a preponderant portion of all the product sold by supplier S and S's rivals. Rather, the conglomerate may merely be buying a large *dollar volume* of the product, a form of buying power that might be exploited most effectively through reciprocity.

3. Regardless of the strength of the monopsony power, a *shift* of its focus might yield quicker, larger, or more lasting profits. For example, the goods S supplies might be components in a product subject to profit regulation, in which case reduced input prices would yield C no profit gain.

4. Supplier S might *itself* have monopsony power in the market where the conglomerate's subsidiary U operates as seller. In this case reciprocity might not represent the exploitation of S by C. Instead, reciprocity might be *mutually* advantageous to both conglomerate C and supplier S. Whereas single market monopsony might lead to seller's price concessions, linked monopsony might find expression in reciprocity.

Whatever the reason for shifting buying power across markets into selling power (from the left-hand side to the right-hand side of Figure 17–2), the market of final resting place may suffer competitively. What are these potentially adverse competitive effects? Basically, there are three possibilities: (1) greater concentration, (2) augmented barriers to entry, and (3) greater price rigidity or higher prices. We have enough space to illustrate the last of these.

Price Effects. General Dynamics is an enormous company best known for its manufacture of major weapon systems. It is also a large and diversified purchaser. In 1957, when it took control of Liquid Carbonic Company (LC), General Dynamics had roughly 80,000 industrial suppliers from whom it purchased about $500 million annually. LC was a manufacturer of carbon dioxide and other industrial gases, with a market share equal to about 35% in 1957. Shortly after LC was taken into General Dynamics' corporate family, a "trade relations" program was instituted in hopes of selling LC gases to General Dynamics' many suppliers. As one LC official put it, "Let's not kid ourselves, the ultimate reason for establishing a trade relations department is to increase sales through the proper application of your purchasing power."[26]

The program proved successful by almost any measure. Over the period 1960–1962, "there was a 33 per cent increase in reciprocity sales, whereas general sales of LC increased only 7 per cent. In addition, prior to merger, LC's market share had declined by about 2.7 per cent. After merger and the reciprocity program, LC's market share regained its earlier position."[27] What is more, these gains were made without price reductions. Quite the contrary. In at least

[26] Erwin A. Blackstone, "Monopsony Power, Reciprocal Buying, and Government Contracts: The General Dynamics Case," *Antitrust Bulletin* (Summer 1972), p. 460.
[27] *Ibid.*, p. 461.

three instances LC gained reciprocity customers at prices *higher* than those charged by its rival gas suppliers. Raytheon, for instance, willingly paid LC $65 per ton for carbon dioxide, which it could have bought from Thermice at only $60 per ton.

Simply stated, prices are affected in the conglomerate's target market because *nonprice* considerations, emanating from other markets, lessen the potency of price as a competitive weapon. For the conglomerate seller pursuing reciprocity, buying power elsewhere is the key weapon. As for the conglomerate's small, specialized competitors who lack reciprocal leverage, they can try to fight back with price cuts. But all the conglomerate needs to do to nullify this effort is stand ready to meet all its rivals' discounts. Price cuts by small specialists would then be futile, since they could never be rewarded with a successful switch of business away from the conglomerate. With price competition rendered needless or unrewarding, prices tend to stabilize or even rise. Ossification then supplants competition. Notice that we have arrived at this conclusion without even mentioning reciprocity's *indirect* contribution to lessened price competition through its potentially adverse affects on concentration and entry barriers. All in all, then, reciprocity may tend to cement trade relations and shrink commercial spaces.

D. Conglomerate Cross-Subsidization

Cross-subsidization includes certain forms of price discrimination and predation (recall IBM versus the plug-compatible producers). It also includes a good deal more. Generally speaking, cross-subsidization is best thought of as a *dynamic* strategy—unlike forbearance and reciprocity, which are rather more static. Short-run losses, covered by short-term intrafirm transfers, may yield *future* power and *future* profits.

Conglomerates may cross-subsidize in a variety of ways for a variety of reasons. Long ago, American Tobacco cross-subsidized advertising for predatory purposes. More recently, Philip Morris Corp. has subsidized a massive advertising campaign for its Miller Brewing Company.[28] Yet Miller apparently wants only the number one spot, not a full-fledged monopoly. Indeed, most modern cross-subsidization might best be thought of as a "power investment" rather than a predatory strategy. Short-run losses may be ultimately profitable because, as William Adams argues, "The power presently enjoyed by a firm depends heavily on the firm's conduct in the past. The greater was yesterday's advertising, the greater is today's product differentiation. The greater was yesterday's research and development activity, the greater is today's patent control. And so on."[29]

Adams goes on to point out that large diversified firms have a significant advantage over small specialized firms because internal funds are the prime source of capital for "power investments," and giants possess the deepest pools

[28] *Business Week,* November 8, 1976, pp. 58–67.
[29] Adams, *op. cit.,* p. 1,287.

of internal funds. Outside capital from banks and other lenders is relatively scarce for these purposes because power investments are especially high in lender's risk. "Since such investments involve little physical asset creation, there may be nothing for the creditors to appropriate if a power bid fails. The prospect of an Edsel trademark as sole surviving asset from a power bid will not attract lending institutions."[30]

Obviously, the main headwaters of internal pools of funds are likely to be those markets where the conglomerate's monopolistic power is well established. You will not be startled to learn that as of the late 1970s, blades and razors accounted for only 30% of Gillette's total *sales* revenue, but blades and razors earned 73% of Gillette's overall *profit.*[31] Nor is it remarkable that in 1958 National Tea, the large retail grocery chain referred to earlier, earned only 0.2% profit "contribution" in cities where its market share was less than 5% but earned close to 7.0% profit "contribution" in cities where its market share exceeded 35%.[32]

Such cross-market disparities do not inevitably indicate power grabs. Indeed, they occasionally reflect an effort at new entry. Gillette used its blade and razor profits to finance ill-fated entries into pocket calculators and digital watches. Still, this seems to be only occasionally true.

Competitive consequences aside, it can also be argued that conglomerate subsidies, intentional or inadvertent, reduce the effectiveness of markets in allocating resources:

> Markets are expected to serve as automatic correctives of misapplied effort—to discourage the production of goods that are not worth their cost and to stimulate the production of profitable goods. . . . So far as conglomerate business structures make the relative costs of different products more uncertain or increase the amount of subsidized production, they make the functioning of markets less adequate.[33]

Conglomerates compound this problem by failing to report their performance openly on a product-by-product basis. Numbers like those cited for Gillette are rarely available. Liberal use of consolidated financial statements masks conditions in individual markets, thereby blinding potential entrants and befuddling investors. Without adequate profit information, the economy's capital markets are not capable of properly allocating resources among various industries.[34]

[30] *Ibid.,* p. 1289.

[31] *Business Week,* February 28, 1977, p. 60.

[32] FTC, *Report on Food Retailing, op. cit.,* p. 89. There are several time-series studies of cross-subsidization, comparing, for example, advertising outlay before and after conglomerate merger and counting instances in which outlay has increased or decreased. The results are usually 50:50. But this does not disprove cross-subsidy. Conglomeracy is merely a necessary condition, not a sufficient one. It gives the *option,* not the achievement. Moreover, subsidy *implies* decrease in one place so as to secure increase in another. Thus 50:50 is not inconsistent with cross-subsidization.

[33] Edwards, Testimony, *op. cit.,* p. 44.

[34] S. E. Boyle and P. W. Jaynes, *Conglomerate Merger Performance: An Empirical Analysis of Nine Corporations* (Washington, D.C.: Federal Trade Commission, 1972), pp. 87–125.

Asking investors to operate in this uncertainty is somewhat like asking surgeons to operate in the dark.

III. MULTINATIONAL CORPORATIONS

Multinational corporations distinguish themselves with wholly owned foreign subsidiaries, partially owned foreign joint ventures, or patent and trademark licensing agreements abroad. Coca Cola, IBM, GM, Exxon, and Mobil are prominent examples among those calling the United States "home." Foreign multinationals include Michelin, Volkswagenwerk, Royal-Dutch Shell, and Unilever. From the perspective of these foreign firms, the U.S. is a "host" country. In aggregate terms, roughly four hundred multinational enterprises produce perhaps as much as one third of the free-world's industrial output. They are, in short, vastly powerful.

A. Why Do Firms Become Multinationals?

Multinational enterprises exist for many reasons. Some, like Rio Tinto Zinc, go abroad to secure raw material supplies. Others, like National Semiconductor, locate assembly plants abroad in order to lower their labor costs. The principal reason of interest to us here, however, is *monopolistic advantages.*[35] In particular, direct foreign investment frequently occurs in industries where monopolistic advantages prevail both at home and abroad. These advantages may be grounded in advanced technology (chemicals and computers for example), potent product differentiation (as in the case of soft drinks and drugs), and economies of scale (as in autos). Note that many of these advantages are protected by "industrial property" rights at home and abroad—that is, patents, proprietary know-how, and trademarks. The basic idea is that these monopolistic advantages give the multinational enterprise an advantage over host country rivals, or at least give the multinational's foreign subsidiaries an equal chance in host country markets. Without such special advantages the foreigner would be at a *dis*advantage because local firms would naturally tend to be more familiar with local market conditions, local laws, local customs, and other local mysteries important to business success. A nice illustration of this is provided by Tandy Corporation, whose Radio Shack store in Holland geared its first Christmas promotion to December 25, unaware that the Dutch customarily exchange holiday gifts on December 6, St. Nicholas Day. They badly missed the market.[36]

Numerous statistical studies support this theory of direct foreign investment by finding high correlations between direct foreign investment on the one hand and four-firm concentration or advertising intensity or R & D expenditure on the other. In Mexico, for instance, foreign firms accounted for 100% of 1970 industry sales in transportation equipment, rubber, electrical equipment, and

[35] Richard E. Caves, *Multinational Enterprise and Economic Analysis* (Cambridge: Cambridge University Press, 1982), pp. 94–97.
[36] "Radio Shack's Rough Trip," *Business Week,* May 30, 1977, p. 55.

office equipment—all of which evince special advantages for member firms. In contrast, 1970 sales of foreign firms accounted for very small percentages in leather, textiles, and apparel—4.6%, 7.1%, and 4.0%, respectively.[37]

From the home country's perspective, multinationals likewise come from oligopolistic industries. Indeed, it has been found that industrial concentration influences U.S. firm foreign investment in a way similar to that shown earlier for advertising in Figure 15–2 (line ABC on page 346). The *timing* of foreign investment and the *intensity* of foreign investment both seem to be keyed to "loose-knit" oligopoly.[38]

B. Adverse Multimarket Conduct

The economic consequences of multinationalism may be viewed from home and host country perspectives. From both perspectives, the consequences are mixed—some good and some bad. We cannot review the entire scene, so we shall limit the discussion to conduct especially pertinent to multimarket spread. In the main, this boils down to several host country adversities.

1. Mutual Forbearance. If firms of potential international scope declined to compete against each other completely, there would be no multinationals, or they would be severely stunted. Becoming a multinational implies thrusts into territories of foreign rivals. So multinationalism is certainly not synonymous with forbearance.

Still, instances of explicit and tacit collusion abound. Formal or informal allocations of territories and price fixing may be the result. The recently documented activities of the International Electrical Association, an international cartel in heavy electrical equipment, illustrates the formal possibilities:

> The cartel comprises over 50 European and Japanese producers and covers sales in most of the markets of the non-Communist world outside the United States, Western Europe, and Japan (amounting to almost $2 billion annually). . . . These cartel arrangements directly harm importing countries because of the onerous markup on cartelized sales as well as common policies among members restricting technology transfers to nonproducing countries. On the basis of data from one product section, it is estimated that successful collusive agreements may raise prices 15 to 25 percent above the competitive rate.[39]

Other examples, both formal and informal, concern tobacco, metal containers, and automobiles.[40]

---

[37] John M. Conner and Willard F. Mueller, "Manufacturing, Denationalization and Market Structure: Brazil, Mexico, and the United States" *Industrial Organization Review* (No. 2, 1978), pp. 86–105.

[38] F. T. Knickerbocker, *Oligopolistic Reaction and Multinational Enterprise* (Boston: Division of Research, Graduate School of Business Administration, Harvard University, 1973); R. E. Caves, M. E. Porter, A. M. Spence, and J. T. Scott, *Competition in the Open Economy* (Cambridge: Harvard University Press, 1980), pp. 86–87.

[39] Barbara Epstein and Richard S. Newfarmer, *International Electrical Association: A Continuing Cartel,* Report for the Committee on Interstate and Foreign Commerce, U.S. House of Representatives (June 1980), p. 12.

[40] See the citations in Caves, *op. cit.,* pp. 104–108.

TABLE 17–1. Percentage of Contracts Studied Imposing Restrictions on Licensees, India, Philippines, and Spain

Type of Restriction	India (pre-1964)	India (1964–1969)	Philippines (1970)	Spain (1950–1973)
Global ban on exports	3.4%	0.9%	19.3%	44.4%
Partial ban on exports	40.0	46.2	13.0	25.9
Tied purchases	14.6	4.7	26.4	30.6
Minimum royalty restriction	5.2	1.2	5.1	N.A.*

* N.A. = not available.
Source: United Nations, Conference on Trade and Development, *Restrictive Business Practices* U.N. doc. TD/B/C.2/104/Rev. 1 (1971); *Major Issues Arising from the Transfer of Technology: A Case Study of Spain,* U.N. doc. TD/B/AC.11/17 (1974).

2. Transfer Pricing. Transfer pricing is like cross-subsidization in that it permits a multinational to vary its earnings across different divisions. The variations are achieved differently here, however, as they arise from transactions among the multinational's various geographic members. In particular, when a subsidiary abroad buys raw materials, technology, or services from its parent multinational company, it is charged an arbitrary intracompany price that might well be exorbitant. For example, the multinational oil companies apparently overcharged their Canadian subsidiaries $3.2 billion on crude oil imported into Canada over the years 1958–1970.[41] Investigations in Colombia for the late 1960s disclosed that drug giant Hoffman-LaRoche was overcharging its subsidiary (as a percentage of world market prices) by 94% for Atelor, by 96% for Trimatoprium, by over 5,000% for Chlordiazepoxide, and by over 6,000% for Diazepam.[42] A major motive for this kind of behavior is taxes. By manipulating intracompany prices, multinationals can cause profits to show up in nations whose tax bite is least burdensome. Moreover, they can take profits out of a host country in a way that evades regulation.

3. "Vertical" Restraints of Trade. "Vertical" restrictions arise in the distribution or licensing process. These include exclusive dealing, tying, and territorial allocations among foreign distributors. Evidence concerning restraints such as these comes from studies of contracts transferring technology from multinational corporations to producers in less developed countries. Table 17–1 summarizes the results of several such studies by the United Nations Conference on Trade

[41] Director of Investigation and Research, Combines Investigation Act, *The State of Competition in the Canadian Petroleum Industry* Vol. I (Ottawa, 1981), pp. 18–19, 61–70.
[42] S. Lall, "The International Pharmaceutical Industry and Less-Developed Countries," *Oxford Bulletin of Economics and Statistics* (August 1974), p. 161.

and Development covering license agreements in India, the Philippines, and Spain. It may be seen that restrictions limiting the exports of licensees have been quite common. Tying provisions requiring licensees to purchase specified materials from the licensor or from other designated suppliers have been less frequent but common nevertheless. Still other restraints, such as minimum royalty payments, post-termination limitations, and restrictions on production methods appear very infrequently, but in certain individual instances they can be important.

SUMMARY

Today's typical large corporation is not limited to a single product and geographic market. It is more like an octopus, with tentacles probing vertical, conglomerate, and multinational crevices. The motives guiding these various forms of expanse may be harmless, and the results may be equally harmless. They may even be beneficial. Still, there are occasional problems.

Vertical integration can be beneficial when it promotes technical efficiency, transaction cost savings, innovation, or new entry. On the other hand, vertical integration, when coupled with high concentration, can produce adverse economic consequences. It may facilitate collusion by simplifying otherwise complex situations and by aiding the detection of "cheaters." It may also permit vertical cross-subsidization, or price squeezes, whereby a large vertically integrated firm can injure its nonintegrated rivals by compressing the prices that separate two stages of the production distribution process.

Conglomerate spread across various product and geographic markets may reduce firm risk, gain efficiencies, and serve as a means of new entry. However, at especially large sizes, these benefits tend to fade and the possibilities of several adverse effects grow. Conglomerates, threatened by multimarket retaliations, may compete in certain markets less vigorously than nonconglomerates, a phenomenon called mutual forbearance. Reciprocal sales, or simply "reciprocity," is another possibility, one that may lessen price competition as nonprice factors become controlling. Finally, cross-subsidization may disadvantage rivals and distort capital flows.

Multinational enterprises gain their multimarket stance through international operations. These firms typically come from highly concentrated industries, such as computers and autos, because their multinationalism often stems from certain monopolistic advantages—e.g., technical prowess, brand image, and economies of scale. Some forms of multinational conduct bear close similarity to forms associated with vertical and conglomerate firm structures, namely, mutual forbearance and cross-subsidy. In addition, multinationals have been found to engage in "vertical" restraints of trade. These include export restrictions and tying provisions imposed on foreign licensees.

397

Part Four:
Performance

18
Introduction to Performance

Winning isn't everything. It's the only thing.
—VINCE LOMBARDI

Just as the last lap of a long race tests the runner's early strategy, so a study of market performance will prove our survey of industrial organization. To be sure, structure and conduct are momentous and memorable in their own right. They are the economic equivalent of anatomy and action. As stated at the outset in Chapter 1, structure and conduct reflect the setting and process by which we obtain answers to the fundamental economic questions of what, how, who, and what's new. And, as we have seen, structure and conduct are sufficiently important to be the focus of many policies—policies whose main objectives are competitive, decentralized structure and fair, unrestrictive conduct.

Given that structure and conduct reflect *how* the game is played, performance reflects *how well* it is played. Performance consists of the achievements, outcomes, and answers provided by the market.

A few economists look upon performance as Vince Lombardi looked upon winning. They see it as the *only* source of thrill.[1] Most industrial organization economists, the present author included, do not share this view.[2] Nevertheless, performance is important, so the remaining six chapters give performance its due. The main topics covered are, in order of their appearance:

1. Allocation efficiency
2. Income distribution

[1] John S. McGee, *In Defense of Industrial Concentration* (New York: Praeger Publishers, 1971).
[2] For elaboration see H. H. Liebhafsky, *American Government and Business* (New York: Wiley & Sons, 1971), Chapter 13; Charles E. Lindblom, *Politics and Markets* (New York: Basic Books, 1977), especially Chapter 19; Corwin Edwards, *Maintaining Competition* (New York: McGraw-Hill Book Co., 1949); and F. M. Scherer, "The Posnerian Harvest: Separating Wheat from Chaff," *Yale Law Journal* (April 1977), pp. 974–1002.

3. Technical efficiency
4. Inflation and full employment
5. Technological progress

The first two items are often measured in profit performance, excessively high profits indicating poor allocation and distorted income distribution. The remaining concepts are largely self-explanatory.

The odd numbered chapters that follow—Chapters 19, 21, and 23—treat these topics theoretically and empirically. Their collective message is simple: *structure and conduct vitally influence performance.* What is more, there is for the most part substantial correlation between good structure, good conduct, and good performance, where "good" means conformity with the value judgments specified in Chapter 1. This is an important message. It means that structures displaying low concentration, easy entry, and well-informed buyers are desirable not only because they in and of themselves further such goals as freedom, decentralized decision making, and equal bargaining power, but because such structures also foster fair and vigorous competitive conduct. In addition, these structures and modes of conduct usually foster appropriate allocation of resources, low-cost methods of production, brisk technological advancement, fairly equitable distributions of income, and minimum wage and price inflation.

Were these blanket statements *always* true, everything would be coming up roses, and the odd numbered chapters would be all that were needed. However, these statements are qualified with words like "usually" and "for the most part," words that warn of exceptions. Unfortunately, for some industries, workably competitive structures do *not* always provide good performance. A classic exception is the so-called "natural monopoly," where economies of scale are so significant that a healthy number of competing rivals could exist only with horrendous inefficiencies. Low-cost performance in such cases requires monopoly structure. Other structural quirks, such as centralized interconnection (for example, telephone service), enormously high capital costs relative to total production costs (for example, sewage disposal), and physical singularities (for example, seaports), also nourish "natural monopolies." Zealous pursuit of competitive structures in these cases would be futile (because their attainment is impossible) or stupid (because, if attained, they yield poor performance). Hence, government typically approaches these unruly beasts by condoning and to some extent even encouraging monopolistic structures. In hopes of serving the public interest, government either (1) *takes over* ownership and operation or (2) *regulates* performance directly if private ownership is permitted. In short, if monopoly is inevitable, it is preferable that such monopoly be publicly owned or publicly supervised. The latter option, which is the subject of Chapter 20, is called "public utility" regulation.

Regrettably, the exceptions are not limited to a few specific industries whose "good" performance requires "bad" structures. Disharmonies between structure and performance arise under other conditions as well. Two broad classes of exceptions concerning specific aspects of performance warrant discussion.

First, governmental awards of *temporary, unregulated monopoly* may be deemed the best way of rewarding and encouraging good performance. Patents provide the main example of this. A patent gives its owner 17 years of monopoly control over an invention. Because unregulated monopoly often yields handsome profits, patents in theory reward deserving inventors, thereby spurring technological progress that would not otherwise occur. This policy is explored in Chapter 24.

Second, certain aspects of good performance may be furthered by competitive structure and conduct, but procompetitive policies may still not be applied. Such policies may be considered *inexpedient;* their vigorous enforcement may be considered *socially and politically impractical or disruptive.* Assume for sake of illustration that labor unions contribute to aggregate inflation or unemployment because they impose anticompetitive restraints on labor markets. We would then have anticompetitive structures (unions) producing bad performance (inflation or unemployment). Assume further that unions bestow no notable economic benefits on society at large (such as increased productivity) that might broadly justify their existence or outweigh their bad aspects. The solution to the performance problem then seems obvious. Break up or totally dissolve unions, right? Right. But for obvious reasons this may be politically impossible (or if not impossible, politically suicidal). Similar assumptions could be made about oligopolistic industries not sufficiently concentrated to draw attack as monopolies but not sufficiently competitive to be free of inflationary biases. How much labor market and product market power actually contribute to inflation will be taken up later (Chapter 21). The point made here is that structures that are *economically* "bad" may nevertheless be considered *politically* "good," or if not exactly "good," then politically impregnable. Under the problem of inflation, this dilemma has led to "wage-price guide posts," "incomes policies," "freezes," and the like, all of which, as will be seen in Chapter 22, can be considered performance policies. Indeed, they are akin to "public utility" regulation but broader in industrial scope and narrower in purpose.

In sum, our passage into performance analysis does not put policy behind us. For a variety of reasons, government does not rest content with whatever desirable aspects of performance may be derived indirectly from its extensive (though often less than diligent) attention to structure and conduct. Government often dabbles and deals in performance directly. Whereas most policies governing structure and conduct may be called "antitrust" or "affirmative disclosure" policies, most of those governing performance typically entail "regulation" or "subsidization." Labels aside, you will find one even-numbered chapter on performance policy for each odd-numbered chapter on performance economics.

Profits, Wages, Technological Efficiency, and Jobs: Theory and Cross-Section Evidence

19

The creation of a monopoly involves a principle which can be generally applied . . . when in need of money.

—ARISTOTLE

Observations on the social ill-effects of market power date back to Aristotle. He tells of a Sicilian who monopolized the iron trade, thereby profiting 100%.[1] More recently, over the past 25 years, there have been more than a hundred empirical studies of the profitability of market power. These modern studies are more sophisticated, more scientific, and more thorough than Aristotle's. But nearly all of them reach the same conclusion—market power boosts profits. The first purpose of this chapter is to review this mountain of empiricism and explain its implications for two measures of economic performance, namely, allocation efficiency and wealth distribution.

The second purpose of this chapter is to show that market power can affect worker wage rates as well as profits. For this purpose we shall explore power in labor markets (as measured by unionization) as well as power in product markets.

As a third consideration, a growing body of empirical literature indicates that market power spawns technical inefficiency or X-inefficiency. X-inefficiency may economically be more costly to society than either excess profits or exorbitant wages.

Finally, this chapter closes with a brief discussion of an aspect of performance that has only recently caught the eyes of economists—job discrimination. As in the case of X-inefficiency, powerful firms appear to have stained records on this score.

---

[1] Ernest Barker (ed.), *The Politics of Aristotle* (New York: Oxford University Press, 1962), p. 31.

I. PROFITS AND MARKET POWER

A. Theory

Figure 19–1 depicts the simple theory of excess profits and resource misallocation under monopoly. With pure competition, industry price would be OP_c, which equals marginal cost. Marginal cost includes a normal profit, one just big enough that investors are content to leave their capital committed to this industry. Competitive quantity Q_c will then be supplied in the long run. Moreover, with price equal to marginal cost, resources are optimally allocated to the production of this commodity. Price indicates resource value "here," whereas marginal cost indicates resource value "elsewhere." Since value here just equals value elsewhere at the margin, any shift of resources will reduce consumer welfare. Consumers' welfare is measured by consumers' surplus, which is the greatest sum consumers are willing to pay for consuming quantity OQ_c less the amount they actually pay. In Figure 19–1, assuming pure competition, $OECQ_c$ is the sum they are willing to pay, whereas OP_cCQ_c is the sum they actually pay. Hence triangle ECP_c is the consumers' surplus associated with pure competition.

Monopolization of the industry has at least two effects. First, **inequity.** The monopolist maximizes profit by producing Q_m, where marginal revenue (MR) matches marginal cost. Price jumps to P_m, and the monopolist takes part of what would be consumers' surplus under pure competition. This area, rectangle P_cP_mAB, is the monopolist's excess profit. How markedly the excess profit contributes to an unequal distribution of income and wealth depends on the relative

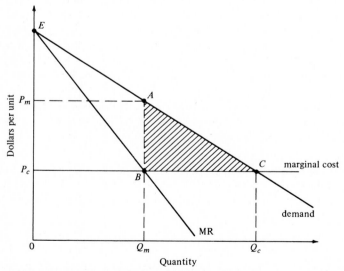

FIGURE 19–1. Social welfare loss due to monopoly.

financial condition of (1) those who pay the higher price and thereby lose the surplus and (2) those who earn the excess profit and thereby gain the surplus. If those who pay are generally poorer than those who receive (in the United States only about 2% of all households control over 50% of all business owner- ship claims), then income distribution is made more unequal than otherwise (Robin Hood in reverse, that is). Regardless of the distribution effect, area P_cP_mAB *should be considered a transfer* from one group to another. It is not a direct measure of allocation inefficiency.

The second effect of monopoly seen here is welfare loss caused by **misalloca- tion of resources.** When price rises above marginal cost to P_m, a portion of what used to be consumers' surplus disappears completely. This is triangular area *ABC*, which is neither retained by consumers nor transferred to the owners. In simple terms, misallocation occurs because monopolization underallocates resources to here, as production is cut back; production cut-backs also force overallocations elsewhere. The fact that price P_m exceeds marginal cost indicates that value here exceeds value elsewhere. And society would therefore be better off if resources were moved from elsewhere into here. But monopolization, with entry barred, prevents the necessary reshuffling. Welfare is lost just as welfare would be lost if seismic violence suddenly obliterated our coal resources. From Figure 19–1 it may be seen that welfare loss will be greater, the greater the divergence between P_m and P_c and between Q_m and Q_c. It is also true that welfare loss is a positive function of profit as a percentage of sales and price elasticity of demand.

In short, if market power does indeed generate excess profit, two adverse economic effects could arise—allocation inefficiency and maldistribution of wealth or income. Notice the "if" and the "could." Nothing is certain about these theoretical effects or the extent of actual harm. Research has tried to dispel some of the uncertainty by focusing on three questions raised by Figure 19–1:

1. Is there a positive association between market power and profitability?
2. Given a yes answer to question 1, what is the total welfare loss due to monopolistic misallocation?
3. Given a yes answer to question 1, what is market power's contribution to the above average wealth of the wealthy?

We shall take up each question in turn. It should be kept in mind throughout that pure monopoly and pure competition are extreme cases. Research actually centers on the varying degrees of market power that lie between these extremes.

B. Does Market Power Increase Profit?

The relationship between market power and profit performance is the most thoroughly studied of all structure-performance relationships. New evidence appears almost monthly. One reason for the intense attention paid to this issue is the immense policy implications it carries. Another is the wide diversity of possible research approaches. "Profit," for example, can be measured in a number of ways, each of which has a variety of data sources.[2]

An ideal measure of "profit" would be comparable across industries and free from biases that varied systematically but irrelevantly with market power. For purposes of comparability, all measures are actually **profit rates,** computed by dividing dollar profit (either pretax or post-tax) by some base figure. There are two broad classes of bases commonly used: (1) balance sheet data and (2) sales revenues. Accordingly, all measures can be divided into two groups.

The first group uses **stockholders' equity or assets** as the base. Indeed, the most widely used measure of profit is the **rate of return on stockholders' equity after tax.** Symbolically, this is $(P - T)/E$, where P is total dollar profit, T is tax on profit, and E is stockholders' equity. This measure has the desirable property of corresponding closely with the profit that stockholders seek to maximize. Moreover, this measure would be the same in the long run for all industries if pure competition prevailed throughout the economy. When assets instead of equity are used as the base, an adjustment must be made because debt capital as well as equity capital stands behind total assets, and debt capital is paid interest rather than profit, which is paid to equity capital owners. Accordingly, the formula for the **rate of return on assets after tax** is $(P - T + I)/A$, where P is dollar profit, T is tax, I is total dollar interest paid, and A is asset value. As compared with return on equity, this measure is probably less affected by irrelevant interindustry variances in debt/equity ratios, but most experts nevertheless consider it to be inferior to $(P - T)/E$. Data for both measures are available from corporation reports or, on a more aggregated level, from Internal Revenue Service documents.

A major problem with this first class of measures is that they may bias all firms toward equal profit rates because the numerator and denominator tend to move together directly rather than independently. Leonard Weiss explains:

> assets are apt to be written up or down according to their profitability. For instance, plant and equipment that have changed hands since they were installed are apt to be valued at their purchase prices rather than at their original costs, and those purchase prices will reflect their income earning prospects. Even when assets do not change hands, investments that turn out badly are sometimes written down to reflect their income potential more realistically. The result of such revaluations is [also] to increase the equity of highly profitable firms and reduce it in unprofitable firms, thus biasing all firms toward equal profit rates.[3]

Another shortcoming of these measures is that available data for them are *firm* specific, not *market* specific. Because many firms are highly diversified, their reported profits are a mix of profits from a number of markets. By contrast, most measures of market power are market specific. The disparity often prevents

[2] For a good review see Leonard W. Weiss, "The Concentration-Profits Relationship," in *Industrial Concentration: the New Learning,* edited by H. Goldschmid, M. Mann, and F. Weston (Boston: Little, Brown, 1974), pp. 196–201.
[3] *Ibid.,* p. 196.

a precise match-up of observations on market structure and observations on profit.

The most obvious of the second group of measures, which use sales, is **profit after tax relative to sales,** or $(P - T)/S$, where S is total sales revenue. This is not the form of profit that stockholders seek to maximize, but it has the advantage of measuring allocation inefficiency more directly than does profit relative to equity or assets. Moreover, it is not biased by asset revaluations. $(P - T)/S$ is not trouble free, however. It varies across industries for reasons wholly unrelated to market power. In particular, $(P - T)/S$ is largely determined by the capital intensity of the production process. Greater capital intensity implies a greater capital investment per unit of sales, and this in turn requires a greater profit per dollar of sales in order to reward investors with a given level of return on their investments. Letting E/S indicate investment per unit of sales, this may be seeen in the following identity:

$$\frac{P - T}{S} = \frac{E}{S} \times \frac{P - T}{E}$$

For a given level of $(P - T)/E$, say 9%, $(P - T)/S$ will be a direct function of E/S. Thus when using $(P - T)/S$, researchers must allow for capital intensity.

To summarize, there is a variety of profit measures and a variety of data sources, but imperfections affect each of them. If these imperfections spuriously generated positive associations between market power and profit, they would seriously reduce the validity of the measurements. Doubt would be cast on the meaning of such positive findings. However, just about all known errors work in the opposite direction. They either lessen the strength of any positive correlation between profits and power or bias it toward zero. Given this direction of error, "we can be pretty sure that if any positive relation does appear there is something there and it is understated. On the other hand, if no relationship is detected, one may still exist."[4]

1. Concentration and Profits. Earlier chapters theorized that concentration fostered market power. They also reviewed evidence of a positive association between concentration and price level. It will not come as a jolt, then, to learn that all but a few of the many statistical studies correlating profit and concentration find a *similar positive and significant relationship*. Figures 19–2(a) and 2(b) depict examples of these results. Such positive effects have been found for all measures of profit, for many different measures of concentration (four-firm and eight-firm ratios plus the Herfindahl–Hirschman index), and for vastly different time periods (from 1936 to the present). Moreover, the positive relationship holds for broad interindustry samples (including all manufacturing industries), narrow interindustry samples (limited to producer goods or food products, for

---

[4] *Ibid.,* p. 201. For statistical demonstration of this conclusion see J. A. Dalton and D. W. Penn, *The Quality of Data As a Factor in Analyses of Structure—Performance Relationships* (Federal Trade Commission Economic Report, 1971).

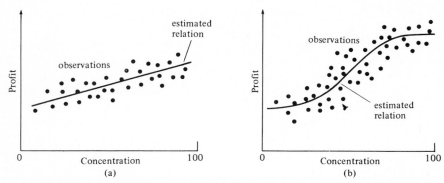

FIGURE 19–2. Positive relationships between profit and concentration.

instance), and intraindustry samples across diverse geographic markets (such as those in banking, grocery retailing, and bread).[5] As if this were not enough, the positive relationship emerges from data gathered from every corner of the world—England, Canada, Japan, Pakistan, India, Mexico, Brazil, Australia, Kenya, and France, as well as the United States.[6] Given this wide variety of tests, the general consistency of a positive concentration-profit relationship is impressive.

[5] For surveys see Weiss, *op. cit.,* and Stephen A. Rhoades, "Structure-Performance Studies in Banking: A Summary and Evaluation," Staff Economic Studies, No. 92 (Board of Governors of the Federal Reserve System, 1977); Rhoades, "Updated," Staff Economic Studies, No. 119 (Board of Governors of the Federal Reserve System, 1982). Among the many studies not mentioned in these surveys are David Qualls, "Concentration, Barriers to Entry, and Long Run Economic Profit Margins," *Journal of Industrial Economics* (April 1972), pp. 146–158; S. A. Rhoades and Joe M. Cleaver, "The Nature of the Concentration—Price/Cost Margin Relationship for 352 Manufacturing Industries: 1967," *Southern Economic Journal* (July 1973), pp. 90–102; James A. Verbrugge and R. A. Shick, "Market Structure and Savings and Loan Profitability," *Quarterly Review of Economics and Business* (Summer 1976), pp. 79–90; A. D. Strickland and L. W. Weiss, "Advertising, Concentration, and Price-Cost Margins," *Journal of Political Economy* (October 1976), pp. 1,109–1,123; Lana Hall, Andrew Schmitz, and James Cothern, "Beef Wholesale-Retail Marketing Margins, and Concentration," *Economica* (August 1979), pp. 295–300.

[6] J. Khalilzadeh-Shiraz, "Market Structure and Price-Cost Margins: A Comparative Analysis of U.K. and U.S. Manufacturing Industries," *Economic Inquiry* (March 1976), pp. 116–128; J. C. H. Jones, L. Laudadio and M. Percy, "Profitability and Market Structure: A Cross-Section Comparison of Canadian and American Manufacturing Industry," *Journal of Industrial Economics* (March 1977), pp. 195–211; Richard E. Caves and Masu Uekusa, *Industrial Organization in Japan* (Washington, D.C.: Brookings Institution, 1976), pp. 92–96; Lawrence J. White, *Industrial Concentration and Economic Power in Pakistan* (Princeton: Princeton University Press, 1974); P. K. Sawhney and B. L. Sawhney, "Capacity-Utilization, Concentration, and Price-Cost Margins: Results on Indian Industries," *Journal of Industrial Economics* (April 1973), pp. 145–153; John M. Conner and Willard F. Mueller, *Market Power and Profitability of Multinational Corporations in Brazil and Mexico,* Report to the Subcommittee on Foreign Economic Policy of the Committee on Foreign Relations, U.S. Senate (1977); William J. House, "Market Structure and Industry Performance: The Case of Kenya," *Oxford Economic Papers* (November 1973), pp. 405–419; F. Jenny and A. P. Weber, "Profit Rates and Structural Variables in the French Manufacturing Sector," *European Economic Review,* (January 1976); Stephen Nickell and David Metcalf, "Monopolistic Industries and Monopoly Profits or, Are Kellogg's Cornflakes Overpriced?" *Economic Journal* (June 1978), pp. 254–268; and David K. Round, "Price-Cost Margins, Industry Structure, and Foreign Competition in Australian Manufacturing" *Industrial Organization Review* (No. 3, 1978), pp. 151–168.

TABLE 19–1. Profit Rates of Food Manufacturing Firms Associated with Levels of Industry Concentration and Advertising to Sales Ratios

Four-Firm Concentration	Advertising to Sales Ratio (%)				
	1.0	2.0	3.0	4.0	5.0
40	6.2	7.4	8.5	9.6	10.7
45	8.0	9.1	10.2	11.3	12.4
50	9.3	10.4	11.5	12.6	13.7
55	10.3	11.4	12.5	13.6	14.7
60	11.0	12.1	13.2	14.3	15.4
65	11.4	12.5	13.6	14.7	15.8
70	11.5	12.6	13.7	14.8	15.9

Source: William H. Kelly, *On the Influence of Market Structure on the Profit Performance of Food Manufacturing Companies* (Federal Trade Commission, 1969), p. 7.

Two brief numerical examples based on United States data convey the message. Robert Kilpatrick computed the correlation between concentration and three different measures of pretax profit for 91 industries using 1963 Internal Revenue Service data. The correlation coefficients are 0.388, 0.442, and 0.506 for profits as a percentage of equity, assets, and sales, respectively.[7] All are statistically significant at the 95% level or better. All indicate a relationship like Figure 19–2(a).

In another study, one limited to 97 firms producing food products, William Kelly used regression analysis to explain interfirm variance in profit rates as a per cent of stockholders equity. A summary of his results is presented in Table 19–1. Reading the table horizontally discloses the estimated impact of advertising on profit. As advertising intensity increases, profit likewise increases, a result explained earlier in Chapter 15. The estimated impact of concentration is seen by scanning down the columns. For example, when advertising is held constant at 1% of sales, a profit rate of 6.3% is associated with concentration of 40, and a profit rate of 11.5% is associated with concentration of 70. Notice that most of the increase in profit occurs in the range of concentration between 40 and 60. Added concentration above 60 adds very little to profit (regardless of advertising intensity). The table does not present results for concentration ratios less than 40 because the sample did not include observations for low levels of concentration. Still, on the basis of other evidence, it can be assumed that profit would not vary greatly over the low range of concentration, in which case these results would trace the pattern depicted in Figure 19–2(b).

[7] Robert W. Kilpatrick, "The Validity of the Average Concentration Ratio as a Measure of Industrial Structure," *Southern Economic Journal* (April 1976), pp. 711–715.

The exact *form* of the concentration-profits relationship is a much debated issue. Some evidence reveals a linear relation like Figure 19–2(a). Other evidence indicates a nonlinear or discontinuous form, one example of which is Figure 19–2(b). The present author is open-minded on the subject of form, but he suspects that a nonlinear form *does* hold under some circumstances, and theory and evidence suggest a form like Figure 19–2(b). That is to say, it is in the *middle* range of concentration that the greatest transformation from competitive to collusive conduct is likely to occur. Therefore it is in the middle range that concentration and profit are most likely to move positively and significantly together, as shown in Figure 19–2(b).[8]

What about the several statistical studies that show *no* significant positive relationship between concentration and profit? Are they not relevant? To be sure, they cannot be ignored. But almost without exception reasonable explanations can be found for their contrary results. It has been found, for example, that the relationship is weak or nonexistent during rapid spurts of economic expansion or price inflation.[9] Studies drawing data from such periods are likely, therefore, to produce contrary results. Another problem is multicollinearity. When a number of variables other than concentration are included in statistical regressions, the effect of concentration is occasionally wiped out. This occurs when concentration and these other variables, such as barriers to entry, are highly correlated. However, this disappearance of concentration does not mean that concentration has no effect. It merely means that computerized statistical procedures cannot sort out the independent contributions that the correlated variables make to profit.[10] Still another group of explicable contrary results arises from the use of limited samples of industries or markets, samples so limited that they do not include observations over a wide range of concentration. As we have just seen, if observations on concentration are limited to either high or low values, positive significant associations are less likely to be detected.[11] The contrary results of studies such as these need not be given great weight.

The fact that contrary results can be explained as aberrations does not silence all skeptics, however. Indeed, there is a small but vocal group of economists

[8] See Norman R. Collins and Lee E. Preston, *Concentration and Price-Cost Margins in Manufacturing Industries* (Berkeley, Calif.: University of California Press, 1968); A. A. Heggestad and J. J. Mingo, "The Competitive Condition of U.S. Banking Markets and the Impact of Structural Reform," *Journal of Finance* (June 1977), pp. 649–661; Ralph M. Bradburd and A. Mead Over, Jr., "Organizational Costs, 'Sticky Equilibria,' and Critical Levels of Concentration," *Review of Economics and Statistics* (February 1982), pp. 50–58.

[9] G. Gambeles. "Structural Determinants of Profit Performance in the United States Manufacturing Industries, 1947–1967," Ph.D. dissertation, University of Maryland, 1969.

[10] The added variable most commonly at fault is economies of scale computed from data entering the concentration ratio. When an independent measure of scalar economics is used, the problem disappears and concentration attains significance. See R. E. Caves, J. Khalilzadeh-Shirazi, and M. E. Porter, "Scale Economies in Statistical Analyses of Market Power," *Review of Economics and Statistics* (May 1975), pp. 133–140.

[11] In the highs see D. R. Fraser and P. S. Rose, "Banking Structure and Performance in Isolated Markets: The Implications for Public Policy," *Antitrust Bulletin* (Fall 1972), pp. 927–947. For examples of lows see Collins and Preston's results for textiles and apparel (*op. cit.,* pp. 94–97).

who acknowledge the existence of a positive correlation between concentration and profit but who claim that it is entirely spurious, that it is due to some fundamental flaw in the data or to factors unrelated to market power that just happen to be positively correlated with both concentration and profit.[12] This is not the proper place to review the entire debate. Still, we should mention some points made by the skeptics and indicate how each has thus far been answered:

1. Skeptics argue that accounting procedures may differ across firms, making the positive association meaningless. It has been shown, however, that accounting practices do not differ systematically between firms in concentrated and unconcentrated industries.[13]
2. Skeptics argue that the positive association is due merely to short-run disequilibrium conditions, that over the long run it disappears under the pressure of dynamic competition brought by new entry, product innovation, and the like. On the other hand, it has been demonstrated repeatedly that the relationship holds across decades of time, not merely months or years.[14] Moreover, study of the market value of firms indicates that investors behave as if firms with market power will keep that power into the distant future. "No indication has appeared that anticipations of entry will erode future excess profits."[15]
3. Skeptics claim that once risk is accounted for, the positive relationship will disappear, partly because risk is a major (and positive) determinant of both profit and concentration. Yet a number of studies have shown that even after profits are adjusted for risk-reward, the positive relationship remains.[16]

[12] John McGee, *In Defense of Industrial Concentration* (New York: Praeger Publishers, 1971), pp. 93–95; Yale Brozen, "The Antitrust Task Force Deconcentration Recommendation," *Journal of Law and Economics* (October 1970), pp. 279–292; Richard B. Mancke, "Causes of Interfirm Profitability Differences: A New Interpretation of the Evidence," *Quarterly Journal of Economics* (May 1974), pp. 181–193; Harold Demsetz, "Two Systems of Belief About Monopoly," in *Industrial Concentration: the New Learning,* edited by H. Goldschmid, M. Mann, and F. Weston (Boston: Little, Brown, 1974), pp. 164–184; Almarin Phillips, "A Critique of Empirical Studies of Relations Between Market Structure and Profitability," *Journal of Industrial Economics* (June 1976), pp. 241–249; George J. Stigler, *Capital and Rates of Return in Manufacturing Industries* (Princeton, N.J.: Princeton University Press, 1963).
[13] Robert L. Hagerman and Lemma W. Senbet, "A Test of Accounting Bias and Market Structure," *Journal of Business* (October 1976), pp. 509–514.
[14] David Qualls, "Stability and Persistence of Economic Profit Margins in Highly Concentrated Industries," *Southern Economic Journal* (April 1974), pp. 604–612; R. H. Litzenberger and O. M. Joy, "Inter-Industry Profitability Under Uncertainty," *Western Economic Journal* (September 1973), pp. 338–349; Dennis Mueller, "The Persistence of Profits Above the Norm," *Economica* (November 1977), pp. 369–380; S. J. Liebowitz, "Measuring Industrial Disequilibria," *Southern Economic Journal* (July 1982), pp. 119–136.
[15] Stavros B. Thomadakis, "A Value-Based Test of Profitability and Market Structure," *Review of Economics and Statistics* (May 1977), pp. 179–185.
[16] William G. Shepherd, *The Treatment of Market Power* (New York: Columbia University Press, 1974), pp. 109–110; James L. Bothwell and Theodore E. Keeler, "Profits, Market Structure and Portfolio Risk," in *Essays on Industrial Organization,* edited by R. T. Masson and P. D. Qualls (Cambridge, Mass.: Ballinger, 1976), pp. 71–88; S. A. Rhoades and R. D. Rutz, "Market Power and Firm Risk," *Journal of Monetary Economics* (1982), pp. 73–85.

4. Skeptics claim that small firms' profits are understated because their owner-officers take profit in the form of salaries. In turn, this allegedly understates the profits of unconcentrated industries. However, proper adjustment for this effect leaves the positive relation unscathed.[17]

5. Skeptics say that the positive relationship is stronger for broadly defined industries than for narrowly defined industries, an anomaly that raises doubts. But careful study of this issue indicates just the opposite—namely, the narrower the definition the better.[18]

6. Skeptics argue that the relationship can be explained by nothing more than luck, luck being the source of both high concentration and high profit. Yet this, too, has been answered by both counter argument and evidence.[19]

7. Skeptics claim that interindustry or intermarket comparisons of profits are irrelevant because they indicate nothing about what would happen to profits if concentration *within* an industry or market *changed.* Policy, they say, brings changes, not comparisons. In reply, it appears that cross-section results are not deceiving. Direct estimates of the effects of change support the positive relationship.[20]

8. Finally, and most important, skeptics claim that the positive relationship arises *not* because concentration *raises prices* relative to costs, but rather because concentration is fostered by *efficiencies* which *reduce costs* relative to prices. This "efficiency hypothesis" is severely undercut by abundant evidence of positive associations between concentration and *price* level, which dovetails with the positive profit effect (see pages 295–301). Still, this hypothesis has received such great attention that two specifics regarding it deserve elaboration.

(a) *First,* there is some evidence that the positive association between profits and concentration holds for large firms but not small firms. If one *assumes* that *all* firms within a given concentrated industry would benefit proportionately from any price collusion, then it can be argued that *all* firms— big and small—should experience a positive association between concentration and profits. The evidence of different profit experiences by size of firm thus allegedly supports the efficiency hypothesis. There are several problems with this line of argument, however: (i) Even if we accept the evidence of differences by size as valid, the assumption of equal proportionate benefit from collusion can be stoutly challenged. Collusion

[17] Robert W. Kilpatrick, "Stigler on the Relationship Between Industrial Profit Rates and Market Concentration," *Journal of Political Economy* (May/June 1968), pp. 479–488.

[18] Frances F. Esposito and Louis Esposito, "Aggregation and the Concentration-Profitability Relationship," *Southern Economic Journal* (October 1977), pp. 323–332.

[19] R. E. Caves, B. T. Gale, and M. E. Porter, "Interfirm Profitability Differences: Comment," *Quarterly Journal of Economics* (November 1977), pp. 667–675; P. S. Albin and R. E. Alcaly, "Stochastic Determinants of Interfirm Profitability Differences," *Review of Economics and Statistics* (November 1979), pp. 615–618.

[20] Keith Cowling and Michael Waterson, "Price-Cost Margins and Market Structure," *Economica* (August 1976), pp. 267–274; Maury N. Harris, "Entry and Long-Term Trends in Industry Performance," *Antitrust Bulletin* (Summer 1976), pp. 295–314.

can reward an industry's big firms with excess profits and simultaneously reward its small firms with only normal profits even if the concentration fostering the collusion is not grounded on big firm efficiencies. Indeed, an industry's small "fringe" firms typically *cannot* earn excess profits without attracting the entry of new, small inefficient firms. Thus price collusion may retard the exit of inefficient small firms or attract the entry of same, yielding size differences in observed profit rates without supporting the efficiency hypothesis.[21] (ii) The profit differences favoring large size may be questioned directly. Most evidence indicates *no* systematic differences by size for most industries. And where the differences do favor the largest firms, concentration does not commonly follow.[22]

(b) A *second* brand of evidence said to support the efficiency hypothesis is the finding that concentration's impact on profits often fades when data for individual firms are used and when *market shares* of the firms are included in the analysis. High market share generates high profits, draining concentration of significance. This suggests that high profits are not due to high concentration but rather to high market shares based on economies of scale, superior products, and good management—i.e., efficiency. However, problems plague this evidence, too: (i) There are, for one thing, numerous excellent studies which reveal positive significance for concentration once market share is taken into account.[23] (ii) The best evidence of market share factors canceling out concentration factors is based on data that show no direct association between firm size and efficiency.[24] (iii) Finally, to the extent larger firm market shares do boost profits (and the boost is apparently substantial), it appears that market share may be measuring *market power,* not efficiency. The market share findings then complement, not supplant, the concentration findings. It

[21] L. Hannah and J. A. Kay, *Concentration in Modern Industry* (London: Macmillan, 1977), p. 21; Robert J. Stonebraker, "Corporate Profits and the Risk of Entry," *Review of Economics and Statistics* (February 1976), pp. 33–39; M. E. Porter, "The Structure Within Industries and Companies Performance," *Review of Economics and Statistics* (May 1979), pp. 214–227; R. T. Masson and J. Shaanan, "Stochastic-Dynamic Limit Pricing: An Empirical Test," *Review of Economics and Statistics* (August 1982), pp. 413–422.

[22] M. Marcus, "Profitability and Size of Firm," *Review of Economics and Statistics* (February 1969), pp. 104–107; Ronald S. Bond and Warren Greenberg, "Industry Structure, Market Rivalry, and Public Policy: A Comment," *Journal of Law & Economics* (April 1976), pp. 201–204; F. M. Scherer, "The Causes and Consequences of Rising Industrial Concentration: A Comment," *Journal of Law & Economics* (April 1979), pp. 191–208; Richard E. Caves and Thomas A. Pugel, *Intraindustry Differences in Conduct and Performance,* Monograph 1980–2, Series in Finance and Economics (New York: New York University, Graduate School of Business Administration, 1980).

[23] See, e.g., Weiss, *op. cit.,* pp. 225–230; Blake Imel, Michael R. Behr, and Peter G. Helmberger, *Market Structure and Performance* (Lexington, Mass.: Lexington Books, 1972); J. A. Dalton and Stanford L. Levin, "Market Power: Concentration and Market Share," *Industrial Organization Review,* (No. 1, 1977), pp. 27–35; D. F. Lean, J. D. Ogur, and R. P. Rogers, *Competition and Collusion in Electrical Equipment Markets: An Economic Assessment* (Washington, D.C.: Federal Trade Commission Staff Report, 1982).

[24] David J. Ravenscraft, "Structure-Profit Relationships at the Line of Business and Industry Level" (mimeo, FTC, June 1981); L. W. Weiss and George Pascoe, "Some Early Results on the Concentration-Profits Relationship from the FTC's Line of Business Data," (mimeo, FTC, September 1981); D. C. Mueller, "Economies of Scale and Concentration" (mimeo, FTC, 1982).

has been shown, for example, that intensive advertising raises product price most dramatically for large firms as opposed to small firms.[25] To be sure, efficiency may be part of the cause, and in some cases the main cause, but, as a general proposition, the efficiency hypothesis cannot overthrow the market power hypothesis on the basis of available evidence.

In short, the positive concentration-profit relationship stands up well under close scrutiny (so Aristotle can rest in peace). This is not to say that high concentration *always* produces high profits. High concentration is merely a necessary, not a sufficient, condition.

2. The Effect of Other Elements of Market Power on Profit.

It has already been shown that, besides concentration, advertising intensity is often positively associated with profits. What about other elements of market power? They too have been tested. They too make big contributions.

BARRIERS TO ENTRY. If entry were perfectly free and easy, excess profits would quickly evaporate regardless of concentration level. Thus, in theory, high barriers should boost profits (everything else being equal).

This expectation has been borne out repeatedly by the data. An early study by Michael Mann, for instance, found that, among 21 highly concentrated industries, those with "very high barriers" averaged 16.4% profit on equity, whereas those with "moderate-to-low" barriers averaged only 11.9% profit on equity.[26] More recent studies have used more refined measures of entry barriers. All in all, they also indicate that high barriers hoist profitability.[27]

One of the most fascinating recent studies is by Robert Stonebraker.[28] He hypothesizes that the risk faced by the small firms occupying market fringes "can be thought of as the vehicle through which entry barriers work." He reasons that "Most entry occurs on a small scale and entrepreneurs are likely to estimate the risk of entering an industry on the basis of the performance of existing small firms." To test this hypothesis Stonebraker devised two measures of risk for the small firms in each of 33 industries: (1) the *per cent* of observed small firm profit rates falling below normal competitive profit, multiplied by the average *distance* these returns fall below the competitive profit rate, and (2) an index of failure frequency. As it turns out, these measures of small firm risk plus industry growth "explain" more than 60% of the interindustry differ-

[25] Paul W. Farris and David J. Reibstein, "How Prices, Ad Expenditures, and Profits Are Linked," *Harvard Business Review* (November 1979), p. 179. See also Dalton and Levin, *op. cit.;* and Bradley T. Gale, "Market Share and Rate of Return," *Review of Economics and Statistics* (November 1972), p. 413.

[26] H. Michael Mann, "Seller Concentration, Barriers to Entry, and Rates of Return in Thirty Industries, 1950–1960," *Review of Economics and Statistics* (August 1966), pp. 296–307.

[27] Harris, *op. cit.;* Caves, Khalilzadeh-Shirazi, and Porter, *op. cit.;* Masson and Shaanan, *op. cit.;* William S. Comanor and Thomas A. Wilson, "Advertising, Market Structure, and Performance," *Review of Economics and Statistics* (November 1967), pp. 423–440; Dale Orr, "An Index of Entry Barriers and its Application to the Structure Performance Relationship," *Journal of Industrial Economics* (September 1974), pp. 39–49.

[28] Robert J. Stonebraker, "Corporate Profits and the Risk of Entry," *Review of Economics and Statistics* (February 1976), pp. 33–39.

ences in large, established firm profits. Simply stated, the *worse* the profit experience of small firms, the *better* the profit experience of their rival large firms. In other words, small firm risk apparently protects large firm profit from entry erosion by serving as a warning beacon to would-be entrants. (Stonebraker also probed the causes of small firm risk. Interestingly enough, advertising intensity was the single most important factor—higher advertising causing greater risk.)

Finally, entry barriers may do more than influence profitability in their own right. They may also *condition* the effect of concentration. In particular, profits ought to rise more rapidly with concentration, the higher the barriers to entry are. Where barriers are low, concentration should have little impact. Where barriers are high, concentration should pack a wallop. Leonard Weiss found this to be so.[29]

IMPORTS. As anyone who has "priced" Japanese television sets or purchased a foreign car knows, imports provide competition for domestic producers. Indeed, they are a form of entry. To see whether such competition affects profit performance, researchers have included import volume in statistical analyses of profits. The results? In general, heavy inbound ocean traffic does seem to mean greater competition because domestic industry profits are inversely related to import volume.[30] (The converse is also true; exports are often positively associated with profit performance.)

BUYER POWER. If the buyers' side of the market is dominated by only a few powerful buyers—as is true for tire cord and primary copper—profits of sellers might be *lower* than otherwise. Theory holds that the monop*sony* power of buyers could negate the mono*poly* power of sellers. Big buyers could play one seller off against another during bargaining or threaten self-supply. Recent tests bear out the theory. Seller profit margins are inversely related to buyer concentration. Moreover, the negative impact of buyer concentration is greatest where seller concentration is greatest, as one would intuitively expect.[31]

Summary. It appears that the answer to our first question is "yes." There is a positive association between market power (variously measured) and profitability. This does *not* mean you should rush to telephone your stockbroker. Your purchase of ownership shares in GM, IBM, or some other behemoth will not guarantee you fantastic returns. More than likely your rate of return will be no more than normal because the prices of powerful firms' stocks are

[29] Leonard W. Weiss, "Quantitative Studies of Industrial Organization," in *Frontiers of Quantitative Economics,* edited by M. D. Intriligator (Amsterdam: North-Holland Publishing Co., 1971), pp. 375–376.

[30] L. Esposito and F. F. Esposito, "Foreign Competition and Domestic Industry Profitability," *Review of Economics and Statistics* (November 1971), pp. 343–353; Gambeles, *op. cit.;* E. Pagoulatos and R. Sorensen, "International Trade, International Investment and Industrial Profitability," *Southern Economic Journal* (January 1976), pp. 425–434; H. P. Marvel, "Foreign Trade and Domestic Competition," *Economic Inquiry* (January 1980), pp. 103–122.

[31] Steven H. Lustgarten, "The Impact of Buyer Concentration in Manufacturing Industries," *Review of Economics and Statistics* (May 1975), pp. 125–132; Douglas G. Brooks, "Buyer Concentration: A Forgotten Element in Market Structure Models," *Industrial Organization Review,* Vol. 1, No. 3 (1973), pp. 151–163; Vincent A. LaFrance, "The Impact of Buyer Concentration—An Extension," *Review of Economics and Statistics* (August 1979), pp. 475–476.

inflated. Expected excess profits are quickly *capitalized* into higher market prices for equity shares.[32] Riches arise mainly in the *process* of this capitalization. Hence, only early bird owners (and their heirs) catch the worm of wealth. However, this *does* mean that the questions still pending concerning allocation efficiency and wealth distribution deserve careful attention.

C. What is the Welfare Loss Due to Monopolistic Misallocation?

When the shaded triangle of Figure 19–1 is calculated for individual industries then tallied across the economy, what is the result? Arnold Harberger, over 25 years ago, was the first to attempt an estimate. Using 1920s data for manufacturing industries and a series of bold assumptions, he concluded that welfare loss amounted to a piddling 0.06% of that portion of gross national product coming from manufacturing. For the economy as a whole, his estimate was a mere 0.1% of GNP.[33] These calculations led many to dismiss the monopoly problem as trifling. As one commentator quipped, this welfare loss would only be "enough to treat every family in the land to a steak dinner at a good (monopolistically competitive) restaurant."[34]

Subsequent researchers have criticized Harberger's procedures and assumptions as being biased downwards. Among other things it has been argued that Harberger's assumed price elasticities of demand were too low, that his assumed normal profit rate of return was too high, that he ignored the transmission of monopoly distortions through the many vertical stages of most production-distribution processes, and that his study was limited to partial equilibrium conditions. Subsequent researchers have attempted to correct these shortcomings in various ways, and virtually all subsequent estimates of welfare loss are substantially greater than Harberger's. Most are 10 to 20 times greater. Yet, Harberger's estimates were so tiny that these multiples likewise yield relatively low numbers. Check the following estimates expressed as a per cent of GNP—Scherer's, 0.5 to 2%; Shepherd's, 2 to 3%; Worcester's, 0.4 to 0.7%; Carson's, 3.2%, at most; and Bergson's, 2 to 4% (as interpreted by Worcester).[35]

These more recent estimates are still small, but they should be qualified by three observations. First, *by its very nature* the percentage computation yields small estimates. Only a *portion* of industry suffers any loss at all. Furthermore,

[32] Timothy G. Sullivan, "A Note on Market Power and Returns to Stockholders," *Review of Economics and Statistics* (February 1977), pp. 108–113.

[33] Arnold C. Harberger, "Monopoly and Resource Allocation," *American Economic Review* (May 1954), pp. 77–87.

[34] F. M. Scherer, *Industrial Market Structure and Economic Performance* (Chicago: Rand McNally, 1970), p. 402.

[35] *Ibid.*, p. 404; William G. Shepherd, *Market Power and Economic Welfare* (New York: Random House, 1970), p. 198; Dean A. Worcester, Jr., "New Estimates of the Welfare Loss to Monopoly, United States: 1956–1969," *Southern Economic Journal* (October 1973), pp. 234–245; R. Carson, D. A. Worcester Jr., and Abram Bergson, "On Monopoly Welfare Losses: Comments and Reply," *American Economic Review* (December 1975), pp. 1008–1031. The highest estimates, 4 to 13% of gross corporate product, are by Keith Cowling and Dennis Mueller, "The Social Costs of Monopoly Power," *Economic Journal* (December 1978), pp. 727–748; see also *EJ* (Sept. 1981), pp. 721–725.

TABLE 19–2. Computation of Welfare Loss in a Hypothetical Industry

	Pure Competition	Oligopoly
Price	$P_c = \$1.00$	$P_m = \$1.25$
Quantity	$Q_c = 1,000,000$	$Q_m = 800,000$
Total Revenue	$P_c \times Q_c = \$1,000,000$	$P_m \times Q_m = \$1,000,000$
Excess profit	zero	$\$0.25 \times Q_m = \$200,000$
Dollar welfare loss	zero	$\frac{1}{2} \times 0.25(Q_c - Q_m) = \$25,000$
Loss as per cent of revenue	zero	2.5%

within the noncompetitive portion, the percentage loss is computed by comparing a fairly small triangle to a typically large total revenue. Table 19–2 presents a numerical example assuming unit elasticity, a price increase of 25% due to oligopoly, and constant costs equal to the purely competitive price of $1.00. Under oligopoly, price is $1.25; quantity is 800,000 units; total industry revenue is $1 million; and excess profit is the price differential, $0.25, times 800,000. The welfare loss triangle is one half of the price differential ($\frac{1}{2} \times 0.25$) times the quantity differential (1,000,000 − 800,000 = 200,000), or $25,000. Dividing this by the oligopoly's total revenue of $1,000,000 to reckon loss in percentage terms yields 2.5%. If this hypothetical oligopoly amounted to as much as half of the total economy, then loss as a per cent of GNP would be only half of that, or 1.25%. Thus the percentage loss is *inherently* small. But our second observation is that a small percentage loss can be quite large when translated into absolute dollars; 1% of a $2 trillion GNP would be $20 billion per year (enough to keep college students, or even their colleges, out of rags). Finally, these are merely *static* losses. The *dynamic* losses due to monopoly power— losses like reduced invention, innovation, and economic growth—could well be much greater.[36] (See Chapter 23.)

D. What is Market Power's Contribution to the Above Average Wealth of the Wealthy?

William Comanor and Robert Smiley have done more than anyone "to estimate the impact of past and current enterprise monopoly profits on the distribution of household wealth in the United States."[37] The task is not an easy one. The distributive consequences of excess profit depend on a number of complex

[36] For a brilliant book on this point see Mancur Olson, *The Rise and Decline of Nations* (New Haven: Yale University Press, 1982).

[37] William S. Comanor and Robert H. Smiley, "Monopoly and the Distribution of Wealth," *Quarterly Journal of Economics* (May 1975), pp. 177–194. See also Smiley's "Survey" in J. J. Siegfried (ed.), *The Economics of Firm Size, Market Structure, and Social Performance* (Federal Trade Commission, July 1980), pp. 90–103; S. A. Rhoades, "Welfare Loss, Redistribution Effect, and Restriction of Output Due to Monopoly in Banking," *Journal of Monetary Economics* (1982), pp. 375–387.

factors—on, among other things, (1) how much profit is excessive, (2) who pays the excess profit, (3) who receives the excess profit, and (4) duration of monopoly. Accordingly, Comanor and Smiley draw heavily upon certain estimates of others and several simplifying assumptions. Examples follow:

1. They borrow Scherer's estimate that excess profit (not welfare loss) amounts to 3% of GNP and assume this to have held since 1890, the first year of their cumulative computation. As an alternative they also use 2%.
2. They make two alternative assumptions concerning who pays: (a) payments are proportional to the distribution of consumption expenditure, or (b) the rich spend relatively *more* of their budget on monopolistic goods.
3. As regards who receives, they assume that monopoly gains are distributed in proportion to the distribution of business ownership claims. This means that wealthy owners are no more or less likely to be monopoly owners than poor owners, a conservative assumption.
4. They assume that the gains are quickly capitalized and are perpetuated to some degree by inheritance.

The results are striking. The wealthiest 2.4% of all households *actually* accounts for slightly more than 40% of total wealth. Under the 3% excess profit assumption, an *absence* of monopoly power would reduce this share to "somewhere between 16.6% and 27.5%, which would represent *a decline of nearly 50 percent* in their share of total household wealth."[38] Under the 2% excess profit assumption, an *absence* of monopoly power would reduce that 40% share to something near 32%, *a decline of roughly 20%*. In addition, an absence of monopoly would elevate the wealth of the poorest families by significant multiples. Comanor and Smiley conclude therefore that "past and current monopoly has had a major impact on the current degree of inequality in this distribution [of wealth]."

Converting these numbers into something concrete, we may note that the monopoly power of the old Standard Oil Company of New Jersey (broken up in 1911) generated a fortune for John D. Rockefeller that in today's dollars would be the equivalent of *$9 billion*.[39]

II. MARKET POWER AND LABOR EARNINGS

A. General Introduction

Excess profits are not the only source of higher prices and lost consumers' surplus. Other price-increasing excesses are associated with market power. Table 19–3 illustrates the point with data from grocery retailing. Column (1) is four-firm concentration in local markets. Columns (2) and (3) give a price index

[38] Comanor and Smiley, *op. cit.,* p. 191, emphasis added.
[39] *Wall Street Journal,* February 11, 1983, p. 38.

TABLE 19–3. Estimated Index of Grocery Prices and Pretax Profit to Sales Ratios Associated with Various Levels of Concentration*

(1) Four-Firm Concentration Ratio	(2) Index of Grocery Prices	(3) Profits as Per Cent of Sales
40	100.0	0.37
50	101.0	0.99
60	103.0	1.22
70	105.3	1.28

* This assumes "relative firm market share" of 10.
Source: B. W. Marion, W. F. Mueller, R. W. Cotterill, F. E. Geithman, and J. R. Schmelzer, *The Profit and Price Performance of Leading Food Chains, 1970–74,* A Study for the Joint Economic Committee, U.S. Congress, 95th Congress, First Session (1977), p. 77.

and profit as a per cent of sales. These last two columns are not perfectly comparable because the data underlying them differ. Nevertheless, to the extent those columns are comparable, they are instructive. Prices clearly rise with concentration. But they rise *much more* than profit. If the price increase of 5.3% associated with an increase in concentration from 40 to 70 were due entirely to profit, then profit would have gone from 0.37 to 5.4% of sales. But this is *not* the case. The observed jump in profit is from 0.37 to 1.28% of sales. Quite clearly, *costs* are rising with concentration as well as *profit*.

The separate cost and profit effects may be illustrated theoretically in Figure 19–3. Let OP_m and OC_m be a monopolist's price and cost per unit, respectively. Then profit per unit is the difference between P_m and C_m. With monopoly output equal OQ_m, total excess profit is area P_mABC_m. The deadweight welfare loss associated with this excess profit is shaded triangle ABH. Thus, in terms of lost consumers' surplus, the combined **profit effect** is represented by trapezoid P_mAHC_m, part of which is transfer and part of which disappears. The preceding sections discussed these profit effects. Were there nothing more in monopoly power, the establishment of competition would merely reduce price to C_m and expand output to Q_n, adding P_mAHC_m to consumers' surplus.

The **cost effect** is seen by first drawing a distinction between monopoly cost C_m and competitive cost C_c. If monopoly power raises costs as well as profits, then establishment of competition will reduce price from P_m to C_c, since competitive price will match competitive cost C_c. This is obviously a much greater price reduction than from P_m to C_m. The social gains from competition are correspondingly greater. Elimination of the excess cost adds to consumers' surplus an area represented by trapezoid C_mHEC_c.

In sum, introduction of competition adds P_mAHC_m from the profit effect *plus* C_mHEC_c from the cost effect. Together these represent a total gain in consumers' surplus amounting to area P_mAEC_c. Stated in terms of loss rather

419

than gain, this area represents the total loss in consumers' surplus due to monopoly, when both cost and profit effects are present. As before, this total welfare loss can be divided into different kinds of losses depending on the *destination* of the loss. Generally speaking, there are four possibilities, two of which should by now be familiar:

1. *Deadweight loss:* First and most obvious is a deadweight loss represented by triangle *ADE* in Figure 19–3. This is much greater than the deadweight loss associated with excess profit alone (which is *ABH*), because there is an additional deadweight loss due to higher cost (represented by trapezoid *BHED*). Estimates of this loss are therefore *under*estimates if based on profit alone. As explained earlier, this deadweight loss arises from *allocation inefficiency*. Quantity Q_m is less than the optimal quantity Q_c.

2. *Profit transfer:* A portion of the lost consumers' surplus again goes to excess profit. This is represented by $P_m ABC_m$. Our earlier discussion and estimates of this effect could be reapplied here. Though a loss to consumers, this represents a gain to owners with *distributive consequences*.

3. *Cost that is transfer:* The added total cost of producing OQ_m, represented by $C_m BDC_c$, can take two possible forms. One is excess factor remuneration. Management or labor (or some other factor) may be overpaid at the expense of owners or consumers or both. The overpayments, or "rents," are analogous to excess profit. They are higher than what is

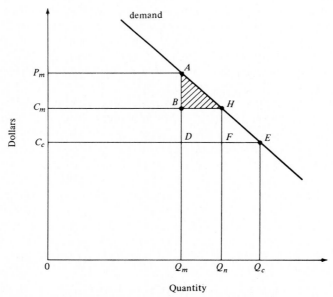

FIGURE 19–3. Cost implications of market power.

necessary to keep the favored factor committed to the industry. Thus, managers may take advantage of the imperfect control stockholders have over the typical large firm to raise managerial salaries or pad expense accounts. On labor's side, it has been argued that unionized workers extract higher pay from concentrated than from unconcentrated industries. As in the case of excess profit, these several excesses may have significant *distributive consequences* depending on the financial strengths of the beneficiaries and the financial weaknesses of owners or consumers who ultimately pay the higher costs.

4. *Cost that is waste:* A second cost element and the final possible destination of lost consumers' surplus is *technical inefficiency* or *X-inefficiency*—that is, the use of more labor, more materials, and more resources than are necessary to produce a given output. This X-inefficiency also shows up in space C_mBDC_c. Monopoly could easily give rise to such waste because, in a word, market power permits "slack." Moreover, it has been argued that monopoly power fosters waste because those who seek such power must expend resources to get it and keep it. Thus resources are burned up when established oligopolists escalate their advertising outlays to fight off new entrants. And labor time spent running cartels is a real cost.

Of these four destinations for lost consumers' surplus, the first two have already been traced. Most of the remainder of this chapter is about the last two, which share area C_mBDC_c in Figure 19–3. Excess wages are taken up first, then X-inefficiency. We shall not explore managerial salaries further, so we should at least mention here that high concentration and high barriers to entry apparently do boost top executives' compensation.[40]

B. Unions, Concentration, and Wages

To some degree labor markets are much like product markets. They have demands and supplies; they have power problems, and so on. What, then, causes the wage rate of a steel worker to exceed the combined hourly earnings of a Greek philosopher and a McDonald's counter attendant? Researchers have uncovered a vast array of variables affecting relative wage earnings. These include skill level, productivity, geographic location, plant size, value of product produced, education, scholastic achievement, work conditions, race, sex, risk to life and limb, and legal regulations. To determine the influence of unionism on the labor supply side or concentration on the labor demand side, these and other factors must first be accounted for. As with price and profit research, there are many ways to skin this cat. Most of them are variants of multiple regression analysis, which allows researchers to control for "other" factors.

The market power hypotheses that have been so tested may be divided into three classes: (1) the wage impact of unionism, (2) the wage impact of product

[40] Oliver E. Williamson, *The Economics of Discretionary Behavior: Managerial Objectives in a Theory of the Firm* (Chicago: Markham Publishing Co., 1967), pp. 129–134.

market concentration, and (3) the *interactive* effect of unions *and* product market concentration.

(1) Impact of Unions on Wages. The hypotheses concerning unionism alone are most obvious. Workers unionize, that is, join together, to speak with one voice, threaten to walk out as one group, and restrict labor supply to one source so that they can demand and obtain higher wages than would otherwise be paid. To the extent unions succeed in raising members' wages they may be simultaneously *reducing* nonunion wages. To gain higher wages, unions restrict the number of people who can compete for available jobs in unionized trades. This restriction forces workers who are excluded to seek work elsewhere. Consequently, the reduced union supply may raise union wages but the increased supply of nonunion workers tends to depress nonunion wages. The usual measure of union impact is therefore *relative* wage, the union wage compared to nonunion wage (everything else held constant).

The most widely cited estimate of union impact is that of H. G. Lewis, who reckoned that for the period 1957–1958 unions enjoyed a relative wage advantage somewhere in the neighborhood of 10–15%.[41] Subsequent studies using better data have estimated still larger union-nonunion wage differentials.[42] One, for example, estimated average differentials for "craftsmen" and "operatives" of about 30%.[43] Another estimated union/nonunion wage differentials ranging between 16 and 25%.[44] Of course not all unions are equally powerful, and these estimates must be qualified by the observation that weak unions, such as the United Farm Workers, tend to gain very little, whereas particularly strong unions, such as the United Steelworkers, may achieve relative wages even above the 25–30% range.

(2) The Wage Impact of Product Market Concentration. The impact of concentration is more complicated. Theories concerning the impact of product market concentration yield ambiguous indications. On the one hand, high concentration might foster high wages for reasons of "ability to pay." These reasons are (1) the ability of concentrated industries to pass excess wage costs on to customers, and (2) the ability to pay excess wages out of excess profits. Some confirmation

[41] H. G. Lewis, *Unionism and Relative Wages in the United States* (Chicago: University of Chicago Press, 1963).

[42] Frank Stafford, "Concentration and Labor Earnings: Comment," *American Economic Review* (March 1968), pp. 174–180; Victor Fuchs, *The Service Economy* (New York: National Bureau of Economic Research, 1968), Chapter 6; and Adrian Throop, "The Union-Nonunion Wage Differential and Cost Push Inflation," *American Economic Review* (March 1968), pp. 79–99.

[43] Leonard W. Weiss, "Concentration and Labor Earnings," *American Economic Review* (March 1966), pp. 96–117.

[44] Sherwin Rosen, "On the Interindustry Wage and Hours Structure," *Journal of Political Economy* (March 1969), pp. 249–273; "Trade Union Power, Threat Effects and the Extent of Organization," *Review of Economic Studies* (April 1969), pp. 185–196. See also Lawrence M. Kahn, "Unionism and Relative Wages: Direct and Indirect Effects," *Industrial and Labor Relations Review* (July 1979), pp. 520–532.

of a positive concentration-wage relation is provided by a number of studies.[45] Charles Haworth and Carol Reuther, for instance, find roughly 8% higher wages where four-firm concentration is 80 as compared to 40 (during 1958). Furthermore, Haworth and Reuther show that, like profits, this positive relation weakens markedly during spurts of expansion or inflation (something to which we shall return in Chapter 21).

On the other hand, "ability to pay" does not necessarily dictate actuality. Many oligopolists may be able but *un*willing to pay extra. In particular, concentration in the product market often means there is concentration on the employer's side of the labor market as well—that is, there are few purchasers of that type of labor. And much conventional theory predicts that such monopsony (or oligopsony) power will *depress* wage rates rather than lift them. Empirically, several studies show that monopsony power has a negative wage impact at least in some instances.[46]

(3) Interactive Impact. A moment's reflection reveals why the preceding discussion of unionism and product market concentration is incomplete. It treats unionism and concentration as wholly independent variables. In fact, they are not independent. They are interactive. The influence of one often depends on the strength of the other. Consider unionization first. *The positive wage impact of unions is likely to be meager where concentration is low but great where concentration is high.* The main reason for this is that competitive firms tend to lack both the ability and the inclination to pay excess wage rates. Unless unionization of the industry is complete, the unionized firm in a competitive industry will go out of business if it pays generous union wages while its rivals do not. Even if all existing firms in a competitive industry are unionized, the threat of fairly easy nonunion entry may check the union's power. Then too, the lack of excess profits may pose a further constraint. Hence, unions are likely to have greater positive wage impact in oligopoly industries, where employers act more nearly in unison, have the financial means to meet union demands, and enjoy substantial protection from interlopers.

Turning things around, the impact of product market concentration probably depends on the presence or absence of a strong union on the labor side. Assuming the incidence of monopsony power is positively associated with product market

---

[45] Leonard Rapping, "Monopoly Rents, Wage Rates, and Union Wage Effectiveness," *Quarterly Review of Economics and Business* (Spring 1967), pp. 31–47; Ira Horowitz, "An International Comparison of the Intranational Effects of Concentration on Industry Wages, Investment, and Sales," *Journal of Industrial Economics* (April 1971), pp. 166–178; Charles T. Haworth and Carol Reuther, "Industry Concentration and Interindustry Wage Determination," *Review of Economics and Statistics* (February 1978), pp. 85–95; and J. A. Dalton and E. J. Ford, Jr., "Concentration and Labor Earnings in Manufacturing and Utilities," *Industrial Labor Relations Review* (October 1977), pp. 45–60.

[46] John H. Landon, "The Effect of Product-Market Concentration on Wage Levels: An Intra-Industry Approach," *Industrial and Labor Relations Review* (January 1970), pp. 237–247; J. H. Landon and R. N. Baird, "Monopsony in the Market for Public School Teachers," *American Economic Review* (December 1971), pp. 966–971.

concentration, high concentration is more likely to depress wages in the absence of a union than in the presence of a union. Substantial buyer power, when unchecked by countervailing seller power, could have this effect. Introduction of a union, however, places power on *both* sides of the labor market. In the extreme, this creates "bilateral monopoly." And, in theory, the resulting wage is logically indeterminant. The union wants a high wage. The monopsonistic employers want a low wage. The resulting wage could be anywhere in between, depending on relative bargaining power. This suggests that the impact of concentration may be largely indeterminant, given union presence. On the other hand, it could be argued that wages will be positively associated with concentration under unionism. For reasons given earlier, such as "ability to pay," high concentration plus unionism is more likely to yield higher wages than is low concentration plus unionism.

Empirical exploration of these complex interactive effects is very difficult. Perhaps the best study to date is that of Wallace Hendricks.[47] He used disaggregated plant-level data on wage rates paid by 450 manufacturing firms in 47 different industries during 1970–1971. The wage rates used were wages per hour for specific occupations (for example, electrician, machinist, and painter). The results were broadly similar for all nine occupations studied, but Hendricks gives janitors special attention because the impact of market power was better isolated for them than for any other group. These results are summarized in Table 19–4. Concentration and unionism are each divided into three groups— low, moderate, and high. The numbers in the body of the table are *per cent* comparisons, where the low concentration and low unionism category is used as the basis for comparison. Thus, where unionism and concentration are both high, wages, are 19.5% higher, on average, than those under low-low conditions. The interactive effects may be seen by comparing the effects of unionism under alternative concentration conditions, then comparing concentration effects under alternative unionization conditions. Thus, unionism generally has a *positive* impact, but the *magnitude* of impact is much smaller where concentration is low than where it is high. High unionism raises wages 9.3 percentage points where concentration is low. But where concentration is high, the difference between high and low unionism is 27.5 percentage points (moving from −8.0 to +19.5).

As for concentration, it carries a positive then ultimately *negative* impact on wages where unionism is low, suggesting that monopsony power dominates where concentration is really high and unionism is low. On the other hand, concentration has an unambiguously *positive influence* on wages where unionism is high. In this latter case, wages are about 10 percentage points greater for high over low concentration (19.5 versus 9.3).

It appears from these data, then, that interactive effects do prevail. Although this makes generalizations hazardous, it can be concluded that *union power*

---

[47] Wallace Hendricks, "Labor Market Structure and Union Wage Levels," *Economic Inquiry* (September 1975), pp. 401–416. For European corroboration see A. P. Jacquemin and H. W. deJong, *European Industrial Organization* (New York: Wiley & Sons, 1977), p. 145.

TABLE 19–4. Impact of Product Market Concentration and
Unionism on Hourly Wage Rates: Per Cent Comparisons

	Unionism		
Concentration	Low	Moderate	High
Low	0 (base)	0.9	9.3
Moderate	7.0	14.1	13.6
High	−8.0	10.6	19.5

Source: Calculated from Wallace Hendricks, "Labor Market Structure
and Union Wage Levels," *Economic Inquiry* (September 1975), pp. 401–416.

usually raises wages. As regards concentration, it can go either way. But because
concentration seems to foster unionism (the positive correlation in manufacturing
runs in the 0.4–0.7 range), and because more often than not concentration's
direct impact is positive, it may also be concluded that, on balance, *high concentration produces relatively high wages* as well as high profits. By one estimate,
7 to 14 per cent of the excess revenue generated by monopoly power in industry
goes to labor in those power laden industries.[48] The gains seem to come largely
at the expense of powerless, nonunionized workers and consumers.

III. X-INEFFICIENCY LOSSES DUE TO MARKET POWER

A. Introduction and Theory

X-inefficiency is a form of deadweight loss. Value is not merely transferred
from one party to another; it is lost to all. This deadweight loss is, in a word,
waste. According to Harvey Leibenstein, who coined the term, **X-inefficiency**
means "the extent to which a given set of inputs do not get to be combined
in such a way so as to lead to maximum output."[49] When inputs are not producing
the maximum output possible, there is error, inertia, spoilage, slovenliness, disor-
der, delay, ineptitude, or something similar. As a result, costs are higher than
otherwise.

It should be stressed that the X-inefficiency concept is not necessarily, or
even usually, applied to cost problems that could be cured by massive alterations
of plant scale, by adoption of new technology, or by invention of new technology.
Think of it rather as a problem of weak motivation and resource misallocation
internal to the firm. Leibenstein points to the vast efficiency gains that plants
and firms have achieved by "simple reorganizations of the production process
such as plant-layout reorganization, materials handling, waste controls, work

---

[48] Thomas A. Pugel, "Profitability, Concentration and the Interindustry Variation in Wages,"
Review of Economics and Statistics (May 1980), pp. 248–253.
[49] Harvey Leibenstein, "Competition and X-Efficiency," *Journal of Political Economy* (May
1973), p. 766.

methods, and payments by results."[50] Viewed more broadly, X-inefficiency could reasonably include all forms of pure resource waste: excessive advertising, superfluous packaging, redundant plant capacity, and so on.

How does this dimension of performance relate to competition? We have already answered the question as it pertains to advertising and nonprice competition generally. As regards other forms of waste, theory postulates on at least two grounds that costs are *lower* whenever firms face intense competition:

> In the first place, the process of competition tends to eliminate high-cost producers, while the existence of substantial market power often allows such firms to remain in business. . . . Second, the process of competition, by mounting pressures on firm profits, tends to discipline managements *and employees* to utilize their inputs, and put forth more energetically and more effectively than is the case where this pressure is absent.[51]

In other words, the "carrot" of greater profits may dangle before all firms seeking to minimize cost, but only the "stick" swung by competition *forces* firms to pursue that objective.

B. Evidence

Tales of business woe constitute some of the most engrossing evidence to this effect. Large, powerful firms often coast merrily along until new entry, flagging demand, or some similar contingency leads to the discovery that costs can be cut drastically without cutting output by so much as one unit. You could build a bulky file of such evidence merely by reading *Business Week,* from which the following examples are taken:

- Suffering from the slap of new entry and slipping profits, Xerox launched a cost cutting drive for the *first time* in its history in 1975. Its Chairman admitted that Xerox was suffering from "sloppy" internal practices and corporate "fat" that had developed during the easy days. Among other things the company fired 8,000 employees; deferred construction of a lush new headquarters; sharpened its inventory control; and scrapped plans for a new plant, all while sales grew.[52]

- When Don Burnham took over as chief executive of Westinghouse in 1963, "the company was languishing on a five-year plateau of $2 billion in sales and earning only 5% on equity. By breaking organizational bottlenecks at the top, introducing more productive manufacturing processes, and slashing overhead, including more than 3,000 people, Burnham doubled Westinghouse's return on equity within two years to 10%."[53]

- Shell Oil Company sustained some profit setbacks on worldwide operations

---

[50] Harvey Leibenstein, *Beyond Economic Man* (Cambridge, Mass.: Harvard University Press, 1976), p. 37.
[51] W. S. Comanor and H. Leibenstein, "Allocative Efficiency, X-Efficiency and the Measurement of Welfare Losses," *Economica* (August 1969), p. 304.
[52] *Business Week,* April 5, 1976, pp. 60–66.
[53] *Business Week,* July 20, 1974, p. 56.

during the 1960s, whereupon it discovered it could eliminate job duplication by consolidating its British and Dutch head offices and reduce its workforce from 214,000 to 170,000 while increasing output. The result: labor cost savings of 32% per barrel.[54]

Further examples of competitive impact come from cartel case studies. A study of price fixing in the gymnasium seating, rock salt, and structural steel industries found cost increases of 10–23% due to competition's strangulation.[55] A massive study of cartel records concluded that available evidence "indicates that the characteristic purposes of cartels point away from efficiency and that their activities tend to diminish efficiency."[56] A research team headed by F. M. Scherer recently uncovered numerous examples of excessive costs due to cartelization in Europe. Citing cases from cigarettes, steel, paint, glass bottles, and cement, Scherer's group concluded, "Our interviews provided *considerable* qualitative evidence that pure X-inefficiency was a *significant* cause of productivity differentials."[57]

Intermarket statistical assessments of X-inefficiency are difficult to devise. Although data on market structure are commonplace, data isolating efficiency are not. Data on costs offer a substitute for data on efficiency, but only a very imperfect substitute because costs are influenced by factors other than efficiency—factors such as wage rates, materials prices, and plant location. Nevertheless, statistical studies have conquered these problems. So far they all indicate that *X-inefficiency is positively associated with market power.* The data shown earlier in Table 19–3 provide one example. Costs of grocery retailing rise with local market concentration, as indicated by the discrepancy between price and profit behavior. And the authors of the study from which those data were taken could find no explanation other than X-inefficiency for the rise in costs.[58] Further examples follow:

[54] *Business Week,* March 8, 1969, pp. 56–57. For further examples involving other major companies see *Business Week* April 13, 1974, pp. 55–58; August 11, 1975, p. 38; August 18, 1975, pp. 80–82; November 3, 1975, pp. 92–93; November 10, 1975, p. 129; December 1, 1975, p. 38; May 10, 1976, p. 66; November 1, 1976, p. 65; June 19, 1978, pp. 116–118; May 7, 1979, pp. 94–97; February 2, 1981, pp. 91–92; December 21, 1981, pp. 69–73; *Washington Post,* February 11, 1973, p. E5; Carl Kaysen, *United States v. United Shoe Machinery Corporation* (Cambridge, Mass.: Harvard University Press, 1956), p. 128; G. Brock, *The U.S. Computer Industry 1954–1973* (Cambridge, Mass.: Ballinger Publishing Co., 1975), pp. 217–218; L. J. White, *The Automobile Industry Since 1945* (Cambridge, Mass.: Harvard University Press, 1971), p. 12; F. M. Scherer, A. Beckenstein, E. Kaufer, R. D. Murphy, *The Economics of Multi-Plant Operation* (Cambridge, Mass.: Harvard University Press, 1975), p. 299; *Fortune,* April 4, 1983, pp. 108–113.
[55] W. Bruce Erickson, "Price Fixing Conspiracies: Their Long-term Impact," *Journal of Industrial Economics* (March 1976), pp. 189–202.
[56] Corwin D. Edwards, *Economic and Political Aspects of International Cartels,* U.S. Senate, Subcommittee on War Mobilization of the Committee on Military Affairs, 78th Congress, Second Session (1944), p. 40.
[57] Scherer, Beckenstein, Kaufer, and Murphy, *op. cit.,* pp. 74–75, 168–169, 314–315 (emphasis added). For further evidence concerning European cartels see D. Swann, D. P. O'Brien, W. P. J. Maunder, and W. S. Howe, *Competition in British Industry* (London: Allen & Unwin, 1974).
[58] Besides the source of Table 19–3 see *Prices and Profits of Leading Retail Food Chains, 1970–74,* Hearings, Joint Economic Committee, 95th Congress, First Session (1977), especially pp. 88–89.

427

• Walter Primeaux carefully compared costs of electricity production in two separate sets of cities—those with electric utility *monopolies* and those with direct competition between *two firms* (of which there were 49 cities). He found "that average cost is reduced, at the mean, by 10.75 percent because of competition. This reflects a quantitative value of the presence of X-efficiency gained through competition."[59]

• Several studies of the commercial banking and savings and loan industries disclose that high concentration raises expenses for excess staff, furniture, equipment, and facilities.[60]

• Measuring X-inefficiency as the extent to which firms make more than justifiable use of capital-intensive means of production, and drawing upon data for Pakistani industries, Lawrence White found that "firms with market power do seem to be 'indulging' in more capital-intensive methods than are firms facing more competition."[61]

Economy-wide estimates of monopoly-induced X-inefficiency can only be very rough approximations. It does not seem unreasonable to assume, however, that such waste may amount to as much as 10% of costs where concentration is very high and 5% of costs where concentration is moderate. Compared with our earlier estimates of deadweight loss due to profit-provoked misallocation, these figures are obviously quite large. Conversion to competition would probably reduce X-inefficiency and thereby improve consumer welfare.

IV. JOB DISCRIMINATION

A. Introduction and Theory

To this point it has been assumed that social welfare is measurable solely in terms of *consumer* welfare. We have been concerned with the size of the consumers' pie (as determined by allocation and technical efficiency) and the sharing of its slices (wealth or income distribution). Although consumer welfare is obviously of critical importance, the experiences people face as *workers* may be equally momentous; many if not most people are preoccupied with their occupation.

[59] Walter J. Primeaux, "An Assessment of X-Efficiency Gained Through Competition," *Review of Economics and Statistics* (February 1977), pp. 105–108.
[60] Franklin R. Edwards, "Managerial Objectives in Regulated Industries: Expense-Preference Behavior in Banking," *Journal of Political Economy* (February 1977), pp. 147–162; C. A. Glassman and S. A. Rhoades, "Owner vs. Manager Control Effects on Bank Performance," *Review of Economics and Statistics* (May 1980), pp. 263–270; T. H. Hannan and F. Mavinga, "Expense Preference and Managerial Control," *Bell Journal of Economics* (Autumn 1980), pp. 671–682; J. A. Verbrugge and J. S. Jahera, Jr., "Expense-Preference Behavior in the Savings and Loan Industry," *Journal of Money, Credit, and Banking* (November 1981), pp. 465–476.
[61] Lawrence J. White, "Appropriate Technology, X-Inefficiency, and A Competitive Environment: Some Evidence from Pakistan," *Quarterly Journal of Economics* (November 1976), pp. 575–589. For still more evidence see R. E. Caves, "Industrial Organization, Corporate Strategy and Structure," *Journal of Economic Literature* (March 1980), pp. 64–92.

Discrimination in employment occurs whenever otherwise extraneous characteristics such as race, sex, or religion influence job placement, promotion, or pay scale. Conventional theory holds that discrimination would *not* arise under perfect competition, at least no more than in surrounding society:

> For firms operating under the constraints of perfect competition any significant indulgence of such preferences would impose extra costs and therefore ultimately be incompatible with the survival of the enterprise. Hiring by firms so constrained would be "neutral;" indeed, if Negro wage rates were relatively low because of discrimination elsewhere, Negroes would tend to be substituted at the margin for white employees with equal qualifications.[62]

As we have seen, market power removes these competitive constraints. Moreover, insofar as oligopolists pay unusually high wages to their workers generally, oligopolists may attract considerably more job applicants of acceptable quality than they can possibly hire. For these reasons the managers of *powerful firms have substantial discretionary power.* Consideration of extraneous characteristics may even be unavoidable. Thus, pretty secretaries are likely to win out over the ugly; well-groomed congenial people over the unkempt and uncouth; and brothers-in-law over the unknown. Whether or not this discretionary power takes socially harmful forms is largely indeterminate, since discretion can be used to *favor or disfavor* disadvantaged minorities:

> With economic constraints eased, and assuming interracial preferences to be negative and significant for at least some managers, then one may expect that . . . employment patterns will embody discrimination. . . . Yet, against this may be set the possibility that managers may exercise their discretion deliberately and "affirmatively" in the social interest, toward open hiring or even "positive" discrimination. The possible social motivation of the modern corporation might prevail in small monopolists as well as in very large oligopolists, and as the rule rather than as the exception. . . . In many cases, the conflicting tendencies within a firm with market power may, at least, yield a standoff between these alternative directions of hiring policy.[63]

B. The Evidence on Racial Discrimination

Which way, in fact, does the evidence indicate? Several studies suggest that during the 1960s and earlier, blacks experienced better chances of being hired in *competitive* industries than *non*competitive industries, other things equal.[64] Moreover, the discrepancies in hiring practices were particularly severe regarding higher skilled occupation categories, such as professionals, managers, and craftsmen (as compared with lower skilled groups such as laborers and sales workers).

[62] William G. Shepherd, *Market Power & Economic Welfare* (New York: Random House, 1970), pp. 213–214.

[63] *Ibid.,* pp. 214–215.

[64] Gary S. Becker, *The Economics of Discrimination* (Chicago: University of Chicago Press, 1957), pp. 31–46; W. S. Comanor, "Racial Discrimination in American Industry," *Economica* (November 1973), pp. 363–378; W. G. Shepherd, "Market Power and Racial Discrimination in White-Collar Employment," *Antitrust Bulletin* (Spring 1969), pp. 141–161; Marshall H. Medoff, "On the Relationship Between Discrimination and Market Structure," *Southern Economic Journal* (April 1980), pp. 1,227–1,234.

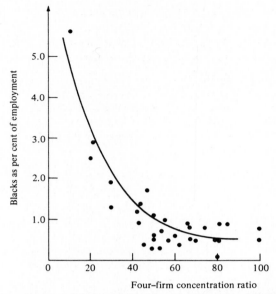

FIGURE 19–4. Industry concentration and black employment as officials, managers, and professionals in nine major cities in 1966. Source: William G. Shepherd, *Market Power and Economic Welfare* (New York: Random House, 1970), p. 221.

Thus, data for the South in 1940 indicate that competitive industries hired *skilled* blacks at a rate *four to eight times* higher than monopolistic industries, whereas competitive industries generally hired *un*skilled blacks at a rate roughly *two times* higher than monopolistic industries. Some findings for 1966 are shown in Figure 19–4. There it may be seen that as concentration rises, the per cent of total official, managerial, and professional employment accounted for by blacks falls.

Since the 1960s, the plight of nonwhites may have improved in virtually all markets, especially noncompetitive markets. Prodded by massive changes in public policy and public opinion, it appears that the discretionary power of noncompetitive firms has pivoted toward improvement.[65]

C. The Evidence on Sex Discrimination

The empirical evidence concerning women is, broadly speaking, similar to that concerning racial minorities. The percentage of females in white collar positions—especially official, management, and professional—*declines* as concen-

[65] See W. G. Shepherd and Sharon G. Levin, "Managerial Discrimination in Large Firms," *Review of Economics and Statistics* (November 1973), pp. 412–422. This paper also shows that on a firm-by-firm basis the effect of concentration is murky. But notice the limited range of size in their sample.

430

tration rises. By some estimates the pattern of decline is nonlinear, as in Figure 19–4.[66]

It must be stressed that these findings on sex and race discrimination relate to *job* discrimination not *wage* discrimination. There are no good theoretical reasons to expect that wages for workers working elbow-to-elbow with each other would differ under market power according to whether those workers were black or white, female or male. And, indeed, research indicates that market power has no impact on wage discrimination, only job discrimination.[67] This, of course, does not make the job discrimination any better.

SUMMARY

This chapter is somewhat like the punchline of a cruel joke. Previous chapters left open the question of market power's impact on *how well* markets work. Now its impact regarding several major measures of performance has been disclosed.

In consumer welfare, market power leads to lost consumer surplus. Surplus is lost because higher prices and lower output prevail under concentration than under competition. The higher prices are due to excess profits, excess wages, excess managerial salaries, and X-inefficiency. The destination of the lost consumers' surplus depends largely on the relative effect of each cause. Excess profits go to those controlling ownership shares. Since roughly 2.4% of the populace controls 50% of all business ownership shares, this transfer from consumers to owners tends to warp the distribution of income and wealth. Excess wages and salaries go to workers and managers in unionized-concentrated industries. These transfers may likewise contribute to maldistribution, but to an unknown extent. Exorbitant costs due to X-inefficiency go to no purpose whatever. They are a form of deadweight loss because they represent resources needlessly consumed.

Yet another form of deadweight loss (and of lost consumers' surplus) is attributable to misallocation of resources. Triangles *ABC* and *AED* in Figures 19–1 and 19–3 signify these losses. Unlike the other losses, these are not directly measurable in dollars, but they are no less real.

If one were to hazard a guess as to how much all these losses of consumers' surplus amounted to, something in the neighborhood of 7–10% of GNP might be reasonable, at least in times past. Individual contributions might be as follows: excess profits, 1–3%; excess wages and salaries, 2–3%; X-inefficiency 3–4%;

---

[66] William A. Luksetich, "Market Power and Sex Discrimination in White-Collar Employment," *Review of Social Economy* (October 1979), pp. 211–224.

[67] William R. Johnson, "Racial Wage Discrimination and Industrial Structure," *Bell Journal of Economics* (Spring 1978), pp. 70–81; E. T. Fujii and J. M. Trapani, "On Estimating the Relationship Between Discrimination and Market Structure," *Southern Economic Journal* (January 1978), pp. 556–567.

and misallocation 0.5–1%. To the extent competition in the economy has recently improved, these numbers might improve.

Finally, market power appears to affect worker equity and welfare as well. In the not too distant past, minorities suffered disproportionate discrimination at the hands of oligopolists and monopolists. Vestiges of this discrimination probably persist. But, again, improvements may be taking place.

20

Profits and Policy: Public Utility Regulation

The Supreme Power who conceived gravity, supply and demand, and the double helix must have been absorbed elsewhere when public utility regulation was invented.

—F. M. SCHERER

Public utility regulation is an industrial halfway house. Its residents are sheltered from the cruelties of all-out competition, yet they are not crushed by total government control. Private firms own and operate enterprises, while state and federal governments police structure, conduct, and performance for purposes other than maintaining competition.

Profit level and price structure are the main concerns of utility regulation. Utility regulation also covers such additional matters as accounting procedures, entry, exit, and quality of service.[1] But these we must neglect. Hence our outline:

- I. What industries are regulated?
- II. Why regulate?
- III. Who regulates?
- IV. How: Price level regulation?
- V. How: Price structure regulation?
- VI. Problems and distortions.

I. WHAT INDUSTRIES ARE REGULATED?

Electricity, natural gas, telecommunications, broadcast communications, and railroading are at present the main industries subject to regulation. Together they account for over $60 billion in business annually, or about 4% of national income. In the recent past, airlines, common carrier trucks, and intercity buses

---

[1] For an excellent complete treatment see Alfred E. Kahn, *The Economics of Regulation,* Vols. I and II (New York: Wiley & Sons, 1970, 1971). At a less advanced level look into Charles F. Phillips, Jr., *The Economics of Regulation* (Homewood, Ill.: R. Irwin, 1969).

433

were also regulated, but *de*regulation has now effectively freed them. Indeed, the railroads have been partially deregulated, so our attention will center on what are often called "utilities"—local electric, gas, and telephone services.

Several characteristics of these industries set them apart from most others. First, they are usually considered **vital** industries. To be sure, food and clothing (and books) are equally vital yet unregulated, but communications and energy are necessities not to be sneezed at.

Second, nearly all regulated industries sell **services** rather than commodities. Unlike commodities, services cannot be stored. Their production and consumption coincide inseparably. Most regulated industries must therefore maintain excess capacity to meet peak periods of consumption. In many cases they must also maintain direct connections by wire or pipe with their customers.

Third, most regulated industries are **capital intensive.** The guts of their operations are cables, turbine generators, switches, steel rails, and road beds rather than mill hands, raw materials, or merchandise.

II. WHY REGULATE?

The selection of industries to regulate rests with government legislatures. State authority is based on "police power." Federal authority is based on the Constitution's commerce clause, which gives Congress the right "to regulate commerce . . . among the several states." Court interpretations of these powers are now quite liberal. Legislatures may impose regulation for just about any reason that strikes their fancy, subject only to the loose constraint that the industries selected must be "clothed with a public interest." Given such flexibility, the regulatory net is woven from diverse strands of reasoning. Despite the rational diversity, the most commonly cited reasons for regulation can be collected under four categories: (1) natural monopoly, (2) conservation of a publicly owned natural resource, (3) destructive competition, and (4) sharp public indignation against "unfairness."

A. Natural Monopoly

In some situations, economic or technical conditions permit only one efficient supplier, leading to "natural monopoly." The most obvious cause of natural monopoly is substantial economies of scale relative to demand. That is, cost per unit of output declines continuously as scale of operations increases. This is shown in Figure 20–1, where, throughout the range of quantity demanded, long-run average and marginal costs fall for a single firm. Two firms could supply the market's requirements at high price P_2, but only at lofty unit costs. A competitive dual between two such firms could be won handily by the largest rival because greater size brings lower cost, enabling the larger firm to price below its competitor's cost. At price P_1 in Figure 20–1, a sole survivor could meet *all* market demand at a point where the unit cost curve is still falling as a function of output. There is, then, room for only one efficient enterprise.

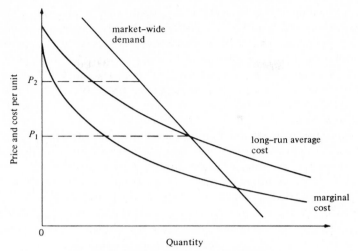

FIGURE 20–1. Decreasing cost industry.

Among regulated industries, costs decline as scale increases for local water, electric power, gas, telephone, and cable TV. The technology of transmission and the physical fact of direct connection are the main causes of this cost effect. Cables, pipelines, and other conduits have transmission capacities that grow *more* than proportionately to size or material makeup. As a consequence, the least expensive way to transmit electricity, gas, water, or telephone communications is through large lines. Furthermore, local distribution of these services requires direct connection to customers. Competition would therefore entail redundant line duplications, something obviously inefficient and wasteful—not to say inconvenient, ugly, and disruptive, given the excessive ditch digging, pipe laying, and wire hanging in which competition would entangle us.

An additional factor contributes to natural monopoly in local telephone service. For one caller to reach another, both must be connected to the same central switch. Almost by definition a central switch must be "central"—that is, monopolistic. With two competing phone companies, there would be *two* central switches. People having only one phone could then call only patrons of the same phone company. Comprehensive interconnection would require either two phones and two lines for everyone or cooperative switching between the central switches of the rival companies.

Although natural monopoly certainly explains much regulation, many natural monopolies are *not* regulated and, conversely, many regulated industries are *not* natural monopolies. Among the former, imagine an isolated small town so sparsely populated that demand can support no more than one movie theater. This might qualify as a natural monopoly. But such movie theaters escape regulation apparently because they offer something less than a "vital" service (there being other, perhaps even more enjoyable, things to do on a Saturday

435

night than watching movies, even in Hatband, Idaho). Among the latter, transportation services have a long history of regulation, but they cannot qualify as natural monopolies. Major air routes can be served efficiently by a flock of airlines. Trucking can be carried on at low cost by very small-scale operators. And, given the competitive potentials of air, truck, and bus transport, railroads cannot be considered natural monopolies either (even though, a century ago, they generally did fit that description). Thus *de*regulation of transportation should be welcomed.

Similarly, certain *segments* of natural monopoly industries are not naturally monopolistic. Telephone service has certain segments where competition is possible, even desirable. Monopoly is unnatural and unneeded when it comes to manufacturing telephone equipment, now a $10 billion business. The gadgetry ranges from Mickey Mouse phones to complicated PBX terminals, all within the low-cost capabilities of dozens of electronics firms besides AT&T. Long-distance telephone service (which, among other things, connects the central switches of separate cities) is another area ripe for competition, especially since the advent of modern microwave and satellite transmission systems. Unfortunately, regulation has stifled competition's full flower in such instances. But deregulation will change this too.

B. Resource Conservation

Regulation of radio and television broadcasting is grounded on a different rationale. Economic efficiency requires no more than small-scale local broadcasting. However, the radio spectrum used by broadcasters is a limited resource, with a limited number of band widths or channels. If broadcasters were granted free and unrestricted entry, they could very well flood the air waves, interfering with each other and garbling the reception of listeners and viewers. Accordingly, access to the spectrum is limited by licensing. Broadcasters, however, are not subject to price or profit control, only to entry restrictions. Moving farther afield, conservation has also served, rightly or wrongly, to justify past regulation in other areas, such as natural gas, oil, and water.

C. Destructive Competition

Certain characteristics of many regulated industries—their ponderous capital intensity and susceptibility to excess capacity in particular—expose them to dangers of destructive competition. At least that is what some defenders of regulation contend. Excess capacity is said to induce reckless price cutting. And heavy capital intensity translates into high fixed costs as a proportion of total cost. So once prices start to fall they can plummet deeply before bottoming at average variable cost. The argument concludes, therefore, that such industries will be plagued by periodic price wars financially destructive to producers and disruptive for consumers.

Notice that this argument cannot rationalize regulation in natural monopoly markets, because natural monopolies, once established, face no competition. Notice, too, that the argument is designed to justify *minimum* price regulation, not *maximum* price regulation (as in the case of natural monopolies). Hence, it is an argument that is vociferously applied to justify minimum price regulation in transportation. Yet, as many economists have pointed out, it is precisely in transportation that this line of argument is least valid. Take trucking for instance:

> Capital costs are relatively small compared to variable costs, so that unregulated truckers would not be likely to operate at prices much below cost. Also, the labor and capital resources employed in trucking can easily be shifted to alternative uses. In other industries with low fixed costs, such as retailing, prices seldom fall much below cost, and adjustments for changing market conditions are made quickly and with little disruption. In fact, this has been the case in trucking's unregulated sector, which ships agricultural products and has been quite free of "ruinous competition."[2]

In short, the argument has limited application.

D. Unfairness

Perhaps the only area where sharp price rivalry can create real problems is railroading. But the main problem is not necessarily bankruptcy. The story begins over a hundred years ago, before trucks and planes, when railroads lorded it over freight transportation. On some routes natural monopolies prevailed (because between any pair of cities railroads experience declining costs up to a point). On these natural monopoly routes, demand was insufficient to support more than one low-cost company. On other routes, such as those between New York and Chicago, traffic volume was big enough to attract and nurture competition. Given railroads' steep fixed costs, conditions on these latter routes were right for rambunctious, if not completely ruinous, price rivalry. During the 1870s, for instance, a price war broke out on eastbound grain shipments between Chicago and New York, causing rates to fall from $0.56 to $0.15 per hundredweight and even lower.[3]

In short, railroading in that era fitted two contrasting models depending on route circumstances—the natural monopoly model or the ruinous competition model. The result was a grossly discriminatory railroad rate structure. Towns without rail competition were charged higher rates than those blessed with two or more railroads. Indeed, in many instances rates on noncompetitive short hauls exceeded those on competitive long hauls, despite one's common sense expectation that rates should rise with distance since costs rise with distance. Moreover, large shippers were able to extract more favorable rates than small shippers. Folks on the unfavorable side of the tracks found these several discrepancies "monstrous," "evil," and "unfair." Their clamor caused Congress to pass the Interstate Commerce Act in 1887, which established the Interstate Commerce Commission and directed that rates approved by the Commission be "just and reasonable." That is, the Act outlawed personal discrimination and prohibited short-haul rates in excess of long-haul rates "under substantially

[2] L. W. Weiss and A. D. Strickland, *Regulation: A Case Approach* (New York: McGraw-Hill Book Co., 1976), p. 6.

[3] Paul W. MacAvoy, *The Economic Effects of Regulation: The Trunkline Railroad Cartels and the Interstate Commerce Commission Before 1900,* (Cambridge, Mass.: MIT Press, 1965).

similar circumstances." The importance of "fairness" in motivating this historic first step toward federal regulation may be seen in the fact that Congress made no explicit provision for the ICC to fix maximum overall rate levels until 20 years later with passage of the Hepburn Act of 1906.

In truth, "fairness," or some variant of it, has probably had a hand in motivating most subsequent regulation as well. A principal proponent of this view is Donald Dewey, who contends that citizens' expectations of regulation go well beyond protection from economic exploitation or resource conservation:

> [First] we expect group therapy—a release of tension and frustrations. . . . Fortunately, plenty of angry people in this world would rather testify at a public hearing—preferably before a TV camera—than blow up buildings or beat their kids.
>
> Second, we expect regulation to protect us from the kind of sharp commercial practice that is generally impossible in competitive industries. . . . The Penn Central Railroad will never refund a nickel for a breakdown in service unless it is compelled to do so by a Utility Commission.
>
> Third, we expect regulation to mitigate some of the consequences of the bureaucratization that comes with great size. To say the obvious, in any organization mistakes are made, and the larger the organization, the more difficult it is to pinpoint the responsibility for error. A complaint to a regulatory body is one way that the consumer has of striking back. . . .

In short, it may well be that "as citizens we wish the regulatory agency to serve as a forum for group therapy, a better business bureau, a check on bureaucracy, and a brake on economic and social change."[4]

III. WHO REGULATES?

The vast bulk of regulatory power rests with independent regulatory commissions. They are neither legislative, judicial, nor administrative. Rather, the duties of these commissions run the gamut of governmental classifications. They make rules and thereby legislate; they hold hearings or adversary proceedings and thereafter adjudicate; they enforce regulatory laws and thereby administer.

Although commission duties are thus typically broad, their scope of jurisdiction is often narrow. One major division of jurisdiction concerns geography. State regulatory commissions govern *intra*state commerce, whereas federal agencies oversee *inter*state commerce. Product or service determines a second division. Many commissions regulate only one type of utility, or a limited class of utilities. As shown in Table 20–1, the Interstate Commerce Commission regulates interstate land transportation (and some waterway carriers); the Federal Energy Regulatory Commission regulates interstate transmission and wholesale price of electricity, and rates and routes of natural gas pipelines; the Federal Communi-

---

[4] Donald J. Dewey, "Regulatory Reform?" in *Regulation in Further Perspective*, edited by Shepherd and Gies (Cambridge, Mass.: Ballinger Publishing Co., 1974), pp. 35–37. See also Bruce Owen and Ronald Braeutigam, *The Regulation Game* (Cambridge, Mass.: Ballinger, 1978), pp. 26–29.

TABLE 20–1. The main Federal Commissions and Selected State Commissions (Circa 1980)

Commission (and year of origin)	Number of Members	Number of Staff Members	Jurisdiction
Federal Commissions			
Interstate Commerce Commission (1887)	11	2,024	Railroads; some water shipping and trucking (with powers diminishing).
Federal Energy Regulatory Commission (formerly the Federal Power Commission, 1934)	5	1,813	Electric power; some gas and pipelines.
Federal Communications Commission (1934)	7	2,088	Telephone; television; radio; telegraph.
Civil Aeronautics Board (1938)	5	745	Airlines (with powers phasing out completely by 1985).
Selected State Commissions			
California (1912)	5	900	Electric, gas, telephone, railroads, buses, docks, water carriers, and more.
Colorado (1913)	3	95	Electric, gas, telephone, telegraph, water, buses, taxis, railroads.
Florida (1887)	5	434	Electric, gas, telephone, telegraph, water, sewer, buses, trucks, railroads, and more.
Indiana (1907)	3	103	Electric, gas, telephone, water, buses, railroads, and more.
Massachusetts (1885)	3	122	Electric, gas, telephone, railroads, buses, trucks, taxis, water.
Pennsylvania (1908)	5	599	Electric, gas, telephone, telegraph, water, sewer, docks, airlines, buses, taxis, railroads, and more.

Source: R. J. Penoyer, *Directory of Federal Regulatory Agencies* (St. Louis: Center for the Study of American Business, Washington University, 1980); National Association of Regulatory Utility Commissioners, *1978 Annual Report on Utility and Carrier Regulation* (1979).

cations Commission licenses broadcasters and regulates interstate (long-distance) telephone and telegraph rates and levels of service; and the Civil Aeronautics Board has jurisdiction over all interstate air passenger service.

State commissions, as shown in Table 20–1, are often less narrowly specialized. With varying scope their main concerns are *local* gas, electric, telephone, water, and transit utilities. State or federal, the U.S. Supreme Court summarized the commission concept when it said that these agencies were "created with the avowed purpose of lodging functions in a body specifically competent to deal with them by reason of information, experience and careful study of the business and economic conditions of the industry affected."[5]

Commission panels usually consist of five to eleven members appointed to fixed terms by either the President (for federal posts) or the Governor (for state posts, although several states *elect* commissioners). With but few exceptions, the commissioners so selected do not fit the ideal image of objective experts. Some appointments are even humorous. A nominee for the Federal Communications Commission was asked during his Senate confirmation hearing about his qualifications in communications. "Senator," he replied, "I don't know anything about communications. I came to Washington expecting to be appointed to the Federal Power Commission."[6]

Commissioners are aided by staffs of civil servants comprising mainly accountants, engineers, lawyers, and economists. Many critics of regulation contend that commissions cannot do an adequate job because both staffers and commissioners are underpaid and overworked. The utilities they regulate can well afford personnel. Hence, control of corporate giants with this feeble machinery has been called herding elephants with flyswatters.[7]

Still, commission personnel do not deserve all the blame for regulation's shortcomings. Many legislative mandates under which commissions work are vague or misguided. What is more, the task of regulation is *inherently* difficult. There is no regulatory cookbook with recipes for every occasion, no utility child-care guide. There are a few principles, plus plenty of questions lacking pat answers. It is to these that we now turn. The discussion is divided into two topics: (1) rate level, and (2) rate structure. **Rate level** refers to *overall* revenues, costs, and returns. **Rate structure** refers to the *specific prices charged* to specific customers for specific services at specific times.

IV. HOW: RATE LEVEL REGULATION

A. Objectives

There are any number of objectives that *could* guide rate level regulation. Among the more obvious possibilities are speedy growth in service, conservation

---

[5] *Federal Trade Commission v. R. F. Keppel and Bros. Inc.*, 291 U.S. 304, 314 (1934).
[6] Louis M. Kohlmeier, Jr., *The Regulators* (New York: Harper & Row, 1969), p. 48.
[7] B. C. Moore, Jr., "AT & T: The Phony Monopoly," in *Monopoly Makers*, edited by M. J. Green (New York: Grossman, 1973), p. 82.

of energy, and optimal allocation of resources in the strict economic sense. For one reason or another, however, *none* of these is the main objective applied in practice. The main objective is to allow the utility sufficient revenues to pay its "full" costs plus a "fair" return on the "fair" value of its capital. Stated differently, *the main objective is to strike a reasonable balance between the interests of consumers* (who should not be gouged by monopoly exploitation) *and the interests of the utility investors and operators* (who should not be cheated by overzealous commissions, or who, in more legalistic language, should not be deprived of their property without "due process of law").

The effort to balance is captured in a simple equation:

$$\text{Total revenue} = \text{operating expenses} + \text{current depreciation}$$

$$+ (\text{capital value} \times \text{rate of return}) \qquad (20\text{--}1)$$

Note that, on the right hand side, operating expenses and current depreciation are both *annual dollar flows.* Capital value is not a dollar flow. It is the asset value of the utility firm at a *given point in time,* also called the **rate base.** However, once this capital value is multiplied by the allowed rate of return (such as 0.10, for 10% per year), the result *is* an annual dollar flow. Thus, the basic problem of rate level regulation is to see to it that the annual flow of total revenue covers the annual flow of "full cost," including depreciation, plus a "fair" or "reasonable" return on capital value, no more and no less.

Generally speaking the owners or operators would like to see "more," which means that their interests lie with *high* estimates of the elements on the right hand side. Consumers, on the other hand, would like to see "less" because their interests are generally served by *low* figures for these elements. It is the job of the commission to balance these conflicting interests—to determine that operating expenses, current depreciation, capital value, and rate of return may be neither too high nor too low, and then to permit a rate level that generates the necessary total revenue. Note that if rates are pressed *too* low, service could suffer and the firm could go bankrupt, injuring everyone involved.

The situation may be seen in Figure 20–2 (which is a total dollar view, not a per unit dollar view as in Figure 20–1). The total payments (or total cost) curve has three components corresponding to the right-hand side of the equation (20–1). Thus, utility payments include a fair or normal profit (which is embodied in rate base × per cent return). An *un*regulated, profit maximizing monopolist would charge an overall price level to yield an output of Q_u, placing the firm at point A on the total revenue curve. Excess profit there would be vertical distance AB. The objective of regulation is to lower price level below the monopolist's profit maximizing price, thereby moving the firm from A to C. At point C, total revenue and total payments, including no more than a fair return, just match. Output is greater at Q_r, and consumers are not exploited. At price levels still lower, output would be still greater but total revenue would fall to unreasonably low levels, hurting the utility's investors. The process does

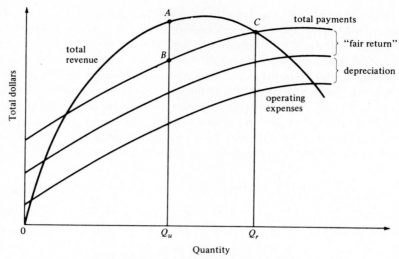

FIGURE 20–2. Rate level regulation.

not exactly simulate competitive results, but it may be helpful to think of it in that way.

Now, to appreciate fully the problems encountered in the regulatory process, each item of rate level decision making needs to be discussed. We begin with operating expenses.

B. Operating Expenses

Operating expenses are to some degree the easiest of all items for a commission to determine. They include such things as fuel costs (for coal, oil, and gas), workers' wages, managers' salaries, materials expense, advertising, and taxes. Together these expenses typically absorb 70–90% of a utility's total operating revenue. They are relatively easy to determine because few such expenses can be padded or faked. Taxes, for example, are beyond the utility's control and therefore unquestioned. Similarly, the costs of fuel are shaped in open markets, and workers' wages are settled by collective bargaining. These, too, are rarely questioned by commissions.

One does not have to go very far down the list of expenses, however, before one encounters snarls. How much should be allowed for advertising? Does a monopolist need to advertise at all? What about public relations advertising, which tells us that little six-year old Suzy is a "typical" AT & T stock holder, that Giant Electric is doing everything possible to clean up the environment but smoke-stack scrubbers ought to be scrubbed, and that *public* ownership of utilities is sinful? Does the tab for these ads belong to consumers or investors? How much should be allowed for executive salaries, executive secretaries, executive jets, and executive travel? Should the gasoline expenses of corporate Cadillacs be approved when economical Pintos would do? Should all worker wage rates be approved? Is it not possible that telephone repairmen could be overpaid? And what about the costs of company lawyers and accountants who represent the utility before the commission? Should consumers pay the company's costs of coping with regulation when these costs support efforts contrary to the consumers' interest? What about donations to charities? Does not "good corporate citizenship" require that community causes be supported? But if it does, what worthy causes should be blessed, in what dollar amounts, and what share of this burden should be borne by consumers?

Answers to these and a stream of similar questions are tricky. Some of these expenses are partly "legitimate," but where does one draw the line? Commissions' answers vary widely, as you might guess.

C. Current Depreciation

Current depreciation is an important item of cost because most utilities have a high capital intensity. For all utilities current depreciation amounts to almost 10% of total sales revenue as against only about 3% for all manufacturing.[8]

No one disputes the necessity of including depreciation as a cost. In one sense, depreciation accounts for the "using up" of capital assets through wear and tear or obsolescence. In another sense, depreciation may be thought of as a payment to capital investors, much as wages, salaries, and materials expenses are payments to other factor suppliers. This means that, of the elements in the summary equation, *both* current depreciation *and* capital value times rate of return go to the investors. As Alfred Kahn explains, "The return to capital . . . has two parts: the return *of* the money capital invested over the estimated economic life of the investment and the return (interest and profit) *on* the portion of the investment that remains outstanding."[9]

Although no one disputes depreciation's inclusion as a cost, its computation is often more controversial than the computation of operating expenses. First, the allowance for depreciation is quite different from operating expenses. Whereas operating expenses entail *actual money outlays,* depreciation does not. It is an *imputed cost.* The portion of total revenues depreciation "permits the company to earn does not, as is the case with normal operating expenses, go out in payments to outside parties—suppliers of raw materials, workers and so on."[10] It goes instead to investors.

Second, since current depreciation is an imputation, there are no hard rules for its reckoning. The actual figure arrived at for any asset in any one year depends on three things: (1) the depreciation base, (2) the asset's estimated life span, and (3) the method of write-off during its life. Each element is judgmental; each is therefore open to dispute.

The depreciation base is the original cost of the asset less any salvage value

---

[8] Internal Revenue Service, *Statistics of Income, Corporation Income Tax Returns 1975* (preliminary) pp. 14–16.
[9] Kahn, *op. cit.,* Vol. I, p. 32.
[10] *Ibid.*

at life's end. Although original cost is straightforward, salvage value is a matter of estimate. Life-span, too, is a matter of estimate. A short life with no assumed salvage value would tend to favor investors over consumers because it would lead to large, early write-offs. Conversely, a long life with high salvage value favors consumers because it leads to small annual write-offs.

As for possible write-off methods, they are too numerous and too complex to summarize here. The major source of difference among them rests with whether the depreciation base is spread *evenly* or *un*evenly over the estimated life span.

It would be nice if there was an Eleventh Commandment to guide commissioners in all these reckonings, but there isn't.

D. Capital Value or Rate Base

Far and away the most controversial part of regulation concerns capital value times rate of return (or rate base × per cent return) because this is the computation that determines profit. The Supreme Court's legal guide to commissions is about as solid as natural gas. Specific estimates or formulas are not so important, says the Court. It's the *end result* that counts. The end result must be "just and reasonable." What is "just and reasonable"? Earnings "which enable the company to operate successfully, to maintain its financial integrity, to attract capital, and to compensate its investors for the risks assumed . . . even though they [the earnings] might produce only a meager return."[11]

This nebulous guide gives commissions great leeway in determining both capital value and rate of return. As regards capital value, there is a wide range of choice concerning (1) accounting devices, and (2) what is counted as real investment. Choice offers opportunities for the exercise of value judgment.

Accounting Devices. At least four methods for computing the rate base have been adopted or proposed:

1. *Original cost* values assets at their "actual" or "book" cost.
2. *Reproduction cost* is the estimated cost of buying, building, and installing the same equipment at today's prices.
3. *Replacement cost* is the estimated cost of replacing the present plant and equipment, much of which may be outdated, with the most efficient and reliable technology available, in amounts sufficient to supply the same service.
4. *Mixed method,* or "fair value," which is some combination, or rough averaging, of the items 1 through 3.

Subtractions for *accumulated* depreciation must be made under any of the options, which expands the horizon for judgment still further.

At present, most federal and state commissions apply the original cost approach, followed in popularity by mixed method. Still, future changes are possible, and the pros and cons of these techniques are endlessly debated. Among

---

[11] *Federal Power Commission v. Hope Natural Gas Co.,* 320 U.S. 591 (1944).

the major points at issue are (1) ease of estimation, (2) inflation, and (3) economic efficiency.

It should be obvious that original cost is the easiest of all methods to estimate (a fact that partly explains its great popularity). The replacement cost approach is undoubtedly the most difficult, because it amounts to little more than a playground for opinion. Reproduction cost lies somewhere in between.

Although original cost is most convenient, it is least competent in accounting for changes over time, especially plant and equipment price changes. During periods of inflation, consumers prefer and investors oppose original cost because it yields a *lower* rate base than the other techniques. On the other hand, during periods of deflation (now about as dated as dinosaurs), producers prefer original cost because it yields a *higher* rate base than the other techniques. What is correct? There is no secure answer, but it can be argued that reproduction cost, which does take inflation into account, might be better economically. Why? Because under the "ideal" of pure competition, industry price will move in the long run to a level that just covers costs plus a normal return on a *new* plant. Moreover, during periods of astounding inflation, original cost valuation might sink the rate base so low as to threaten the firm's viability.

Actually, on grounds of allocation efficiency, the replacement cost approach seems most attractive because the *new* plant alluded to should be one *incorporating the latest in new technology*. Although certainly favorable to replacement cost, this argument is undercut by the fact that the main purpose of regulation is *not* allocation efficiency. Commissions make no attempt to see that utility prices always match marginal cost. They only seek a "fair" balance between opposing parties.

Asset Inclusion. Regardless of accounting technique, there remains the question of what is to be included in the rate base. Buildings, cables, trucks, dams, generators, switches and the like obviously qualify. But what about the $1 billion nuclear power plant completed only a year ago but now shut down because geologists have just discovered an earthquake fault within one half mile of it? Who ought to pay for it? If the dead plant is included in the rate base, consumers will howl. If excluded, it would surely thrash investors. How would you decide as a commissioner? What, further, about *intangible* assets? Would you permit the cost of patents, franchise papers, licenses, and purchase options to enter the rate base? Some commissions do permit them—to some extent.

E. Per Cent Return

Utility investors own utility bonds, preferred stock, and common stock. Each instrument's rate of return differs because each differs in "priority" of pay-out, with bonds enjoying top priority and earning the lowest return. Thus, the per cent rate of return referred to in the regulatory equation is actually a *weighted average* rate. Reducing the return to its components, most commissions allow the interest actually paid on bonds, the dividends actually paid on preferred stock, and then they add a "fair" return for stockholders' equity.

Equity Returns. On the whole, equity returns average about 11–12%, which is pretty close to the all-manufacturing average. However, the average masks considerable variety because there is no single scientifically correct rate of return. At best, there is (as with Miss America's measurements) a "zone of reasonableness," within which judgment (and imagination) may roam. What are the limits of this zone? The *bottom* limit would be a rate just high enough to attract continuing investor commitments of capital. The *upper* limit would be considerably more generous but not lavish. Obviously, the zone itself is rather elastic.

Perhaps the best way to appreciate this problem is to imagine yourself as the typical investor whose capital the utility is trying to attract. What rate of return would the company have to pay (and the commission have to approve) to get you to bite? If you are shrewd, that rate would depend on the following:

1. The rate you could earn if you put your money elsewhere.
2. The risk of losing your investment (here and elsewhere).
3. The extent to which the company's earnings fluctuate, which in turn may depend on its debt/equity ratio, dividend pay-out policy, general economic condition, and so on.
4. The recent trend in the company's stock price.
5. Your expectations of political changes that may alter regulation.

These would be churning in your head, but the commission cannot read your mind. It therefore has no way of knowing precisely what minimum rate would attract your captial, or that of others. For this reason, commissions must exercise a good bit of judgment, taking these various factors into account because you take them into account.

V. HOW: RATE STRUCTURE REGULATION

The duty of commissions does not stop once overall revenue is set. The question of what *specific* prices or rates to charge remains. According to judicial and legislative instructions, commissions may permit rates that jump around with time, place, type of buyer, and size of transaction. However, the jumps cannot be "unduly discriminatory"; the differences in rates charged various customers or classes of service must be "just and reasonable." In carrying out this vague mandate, commissions have permitted rates to vary with *cost-of-service* and *value-of-service*. Each is worth illustrating.

A. Costs and Peak-Load Pricing[12]

For years now we have had to pay more to call long distance during weekday daylight hours than to call during nights and weekends. Likewise, many large buyers of natural gas are charged low prices for "interruptible" service, meaning that they can be cut off if the demand of noninterruptible buyers burgeons.

---

[12] This section is based primarily on Weiss and Strickland, *op. cit.*, pp. 18–21.

446

Traditionally, electric power companies have not charged such time based rates, but now there is a definite trend toward them. In 1977, for instance, Wisconsin Power & Light Company began charging business customers 2.03 cents per kilowatt-hour between 8 A.M. and 10 P.M., and just 1.013 cents per kilowatt-hour at other times. Rates may also vary with the seasons. All these are examples of **peak load pricing,** because rates are higher to peak users.

The main justification for higher prices during peak periods is that the costs of providing peak service are greater than those of providing off-peak service. One such cost is plant and equipment. Because a utility must have on hand capacity to satisfy total peak demand, capacity costs can be blamed mainly on those who tap into the utility during peak hours. As for off-peak customers, *the plant and equipment are already there for the peak,* so capacity costs of serving them do not apply, although off-peak users do create costs for fuel and other variable inputs. Indeed, even fuel costs per unit tend to vary with time of demand because utilities usually fire up their least efficient, high-cost plants only during peak periods. The differences between plants can be substantial. In 1973, for instance, a major eastern electric company experienced fuel costs of 3.3 mills/kWh in its most efficient plant and 9.51 mills/kWh in its least efficient plant.[13] (Note that these cost experiences do not contradict the economies of scale mentioned earlier. These are *short-run* cost comparisons, not long-run scalar comparisons).

Figure 20–3 shows peak and off-peak demands set against the short-run marginal cost curve of a hypothetical utility. If a uniform price of P_2 were charged to both peak and off-peak demands, capacity would have to equal OQ_2, which is peak quantity demanded at P_2. Off-peak demand would be OQ_0 given price P_2. Since OQ_2 greatly exceeds OQ_0, it is easy to see that peak demand would be responsible for the plant necessary to produce OQ_2 (even if off-peak demand were nonexistent). Moreover, a uniform price of P_2 would cause inefficient plant usage, because there would be tremendous excess capacity during off-peak periods. In short, such a uniform price is *too low* for peak demand (producing a state of overbuilding) and *too high* for off-peak demand (causing off-peak underutilization). Indeed, off-peak demand is to some extent subsidizing peak demand, since the shaded area in Figure 20–3 indicates the amount by which off-peak revenues exceed off-peak costs.

With a more sensible rate structure, peak customers would be charged P_3 and offpeak customers would be charged P_1. At P_3, peak demand would be curtailed to OQ_3, eliminating the need for capacity over the Q_3-Q_2 range. (It has been estimated that $13 *billion* of electric utility capital spending would be avoided over the years 1977–1985 if all United States electric companies were using such peak-load pricing.[14])

As already suggested, a rate structure that fully reflected costs would entail more than charges sufficient to cover whatever capacity various classes of custom-

[13] E. Berlin, C. J. Cicchetti, and W. J. Gillen, *Perspective on Power* (Cambridge, Mass.: Ballinger Publishing Co., 1975), p. 35.
[14] *Wall Street Journal,* August 12,1977, p. 1.

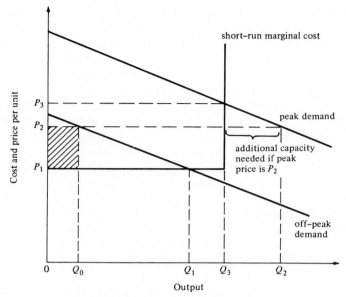

FIGURE 20–3. Peak-load pricing.

ers were responsible for. Rates would also have to include: (1) A charge per unit of service (for example, per kilowatt-hour, or per phone call) to meet the costs that vary with output (fuel especially). (2) A fixed charge for connection. (3) A fixed charge per month to cover the costs of metering, billing, and the like, costs which do not vary with consumption level or timing.

B. Value-of-Service Pricing

In the main, utility prices are not based strictly on cost of service. Price discrimination of second and third degrees (as defined and explained in Chapter 13) runs rampant. A common feature of such price discrimination is that those customers or classes of service having *in*elastic demands are typically charged more than those having elastic demands. In 1978, for instance, average electric rates to residential customers were about 4.03 cents per kWh, whereas those charged to industrial customers were only 2.59 cents per kWh.[15] To be sure, supplying a big factory often costs less per unit than supplying a home because many industrial buyers provide their own transformers and other equipment. Still, the main explanation for the higher household rate is found in price elasticity of demand. Industrial elasticity appears to be about 1.9, whereas residential elasticity is closer to 1.2.[16] The difference is due to the greater energy options

[15] U.S. Department of Commerce, *Statistical Abstract of the United States 1979*, pp. 613, 614.

[16] For a survey of elasticity estimates, see L. D. Taylor, "The Demand for Electricity: A survey," *Bell Journal of Economics* (Spring 1975), pp. 74–110.

open to industrial buyers. Indeed, many of them economically generate their own electricity.

Another form of discrimination in electricity is the so-called block rate, that, until recently, confronted virtually every residential consumer in the United States. Under a block-rate schedule, price falls as additional "blocks" of electricity are consumed during the month. The idea is that a high rate could be charged for basic uses like lighting, which lacks energy substitutes, whereas a lower rate could apply to electricity used for cooking and heating, where natural gas might be used instead. Of late, many commissions have abandoned block rates in hopes of encouraging energy conservation.

Telephones further illustrate value-of-service pricing. Business users have traditionally been charged *more* than residential users on the theory that phone service is indispensable to businesses but more or less optional in the home. Within the home, it appears that for years AT & T imposed equipment rental charges that greatly exceeded the costs of supplying equipment. Conversely, basic phone service was apparently under-priced, drawing a subsidy from equipment. Once people were permitted to *buy* their own phones, beginning in the late 1970s, AT & T said rates on basic phone service would have to go up because it could no longer count on lucrative equipment rentals.

Perhaps an even more striking example of AT & T's price discrimination concerns interstate services of various kinds. AT & T's "Seven-Way Cost Study" in the mid-1960s disclosed a pattern of discrimination generated by competition. Profits as a per cent of investment were 9.7% and 13.4% on message toll telephone and WATS services, where the company faced no competition to speak of. In contrast, profits were a piddling 0.3% and 1.4% on TELPAK and private line telegraph services, where rivals posed a threat.[17] Clearly, Ma Bell's elasticity of demand was higher with competition than without.

Presentation of these examples is not meant to imply that utility price discrimination is always "bad" or "unfair." It may seem unfair because some pay high and some pay low, relative to costs. But there are instances of beneficial price discrimination, "beneficial" in that it can lead to a *lower overall average price* for the company and even allow a *reduction in the high price paid* by those with relatively inelastic demand.

In short, rate structure regulation is complex. Cost-of-service pricing is not the only option. Value-of-service pricing may sometimes be socially valuable.

VI. PROBLEMS AND DISTORTIONS

As if we have not hung enough problems around regulators' necks, a few more must be mentioned. First, it would be nice if commissions could reward utilities that operate efficiently and progressively and penalize those putting out poorly.

---

[17] Harry M. Trebing and William H. Melody, "An Evaluation of Domestic Communications Pricing Practices and Policies," Staff Paper No. 5, *The Domestic Telecommunications Carrier Industry,* President's Task Force on Communications (1968), p. 217.

But no tidy incentive techniques have yet been devised. Measurement of efficiency and progressiveness is imprecise at best. And deviations from whatever measures are adopted may be as much the fault of regulators as managers. Assume, for example, that low profit earnings are taken to signal poor performance. Such a predicament might, in fact, be the result of some commission decision. Even if it were not, it is hard to see how a penalty of *still lower* earnings would allow the utility to improve its efficiency and maintain its financial soundness. Perhaps the only present source of proper incentive is regulatory "lag." Earnings that rise inordinately from efficiency remain with the firm until regulators act to reduce rate levels, but they act only after a long lag. Conversely, earnings that fall with inefficiency must be borne by the firm until requests for rate increases are answered, which procedure likewise entails some lag. Thus the lag imperfectly and temporarily rewards "goodness" and punishes "badness."

Second, some regulatory theorists argue that profit regulation contains some particularly unfavorable incentives. Because profit is keyed to the rate base, *there is an incentive to expand the rate base* (to substitute capital for labor) beyond the point that would be optimal in the absence of regulation.[18] Just how serious this so-called "Averch-Johnson effect" actually is no one can say. Empirical tests of the hypothesis have been mixed, half confirming and half refuting it.[19] Even if the effect does exist, it may not be as bad as it might seem. Although in *static* terms the bias favoring capital over other inputs may lift costs undesirably, the *dynamic* result may be *lower* costs through *improved technological progress,* given that most technological change tends to favor capital intensity.[20]

A third problem is what James McKie aptly calls the "tar-baby" effect.[21] Each swipe regulators take at some supposed utility sin seems to ensnare regulators in ever deeper difficulties. The innocent and well meaning souls who first devised regulation imagined it to be a rather simple matter. What could be easier, they must have asked, than restricting a natural monopolist's profit to some "just" percentage? Yet, as we have already seen, it is not so easy. Taking a punch at profit may mean a bulge in costs; striking at excess cost may hurt quality; close control of quality entails details demanding nearly one bureaucrat for every hard-hat; and so on. Pretty soon regulators are attempting to cover everything from plant purchases to billing frequencies, and in the process they get covered with tar.

---

[18] Harvey Averch and Leland L. Johnson, "Behavior of the Firm under Regulatory Constraint," *American Economic Review* (December 1962), pp. 1052–1069; Stanislaw H. Wellisz, "Regulation of Natural Gas Pipeline Companies: An Economic Analysis," *Journal of Political Economy* (February 1963), pp. 30–43.

[19] See L. L. Johnson's survey, "The Averch-Johnson Hypothesis after Ten Years," in *Regulation in Further Perspective,* edited by Shepherd and Gies (Cambridge, Mass.: Ballinger Publishing Co., 1974), pp. 67–78; plus Charles W. Smithson, "The Degree of Regulation and the Monopoly Firm," *Southern Economic Journal* (January 1978), pp. 568–580, and Robert W. Spann, "Rate of Return Regulation," *Bell Journal of Economics* (Spring, 1974), pp. 38–52.

[20] Kahn, *op. cit.,* Vol. II, pp. 106–107.

[21] James W. McKie, "Regulation and the Free Market: The Problem of Boundaries," *Bell Journal of Economics* (Spring, 1970), pp. 6–26.

Finally, consequently, and most important, the main problem with regulation is that, once it gets rolling, it does not stop with appropriate control of natural monopoly or grossly unfair price discrimination. It keeps right on rolling, crushing many fine opportunities for competition. As Walter Adams once remarked, "Regulation breeds regulation. Competition, even at the margin, is a source of disturbance, annoyance, and embarrassment to the bureaucracy. . . . From the regulator's point of view, therefore, competition must be suppressed wherever it arises."[22]

This is, to say the least, unfortunate. If you have learned nothing else to this point, you should have learned that regulation is but a very poor substitute for competition (even though it may be a lesser of two evils substitute for unregulated natural monopoly). No one has expressed this sentiment better than Clair Wilcox:

> Regulation, at best, is a pallid substitute for competition. It cannot prescribe quality, force efficiency, or require innovation, because such action would invade the sphere of management. But when it leaves these matters to the discretion of industry, it denies consumers the protection that competition would afford. Regulation cannot set prices below an industry's costs however excessive they may be. Competition does so, and the high-cost company is compelled to discover means whereby its costs can be reduced. Regulation does not enlarge consumption by setting prices at the lowest level consistent with a fair return. Competition has this effect. Regulation fails to encourage performance in the public interest by offering rewards and penalties. Competition offers both.[23]

The proper and improper application of regulation may be seen in the starkly contrasting results of regulation's impact on prices that empiricists have uncovered. For electric power and telephone service, regulation seems to have pressed prices *lower* than they would otherwise be, perhaps by as much as 6–10%.[24] But notice, these markets fit the natural monopoly model fairly well. In contrast, empirical studies show exactly opposite results in transportation, where natural monopoly does *not* prevail and where in the past competition has suffered the greatest official suppression through entry restriction and minimum price control. Regulation there *raised* prices. Before deregulation, as of the mid 1960s, ICC regulation of railroads, trucks, and water carriers cost the American public perhaps as much as $4–$9 *billion* a year in higher rates.[25] Similar conclusions have been reached regarding airline regulation. Over the period 1969–1974, CAB regulation is estimated to have inflated airfares by an average of 22–52%.

[22] Walter Adams, "Business Exemptions from the Antitrust Laws: Their Extent and Rationale," in *Perspectives on Antitrust Policy,* edited by A. Phillips (Princeton, N.J.: Princeton University Press, 1965), p. 283.

[23] Clair Wilcox, *Public Policies Toward Business* (Homewood, Ill.: Irwin 1966), pp. 476.

[24] William S. Comanor, "Should Natural Monopolies Be Regulated?" *Stanford Law Review* (February 1970), pp. 510–518; Kahn, *op. cit.,* Vol. II, pp. 108–111.

[25] Thomas G. Moore, "Deregulating Surface Freight Transportation," in *Promoting Competition in Regulated Markets,* edited by A. Phillips (Washington, D.C.: Brookings Institution, 1975), pp. 55–98.

TABLE 20–2. Comparison Between Interstate and Intrastate
Air Fares, 1975

City-Pair	Miles	Fare ($)
Los Angeles–San Francisco	338	18.75
Chicago–Minneapolis	339	38.89
New York–Pittsburgh	335	37.96
Los Angeles–San Diego	109	10.10
Portland–Seattle	129	22.22
Dallas–Houston	239	13.89*
Las Vegas–Los Angeles	236	28.70
Chicago–St. Louis	258	29.63

* This is the night and weekend rate. Day-time week-day rate was $23.15.
Source: *Civil Aeronautics Board Practices and Procedures*, Report of the Subcommittee on Administrative Practice and Procedure, U.S. Senate (1975), p. 41.

In annual dollars, that amounted to between $1.4 and $1.8 *billion*.[26] The major causes of these exorbitant rates are various forms of X-inefficiency.

Lest the reader think that these rather shocking estimates are fabricated from thin air, or unnatural gas, he or she should recognize that some sectors of transportation have always escaped tight regulation, and the experience of these fairly competitive sectors guided the estimates. On the ground, agricultural trucking and private trucking have always been beyond the ICC's reach. In the air, travel within California and Texas was not controlled by the CAB. A comparison of *intra*state air fares and *inter*state regulated air fares in 1975 is shown in Table 20–2. It does not take a pilot's eyes to see that, for routes of similar length and paired-city size, the *intra*state fares were substantially lower.

Fortunately, deregulation of transportation is now well under way. Airlines, for example, have been given greater freedom to cut prices and select their routes. The result has been lower fares, but no drastic financial danger to the airlines. Nevertheless, many airlines are squirming under the competitive pressure and squealing for regulatory protection. A blunt answer to the airlines' resistance is contained in a letter written by former CAB Chairman Alfred Kahn, replying to protestations of doom put out by Continental Airlines. Kahn expressed doubts that Continental would suffer, but added, "if every other carrier . . . will feast on Continental, does the public interest demand that we protect you?"[27]

[26] Theodore E. Keeler, "Airline Regulation and Market Performance," *Bell Journal of Economics* (Autumn, 1972), pp. 399–424; see also GAO Report CED-77-34, "Lower Airline Costs Per Passenger Are Possible In the United States Could Result in Lower Fares" (February 18, 1977).
[27] *Wall Street Journal,* May 9, 1978. For more on deregulation see Douglas W. Caves, L. R. Christensen, and M. W. Tretheway, "Airline Productivity under Deregulation," *Regulation* (November 1982), pp. 25–28; David R. Graham, and Daniel P. Kaplan, "Airline Deregulation Is Working," *Regulation* (May 1982), pp. 26–32; "Rough Road," *Wall Street Journal,* March 31, 1983, p. 50.

SUMMARY

Regulation governs major segments of energy and communications, which account for about 4% of GNP. These industries tend to be more capital intensive than others, some experiencing asset/sales ratios of three to one. Moreover, they provide "vital" services, often reaching consumers directly through pipes, wires, and conduits.

Regulation is grounded on several rationales. Natural monopoly justifies regulation of local electricity, water, gas, and telephone service, where economies of scale seem to stretch the full range of demand. Resource conservation vindicates some entry regulation of the air waves. These and other areas of regulation may also be based on fairness. Another rationale—destructive competition—provides a very weak peg on which to hang regulation, especially in transportation, where it is most frequently invoked.

State and federal commissions with broad powers actually do the regulating. Their procedures are legalistic and their personnel bureaucratic. Among the many criticisms of commissions, the most commonly voiced are incompetence and inadequacy. Although there may be some validity to these charges, it should be acknowledged that the task of regulation is *inherently* difficult.

Profit, or rate level, regulation focuses on the following equation: total revenue = operating expense + current depreciation + (capital value × rate of return). Each element on the right hand side must be determined to reckon the total revenue needed. The appraisal entails quantities of pure judgment because there are no scientifically established "rights" and "wrongs." There are certain principles, such as the need for a rate of return sufficient to attract capital, but nothing definite. As for objectives, commissions pursue a "balancing act," forever making compromises between the interests of investors and customers. Much the same could be said of rate structure regulation.

Probably the biggest problem with regulation is its potentially anticompetitive effect. To quote a noted economist: "Regulation is like growing old: we would rather not do it, but consider the alternative." Where *un*regulated natural monopoly (or government ownership) is the alternative, this may be correct. Youthful death and unfettered monopoly are both undesirable. But where *competition* is the alternative, it ought to be tried.

21

Inflation and Macroeconomic Stability: Theory and Evidence

Inflation is like toothpaste. Once it's out, you can hardly put it back in.

—KARL-OTTO PÖHL

Rapid inflation is bad. High unemployment is bad. When these two hit us at the same time, as they have since the mid-1970s, the economy reels. The contribution market power makes to inflation and unemployment, whether they occur separately or together, is disputed. Some believe oligopolists and labor unions are innocent as new born lambs; others claim the two are venal as polecats. This entire chapter could be devoted to a blow-by-blow account of the controversy, but the approach would be confusing. Instead, a brief *synthesis* of views is offered.

Previous chapters have discussed the likelihood that market power will lead to higher and relatively more stable market prices than would be the case under competition. The focus was on individual markets at the *micro*economic level. Thus we begin this chapter by distinguishing between the issue of aggregate or *macro*-level inflation and unemployment on the one hand, and the issue of high and stable prices in *micro*-markets on the other. Next, we explore theoretically the inflation-unemployment relationship in terms of three major possible causes of inflation—demand-pull, market-power push, and exogenous shock. Finally, we review some empirical evidence on the roles these possible causes have played in recent economic events in the United States and, with less emphasis, in other countries as well.

I. DELINEATION OF THE PROBLEM

A. Price and Wage Levels

Up to this point our analysis has focused on the structure, conduct, and performance of *individual* markets for products and services. It was shown

454

that product market power (as measured by concentration or barriers to entry) is positively associated with relatively high and relatively stable prices. In labor markets, unionization is the means by which market power is attained, and union wage rates tend to be both higher and cyclically more stable than nonunion wage rates.[1]

Although it may seem that these micro-level findings have some direct and easy application to the question of macro-level inflation, they do not. The micro-level findings relate to *relative* price and wage levels at a given point in time and *relative* price and wage changes over the business cycle—for example, the price of autos (under oligopoly) relative to the price of lumber (under atomistic competition), and the cyclical stability (up and down) of steel prices relative to the cyclical stability of textile prices. In contrast, **inflation** is a macro issue; it refers to increases in the *average* level of *all* prices and wages in the economy over time, and for our purposes it may be defined as being a substantial increase in the consumer price index (CPI) or overall wage index. **Deflation** is the opposite—a decrease in the average level of prices and wages.

To be sure, the overall average price level is derived from prices in individual markets. But to understand the possible contribution market power makes to inflation, we must begin thinking in macroeconomic terms instead of microeconomic ones. Our earlier analysis showed that, if an industry's structure changes from pure competition to oligopoly or monopoly, the price of this industry's product is likely to rise. Thus substantial *changes* in market structure toward greater concentration could be a source of inflationary changes in prices.[2] But this is a purely microeconomic view of the possible contribution of market power. Its implications are quite limited. The static theory and empirical evidence of earlier chapters gave no indication that prices would rise *continually* under monopoly or oligopoly. That analysis applied solely to *relative* prices, and a monopolist's price should *not* rise continually relative to costs or relative to prices of other goods solely by virtue of the monopolist's having market power. Moreover, if increased seller's control raises price in one market—that for autos, say—the overall *average* level of prices need not change because this increase may be offset by price reductions in other markets, particularly in those markets becoming more competitive. Indeed, over the past three decades, there has been no clear cut trend toward greater concentration in most individual product markets, so *changes* in market power cannot explain the substantial inflation we have experienced since World War II. Instead of looking at the inflationary impact of changes in structure, we shall be concerned here with the *mere existence* of market power in both product and labor markets.

[1] For evidence see H. G. Lewis, *Unionism and Relative Wages in the United States* (Chicago: University of Chicago Press, 1963); Daniel Hamermesh, "Market Power and Wage Inflation," *Southern Economic Journal* (October 1972); O. C. Ashenfelter, G. E. Johnson, and J. H. Pencavel, "Trade Unions and the Rate of Change of Money Wages in the United States Manufacturing Industry," *Review of Economic Studies* (January 1972); Wallace Hendricks, "Unionism, Oligopoly and Rigid Wages," *Review of Economics and Statistics* (May 1981).

[2] For evidence to this effect with respect to wages and the spread of unionism see A. G. Hines, "Trade Unions and Wage Inflation in the United Kingdom 1893–1961," *Review of Economic Studies* (October 1964).

B. Cyclical Stability and Inflation

The same limitations apply to the evidence cited earlier that high market concentration and unionism are associated with greater cyclical stability of prices and wages. Contrary to appearances, these findings do not necessarily imply that market power is irrelevant to inflation or that market power tends to reduce inflation. The extent to which a product's price moves up and down with cyclical increases and decreases of demand gives no indication of the *average* or *net* change in the product's price over the entire span of the business cycle or over the span of numerous business cycles. The same is true of wage rates.

Figure 21–1 illustrates this point as it applies to product prices. The horizontal axis measures excess demand and supply, with quantity demand exceeding quantity supply to the right of the origin and supply exceeding demand to the left. The vertical axis measures the *rate of change* in market price (positive or negative change over one year's time), with the rate of change being a positive function of the extent to which demand exceeds supply. If line *CC* represents price behavior throughout the cycle under competitive conditions, and if line *MM* represents price behavior under oligopolistic conditions, prices will be more flexible in the former case than in the latter—ranging between plus and minus 10% compared to plus and minus 4%, respectively. Still, the *average* extent of change in both instances would be zero, indicating no net inflation. The only way inflation could occur under such circumstances would be for demand

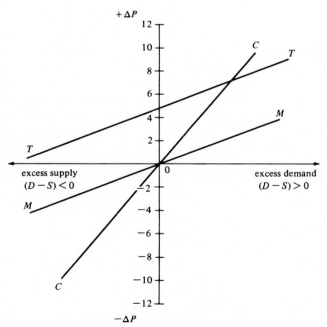

FIGURE 21–1. Relationship between excess demand, excess supply, and the rate of change in market prices.

to exceed supply rather persistently in most industries, confining us on average to the right of the origin. This describes **demand pull inflation.**

Notice next that line *TT* has the same slope as *MM,* so that both *TT* and *MM* represent the same degree of price flexibility (or inflexibility). The intercept of *TT* is much greater than that of *MM,* however, indicating a positive rate of change in price *even in the absence of excess demand.* Thus if *TT* represented oligopolistic price behavior and *CC* represented competitive price behavior, market power would contribute substantially to inflation even though the oligopolist's prices were cyclically less flexible than those of competitive firms. This could be called **market power inflation.**

Testing for this type of inflation may look easy. Data on price changes and excess demand in oligopoly industries could be compared with similar data for competitive industries to see if the former industries displayed a *TT* pattern and the latter displayed a *CC* pattern. Unfortunately, the task is not so easy for several reasons. First, no wholly reliable measure of excess demand is available for product markets. Second, this test would not be a fair test of the market power hypothesis because a *TT* pattern versus a *CC* pattern would imply that, on average, prices in oligopoly and monopoly industries always and continuously rise *relative* to prices in competitive industries, even without structural change. However, as already noted, such a perpetually growing divergence in relative prices is highly unlikely and theoretically unjustifiable.

The only way market power can cause perpetual changes in *relative* prices is to have perpetual *changes* in market power. Intermarket equilibrating forces of supply and demand tend to erase any changes in relative prices (or changes in their rates of change) based solely on the (long-standing) existence of market power. Thus a fairer test would allow for the possibility that market power contributes to inflation in such a way that no substantial divergence over time is observed. If market power were to produce a *TT* pattern for oligopoly, and if these intermarket equilibrating forces were to shift the competitive *CC* line upward to share the same average and the same intercept as the *TT* line, then market power would contribute to inflation without divergence over time. Unfortunately, an empirical test for this form of contribution would be even more difficult than the test considered earlier comparing *TT* and *CC* as they stand because factors *other* than market power may also cause prices in all industries to rise, on average and over time, even without excess aggregate demand.

C. The Phillips Curve

Before we take up detailed consideration of these other inflationary forces and their relation to market power inflation, we should first gain some familiarity with the **Phillips curve,** which depicts the relationship between inflation and unemployment.[3] Familiarity with the Phillips curve (named after its inventor) will allow us to center attention on labor markets as opposed to product markets, a focus that has the following advantages:

[3] A. W. Phillips, "The Relationship between Unemployment and the Rate of Change of Money Wage Rates in the United Kingdom, 1861–1957," *Economica* (November 1958).

1. A good measure of excess demand in labor markets is both readily available and easily understandable—namely, the unemployment rate.
2. It can be argued that market power inflation is more likely to originate with wage inflation as opposed to product price inflation because labor's wage demands are governed by motives quite different from the profit maximizing motive of firms, which tends to limit discretionary increases in relative prices.
3. If market power inflation does indeed originate with wage changes, it should be more readily observable because, unlike most product prices, union wage rates change only intermittently at well-defined, contractually determined times.
4. There is high positive correlation between the extent of labor unionism within industries and the degree of product market concentration. Thus, evidence reflecting the wage impact of one of these measures of market power will not likely be contradicted by evidence concerning the other measure. Indeed it can be argued that a *combination* of product and labor market power confers the greatest degree of discretion over wage rates and is thereby most inflationary.

In sum, the labor market is worthy of our attention, for it is there that market power inflation is most likely to arise and, if it does, most readily observable.

Assuming the aggregate rate of unemployment is a good overall index of excess demand or "labor shortage" in the labor market, the Phillips curve states that annual percentage rates of change in money wages are a negative, nonlinear function of unemployment. As shown in Figure 21–2, low levels of unemployment (indicating excess aggregate demand) are associated with high rates of

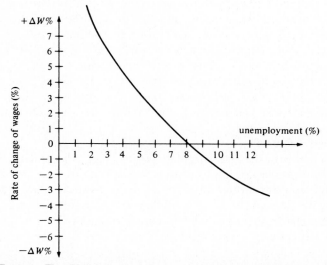

FIGURE 21–2. The Phillips curve relating unemployment and wage change.

wage inflation. The curve does not cross the vertical axis because the unemployment rate cannot be less than zero. Moreover, even with very high aggregate demand and rapidly rising wages, some workers will quit work and accept temporary unemployment while they seek better jobs. Conversely, at high levels of unemployment there is much involuntary unemployment and wages tend to be stable or declining slightly.

This wage-unemployment relationship is important to the issue of product *price* inflation because it can easily be converted into a similar relationship between prices and unemployment. In general, (1) price per unit of product increases in response to an increase in labor cost per unit; and (2) labor cost per unit is a function of the number of units that are produced by one man-hour (labor productivity) as well as the wage cost of one hour of work.

Specifically, the rate of change of prices, $\Delta P\%$, can be depicted as the difference between the rate of change of money wages, $\Delta W\%$, and the constant trend rate of increase of man-hour productivity, $\Delta Q\%$, such that

$$\Delta P\% = \Delta W\% - \Delta Q\%.$$

A simple example may help: If the hourly-wage of tee-shirt painters doubled from $3.00 to $6.00, the cost (and price) of painted tee-shirts need not also rise if a new application of stencils doubled the hourly output of each painter from two to four shirts per hour. Labor cost per tee-shirt both before and after is $1.50 ($3/2 and $6/4). Thus, a Phillips curve for price change is obtained merely by relabeling the vertical axis of Figure 21–2 to indicate annual percentage rate of change of prices instead of wages, and by shifting the curve of Figure 21–2 downward a few percentage points to account for productivity growth.

These adjustments are made in Figure 21–3, where annual productivity growth is assumed to be 3%. In this illustration wages can increase at an annual rate of 3% without causing any increase in the overall level of product prices. At rates of wage increase greater than 3% per year, wages tend to "push up" prices. Whether such inflationary rates of wage increase can be attributed to excess demand in labor and product markets (demand-pull), or to the mere exercise of market power on the part of firms and labor unions (market-power push) is an issue that will be explored later. At this point it is important to recognize the two-way causal relationship between price inflation and wage inflation: (1) Wage increases, via their effect on suppliers' cost of production, can cause prices to increase. (2) Product price increases, via their effect on consumers' (workers') cost of living, can cause wages to increase.

One final preliminary step is necessary before discussing causality further. We need to distinguish three different forms of wage-price increase:

1. A once-and-for-all or "one-shot" aggregate increase.
2. Secular inflation, a roughly constant rate of increase over time.
3. Accelerating inflation, with prices and wages increasing at an ever increasing rate.

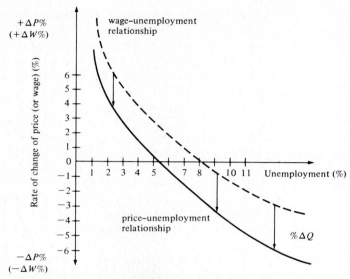

FIGURE 21–3. The Phillips curve for product price inflation.

Each of these is conceptually distinct. Moreover, each is functionally independent: one-shot inflation does not inevitably produce secular inflation, and secular inflation does not inevitably produce accelerating inflation. Under certain circumstances, however, progression up the scale of severity is possible.

II. THE PRINCIPAL CAUSES OF INFLATION

For our purposes, three possible causes of inflation may be considered important: (A) demand-pull or money supply, (B) market-power push or cost-push, and (C) exogenous shock. These are deep, abstract theories, so to avoid drowning we had better begin with a simple wading-pool example. Suppose it is hot. A child's pleasure from a wading pool will depend on three things—the size of the pool, the level of the water in it, and the behavior of the other children in it. If water overflow is thought of as inflation, and low water is equated with unemployment, then: (A) Running water into the pool continually will prevent low water (unemployment) but cause overflow (inflation)—unless the pool expands over time or something else happens to accommodate the influx. This is analogous to the demand-pull or money supply model if money is thought of as water and pool size is thought of as real income. (B) Next, imagine that a gang of quarrelsome "big kids" occupies the pool instead of a few docile toddlers. As these louts fight over space and splash about, water will overflow (inflation) unless the hose is withdrawn, allowing the water level to fall (unemployment). The situation is analogous to the market-power cost-push model,

460

if the demands of the "big kids" are likened to the money-wage demands of unionized labor or the money-profit demands of powerful oligopolists. (C) Overflow (inflation) would also occur if the pool suddenly shrank or the lip of one edge were bent down or some similar catastrophe hit. These possibilities are analogous to exogenous shock inflation if the size and strength of the pool are thought of as "real" income. (Notice for later application that an enlarged pool permits more water and more splashing without overflow.) Now that our toes are wet, we are ready for technical discussions of causes A, B, and C.

A. Cause A: A Growth in the Money Supply that Exceeds Growth in Real Income

In short, this is the "monetarist" view of inflation,[4] and there is much validity to it. This view can be captured in a single equation:

$$M \cdot V = P \cdot Y \qquad (21\text{--}1)$$

where M = money supply (a dollar stock value comprised of currency, demand deposits in banks, and savings deposits)

V = average income velocity (the number of times money supply circulates per year)

P = average price level

Y = real output or income (the aggregate annual quantity flow of goods and services)

Since $\Delta(P \cdot Y)$ is approximated by $Y \cdot \Delta P + P \cdot \Delta Y$, which becomes $\Delta P/P + \Delta Y/Y$ if divided by $P \cdot Y$, equation (21–1) can easily be transformed into annual percentage rates of change:

$$\Delta M\% + \Delta V\% = \Delta P\% + \Delta Y\% \qquad (21\text{--}2)$$

To simplify matters we assume, not too unrealistically, that $\Delta V\%$ is zero in the long run and that growth in real income $\Delta Y\%$ is determined by long-run growth of productivity and labor force size (or population). It follows, then, that, if $\Delta M\%$ is set by the monetary authorities to equal $\Delta Y\%$, average price change $\Delta P\%$ would be zero. On the other hand, if the growth rate of nominal money stock accelerates in excess of the growth rate of real income, accelerating inflation ensues. Correspondingly, if the growth rate of money persistently exceeds the growth rate of real income by some constant amount, secular inflation ensues. With $\Delta M\% = 9\%$ and $\Delta Y\% = 4\%$, for example, $\Delta P\%$ would be 5%, which is 9% $-$ 4%. Finally, this theory predicts that a one-shot inflation would result from an appropriate combination of short-run monetary overflow and underflow relative to $\Delta Y\%$.

[4] See for instance Milton Friedman, "The Role of Monetary Policy," *American Economic Review* (March 1968); and John T. Boorman and Thomas M. Havrilesky, *Money Supply, Money Demand, and Macroeconomic Models* (Boston: Allyn and Bacon, 1972), Chapter 5.

According to the monetarists, secular and accelerating inflation cannot be illustrated by the single Phillips curves of Figures 21–2 and 21–3 because each such negatively sloped curve depicts only a single *short-run* relationship between inflation and unemployment. To develop the monetarists' *long-run* view of the Phillips relation three new concepts are necessary:

1. First, we must distinguish between **money wages,** which are simply dollar and cents wages, and **real wages,** which are money wages translated into the real goods and services that they can buy—that is, money wages relative to consumer goods prices. Monetarists hold that workers think and act in terms of their real wages, not their money wages. In other words, if overnight all prices and all incomes double in nominal money terms, and all other money values double, people will *not* feel better or worse off than before. They do not suffer "money illusion."
2. Second, people's **expectations** must be taken into account. If prices have been going up 5% every year for the past 10 years, they will logically expect them to go up 5% next year as well. And in light of point 1, they will adjust their money wage demands upward accordingly.
3. Third, there is a **natural rate** of unemployment that coincides with a condition of aggregate economic equilibrium, implying an absence of either excess demand or excess supply at the aggregate level. This natural rate is determined by such "real" factors as worker mobility, labor market information, and institutional conditions.

If we assume a condition of pure competition all round, application of these three concepts yields numerous short-run Phillips curves stacked vertically above the natural rate of unemployment, each one of which is associated with a different rate of *expected* price inflation. Put differently, the short-run Phillips curve shifts up or down with price expectations. This family of curves is depicted in Figure 21–4.

Assume initially that the economy is at point *A,* with unemployment at the natural rate and no actual or expected inflation. The monetary authorities could increase money supply ($\uparrow \Delta M\%$) and consequently cause price inflation ($\uparrow \Delta P\%$), but, because in the *short run* money wages would be set under expectations of zero price change, real wages would fall. As real wages fall, businesses would hire more workers because they are cheaper, reducing unemployment to point *B* in Figure 21–4 and boosting real output ($\uparrow \Delta Y\%$), both of which are beneficial. However, money supply is now growing more rapidly than before, and this increase in the *rate* of increase ($\uparrow \Delta M\%$) cannot keep unemployment below the natural rate of unemployment over the *long run* because the 3% inflation experienced at point B will eventually modify expectations, causing a *shift* to point C, which coincides with a new Phillips curve that embodies expectations of 3% price *and* wage inflation. With real wages retured to normal, the natural rate of unemployment prevails, and real income returns to its exogenously determined long-run growth rate ($\downarrow \Delta Y\%$).

One major conclusion to be derived here is that inflation at point *C* is sustained by expectations, even in the absence of excess aggregate demand: workers and firms continue to raise their own wages and prices without injuring their competitiveness because their competitors are raising their wages and prices too. This situation corresponds to an important earlier observation concerning Figure 21–1—namely, lines *MM* and *CC* in that diagram can both shift upward in response to forces other than a market-power push led by *MM*. A second major conclusion is that continued unemployment below the "natural" level cannot be gained by engineering a given, steady state (secular) rate of inflation. It can only be gained by accelerating inflation. Point *B* in Figure 21–4 was attained only by having actual inflation (3%) exceed expected inflation (0%). As expectations rise to 1%, 2%, 3%, and so on, the actual rate of inflation must accelerate ahead at 4%, 5%, 6%, and so on, if unemployment is to be held at *B* level. This moves the economy toward point *D*.

The reverse holds true on the down side. Deflation ($\downarrow \Delta P\%$) will follow a substantial drop in the growth of money supply ($\downarrow \Delta M\%$), as indicated by a movement from point *D* to point *E* in Figure 21–4, but only at the expense of greater unemployment, which, if sustained, will lead to still further deflation, as illustrated by movement from *E* to *F*. Eventually, we could return to point

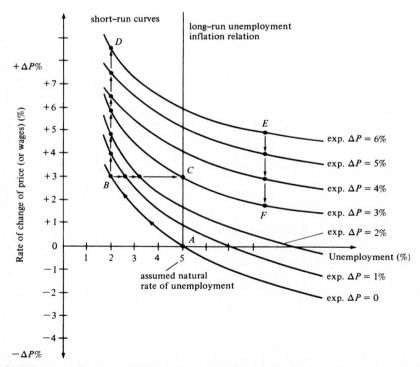

FIGURE 21–4. Short-run Phillips curves relative to the long-run natural rate curve.

A by bringing actual inflation down to zero and holding the rate there until expectations caught up.

Finally, the most important conclusion to be drawn here is that "full-employment" (that is, zero excess aggregate demand) may be defined in terms of this Cause A and the "natural rate." At **full-employment,** the *rate of change* of price is constant, though perhaps positive (that is, 5% year-in and year-out). Full-employment is that level of employment yielding neither acceleration nor deceleration of prices in *direct* response to variations in the money supply. The qualifying word "direct" indicates an assumed "neutrality" or "passivity" in the other possible causes of inflation, a state that can be fully understood only after we have discussed these other causes.

B. Cause B: The Exercise of Labor and Product Market Power

In major segments of the economy both labor and management possess enough market power to exercise discretionary control over wages and prices, at least in the short run. This ability to control was shown in previous chapters. Whether or not this market power results in inflation depends on how it is exercised and the nature of the monetary policy accompanying its exercise. It does not necessarily depend on changes in market power.

This feature of market power may be seen by modifying equation (21–1).[5] Broken down into components of national income, price is

$$P = k \cdot W \cdot E \qquad (21–3)$$

where P = average price

W = average wage and salary per man-year

E = man-year input per unit of output, that is, the inverse of labor productivity

k = mark-up of prices over unit labor costs $(W \cdot E)$ to cover profits, rents, and interest, for example $k = 1.20$.

Substituting this expression for P into equation (21–1) yields

$$M \cdot V = k \cdot W \cdot E \cdot Y \qquad (21–4)$$

which in terms of annual percentage change is

$$\Delta M\% + \Delta V\% = \Delta k \cdot W\% + \Delta E\% + \Delta Y\% \qquad (21–5)$$

If we assume $\Delta V\%$ is zero and k is constant (in the absence of structural change) this further reduces to

$$\Delta M\% = \Delta W\% + \Delta E\% + \Delta Y\% \qquad (21–6)$$

[5] This formulation is derived from Sidney Weintraub, "Incomes Policy: Completing the Stabilization Triangle," *Journal of Economic Issues* (December 1972).

Note that $\Delta E\%$ will normally be negative because labor requirements per unit of output fall as productivity rises over time. Thus wages can increase ($+\Delta W\%$) at a rate matching that of productivity growth ($-\Delta E\%$) without increasing prices ($\Delta P\% = 0$), and full employment (as embodied in $\Delta Y\%$) may be maintained by equating $\Delta M\%$ and $\Delta Y\%$ as before. If however $+\Delta W\%$ *exceeds* $-\Delta E\%$, then $\Delta Y\%$ and employment can be maintained only if $\Delta M\%$ exceeds $\Delta Y\%$ by a similar amount, implying inflation.

One-Shot Inflation. A one-shot market-power inflation would result from the following sequence of events. First, monetary policy is aimed at maintaining full-employment as defined previously. Second, unionized labor attempts to gain a once-and-for-all increase in its long-run share of real income by accelerating its wage level to a growth rate that exceeds average productivity growth. The attempt, however, is eventually thwarted by a commensurate rise in the rate of change of all other prices and wages (a change attributable to **spill-overs** or the long-run intermarket equilibrating forces that restore all preexisting *relative* wages and prices, or their rates of change, in the absence of any significant changes in market power). And third, the unionized sector then abandons its attempt by *decelerating* its wage claims to a rate of increase again matching average productivity growth, whereupon this reverse movement in the rate of increase is followed commensurately in all other sectors.

A numerical example of this one-shot market power inflation is presented in Table 21–1, in which it is assumed for simplicity that the unionized or monopolized sector accounts for 50% of all wages and prices ($0.5 \cdot k \cdot W \cdot E$); that the competitive sector's prices and wages are set over the course of each time period according to events during the preceding period; and that productivity growth is zero throughout. In period 1, wages in the unionized sector jump to a 10% rate of increase, causing aggregate inflation of 5%. In subsequent periods the competitive sector adjusts under the influence of two factors: (1) the drive to regain real wages lost by aggregate price increases (as in the monetarist model), and (2) spill-over, the forces that tend to return *relative* wages and prices to initial levels. By assumption, the 10% spill-over effect is made up entirely in period 2, but the influence of the aggregate price level is spread over numerous periods due to lagged adjustment. By period 10, all prices and wages are rising at a 10% rate. Thereafter, the sequence of percentage increases is reversed. By period 20, this reversal yields no change in relative prices or wages or real income shares, but this process has resulted in a one-shot increase in all money values of 157.3% (see the index numbers), which remains even after the process has ended.

Secular Inflation. It should be clear from the foregoing that secular rather than one-shot inflation would result if the same "passive" monetary policy were followed (keyed to maintenance of full-employment) and a similarly frustrated attempt were made by the union sector to raise its long-run share of real income, *but no voluntary discretionary deceleration occurred after the attempt was aban-*

465

TABLE 21–1. Illustration of an Attempt to Enhance Share of Real Income that is Unsuccessful in the Long Run but Inflationary

Time Period	Union Sector Wage Change (%)	Union Sector Wage Index	All Other Wages and Prices Change (%)	All Other Wages and Prices Index	Overall Price Level Change (%)	Overall Price Level Index
0	0	100	0	100	0	100
1	10	110	0	100	5	105
2	10	121	10 + 5	115	12.5	118
3	10	132.1	12.5	129.4	11.2	130.7
4	10	145.3	11.2	143.9	10.6	144.6
5	10	159.8	10.6	159.2	10.3	159.5
⋮	⋮	⋮	⋮	⋮	⋮	⋮
⋮	⋮	⋮	⋮	⋮	⋮	⋮
10	10	257.3	10.0	257.3	10.0	257.3
11	0	257.3	10.0	283.1	5.0	270.2
12	0	257.3	−10 + 5	268.9	−2.5	263.1
13	0	257.3	−2.5	262.2	−1.2	259.8
14	0	257.3	−1.2	258.9	−0.6	258.1
⋮	⋮	⋮	⋮	⋮	⋮	⋮
⋮	⋮	⋮	⋮	⋮	⋮	⋮
20	0	257.3	0	257.3	0	257.3

doned. The secular inflation process would leave the *rate of change* of money wages and prices at a new and higher level. In Table 21–1, this movement is illustrated by events between periods 0 and 10, but the period 10 situation would then be *perpetuated,* with all money values rising at 10% per period.

Thus, the secular inflation process results in (1) *a short-run* transfer of real income from the competitive sector to the monopolistic sector (for example, the index *levels* of period 2 are 121 versus 115), (2) an increase in the rate of change of all money values, (3) no *long-run* change in relative prices, wages, or income shares, (4) no change in employment, and (5) no further progression to accelerating inflation. Notice that all the basic components of the monetarists' model are retained here. The only concepts that have been added are short-run discretionary power, the long-run constancy of relative wages and prices in the absence of structural change, and spill-overs of rates of change from

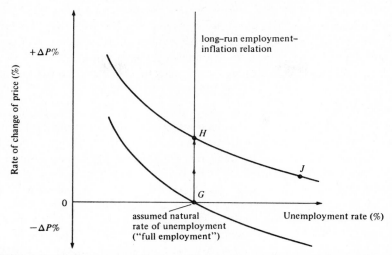

FIGURE 21–5. Market-power inflation with monetary policy geared to maintenance of "full employment."

the monopolistic to the competitive sectors—a consequence of this tendency toward constant relative wages and prices.

In Phillips curves, this kind of secular inflation is illustrated by a single upward shift of the short-run Phillips relation at the natural rate of unemployment, as shown by a movement from point G to point H in Figure 21–5 (corresponding to a combined upward shift of MM and CC in Figure 21–1, led by MM). Progression to accelerating inflation (continuing above point H) would result from *persistently* repeated attempts by the monopolistic decision makers to raise their real income share while monetary policy was pegged to the maintenance of full-employment and intermarket equilibrating forces prevented the radical changes in relative prices and wages necessary to reward these efforts.

Labor's Motives. It should be stressed that these Cause B inflations are not due to a growth in market power over time. The mere existence of substantial market power *enables* (and rational behavior encourages) a short-run reach for greater real-income share even in the absence of the structural alterations that would in fact permit the long-run realization of this goal. Among the many *motives* that might translate this ability into action, the following are probably most important in labor's behavior:

1. In contrast to the once-and-for-all attainment of a "monopoly wage" that might be suggested by static theory, unions may strive to maximize their *annual* rate of wage *increase.*[6]

[6] Gottfried Haberler, *Incomes Policies and Inflation* (Washington, D.C.: American Enterprice Institute, 1971), p. 14.

2. They may also strive to enhance interindustry wage inequality.
3. In industries experiencing above average productivity growth, unions will press for money wage increases that also exceed average productivity growth rather than press for product price reductions because the higher wages are of immediate, tangible, and measurable benefit to their members and provide the basis for union-leader reelection.[7]

Empirical research has shown that this type of inflation proceeds without a perpetually growing disparity of money wage rates and income shares between union and nonunion sectors—without, that is, any substantial structural alterations over time.[8] Some evidence even suggests that the general wage level rises faster in countries where wages in different sectors move more closely together and where there is relatively little interindustry dispersal of wage growth rates.[9]

Role of Product Market Power. The role of product market power in this wage-push inflation could be substantial because union motives are likely to be most effectively expressed in highly concentrated industries with barriers to new (nonunion) firm entry.[10] The higher profits of such industries provide a "target" for unions to "shoot at." Moreover, firms in these industries may be less resistent than competitive firms to union demands because (1) they can more easily raise prices, (2) they may want to maintain labor queues in anticipation of fluctuations in production, and (3) they may gain some prestige from paying premium wages. Under these circumstances, product market power would have an indirect inflationary effect through wages. It is also conceivable that some "profit inflation" may occasionally occur among oligopolists with consequences similar to those outlined above for union wage inflation. In equations (21–4) and (21–5), profit inflation would involve an increase in business mark-up over labor cost, *k,* that is eventually eliminated in the long run by the equilibrating effect of spill-overs.

Role of Money Adjustments. It must also be stressed that these Cause B inflations need validation by passive, full-employment monetary adjustments. Strict monetary restraint could probably nullify these inflations, but only by generating sufficient unemployment to negate the inflationary bias at the aggre-

[7] Alfred Kuhn, "Market Structures and Wage-Push Inflation," *Industrial and Labor Relations Review* (January 1959); Thomas Wilson, *Inflation* (Cambridge, Mass.: Harvard University Press, 1961), Chapter XV. For more on motives (and mechanics) see J. E. Meade, *Wage-Fixing* (London: Allen & Unwin, 1982).

[8] Douglas Greer, "Market Power and Wage Inflation," *Southern Economic Journal* (January 1975).

[9] H. A. Turner and D. A. S. Jackson, "On the Determination of the General Wage Level—A World Analysis; or 'Unlimited Labor Forever,'" *Economic Journal* (December 1970).

[10] James R. Schlesinger, "Market Structure, Union Power and Inflation," *Southern Economic Journal* (January 1958); Martin Segal, "The Relation Between Union Wage Impact and Market Structure," *Quarterly Journal of Economics* (February 1964); Harold M. Levinson, *Determining Forces in Collective Bargaining* (New York: John Wiley & Sons, 1966), Chapter 6; George de Menil, *Bargaining: Monopoly Power versus Union Power* (Cambridge, Mass.: MIT Press, 1971); Tibor Scitovsky, "Market Power and Inflation," *Economica* (August 1978).

gate level, as indicated by a movement from point H to point J in Figure 21–5. To stem secular and accelerating inflations attributable to Cause B, monetary restraint could mean higher unemployment in the long run. For, only if there was a voluntary discretionary deceleration by the monopolistic sectors, with a short-run transfer of real income share from the monopolistic sector to the competitive sector (like that occurring over time periods 10 through 20 in Table 21–1), would monetary stringency alone be able to curtail these inflations with only a temporary loss of employment and output.

At this point we can explain the phrase **neutrality** or **passivity** in the other possible causes of inflation that was used to qualify our Cause A monetarist discussion. Just as we here had to assume passivity on the part of official money supply managers in order to describe the process by which market power caused inflation, so too we had to assume passivity on the part of monopolistic powers in order to develop the purely "monetarist" model of inflation and deflation, although this assumption was not explicitly discussed for the monetary theory. It should now be clear that passivity of private market power means either an absence of such power or a willingness on the part of those possessing such power to behave as if they do not have it. Those possessing power over wages and prices use it passively if they vary prices and wages only and precisely to achieve a full, "natural-competitive" level of unemployment. This behavior would emulate purely competitive behavior. The extent to which passivity is actually practiced by those with market power or the official monetary authority (in the United States this is the Board of Governors of the Federal Reserve System) is an *empirical* issue, and it will be discussed at length later. Still, a few preliminary comments are appropriate here.

Given the elementary background knowledge provided so far, we can hypothesize *asymmetry* in applications of the passivity assumption. Monopolistic sectors will probably be passive to money supply *inflation* but not pliably passive to money supply *deflation* since in the latter case the monopolistic sector would suffer a temporary but perhaps sizable loss of real income to the competitive sector. Failure of the monopolistic sector to "permit" or "endorse" this deflation passively would increase unemployment. Contrarywise, monetary officials will probably be passive to monopolistic *deflation* (which deflation is unlikely in practice but possible in principle), though not pliably passive to monopolistic *inflation*, particularly an accelerating inflation. Failure of the monetary authority to "permit" or "endorse" this inflation passively would increase unemployment.

The monetary authority, therefore, does *not* have simultaneous control over both the wage-price level *and* employment, and neither does the monopolistic sector.[11] Either power center can play the passive role by bending all its efforts to the task of maintaining the "natural rate" of employment, but in so doing it relinquishes control over the wage-price level to the other power center. Since both centers seek to exercise at least some power over prices-wages, even though

[11] M. W. Reder, "The Theoretical Problems of a National Wage Price Policy," *Canadian Journal of Economics and Political Science* (February 1948).

this can only be partial power, each intentionally abandons the full-employment objective whenever it wants to assert itself actively. In light of this fact, and in light of the asymmetry just mentioned, simultaneous passivity is rather unlikely. Simultaneous activity in opposite directions (Cause B inflation, Cause A deflation) can and apparently does occur, resulting in high "unnatural" unemployment coupled occasionally with inflation. But more often an active-passive seesaw prevails, one that generates unstable, negatively sloped *short-run* Phillips curves that overlap an L-shaped *long-run* Phillips curve (which is vertical at a low "natural rate" of unemployment and horizontal, at least at zero inflation, over a moderately high range of unemployment above that).[12] Finally, because deflationary activity by monopolists is a remote possibility in the event of active money supply inflation, monetarist inflations can easily become "runaway" inflations, and historically almost all "runaway" inflations are attributable to "runaway" monetary growth.

C. Cause C: Exogenous Shocks

Exogenous shocks (that is, changes in $\Delta Y\%$ outside the control of domestic decision makers, official or otherwise) can cause one-shot, secular, or accelerating inflation, depending on whether they are temporary, permanent and stable, or of increasing intensity. Assuming passivity among other possible causes, we can illustrate this point with a timely example.[13]

Suppose that wages are rising at the same rate as average productivity advance and there is full-employment. Next, suppose this pleasant situation is disrupted when a powerful foreign oil cartel (like the Organization of Petroleum Exporting Countries) raises the price of crude oil from $3 to $12 per barrel. An aggregate increase in the domestic transactions demand for nominal money and a loss of real domestic income ensue. Both results may be either temporary or permanent. It is a temporary loss of real income if, first, oil prices shortly thereafter fall back to $3 while all other prices and wages remain unchanged, or, second, if the price of oil remains at $12 and all other prices and wages also rise fourfold to restore all former levels of *relativity*.

The first temporary case amounts to an inflation-deflation attributable to Cause C, with only a temporary increment in money demand, and it suggests a definition of "passivity" in the context of Cause C. **Passivity** in this case requires an absence of such exogenous shocks (that is, constant productivity growth), compensatory positive-negative shocks, or, with respect to an "open" economy, variations in rates of currency exchange designed to assure a balance of international accounts—that is, floating exchange rates.[14] In the second tempo-

---

[12] Otto Eckstein and R. Brinner, *The Inflationary Process in the United States,* U.S. Congress, Joint Economic Committee Study, Washington, D.C., 1972.

[13] For detailed discussion of this example see J. L. Pierce and J. J. Enzler, "The Effects of External Inflationary Shocks," *Brookings Papers on Economic Activity,* No. 1 (1974).

[14] For a good explanation of this last point, see T. J. Courchene, "Stabilization Policy: A Monetarist Interpretation," in *Issues in Canadian Economics,* edited by L. H. Officer and L. B. Smith (Toronto: McGraw-Hill Ryerson, 1974).

rary case, where all other prices and wages rise fourfold, we have one-shot inflation with a permanent increment in money demand.

If the shock is not temporary, the loss of real income is permanent. Cause C exogenous shock then produces at least one-shot inflation. For example, the monetary authority could try to suppress this inflation by curtailing the money supply, but this action would violate passivity because it would raise unemployment in the course of restoring the old aggregate price level, and it would not regain the lost real income. More important for present purposes is the likely action of those possessing market power. In violation of their passivity, domestic monopolistic elements may attempt to restore their real income by boosting their prices and wages (to cover the higher costs of oil), but this too would not regain the lost real income. Assuming passive money supply, this effort would only cause progression to secular inflation.

Because the shock is assumed to be *permanent,* the oil cartel will maintain its receipts in real terms; hence, once the new relative price ratios are established in its favor, the ratios will be maintained by a rate of *further* oil price inflation matching the discretionary "recoupment" inflation of the domestic price-wage setters. We are then on an escalating merry-go-round. Only a fairly long lag pattern would prevent secular inflation from progressing to accelerating inflation under these conditions. Efforts on the part of the monetary authority to stifle these inflations would most likely result in perpetual and "unnatural" unemployment because passivity does not hold for either Cause B or Cause C in this instance. Both Causes B and C are working to increase prices and wages rather than maintain full-employment.

In brief, the problem of exogenous shock is analogous to the problem of flooded farmland or technological stagnation. If it is temporary and passivity holds for the other causes, the lost real income is temporary and the shock is "neutral." If it is permanent to the extent, say, of half our farmland sliding into the sea, or half our productivity growth suddenly disappearing, then the lost real income is a *permanent* loss, and inflations of varying degrees of severity are likely to ensue as people fight for greater shares of a smaller national real income.

D. Other Possible Causes and a Qualification

Other causes of inflation could be identified, but for present purposes they can either be subsumed under one of the preceding causes or merely acknowledged as potential qualifications to certain aspects of the analysis. Deficit spending at the federal level, for example, is often mentioned as a cause of inflation, but it is not fully distinct from Cause A.[15] Variations in the velocity of money ($\Delta V\%$) can also be considered a cause of inflation, but these too can be subsumed

[15] Abba Lerner, *Flation* (Baltimore: Penguin Books, 1972), p. 33; G. P. Dwyer, Jr., "Inflation and Government Deficits," *Economic Inquiry* (July 1982).

under Cause A. Empirically, velocity inflations seem to be rare and unimportant.[16]

In reality, the operations of Causes A through C are neither as simple nor as direct as our outline suggests because numerous factors may increase or abate their influence. Most of the necessary qualifications are beyond our scope, but one qualification is particularly worthy of mention. A major assumption of our Cause B (monopolistic) discussion is that prices of goods, services, productive factors, and assets outside the monopolistic sectors are all flexible enough over the long run to move in step with prices inside the monopolistic sectors (provided structural change is absent). However, such flexibility does not prevail universally. Many prices and rates of remuneration are inflexibly fixed by long-term contract, regulation, or legislation. To the extent inflexibility applies (and historically its importance seems to be lessening), variations in aggregate inflation and unemployment will be attenuated.

III. THE EVIDENCE CONCERNING CAUSES

In theory, the three causes of inflation appear to be quite different. In practice, however, we encounter numerous difficulties when we try to attribute any specific real-world inflation to one of these three causes. The trick is to determine the *unique earmarks* of each cause, and then look for them in instances of inflation. Earmarks that may be associated with more than one cause don't help much, yet most earmarks isolated so far seem to have this failing. For example, if wages were rising more rapidly than productivity during some inflation, one might be tempted to conclude that "market-power push" by unions in concentrated industries was the cause. However, this pattern is also symptomatic of money-supply and exogenous shock inflations; money wages almost always rise with inflated prices.

Another example is illustrated in Figure 21–6. Believers in market-power inflation often claim that rising rates of price increase coupled with rising unemployment, as indicated by the movement from R to S in that diagram, can only be attributed to market-power push (Cause B). But the validity of this attribution depends on what constitutes full-employment. A monetarist could claim that the R to S movement is compatible with Cause A, given a true full-employment level of 9% instead of 5% (see Figure 21–6). Indeed, even if 5% were the true full-employment level (ruling out Cause A), this R to S movement might be due to Cause C (exogenous shock) rather than Cause B.

None of the evidence presented in the following subsections is completely free of this identification problem, and in some instances the doubts will be

---

[16] Phillip Cagen, "The Monetary Dynamics of Hyperinflation," in *Studies in the Quantity Theory of Money,* edited by Milton Friedman (Chicago: University of Chicago Press, 1956); Tibor Scitovsky and Anne Scitovsky, "Inflation versus Unemployment: An Examination of their Effects," in *Inflation Growth and Employment,* Commission on Money and Credit (Englewood Cliffs, N.J.: Prentice-Hall, 1964).

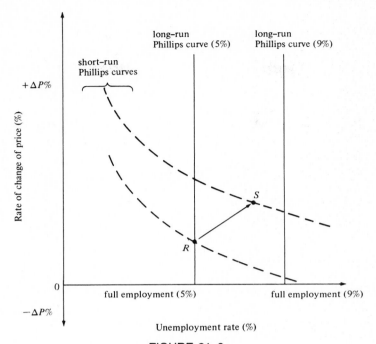

FIGURE 21–6.

acknowledged explicitly. Unfortunately, space limitations prevent "full disclosure" in every instance.

A. Cause A Inflation: What to Look for? What's Been Found?

The most obvious way to test the monetarist theory, that is, the effect of money supply, is to check the relationship between changes in money supply and changes in aggregate price level. This has been done repeatedly and variously by numerous investigators using data from many diverse time periods and many different countries. And the answer is almost always the same—prices and money supply do indeed move closely together, especially in the long run.[17] United States experience in this respect between 1961 and 1981 is plotted in Figure 21–7, where the vertical axis measures percentage price change for each year and the horizontal axis measures percentage change in money supply during the preceding year. A positive line depicting the relation $\Delta P\% = \Delta M\%$ is included, highlighting the positive association between these variables. (The negative lines are discussed later.)

[17] To list but a few examples, see Anna Schwartz, "Secular Price Change in Historical Perspective," *Journal of Money Credit and Banking* (February 1973), Part II; P. Cagan, *Determinants and Effects of Change in the Stock of Money, 1875–1960* (New York: National Bureau of Economics Research, 1965); R. C. Vogel "The Dynamics of Inflation in Latin America," *American Economic Review* (March 1974).

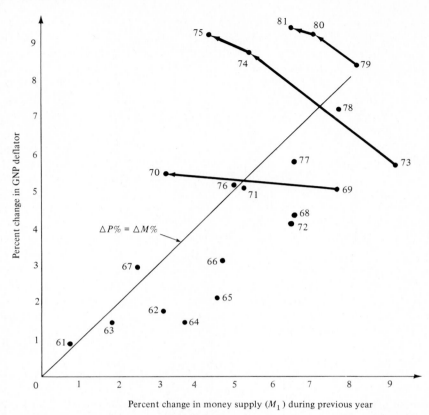

FIGURE 21-7. U.S. price changes and money supply changes, 1961–1981. Source: *Economic Report of the President,* 1983.

Although findings like these support monetarist theory, they do *not* provide ironclad evidence that *all* inflations *originate* from Cause A. Many inflations can be directly attributed to excessive monetary expansion, but other inflations appear to be initiated by Causes B or C, only later to be "permitted" or "endorsed" by passive monetary action designed to maintain full-employment (or prevent excessive unemployment). A further and more rigorous test of whether all inflations are directly attributable to monetary expansions of Cause A, one that acknowledges this lead-lag problem, rests on the observed value of a_3 in the following simplified depiction of the Phillips relation for aggregate wage change:

$$\Delta W\%_t = a_1 + a_2 1/U_t + a_3 \Delta P\%_{t-1} \qquad (21-7)$$

Where $\Delta W\%_t$ = percentage change in wage level during year t

$1/U_t$ = the inverse of the unemployment rate during year t

$\Delta P\%_{t-1}$ = percentage change in price level during the *prior* year

474

This is merely an algebraic expression for a family of Phillips curves, such as shown earlier in Figure 21–4, that illustrate monetarist theory. If the coefficient a_3 has a value of 1, the short-run negatively sloped Phillips curve shifts up or down to the full extent (one-for-one) that overall prices change up or down. Thus a value of 1 for a_3 tends to indicate Cause A at work. On the other hand, a value of a_3 substantially less than 1, say 0.5, would be observed if wages in monopolistic sectors rose (they almost never fall) *before* the rise in overall price level, a timing implying Cause B.[18]

In fact, statistical estimates of a_3 vary greatly across countries and within countries over different time periods. As regards foreign countries, for example, estimates of a_3 (or its equivalent) are close to or slightly greater than 1 for Austria, Belgium, France, and Italy based on inflation data from the 1950s and early 1960s.[19] Working independently of these estimates and using other criteria, an international team of experts studying European events during this period concluded that these four countries had experienced excess-demand monetary inflation (Cause A).[20] In contrast, estimates of a_3 for England, Ireland, Norway, Sweden, and Denmark during the same period are substantially less than 1, and the experts think "wage-push" (Cause B) played the major inflationary role in these instances. The experts' verdict on West Germany for these years is mixed. During the 1950s West Germany seems to have experienced very mild wage-push inflation, but significant demand-pull pressures developed during the early 1960s. As an apparent consequence, its a_3 coefficient rose from substantially less than 1 to approximately 1.[21]

United States experience since the Korean War is somewhat similar to that of West Germany. Estimates of a_3 based on United States data for the 1950s and early 1960s are substantially less than 1,[22] suggesting a poor fit for the monetarist model during that period. Aggregate statistics for these years also

---

[18] Despite appearances, a value of a_3 less than 1 for aggregate data does not necessarily imply the presence of money illusion. Still, money illusion could have such an effect, so this test is not airtight.

[19] R. G. Bodkin, *et al.*, *Price Stability and High Employment: The Options for Canadian Economic Policy,* Economic Council of Canada (Ottawa: Queens Printer, 1967); R. J. Flanagan, "The U.S. Phillips Curve and International Unemployment Rate Differentials," *American Economic Review* (March 1973); Economic Commission for Europe, *Incomes in Postwar Europe: A Study of Policies Growth and Distribution,* United Nations, 1967 (Sales No. 66 II.E.14); L. Ulman and R. Flanagan, *Wage Restraint: A Study of Income Policies in Western Europe* (Berkeley, Calif.: University of California Press, 1971).

[20] W. Fellner, M. Gilbert, B. Hansen, R. Kahn, F. Lutz, and P. de Wolf, *The Problem of Rising Prices,* Organization for European Economic Co-operation, 1961, p. 46.

[21] Ulman and Flanagan, *op. cit.,* pp. 180–181. It should be noted that these international estimates of a_3 are not positively related to the rate at which prices rose during the period the data apply. For example, recent estimates for the United States, Canada, Germany, United Kingdom, France and Japan based on the 1959–1969 period reveal that the first three had the lowest average annual rate of price increase (2.4 compared to 4.2), yet, on average, their a_3 were higher than those of the last three countries (0.63 versus 0.54). Organization for Economic Co-operation and Development, *Inflation: The Present Problem,* December 1970.

[22] For examples, see G. L. Perry, *Unemployment, Money Wage Rates and Inflation* (Cambridge, Mass.: MIT Press, 1966); and the papers by A. Hirsch and S. Hymans in *The Econometrics of Price Determination* (Washington, D.C.: Board of Governors of the Federal Reserve System, 1972).

suggest a poor fit for the monetarist model—average annual growth in money supply ($\Delta M\%$) and real GNP ($\Delta Y\%$) were very close at 4.5 and 4.3%, respectively, whereas average unemployment was held moderately high at 4.8%. Even so, the consumer price index rose by 2% per year. Things changed dramatically, however, with the eruption of hostilities in Vietnam. Between 1965 and 1969 $\Delta M\%$ rose from 7 to 10%, unemployment fell from 4.5 to 3.5%, and $\Delta P\%$ as measured by the CPI rose from 2 to 6% per year. Coincidentally, estimates of the a_3 coefficient for these years jumped toward 1.[23] Taken together, these facts point to a clear-cut case of excess-demand Cause A inflation during the war years.

The record for Cause A thus indicates that virtually all inflations are *accompanied* by money supply expansion but not all inflations are *caused* by it. Mere accompaniment involves no more than a "passive," full-employment monetary policy when confronted with *non*monetary inflationary forces.[24] Direct causation involves active stimulation of excess employment and demand.

B. Cause B Inflation: What to Look for? What's Been Found?

There are several earmarks of market-power inflation besides the low a_3 coefficient mentioned previously. These include (1) differing discretionary behaviors varying with the strength of market power, (2) spill-over effects, (3) perverse movements in aggregate variables, and (4) severe political and social disputes over income distribution.

1. Discretionary Behavior. With respect to differences in discretionary behavior, a number of studies have shown wages increasing more rapidly over fairly long periods in highly unionized, highly concentrated industries than in other industries.[25] These results are impressive, but they run counter to other evidence and to theory, both of which suggest no *long-run* decades of divergence in wages based solely on the existence of market power. Thus, this author attributes these results either to *changes* in structure (inadvertently reflected in the power variables these studies used), or to a dominance of cyclical effects during the time periods tested in these studies. Once long-run divergence is precluded and spill-overs are accepted, detection of a genuine long-run inflationary bias is much more difficult, for then it must be shown that market power (and not money supply) is responsible for an *overall* inflationary wage pattern, even with-

---

[23] Eckstein and Brinner, *op. cit.,* C. L. Schultze, "Has the Phillips Curve Shifted? Some Additional Evidence," *Brookings Papers of Economic Activity* No. 2 (1971). For a different interpretation concerning this shift see G. L. Perry, "Changing Labor Markets and Inflation," *Brookings Papers of Economic Activity,* No. 3 (1970).

[24] Robert J. Gordon, "The Demand for and Supply of Inflation," *Journal of Law & Economics* (December 1975).

[25] These include J. Garbarino, "A Theory of Interindustry Wage Structure Variation," *Quarterly Journal of Economics* (May 1950); W. G. Bowen, *Wage Behavior in the Postwar Period* (Princeton, N.J.: Industrial Relations Section Princeton University, 1960); M. Segal, "Unionism and Wage Movements," *Southern Economic Journal* (October 1961); and B. Allen, "Market Concentration and Wage Increases: U.S. Manufacturing 1947–1964," *Industrial and Labor Relations Review* (April 1968).

out excess demand—that is, responsible for an upward shift of the Phillips curve as in Figures 21–5 and 21–6. For this overall pattern, several types of evidence are available.

First, an analysis of 118 wage contracts entered into by 14 major firms during 1954–1970 discloses a significant ratchet effect in wage increases granted by firms in highly concentrated, highly unionized industries, despite the fact that, on average, wages paid by these firms rose no more rapidly over the long run than those paid by firms in competitive labor and product markets.[26] It was estimated that a rise *and* fall of unemployment by 1 percentage point would cause *competitive* wages to rise and fall with *no* net change, that is, no ratchet. On the other hand, with four-firm concentration equal 100%, the same rise and fall of unemployment yields a positive net change of 0.77 in the percentage rate of wage inflation.

A second type of evidence concerns discretionary deflation rather than inflation, but carries similar implications. The deflation occurred under the Kennedy Administration's wage-price "guidepost" program. As will be explained in the following chapter on policy, this was a *voluntary* program exhorting both business and labor to abide by certain noninflationary guideposts when setting prices and wages. Any interindustry differentials in deflation under the program could therefore be attributed to discretionary power. And several studies show that, indeed, the guide posts had greater impact on the wages of highly concentrated, highly unionized industries than on other wages.[27] Graphically, these results would be depicted by a downward shift of the short-run Phillips curve led by those possessing substantial market power. Periods 10 through 20 of Table 21–1 illustrate such an experience.

2. Spill-overs. Spill-overs, a second identifying feature of market-power push, are wage increases (or decreases) obtained by one powerful group of workers that spill-over into other less powerful sectors of the labor market because other workers attempt to maintain their relative position in the wage structure. In particular, highly concentrated, highly unionized industries that happen to be blessed with above average productivity growth have the option of (1) passing their cost savings on to customers in the form of lower product prices, (2) keeping prices stable and raising wages at a rate that exceeds overall average productivity growth, or (3) raising prices *and* wages. To the extent one of the latter two options prevails, and to the extent the excessive wage increases spill-

---

[26] D. Greer, "Market Power and Wage Inflation: A Further Analysis," *Southern Economic Journal* (January 1975). It is also shown in this paper that there is good reason to believe that wage increases of monopolistic firms *led* the aggregate price increases of the 1950s and 1960s, contributing to a low aggregate a_3 coefficient and fostering market-power inflation. For related evidence see W. C. Riddell, "The Empirical Foundations of the Phillips Curve," *Econometrica* (January 1979).

[27] Greer, *op. cit.*, S. Wallack, "Wage-Price Guidelines and the Rate of Wage Changes in U.S. Manufacturing, 1951–1966, *Southern Economic Journal* (July 1971); G. L. Perry, "Wages and the Guideposts," *American Economic Review* (September 1967); G. Pierson, "The Effect of Union Strength on the U.S. Phillips Curve," *American Economic Review* (June 1968).

over into other sectors, wages overall tend to exceed average productivity growth, thereby contributing to inflation.

Otto Eckstein and T. A. Wilson were among the first to demonstrate the presence of spill-overs in the United States, and their "pace-setting" wage leaders were highly concentrated, highly unionized industries such as autos, steel, rubber, and electrical machinery.[28] In a still broader study, J. Eatwell, J. Llewellyn, and R. Tarling analyzed wage and productivity trends in the manufacturing industries of 15 countries for 1958–1967.[29] They found that earnings across industries, within each country, rose more uniformly than productivity across industries. Moreover, the *average* rate of earnings inflation in each country did not equal average productivity growth among all industries in each country. Instead, average earnings rose at approximately the same rate as productivity in the *three* industries with *greatest* productivity growth in each country, suggesting spill-overs from these three industries down to others.

How spill-overs occur is a separate issue. Within unionized sectors there is no doubt but that the wage aspirations of weaker unions are stimulated by inflationary gains of powerful unions. It has been shown that strike activity tends to increase in an industry that deviates substantially from its traditional place in the interindustry wage structure.[30] ("No money, no bunny," shouted workers striking for spill-over wages at VW's Rabbit plant in Pennsylvania in 1978.)[31] As for the other workers toward the bottom end of the spill-over, it can be argued that these workers need not be organized in unions to express their dissatisfaction if their wages fail to keep up with the general pattern.[32] Much spill-over is even governmentally imposed, as when for example the legal minimum wage rate is periodically raised in response to wage-price inflation, or when wages paid by government and its contractors are by law keyed to "comparable" earnings in the private sphere. Spill-overs thus tend to draw competitive wages up, rather than bring noncompetitive wages down, erecting a general inflationary bias grounded on what amounts to short-run discretionary power.

[28] O. Eckstein and T. A. Wilson, "The Determination of Money Wages in American Industry," *Quarterly Journal of Economics* (August 1962). Two related studies are A. G. Hines, "Wage Inflation in the United Kingdom 1948–1962: A Disaggregated Study," *Economic Journal* (March 1969); and M. Wachter, "Relative Wage Equations for U.S. Manufacturing Industries 1947–1967," *Review of Economics and Statistics* (November 1970).

[29] J. Eatwell, J. Llewellyn, and R. Tarling "Money Wage Inflation in Industrial Countries," *Review of Economic Studies* (October 1974). For further evidence see, e.g., L. N. Christofides, R. Swidinsky, and D. A. Wilton, "A Microeconometric Analysis of Spillovers within the Canadian Wage Determination Process, "*Review of Economics and Statistics* (May 1980).

[30] J. Shorey, "An Analysis of Strike Activity in Britain," unpublished Ph.D. thesis, University of London, 1974, cited by D. Metcalf, "Inflation: The Labor Market," Working Paper No. 61 (Industrial Relations Section, Princeton University 1975).

[31] *Wall Street Journal,* October 13, 1978, p. 1.

[32] C. L. Schultze, *Recent Inflation in the United States,* Study for the Joint Economic Committee, U.S. Congress, 1959, p. 68; "The Soaring Cost of Employee Compensation," *Business Week,* September 7, 1974, pp. 42–44; "A Boom in White-Collar Salaries," *Business Week,* September 11, 1978, pp. 50–51.

3. **Aggregate Variables.** Aggregate economic events that cannot logically be accounted for by Cause A theory may also indicate Cause B (monopoly power) at work. Three time periods characterized by such anomalies are identified by the three negatively sloped lines of Figure 21–7, which show price inflation *rising* despite substantial *drops* in money supply growth. The 1973–1974 episode is best explained by exogenous shock, so it will be discussed in the following section. Cause B monopoly power best explains the two remaining anomalies. Here we focus on the 1969–1970 episode.

Shortly after taking office in 1969, President Nixon announced that he would not rely on "guideposts" or "controls" to bring price and wage inflation down from their lofty Vietnam War levels. Instead, he said he would achieve stability by deliberately reducing aggregate demand through balanced budgets and curtailed monetary growth. Money supply was cut back from an annual growth rate of 10% in 1968 to a 2% annual growth rate during the first half of 1970. And, as shown in Table 21–2, the unemployment rate advanced from 3.3 to 4.8% over the same period, advancing thereafter to 6.0%. Nevertheless, union wages not only *continued* to increase, their *rate of increase increased,* as also indicated in Table 21–2. Nonunion wages continued to increase, too, but they did not accelerate like union wages. Graphically, the situation is illustrated by the *R* to *S* movement in Figure 21–6 with a 5% "natural rate" of unemployment.

TABLE 21–2. Unemployment and Rates of Change of Union and Non-union Money Wages: 1969–1971

Year and Quarter	Unemployment (%) (Seasonally Adjusted)	Wage Changes Annual Rate %	
		Union	Nonunion
1969 I	3.3	6.7	5.5
1969 II	3.5	7.6	5.8
1969 III	3.7	7.9	6.2
1969 IV	3.6	7.5	7.2
1970 I	4.2	7.6	5.4
1970 II	4.8	8.2	5.2
1970 III	5.2	8.3	6.1
1970 IV	5.8	6.9	5.9
1971 I	6.0	8.0	5.5
1971 II	6.0	8.6	5.6
1971 III	6.0	12.9	5.6

Sources: *Economic Report of the President,* various issues; Marten Estey, "Union and Non-union Wage Changes, 1959–1972" in *Price and Wage Control: An Evaluation of Current Policies* Part 2, Joint Economic Committee, U.S. Congress, 1972, p. 328.

Confronted with these facts, those who see no inflationary harm whatever in market power might argue that Cause A "expectations" of inflation fed the continuing and accelerating inflation. In other words, they could argue that the "natural rate" of unemployment must have shifted from its prior estimated level of 4 or 5% to 7 or 8%, which would then allow the facts to fit a purely competitive Cause A theory of these events. This argument contains several flaws, however. Consider first the inconsistency implied by postulating a long-run "natural rate" of unemployment that shifts abruptly about in the short run. Second, a purely competitive seller's expectation that he can actually sell his labor or product at ever higher prices needs to be confirmed by continued brisk sales or full-time employment to warrant the proper Cause A price "expectations." If not confirmed, the seller will begin to expect the loss of his business or job and consequently act more in accord with these distressing expectations than with his price "expectations." Thus, expectations alone cannot explain *accelerating* wages when unemployment climbs to unusual heights. In any event, the Nixon administration foresook its purely monetarist approach by instituting a 90 day wage-price freeze on August 15, 1971.

4. Political and Social Disputes. Put bluntly, Cause B inflation amounts to no more than a struggle over income shares, a struggle that may occasionally provoke serious social and political conflict. To illustrate this as briefly as possible we borrow liberally from an analysis of "strato-inflation" in Chile after World War II:

> a wage fixing process developed by which government decreed annually an increase in minimum wages (and salaries) equivalent to the previous year's rise in living costs. On this base, the more powerful unions would proceed to bargain for *additional increases to cover increased productivity, plus* some part of the anticipated future rise in prices. Farm prices were guaranteed so as to protect farmers' real income against the consequent rise in industrial prices, and industrial prices were fixed (often by legal controls) to cover the anticipated increases in wages and raw materials charges and to protect profits in real terms. The system inherently involved—granted an initial instability and the large monetary increases that were required to protect the position of individual groups—a cumulative inflation.[33]

The upshot: money claims to national income exceeded 100% of real income. Notice in particular the three part *money* wage demands of unions: (1) an increment for past price inflation (to preserve existing real income), (2) a further increment for productivity growth, plus (3) something extra for *anticipated* price increases. If achieved in *real* terms, union members would have obviously gained appreciable income share at the expense of others. The resulting strato-inflation ranging between 20 and 50% prevented such a realization but became intolerable, so the Chilean government made "periodic attempts at 'stabilization,' by severe

[33] D. Jackson, H. A. Turner, and F. Wilkinson, *Do Trade Unions Cause Inflation?* (Cambridge, U.K.: Cambridge University Press, 1972), p. 34.

deflations, credit squeezes, wage freezes and the like." However, the Cause B monopolistic powers were not forced into passivity. These measures

> induced violent social conflict—there was a general strike in 1954. And every such attempt at stabilization was finally defeated because the reaction of particular groups to the measures of control or deflation involved was so violent that the government abandoned the effort.[34]

Thus money supply growth does not tell the whole story, even about certain "strato-inflations."

5. Market-Power Profit Inflation. In this section we have concentrated on market-power *wage* inflation to the neglect of market-power *profit* inflation simply because the available cross-section evidence concerning the latter is sketchy.[35] Disaggregate behavior of profits is similar to that of wages, but the complete step of showing conclusively that beneath this behavior lie long-run inflationary forces has not, in my judgment, been taken. Half this step has apparently been made because the observed behavior is consistent with several plausible theories of such inflationary elements.[36] Some interesting case history evidence is also available, part of which will be reviewed in the next chapter. In any event, we need not stretch this present knowledge into a whole step to establish the existence of market-power inflation. The available evidence on profits supports all that needs to be said given the labor market evidence just reviewed: discretionary power in product markets is sufficient to enable capitalists to protect their income share from wage inflation and, as already mentioned, such power apparently fosters wage inflation. At the very least, product market power acts as a *transmission belt* to relay labor market wages on to consumer prices.[37]

C. Cause C Inflation: What to Look for? What's Been Found?

As already noted, the unusual episode of 1973–1974 (see Figure 21–7) can largely be attributed to exogenous shock, the principal identifying characteristic in this case being abrupt and violent changes in the prices of a few crucial commodities evincing shortages of supply and low price elasticities of demand. Between November 1972 and August 1973, an estimated 64% of the increase

---

[34] *Ibid.* Later on the authors note that "the incidence of *recorded* strikes in Chile in the 1960s was ten times higher than that in Britain—for an approximately ten times faster rate of general price increases." For a related but more recent report on Brazil see the *Wall Street Journal*, August 13, 1982, p. 36. And on Argentina, Guido Di Tella, "Price Oscillation, Oligopolistic Behavior and Inflation: The Argentine Case," *World Development* (1979), pp. 1,043–1,052.

[35] F. M. Scherer, *Industrial Market Structure and Economic Performance* (Chicago: Rand McNally, 1970), pp. 284–303; R. E. Beals, "Concentrated Industries, Administered Prices, and Inflation: A Survey of Recent Empirical Research," Report to the Council on Wage and Price Stability (processed, June 17, 1975); S. Lustgarten, *Industrial Concentration and Inflation* (Washington, D.C.: American Enterprise Institute, 1975).

[36] C. L. Schultze, *op. cit.*; A. S. Eichner, *The Megacorp and Oligopoly* (Cambridge, U.K.: Cambridge University Press, 1976).

[37] Alfred E. Kahn, "The Relevance of Industrial Organization," in *Industrial Organization, Antitrust, and Public Policy* edited by John V. Craven (Boston: Kluwer-Nijhoff Publishing, 1983).

in the wholesale price index was accounted for by increases in agricultural prices alone. Another 14% arose from imported commodities, largely because of devaluation. Then, from the fall of 1973 to the end of 1974, domestic prices of all fuels and related products shot up 70%, thereby replacing food as the major inflationary factor. Since our earlier discussion of shocks (particularly OPEC's shocking price behavior) dealt with these events, only a few points need emphasis here.

First, these shocks noticeably reduced the *real* income and wealth of people who had come to take rising real incomes for granted and who were, therefore, unprepared for such contingencies. Sufficient discretionary power was spread among corporate and labor groups to enable them to try to regain that lost real income through escalated wage, salary, and profit demands. These demands in turn raised the costs and prices of most other commodities, converting what might otherwise have been a simple one-shot, exogenous shock inflation into a continuing market-power push inflation.

Second, these inflationary recoupment efforts may have caused some domestic redistribution of the remaining real income in favor of those having the greatest market power. Over the long run, spill-overs into the competitive sectors could restore initial distributive shares.

Finally, in their effort to keep the inflation of 1973–1974 below "double-digit" levels, United States monetary authorities had to abandon whatever "passive" full-employment objectives they may have held. Their resulting meager expansion of the money supply forced unemployment up to heights not seen since the Great Depression—a fact suggestive of the situation's severity.

SUMMARY

There seem to be three basic causes of inflation: (A) monetary-fiscal stimulation, which operates on the principle of aggregate excess demand; (B) discretionary power in labor and product markets, which involve wage and profit claims that add up to more than 100% of real income; and (C) exogenous shocks, which are either capricious or attributable to premeditated acts in the international sphere (unlike the other causes, these shocks are the primary determinants of radical changes in aggregate real income).

These causes are interdependent in that the pure operation of each is dependent on the passivity or neutrality of the others. Cause A passivity is monetary-fiscal policy maintaining the natural-competitive rate of full-employment. Cause B passivity is purely competitive structure or behavior in all markets, something that assures that the natural rate of employment is the *only* equilibrium rate. Cause C passivity is an absence of exogenous shock (or temporary cross-cancelling shocks) plus floating exchange rates. If passivity holds in all these respects, there can be no accelerating inflation and the other types of inflation can be avoided. If passivity holds with respect to any two causes, the remaining cause can generate inflation of any type by becoming an active inflationary force.

Whether one cause can act in a deflationary manner to counter an inflation initiated by another cause depends solely on whether the inflationary cause can be *converted* to passivity (to be a cause it had to be an active cause at some point). If the inflationary cause cannot be so converted, then deflation can be achieved only through greater unemployment. This is as true for Cause A countering a Cause B inflation as it is for the less realistic cases of Causes B or C countering a Cause A inflation. Thus full-employment depends entirely on passivity, and the price level depends on whether the deflationary or the inflationary force is pacified first.

Empirically, there is evidence of all three causes. Indeed, recent United States economic history provides examples of each. From 1954 to about 1967, a period of only mild inflation, Cause B seems to have prevailed. Between 1967 and 1970, the Vietnam War occasioned a serious Cause A inflation. Reversal by means of Cause A (monetary deflation) was prevented in 1970 and 1971 by Cause B developments. More recently, Cause C touched off an even more serious inflation, and once again Cause A deflationary efforts have been hampered by Cause B inflationary forces, which this time spring from a quest to recoup lost real income.

22 Inflation and Macro-Stability: Wage and Price Controls

We have learned a lot about wage and price controls but not how to control wages and prices.

—Sidney L. Jones

Panic, chaos, disillusion—all are possible if inflation gets out of hand. Rapid inflation drastically reshuffles people's real incomes, as some keep up and others fall behind. It ambushes savings, disrupts corporate finance, and undermines long-term projects.

Wage-price control is an attempt by governments to deal directly with inflation. It has been tried at various times in the U.S. and Europe, and is likely to be tried again in one form or another. Our review of wage-price control covers several questions. How might wage-price control help fight inflation? What does wage-price control entail? What has experience taught us? What improvements might be made in the policy if it is ever tried again?

I. THE PROBLEM

A. The Causes of Inflation

As argued in Chapter 21, there are essentially three causes of inflation: (1) demand-pull, (2) market-power push (also called cost-push in some forms), and (3) exogenous shock. The price effect of the first two may be seen in Figure 22–1, which shows simple shifts in demand and supply.

1. *Demand-pull* operates on the principle of excess aggregate demand. As demand increases from D_1 to D_2 in Figure 22–1, price level is pulled up from P_1 to P_2 and equilibrium shifts from point F to point E. A jump in the supply of money could cause such a demand-pull inflation. This is immortalized in the old saying that inflation is just "too much money chasing too few goods."

2. *Market-power push* operates on the supply side. Prices are pushed up by wage escalations that exceed productivity growth or by higher profit markups.

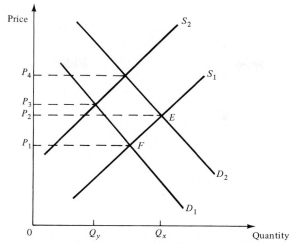

FIGURE 22–1. Inflation from shifts of demand and supply

The guilty parties here are powerful labor unions and/or large corporations. In Figure 22–1, the higher cost per unit would shift supply up from S_1 to S_2, which relative to D_1 boosts price from P_1 to P_3.

B. The Ultimate Role of the Money Supply

It should be noted that exogenous shocks and market-power pushes erupt from certain sectors of the economy, say food in the case of a drought or steel in the case of excessive steelworker wage increases. These sectoral jumps in prices need not result in overall inflation of the *average* price level if elsewhere in the economy prices are falling. Thus exogenous shocks and market-power pushes do not generate general inflation unless "endorsed" at the aggregate level by money supply expansion, responsibility for which rests with the Federal Reserve Board. Stated differently, virtually all aggregate inflations are *accompanied* by money supply expansion but not all inflations are *caused* by it. Exogenous shock and market-power push stand as separate causes.

The critical role of aggregate money supply works in the opposite direction as well. Virtually all inflations can be stopped dead in their tracks by sufficiently stringent money supply curtailment. This works through lessened aggregate demand, and may be illustrated simply by referring again to Figure 22–1. If at the start demand is D_2, a market-power push that shifted supply from S_1 to S_2 would lift price from P_2 to P_4. But a drop in demand from D_2 to D_1 by monetary restraint could press price level back down to P_3, nearly wiping out the inflationary effect.

The great importance of money supply to inflation has spawned an entire school of economic thought, members of which are called *monetarists*. Monetarists are the chief critics of wage-price controls because, as they see it, monetary

485

restraint is both necessary and sufficient to achieve price and wage stability. Moreover, in this view, direct controls are not merely worthless. They are oppressive, wasteful, and economically deadly. They create artificial shortages and black markets, crimp freedom, and lead to misallocations of resources.[1]

C. The Problem: Where Controls May Help

Those who advocate the use of wage-price controls concede that money supply is crucial. Indeed, they even concede that tight monetary constraint could stop any inflation if sufficiently tight. Where, then, do advocates of controls differ from the monetarists? First, they draw a distinction between demand-pull inflation caused by excess money supply growth and other kinds of inflations. Second, they believe that money supply reductions *alone* are a proper remedy to cure only excess demand inflation. Third, they argue that combat against market-power push inflation is best conducted by a two-pronged attack—monetary restraint *plus* wage-price control. Fourth, they contend that in this context monetary curtailment alone is too blunt an instrument, one that creates very high costs in unemployment and excess capacity. Thus, in short, procontrols people arrive at their position by weighing perceived benefits and costs. They advocate controls as a low-cost means of countering market-power push inflation.

In terms of Figure 22–1, the basic idea can be appreciated by looking again at what happens when demand is pressed down from D_2 to D_1 in the effort to counter the shift of supply from S_1 to S_2. Price, as we noted, falls from P_4 to P_3. At the same time, however, quantity falls toward Q_y, resulting in an overall drop in quantity from Q_x to Q_y. With quantity down, unemployment rises and idle capacity emerges—the costs of concern to advocates of controls. Would it not be better, procontrols people ask, if instead of shifting demand from D_2 to D_1, we simply shifted supply from S_2 to S_1 through the application of wage-price controls?

Monetarists concede that when money supply curbs depress demand, unemployment and idle capacity ensue. But they are not overly concerned about these costs because they consider them to be mild and temporary. Moreover, monetarists scoff at the theory of controls, saying that the shift from S_2 to S_1 would occur even without controls if monetary restraint substantially raised unemployment for a sufficient spell. (Granting this, a more sophisticated theory of controls would hold that controls can achieve a *quicker* shift than monetary policy alone can attain.) In short, the monetarists do not see powerful unions and large corporations as being much of a problem. If those possessing market power do not respond immediately to recessionary forces, they will *eventually* be beaten into submission by the penalties of low profits and high unemployment.

D. The Problem: Concrete Examples

However lightly monetarists may regard it, there is enough of a problem with market-power push inflation to cause politicians to take wage-price controls

[1] For a good statement of the monetarist position, see Samuel Brittan and Peter Lilley, *The Delusion of Incomes Policy* (New York: Holmes & Meier, 1977).

seriously. Some evidence indicates that highly unionized and highly concentrated sectors of the economy occasionally cause inflation directly. Even if this evidence is discarded, there is other evidence indicating that inflations started by other causes are perpetuated and aggravated by market power. Market power seems to make prices and wages unresponsive to downward demand pressures.

The steel industry provides several classic examples. Between 1955 and 1958 capacity usage in steel fell sharply from 92.1% to 59.1%; at the same time the price of steel mill products rose roughly 23%. Between 1973 and 1976 capacity usage dipped markedly again; yet prices simultaneously soared over 60%. A major contributing factor to these and similar experiences was ever rising steelworker wages and fringe benefits. Between 1952 and 1977 average hourly employee costs in steel rose 450%, which was much more than the 297% increase in all of manufacturing.[2]

A broader example is more recent. Beginning in late 1979 officials at the Federal Reserve System vowed to reduce inflation by curtailing money supply growth. Accordingly, the growth of "M1" slowed to 5% during 1981, down from 8% in 1979. Prices and wages were slow in responding, with union wages continuing to rise at annual rates exceeding 1979's rate of 9% until they dropped to 7.4% growth in 1982. The cost of the eventual price-wage de-escalation? The worst recession since the great depression: unemployment brushing 11%; capacity utilization falling below 70%; and business failures spreading like brushfire.[3]

II. WAGE-PRICE CONTROLS

A. Background

Monetarists like to point out that wage-price controls have a long and unclean record. They contend that all control efforts have been failures since as early as Roman times, when the Emperor Diocletian fixed the value of 900 goods, 130 grades of labor, and 41 freight rates. The death penalty was prescribed for breaches, of which there were apparently many. According to one historian of the day, Lactantius, much blood was shed "upon very slight and trifling accounts." Even so, failure of the policy lay more in the shortages and disruptions it seems to have caused than in the official savagery. People stopped bringing goods to market "because they could not get a reasonable price for them."[4] History is littered with hundreds of further attempts at direct control that

---

[2] Council on Wage and Price Stability, *Prices and Costs in the United States Steel Industry* (October 1977); R. M. Duke, R. L. Johnson, Hans Mueller, P. D. Qualls, C. T. Roush, and D. G. Tarr, *The United States Steel Industry and Its International Rivals* (Federal Trade Commission, 1977).

[3] Andrew F. Brimmer, "Monetary Policy and Economic Activity: Benefits and Costs of Monetarism," *American Economic Review* (May 1983), pp. 1–12. A similar experiment with monetarism in England produced similar results. See, e.g., *Wall Street Journal,* October 21, 1981, p. 27; November 3, 1981, p. 27; November 5, 1981, p. 27.

[4] Brittan and Lilley, *op. cit.,* p. 73.

monetarists consider no more than temporary successes (unless one wants to count totalitarian control programs as long-term successes). Of course procontrols people disagree with this interpretation. They argue in rebuttal that success often needs to be no more than "temporary," as in time of war. They argue further that crude ancient schemes imposed to counter money supply inflations cannot be fairly compared to our more sophisticated modern versions, which are designed to check market-power push inflations.

In fact, there is a spicy variety of "control" policies. Their common element is some form of **direct government supervision** of wages, salaries, prices, and perhaps profits, interest rates, and rents as well. The usual purpose of such controls is to stem inflation, although they have also been aimed at balance of payments improvement and income redistribution. Of present interest are control policies designed to check market-power push inflation.

Such control policies vary in four major respects: (1) coverage, (2) the nature of wage-price standards, (3) methods of enforcement, and (4) duration.[5] The scope of **coverage** may be very broad, in which case the program includes virtually all industrial sectors and most income variables—wages, salaries, prices, rents, and so on. Conversely, a program of limited coverage may focus on just a few industries (especially those thought to be sources of inflation) and a few economic figures (wages and prices, say). Between these extremes are countless combinations.

As for **standards,** every control policy must define what behavior is "proper." Standards may be simple or complex, vague or specific. An example of a fairly simple standard is a wage-price freeze. Usually, control policies have rather simple and vague *overall* standards, such as "wage restraint" or "increases matching productivity," applying to everyone covered. These standards are then augmented in the course of enforcement by more *specific* standards applying to certain industries or companies.

One extreme of **enforcement** has already received mention—Diocletian's death penalty. At the other extreme are official "urging," "jaw-boning," and "exhortation." These latter means of compliance obviously play on peoples' feelings of patriotism or fairness as opposed to their fear of oblivion. They are also the means western democracies rely on most heavily; so voluntary compliance is essential to the success of their control. Even where fines, or worse, serve as penalties, widespread support or acquiescence is necessary. (Otherwise the authorities would quickly run out of jail space.) As you might guess, there are some strong links between compliance method and program coverage. Jawboning can only work with limited coverage because it works on the spotlight principle, wherein public opinion is mobilized against offenders. Just as it is impossible for everyone to be famous, it is impossible to spotlight every corner

[5] Arnold R. Weber, *In Pursuit of Price Stability* (Washington, D.C.: Brookings Institution, 1973), pp. 10–14. See also *Wage and Price Policies in Australia, Austria, Canada, Japan, The Netherlands, and West Germany,* Congress of the U.S., Joint Economic Committee, 97th Congress, 2nd session (June 1982).

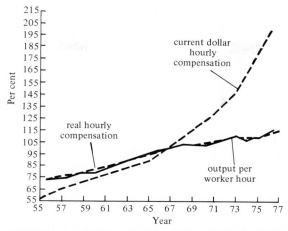

FIGURE 22–2. Indexes of output per worker and real and nominal compensation, private nonfarm business, for all persons. Source: U.S. Department of Labor, Bureau of Labor Statistics. 1967 = 100.

grocer and auto repair shop. Programs of broad coverage consequently require specific legal sanctions.

Regarding **duration,** most control policies have no set lifespan. A few, however, do, most notably policies that freeze wages and prices. In such cases the duration is always short—60 to 90 days or so. Longer freezes would petrify the economy until brittle.

With this background we are prepared to survey two United States control programs—Kennedy's wage-price "guideposts" and Nixon's Phases I through IV. A brief rundown of European experience then follows.

B. The Guidepost Program (1962–1966)

Well aware of the wage-price antics in steel and other power-laden industries during the late 1950s, President Kennedy's Council of Economic Advisors introduced an informal "guidepost" program in 1962. As stated in the *Economic Report of the President* the standard for noninflationary wage behavior was that wage increases in each industry should not exceed the rate of *overall* productivity increase.[6] Later, the vagueness of "overall productivity increase" was removed by specifying one number for wage increases, 3.2%, which was an average estimate of the previous 5 years' productivity growth. The theory underlying this standard derives from conditions pictured in Figure 22–2. Regardless of what happens to hourly compensation in dollars and cents, *real* income follows a narrow path cleared by output per worker hour, that is, productivity.

[6] *Economic Report of the President,* 1962, p. 189.

Hence the growth of *money* income might as well match the growth of *real* income as determined by productivity improvement. Moreover, if these two figures do match, producers' labor cost per unit will not increase on average because additions to labor cost will be offset by additions to output. With unit labor cost steady, *prices need not climb* (unless pushed up by raw materials costs). In short, the guideposts were designed so the productivity dividend could go to consumers (everybody) without rising prices.

Prices, that is, need not rise *overall*. The guidepost standard for *individual* industry price changes could not be zero because productivity advance *varies* from industry to industry. Given wage increments of 3.2% for all workers, unit labor costs will *fall* in those industries experiencing above average productivity growth and *rise* in those industries languishing with below average productivity growth. Accordingly, the guidepost standard for prices was that prices fall where productivity improvement was unusually brisk and rise where it was unusually slow. Given uniform wage increases, this price behavior would prevail under competitive conditions.

Figure 22–3 conveys the idea because it shows price changes plotted against productivity changes in 139 industries over 1958–1968. On average, prices rose, so declines did not offset increases. But the broadly negative relation is plain to see. If price changes had averaged out to zero, the price reductions would clearly have come chiefly from particularly progressive industries.

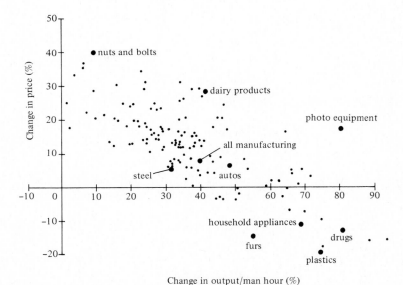

Change in output/man hour (%)

FIGURE 22–3. Per cent of change in output per man-hour and prices, for 139 manufacturing industries, 1958–1968. Source: Bureau of Labor Statistics Bulletin 1710, Productivity and the Economy (1971), p. 29.

These general wage and price standards were qualified by certain "exceptions." Wage increases, for example, could be above standard if necessary "to attract sufficient labor." And prices could rise above an industry's standard if necessary "to finance a needed expansion in capacity." Although economically defensible, these exceptions offered loopholes that complicated enforcement.

Jaw-boning, ear-stroking, and related anatomical incantations provided the main firepower of enforcement, although President Kennedy and later President Johnson were by no means averse to harsher measures. Various threats—ranging from prospective antitrust suits to massive sales from government stockpiles—were occasionally brought in for reinforcements. Still, the program was "voluntary," so the focus of its coverage remained rather narrowly fixed on the biggest, most highly concentrated, and most thoroughly unionized industries. Moreover, no bureaucracy was created to implement the program.

Because most control policies are based on the same economic principles as those guiding the guideposts, the problems arising under this program carry special significance.[7] High on the list of difficulties was the necessity of relying on *past* productivity performance to channel *future* wage settlements. In fact, productivity growth in 1963–1965 exceeded the 3.2% standard while wages generally met the standard. As a consequence, profits ballooned, angering organized labor. The Council of Economic Advisors considered raising the wage standard to 3.6%, which union leadership advocated, but stuck with 3.2% in the end. A measure of the delicacy of labor's support is the explosion of tempers caused by this little 0.4 percentage point difference of opinion. Unfortunately, it is not possible to solve the problem of finding a correct standard by adopting a short-run estimate based on current experience because productivity is whipped about rather wildly by the short-run business cycle. The problem is thus endemic to all control programs.

A major problem concerning prices lay in getting price reductions in industries experiencing especially favorable productivity growth. Competition would normally *force* price reductions in such cases, but of course competition was (and is) lacking in many industries. In particular, the auto industry gained substantial profit increases by refusing to cut prices in the face of above average productivity growth. Auto workers then felt free to press for wage increases that would break the 3.2 ceiling, and their success undermined the program. A similar situation arose in the airline industry in 1966. This latter breach in the ceiling damaged the program's foundation, heralding collapse shortly thereafter.

The guideposts might have been able to outlast these difficulties. They could not, however, endure the forces of economic boom that began building in 1966 and 1967 with the escalating war in Vietnam. As demand-pull inflation raised prices in competitive sectors outside the guidepost program, the 3.2% wage standard, which was barely acceptable to organized labor even assuming zero inflation, became intolerable. The moral is simple: *strong demand-pull pressure*

[7] For a thorough discussion, see John Sheahan, *Wage-Price Guideposts* (Washington, D.C.: Brookings Institution, 1967).

will crush any such voluntary program. By extension, a substantial exogenous shock inflation would also have destroyed the modicum of social consensus sustaining the program.

It is of course impossible to "prove" whether or not a given controls policy successfully stems inflation (or reduces unemployment) because one can never be sure what conditions would have been like without the policy. Nevertheless, deviations from prepolicy trends can be estimated statistically. A number of tests by this method show that, despite their several failings, the guideposts were moderately successful, at least temporarily. Overall wage and price inflation were trimmed by 1 or 2 percentage points between 1962 and 1966.[8] Moreover, the bulk of curtailment seems to have been achieved in those sectors receiving greatest policy attention—that is, highly unionized and highly concentrated industries such as machinery, chemicals, rubber, and petroleum.[9]

C. The Wage-Price Freeze of 1971, or Phase I[10]

The guideposts were just a teaser. They were so informal that Council economists learned of price increases through the newspapers. The guideposts likewise had no congressional authorization, no biting sanctions. It could be said, then, that on August 15, 1971, the United States really lost its virginity in this area of peacetime wage-price controls. On that day President Nixon, acting under standby authority granted by Congress in 1970, imposed a 90-day wage-price freeze. The freeze replaced his unsuccessful two and a half year effort to curb inflation by monetary restraint and deliberate recession. Most folks were by that time growing weary of inflation *plus* unemployment. There was consequently tremendous pressure on Nixon to "do something." Immediately after the freeze began, opinion polls showed 75% approval, including several expressions of near ecstasy from businessmen.[11]

The freeze was supposed to be a short and simple surprise. It was short because it was meant to be no more than a stopgap until a more elaborate Phase II control program could be devised. The element of surprise was necessary because prices and wages in power-laden sectors would have gone up like a gas tank inspected by match illumination had everyone known in advance that controls were in the offing. As for simplicity, a zero rate of change implies a clarity and purity unequalled by any other standard imaginable.

Yet, the freeze was anything but simple. A listing of its complexities could

---

[8] Ibid., pp. 79–95; Norman Keiser, *Macroeconomics* (New York: Random House, 1975), pp. 324–333; Otto Eckstein and R. Brinner, *The Inflationary Process in the United States,* U.S. Congress, Joint Economic Committee Study, 1972. On the other hand, see S. W. Black and H. H. Kelejian, "A Macro Model of the U.S. Labor Market," *Review of Economics and Statistics* (September 1970), pp. 712–741.

[9] Stanley S. Wallack, "Wage-Price Guidelines and the Rate of Wage Changes in U.S. Manufacturing 1951–66," *Southern Economic Journal* (July 1971), pp. 33–47; D. F. Greer, "Market Power and Wage Inflation: A Further Analysis," *Southern Economic Journal* (January 1975), pp. 466–479; George L. Perry, "Wages and the Guideposts," *American Economic Review* (September 1967), pp. 897–904.

[10] This section is based largely on Arnold Weber, *op cit.*

[11] *Business Week,* August 21, 1971, pp. 21–22.

fill a big book. Such a book would be instructive, however, because its message would be (quite simply) that even the simplest of control programs is a rat's nest. No less than four government agencies got their fingers in the enforcement stew. In the short span of 90 days, these agencies had to answer no fewer than 800,000 inquiries at field office level, 2,435 special exemption requests, 400 executive-level questions, and 75 key policy issues. Among the policy issues were the following:

1. What should be covered besides wages and prices? Rents, interest rates, dividends, and profits? What about country club dues, college tuition, social security payments, and the like? Raw agricultural products were exempt from the start, but when are honey and peanuts transformed from raw to processed? What about exports and imports? Are their prices to be frozen?
2. The freeze applies in comparison to what? Prices and wages prevailing on August 15, 1971? If so, what about the many items that were "on sale" that day? What about goods whose prices are seasonal—normally rising or falling during the freeze period? Given an exemption for seasonal goods (which was granted), is Halloween candy a seasonal good?
3. There has to be some means of preventing evasion through quality change, but what is a quality change? Are grocery store trading stamps part of quality? And so on, ad infinitum.
4. What about price and wage changes that are by contract due to occur during the freeze? Should they be allowed? What about price increases that were posted and paid for *prior* to 8/15/71, but on goods and services not yet delivered? For example, should those who in July bought season tickets to see the Atlanta Falcons play football in the fall be reimbursed for the increase over prior year's prices?

The actual answers were stringent enough to decelerate prices and wages substantially. Between August and November 1971 the consumer price index rose at an annual rate of 1.6%, well below the 4.0 rate of increase during the 6 months preceding the freeze. Greater reductions were registered in the wholesale price index and various wage indexes. Whether the freeze had any lasting impact, however, is debatable. A big "bulge" of increases occurred just after the thaw on November 14.

D. Phase II (November 1971 to January 1973)

The freeze gave way to what turned out to be protracted controls of varying coverage and stringency. Table 22–1, which is a terse summary, conveys the content and complexity of these regulations.

During Phase II, statutory controls limited price increases on a firm-by-firm basis to a per cent pass-through of cost increases, meaning, for example, that prices could rise 10% if costs rose 10%. Since *increases* rather than *absolute levels* were being controlled, there had to be some base period against which the current costs could be compared, and the period varied. It could be either

TABLE 22-1. Regulations of the Control Program, Phases II, III, and IV

Program	Phase II 14 November 1971 to 11 January 1973	Phase III 11 January 1973 to 13 June 1973	Phase IV 12 August 1973 to 30 April 1974
General Standards			
Price increase limitations	Percentage pass-through of allowable cost increases since last price increase, or 1 Jan. 1971, adjusted for productivity and volume offsets. Term limit pricing option available.	Self-administered standards of Phase II.	In most manufacturing and service industries dollar-for-dollar pass-through of allowable cost increase since last fiscal quarter ending prior to 11 Jan. 1973.
Profit margin limitations	Not to exceed margins of the best 2 of 3 fiscal years before 15 August 1971. Not applicable if prices were not increased above base level, or if firms "purified" themselves.	Not to exceed margins of the best 2 fiscal years completed after 15 August 1968. No limitations if average price increase does not exceed 1.5%.	Same years as Phase III, except that a firm that has not charged a price for any item above its base price, or adjusted freeze price, whichever is higher, is not subject to the limitation.
Wage increase limitations	General standard of 5.5%. Exceptions made to correct gross inequities, and for workers whose pay had increased less than 7% a year for the last 3 years. Workers earning less than $2.75 per hour were exempt. Increases in qualified fringe benefits permitted raising standard to 6.2%.	General Phase II standard, self-administered. Some special limitations. More flexibility with respect to specific cases. Workers earning less than $3.50 per hour were exempted after 1 May.	Self-administered standards of Phase III. Executive compensation limited.

Prenotification			
Prices	Prenotification required for all firms with annual sales above $100 million, 30 days before implementation, approval required.	After 2 May 1973, prenotification required for all firms with sales above $250 million whose price increase has exceeded a weighted average of 1.5%.	Same as Phase II except that prenotified price increases may be implemented in 30 days unless CLC requires otherwise.
Wages	For all increases of wages for units of 5,000 or more; for all increases above the standard regardless of the number of workers involved.	None.	None.
Reporting			
Prices	Quarterly for firms with sales over $50 million.	Quarterly for firms with sales over $250 million.	Quarterly for firms with sales over $50 million.
Wages	Pay adjustments below standard for units greater than 1,000 persons.	Pay adjustments for units greater than 5000 persons.	Same as Phase III.
Special Areas	Health, insurance, rent, construction, public utilities.	Health, food, public utilities, construction, petroleum.	Health, food, petroleum, construction, insurance, executive and variable compensation.
Exemptions	Raw agricultural commodities, import prices, export prices, firms with 60 or fewer employees.	Same as Phase II plus rents.	Same as Phase III plus public utilities, lumber, copper scrap, and long-term coal contracts, initially with sector-by-sector decontrol of prices and wages until 30 April 1974.

Source: Cost of Living Council and *Economic Report of the President, 1974*, p. 91.

495

the time of the "last" price increase or January 1, 1971, whichever was more recent. But there was a catch. Price increases by this standard could not be such as to generate "excess" profits, which were defined in historic terms particular to each firm. The *overall* goal was to hold price inflation to 2.5% per year.

The general standard for wage increases was 5.5% per year. This standard was based on the theory that, assuming a 3% rate of productivity advance, 5.5% wage inflation would attain the 2.5% target level of price inflation. The ghost of the old guideposts should be obvious here. Unfortunately, organized labor was disenchanted with this standard (thinking it was too low, of course), so an additional 0.7 percentage point was added for fringe benefits, resulting in a total compensation standard of 6.2%. Furthermore, a major exception for additional increments was granted to workers earning "substandard" wages. Interpretation of "substandard" proved a problem because the Cost of Living Council, whose administrative responsibility carried over from the freeze, wanted a threshold figure of $1.90 per hour, whereas organized labor insisted it be higher. A compromise of $2.75 settled the dispute.

While the Cost of Living Council had overall policy authority, responsibility for direct supervision of prices and wages was split between a Price Commission (for prices) and a Pay Board (for wages and salaries), both of which ranked below the Cost of Living Council. To aid their enforcement efforts, these agencies developed rules for business notification of intended changes and for reporting of actual changes. Their basic scheme divided all covered firms into three tiers:

1. **Tier I firms** had sales exceeding $100 million or collective-bargaining units of 5000 or more employees. These firms had to obtain *prior approval* before implementing price and wage increases.
2. **Tier II firms** had sales between $50 million and $100 million or collective-bargaining units of 1,000 to 5,000 employees. These firms did not need prior approval for their actions, but they had to *submit regular reports* of behavior.
3. **Tier III firms,** with sales and employees below those of tier II firms, had no prenotification or reporting requirements.

Beyond these generalities lay hordes of exemptions, special treatments, and individual cases. Major exemptions were raw agricultural commodities, exports, imports, and small firms. One of the main special treatments concerned public utilities. Rather than duplicate the efforts of public utility commissions, the Price Commission delegated its authority to control prices in those areas to existing regulatory authorities. A memorable hint of the program's burial beneath detail arose in this regard when the Price Commission received a letter from a legal brothel in Nevada that was regulated by health authorities. The letter asked whether the Pay Board considered prostitution a service industry or regulated utility.[12]

---

[12] Jackson Grayson, "A View from the Outside of the Inside of Upside Down," in *The Illusion of Wage and Price Control,* edited by M. Walker (Vancouver, B.C.: The Fraser Institute, 1976), p. 169.

Problems with Phase II. Administrators of the Phase I freeze passed a 400 page book of problems on to the officials who took over for Phase II. On top of this, Phase II produced its own brands of perplexity.

A problem now acknowledged even by former price control officials might be called the "great grocery gaffe." During the Phase I freeze, grocery stores were required to post prices conspicuously so that shoppers could compare posted prices with actual prices and blow the whistle on any grocer with gross discrepancies. However, the freeze was so short and the signs so difficult to compile that the signs could not be posted until a few days before the end of the freeze. Rather than rub grocers the wrong way by scrapping the signs at the start of Phase II, they were kept for reporting "base prices." But the main technique of Phase II was to allow price increases for cost increases, not to freeze prices. So, as grocery prices climbed above posted prices, great confusion ensued. Many consumers thought the posted prices were the only legal prices, but unless the consumer knew specific margins of markup above cost, he could detect no violations by the signs, even if he understood what the signs represented. Hence the signs provoked many groundless complaints, and led many folks to think that Phase II was fake.[13] Indeed, it was probably a mistake to try to regulate retail food prices in the first place because raw agricultural products were exempt and grocery retailing is largely competitive.

The fundamental method of percentage cost pass-through has also been attacked. With few exceptions, price increases were permitted to cover increased costs *plus* a customary profit margin on those added costs. By this method profits could increase with added cost, leading to charges that inefficiency was rewarded. It has been argued in defense of the program that the adverse effect was not as bad as it might seem.[14] Still, it can also be argued that a scheme of *partial* cost pass-through might have served better.[15]

Economic distortions provide the most sensational problems of any controls program, including Phase II. The lumber industry, where distortions stemmed from evasion efforts, is perhaps the best example to emerge from Phase II:

- First, since the regulations permitted higher prices when services were added to products, plywood producers performed the "service" of cutting ⅛ inch off plywood sheets and sold the sheets for substantially higher prices. The dimensions of lumber products were also shaved as a device to obtain effective price increases.

- Second, since the Price Commission could not control foreign producers and import prices were thus uncontrolled, producers in the Pacific Northwest exported lumber to Canada and reimported it at substantially higher prices.

---

[13] Robert F. Lanzillotti, Mary T. Hamilton, and R. Blaine Roberts, *Phase II in Review* (Washington, D.C.: Brookings Institution, 1975), pp. 54–55.

[14] Ibid., pp. 80–97.

[15] A. Bradley Askin, "Wage-Price Controls in Administrative and Political Perspective," in *Wage and Price Controls: The U.S. Experiment*, edited by John Kraft and Blaine Roberts (New York: Praeger, 1975), pp. 26–27.

- Third, Price Commission regulations that permitted normal markups at each stage of distribution spawned shipments of lumber from one wholesaler to another; each added a normal markup but did not perform all of the usual wholesaler functions.

- Finally, at least for a time, the regulated price on two-by-fours was relatively high as compared with boards; thus, logs were turned into two-by-fours and a shortage of boards developed.[16]

On the *wage* side of Phase II, the biggest problem with the Pay Board was that it leaned toward leniency, especially where strong unions were involved. As compared to the 5.5% wage standard, the average rate of approved increases in major collective bargain agreements was 7.0% during 1972. Nonunion wage increases were considerably lower, however, largely as a result of continued slack in aggregate demand during 1972. These substandard increases in the nonunion sector permitted overall average hourly earnings to rise at a 5.6% rate during the year, running just shy of the 5.5 target.

These many sour spots in Phase II would leave less aftertaste today if it could be shown that Phase II allayed wage-price inflation significantly. But econometric studies yield no consensus that it did. Several estimates reveal absolutely no effect for either prices or wages. Several others suggest a downshift of 0.5 to 2.0 percentage points in price inflation plus some lesser consequences for wage inflation. The one thing that seems certain is that *if* there was any effect at all, prices were restrained more than wages.[17]

E. Phases III and IV, Plus Another Freeze

President Nixon terminated Phase II on January 11, 1973, replacing it with Phase III. As shown in Table 22–1, Phase III retained the standards of Phase II but removed most prenotification and reporting requirements. The Pay Board and Price Commission were abolished, leaving only the Cost of Living Council. In addition, exemptions were broadened to free rents and free more workers earning "substandard" wages. (Remarkably, the new low-wage exemption was set at $3.50, which was only slightly below average hourly earnings for *all* nonfarm workers.[18]) The stated purpose of the changes was to reduce administrative burdens while continuing controls. Compliance was to be "voluntary." In fact, most people saw Phase III as a *relaxation* of controls rather than a mere *reorganization*.

Price behavior during the next six months seemed to confirm people's impression of an economic dam-break: the wholesale price index leaped to a 22.3% annual rate of increase, and the consumer price index rose to an 8.0% annual pace of advance. Actually, conversion to Phase III had little to do with this

[16] William Poole, "Wage-Price Controls: Where Do We Go From Here?" *Brookings Papers on Economic Activity*, No. 1 (1973), p. 292.

[17] For reviews, see Kraft and Roberts, *op. cit.*, pp. 143–149; Jerry E. Pohlman, *Inflation Under Control?* (Reston, Va.: Reston Publishing Co., 1976), pp. 221–226; Brittan and Lilley, *op. cit.*, pp. 146–150.

[18] Albert Rees, *Wage-Price Policy* (General Learning Press, 1974), p. 16.

surge, for it came mainly from sectors uncontrolled from the beginning. In particular, wholesale prices of farm products exploded, elevating at close to a 60% annual rate of increase during the first six months of 1973. This jump was due to domestic shortages of agricultural commodities relative to an extremely strong surge of worldwide demand for our exports. Prices for timber and petroleum leaped for similar reasons.[19] On top of these exogenous shocks, the aggregate economy moved into high gear, responding to expansionary monetary and fiscal policies launched with the Phases. Unemployment fell from 6.0% at the start of Phase II in November 1972 to 4.8% in June 1973. In short, the timing of Phase II's demise was a public relations catastrophe.

Amid public pressure to reinstate tough controls, Phase III was abandoned while still in its infancy. A second freeze descended over the land. Like the first freeze, this one hit during the summer, lasting from mid-June to mid-August. *Unlike* the first one, this one hit just when the main inflationary forces at work were chiefly exogenous shock and demand-pull. What is more, this freeze was followed by Phase IV, which, as shown in Table 22–1, was in many respects even more stringent than Phase II. In particular, the new price standards permitted pass-through of cost increases only on a dollar-for-dollar basis, not on a percentage basis. (That is, if one's cost rose by 50¢ a widget, price per widget could rise only 50¢, not 50¢ plus some percentage markup.)

The results of Freeze II and Phase IV added up to more than a public relations catastrophe. Their inappropriateness produced some genuine economic catastrophes:

> When prices of more and more commodities were held below market clearing levels in late 1973, symptoms of inefficiency became increasingly widespread and diverse. Curtailment of domestic supply was sometimes threatened by increased exports, reduced production to avoid losses, and failure to expand production through use of marginal production capacity. Lack of availability and wide differences in prices of material inputs complicated production planning and threatened to disrupt production schedules. Distribution and purchasing operations were complicated by multiple prices and instances of bartering in order to reduce costs or obtain scarce materials, and black markets were frequently reported. Shortages were perhaps the most commonly reported symptom of inefficiency. . . .[20]

Under these burdens, people quickly became weary and disenchanted. Phase IV officially died on April 30, 1974. Whereas controls were greeted with rousing cheers in August 1971, no wailing over Phase IV's death could be heard the first day of May 1974. The contrast of public emotions seems odd when set against the fact that consumer prices were rising *three times faster toward the end of Phase IV than they were rising before imposition of Phase I.* Of course the explanation is very simple. People began to look upon controls as a sham and a burden. That is, they learned two lessons: (1) controls cannot suppress

[19] Ross E. Azevedo, "Phase III—A Stabilization Program That Could Not Work," *Quarterly Review of Economics and Business* (Spring 1976), pp. 7–21.

[20] Marvin Kosters, *Controls and Inflation* (Washington, D.C.: American Enterprise Institute, 1975), pp. 94–95.

a chronic inflationary trend, especially not one "goosed" by exogenous shocks, and (2) if controls are given an earnest try, they create distortions, inefficiencies, and inequities that may even aggravate the inflation in the long run.

F. European Experience

European experience with controls, usually called "incomes policies," is greater than the United States experience. Although a few observers look favorably on European policies,[21] most agree that on balance they have failed.[22] Thus, Lloyd Ulman and Robert Flanagan conclude their study of seven European countries by saying that "in none of the variations so far turned up has incomes policy succeeded in its fundamental objective, as stated, of making full employment consistent with a reasonable degree of price stability."[23] Walter Galenson's view is also representative: "Great Britain, Sweden, and Holland have had indifferent success with bouts of formal incomes policy."[24] Even proponents of controls, like Jerry Pohlman, admit that the European record is bleak:

> Certainly, one who attempts to find strong support for the effectiveness of wage and price restraints by looking abroad will be disappointed. Without exception, market controls have broken down at some time or another in all the free economies that have tried them.[25]

It may seem odd, then, that experience has not discouraged advocates of controls. They argue that controls are sound in principle; that failures occur only because of faulty application. They explain away failures as results of (1) inadequate sanctions, (2) lack of public support, (3) failure to constrain money supply in the course of control effort, (4) inappropriate application to money supply inflations, (5) over ambitious coverage and duration, and (6) unsatisfactory supervision of relative income shares.

III. PROPOSED IMPROVEMENTS

Can controls be patched up? Can they be made to succeed? Mention of a few proposed improvements (short of totalitarianism) concludes this review.

Limited coverage is one of the most common corrections called for. The

---

[21] For example, Organization for Economic Co-operation and Development, *Socially Responsible Wage Policies and Inflation* (1975); Ann R. Braun, "The Role of Incomes Policy in Industrial Countries Since World War II," *International Monetary Fund Staff Papers* (March 1975), pp. 1–36.

[22] For example, Brittan and Lilley, *op. cit.*; Lloyd Ulman and Robert J. Flanagan, *Wage Restraint: A Study of Incomes Policies in Western Europe* (Berkeley, Calif.: University of California Press, 1971); David C. Smith, *Incomes Policies* (Ottawa: Economic Council of Canada, 1966); Walter Galenson (ed.), *Incomes Policy: What Can We Learn from Europe?* (Ithaca, N.Y.: Cornell University School of Industrial and Labor Relations, 1973); Michael Parkin and Michael T. Sumner (eds.), *Incomes Policy and Inflation* (Toronto: University of Toronto Press, 1972).

[23] Ulman and Flanagan, *op. cit.*, p. 216.

[24] Galenson, *op. cit.*, p. xiv.

[25] Pohlman, *op. cit.*, p. 187.

idea is to focus stringent controls solely on big business and big labor, ignoring competitive areas, such as food and lumber, which have been reduced to chaos by past control efforts. There is a problem here, however. Defenders of limited coverage have yet to explain why this narrow lunge at largeness is politically more realistic than a policy of competitive restructuring, or why, if it is equally realistic, controls are superior to competition.

Another modification would be to keep controls temporary, to apply them only occasionally. Although this view has its merits, it seems tantamount to applying a band-aid to cure a malignant tumor. Temporary application of controls may even have the adverse side effect of delaying implementation of more effective long-lasting treatments.

Others see past controls as not being permanent enough. If controls collapse because of disputes over relative income shares, then the solution is to draw up a massive schedule of formulas "fairly" fixing everyone's wage relative to everyone else's wage. There are two problems with this approach, however. First, if the wage-relatives decided upon do not correspond to those that would be cranked out by the market (and there is no reason to think that they would so correspond), economic chaos will ensue. Second, the approach is politically unrealistic. As explained by Samuel Brittan and Peter Lilley:

> However resentful they are about it, people will in the last resort accept a relatively low position in the pecking order if it is due to the luck of the market. . . . If, on the other hand, their low position seems to result from a moralistic evaluation of their merits made by their fellow citizens through some political process, they will stop at nothing to get the judgment withdrawn. No one likes being consigned to the rubbish heap by a body of wise men appointed to express the supposed moral evaluations of society.[26]

Finally, a number of economists, most notably Sidney Weintraub and Henry Wallich, advocate a "taxed-based incomes policy," or TIP.[27] The basic idea is to stiffen the backbone of businessmen against labor's inflationary wage demands. This would be achieved by heavily taxing those businesses that grant wage increases above some specified standard. An alternative approach would provide tax breaks for those who voluntarily limit their wage increases to a specific amount. In essence, these plans provide streamlined enforcement mechanisms for a guidelines policy. They have the advantage of relying on market forces more than most incomes policies. Yet they, too, are not without deficiencies and distortions.[28]

Assuming market-power push inflation is a problem, this analysis paints a rather bleak picture. Our alternatives seem to be limited to (1) trying a tax-based incomes policy, which at least theoretically is the best of the wage-price

---

[26] Brittan and Lilley, op. cit., p. 186.
[27] Henry Wallich and Sidney Weintraub, "A Tax-Based Incomes Policy," Journal of Economic Issues (June 1971), pp. 1–19.
[28] Perhaps the best plan is the invention of Abba P. Lerner and David C. Colander, MAP: A Market Anti-inflation Plan (New York: Harcourt Brace Jovanovich, Inc., 1980). But it is too complex to describe here.

control policies, (2) going through the wringer of tight monetary restraint now and again with every substantial exogenous shock, or (3) learning to live with inflation, nasty though it is. Actually, there is another alternative. We could strike at the root of the problem by lessening market power itself. This would be achieved by curbing union power and restructuring industry through more vigorous antitrust. Greater competition would also follow from less anticompetitive government intervention, as occurred in transportation deregulation. Unfortunately, political realities seem to bar significant achievements in these respects, so alternatives (1), (2), and (3) above probably exhaust the possibilities.

SUMMARY

Inflation has essentially three causes—(1) demand-pull, (2) exogenous shock, and (3) market-power push. Under the last of these, prices are pushed up by wage escalations that exceed productivity growth or by higher profit markups— the work of powerful labor unions and/or large corporations.

The chief purpose of wage-price controls is to curb inflations that are either caused or aggravated by market-power forces *while at the same time* minimizing the adverse effects on unemployment and idle capacity. Advocates of wage-price controls agree with monetarists that monetary restraint is also desirable. Indeed, they generally concede that inflation could be halted by monetary policy alone. But they look upon controls as a means of minimizing the economic casualties inflicted by monetary restraint alone. Review of specific evidence indicates that the advocates of controls may well be right in that there *is* a problem. But review of past control policies indicates that these policies may not be the best solutions.

Such policies vary in their coverage, standards, enforcement method, and duration. In coverage, they can broadly include most everything from dog license fees to ballplayer salaries, or they can focus narrowly on sectors where problems of market power are most pronounced. In standards, the growth rate in labor productivity has served as a key benchmark because if wages on average rose no faster, they would not be inflationary. In enforcement, programs have been voluntary and compulsory, with blends in between. In duration, they have been brief when harsh and long when lax.

Aside from wartime, controls in the U.S. first blossomed in the 1960s and 1970s. The Kennedy administration launched wage-price "guideposts" in 1962. Though casual, with little bureaucracy and rubbery enforcement, the program was partially successful until demand-pull pressures pulled the program apart in 1966.

Nixon's multiple "Phases" began with a 90-day freeze in 1971 and evolved into a program of protracted controls of varying coverage and stringency. The massive complexity of this effort is nicely illustrated by the freeze because that would intuitively seem to be the easiest of all kinds of control programs. The freeze was anything but simple, however. The adverse consequences of the Nixon effort are perhaps best illustrated by the experience of lumber under Phase II. Shortages, distortions, evasions, and other unsavory effects arose. Overall, the benefits of the "Phases" were less than outstanding.

European experience with controls has not been notably better than ours. A key problem in the failure of many of these attempts is their tendency to shatter when hit by exogenous shocks, such as fuel shortages.

Improvements have been proposed. Of these, tax-based incomes policies are most favored by economists who favor controls. Whether these will ever be tried is uncertain. But the problem will not go away as long as monopoly power and anticompetitive government policies endure. Thus we may one day witness a tax-based incomes policy or some first cousin of such.

23 Technological Change: Theory and Cross-Section Evidence

What laws govern the growth of man's mastery over nature?
—JACOB SCHMOOKLER

From the first squawky telephone to the latest supersonic transport, technological change has done more than anything else to shape our modern economy and everyday life. Innovation spurs growth, boosts productivity, lifts profits, lengthens lives, generates jobs, and enriches experiences. Nearly half of all this century's gains in real income can be attributed to technological progress. The lion's share of the products we now use and take for granted simply did not exist as little as three generations ago—television, frozen food, zippers, computers, air conditioning, penicillin, nylon, refrigerators, synthetic detergents, Frisbees, and so on. Society's investment in research and development (R & D) yields a fantastic return of 30–50%.[1]

What is the role of industry in all this? During 1981 private companies spent more than $32 billion on R & D. Roughly 60% of this expenditure went for improvement of existing products, 30% for development of new products, and 10% for developing new processes of production. On top of this, private industry conducted the lion's share of government funded R & D, which amounted to several tens of billions of dollars more.[2]

In this light, questions concerning industry's performance for progress take on a serious cast. Does high concentration help or hinder technological advance? What sorts and sizes of firms put forth the greatest R & D effort? Are there still active independent inventors of the type of Thomas Edison and the Wright brothers? These queries now occupy our focus. We begin by filling in some background. The remainder of the chapter is then divided into two major por-

---

[1] Edwin Mansfield, "Federal Support of R & D Activities in the Private Sector," *Priorities and Efficiency in Federal Research and Development,* Joint Economic Committee of the U.S. Congress, 94th Congress, Second Session (October 29, 1976), pp. 95–99.

[2] *Business Week,* July 5, 1982, p. 54; June 27, 1977, pp. 62–63.

tions, one covering the impact of firm size, the other discussing the effect of market structure. It will be seen that bigness comes out looking better than it has in previous chapters, but only to a limited degree.[3]

I. CONCEPTS AND CONDITIONS

A. Definitions

Edison was undoubtedly right when he said that invention is the product of "one percent inspiration and ninety-nine percent perspiration." But for present purposes, **invention** is best defined as "*the first confidence that something should work, and the first rough test that it will, in fact, work.*"[4] It requires an *initial concept* and *crude proof.* Furthermore, a common caveat is that an invention must possess *utility,* not inanity.

Although invention is surely the seed of technical progress, it is only the seed. In monetary weight invention accounts for no more than about 5–15% of the total cost of bringing most new products to market or placing new production processes into service for the first time. By far the greatest amount of time and expense goes into what may be called innovation. **Innovation** *is the first commercial application of an invention.* It entails refinement of the basic idea, testing prototypes, debugging, development, engineering, initial production, and perhaps initial marketing as well.

In many cases there is no clear boundary between invention and innovation. Conceptually, however, "Invention is the stage at which the scent is first picked up, development the stage at which the hunt is in full cry."[5] Whereas about 5–15% of a successful new product's cost goes into invention, about 10–20% goes into engineering and design, 40–60% is spent on tooling and manufacturing set-up, 5–15% into manufacturing start-up, and 10–25% covers initial marketing expenses.[6] A similar pattern is revealed by a breakdown of industrial R & D outlays for 1979, as estimated by the National Science Foundation:

- $886 million, or 3.5%, went toward *basic research,* for the advancement of *general* scientific knowledge;

- $5,627 million, or 22.1%, went for *applied research,* pursuing what could be called inventions;

---

[3] Excellent surveys guiding this one include F. M. Scherer, *Industrial Market Structure and Economic Performance,* 2nd ed. (Chicago: Rand McNally, 1980), Chapter 15; Morton I. Kamien and Nancy L. Schwartz, "Market Structure and Innovation: A Survey," *Journal of Economic Literature* (March 1975), pp. 1–37.

[4] John Jewkes, David Sawers, and Richard Stillerman, *The Sources of Invention,* 2nd ed. (New York: Norton, 1969), p. 28.

[5] *Ibid.*

[6] U.S. Department of Commerce, *Technological Innovation: Its Environment and Management* (Washington, D.C., 1967), p. 9.

- $18,980 million, or 74.4%, went into *development*, that is, innovative activities concerned with translating research findings into commercial products or processes.[7]

Innovation also consumes a tremendous amount of time, further separating the first flash of insight from the marketing debut. John Enos estimated the interval between invention and innovation for 44 major discoveries, finding that, on average, the interval was about 13 years. To mention a few examples: radio was 8 years maturing; jet engine, 14 years; catalytic cracking of petroleum, 9 years; ballpoint pen, 6 years; magnetic recording, 5 years; mechanical cotton picker, 53 years; television, 22 years; and dacron, 12 years.[8] In short, innovation is indispensible; an invention without innovation is like an unsung song.

But advance requires still more, a third stage called **diffusion.** The innovation may flop, or it may spread. Clearly, *the extent and speed of any spread can be very important to overall progress.* Like the earlier stages, diffusion usually takes time and money because it, too, is essentially a learning process. Unlike the earlier stages, however, this learning process is not confined to a single research laboratory or a few firms; it can involve multitudes of producers and users. The digital watch provides a timely example of diffusion. Introduced in 1972 at $2,000 apiece, it was at first more a curiosity than a chronometer. But then it caught on. With improvements, climbing sales, longer production runs, and cost reductions, prices fell from $2,000 to $10 in just 5 years ($10 being the bottom of the line, of course). Now more than half of all watches sold are digital.[9]

It may be concluded that a full assessment of progressive performance must take into account *invention, innovation,* and *diffusion.* Each is different. Yet each is crucial to progress. And it will be shown that, to some degree, certain firm sizes and certain market structures perform better at one stage than others. These distinctions should therefore be put in warm storage.

B. Measurement

One more preliminary comment needs mention. Good performance in these several respects cannot be measured in absolute terms. Given that IBM spends $1,612 million on R & D and Amdahl spends $75 million, as they did in 1981, one cannot conclude therefrom that IBM is necessarily the more progressive of the two. *Relative to sales,* Amdahl spent 17.0% as against IBM's 5.5%. *Relative to profits* Amdahl spent 281% to IBM's 49%. The implication should

---

[7] National Science Foundation, *Research and Development in Industry 1979* (NSF 81–324), p. 42.

[8] John L. Enos, "Invention and Innovation in the Petroleum Refining Industry," reprinted in *Economic Concentration Hearings,* Part 3, U.S. Senate 98th Congress, First Session, Subcommittee on Antitrust and Monopoly (1965), pp. 1,486–1,491.

[9] *Business Week,* October 27, 1975, pp. 78–92; January 26, 1976, pp. 27–28; May 2, 1977, pp. 78–80.

be obvious. Accordingly, subsequent analysis places heavy reliance on a varied assortment of *relative* measures.

Unfortunately, the problem cuts even deeper than can be controlled by converting all statistics to percentage or per unit values. Let private R & D spending as a percent of sales be 5.3% for drugs and 0.4% for textiles, as shown in Table 23–1. One is tempted to deduce from this marked disparity that performance in drugs is better than in textiles. But such a supposition might be wrong. Although relative outlays are plainly higher for drugs, the *opportunity* for technical progress is also much greater for drugs than for textiles. One reason is that drug products tend to occupy earlier stages of their *life cycle* as compared to textiles.

Given a greater opportunity, the profitability of R & D will be greater over a larger range of expenditure. It is only natural to expect, then, that industries and firms with richer opportunities will outspend and outinnovate those with relatively impoverished prospects. Much of the interindustry variation in outlays observed in Table 23–1 can probably be pinned on just such differences. At the top of the list we find semiconductors, computers, drugs, aerospace, instruments, motor vehicles, electronics, and chemicals. All enjoy dazzling opportunities and spend accordingly. Indeed, these industries alone account for over 80% of all industrial R & D. Toward the bottom of the list are food, textiles, apparel, and paper. Centuries of attention paid to their design and production undoub-

TABLE 23–1. Selected Data for R & D Performing Companies: By Industry 1981

Industry	Company R & D Funds as a Per Cent of Sales (%)	Company R & D Funds ($ millions)
Semiconductors	7.1	713.5
Computers	6.4	3,845.5
Drugs	5.3	2,450.6
Office equipment	5.0	729.2
Aerospace	4.8	2,363.2
Instruments	4.6	647.5
Cars & trucks	3.7	4,545.1
Electrical, electronics	2.9	2,328.4
Chemicals	2.5	2,635.2
Machinery	2.4	1,221.4
Tires, rubber	2.0	451.2
Building materials	1.2	175.3
Paper	0.9	255.9
Food, beverage	0.7	578.1
Textiles, apparel	0.4	47.8

Source: *Business Week*, July 5, 1982, pp. 54–74.

tedly curtails present-day leeway for change. Hence progressiveness ought to be measured *relative to the potential for progress*. Full exploitation of an industry's opportunities would then be good performance. Failure to reach full potential would mean defective performance, even though observed progress may give impressive appearances.

It is of course difficult to know exactly where full potentials of this sort lie. In fact, it was at one time thought that meaningful economic research in this area was impossible, that ignorance of true technological opportunities was fatal to the undertaking.[10] Luckily, this is not so. Ways around the problem have been devised. These ways should therefore be noted.

First, and most obviously, federal contributions to R & D have to be excluded when calculating private industry performance. Otherwise, those few industries benefitting from federal largess—aircraft, electronics, and communications, in particular—would have an unfair edge. The data in Table 23–1 thus exclude federal funds.

Second, much can be learned by comparing the progressiveness of individual firms *within a single industry*. All such firms presumably face the *same* opportunities, whatever they may be. Hence we shall review more evidence concerning individual firms here than anywhere else in the book. This evidence is not only intriguing, it is also pertinent; if an industry's small firms outdo their bigger brethren, it might pay to slice the big ones smaller. Then again, the evidence might suggest the opposite conclusion.

Finally, *inter*industry comparisons of progressiveness are possible if potentials are accounted for in some fashion. The techniques tried thus far include use of "dummy" variables in regression analysis and international comparisons. The latter are easiest to explain. French steel and American steel industries presumably face the same opportunities, but one may be more highly concentrated than the other, in which case any differences in progressiveness between them might be due to this structural difference. Still another approach can be used for diffusion. If a single innovation is useable in several industries but adopted at different rates in different industries, one can test whether market structure helps to explain those different rates of adoption. Numerically controlled machine tools is one such innovation.

Within the confines of these various techniques, it will be assumed that more progressiveness means better performance. This, too, has its problems. Sensitive readers need no prodding to realize that "more" is not necessarily "better." They may object that newness can be unsettling and even dangerous. Faster cars and deadlier pesticides might mark progress in terms of "more," but they might also raise costs of safety and pollution. This particular objection to progressiveness certainly has its merits. But we shall simply assume that "more" R & D, "more" patents, "more" innovations, and "more" rapid diffusion are indeed for the better.

[10] Joe Bain, *Industrial Organization* (New York: Wiley & Sons 1968), p. 460.

II. FIRM SIZE AND PROGRESSIVENESS

A. Theory

Confident that big firms were more progressive than small, J. K. Galbraith wrote some time ago that "a benign Providence . . . has made the modern industry of a few large firms an excellent instrument for inducing technical change."[11] He was not alone in his praise of bigness. Others, like Joseph Schumpeter, have expressed the same sentiment. They rest their case on a chain of arguments.

1. *Absolute size:* It is alleged that big firms can better afford R & D outlays. They have bigger bank balances and richer cash flows than smaller firms. Given the immense expense of R & D projects, small firms simply cannot compete.
2. *Economies of scale:* Invention and innovation often require costly specialized equipment—wind tunnels, test tracks, electron microscopes, and so on. Researchers themselves are growing ever more specialized, necessitating teamwork. These R & D inputs can be used more efficiently by large scale enterprises, or so it is argued.
3. *Risk:* Every project is a gamble. Large size enables numerous projects, so the hits can offset the misses. Risk thus diminishes with added size.
4. *Time horizon:* It is contended that a larger firm can wait longer for a payoff than a smaller firm. This argument presumably gives larger firms longer time horizons, and innovation is time consuming.
5. *Diversification:* R & D often yield unexpected outcomes. Search for a synthetic fiber may turn up a new paint. Since bigger firms tend to be more diversified than smaller firms, the giants can better exploit these happenstances.

Though plausible, these arguments are not unassailable. Those who question the view that bigness is better quarrel with these theoretical assertions. It can be argued that, although many projects are indeed costly and require large absolute size, many are not. Some run into the millions, some into the thousands. The range leaves ample room for smaller firms, and, on average, the cost of a typical project is not gargantuan. By one estimate, "the median project in the combined R & D project portfolio of all sizeable U.S. industrial corporations in 1976 would have a total R & D cost of less than $500,000."[12]

As for economies of scale, a small firm may be able to overcome a handicap by hiring the services of a large independent R & D outfit, whose sole activity is research and whose costs are spread over its many contract customers. The fact that most contracted R & D is done for large firms does not negate this

---

[11] John Kenneth Galbraith, *American Capitalism* (Boston: Houghton Mifflin, 1956), p. 86.
[12] F. M. Scherer, *The Economic Effects of Compulsory Patent Licensing* (New York: New York University Graduate School of Business Administration, 1977, Monograph 1977–2), p. 15.

possibility. Moreover, it can be argued that since R & D is a *creative* activity, the bureaucratic tangles that bigness inevitably brings may be stifling rather than liberating, inefficient rather than efficient.

Risk, too, may be questioned as a force favoring bigness. To be sure, the bigger firm may be able to back more projects and thereby assure itself success in some of them, just as "the richer gambler who backs more horses in the race is, other things being equal, more likely to pick the winner."[13] However, it may be doubted whether the returns from this strategy are *more than proportionate* to the outlay. If they are not, then great size gives no particular advantage.

Moreover, it may be questioned whether the risk in funding only a few projects intimidates the smaller firms. Do race tracks draw only the wealthy who can wager on a number of horses each time round? Don't bet on it. There are countless little guys who *really* gamble; there are countless small firms accepting great risks. Conversely, there are many large firms whose bureaucrats seem to shun almost everything short of a sure thing. Approval of projects in big firms typically requires clearance of several managerial layers, something that heightens the chances that uncertain undertakings will be vetoed by "an abominable no-man."[14] IBM repeatedly rejected opportunities to develop and produce the Xerox machine, saying it was too risky. But it was not too risky for Haloid, the half-pint company that actually undertook the task and later changed its name to Xerox. IBM management also ordered IBM researchers to drop development of disk memories, one of the most significant of all computer inventions. Although IBM later claimed credit for these devices, it could do so only because several unruly IBM researchers ignored orders, endangered their jobs, secretly persisted, and eventually succeeded.[15]

Several studies by Edwin Mansfield indicate that the risks of R & D may not be as awesome as commonly supposed. His most recent study summarizes the 1968–1971 experience of 16 firms in the chemical, drug, petroleum, and electronics industries.[16] Mansfield quantifies the probabilities of success at three stages that roughly correspond to invention, innovation, and diffusion but go by different labels. He finds considerable variation, but the average probability of successful "technical completion" was 57%. Of those projects passing "technical completion," 65% were "commercialized." And of those "commercialized," 74% returned a profit. In other words, the probability of prize-winning was better than 50:50 at the purely technical level. These good odds seem "to be due to the fact that the bulk of R & D projects are aimed at fairly modest advances in the state of the art." Eventual profitability is much more precarious, however. Of all projects entering the front end of the R & D pipeline, only about 27% emerge profitably at the rear end (a figure attained by multiplying

[13] Jewkes, Sawers, and Stillerman, *op. cit.,* p. 130.

[14] C. Northcote Parkinson's expression, cited by Scherer, *Industrial Market Structure and Economic Performance* (Chicago: Rand McNally, 1970), p. 354.

[15] *Economic Concentration Hearings, op. cit.,* p. 1,217.

[16] Edwin Mansfield, J. Rapoport, A. Romeo, E. Villani, S. Wagner, and F. Husic, *The Production and Application of New Industrial Technology* (New York: Norton, 1977), pp. 21–43.

the several probabilities, $0.57 \times 0.65 \times 0.74 = 0.27$). Still, 27% is not dreadfully risky. The odds do not imply a game of utterly foolish gambles. It may therefore be a game that small firms can play without suffering nightmares.

The remaining arguments favoring large size—time horizon and diversification—are equally vulnerable to counterargument. But the debate will now be dropped. Resolution cannot be reached without recourse to the facts. So let's now turn to the facts as they relate to invention, innovation, and diffusion (keeping in mind that the statistics often blur these stages). Truth on both sides will be revealed.

B. Firm Size and Invention: The Evidence

The facts concerning invention are best kept in three separate compartments: (1) inputs, (2) outputs, and (3) outputs/inputs, or efficiency. Inputs of R & D money and personnel obviously reflect *effort*, but they may indicate nothing about *results achieved*. The most common and convenient measure of results, or R & D output, is patents. In lieu of patents, which fail to discriminate between marvelous and mundane discoveries, some students of the subject have tried to measure output by selecting only "significant" inventions then tracing their sources. Finally, systematic comparison of outputs and inputs yields a measure of efficiency, such as patents *per dollar* of R & D investment. Such a measure is needed to test the presence of scalar economies.

1. Inputs. At first glance, statistics reflecting effort overwhelmingly favor the big firms as being most progressive. R & D expenditures are tightly concentrated. In 1972, for example, U.S. firms with 5,000 or more employees accounted for 53% of all manufacturing employment. At the same time they made 87% of all privately financed expenditures on R & D performed by manufacturing companies.[17] One of the main reasons R & D effort is so dramatically concentrated is that virtually all large firms undertake some R & D, whereas most small firms have no formal R & D program whatsoever. Over 90% of all firms with more than 5,000 employees engage in some R & D, but below this, as firm size drops, the proportion of firms engaging in R & D sinks. The result: about 600 companies account for 90% of all private R & D spending.[18] Thus there is some element of truth to the claim that bigness is better.

These aggregate statistics, however, exaggerate the prominence of the largest enterprises. They take no account of differing technical opportunities across industries, and they make no distinction between what could be considered large middle-sized firms and the genuine giants among those who do have R & D programs. The most pertinent question is this: *Within* a given industry or a cluster of industries of given technological opportunity, is the effort of the largest firms greater, *relative to their size,* than the effort of medium-sized firms? The question is diagrammed in Figure 23–1. The vertical axis is

[17] Scherer *op. cit.* (1980), p. 418.
[18] *Business Week,* June 27, 1977, p. 62.

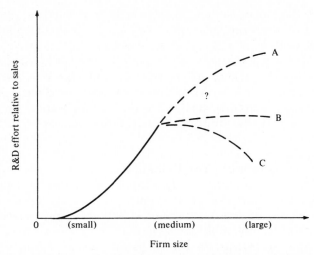

FIGURE 23–1. Effort and firm size within a given industry.

R & D outlay per dollar of sales or some other measure of *relative* effort. The horizontal axis is firm size. The solid line indicates what we already know, namely, the effort of really small firms *is* relatively small. The dashed lines indicate the possibilities among the medium and large sizes. If relative effort always rose with size, pattern *A* would prevail. If medium and large firms put forth the *same* relative effort, pattern *B* would be observed. Finally, pattern *C* would hold if relative effort dwindled beyond the middle range.

There have been at least twelve statistical studies of this question.[19] They vary in number of industries and firms included, time periods, and measures

[19] J. S. Worely, "Industrial Research and the New Competition," *Journal of Political Economy* (April 1961), pp. 181–186; D. Hamberg, "Size of Firm, Oligopoly and Research: The Evidence," *Canadian Journal of Economics and Political Science* (February 1964), pp. 62–75; Edwin Mansfield, *Industrial Research and Technological Innovation* (New York: Norton, 1968), pp. 38–40; William S. Comanor, "Market Structure, Product Differentiation, and Industrial Research," *Quarterly Journal of Economics* (November 1967), pp. 639–657; F. M. Scherer, Testimony, *Economic Concentration Hearings, op. cit.,* pp. 1,194–1,196; H. G. Grabowski, "The Determinants of Industrial Research and Development: A Study of the Chemical, Drug, and Petroleum Industries," *Journal of Political Economy* (March 1968), pp. 292–306; Ronald E. Shrieves, "Firm Size and Innovation: Further Evidence," *Industrial Organization Review,* Vol. 4, No. 1 (1976), pp. 26–33; John E. Tilton, "Firm Size and Innovative Activity in the Semiconductor Industry" (mimeo, April 1972); Douglas W. Webbink, *The Semiconductor Industry* (Washington, D.C., Federal Trade Commission Economic Report, 1977), pp. 103–108; Peter D. Loeb and Vincent Lin, "Research and Development in the Pharmaceutical Industry," *Journal of Industrial Economics* (September 1977), pp. 45–51; W. F. Mueller, J. Culbertson, and B. Peckham, *Market Structure and Technological Performance in the Food-Manufacturing Industries* (Madison: Research Division, College of Agricultural and Life Sciences, University of Wisconsin, 1982); F. M. Scherer, "Technological Change and the Modern Corporation" (mimeo, November 1982). It must be noted, however, that big firms perform better when spending on *basic* research. E. Mansfield, "Composition of R & D Expenditures," *Review of Economics and Statistics* (November 1981), pp. 610–614; Albert N. Link, *Research and Development Activity in U.S. Manufacturing* (New York: Praeger, 1981).

of size and effort. Yet there is substantial agreement among them. Patterns *B* and *C* prevail in all but a few industries, chemicals being the most prominent exception. That is to say, inventive and innovative effort tends to increase *more* than proportionately with firm size *only over the small to medium range* ("medium" varying from industry to industry). For still larger firms, intensity of effort is either *constant or decreasing* with size. Hence bigness is better only up to a point; thereafter it is often worse.

2. Outputs. Patents and R & D spending are highly correlated, so observations concerning outputs generally conform with those concerning inputs. Still, there are significant differences, and all the differences tend to favor smallness. Take simple patent statistics for instance. Whereas 90% of all private R & D funds can be credited to about 600 firms, they cannot claim the same percentage of patents; 78% of all patents issued nowadays go to corporations, both big and small, while 22% go to *individuals.*[20]

Moreover, *within* the corporate sector itself, patents are nowhere near as highly concentrated as R & D dollars. Detailed data from the mid-1970s on 443 of the largest manufacturing corporations reveal their shares to be:

- share of industrial R & D expenditure. . . . 73%

- share of industrial corporate patents. . . . 61%

The same data, when studied industry-by-industry, disclose that nearly 90% of the industries follow a *B* or *C* pattern in Figure 23–1 when it comes to *patents,* whereas 80% of them follow a *B* or *C* pattern in R & D expenditure.[21] Thus the B and C patterns unfavorable to large firms are even more prevalent for *outputs* than they are for *inputs.*

A defender of large corporations might at this point like to explain the discrepancy in output and input by claiming that the *quality* of large firm inventions is superior to that of small-firm or individual inventions. But the claim would collapse for lack of evidence. One index of quality is commercial utilization, and several studies show that a greater percentage of small-firm patented inventions are used commercially than large-firm patented inventions.[22] Moreover, as Scherer notes, "Interview studies also reveal that large corporations with an active staff of patent attorneys are less discriminating in their choice of inventions on which patent protection is sought."[23]

As for the inventions of individuals, the evidence is almost astounding. John Jewkes, David Sawers, and Richard Stillerman carefully compiled case histories for seventy momentous twentieth century inventions and found that only 24 of them, or one third, were the work of corporate research laboratories. In contrast, 38, or more than half, "can be ranked as individual invention in the

[20] U.S. Department of Commerce, *Statistical Abstract 1979,* p. 573.
[21] Scherer *op. cit.* (1982), pp. 16–27.
[22] Jacob Schmookler, *Invention and Economic Growth* (Cambridge, Mass.: Harvard University Press, 1966), pp. 48–51.
[23] Scherer *op. cit.* (1970), p. 358.

sense that much of the pioneering work was carried through by men who were working on their own behalf without the backing of research institutions and usually with limited resources."[24] Among these individual discoveries are: air conditioning; jet engine; Kodachrome; penicillin; "Polaroid" Land camera; power steering; automatic transmissions; safety razor; cyclotron; xerography; titanium; helicopter; electron microscope; gyro-compass; and Cellophane.

Corroborating these results, Daniel Hamberg found that of 27 major inventions made during the decade 1946–1955, only seven (26%) came from large industrial laboratories. The remainder came from independent inventors, small firms, and universities. Hamberg also found that of 13 major steel inventions he studied, seven were concocted by individual inventors.[25] Moreover, after study of seven major inventions for the refining and cracking of petroleum, John Enos determined that all seven were made by independent inventors.[26] However instructive (and inspirational) these statistics might be, it nevertheless seems to be true that, *over time,* the *relative* importance of individual inventors seems to be shrinking. Whereas today 20% of all patents go to individuals, at the turn of the century individuals garnered 80%.[27]

3. Output/Input. When the input and output records of the largest firms are compared, it appears that their inventive output is much the weaker. For this, there are two main explanations. First, the inputs are probably more imperfectly measured than the outputs, and the imperfections shift as a function of firm size. In particular, data on R & D spending tend to understate the inventive effort of small firms and individuals. Such efforts tend to be more casual, less formal, and therefore less fully reported than the efforts of large firms. Conversely, R & D spending data may somewhat overstate the inventive efforts of larger firms because most of the larger firms' money goes into *innovation* rather than invention. And in the area of innovation, many large firms make up for their embarrassing record regarding invention. Thus, for example, virtually all the inventions credited to *individuals* by Jewkes, Sawers, and Stillerman were not innovated by individuals but rather by industrial firms, many of which are immense.[28] Not to much should be made of this qualification, however, because "development" and "innovation" do produce patents, the main measure of invention.

The second explanation for the discrepancy shows bigness in a less praiseworthy light. That is, output/input tends to fall directly with increased size, everything else being equal, because of *diseconomies of scale in invention.* Telling statistics demonstrating these diseconomies were gathered by Jacob Schmookler. They may be seen in Table 23–2, which reports the number of patents pending

---

[24] Jewkes, Sawers, and Stillerman, *op. cit.,* p. 73.
[25] Daniel Hamberg, "Invention in the Industrial Research Laboratory," *Journal of Political Economy* (April 1963), pp. 96–98.
[26] Enos, *op. cit.,* pp. 1,481–1,486.
[27] Schmookler, *op. cit.,* p. 26.
[28] Richard R. Nelson, *Economic Concentration Hearings, op. cit.,* p. 1,145.

TABLE 23–2. Number of Patents Pending per Million Dollars Spent on R & D, 1953

| Industry | Size of Firm | | |
	Under 1,000 Employees	1,000 to 4,999 Employees	5,000 or more Employees
Machinery	117.6	70.4	41.3
Chemicals	89.3	50.0	42.4
Electric equipment	63.7	79.4	39.1
Petroleum	100.0	119.0	64.1
Instruments	63.3	69.4	26.7
All other industries	64.9	140.8	35.9
Average all industries	78.1	74.6	39.1

Source: Derived from Jacob Schmookler, *Economic Concentration, Hearings,* Part 3, U.S. Senate Subcommittee on Antitrust and Monopoly, 89th Congress, First Session (1965), p. 1,258.

per million dollars of R & D outlay for firms formally engaged in R & D, broken down by size classes. In short, the data are patent output ÷ million dollars R & D input. Reading across the rows, you will spy a fairly consistent pattern. Patent productivity is always *lowest in the largest size class.* In four of the industry groups it is highest among medium-sized firms. And in two industries—machinery and chemicals—the *smallest* firms display the greatest patent productivity. The smallest firms, in fact, are rarely far below the medium firms, and the smallest are typically twice as efficient as the largest. Using different data drawn from the petroleum, chemical, and steel industries, plus a different analytical technique, Mansfield came up with similar results. He concluded that, "contrary to popular belief, the inventive output per dollar of R & D expenditure in most of these cases seems to be lower in the largest firms than in large and medium-sized firms."[29]

Stated differently, costs per patent rise with size. The obvious next question is why? There is of course no answer universally propounded by all observers, but most seem to agree with the answer derived by Arnold Cooper, whose comparative study of large and small research organizations is widely cited:

Large firms, he found, seem to become enmeshed in bureaucracy and red tape, resulting in a less hospitable atmosphere for creative contributions by operating personnel. Superior technical personnel tend to be attracted to smaller companies where greater latitude may be afforded them. The larger the firm, the more difficult it may be to recognize the problems needing solution. Finally there is evidence of greater cost consciousness in smaller firms.[30]

[29] E. Mansfield *op. cit.* (1968), p. 42. See also Tilton, *op. cit.* and Scherer *op. cit.* (1982). A major exception is drugs: J. M. Vernon and Peter Gusen, "Technical Change and Firm Size: The Pharmaceutical Industry," *Review of Economics and Statistics* (August 1974), pp. 294–302.
[30] Kamien and Schwartz, *op. cit.,* p. 10.

Because big firms are often frustrated when trying to hire creative personnel, they sometimes try to compensate by *acquiring* the small *firms* they work for, but the result is frequently the same:

> Xerox . . . saw the founders of two of its key data processing acquisitions of the 1970s—Diablo Systems and Shugart Associates—walk out to start companies that became major competitors. "There is a natural temptation to go in and overlay your reporting procedures, your own benefit plans, sometimes even your own management people," says Wayland R. Hickes, a Xerox vice-president. "You create frustration, and to an extent you stifle creativity."[31]

It seems then that "nothing is more characteristic of the individual inventor than this disposition to fold his tent and quietly steal away to other territory when large-scale organized research comes into his field."[32]

To sum up, inventive inputs, outputs, and output/input ratios all seem to be positively associated with size only among very small and medium-sized firms. Beyond that, no additional gains from size are evident. If anything, losses are thereafter more likely than gains. There is, moreover, still a place for the individual inventor.

C. Firm Size and Innovation: The Evidence

A rather forceful case can be made that *innovation* is affected by size much as invention is. Observe first that the bulk of R & D money goes to "development," and that many if not most corporate patents are offspring of "development" instead of "research." So the preceding section's message necessarily overflows to cover much present ground.

Second, there is certainly no shortage of "hare and tortoise" stories, wherein the unlikely little firm outraces the unsuspecting, seemingly swift, all-powerful, large firm, whose brash overconfidence or lackadaisical attitude instills sloth:

- In 1926, Western Electric offered sound equipment to the major movie companies, all of whom rejected it. Warner Brothers, then a minor company, gambled on the sound equipment. The major companies decided to fight the adoption of sound; acceptance would make much of their equipment obsolete; long-term contracts with silent-picture stars might become costly liabilities, techniques would be revolutionized; conversion to sound would require an embarrassing payment of royalties to tiny Warner. Warner won.[33]

- It was not the Big Three who innovated small cars in the United States after World War II, but rather Kaiser, Willys, American Motors, and Studebaker. The Big Three resisted, fearing dilution of their large-car sales.[34]

---

[31] *Business Week,* April 18, 1983, p. 88. See also "Can Semiconductors Survive Big Business?" *Business Week,* December 3, 1979, pp. 66–85.

[32] Jewkes, Sawers, and Stillerman, *op. cit.,* p. 99.

[33] William F. Hellmuth, Jr., "The Motion Picture Industry," in W. Adams, *The Structure of American Industry,* 3rd ed. (New York: Macmillan Publishing Co., 1961), p. 398.

[34] Lawrence J. White, "The American Automobile Industry and the Small Car, 1945–70," *Journal of Industrial Economics* (April 1972), pp. 179–192.

- Much the same could be said of unit-body construction, dual-braking systems, crash panels, auto air conditioning, pollution control equipment, and so on. Some claim that, aside from automatic transmissions, the crowning achievements of GM are tail fins, opera windows, and landau roofs.[35]

- When inventors of the digital watch offered it to the major old-line watch companies for development, they ran into a brick wall. Innovation thus fell to electronics companies like Time Computer, Fairchild, and Texas Instruments.[36]

- Stephen Wozniak tried to persuade his bosses at Hewlett-Packard Company to back his efforts to build a personal computer. He "couldn't get anybody to listen," so in 1977 he founded Apple Computer. Now, Hewlett-Packard is struggling to catch up to Apple.[37]

The foot-dragging behavior of leading firms is so common that theorists have dubbed it "the fast-second strategy." Briefly, the idea is that, for a large firm, *innovation* is often costlier, riskier, and less profitable than *imitation*. A large firm can lie back, let others gamble, then respond quickly with a "fast second" if anything started by their smaller rivals catches fire. Being large to begin with minimizes any eventual market share losses, as explained by William Baldwin and Gerald Childs: "The dominant firm is likely to be favored as an imitator because of such factors as its ability to distribute a new product far more widely and in a shorter period of time than a smaller innovator, its current reputation among a large number of customers, ability to engage in more extensive advertising than its rivals and, conceivably, because its leading position in current markets is attributable to greater efficiency and the general ability to produce better products at lower costs than any of its rivals."[38] In short, "A firm with a dominating position, conscious of its power to pounce if its position should suddenly be put in jeopardy, may be so confident of being able to deal with incipient competition as to become sluggish."[39]

For fairly obvious reasons, the strategy would pay off best (1) where the innovations in question are easily copied, both technically and legally, and (2) where the leading firm faces an inelastic demand and the innovations in question

---

[35] Blair, *Economic Concentration Hearings, op. cit.,* pp. 1,123–1,124; Lawrence J. White, *The Automobile Industry Since 1945* (Cambridge, Mass.: Harvard University Press, 1971).

[36] *Business Week,* October 27, 1975, pp. 78–92.

[37] *Business Week,* December 6, 1982, p. 75.

[38] William L. Baldwin and Gerald L. Childs, "The Fast Second and Rivalry in Research and Development," *Southern Economic Journal* (July 1969), p. 24.

[39] Jewkes, Sawers, and Stillerman, *op. cit.,* p. 166. To illustrate, Royal Crown is the most innovative firm in the soft drink industry. Its credits include the first decaffeinated cola, the first use of cans, the first with 16-ounce returnable bottles, the first to introduce diet cola, and the first cola company to carry ginger ale and other flavors in its line. "At each stage, the industry pooh-poohs what we consider a breakthrough, then follows our lead," says RC's vice president. Yet the followers end up with most of the spoils. *Wall Street Journal,* May 24, 1982, p. 21; *Forbes,* August 16, 1982, pp. 50–51. For other such stories see *Wall Street Journal,* September 13, 1982, pp. 1, 16.

are "durable" or "economy" models, representing substantial price cuts. (Thus the stainless steel blade was not Gillette's baby.)

On the other hand, there are several good reasons to doubt that the last section's conclusions on invention carry over to innovation. The evidence concerning R & D and patented inventions, although instructive, is only loosely applicable to innovation. Given the significant differences between invention and innovation, bigness may well be better for innovation. Moreover, casual empiricism concerning sound-movies and compact cars lacks resolve, even when it is backed up by plausible theories. Counterexamples and counterarguments are available to defenders of giant enterprises. RCA's color television, Du Pont's nylon, AT & T's transistor, GM's diesel locomotive, and IBM's "Selectric" typewriter are just a few instances of large firm innovation involving vision, risk, and voluminous cost.

What is needed, then, is some *systematic* analysis of the question. To this end, Edwin Mansfield and his associates have conducted detailed studies of innovation in the steel, petroleum, coal, drug, and chemical industries. Their approach was, first, to obtain information on *what* innovations had been made, *which* were the most important, and *who* was most responsible for the pioneering. This information was obtained by canvassing knowledgeable experts on these industries—engineers, scientists, trade associations, and so on. All told, 325 major innovations were included. Next, economic data on each industry were assembled, such as firm size and market concentration. Finally, the innovation information and economic data were compared. Because long time spans were involved, an "early" period and "late" period was selected for each industry within the data's limitations—for example steel was 1919–1938 early, 1939–1958 late; chemicals 1930–1950 early, 1951–1971 late.

The results are reported in Table 23–3. Market shares for the top four firms in each case are given in italics. The top four's percentage share of innovations—weighted and unweighted for estimated importance—is given in regular type. If the largest firms were extraordinarily innovative, their share of innovations would exceed their share of the market. Conversely, if they were relatively slow and staid, their share of innovations would fall short of their market shares. A simple tally tells us that, when innovations are weighted by their importance, the top four's share of innovations exceeded their market share eight times and fell short eight times. Using unweighted raw shares, the top-four performed favorably seven times and unfavorably nine times. These results suggest a toss-up. The largest firms are neither disproportionately innovative nor disproportionately slothful. There is substantial variance across industries, however. The top four petroleum and coal companies performed especially well, whereas the top four steel and chemical companies produced rather embarrassing records.

Though not strictly comparable, available data on the aluminum industry paint a picture even worse than steel, thereby tipping the balance of available evidence in favor of lesser sized firms. Over the years 1946–1957, the aluminum industry was dominated by the "Big Three"—Alcoa, Kaiser, and Reynolds—which then accounted for over 90% of ingot sales and 40% of fabrications.

TABLE 23–3. Per Cent Share of Innovations and of Market Accounted For by Largest Four Firms in Steel, Petroleum, Coal, Drugs, and Chemicals

Item	Steel		Petroleum		Coal		Drugs		Chemicals	
	Weighted	Raw	Weighted	Raw	Weighted	Raw	Weighted	Raw	Weighted	Raw
Early period										
Product innovations	20	20	60	71	n.a.	n.a.	45	37	63	61
Process innovations	39	41	34	36	27	18	n.a.	n.a.	56	58
Market share	62	62	33	33	11	11	50	50	67	67
Late Period										
Product innovations	27	27	40	34	n.a.	n.a.	48	27	60	61
Process innovations	58	64	58	57	30	27	n.a.	n.a.	41	43
Market share	63	63	39	39	13	13	33	33	57	57

n.a.: Not available.
Sources: Edwin Mansfield, Industrial Research and Technological Innovation (New York: Norton, 1968), p. 91; E. Mansfield, J. Rapoport, J. Schnee, S. Wagner, and M. Hamburger, Research and Innovation in the Modern Corporation (New York: Norton, 1971), Chapter 8; E. Mansfield, J. Rapoport, A. Romeo, E. Villani, S. Wagner, and F. Husic, The Production and Application of New Industrial Technology (New York: Norton, 1977), Chapter 3.

Yet at the same time these firms accounted for only 11% of 155 innovations in fabricating, finishing, and joining.[40] Over the later period 1958–1968, the Big Three controlled more than 75% of ingot capacity; at the same time they "only accounted for 18 percent of the listed innovations."[41] The only area in which the Big Three might be patted on their backs (one pat each) was alloy innovation. They accounted for 69% of those during 1946–1957, and 35% during 1958–1968.

This presentation of the evidence merely indicates whether, *as a group*, the largest firms could claim a disproportionately large share of innovations. Mansfield and his friends went further, however. They estimated the distribution of performance across *all* innovating firms in each of their studied industries to determine what size of firm was *the* best for innovation. To appreciate this effort refer back to Figure 23–1 and mentally relabel the vertical axis "Innovative performance relative to sales," or "Number of innovations per sales dollar." An *OA* pattern of performance across all firms would obviously give the top four a disproportionately large share of the innovations. But an *OC* pattern also could, in which case the biggest four firms would be good but *not* the best. The fifth through eighth firms, say, would then be better than the top four. And perhaps the seventh firm would be best of all. If the seventh were best, the peak in the *OC* curve would occur at the seventh firm's size level.

Well then, what are the innovation distribution patterns for these industries? Only chemicals had an *OA* pattern, mainly because the largest firm, DuPont, was also the most intensive innovator of all chemical producers. The other four industries delivered *OC* patterns, wherein the biggest were not the best. The best (or peak) in coal was ranked fourth; in petroleum, sixth; in drugs, twelfth; and in steel, the peak was always found "among very small firms."

It would thus appear that our previous conclusions concerning invention apply here after all. Innovative vigor typically rises with size only from small to medium-sized firms. Beyond some point, which varies, the zeal fizzles relative to size. The only apparent exception is chemicals.

D. Firm Size and Diffusion

Diffusion typically traces a path similar to a "logistic" curve, as it is called. Three such S-shaped curves are captured in Figure 23–2, where zero represents the date of innovation. As time passes (on the horizontal axis), the per cent of firms adopting the innovation rises slowly at first, picks up steam over the middle stretch, and then tapers off as the stragglers finally convert. Curves I and II show cases of complete conversion by all members of the industry. Of

[40] Merton J. Peck, *Competition in the Aluminum Industry 1945–1958* (Cambridge, Mass.: Harvard University Press, 1961), pp. 183–197.

[41] Bruce Smith, "Technological Leadership in the Aluminum Industry," in *Technological Development and Economic Growth,* edited by G. W. Wilson (Bloomington, Ind.: Indiana University Press, 1971), pp. 209–229. The computer industry tips the balance still further away from large firms. A study of 21 major computer innovations found that IBM came up with only 28 per cent of them while its market share ranged between 66 and 78 per cent. Gerald W. Brock, *The U.S. Computer Industry* (Cambridge, Mass.: Ballinger, 1975), pp. 185–207.

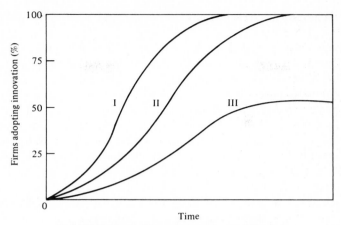

FIGURE 23–2. Three patterns of diffusion.

the two, curve I depicts the more rapid diffusion. Curve III illustrates a case where the innovation is very slow to spread and is never fully adopted by all. Nuclear power illustrates partial adoption, as it seems highly unlikely that nuclear reactors (as we know them today) will ever be universally accepted.

Whether an innovation spreads quickly or slowly, completely or partially, depends on many factors.[42] Market growth, capital cost magnitude, risk, patent protection, and the technical competency of management are among them. Most important, however, is the potential profitability of the innovation. If it promises remarkable cost savings or skyrocketing sales, converts will not timidly hesitate. Dim profit prospects have the opposite effect. Both ups and downs are illustrated by the textile industry. High speed shuttleless looms were innovated in the 1950s, but United States textile manufacturers delayed extensive adoption until the 1970s when rising labor costs made the new looms significantly more profitable than the older, relatively labor-intensive looms. In 1973, an old-style loom cost $8,000 as against $35,000 for a new shuttleless loom. Conversion at that time was nevertheless "the only way to go," according to one textile executive, because the new looms could "get 70% more output with 15% less manpower."[43]

Firm size also has a bearing, and its influence has been measured two ways. The first is merely a matter of positioning. Which firms are the *quickest to begin* using an innovation? Mansfield's studies of diffusion in the coal, brewing, steel, and railroad industries led him to conclude that larger firms were quicker to adopt innovations. He estimated that a 10% increase in firm size would, on the average, reduce delay time 4%.[44] Other results indicating a favorable influence of firm size have been found for the diffusion of numerically controlled

---

[42] Bela Gold, "Technological Diffusion in Industry," *Journal of Industrial Economics* (March 1981), pp. 247–269.
[43] *Business Week,* October 27, 1973, p. 124.
[44] Mansfield *op. cit.* (1968), pp. 155–172.

machine tools in a number of industries,[45] and diffusion in the British textile industry.[46]

Although these results seem to conflict with those concerning invention and innovation, they do not. Several qualifications attend them. For one thing, as a matter of sheer statistical probability, one would expect big firms to be quicker, on the average, than small firms. But it does not appear that they are *disproportionately* quicker. Mansfield explains the difference nicely: "To illustrate this, consider an industry with two firms, one large (80 percent of the market), one small (20 percent of the market). If the large firm does its share of the innovating (no more, no less), it will be first in 80 percent of the cases— and it will be quicker on the average than the small firm."[47] There is, indeed, some evidence of diminishing returns to size.[48]

For another thing, one would expect the effect of firm size to emerge only or mainly where the costs of introduction are particularly high or risky because the big firms should be at their best in such instances. In fact, a study of numerous innovations in chemicals turned up just such differential effects. Firm size had a favorable impact only for high-cost innovations.

Finally, there are many cases where firm size appears to have had *no* effect or an *adverse* effect on the speed of adoption, even where high costs are involved. Examples of these innovations and their industries include "special presses" in Canadian paper,[49] nonflammable dry cleaning in British dry cleaning,[50] basic oxygen process in United States steel,[51] and Sulzer shuttleless looms in United States textiles.[52]

There is thus some sketchy evidence favorable to firm size regarding firm-by-firm diffusion. However, the evidence regarding *intra*firm diffusion, the second measure of diffusion, is definitely stacked on the side of small firms. That is to say, small firms may be somewhat slower to take up an innovation once it is introduced, but, once they do pick it up, they adopt it *throughout their operations* more quickly than large firms. Thus, although small firms may be "late

[45] Anthony A. Romeo, "Interindustry and Interfirm Differences in the Rate of Diffusion of an Innovation," *Review of Economics and Statistics* (August 1975), pp. 311–319; Steven Globerman, "Technical Diffusion in the Canadian Tool and Die Industry," *Review of Economics and Statistics* (November 1975), pp. 428–434.

[46] J. S. Metcalfe, "Diffusion of Innovation in the Lancashire Textile Industry," *Manchester School* (June 1970), pp. 145–159.

[47] Mansfield *op. cit.* (1968), pp. 171–172.

[48] Anita M. Benvignati, "Interfirm Adoption of Capital-Goods Innovations," *Review of Economics and Statistics* (May 1982), pp. 330–335.

[49] Steven Globerman, "New Technology Adoption in the Canadian Paper Industry," *Industrial Organization Review*, Vol. 4, No. 1 (1976), pp. 5–12.

[50] R. W. Shaw and C. J. Sutton, *Industry and Competition* (London: Macmillan Publishing Co., 1976), pp. 108–119.

[51] Joel Dirlam and Walter Adams, "Big Steel, Invention, and Innovation," *Quarterly Journal of Economics* (May 1966), pp. 167–189; James B. Sumrall, Jr., "Diffusion of the Basic Oxygen Furnace in the U.S. Steel Industry," *Journal of Industrial Economics* (June 1982), pp. 421–437.

[52] *Business Week*, October 27, 1973, p. 124. See also Jewkes, Sawers, and Stillerman, *op. cit.*, pp. 303–304.

starters," they also tend to "catch up" with *internal* rates of diffusion exceeding those of large firms. (Now *that* really is playing tortoise to the big firms' hare.) The phenomenon has been observed in railroading, paper manufacturing, chemicals, and in ten industries using numerical machine tools.[53] The main explanations for small-firm speed here seem to be (1) that their nonbureaucratic nature enables quicker, more comprehensive decision making, and (2) the later they start, the more certain they are of the innovation's good value, having the benefit of positive experiences among their adopting predecessors.

To summarize, there is some evidence that large firms adopt innovations earlier than small firms, all else being equal. But the big ones may not be disproportionately faster. Indeed, other evidence indicates no differential at all. Moreover, where the small-fry have been slow to pick up a new ball, they run with it faster toward complete internal conversion.

E. Firm Diversification and Progress

The diversification aspect of the topic has been explored very little. Theoretically, firm diversification is often said to have a favorable impact on invention and innovation.[54] Yet empirical tests have neither confirmed nor refuted this hypothesis. Some studies, especially those concerning *basic* research, find a positive effect of diversification on R & D input and output. Others find a negative impact. Still others find nothing. A definite answer thus awaits further study.[55]

F. Firm Size: An Overview

Overall, medium-sized firms emerge as the most willing and able to spur advance. A little bit of bigness is good; too much often seems bad. Still, a *range* of sizes may be best for an industry, just as they are for a basketball team. Invention, innovation, and diffusion each demand talents and resources. Projects vary widely in size and scope. "All things considered," Scherer aptly concludes, "the most favorable industrial environment for rapid technological progress would appear to be a firm size distribution which includes a preponderance of companies with sales below $500 million, pressed on one side by a horde of small technology-oriented enterprises bubbling over with bright new ideas and on the other by a few larger corporations with the capacity to undertake exceptionally ambitious developments."[56]

---

[53] Romeo, *op. cit.;* Globerman *op. cit.* (1976); and Mansfield *op. cit.* (1968), Chapter 9; Mansfield, *et. al. op. cit.* (1977), p. 118 (referring to a study by Peter Simon).

[54] Richard R. Nelson, "The Simple Economics of Basic Research," *Journal of Political Economy* (June 1959), p. 320.

[55] For a survey see Kamien and Schwartz, *op. cit.,* pp. 26–27. For new evidence see Mueller, et al, *op. cit.* (1982); Scherer, *op. cit.* (1982); and Albert N. Link and James E. Long, "The Simple Economics of Basic Scientific Research," *Journal of Industrial Economics* (September 1981), pp. 105–109.

[56] Scherer, *op. cit.* (1980), p. 422.

III. MARKET STRUCTURE AND PROGRESS

A. Theory

Theories on the impact of market structure on progress differ from those on firm size by giving greater consideration to *rivalry,* or the lack thereof. Early theorists, like Galbraith, argued that high concentration and high barriers to entry would foster progressiveness. They reasoned that the *lack* of rivalry implied by these conditions would (1) boost profits, thereby supplying abundant monetary wherewithal to engage in risky R & D, and (2) protect inventors and innovators from imitators, poachers, and like-minded creatures who would "steal" the pioneers' ideas, thereby discouraging the initiation of progressive efforts by jeopardizing the chance of just rewards.

Of course these arguments are no more overpowering than those defending large firm size. We have already seen that much, if not most, R & D is neither as risky nor as expensive as one might think. Counterargument concerning blood-sucking imitators and interlopers is even easier. The whole idea behind patents is to protect technical frontiersmen from just such discouraging fates. Patents are an even more efficient protection than indiscriminate approval of monopoly because patents grant *temporary* monopoly control *after* the birth of an invention rather than *permanent* power *before*.

More recent and more complicated theories cast added doubt on the notion that progressiveness is necessarily positively associated with monopoly power. Unfortunately, these theories defy compact discussion because they bend and branch with each varying assumption about the ease of imitation, cost contours, technological opportunity, risk, price elasticity of demand, and time horizon.[57] If one were to hazard a crude summary of what appears to be the emerging theoretical consensus, however, it might go something like this:

Two elements are imperative to vigorous progressiveness—ability and incentive. **Ability** includes some modicum of financial treasure that can be sunk into long-term risky projects, and some freedom from the pressures that arise from daily uncertainty about survival. We naturally could not expect a firm whose vitality was flickering to take on extra burdens that a secure firm might assume without strain. Quite obviously, monopolies are usually strong enough to shoulder the added load, for they enjoy both wealth and security. It is indeed these attributes that are emphasized by those who believe that monopolies are ideal for spearheading technical advance.

On the other hand, **incentive** includes prospects of profit and loss. The larger the prospective profit from some endeavor, the greater the incentive to undertake it. Conversely, the larger the prospective loss from stagnation, the greater the incentive to get moving. For various reasons, competition probably heightens both incentives. The greater the competition, the greater the industry's output

---

[57] Examples include Douglas Needham, "Market Structure and Firms' R & D Behavior," *Journal of Industrial Economics* (June 1975), pp. 241–255, Raymond Jackson, "Market Structure and the Rewards for Patented Inventions," *Antitrust Bulletin* (Fall 1972), pp. 911–926, plus those cited by Kamien and Schwartz, *op. cit.*

and the greater the expansion opportunities for any one firm that gets a jump on the others. Likewise, the greater the profit prospects will be for any technical breakthrough. As for considerations on the loss side, the greater the competition, the greater the chances are that stagnant firms will be outdistanced by their rivals. Competition thus propels movement with fear.

All told, it appears that monopolies probably have a great deal of ability but very little incentive, whereas purely competitive firms probably have little ability but ample incentive. Neither structural extreme is therefore particularly conducive to progress. However, the elements blend in intermediate structures, where market power is sufficient to secure ability but not so strong as to eradicate the incentives brought by rivalry. With both ability and incentive present, intermediate ranges of oligopoly may be expected to display the least lassitude.

Elaborations on this theme could generate additional arguments for the same conclusion. For example, more than half of all private R & D effort is aimed at "product improvement," which of course is one form of product differentiation, a form that extends to producer goods as well as consumer goods. The vigor of such product–improvement differentiation could well be most spirited in some middle range of concentration, just as advertising is, and for many of the same reasons. As concentration rises from low to moderate levels, price competition becomes less and less attractive while *nonprice* competition, including competition on the technology front, becomes more and more attractive. However, *further* increases in concentration, above oligopolistic levels, are not likely to continue intensification of R & D aimed in the nonprice direction. Approach toward monopoly tends to subdue rivalry of all forms, especially if under oligopoly that rivalry is excessive from the market-wide, profit maximizing point of view. This restraint at particularly high levels of concentration may obtain despite the fact that collusive agreements restricting R & D could probably never be more than nebulous understandings, given the complexities involved and generous opportunities for double-crossing one's collaborators. Comparing concentration ratios of 60 and 100, then, invention and innovation are likely to be about the same, or the 100 could pump out the inferior record, all else being equal. Pictorially, curves *ABC* and *AC* in Figure 15–2 (of Chapter 15) would depict this hypotheses if the horizontal axis there were relabeled "R & D intensity."[58]

Complicating matters a bit is the possibility that causation may not run just one way, from structure to performance. Particularly rapid technical change, where it is attributable mainly to an independent march of science, could *cause* high concentration. Firms that fail to keep step with the march will fall to the wayside, dying from self-destructive mistakes—such as delays that are never overcome or costly trips down blind alleys. These possibilities appear to be the explanation for rising concentration in aircraft manufacturing,[59] and they

[58] More sophisticated theories to roughly the same effect may be found in Scherer, *op. cit.* (1980), pp. 426–430; Kamien and Schwartz, *op. cit.*, pp. 30–31.

[59] Almarin Phillips, *Technology and Market Structure* (Lexington, Mass.: Lexington Books, 1971).

could apply to other industries. Patents constitute another mechanism that encourages concentration. Historically, they have contributed to concentration in such fields as electric lamps, aluminum, synthetic fibers, and telephone equipment. On this empirical note we now leave theory behind.

B. Market Structure and R & D Effort: The Evidence

The evidence of structure's impact is best collected into three classes—one each for R & D effort, innovative output, and diffusion. These classes of evidence present nowhere near as clear a pattern as that traced for firm size. Perhaps interindustry differences in technical opportunity cannot be sufficiently accounted for. Perhaps the available measures of technical vigor are less reliable in the interindustry context. Whatever the reason, the present picture is at best murky. ("Our test tubes are dirty," Richard Miller would say.)

As regards R & D effort, there are at least fifteen statistical studies exploring the relationship between concentration or barriers to entry and R & D intensity. Most studies measure intensity by R & D expenditure relative to sales, but a few use counts of scientific personnel relative to total employment or patents relative to sales. Unfortunately, the results lack consistency. Several studies find a positive relationship between concentration and R & D intensity.[60] One discloses a negative association.[61] Five detect no significant relationship whatever or wobble between positive and negative relationships.[62]

Finally, the results of seven other studies more-or-less support the nonlinear hypothesis developed earlier. These last tentatively reveal a *positive* relationship between concentration and R & D intensity over a low to medium range of concentration, plus a *negative* relationship over a medium to high range of concentration.[63] I say "tentatively" because in some of these studies the effect

[60] D. Hamberg *op. cit.* (1964); F. M. Scherer, "Market Structure and the Employment of Scientists and Engineers," *American Economic Review* (June 1967), pp. 524–531; Blake Imel, Michael R. Behr, and Peter G. Helmberger, *Market Structure and Performance* (Lexington, Mass.: Lexington Books, 1972), pp. 65–75; F. M. Scherer, "Concentration, R & D, and Productivity Change" (mimeo, 1980).

[61] Robert W. Wilson, "The Effect of Technological Environment and Product Rivalry on R & D Effort and Licensing of Inventions," *Review of Economics and Statistics* (May 1977), pp. 171–178.

[62] F. M. Scherer, "Firm Size and Patented Inventions," *American Economic Review* (December 1965), pp. 116–121; Richard E. Caves and Masu Uekusa, *Industrial Organization in Japan* (Washington, D.C.: Brookings Institution, 1976), p. 128; Comanor *op. cit.* (1967); Stephen Farber, "Buyer Market Structure and R & D Effort," *Review of Economics and Statistics* (August 1981), pp. 336–345; Albert N. Link, "An Analysis of the Composition of R & D Spending," *Southern Economic Journal* (October 1982) pp. 342–349.

[63] Scherer *op. cit.* (1967); T. M. Kelly, "The Influences of Firm Size and Market Structure on the Research Efforts of Large Multiproduct Firms," Ph.D. dissertation, Oklahoma State University, 1970 (as summarized in Kamien and Schwartz, *op. cit.*); F. T. Knickerbocker, *Oligopolistic Reaction and Multinational Enterprise* (Boston: Graduate School of Business Administration, Harvard University, 1973), pp. 141–142; S. Globerman, "Market Structure and R & D in Canadian Manufacturing Industries," *Quarterly Review of Economics and Business* (Summer 1973), pp. 59–67 (assuming the high technology industries are highly concentrated, as in Scherer); William J. Adams, "Firm Size and Research Activity: France and the United States," *Quarterly Journal of Economics* (August 1970), pp. 386–409; Ronald E. Shrieves, "Market Structure and Innovation: A New Perspective," *Journal of Industrial Economics* (June 1978), pp. 329–347; Mueller, Culbertson, and Peckham, *op. cit.,* pp. 33–43.

of concentration is obscured by the authors' attempts to account for technical opportunity. In one study, for instance, the sample of industries is divided into "low" and "high" technology groups.[64] Concentration and R & D intensity are positively associated in the "low" group and negatively associated in the "high" group. However, average concentration tends to be high in the "high" group and low in the "low" group. So the hypothesized nonlinear relation emerges, but only indirectly and uncertainly.

Still, there are several grounds for accepting the nonlinear results as more than merely tentative. Scherer's study of this issue is among the best, and he concluded that "technological vigor appears to increase with concentration mainly at relatively low levels of concentration." In the higher ranges, he felt that "additional market power is probably not conducive to more vigorous technological efforts and may be downright stultifying."[65] Furthermore, William Adams' study produces a nonlinear relation, and his is perhaps the best in controlling for technical opportunity. He compared R & D intensity and concentration *industry-by-industry* between the United States and France. For 5 of the 14 industries so studied he found R & D intensity to be higher in the country where concentration was higher. One such industry is textiles: the R & D outlay/sales ratio for textiles was 2.4 in France and 0.5 in the United States, whereas concentration was 30 in France and 19 in the United States. In *all* such cases the concentration comparison was over a low range of concentration. The concentration ratios in these comparisons averaged 19 on the low side of the Atlantic and 31 on the high side. Conversely, seven of the industries compared revealed an opposite tendency, and they were generally more concentrated. That is to say, there were seven instances in which the country with the *higher* concentration had the *lower* R & D intensity, and, for these, topside concentration averaged 54 as against 42 on the bottom. Combining the averages of these two sets, R & D rose when concentration rose from 19 to 31, but R & D *fell* as concentration rose from 42 to 54. For two industries there were no inter-country differences in R & D or concentration, precluding their comparison.

The notion that R & D intensity is most feverish in the intermediate values of market structure is buttressed by still further tidbits like the following: Analysis of the impact of entry barriers led William Comanor to the conviction that "Where technical barriers either effectively foreclose the entry of new firms or where they are quite low, research spending tends to be limited. Where barriers are moderate, however, and where prospects for some entry exist, research spending is greater."[66]

---

[64] Globerman, *op. cit.;* see also Shrieves, *op. cit.* Note, too, that Farber, *op. cit.,* finds a quadratic with "unadjusted" data.

[65] Scherer *op. cit.* (1967).

[66] Comanor, *op. cit.* (1967), p. 657. Farber, *op. cit.,* also finds that high barriers have an adverse affect.

527

C. Market Structure and Innovative Output: The Evidence

Measurement and data problems make interindustry studies of innovative output extremely difficult. About all that can be said with certainty is that, once again, few if any gains in progressiveness would probably be obtained by transforming all our industries into near monopolies or tight-knit oligopolies.

This conclusion is suggested, first of all, by reexamining the innovation data compiled by Mansfield and his associates—data reported above in Table 23–3. Those data plotted produce Figure 23–3. The vertical axis is market share of the top four firms, and the horizontal axis is their share of significant innovations. A diagonal line, on which the two shares would be equal, divides the diagram. Thus, all instances of market share exceeding innovation share are plotted in the top left half. On the other hand, all instances of market share falling below innovation share end up in the bottom right half. Put differently, the upper left half is the home for observations that reflect *un*favorably on the performance of the leading firms, whereas the lower right half houses favorable observations.

Now, if concentration had *no* influence on the relative performance of leading firms, the plotted points would present no clear pattern relative to concentration. Notice, however, that above a concentration level of 45%, 15 of the 18 observations appear in the *un*favorable region. Conversely, below a concentration level of 45%, only 2 points appear in the unfavorable region whereas 12 cast reflections of favorable performance. The relative performance of leading firms is therefore markedly better where concentration is lower and competition keener.

Oliver Williamson, who first recognized this pattern, explains it thus,

> in the short run, monopoly advantages may permit the largest firms to neglect the behavior of their rivals, while over the long run the recognized degree of interdependence among the principal rivals may lead to calculated efforts to restrain innovation and thereby preserve stable interfirm relations. Lacking compulsion to innovate in the short run and anxious to moderate competition in the long run, *the relative innovative performance of the largest firms may decline as monopoly power increases.* This is contrasted with circumstances in a competitive industry where differential advantages may be available only to the extent that a firm is a successful innovator. Hence, *the incentives to innovate are held to be particularly keen where competitive conditions prevail.* [67]

The *relatively* poor showing of leading firms in highly concentrated industries suggests that, *in general,* highly concentrated industries perform less laudably than competitive industries when it comes to innovation (other things being equal). By definition the leading firms account for more of the performance where concentration is high than where it is low. So, if their performance is relatively poor, it reflects adversely on the entire industry. Even so, this deduction is not based on hard data.

As regards hard data, statistical studies of concentration and technological

---

[67] Oliver E. Williamson, "Innovation and Market Structure," *Journal of Political Economy* (February 1965), p. 68 (emphasis added).

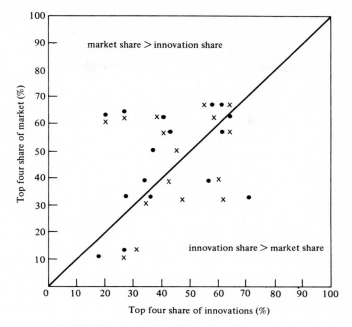

x = weighted for importance
• = unweighted for importance

FIGURE 23–3. Concentration and innovation.

outputs yield mixed results.[68] But there is one area where recent evidence reflects quite favorably on bigness. Several recent studies find a significant positive association between concentration and growth in labor productivity.[69] Moreover, it appears that this positive effect on innovative output may be due to a positive association between concentration and R & D inputs. As the most recent of these studies puts it:

> The more concentrated an industry is, the larger will be the market shares of its representative sellers. And the larger a seller's market share is, the larger will be the share of cost savings from process innovations it can appropriate, *assuming* that licensing the process to competitors is either unattractive or entails high transactions costs. The firm able to appropriate a large share of benefits should in turn have a stronger incentive to perform process R & D, all else (such as technological opportu-

[68] For example, Mueller, Culbertson, and Peckham find no association whatever between concentration and patents in food manufacturing (*op. cit.*). C. D. Sveikauskas and L. Sveikauskas find both positive and negative ties between concentration and productivity growth, *Southern Economic Journal* (January 1982), pp. 769–774.

[69] Douglas F. Greer and Stephen A. Rhoades, "Concentration and Productivity Changes in the Long and Short Run," *Southern Economic Journal* (October 1976), pp. 1031–1044; F. M. Scherer, "Concentration, R & D, and Productivity Change," (mimeo, October 1982). For evidence that the positive relation may turn negative at very high levels of concentration see Karin Wagner, "Competition and Productivity," *Journal of Industrial Economics* (September 1980), pp. 32–33.

nity and competitive stimulus) held equal. And this in turn could lead to more rapid productivity growth.[70]

D. Market Structure and Diffusion: The Evidence

Hampered by data difficulties, early tests of structure's impact on diffusion were no more than makeshift. These tests nevertheless suggested that competition was stimulating and monopoly power encumbering. Thus, early analysis of diffusion in the coal, steel, brewing, and railroad industries led to a qualified conclusion: "We have too few industries to test accurately the hypothesis often advanced that the rate of imitation is faster in more competitive industries, but the differences seem to be generally in that direction."[71]A book-length study of international diffusion in the semiconductor industry arrived at a similar spot: "The evidence presented in this study about the market structure characteristics conducive to the rapid diffusion of new technology shows that easy entry conditions and new firms were very instrumental in the rapid utilization of new semiconductor techniques and devices in the American market."[72]

More recently, Anthony Romeo has confirmed these suggestions with a convincing test.[73] The power of his test derives from his choice of a single innovation, numerically controlled machine tools, that many industries of varying structure use. These tools are controlled by specially coded cards or tapes, which guide them through their paces. The machines can produce simple or intricate metal parts faster, cheaper, and more flawlessly than old methods. Wide potential usage of the innovation permitted Romeo to gather adoption data from 140 firms in 10 manufacturing industries—aircraft engines, airframes, coal mining machinery, digital computers, farm machinery, industrial instruments, large steam turbines, machine tools, printing presses, and tools and dies. Employing two alternative measures for speed of numerical control diffusion within each of these industries, Romeo discovered that the *less* concentrated among them adopted the innovation significantly *more quickly* than the more highly concentrated. Thus he had good reason to write that "competitive pressures do seem to lead to higher rates of diffusion."

E. Market Structure: An Overview

All in all, the evidence concerning market structure is in harmony with that on firm size. Whether the measure of performance is R & D effort, innovation, or diffusion does not seem to matter. Towering concentration ratios and obstructive barriers to entry stifle progress. At the same time, there are grounds for arguing that structures of the opposite extreme—atomistic structures with fluid firm turnover—might be less than ideal, especially for R & D effort. Interme-

[70] Scherer, *op. cit.* (1982), p. 3 (emphasis in original).
[71] Mansfield *op. cit.* (1968), p. 154.
[72] John E. Tilton, *International Diffusion of Technology: The Case of Semiconductors* (Washington, D.C.: Brookings Institution, 1971), p. 166.
[73] Romeo *op. cit.* (1975); and A. A. Romeo, "The Rate of Imitation of a Capital-Embodied Process Innovation," *Economica* (February 1977), pp. 63–69.

diate structures, leaning toward the competitive side of the continuum, seem best. The one exception might be for productivity growth.

SUMMARY

Our progress through this discussion took three steps. First, by way of background, it was explained that technological progress itself entails three steps— invention, innovation, and diffusion. Invention is the first realization and crude proof that something will work. Innovation is the first commercial application of the invention. And diffusion is the spread of its adoption. Each step demands somewhat different talents and resources. A surprising amount of invention can still be carried out in basements and garages, although the relative importance of truly independent inventors is waning. Innovation requires refinement, testing, sometimes further invention, and initial production, all of which can be costly. Diffusion involves some risk-acceptance on the part of buyers. Since progress in these three categories is partly determined by technological opportunities, as dictated by divergent growth rates in different branches of science, the impact of market conditions is both limited and difficult to measure. Nevertheless, measurement is not impossible because firms within a given industry face similar opportunities and interindustry comparisons can be devised.

Early theorizing on the relation between progress and *firm size* stressed the virtues of bigness. But two decades of subsequent study have shown that emphasis to be misplaced. In the aggregate, R & D effort is concentrated in the hands of the top 600 firms, but inventive output is not commensurate with the input of these firms. Within specific industries there is no evidence indicating that R & D intensity, relative to firm size, increases beyond medium-sized firms. Indeed, the largest firms are much less spirited than medium-sized firms in many industries. Moreover, within most industries, inventive output does not match measured input, apparently because diseconomies of scale occur beyond moderate size levels.

The record regarding innovation and firm size is much the same. The largest firms cannot claim credit for a disproportionate share of the innovations. Except in chemicals, firms of less than ponderous proportions are the best. The largest firms in some industries lead in diffusion. But their showing in that respect is tarnished by several qualifications, the most important of which is the more rapid *internal* diffusion displayed by small firms.

The influence of market structure is still somewhat uncertain because test results conflict. Nevertheless, several faint outlines seem discernable. First, it is perhaps most plausible to suppose that neither monopoly nor pure competition (nor the nearby neighboring structures of either) are very good for vigorous advance. Incentive and ability blend in the middle ranges of structure, as evidence on R & D effort seems to bear out. Second, the facts concerning innovation indicate that the relative performance of leading firms diminishes as concentration increases. Data on productivity change are mixed, but concentration apparently does make some positive small contribution. Finally, several studies of diffusion testify to the benefits of competitive structures. Other things being equal, high concentration and lofty entry barriers hinder the spread of technological breakthroughs.

Technological Change: Public Policy

The patent system added the fuel of interest to the fire of genius.

—ABE LINCOLN

The list of 17 innovations was unimpressive—a stain remover, a construction material, and a sewing thread were highlights. Yet the list produced amazing results when assessed by Edwin Mansfield and his associates. They sought to estimate the private and social rates of return generated by run-of-the-mill innovations. The *private* rate of return is the *innovator's* reward, or profit before tax. The *social* rate of return is the *users'* prize, namely, the cost savings or added consumers' surplus that users of innovations gain.

The difference between private and social reward can best be illustrated with an extreme case not included on Mansfield's list: Dr. Jonas Salk donated his discovery of polio vaccine to the public, declining patent monopoly and with it a staggering fortune, thereby minimizing his return. But the public's return was stupendous, amounting to untold millions, perhaps billions, of dollars in reduced medical bills, a more productive populace, and relieved suffering. Although none of the 17 innovations on Mansfield's list could match the polio vaccine, and although none were charitably donated to the public, the median social rate of return for the group was a bountiful 56% as compared to the median private rate of 25%.[1] That is a gap of 2 to 1! For one reason or another—imitators' poaching, "satisficing" rather than profit maximizing prices, and so on—the innovators did not capture all the benefits society received. They shook the tree while others ran off with most of the apples.

Of course we would not want to arrange the world so that every discoverer appropriated the full value of his discovery. Such is not needed to motivate trailblazers, given the alternative inducements of fame and psychic pleasure.

[1] E. Mansfield, J. Rapoport, A. Romeo, E. Villani, S. Wagner, and F. Husic, *The Production and Application of New Industrial Technology* (New York: Norton, 1977), pp. 144–166.

Such is not even desirable, given the crazy implications full reward would have for income and wealth distribution. (Imagine the consequences to us and the heirs of Columbus if he could have claimed America as his private property.) Nevertheless, the gap between private and social gain does suggest that reliance on private markets, plain and simple, may lead individuals and enterprises to invest *too little* in research, development, and innovation as compared to a socially optimal investment. Thus, we do not rely on private markets plain and simple. Government intervenes to encourage invention and innovation. Two government policies having this purpose—patents and R & D funding—are the focus of this chapter.

Our discussion of patents answers such questions as: What is a patent? What can be patented? Why have patents? What are the benefits and costs of patents? Our discussion of government funding of research and development covers two basic questions: What amounts of money are involved? Why is such funding needed?

We conclude with a brief review of other policies that promote progress.

I. THE PATENT SYSTEM: NATURE AND SCOPE

A. Background

A patent is a **monopoly right** to make and sell some product, or use some process, that is governmentally granted for a limited number of years as a reward for invention. The character and duration of this right differs from country to country. United States law grants "for the term of seventeen years [from the patent's date] . . . the right to exclude others from making, using, or selling the invention throughout the United States."[2] The right is a form of private property that can be bought and sold, traded, given away, and leased or licensed for the use of others (who pay a "royalty" for the privilege). The invention covered can even go unused if the owner wishes. Moreover, although only individuals can be awarded patents, corporate employees typically "assign" their patents to their employers, and independent inventors often sell or license their patents to others for commercial application.

Regardless of ultimate ownership, roughly half of all patents go unused because the inventions they cover are too far ahead of their time, too costly to develop relative to the potential profit, or too unsettling to the ultimate owner's old way of doing things. Many go unused because close substitutes for the invention are available. Thus, the monopoly granted may be only a measly one.

Indeed, more than four million patents have been issued since inception of the system. Of late, the annual flow tops 70,000. If these figures are not big enough to suggest to you that many if not most patented inventions are rather pedestrian, consider the following: Patent 2,882,858, awarded in 1959, covers

[2] U.S.C. Section 154 (1970).

534

a diaper for parakeets. A vibrating toilet seat won patent No. 3,244,168 in 1966.[3]

Fortunately, enforcement of any patent is left up to the patent holder. Accused infringers must be hauled into court by patentees. The original Bell telephone patents, for instance, were enforced with more than six hundred infringement suits initiated by Bell interests. What is more, the patent office does not have final say as to what constitutes a valid patent. The federal courts have final say. So, once in court, an infringer almost always defends himself against a patentee's attack by claiming the patent is invalid. This defense is by no means futile because court judges generally hold more stringent standards of patentability than the patent office. Approximately 60% of all patents coming under court review are declared invalid and unenforceable. In three out of four cases the chief cause for rejection is a lack of "inventiveness."[4] The remaining reasons for invalidation can be understood only after an explanation of what can and cannot be patented.

B. Patentability

According to statute law, "Whoever invents or discovers any new and useful process, machine, manufacture, or composition of matter, or any new and useful improvement thereof, may obtain a patent therefor." Embedded in the language are four criteria for patentability: (1) inventiveness, (2) novelty, (3) utility, and (4) subject matter.

To cross the threshhold of **inventiveness** the discovery must be "nonobvious" at the time "to a person having ordinary skill in the art." There must, in other words, be some creativity. Just how much creativity is required and how much creativity went into any claimed invention are often difficult to judge. The uncertainties in the "nonobvious" standard are, in fact, almost vague and various enough to call for discriminating "creativity" on the part of patent examiners. To restate the problem more concretely, do you think the following should qualify? Putting a rubber erasure on the end of a pencil? Making doorknobs of clay rather than metal or wood? Devising a motorized golf-bag cart? All three were in fact awarded patents, but when tested in court two were found wanting. Given the nature of the problem, it is hard to disagree with Judge Learned Hand, who once grumbled that the test of invention was little more than a vague and fugitive "phantom."[5]

As for **novelty**, the invention must not be previously known or used. This standard is fairly straightforward, but it takes patent examiners a long time to review past patents and published scientific papers in search of duplication. Of all standards, **utility** is certainly the least demanding. As the extravagant examples given earlier and Figure 24–1 illustrate, many approved inventions are empty of all but the most fantastic applications.

---

[3] Stacy V. Jones, *The Patent Office* (New York: Praeger, 1971), pp. 64–69.
[4] Ibid., pp. 43–44.
[5] *Harries* v. *Air King Prods. Co.,* 183 F. 2d 158, 162 (2d Cir. 1950).

THE TWIDD

FIGURE 24–1. The Twidd, a device that facilitates thumb twiddling, won patent number 4,227,342 in 1979. The patent states: "To those twiddlers who lack sufficient coordination, not only is the repose and peace of mind which thumb twiddling normally brings not available, but the inability to carry out the twiddling successfully, including inadvertent bumping of the thumbs . . . causes additional frustration." Source: *Wall Street Journal,* January 19, 1983, p. 25.

Because patentable **subject matter** is limited to mechanical or chemical processes and compositions, much is excluded. Discovery of fundamental laws of nature, such as $E = mc^2$, may not be patented, however brilliant or useful their discovery may be. The same holds for mathematical formulas, managerial strategies, teaching methods, and the like. Products of nature are likewise unpatentable, although this rule has exceptions.

In 1980, the Supreme Court made headlines by deciding that manmade living organisms could be patented. The organism at issue was a new bacterium capable of "eating" crude oil, making it useful in cleaning up oil spills. But the decision had broad implications because it opened the door for patents on all kinds of newly created microbes. Indeed, shortly thereafter, the first U.S. patent covering techniques of recombinant DNA, or genesplicing, was awarded for work done at Stanford University and the University of California. These developments sparked controversy because to some people they gave birth to a Brave New World. One overwrought group claimed that such patenting "lays the groundwork for corporations to own the processes of life in the centuries to come."[6]

C. Obtaining a Patent

The rules and regulations of patentability give appearances of an imposing thicket, blocking all but a privileged few. But of the more than 100,000 patent applications filed annually, 50% or so gain patent office approval. Applicants are aided not only by lenient standards of invention and utility but also by an army of clever, well-heeled patent attorneys. Indeed, these attorneys are often more crucial to obtaining a patent than an invention is.[7]

[6] *Wall Street Journal,* June 17, 1980, p. 3; December 31, 1980, pp. 1, 8.

[7] Specific evidence is provided by F. M. Scherer, "Firm Size, Market Structure, Opportunity, and the Output of Patented Inventions," *American Economic Review* (December 1965), p. 1111, note 20. See also Corwin D. Edwards, *Maintaining Competition* (New York: McGraw-Hill Book Co., 1964 edition), p. 218.

The point is driven home by citing Patent 549,160, which a patent attorney obtained for himself in 1895, and which covered what later proved to be the wonder machine of our modern age—the automobile. According to legend, George Selden stole ideas from genuine auto engineers and bluffed his way far enough along to see his auto patent earn $5.8 million in royalties and gain the approval of a U.S. District Court. The only person willing and able to challenge the validity of Selden's patent was Henry Ford, who eventually won his case in Circuit Court.[8]

II. TWO CASE STUDIES

At its best, the patent system stimulates progress, rewards deserving inventors and innovators, and arouses competition. At its worst, it fosters opposite tendencies. Each extreme may be vividly depicted by a case history.

A. United States Gypsum and Wallboard[9]

There is nothing especially clever about wallboard, looking at it with today's familiarity. It is plaster sandwiched between two sheets of paper. At the turn of the century, all wallboard was produced with open edges that exposed the plaster filler. Exposure caused the edges to chip and crumble when bumped in transit. The obvious remedy for this problem—paper covering for the edges as well as the body of the wallboard—was hit upon in 1912 and won for its discoverer, one Utzman, patent No. 1,034,746. This patent covered the process of closing the edges of wallboard by folding the bottom cover sheet over the edge and then affixing the top cover sheet.

Realizing its great value, United States Gypsum Corporation (called U.S. Gypsum), the leading wallboard producer of the day, acquired the Utzman patent and then used it as a springboard to four decades of industry dominance. On the face of it, the odds against U.S. Gypsum's conquest were rather large, for it was based on a brittle springboard. Aside from the fact that the Utzman patent lasted only seventeen years, competitors could easily "invent around" it by closing wallboard edges in other, equally obvious ways. The top cover sheet could fold toward the bottom; the two cover sheets could *both* fold to overlap the edge; the two cover sheets could be imbedded in the center of the plaster edge; a separate sheet could cap the edge, and so on. U.S. Gypsum, however, was able to control the competition these options offered its smaller rivals by tenaciously suing for infringement at every fold. After thus "softening" up its competitors, U.S. Gypsum bought their renegade patents.

In exchange for the cooperation of its rivals, U.S. Gypsum licensed them

---

[8] Jones, *op. cit.*, pp. 77–79; Irene Till, "The Legal Monopoly," in *The Monopoly Makers*, edited by M. J. Green (New York: Grossman, 1973), pp. 293–294.

[9] This section is based primarily on *United States* v. *United States Gypsum Co.* 333 U.S. 366 (1947); and Clair Wilcox, *Competition and Monopoly in American Industry*, Monograph No. 21 of the Temporary National Economic Committee, U.S. Congress (1940), pp. 161–163.

to use its accumulated patents through agreements that fixed the prices all parties charged for their wallboard. While building these arrangements, U.S. Gypsum seems to have avoided court and favored nontrial settlements as often as possible, perhaps out of fear that its patents would be found invalid if ever truly tested. In other words, competitors were sufficiently strong and U.S. Gypsum's patents were sufficiently weak that the company could not monopolize the trade. At best, it attained a 57% market share. Even so, U.S. Gypsum was resourceful enough to construct a network of license agreements that effectively cartelized the industry. "According to the plans we have," an optimistic executive said at one point, "we figure that there is a possibility of us holding the price steady on wallboard for the next fourteen or fifteen years which means much to the industry."[10] How much it meant is measured by the fact that in 1928, U.S. Gypsum reportedly earned a profit of $11.09 per 1,000 square feet of wallboard over the manufacturing cost of $10.50.

Subsequent patents on wallboard became the basis of subsequent cartelization. But the cartel's life was cut short by action of the Antitrust Division of the Department of Justice. Attacked for violating the Sherman Act, the cartel was dissolved after the Supreme Court decided in 1947 that "regardless of motive, the Sherman Act bars patent exploitation of the kind that was here attempted."[11]

B. Chester Carlson and Xerox[12]

Born to the wife of an itinerant barber and raised in poverty, Chester Carlson invented xerography. Various family tragedies compelled Carlson to work unceasingly from age twelve to support his family and his education. His dire boyhood circumstances induced dreams of escape. In his own words:

> At this stage in my life, I was entranced by the accounts I read of the work and successes of independent inventors and of the rewards they were able to secure through the patents on their inventions. I, too, might do this, I thought; and this contemplation gave stimulus and direction to my life.

After working his way through to a physics degree at the California Institute of Technology, Carlson accepted a research position at Bell Telephone Laboratories in 1930, a position made temporary by the Great Depression. Though plagued by financial difficulties during the depression, he found a job in the patent department of another company. His tasks there impressed upon him the need for quick, inexpensive copies of drawings and documents. Thus it was that in 1935 Carlson began a spare-time search for a copy machine. Although

---

[10] *U.S.* v. *U.S. Gypsum, op. cit.,* 374.

[11] Ibid., p. 393.

[12] This section is based on J. Jewkes, D. Sawers, and R. Stillerman, *The Sources of Invention* (New York: Norton, 1969), pp. 321–323; D. V. DeSimone, Testimony, *Economic Concentration,* Part 3, U.S. Senate Subcommittee on Antitrust and Monopoly, (1965), pp. 1,108–1,111; E. A. Blackstone, "The Copying-Machine Industry: Innovations, Patents, and Pricing," *Antitrust Law & Economics Review* (Fall 1972), pp. 105–122; and F. M. Scherer, *The Economic Effects of Compulsory Patent Licensing* (New York: New York University Graduate School of Business Administration, 1977), p. 9.

he was working full time and attending law school at night (in hopes of becoming a patent attorney!), his research and experimentation were extensive, leading eventually to his key idea of combining electrostatics and photoconductive materials. The first successful demonstration of Carlson's ideas took place in a room behind a beauty parlor in Astoria, Long Island, on October 22, 1938. He used a crude device to copy the message "10–22–38 Astoria."

Four patents awarded to Carlson between 1940 and 1944 covered his basic concepts. During the same years he tried to find a firm that would develop his invention for commercial use, but he encountered a stream of rejections, including those of twenty large firms—IBM, Remington Rand, and Eastman Kodak among them. The project was finally picked up for experimentation by Battelle Memorial Institute, a nonprofit research outfit, which thereby gained partial rights to any future earnings on the patents. Battelle devised a number of major patentable improvements, including use of a selenium plate, which allowed copies to be made on ordinary as opposed to chemically coated paper. But Battelle did not have the resources to manufacture and market the machine.

Quest for a commercial innovator led to another round of rejections from big companies, whereupon, in 1946, the task was undertaken by Haloid Company, a small firm earning an annual net income of only $101,000. Motivated by partial rights to potential earnings and led by a bright, enthusiastic fellow named Joseph Wilson, Haloid pushed the project to fruition. Among the landmarks on the long road that followed were (1) the first marketing of an industrial-use copier in 1950; (2) a change of company name from Haloid to Xerox; (3) first profit earnings in 1953; (4) development by 1957 of a prototype office copier, the cost of which nearly bankrupted the company; and (5) commercial introduction of the famous 914 console copier in 1959, more than 20 years after Carlson began his initial experiments.

All told, over $20 million was spent on the development of xerography before 1959. It is doubtful whether such a large financial commitment would ever have been made by the people who made it without patent protection. Besides Carlson's first four patents, the project generated well over one hundred improvement patents for various machine designs, selenium drums, paper feeding devices, copy counters, powder dispensers, and so on. The significance of patents to Xerox is summarized by Joseph Wilson:

> We have become an almost classic case for those who believe the (patent) system was designed to permit small, weak companies to become healthy. During the early years of xerography we were investing almost as much in research as we were realizing in profit. Unless the first faltering efforts had been protected from imitators, the business itself probably would have foundered, thus obliterating opportunities for jobs for thousands throughout the world.[13]

(Carlson, Battelle, and Wilson were each eventually rewarded with eight-digit earnings.)

[13] DeSimone, *op. cit.*, p. 1,111.

III. WHY PATENTS?

The Xerox story implies several justifications for the patent system that now ought to be openly stated. At bottom, support rests on three legs: "natural law" property, "exchange-for-secrets," and "incentives."

A. Natural Law

The natural law thesis asserts that inventors have a natural property right to their own idea. "It would be a gross immorality in the law," John Stuart Mill argued, "to set everybody free to use a person's work without his consent and without giving him an equivalent."[14] Although this view appeals to our sense of fairness, it is not without its practical problems. For one thing, it implicitly assumes that invention is the work of a single, identifiable mind, or at most a few minds. But today invention is usually the product of a faceless corporate team, and any resulting patent rights rest with the corporation, not with the deserving inventors, individual or otherwise. Of course corporations may fund the research and thereby accept the risks, so the property argument could be extended to corporate research on grounds of "just" compensation.

This extention does not square with the fact that corporations doing research for the U.S. Department of Defense get exclusive patent rights on their defense work without bearing any financial risk. The property rationale is further undermined by the fact that patents protect only a few classes of ideas. If one is seriously concerned about the fair treatment of thinkers, why forsake those who push back the frontiers of knowledge in areas excluded from patent eligibility—such as pure science, mathematics, economics, and business administration? Is the inventor of parakeet diapers more deserving than the inventor of double-entry bookkeeping?

B. Exchange-for-Secrets

Patent law requires that inventors disclose their invention to the public. Without patent protection it is a pretty safe bet that inventors would try to rely on secrecy more than they now do to protect their ideas from theft. Thus the exchange-for-secrets rationale "presumes a bargain between inventor and society, the former surrendering the possession of secret knowledge in exchange for the protection of a temporary exclusivity in its industrial use."[15] Widespread public knowledge is assumed to be more beneficial than secret knowledge because openness fertilizes technological advance. One discovery may trigger dozens of others among many inventors. And, although the initial discovery cannot be used freely for seventeen years, secrecy might prevent full diffusion of its application for an even longer duration. Just how well society comes out in

[14] Cited by Floyd L. Vaughan, *The United States Patent System* (Norman, Okla.: University of Oklahoma Press, 1956), p. 27.
[15] Fritz Machlup, *An Economic Review of the Patent System*, Study No. 15, U.S. Senate, Subcommittee on Patents, Trademarks, and Copyrights, 85th Congress, Second Session (1958), p. 21.

the bargain is impossible to say. The benefits of openness and the costs of temporary monopoly defy accurate estimation, especially the former. About all that can be said with confidence is that abolition of the patent system would cause the burial of *some* knowledge currently revealed in patent applications.[16]

C. Incentive

The justification most solidly illustrated by the story of Xerox, and the justification most supportive of the patent system, is that it provides incentive to invent and innovate. This rationale rests on two propositions: first, that more invention and innovation than would occur in the absence of some special induce-ment are desirable, and second, that giving out patents is the best method of providing such special inducement. In other words, discoveries would surely occur without patents, but it is believed that their unearthing will be appreciably hastened, or that more of them will be obtained, if the vast profit potential exclusive patents provide is used to lure inventors and innovators into action.

There can be no doubt that many inventions and innovations depend on patents for their existence or early arrival. Stories of people like Chester Carlson tell us that garrets and garages shelter thousands of inventors so inspired. As for innovation, which is the commercial application of an invention rather than the invention itself, evidence shows patents providing further incentive. A good test of this incentive would compare the commercial development of inventions *with* and *without* patent protection. The inventions that emerge from government funded research and development yield data for such a test because those doing the research sometimes get exclusive patent rights and sometimes not. (When not, the patent is publicly available to anyone.) These data show that commercial development of inventions (i.e., innovation) is two to three times more common *with* exclusive patent protection than without.[17] Results like these prompted a change in policy in 1980. Amendments to patent law now allow universities and small businesses to patent all technology developed with federal funds.

Still, the incentive thesis needs qualification at two levels. First, social benefits of cost savings and added consumer surplus may be rightly credited to the patent system for fathering "patent-dependent" inventions and innovations, but patent protection of these discoveries also creates social costs. These costs are the usual ones associated with monopoly—such as higher prices than otherwise. When these costs are deducted from the social benefits provided by these patent-dependent discoveries, the *net result* is considerably smaller than that suggested by brash talk of the gross benefits. This qualification of the incentive thesis is nevertheless not very serious because theory can demonstrate that the social benefits of these patent-dependent discoveries nearly always exceed those social costs to yield a positive net social benefit.[18] (See Appendix to this chapter.)

[16] C. T. Taylor and Z. A. Silberston, *The Economic Impact of the Patent System* (Cambridge, U.K.: Cambridge University Press, 1973), p. 352.

[17] U.S. House of Representatives, Subcommittee on Domestic and International Scientific Planning and Analysis, *Background Materials on Government Patent Policies,* Vol. II, 94th Congress, 2nd Session (1976), p. 97.

[18] For a review, see Scherer, *op. cit.,* (1977), pp. 25–34.

The second and higher level qualification is critical, however. We may comfortably assume that patent-dependent inventions and innovations are always, on balance, beneficial. But we *cannot* jump from there to conclude that the *patent system itself* is, on balance, always beneficial. Inability to make this leap weakens the incentive thesis. Thus a more thorough discussion of the patent system's costs and benefits is needed.

IV. BENEFITS AND COSTS OF PATENTS

If the net social benefits of patent-dependent discoveries and developments were all that counted, the value of patent systems could not be questioned. However, patents are extended to *all* inventions that meet the legal qualifications, including inventions that are *not* dependent on the patent system for their existence. Whatever social benefits may be claimed for these *non*patent-dependent inventions, they cannot be attributed to the patent system for the simple reason that their existence does not hinge on patent protection. Patent protection for these nondependent inventions does create social costs, however, costs of the monopoly kind. So in such cases there will *always be net social costs* from patents. Given that (1) patent dependency always yields net social benefits and (2) *non*patent dependency of patented inventions always yields net social costs, economists have devised the following criterion for judging the value of the patent system. As stated by F. M. Scherer, one "must weigh the *net* benefits associated with inventions which would not have been available without patent protection against the *net* social losses associated with patented inventions that would be introduced even if no patent rights were offered."[19]

Unfortunately, balance scales capable of this weighing have not yet been invented (patentable or otherwise). Some have even said the task is and always will be impossible because there is no sure way of telling whether a given invention is, or is not, patent dependent. Still, the major considerations that would guide educated guesswork on the issue have been sketched, and they include the following:

A. Tallies of Patent Dependency

Rough approximations have occasionally been made about the number of patent-dependent versus nonpatent-dependent inventions, on the assumption that, if the former number falls considerably short of the latter, the net benefits of the former are also likely to fall short of the net costs of the latter. For example, these two figures have been crudely estimated by classifying discoveries of individual inventors (and perhaps those of small firms too) in the patent-dependent group and relegating those of corporations (or *large* corporations) into the nonpatent-dependent group. Questionnaire surveys of patentees rather

---

[19] F. M. Scherer, *Industrial Market Structure and Economic Performance* (Chicago: Rand McNally, 1970), p. 384.

consistently reveal that, in general, individual inventors rely heavily on patent protection to sustain their efforts, whereas most corporations claim that patents are neither the chief goal nor principal determinant of their innovative efforts.[20]

By this broad measure it would appear that *non*patent-dependent inventions easily outnumber patent-dependent inventions by a ratio somewhere in the neighborhood of 3 or 4 to 1. However, the very rough nature of this approximation is underscored by substantial differences of patent-dependency across industries. Chemical and pharmaceutical companies claim to lean more heavily on patents than do other corporate classes. A West German study arrived through opinion surveys at the following estimates of patent-dependent inventions as a per cent of all patented inventions in West Germany: chemicals and drugs, 36%; electrical equipment, 21%; instruments and optical, 21%; machinery, 3%; and iron and steel, 0%.[21]

Patent dependency has also been examined by study of situations in which patents have not been available. Neither Switzerland nor the Netherlands had patent systems during the latter half of the nineteenth century and the first decade of this century. Yet the absence of patents failed to petrify industry in either.[22]

If, on the whole, patents are no more forceful in stimulating invention and innovation than is indicated by these items of evidence, obviously there must be other sources of incentive, other factors propelling progress. In the first place, to the extent *secrecy* can be maintained, it provides protection in lieu of patent protection. Second, many companies engage in progressive activities to remain *competitive* or gain competitive leadership. Introduction of new products or product improvements is a form of product differentiation, much like advertising. Natural lags, including temporary secrecy and retooling requirements, prevent immediate imitation of these efforts, gaining prestige and customer loyalty for the innovators. Third, even where imitation is not substantially delayed, innovative investments are not always or even usually flushed down the drain by the price competition of imitators. High concentration, stiff barriers to entry, and similar sources of *market power other than patents* furnish a basis for postimitation price discipline in many industries. Finally, even when R & D does not on average pay its own way, it may nevertheless persist. Like gamblers, inventors and innovators often have distorted visions. They tend to see the Chester Carlsons more clearly than the Feckless Floyd failures. They *overrate their chances* of winning the spectacular treasures, and, as a consequence, they often subsidize their R & D efforts from unrelated earnings.

Note that most of these nonpatent inducements probably apply most strongly to medium-sized or large firms. Secrecy cannot be maintained by a small individual inventor who must go around displaying his ideas in hopes of finding a firm that will commercialize them. A small, newly entering enterprise that dares

[20] For a survey of the surveys, see Scherer, *op. cit.*, (1977), pp. 50–56.

[21] Ibid., p. 53.

[22] Eric Schiff, *Industrialization without Patents* (Princeton, N.J.: Princeton University Press, 1971).

to threaten the established position of existing behemoths cannot count on the restraint of their price discipline should they elect to crush the newcomer. A small company cannot gain much of a jump on its rivals if its brand name is less entrenched and its distribution channels are shallower and thinner than those of its larger rivals. A small company likewise tends to be less diversified than its larger foes, so it may have fewer opportunities to subsidize its R & D during periods of financial drought. Perhaps these considerations explain why individual inventors and small firms profess greater reliance on the patent system, and claim a keener interest in its perpetuation, than big firms. (This does not necessarily mean that the patent system is, on balance, procompetitive. The story of U.S. Gypsum should dispel hasty conclusions of that kind.)

To summarize, various empirical tallies of patent dependency indicate that the system provides life-support for only a minority of inventions and innovations, a minority whose origins are of usually humble size. This minority wins credit for the system. But since patents are also showered indiscriminately on the nonpatent-dependent majority of inventions, it would appear from tally-type evidence that the net costs of the majority exceed the net benefits of the minority, and the system should therefore be reformed or abolished. However, we must hold off the executioners, at least momentarily.

B. The Economic Significance of Patent-Dependent Inventions

Although the weight of numbers suggests the patent system is economically unfit, that measure may be misleading. What if the relatively few inventions that are patent-dependent include the relatively few inventions that are truly revolutionary, whereas, at the same time, the relatively numerous nonpatent-dependent inventions include only simple improvements or inanities? It has been argued that, to some extent, there is a direct relationship between the economic significance of inventions and their patent dependency. F. M. Scherer speaks for this view:

> It is conceivable that without a patent system some of the most spectacular technical contributions—those which effect a genuine revolution in production or consumption patterns—might be lost or (more plausibly) seriously delayed. . . . Such innovations may lie off the beaten paths of industrial technology, where no firm or group of firms has a natural advantage, and the innovator may be forced to develop completely new marketing channels and production facilities to exploit them. They may entail greater technological and market uncertainties, higher development costs, and longer inception-to-commercialization lags than the vast bulk of all industrial innovation. Entrepreneurs may be willing to accept their challenge only under highly favorable circumstances—notably, when it is anticipated that if success is achieved, it can be exploited to the fullest through the exercise of exclusive patent rights.

> That such cases exist is virtually certain. Black-and-white television and the development of Chester Carlson's xerographic concepts are probable examples.[23]

---

[23] Scherer, *op. cit.*, (1970), p. 388.

Undoubtedly it is this possibility, coupled with notions of "natural law" property, that persuades politicians to keep the patent system intact. At a bare minimum, such crude *qualitative* accounting raises serious doubts about the accuracy of negative conclusions derived from simple *quantitative* tallies.

C. The Social Cost of Nondependent Inventions

But the qualifications cannot end there, not in fairness to those critical of patents, anyway. Just as the net benefits of dependent cases need qualification, so too the net costs of granting patents in nondependent cases need amplification—an exercise that tips the balance back in the negative direction, especially where revolutionary innovations of this nondependent stripe are concerned.

First, granting monopoly rights over knowledge that is not dependent on patents artificially restricts use of that knowledge below what is socially optimal. The marginal cost of using technical knowledge is zero in the sense that knowledge can be used over and over and over again, by one person or many, without even the slightest danger of exhaustion through wear and tear. No one is compelled to get less of it when anyone else gets more. Ideally, therefore, technology should be *freely* available to all potential users because the "pure" marginal cost of its dissemination and application is zero. But the grant of monopoly leads to exclusions, either directly or by the extraction of a royalty-price that exceeds zero.[24]

A second social cost, one stemming from that just mentioned, is a blocking effect. Potential inventors who might like to use a patented invention to further their research in different or related fields may be blocked from doing so, in which case the patent would not be fostering progress but rather inhibiting it.

Third, if a patent is extended to a firm with a preexisting monopoly position, then suppression of the patented invention is possible under certain circumstances.[25]

Fourth, patents give rise to monopoly powers and restrictive practices that go well beyond those inherent in patents themselves.

It is at this last point that patent policy collides with antitrust policy. Pure and simple patent monopoly escapes antitrust attack for obvious reasons. But, as seen earlier in the story of U.S. Gypsum, patents may be cleverly accumulated and manipulated to construct fortresses of monopoly power or networks of price-fixing agreements. The line between proper use and malevolent abuse of patent rights is difficult to draw, but the antitrust authorities and federal courts have over time made the attempt. As a result, the following practices, among others, have been declared illegal:

Restrictive Licensing. If a number of patent licensees are restricted to charging prices specified by the patent holder, or if a number of licensees collude

---

[24] Wassily Leontief, "On Assignment of Patent Rights on Inventions Made Under Government Research Contracts," *Harvard Law Review* (January 1964), pp. 492–497.

[25] For a review of suppression cases, see Vaughan, *op. cit.*, pp. 227–260.

to allocate markets using patent licenses to formalize their agreement, violation is likely, as in the *Gypsum* case.[26]

Cross-licensing. Two or more patent holders may exchange rights of access to each other's patents, something which is often desirable in light of the fact that several firms may contribute to the technology of a single item, such as a TV set. However, patent "pools" that exclude others, or fix prices, or otherwise restrain trade are illegal.[27]

Acquisition of Patents. Monopoly power built on the acquisition of many patents (as opposed to relying on one's own inventiveness) may be attacked under Section 7 of the Clayton Act.[28]

Tying. Tying the sale of an unpatented product (like salt) to a patented product (a salt dispensing machine used in food processing) is virtually per se illegal.[29]

In brief, antitrust policy permits patent holders to earn their "legitimate" reward for invention, a reward that may be monopolistically plump. But patent rights cannot be stretched beyond "legitimate" rights. Tight interpretation of legitimacy has held down the social costs of the patent system, but not to the point of quieting cries for reform.

V. PROPOSALS FOR REFORM

A. Proposals to Weaken the System

Ideology and evidence lead few folks to advocate complete abolition of the United States patent system. The natural law property thesis rests on strongly held value judgments unrelated to economic benefits and costs. There is also enough incentive provided by the system to produce some social benefits. Whether these benefits exceed the social costs is, as we have seen, uncertain, but the benefits are large enough that abolition of the system might give appearances of throwing the baby out with the bath water. Hence critics who want the system weakened usually advocate reform, not abolition.[30]

One of the most obvious improvements that could be made in the system is the elimination of improvident patent grants. The test of inventiveness could be tightened substantially.

[26] *U.S.* v. *United States Gypsum Co.* 333 U.S. 364 (1948); *U.S.* v. *Masonite Corp.,* 316 U.S. 265 (1942); *Newburgh Moire Co.* v. *Superiors Moire Co.,* 237 F.2d 283 (3d Cir. 1956).

[27] *U.S.* v. *Line Material Co.,* 333 U.S. 287 (1948); *U.S.* v. *Singer Manufacturing Co.,* 374 U.S. 174 (1963).

[28] *U.S.* v. *Lever Bros. Co.,* 216 F. Supp. 887 (S.D.N.Y. 1963); *Kobe, Inc.* v. *Dempsey Pump Co.,* 198 F.2d 416 (10th Cir. 1952).

[29] *International Salt Co.* v. *U.S.,* 332 U.S. 392 (1947).

[30] Patent systems in less-developed countries are an entirely different matter, though: D. F. Greer, "The Case Against Patent Systems in Less-Developed Countries," *Journal of International Law and Economics* (December 1973), pp. 223–266.

A number of other proposed changes would lessen the monopoly power of patents. These include such things as shorter patent life and compulsory licensing. Reducing patent life below seventeen years would reduce monopoly's duration. Compulsory licensing would simply require patent holders to license their patents to all who wanted to use them at a "reasonable" royalty fee. This would reduce monopoly power because it would end the exclusiveness that patents presently bestow. Empirical studies of compulsory licensing indicate that it would also substantially deflate the system's incentives, but by less than abolition would.[31]

B. Proposals to Strengthen the System

As the U.S. economy grew sluggish in the late 1970s, our technological superiority was called increasingly into question. This spurred proposals to *strengthen* the patent system rather than weaken it. The result was a new patent law in December 1980. The law gives small businesses and universities exclusive patent rights to products invented with federal research funding.

Another provision of the new law reduced the likelihood that courts would declare patents invalid. Unlike before, the Patent Office can now recheck on the validity of a challenged patent. The results of the recheck, if favorable to the patent, solidify its validity.

Another piece of strengthening legislation seems to be moving toward passage. This bill would, in effect, lengthen the life of many patents, especially those covering drugs, chemicals, and medical devices. The problem addressed by the bill is this: some products, like drugs, cannot be marketed without prior government approval. But that approval can take a long time, as long as ten years. Thus new product "X" might be patented shortly after invention in 1980, but not be sold until after 1990. With the patent expiring in 1997, there would be only seven years of legal monopoly in the market instead of the seventeen accorded products not needing premarket clearance. The intent of the proposed legislation, then, is to extend patent life by the amount of time the product is under premarket regulatory review.[32] If this proposal gives any indication, the prevailing mood portends future reforms that would build up rather than tear down the patent system.

VI. FEDERAL FUNDING OF R & D

A. Trends

The federal government has seated itself at the dining table of technology, supped gluttonously, and has begun picking up the tab. Back in 1940 federal expenditures on R & D amounted to no more than $74.1 million, which was 0.8% of the total federal budget and barely 0.07% of GNP. A further mark of that era is the fact that federal spending on *agricultural* R & D exceeded *defense* R & D spending. World War II, the Cold War, the Space Race, and

---

[31] Taylor and Silberston, *op. cit.;* Scherer, *op. cit.,* (1977).
[32] *Business Week,* February 16, 1981, p. 29.

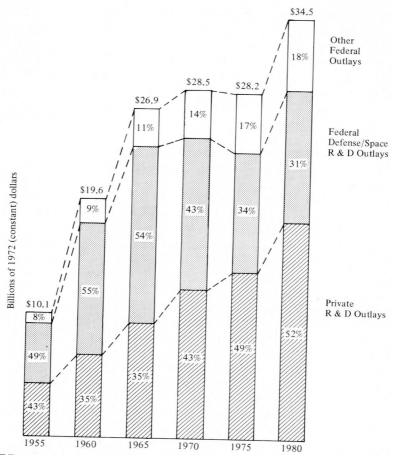

FIGURE 24–2. Trend in private and federal R & D outlays, constant dollars (1972).
Source: U.S. Department of Commerce, *Statistical Abstract of the United States,*
1981, p. 598.

the Vietnam War conspired to change all that. By the mid-1960s federal R &
D spending had soared to exceed $14 *billion,* which relative to total federal
spending of all kinds topped 12%, and compared to GNP exceeded 2%. Defense
R & D spending exploded to 41 times the size of agricultural outlays.[33]

The contribution this jump in federal R & D funding made to overall R
& D may be seen in Figure 24–2, which shows total outlays in constant (1972)
dollars over the period 1955 to 1980. Between 1955 and 1965, federal funding
tripled in real terms. Private expenditures, though also growing in real terms,

[33] National Science Foundation, *Federal Funds for Research, Development, and Other Scientific
Activities* (NSF 77–301, 1977), p. 4; Edwin Mansfield, *The Economics of Technical Change* (New
York: Norton, 1968), p. 163.

slipped as a percentage of the total to 35% in 1965. Since 1965 federal outlays have remained fairly steady in real terms except for a temporary dip in the mid-1970s. Thus the latest spurt shown in Figure 24–2, from 1975 to 1980, is due mainly to a rather healthy jump in "real" private expenditures. The overall total R & D outlay is now split fairly evenly between private and federal sources.

Figure 24–2 also shows that defense and space were big beneficiaries of the spurt in federal outlays over 1955–1965. Defense and space, especially space, then experienced a real and relative decline in support between 1965 and 1975.

More recent and more detailed trends in the composition of federal expenditures are depicted in Table 24–1. Space has continued to slide as a percentage of total federal outlays, but defense has experienced a revival. Indeed, defense is far and away the largest single category of expenditure with nearly 60% of the total.

While space has been falling, energy has been rising. Increasing more than seven-fold in absolute expenditure and more than three-fold in relative share, energy R & D now hovers around $5 billion annually and is second only to defense in overall ranking. By far the biggest chunk of energy money has in the past gone to support the development of nuclear power—projects like the liquid metal fast breeder reactor, uranium enrichment processing, magnetic fusion, and laser fusion. In 1969 these efforts took 93% of the energy outlay. These efforts still take a hefty portion, more than a third, but other energy sources are now getting greater attention, including coal gasification, oil shale, and solar power.

TABLE 24–1. Federal R & D Funding by Function: 1973 and 1983

Function	Millions of Dollars		Per Cent of Total	
	1973	1983*	1973	1983*
National defense	$ 9,002	$23,179	53.6%	59.6%
Space	2,824	2,506	16.8	6.4
Health	1,585	4,316	9.4	11.1
Energy	630	4,922	3.8	12.7
General science	658	1,060	3.9	2.7
Natural resources and environment	554	614	3.3	1.6
Transportation	572	393	3.4	1.0
Agriculture	308	850	1.8	2.2
Other	667	1,020	4.0	2.6
Total	16,800	38,860	100.0	100.0

* Estimate
Source: U.S. Department of Commerce, *Statistical Abstract of the United States* 1981, p. 600; Office of Management and Budget, *Budget of the United States:* Fiscal Year 1984, Special Analyses, p. K5.

PERFORMANCE

B. The Reasons for Federal Funding

Why has the government opened its purse so widely to these pursuits? Why has the distribution of money moved around so much? What guides Washington in these matters? There are no really solid answers because noneconomic value judgments play a crucial role in the decision making. Which will reduce the threat of death more—a billion dollars spent for a new military weapon or for a cure for cancer? Which will do more to relieve the energy crisis by the year 2000—a billion dollars spent on nuclear or on solar power? No one knows for sure; speculation reigns amidst the inherent uncertainties. Hence, value judgments are inescapable, and these shift under the press of political, social, international, and technical developments.

Still, there are a few broad economic foundations for this effort.[34] To begin with, most federal R & D is allocated to areas where the federal government stands as the sole or chief consumer of the ultimate product. National defense and space are the most obvious instances. Because the federal government has prime responsibility for provision of these "public goods" (a responsibility recognized by even the most miserly conservatives), it is strongly felt that the government should also take responsibility for technological advance in these areas, the advances themselves being "public goods."

Other R & D programs are grounded on the belief that private incentives are lacking. That is, the social benefits of advancement greatly exceed the benefits that can be privately captured, or if they can be captured, such would be undesirable. Research in basic science, health, environmental protection, and crime prevention probably fit this justification.

Still other programs can be defended as offsets to market imperfections of somewhat different sorts. Single R & D projects in such areas as nuclear power and urban mass transportation couple costs of billions of dollars with risks of ominous magnitudes, so much so that even our largest and most courageous private companies are scared to undertake them without government support. The necessity for government R & D funding in agriculture, housing, construction, and coal is often defended because these industries tend to be populated with firms too small and too scattered to shoulder the burdens of even medium-sized R & D projects.

Whatever the reason, federal R & D outlays now exceed those of private industry by a fat margin. Accordingly, our survey of policy would have been woefully lacking had it concealed this contribution.

---

[34] For details see Mansfield, *op. cit.*, pp. 186–187; *Priorities and Efficiency in Federal Research and Development*, A Compendium of Papers, Subcommittee on Priorities and Economy in Government of the Joint Economic Committee, U.S. Congress, 94th Congress, Second Session (1976); John E. Tilton, *U.S. Energy R & D Policy* (Washington, D.C.: Resources for the Future, 1974); Paul Horwitz, "Direct Government Funding of Research and Development," in *Technological Innovation for a Dynamic Economy*, edited by C. T. Hill and J. M. Utterback (New York: Pergamon Press, 1979), pp. 255–291.

VII. MISCELLANEOUS POLICIES

The government's influence on technological progress reaches well beyond patents and R & D funding. Indeed, the government's influence may be negative as well as positive. Regulations concerning consumer safety and health, or worker safety and health, may occasionally have adverse impacts. For example, changes in regulations governing new drug introductions during the early 1960s apparently contributed to a dramatic decline in the number of subsequent drug innovations.[35] Accentuating the positive, we shall briefly mention three possibilities: (1) competition, (2) procurement, and (3) taxes.[36]

1. Competition. As suggested by the analysis of the previous chapter, competition spurs technological change, so government would do well to pursue policies that maintain competition. Such policies include, most obviously, antitrust. The antitrust need not be of the traditional type, but it can make a big contribution.[37] In a similar vein, we should not smother the competition that foreign firms can provide through imports. We should, in other words, avoid protective tariffs and quotas. Were it not for imports, the auto industry, for one, would be a lot less progressive than it is today.

2. Procurement. Although parakeet diapers might be contrived without much of a prospective market to promote the effort, heavy commitments of resources to most innovations would disappear without visions of buyers at the ready. The government can serve as a buyer, indeed a very big buyer. Hence government procurement policy has been successfully used in the past to stimulate innovation. Semiconductor technology, among others, received a tremendous boost from this quarter:

> the importance of the government's role as a high-volume purchaser of quality goods at premium prices cannot be exaggerated. The presence of government demand reduced the risks of investment in new technology, and the government's willingness to purchase large volumes at premium prices permitted the accumulation of production experience necessary for the realization of dynamic economies and the penetration of the commercial markets.[38]

---

[35] H. G. Grabowski and J. M. Vernon, "Consumer Protection Regulation in Ethical Drugs," *American Economic Review* (February 1977), pp. 359–364; H. G. Grabowski, *Drug Regulation and Innovation* (Washington D.C.: American Enterprise Institute, 1976).

[36] For a more complete survey see J. Herbert Hollomon, "Policies and Programs of Governments Directed Toward Industrial Innovation," in *Technological Innovation for a Dynamic Economy, op. cit.*, pp. 292–317.

[37] Burton H. Klein, "The Slowdown in Productivity Advances: A Dynamic Explanation," in *Ibid.*, pp. 66–117.

[38] Richard C. Levin, "The Semiconductor Industry," in *Government and Technical Progress,* edited by R. R. Nelson (New York: Pergamon Press, 1982), p. 94.

PERFORMANCE

3. Taxes. Because small, new, high-technology firms (such as those in California's "Silicon Valley") are especially good sources of innovation, tax policies that encourage the formation of such companies would stimulate innovation. In particular, startup companies need "venture" capital to get off the ground—that is, money from venturesome investors willing to take big risks in sprouting companies. Taxes influence the expected return on such "venture" investment, thereby also influencing its availability. As if to illustrate this point, venture capital has burgeoned since 1978: "Spurring this shower of investment are tax-law changes starting in 1978 that cut the maximum capital gains tax bite to 20% from nearly 50% for individuals. The corporate rate was eased to around 28% from about 30%."[39] Changes in tax treatment of losses (carried forward) and tax treatment of R & D expenditures could also serve as stimulants to startups.[40]

SUMMARY

The United States government's promotion of technical progress dates from the days of the Founding Fathers. Patents originate in the Constitution, which authorizes legislation to "promote the progress of science and useful arts, by securing for limited times to authors and inventors the exclusive right to their respective writings and discoveries." Under present law, patents last 17 years and cover discoveries that pass fairly lenient standards of inventiveness, novelty, and utility. Admissible subject matter is essentially limited to mechanical and chemical products or processes, thereby excluding fundamental laws of nature and other worthwhile discoveries.

At its best, the patent system stimulates progress, rewards deserving inventors and innovators, and arouses competition by nourishing small firms. The history of Xerox illustrates these beneficent effects. On the other hand, deserving and getting do not always coincide under the system, with the result that patents protect discoveries that would be available anyway. Moreover, patents often provide hooks on which to hang restrictive practices, and they occasionally even stifle technical progress. Many of these blemishes in the system were underscored by the story of wallboard.

The main justifications for the patent system are "natural law" property, "exchange-for-secrets," and "incentives." Each has appeal; each has problems. As the law presently stands, too much is arbitrarily excluded to make the natural law argument natural, and society gets in on too few of the secrets it bargains for. That patent incentives pull some discoveries from the nether world cannot be doubted, but this effect is easily exaggerated.

Ideally, a benefit-cost analysis would compare the net benefits of patent-dependent inventions with the net costs of extending patents to nonpatent-dependent inventions. Unfortunately, data deficiencies permit no more than speculation

[39] *Business Week*, April 18, 1983, p. 79.
[40] Hollomon, *op. cit.*, p. 305.

552

on this score. What little evidence is available indicates that net benefits have the best chance of exceeding net costs on those patents that are extended to individual inventors and small firms. Chemicals and pharmaceuticals might also enjoy favorable balances. These findings have led reformists to call for changes in the system.

Federal funding of R & D has grown from little more than a teenager's weekly allowance to amounts in excess of $35 billion. In recent years, defense and space R & D have been deemphasized in favor of civilian R & D, but defense is staging a comeback. Noneconomic value judgments play a particularly prominent role in this policy area.

Other policies promoting progress focus on competition, procurement, and taxes.

APPENDIX TO CHAPTER 24:
The Economic Benefits of Cost-Reducing Inventions

In cases where patents bring forth new *products,* the net social benefits are easy to imagine because new products yield new consumer surpluses even when priced at monopoly levels. Less intuitively plausible are the net benefits associated with *production process* innovations, where no new product is involved and where the monopoly control granted by the patent can convert a purely competitive industry into a monopoly. Figures 24–3 (a) and (b) illustrate the two possibilities in this regard.

If, as in Figure 24–3 (a), production costs per unit drop substantially from C_1 under pure competition to C_2 under monopoly, then buyers will gain an immediate benefit from the invention—namely, a price reduction from P_1 to P_2, which increases quantity from Q_1 to Q_2. Under pure competition, price equals marginal cost, as P_1 equals C_1 in Figure 24–3 (where marginal cost is

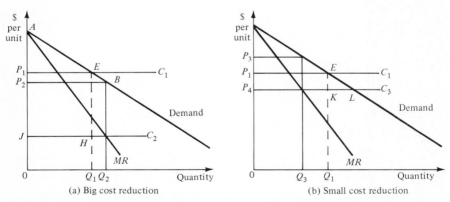

(a) Big cost reduction   (b) Small cost reduction

FIGURE 24–3. The Economic Effects of Patent-Dependent Cost-Reducing Inventions

assumed constant and therefore also equal to average cost). When cost falls from C_1 to C_2 because of the invention, price will not fall as much because patent monopoly prevails as well as cost C_2, and the monopolist's price, P_2, will be above C_2. Still, the price reduction increases consumers' surplus from AEP_1 to ABP_2.

Aside from the price reduction, society also gains by the fact that, after the invention, fewer resources are used to produce Q_1, a savings represented by the area JP_1EH. Although most of these savings are pocketed by the monopolist in the form of excess profits, they are nevertheless genuine and the monopolist is, after all, a member of society, not a Martian. Once the patent expires the industry could return to a purely competitive structure (assuming favorable conditions), at which time price will drop to C_2 and all gains then pass to buyers (consumers).

The cost reduction in panel (b) of Figure 24–3 is smaller, C_1 to C_3. Indeed, it is small enough to suggest that, with conversion to monopoly, price could actually rise from P_1 to P_3, given that marginal revenue MR equals marginal cost C_3 at quantity Q_3, which is less than Q_1. However, the monopolist's price cannot rise above P_1 because the pure competitors can sell at P_1, and they would be encouraged to do so at any price above P_1. Thus in this case price is likely to remain at P_1, implying no immediate gain for buyers. All the immediate social gains take the form of reduced resource use in the production of Q_1, a reduction represented by area P_1EKP_4. These savings go to the monopolist (still a member of society). If pure competition returns after expiration of the patent, buyers then reap the benefits when price falls to P_4 from P_1. The gain in consumer surplus then equals P_4P_1EL, because triangle ELK is added to the cost savings of P_1EKP_4 just mentioned. Thus in this case, too, a patent dependent invention yields net social benefits even though the patent creates a seventeen year monopoly.[41]

[41] For further discussion, see Dan Usher, "The Welfare Economics of Invention," *Economic* (August 1964), pp. 279–287; William D. Nordhaus, *Invention, Growth and Welfare* (Cambridge, Mass.: MIT Press, 1969); F. M. Scherer, *Industrial Market Structure and Economic Performance* (2nd ed.) (Chicago: Rand McNally, 1980), pp. 442–444.

Index of Authors

INDEX OF AUTHORS

Index of Major Companies

Index of Industries

Index of Legal Cases

Subject Index

569